W9-COI-667

SOLUTIONS MANUAL

To accompany Raymond A. Barnett and Michael R. Ziegler
FINITE MATHEMATICS for Management, Life and Social Sciences
Fourth Edition

Dellen Publishing Company
San Francisco
Collier Macmillan Publishers
London
divisions of Macmillan, Inc.

PREFACE

"It is by solving problems that mathematics keeps alive."

—DAVID HILBERT

This supplement accompanies *Finite Mathematics for Management, Life, and Social Sciences*, Fourth Edition, by Raymond A. Barnett and Michael R. Ziegler.

The manual contains the solutions to the odd-numbered problems in each of the exercise sets, and the solutions to all of the problems in the Chapter Reviews. Each of the sections begins with a list of important terms and formulas, given under the heading "Things to Remember." While sufficient details are given for each solution, the first few solutions in each section are more detailed than the remaining ones.

CONTENTS

APPENDIX A   SPECIAL TOPICS

CHAPTER 0　PRELIMINARIES

Things to remember:

1. $a \in A$ means "a is an element of set A."
2. $a \notin A$ means "a is not an element of set A."
3. $\emptyset$ means "the empty set or null set."
4. $S = \{x \mid P(x)\}$ means "S is the set of all x such that $P(x)$ is true."
5. $A \subseteq B$ means "A is a subset of B."
6. $A \subset B$ means "A is a proper subset of B," or A and B have exactly the same elements.
7. $A = B$ means "$A \subseteq B$ and $B \subseteq A$."
8. $A \cup B = A$ union $B = \{x \mid x \in A \text{ or } x \in B\}$.
9. $A \cap B = A$ intersection $B = \{x \mid x \in A \text{ and } x \in B\}$.
10. $A' = $ complement of $A = \{x \in U \mid x \notin A\}$, where U is a universal set.

1. T　　3. T　　5. T　　7. T

9. $\{1, 3, 5\} \cup \{2, 3, 4\} = \{1, 2, 3, 4, 5\}$

11. $\{1, 3, 4\} \cap \{2, 3, 4\} = \{3, 4\}$

13. $\{1, 5, 9\} \cap \{3, 4, 6, 8\} = \emptyset$

15. $\{x \mid x - 2 = 0\}$
$x - 2 = 0$ is true for $x = 2$.
Hence, $\{x \mid x - 2 = 0\} = \{2\}$.

17. $x^2 = 49$ is true for $x = 7$ and -7.
Hence, $\{x \mid x^2 = 49\} = \{-7, 7\}$.

19. $\{x \mid x$ is an odd number between 1 and 9 inclusive$\} = \{1, 3, 5, 7, 9\}$.

21. $U = \{1, 2, 3, 4, 5\}$; $A = \{2, 3, 4\}$
Then $A' = \{1, 5\}$.

23. From the Venn diagram, A has 40 elements.

25. A' has 60 elements.

1

27. $A \cup B$ has 60 elements
$(35 + 5 + 20)$.

29. $A' \cap B$ has 20 elements
(common elements between A' and B).

31. $(A \cap B)'$ has 95 elements.
(Note that $A \cap B$ has 5 elements.)

33. $A' \cap B'$ has 40 elements.

35. (A) $\{x \mid x \in R \text{ or } x \in T\}$
$= R \cup T$ ("or" translated as
$\cup$, union)
$= \{1, 2, 3, 4\} \cup \{2, 4, 6\}$
$= \{1, 2, 3, 4, 6\}$

(B) $R \cup T = \{1, 2, 3, 4, 6\}$

37. $Q \cap R = \{2, 4, 6\} \cap \{3, 4, 5, 6\}$
$= \{4, 6\}$

$P \cup (Q \cap R) = \{1, 2, 3, 4\} \cup \{4, 6\}$
$= \{1, 2, 3, 4, 6\}$

39. $A \cup B = B$ can be represented by
the Venn diagram

From the diagram we see that
$A \cup B = B$. Thus, the given
statement is *true*.

41. The given statement is always *true*.
To understand this, see the following Venn diagram.

$A \cap B \subset B$

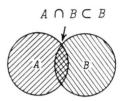

43. The given statement is *true*.
To understand this, see the
following Venn diagram.

 $x \in A$

From the diagram we conclude
that $x \in B$.

45. (A) Set $\{a\}$ has two subsets:
$\{a\}$ and $\emptyset$

(B) Set $\{a, b\}$ has four subsets:
$\{a, b\}$, $\emptyset$, $\{a\}$, $\{b\}$

(C) Set $\{a, b, c\}$ has eight subsets:
$\{a, b, c\}$, $\emptyset$, $\{a\}$, $\{b\}$, $\{c\}$,
$\{a, b\}$, $\{a, c\}$, $\{b, c\}$

Parts (A), (B), and (C) suggest the
following formula:

The number of subsets in a set with
n elements $= 2^n$.

47. The Venn diagram that corresponds
to the given information is shown
at the right. We can see that $N \cup M$
has $300 + 300 + 200 = 800$ students.

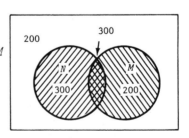

49. $(N \cup M)'$ has 200 students
[because $N \cup M$ has 800 students
and $(N \cup M)' = 1000 - 800 = 200$.].

51. $N' \cap M$ has 200 students.

53. The number of commuters who listen to either news or music = number of commuters in the set $M \cup N$, which is 800.

55. The number of commuters who do not listen to either news or music = number of commuters in the set $(N \cup M)'$, which is $1000 - 800 = 200$.

57. The number of commuters who listen to music but not news = number of commuters in the set $N' \cap M$, which is 200.

59. The six two-person subsets that can be formed from the given set $\{P, V_1, V_2, V_3\}$ are:

$\{P, V_1\}$ $\{P, V_3\}$ $\{V_1, V_3\}$
$\{P, V_2\}$ $\{V_1, V_2\}$ $\{V_2, V_3\}$

61. From the given Venn diagram, $A \cap Rh = \{A+, AB+\}$.

63. Again, from the given Venn diagram, $A \cup Rh = \{A-, A+, B+, AB-, AB+, 0+\}$.

65. From the given Venn diagram, $(A \cup B)' = \{0+, 0-\}$.

67. $A' \cap B = \{B-, B+\}$.

69. Statement (2): For every $a, b \in C$, aRb and bRa means that everyone in the clique relates to one another.

EXERCISE 0-2

Things to remember:

1. There is a one-to-one correspondence between the set of real numbers and the set of points on a line. A line with a real number associated with each point, and vice versa, as in the figure, is called a REAL NUMBER LINE or REAL LINE. The real number r associated with a given point is called the COORDINATE of the point. The point with coordinate 0 is called the ORIGIN. The arrow indicates the positive direction.

Let a, b, and c be real numbers. Then

2. If $a = b$, then (a) $a + c = b + c$
(b) $a - c = b - c$
(c) $ac = bc$
(d) $\dfrac{a}{c} = \dfrac{b}{c}$ $c \neq 0$

3. If $a > b$, then (a) $a + b > b + c$
(b) $a - c > b - c$

(c) $ac > bc$ $\bigg\}$ if c is positive
(d) $\dfrac{a}{c} > \dfrac{b}{c}$

(e) $ac < bc$ $\bigg\}$ if c is negative
(f) $\dfrac{a}{c} < \dfrac{b}{c}$

Note: Similar properties hold if each inequality is reversed, or if $>$ is replaced by $\geqslant$ and $<$ is replaced by $\leqslant$.

4. The double inequality $a \leqslant x \leqslant b$ means that $a \leqslant x$ and $x \leqslant b$. Other variations, as well as a useful interval notation, are indicated in the following table.

INTERVAL NOTATION	INEQUALITY NOTATION	LINE GRAPH
$[a, b]$	$a \leqslant x \leqslant b$	
$[a, b)$	$a \leqslant x < b$	
$(a, b]$	$a < x \leqslant b$	
(a, b)	$a < x < b$	
$(-\infty, a]$	$x \leqslant a$	
$(-\infty, a)$	$x < a$	
$[b, \infty)$	$x \geqslant b$	
(b, ∞)	$x > b$	

Note: An endpoint on a line graph has a square bracket through it if it is included in the inequality and a parenthesis through it if it is not.

1.
$$2m + 9 = 5m - 6$$
$$2m + 9 - 9 = 5m - 6 - 9 \quad [\text{using } \underline{2}(b)]$$
$$2m = 5m - 15$$
$$2m - 5m = 5m - 15 - 5m \quad [\text{using } \underline{2}(b)]$$
$$-3m = -15$$
$$\frac{-3m}{-3} = \frac{-15}{-3} \quad [\text{using } \underline{2}(d)]$$
$$m = 5$$

3.
$$x + 5 < -4$$
$$x + 5 - 5 < -4 - 5 \quad [\text{using } \underline{3}(b)]$$
$$x < -9$$

5.
$$-3x \geqslant -12$$
$$\frac{-3x}{-3} \leqslant \frac{-12}{-3} \quad [\text{using } \underline{3}(f)]$$
$$x \leqslant 4$$

7.
$$-4x - 7 > 5$$
$$-4x > 5 + 7$$
$$-4x > 12$$
$$x < -3$$

Graph of $x < -3$ is:

9.
$$2 \leqslant x + 3 \leqslant 5$$
$$2 - 3 \leqslant x \leqslant 5 - 3$$
$$-1 \leqslant x \leqslant 2$$

Graph of $-1 \leqslant x \leqslant 2$ is:

11. $\frac{y}{7} - 1 = \frac{1}{7}$

Multiply both sides of the equation by 7. We obtain:

$$y - 7 = 1 \quad [\text{using } \underline{2}(c)]$$
$$y = 8$$

13. $\frac{x}{3} > -2$

Multiply both sides of the inequality by 3. We obtain:

$$x > -6 \quad [\text{using } \underline{3}(c)]$$

15. $\frac{y}{3} = 4 - \frac{y}{6}$

Multiply both sides of the equation by 6. We obtain:

$$2y = 24 - y$$
$$3y = 24$$
$$y = 8$$

17.
$$10x + 25(x - 3) = 275$$
$$10x + 25x - 75 = 275$$
$$35x = 275 + 75$$
$$35x = 350$$
$$x = \frac{350}{35}$$
$$x = 10$$

19.
$$3 - y \leqslant 4(y - 3)$$
$$3 - y \leqslant 4y - 12$$
$$-5y \leqslant -15$$
$$y \geqslant 3$$

(note division by a negative number, -3)

21. $\frac{x}{5} - \frac{x}{6} = \frac{6}{5}$

Multiply both sides of the equation by 30. We obtain:

$$6x - 5x = 36$$
$$x = 36$$

23. $\frac{m}{5} - 3 < \frac{3}{5} - m$ Multiply both sides of the inequality by 5. We obtain:

$$m - 15 < 3 - 5m$$
$$6m < 18$$
$$m < 3$$

25. $0.1(x - 7) + 0.05x = 0.8$
$0.1x - 0.7 + 0.05x = 0.8$
$0.15x = 1.5$
$$x = \frac{1.5}{0.15}$$
$$x = 10$$

27. $2 \leqslant 3x - 7 < 14$
$7 + 2 \leqslant 3x < 14 + 7$
$9 \leqslant 3x < 21$
$3 \leqslant x < 7$

Graph of $3 \leqslant x < 7$ is:

29. $-4 \leqslant \frac{9}{5}C + 32 \leqslant 68$

$-36 \leqslant \frac{9}{5}C \leqslant 36$

$-36\left(\frac{5}{9}\right) \leqslant C \leqslant 36\left(\frac{5}{9}\right)$

$-20 \leqslant C \leqslant 20$

Graph of $-20 \leqslant C \leqslant 20$ is:

31. $3x - 4y = 12$
$3x = 12 + 4y$
$3x - 12 = 4y$
$$y = \frac{1}{4}(3x - 12)$$
$$= \frac{3}{4}x - 3$$

33. $Ax + By = C$
$By = C - Ax$
$$y = \frac{C}{B} - \frac{Ax}{B}$$
or $y = -\left(\frac{A}{B}\right)x + \frac{C}{B}$

35. $F = \frac{9}{5}C + 32$

$\frac{9}{5}C + 32 = F$

$\frac{9}{5}C = F - 32$

$C = \frac{5}{9}(F - 32)$

37. $A = Bm - Bn$
$A = B(m - n)$
$$B = \frac{A}{m - n}$$

39. $-3 \leqslant 4 - 7x < 18$
$-3 - 4 \leqslant -7x < 18 - 4$

and $-7 \leqslant -7x < 14$.

Dividing by -7, and recalling 3(f), we have

$1 \geqslant x > -2$ or $-2 < x \leqslant 1$

The graph is:

41. Let x = number of \$6 tickets. Then the number of \$10 tickets = $8,000 - x$.

$6x + 10(8,000 - x) = 60,000$

Thus,

$6x + 80,000 - 10x = 60,000$
$-4x = 60,000 - 80,000$
$4x = 20,000$
$x = 5,000$

Therefore, $x = 5,000$ \$6 tickets and $8,000 - x = 3,000$ \$10 tickets were sold.

43. Let x = amount invested at 10%. Then $12,000 - x$ is the amount invested at 15%.

Required total yield = 12% of $12,000 = 0.12 \cdot 12,000 = \$1,400$. Thus,

$$0.10x + 0.15(12,000 - x) = 0.12 \cdot 12,000$$
$$10x + 15(12,000 - x) = 12 \cdot 12,000 \quad \text{(multiply both sides by 100)}$$
$$10x + 180,000 - 15x = 144,000$$
$$-5x = -36,000$$
$$x = \$7,200$$

Thus, we get $7,200 invested at 10% and $12,000 - 7,200 = \$4,800$ invested at 15%.

45. $\dfrac{\text{Car sold for in 1980}}{\text{Car sold for in 1965}} = \dfrac{\text{Consumer price index in 1980}}{\text{Consumer price index in 1965}}$

$$\frac{x}{3000} = \frac{247}{95} \quad \text{(refer to Table 2, Example 13)}$$
$$x = \frac{3000 \times 247}{95}$$
$$= \$7,800$$

47. Let x = number of rainbow trout in the lake. Then,

$$\frac{x}{200} = \frac{200}{8} \quad \text{(since proportions are the same)}$$
$$x = \frac{200}{8}(200)$$
$$x = 5000$$

49. $\text{IQ} = \dfrac{\text{Mental age}}{\text{Chronological age}}(100)$

$$\frac{\text{Mental age}}{9}(100) = 140$$
$$\text{Mental age} = \frac{140}{100}(9)$$
$$= 12.6 \text{ years}$$

EXERCISE 0-3

Things to remember:

1. A quadratic equation in one variable is an equation of the form

   (A) $ax^2 + bx + c = 0$,

   where x is a variable and a, b, and c are constants, $a \neq 0$.

2. Quadratic equations of the form $ax^2 + c = 0$ can be solved by the SQUARE ROOT METHOD. The solutions are:

   $$x = \pm\sqrt{\frac{-c}{a}} \quad \text{provided} \quad \frac{-c}{a} \geq 0;$$

   otherwise, the equation has no real solutions.

PRELIMINARIES

3. If the left side of the quadratic equation (A) can be FACTORED,

$$ax^2 + bx + c = (px + q)(rx + s),$$

then the solutions of (A) are

$$x = \frac{-q}{p} \quad \text{or} \quad x = \frac{-s}{r}.$$

4. The solutions of (A) are given by the QUADRATIC FORMULA:

$$x = \frac{-b \pm \sqrt{b^2 - 4ac}}{2a}$$

The quantity $b^2 - 4ac$ is called the DISCRIMINANT and:

(i) (A) has two real solutions if $b^2 - 4ac > 0$;

(ii) (A) has one real solution if $b^2 - 4ac = 0$;

(iii) (A) has no real solutions if $b^2 - 4ac < 0$.

---

1. $x^2 - 4 = 0$
$x^2 = 4$
$x = \pm\sqrt{4} = \pm 2$

3. $2x^2 - 22 = 0$
$x^2 - 11 = 0$
$x^2 = 11$
$x = \pm\sqrt{11}$

5. $2u^2 - 8u - 24 = 0$
$u^2 - 4u - 12 = 0$
$(u - 6)(u + 2) = 0$

$u - 6 = 0 \quad \text{or} \quad u + 2 = 0$
$u = 6 \quad \text{or} \quad u = -2$

7. $x^2 = 2x$
$x^2 - 2x = 0$
$x(x - 2) = 0$

$x = 0 \quad \text{or} \quad x - 2 = 0$
$= 2$

9. $x^2 - 6x - 3 = 0$

$$x = \frac{-b \pm \sqrt{b^2 - 4ac}}{2a}, \quad a = 1, \ b = -6, \ c = -3$$

$$= \frac{-(-6) \pm \sqrt{(-6)^2 - 4(1)(-3)}}{2(1)}$$

$$= \frac{6 \pm \sqrt{48}}{2} = \frac{6 \pm 4\sqrt{3}}{2} = 3 \pm 2\sqrt{3}$$

11. $3u^2 + 12u + 6 = 0$

Since 3 is a factor of each coefficient, divide both sides by 3.

$u^2 + 4u + 2 = 0$

$$u = \frac{-b \pm \sqrt{b^2 - 4}}{2a}, \quad a = 1, \ b = 4, \ c = 2$$

$$= \frac{-4 \pm \sqrt{4^2 - 4(1)(2)}}{2(1)} = \frac{-4 \pm \sqrt{8}}{1} = \frac{-4 \pm 2\sqrt{2}}{2} = -2 \pm \sqrt{2}$$

13.
$$2x^2 = 4x$$
$$x^2 = 2x \quad \text{(divide both sides by 2)}$$
$$x^2 - 2x = 0 \quad \text{(solve by factoring)}$$
$$x(x - 2) = 0$$
$$x = 0 \quad \text{or} \quad x - 2 = 0$$
$$x = 2$$

15.
$$4u^2 - 9 = 0$$
$$4u^2 = 9 \quad \text{(solve by square}$$
$$u^2 = \frac{9}{4} \quad \text{root method)}$$
$$u = \pm\sqrt{\frac{9}{4}} = \pm\frac{3}{2}$$

17.
$$8x^2 + 20x = 12$$
$$8x^2 + 20x - 12 = 0$$
$$2x^2 + 5x - 3 = 0$$
$$(x + 3)(2x - 1) = 0$$
$$x + 3 = 0 \quad \text{or} \quad 2x - 1 = 0$$
$$x = -3 \quad \text{or} \quad 2x = 1$$
$$x = \frac{1}{2}$$

19.
$$x^2 = 1 - x$$
$$x^2 + x - 1 = 0$$
$$x = \frac{-b \pm \sqrt{b^2 - 4ac}}{2a}, \quad a = 1, \ b = 1, \ c = -1$$
$$= \frac{-1 \pm \sqrt{(1)^2 - 4(1)(-1)}}{2(1)} = \frac{-1 \pm \sqrt{5}}{2}$$

21.
$$2x^2 = 6x - 3$$
$$2x^2 - 6x + 3 = 0$$
$$x = \frac{-b \pm \sqrt{b^2 - 4ac}}{2a}, \quad a = 2, \ b = -6, \ c = 3$$
$$= \frac{-(-6) \pm \sqrt{(-6)^2 - 4(2)(3)}}{2(2)}$$
$$= \frac{6 \pm \sqrt{12}}{4} = \frac{6 \pm 2\sqrt{3}}{4} = \frac{3 \pm \sqrt{3}}{2}$$

23.
$$y^2 - 4y = -8$$
$$y^2 - 4y + 8 = 0$$
$$y = \frac{-b \pm \sqrt{b^2 - 4ac}}{2a}, \quad a = 1, \ b = -4, \ c = 8$$
$$= \frac{-(-4) \pm \sqrt{(-4)^2 - 4(1)(8)}}{2(1)} = \frac{4 \pm \sqrt{-16}}{2}$$

Since $\sqrt{-16}$ is not a real number, there are no real solutions.

25.
$$(x + 4)^2 = 11$$
$$x + 4 = \pm\sqrt{11}$$
$$x = -4 \pm \sqrt{11}$$

27.
$$A = P(1 + r)^2$$
$$(1 + r)^2 = \frac{A}{P}$$
$$1 + r = \sqrt{\frac{A}{P}}$$
$$r = \sqrt{\frac{A}{P}} - 1$$

29. $d = \dfrac{3000}{p}$ and $s = 1000p - 500$

Let $d = s$. Then,

$\dfrac{3000}{p} = 1000p - 500$ or $3000 = 1000p^2 - 500p$ and $1000p^2 - 500p - 3000 = 0$.

Divide both sides by 500.

$\quad 2p^2 - p - 6 = 0$ (solve by factoring)
$(2p + 3)(p - 2) = 0$

$2p + 3 = 0 \quad$ or $\quad p - 2 = 0$
$\quad p = -\dfrac{3}{2} \quad$ or $\quad\quad p = 2$

Since the price, p, must be positive, we have $p = \$2$ as the equilibrium point.

31. $v^2 = 64h$

For $h = 1$, $v^2 = 64(1) = 64$. Therefore, $v = 8$ ft/sec.

For $h = 0.5$, $v^2 = 64(0.5) = 32$. Therefore, $v = \sqrt{32} \approx 5.66$ ft/sec.

EXERCISE 0-4

Things to remember:

1. The graph of any equation of the form $Ax + By = C$ (standard form), where A, B, and C are constants (A and B not both zero) is a straight line. Every straight line in a cartesian coordinate system is the graph of an equation of this type.

2. The slope, m, of a line through the two points (x_1, y_1) and (x_2, y_2) is given by:

$m = \dfrac{y_2 - y_1}{x_2 - x_1}$,

$x_1 \neq x_2$.

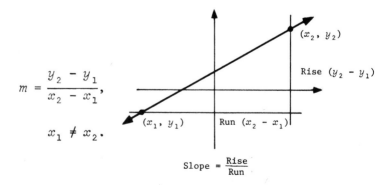

$\text{Slope} = \dfrac{\text{Rise}}{\text{Run}}$

3. In general, the slope of a line may be positive, negative, 0, or not defined. Each of these cases is interpreted geometrically as illustrated in the following table.

Going from left to right:

He went over this in class during review class #2

Line	Slope	Example
Rising	Positive	
Falling	Negative	
Horizontal	0	
Vertical	Not defined	

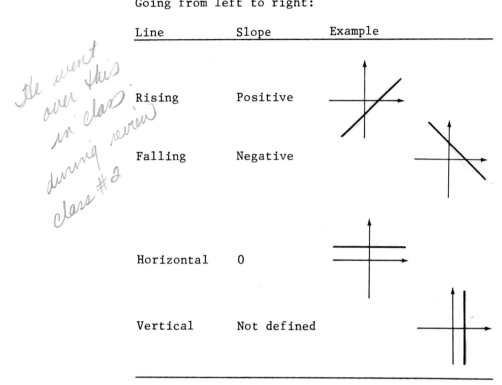

4. The equation

   $$y = mx + b \qquad \begin{array}{l} m = \text{slope} \\ b = y \text{ intercept} \end{array}$$

   is called the SLOPE-INTERCEPT form of an equation of a line.

5. An equation for the line that passes through (x_1, y_1) with slope m is:

   $$y - y_1 = m(x - x_1)$$

   This equation is called the POINT-SLOPE FORM.

6. The horizontal line with y intercept c has the equation: $y = c$
   The vertical line with x intercept c has the equation: $x = c$

---

1. $y = 2x - 3$

x	y
0	-3
1	-1
4	5

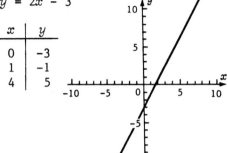

3. $2x + 3y = 12$

x	y
0	4
6	0
9	-2

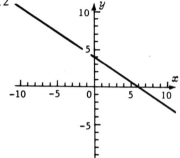

5. Slope $m = 2$

y intercept $b = -3$

7. Slope $m = -\dfrac{2}{3}$

y intercept $b = 2$

9. $m = -2$

$b = 4$

Using <u>4</u>, $y = -2x + 4$

11. $m = -\dfrac{3}{5}$

$b = 3$

Using <u>4</u>, $y = -\dfrac{3}{5}x + 3$

13. $y = -\dfrac{2}{3}x - 2$

$m = -\dfrac{2}{3}$, $b = -2$

x	y
0	-2
3	-4
-3	0

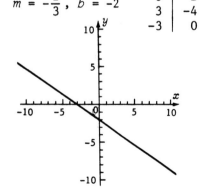

15. $3x - 2y = 10$

x	y
0	-5
10	10
-4	-11

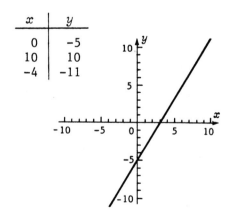

17.

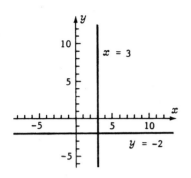

19. $3x + y = 5$
$$y = -3x + 5$$
$$m = -3 \quad \text{(using } \underline{4})$$

21. $2x + 3y = 12$
$$3y = -2x + 12$$

Divide both sides by 3:

$$y = -\frac{2}{3}x + \frac{12}{3} = -\frac{2}{3}x + 4$$

$$m = -\frac{2}{3} \quad \text{(using } \underline{4})$$

23. $m = -3$

For the point $(4, -1)$, $x_1 = 4$ and $y_1 = -1$. Using $\underline{5}$, we get:

$$y - (-1) = -3(x - 4)$$
$$y + 1 = -3x + 12$$
$$y = -3x + 11$$

25. $m = \frac{2}{3}$

For the point $(-6, -5)$, $x_1 = -6$ and $y_1 = -5$. Using $\underline{5}$, we get:

$$y - (-5) = \frac{2}{3}(x - (-6))$$
$$y + 5 = \frac{2}{3}(x + 6)$$
$$y + 5 = \frac{2}{3}x + 4$$
$$y = \frac{2}{3}x - 1$$

27. The points are $(1, 3)$ and $(7, 5)$. Let $x_1 = 1$, $y_1 = 3$, $x_2 = 7$, and $y_2 = 5$. Using $\underline{2}$, we get:

$$m = \frac{5 - 3}{7 - 1} = \frac{2}{6} = \frac{1}{3}$$

29. Let $x_1 = -5$, $y_1 = -2$, $x_2 = 5$, and $y_2 = -4$. Using $\underline{2}$, we get:

$$m = \frac{-4 - (-2)}{5 - (-5)} = \frac{-4 + 2}{5 + 5}$$
$$= \frac{-2}{10} = -\frac{1}{5}$$

31. First, find the slope using $\underline{2}$:

$$m = \frac{y_2 - y_1}{x_2 - x_1} = \frac{5 - 3}{7 - 1} = \frac{2}{6} = \frac{1}{3}$$

Then, by using $\underline{5}$, $y - y = m(x - x)$, where $m = 1/3$ and $(x_1, y_1) = (1, 3)$ or $(7, 5)$, we get:

$$y - 3 = \frac{1}{3}(x - 1) \quad \text{or} \quad y - 5 = \frac{1}{3}(x - 7)$$

These two equations are equivalent. After simplifying either one of these, we obtain:

$$-x + 3y = 8 \quad \text{or} \quad x - 3y = -8$$

33. First, find the slope using $\underline{2}$:

$$m = \frac{-4 - (-2)}{5 - (-5)} = \frac{-4 + 2}{5 + 5} = \frac{-2}{10} = -\frac{1}{5}$$

By using $\underline{5}$, and either one of the points, we obtain:

$$y - (-2) = -\frac{1}{5}(x - (-5)) \quad \text{[using } (-5, -2)\text{]}$$

$$y + 2 = -\frac{1}{5}(x + 5)$$

$$5(y + 2) = -x - 5$$
$$5y + 10 = -x - 5$$
$$x + 5y = -15$$

35. Using $\underline{6}$ with $c = 3$ for the vertical line and $c = -5$ for the horizontal line, we find that the equation of the vertical line is $x = 3$ and the equation of the horizontal line is $y = -5$.

37. Using $\underline{6}$ with $c = -1$ for the vertical line and $c = -3$ for the horizontal line, we find that the equation of the vertical line is $x = -1$ and the equation of the horizontal line is $y = -3$.

39. $m = -\frac{1}{2}$ and $(x_1, y_1) = (-2, 5)$.

Using $\underline{4}$:

$$y - 5 = -\frac{1}{2}(x - (-2))$$

$$y - 5 = -\frac{1}{2}(x + 2)$$

$$y - 5 = -\frac{1}{2}x - 1$$

$$y = -\frac{1}{2}x + 4$$

41. The straight line L whose equation is $y = (-1/2)x + 5$ has slope $m = -1/2$.

(A) The line through $(-2, 2)$ which is parallel to L has slope $m = -1/2$. Thus, an equation for this line is:

$$y - 2 = -\frac{1}{2}(x - (-2))$$

$$y - 2 = -\frac{1}{2}(x + 2)$$

$$y - 2 = \left(-\frac{1}{2}\right)x - 1$$

$$y = \left(-\frac{1}{2}\right)x + 1$$

(B) The line through $(-2, 2)$ which is perpendicular to L has slope $m = (-1)/(-1/2) = 2$. Thus, an equation for this line is:

$$y - 2 = 2(x - (-2))$$
$$y - 2 = 2x + 4$$
$$y = 2x + 6$$

43. Writing the equation $x - 2y = 4$ in slope-intercept form, we have $y = (1/2)x - 2$. Therefore, the slope of this line L is $m = 1/2$.

(A) The line through (−2, −1) which is parallel to L has slope $m = 1/2$. Thus, an equation for this line is:

$$y - (-1) = \frac{1}{2}(x - (-2))$$

$$y + 1 = \frac{1}{2}(x + 2)$$

$$y + 1 = \frac{1}{2}x + 1$$

$$y = \frac{1}{2}x$$

(B) The line through (−2, −1) which is perpendicular to L has slope $m = (-1)/(1/2) = -2$. Thus, an equation for this line is:

$$y - (-1) = -2(x - (-2))$$
$$y + 1 = -2(x + 2)$$
$$y + 1 = -2x - 4$$
$$y = -2x - 5$$

45. $y = mx - 2$.

Using 2 with y intercept = −2 and the given slopes 2, 1/2, 0, −1/2, and −2, we have:

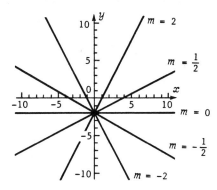

47. (2, 7) and (2, −3)

Since each point has the same x-coordinate, the graph of the line formed by these two points will be a *vertical line*. Then, using 6, with $c = 2$, we have $x = 2$ as the equation of the line.

49. (2, 3) and (−5, 3)

Since each point has the same y-coordinate, the graph of the line formed by these two points will be a *horizontal line*. Then, using 6, with $c = 3$, we have $y = 3$ as the equation of the line.

51. $A = Prt + P$ (1)

Rate $r = 0.06$

Principal $P = 100$

Substituting in (1), we get:

$A = 6t + 100$ (2)

(A) Let $t = 5$ and $t = 20$ and substitute in (2). We get:

$$A = 6(5) + 100 = \$130$$
$$A = 6(20) + 100 = \$220$$

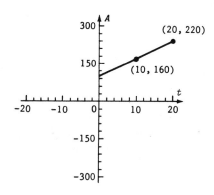

(B)

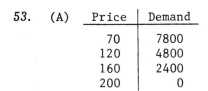

t	A
0	100
10	160
20	220

(C) Consider two points (10, 160) and (20, 220). Using $\underline{2}$, we have:

$$m = \frac{220 - 160}{20 - 10} = \frac{60}{10} = 6$$

53. (A)

Price	Demand
70	7800
120	4800
160	2400
200	0

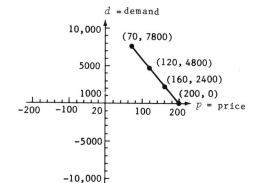

(B) We observe that the points in part (A) lie along a straight line. Consider two points, (120, 4800) and (160, 2400). Using $\underline{1}$, we have:

$$m = \frac{2400 - 4800}{160 - 120} = -\frac{2400}{40} = -60$$

The equation of the line, which has slope −60 and passes through (120, 4800), is:

$$(d - 4800) = -60(P - 120)$$
$$d - 4800 = -60P + 7200$$
$$d = -60P + 12{,}000$$

Slope = −60

The slope of the line indicates that the demand will decrease by 60 power mowers for each dollar increase in price.

55. Mix A contains 20% protein.
Mix B contains 10% protein.

Let x be the amount of A used and y be the amount of B used. Then $0.2x$ is the amount of protein from mix A and $0.1y$ is the amount of protein from mix B. Thus, the linear equation is:

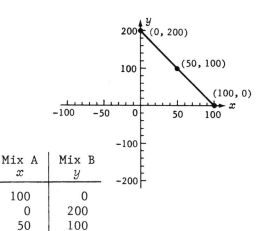

$0.2x + 0.1y = 20$

The table shows different combinations of mix A and mix B to provide 20 grams of protein. [**Note:** We can get many more combinations. In fact, each point on the graph indicates a combination of mix A and mix B.]

Mix A x	Mix B y
100	0
0	200
50	100
10	180

57. $p = -\frac{1}{5}d + 70$, $30 \leqslant d \leqslant 175$, where d = distance in centimeters
p = pull in grams

(A) $d = 30$ $\qquad\qquad\qquad\qquad$ $d = 175$

$p = -\frac{1}{5}(30) + 70 = 64$ grams $\qquad p = -\frac{1}{5}(175) + 70 = 35$ grams

(B)

d	p
30	64
50	60
175	35

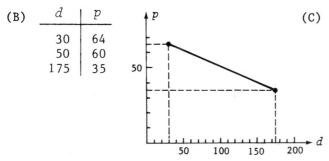

(C) Select two points (30, 64) and (50, 60) as (x_1, y_1) and (x_2, y_2), respectively, from part (B). Using $\underline{2}$:

$$\text{slope } m = \frac{y_2 - y_1}{x_2 - x_1} = \frac{60 - 64}{50 - 30}$$

$$= -\frac{4}{20}$$

$$= -\frac{1}{5}$$

EXERCISE 0-5

Things to remember:

$\underline{1.}$ A FUNCTION is a rule (process or method) that produces a correspondence between one set of elements, called the DOMAIN, and a second set of elements, called the RANGE, such that to each element in the domain there corresponds one and only one element in the range.

$\underline{2.}$ EQUATIONS AND FUNCTIONS:

Given an equation in two variables. If there corresponds exactly one value of the dependent variable (output) to each value of the independent variable (input), then the equation specifies a function. If there is more than one output for at least one input, then the equation does not specify a function.

$\underline{3.}$ AGREEMENT ON DOMAINS AND RANGES:

If a function is specified by an equation and the domain is not given explicitly, then assume that the domain is the set of all real number replacements of the independent variable (inputs) that produce real values for the dependent variable (outputs). The range is the set of all outputs corresponding to input values.

<u>4.</u> FUNCTION NOTATION:

Let f be a function. For each element x in the domain of f, the symbol $f(x)$ represents the unique element in the range of f which corresponds to x. That is, if x is an input value, then $f(x)$ is the corresponding output value; symbolically $f : x \to f(x)$. The ordered pair $(x, f(x))$ belongs to the function f.

<u>5.</u> The function f specified by the equation

$$f(x) = mx + b \quad \text{or} \quad y = mx + b,$$

where m and b are constants, is a LINEAR FUNCTION. The graph of $f(x) = mx + b$ is a nonvertical straight line with slope m and y intercept b.

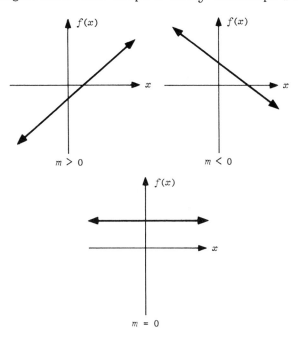

<u>6.</u> The function f specified by the equation

$$f(x) = ax^2 + bx + c \quad \text{or} \quad y = ax^2 + bx + c,$$

where a, b, and c are constants and $a \neq 0$, is called a QUADRATIC FUNCTION. The graph of a quadratic function   is a parabola whose AXIS (line of symmetry) is parallel to the vertical axis (or y axis). It opens upward if $a > 0$ and downward if $a < 0$. The intersection point of the parabola and its axis is called the VERTEX.

18

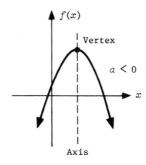 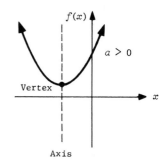

7. Given the quadratic function $f(x) = ax^2 + bx + c$.

(i) Axis (of symmetry) of the parabola:

$$x = \frac{-b}{2a}$$

(ii) Maximum or minimum value of $f(x)$:

$$f\left(\frac{-b}{2a}\right) \quad \begin{array}{l} \text{Minimum if } a > 0 \\ \text{Maximum if } a < 0 \end{array}$$

(iii) Vertex of the parabola:

$$\left(\frac{-b}{2a}, \ f\left(\frac{-b}{2a}\right)\right)$$

---

1. The table specifies a function, since for each domain value there corresponds one and only one range value.

3. The table does not specify a function, since more than one range value corresponds to a given domain value. (Range values 5, 6 correspond to domain value 3; range values 6, 7 correspond to domain value 4.)

5. This is a function.

7. The graph specifies a function; there is one and only one value of y corresponding to each value of x.

9. The graph does not specify a function.

11. The graph specifies a function.

13. $f(x) = 3x - 2$
    $f(2) = 3(2) - 2 = 4$

15. $f(-1) = 3(-1) - 2$
    $= -5$

17. $g(x) = x - x^2$
    $g(3) = 3 - 3^2 = -6$

19. $f(0) = 3(0) - 2$
    $= -2$

21. $g(-3) = -3 - (-3)^2$
    $= -12$

23. $f(1) + g(2)$
    $= [3(1) - 2] + (2 - 2^2) = -1$

25. $g(2) - f(2) = (2 - 2^2) - [3(2) - 2]$
$= -2 - 4$
$= -6$

27. $g(3) \cdot f(0) = (3 - 3^2)[3(0) - 2]$
$= (-6)(-2)$
$= 12$

29. $\dfrac{g(-2)}{f(-2)} = \dfrac{-2 - (-2)^2}{3(-2) - 2} = \dfrac{-6}{-8} = \dfrac{3}{4}$

31. $f(x) = 2x - 4$
Slope $m = 2$
y intercept $b = -4$

x	$f(x)$
0	-4
1	-2
2	0

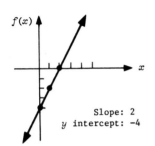

Slope: 2
y intercept: -4

33. $h(x) = 4 - 2$
Slope $m = -2$
y intercept $b = 4$

x	$h(x)$
0	4
2	0

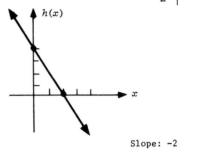

Slope: -2
y intercept: 4

35. $g(x) = -\dfrac{2}{3}x + 4$

Slope $m = -\dfrac{2}{3}$

y intercept $b = 4$

x	$g(x)$
0	4
3	2
6	0

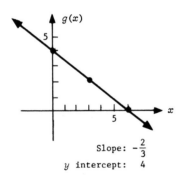

Slope: $-\dfrac{2}{3}$
y intercept: 4

37. $f(3) + g(-2)$
$= [2(3) + 1] + [(-2)^2 - (-2)]$
$= 7 + 6 = 13$

39. $k(9) - g(-2)$
$= \sqrt{9} - [(-2)^2 - (-2)]$
$= 3 - 6 = -3$

41. $k(4) = \sqrt{4} = 2$
$f[k(4)] - f(2) = 2(2) + 1 = 5$

43. $g(2) = 2^2 - 2 = 2$
$k[g(2)] = g(2) = \sqrt{2}$

45. $g(e) = e^2 - e$

47 $k(u) = \sqrt{u}$

49. $g(2 + h) = (2 + h)^2 - (2 + h)$
$= 4 + 4h + h^2 - 2 - h$
$= h^2 + 3h + 2$

51. $f(a + h) = 2(a + h) + 1$
$= 2a + 2h + 1$

53. $\dfrac{f(2 + h) - f(2)}{h} = \dfrac{[2(2 + h) + 1] - [2(2) + 1]}{h}$

$= \dfrac{4 + 2h + 1 - 4 - 1}{h} = \dfrac{2h}{h} = 2$

55.
$$\frac{g(2 + h) - g(2)}{h} = \frac{[(2 + h)^2 - (2 + h)] - [2^2 - 2]}{h}$$

$$= \frac{4 + 4h + h^2 - 2 - h - 2}{h} = \frac{3h + h^2}{h} = \frac{h(3 + h)}{h} = 3 + h$$

57. The domain of $f(x) = \sqrt{x}$ is all nonnegative real numbers (the square root of a negative number is not a real number).

59. The domain is all real numbers except $x = -3$ and $x = 5$. The function is not defined at $x = -3$ and $x = 5$.

61. Since the square root of a negative number is not real, we must have:

$$x + 5 \geqslant 0 \quad \text{or} \quad x \geqslant -5$$

Thus, the domain of $f(x) = \sqrt{x + 5}$ is the set of all real numbers such that $x \geqslant -5$ or $[-5, \infty)$.

63. $f(x) = x^2 + 8x + 16$;
$a = 1$, $b = 8$, $c = 16$.
Using 7, the axis (of symmetry) of the parabola is:

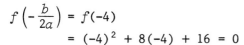

x	$f(x)$
0	16
-3	1
-5	1
-4	0

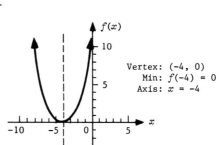

Vertex: $(-4, 0)$
Min: $f(-4) = 0$
Axis: $x = -4$

$$x = -\frac{b}{2a} = \frac{8}{2 \cdot 1} = -4$$

Since $a = 1 > 0$, the minimum value of $f(x)$ is:

$$f\left(-\frac{b}{2a}\right) = f(-4)$$

$$= (-4)^2 + 8(-4) + 16 = 0$$

The vertex of the parabola is: $\left(-\frac{b}{2a},\ f\left(-\frac{b}{2a}\right)\right) = (-4,\ 0).$

65. $f(u) = u^2 - 2u + 4$; $a = 1$, $b = -2$, $c = 4$.
Using 7, the axis (of symmetry) of the parabola is:

$$u = -\frac{u}{2a} = \frac{2}{2 \cdot 1} = 1$$

The minimum value of $f(u)$ is:

u	$f(u)$
0	4
-1	7
2	4
1	3

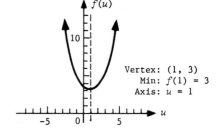

Vertex: $(1, 3)$
Min: $f(1) = 3$
Axis: $u = 1$

$$f\left(-\frac{b}{2a}\right) = f(1) = 1 \quad - 2 \quad 1 + 4 = 3$$

$$= 1^2 - 2 \cdot 1 + 4 = 3$$

The vertex of the parabola is: $\left(-\frac{b}{2a},\ f\left(-\frac{b}{2a}\right)\right) = (1,\ 3)$

67. $h(x) = 2 + 4x - x^2$; $a = -1$, $b = 4$, $c = 2$.
Using 7, the axis (of symmetry) of the parabola is:

$$x = -\frac{b}{2a} = -\frac{4}{2(-1)} = 2$$

Since $a = -1 < 0$, the maximum value of $h(x)$ is:

$$h\left(-\frac{b}{2a}\right) = h(2)$$
$$= 2 + 4 \cdot 2 - 2^2 = 6$$

The vertex of the parabola is:

$$\left(-\frac{b}{2a},\ h\left(-\frac{b}{2a}\right)\right) = (2,\ 6)$$

x	$h(x)$
0	2
1	5
2	6
3	5

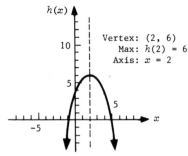

Vertex: $(2,\ 6)$
Max: $h(2) = 6$
Axis: $x = 2$

69. $f(x) = 6x - x^2$; $a = -1$, $b = 6$, $c = 0$.
The axis of symmetry is:

$$f = -\frac{b}{2a} = -\frac{6}{2(-1)} = 3$$

The maximum value of $f(x)$ is:

$$f\left(-\frac{b}{2a}\right) = f(3) = 6 \cdot 3 - 3^2 = 9$$

The vertex is:

$$\left(-\frac{b}{2a},\ f\left(-\frac{b}{2a}\right)\right) = (3,\ 9)$$

x	$f(x)$
0	0
1	5
2	8
3	9
4	8
5	5

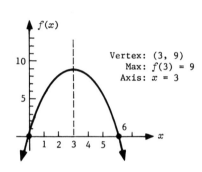

Vertex: $(3,\ 9)$
Max: $f(3) = 9$
Axis: $x = 3$

71. $F(s) = s^2 - 4$; $a = 1$, $b = 0$, $c = -4$.
The axis of symmetry is:

$$s = -\frac{b}{2a} = \frac{0}{2 \cdot 1} = 0$$

The minimum value of $F(s)$ is:

$$F\left(-\frac{b}{2a}\right) = F(0) = -4$$

The vertex is:

$$\left(-\frac{b}{2a},\ F\left(-\frac{b}{2a}\right)\right) = (0,\ -4)$$

s	$F(s)$
0	-4
-1	-3
1	-3
-2	0
2	0

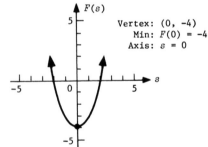

Vertex: $(0,\ -4)$
Min: $F(0) = -4$
Axis: $s = 0$

73. $F(x) = 4 - x^2$; $a = -1$, $b = 0$, $c = 4$.
The axis of symmetry is:

$$x = -\frac{b}{2a} = \frac{0}{2(-1)} = 0$$

The maximum value of $F(x)$ is:

$$F\left(-\frac{b}{2a}\right) = F(0) = 4$$

The vertex is:

$$\left(-\frac{b}{2a},\ F\left(-\frac{b}{2a}\right)\right) = (0,\ 4)$$

x	$F(x)$
0	4
-1	3
1	3
-2	0
2	0

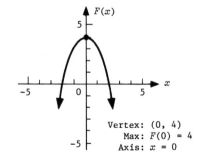

Vertex: $(0,\ 4)$
Max: $F(0) = 4$
Axis: $x = 0$

75. $f(x) = \begin{cases} x^2 \text{ when } x < 1 \\ 2x \text{ when } x \geqslant 1 \end{cases}$

(A) $f(-1) = (-1)^2 = 1$ using $f(x) = x^2$ since $x = -1 < 1$.

(B) $f(0) = (0)^2 = 0$ using $f(x) = x^2$ since $x = 0 < 1$.

(C) $f(1) = 2(1) = 1$ using $f(x) = 2x$ since $x = 1 \geqslant 1$.

(D) $f(3) = 2(3) = 6$ using $f(x) = 2x$ since $x = 3 \geqslant 1$.

77. $f(x) = x^2 - 7x + 10$;
$a = 1$, $b = -7$, $c = 10$.
The axis of symmetry is:

$x = -\dfrac{b}{2a} = -\dfrac{(-7)}{2 \cdot 1} = \dfrac{7}{2} = 3.5$

Since $a = 1 > 0$, the minimum value of $f(x)$ is:

$f\left(-\dfrac{b}{2a}\right) = f(3.5)^2$

$\quad = (3.5) - 7(3.5) + 10$

$\quad = -2.25$

The vertex is: $\left(-\dfrac{b}{2a}, \ f\left(-\dfrac{b}{2a}\right)\right) = (3.5, -2.25)$

x	$f(x)$
0	10
1	4
2	0
3	-2
3.5	-2.25
4	-2
5	0

Vertex: (3.5, -2.25)
Min: $f(3.5) = -2.25$
Axis: $x = 3.5$

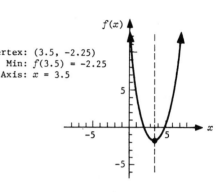

79. $g(t) = 4 + 3t - t^2$;
$a = -1$, $b = 3$, $c = 4$.
The axis of symmetry is:

$t = -\dfrac{b}{2a} = \dfrac{-3}{2(-1)} = \dfrac{3}{2} = 1.5$

Since $a = -1 < 0$, the maximum value of $g(t)$ is:

$g\left(-\dfrac{b}{2a}\right) = g(1.5) = 4 + 3(1.5) - (1.5)^2 = 6.25$

The vertex is: $\left(-\dfrac{b}{2a}, \ g\left(-\dfrac{b}{2a}\right)\right) = (1.5, 6.25)$

t	$g(t)$
0	4
1	6
1.5	6.25
2	6
3	4

Vertex: (1.5, 6.25)
Max: $g(1.5) = 6.25$
Axis: $t = 1.5$

81. Cost equation: $C = g(n) = 96,000 + 80n$

This is a linear function, the slope $m = 80$ and the intercept on the C axis $= 96,000$.

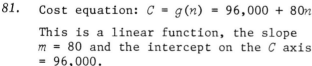

n	C
0	96,000
50	100,000
500	136,000
1000	176,000

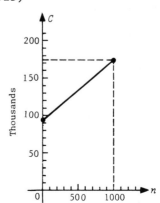

83. (A)

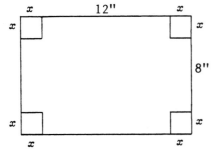

$$V = (\text{length})(\text{width})(\text{height})$$
$$V(x) = (12 - 2x)(8 - 2x)(x)$$

or $\quad V(z) = x(8 - 2x)(12 - 2x)$

(B) Domain = $0 < x < 4$

(C) $V(1) = (12 - 2)(8 - 2)(1)$
$\quad\quad\quad = (10)(6)(1) = 60$
$\quad V(2) = (12 - 4)(8 - 4)(2)$
$\quad\quad\quad = (8)(4)(2) = 64$
$\quad V(3) = (12 - 6)(8 - 6)(3)$
$\quad\quad\quad = (6)(2)(2) = 36$

Thus,

x	$V(x)$
1	60
2	64
3	36

85. Demand equation: $x = 9000 - 30p$ (1)
Cost equation: $C(x) = 90,000 + 30x$ (2)
Substituting x from (1) into (2), we get:

(A) $C = 90,000 + 30(9000 - 30p)$
$\quad\quad = 360,000 - 900p$

(B) Revenue = $xp = (9000 - 30p)p$
$\quad\quad R = 9000p - 30p^2$

(C) The graphs of the cost function and
the revenue function are shown at
the right; they have been constructed
following the usual graphing technique. Profit and loss regions are
also shown.

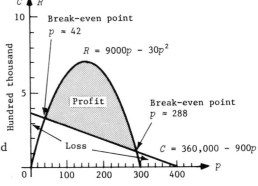

(D) At the break-even point, $R = C$:
$$9000p - 30p^2 = 360,000 - 900$$
$$30p^2 - 9900p + 360,000 = 0$$
$$p^2 - 330p + 12,000 = 0$$
$$(p - 42)(p - 288) \approx 0$$

Thus, the break-even points are
(approximately) $p = \$42$, $p = \$288$.

(E) The maximum revenue occurs at
$$p = -\frac{b}{2a} = \frac{-9000}{2(-30)}$$
$$= \frac{-9000}{-60} = 150$$

or $p = \$150$.

87. $\dfrac{\Delta s}{s} = k$. For $k = \dfrac{1}{30}$, $\dfrac{\Delta s}{s} = \dfrac{1}{30}$ or $\Delta s = \dfrac{1}{30}s$.

(A) When $s = 30$, $\Delta s = \dfrac{1}{30}(30) = 1$ pound.

When $s = 90$, $\Delta s = \dfrac{1}{30}(90) = 3$ pounds.

(B) $\Delta s = \dfrac{1}{30}s$.

Slope $m = 30$

y intercept $b = 0$

(C) Slope $m = \dfrac{1}{30}$

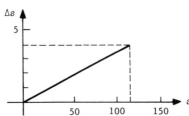

Things to remember:

1. $f(x) = b^x$, $b > 0$, $b \neq 1$ is an EXPONENTIAL FUNCTION. The domain of f is the set of all real numbers and the range of f is the set of positive real numbers. The x axis is a horizontal asymptote of the graph of f.

2. The most frequently used exponential function is $f(x) = e^x$, where $e \approx 2.71828$.

---

1. $y = 3^x$

x	y
-3	0.03
-2	0.11
-1	0.33
0	1
1	3
2	9
3	27

3. $y = \left(\dfrac{1}{3}\right)^x = 3^{-x}$

x	y
-3	27
-2	9
-1	3
0	1
1	0.33
2	0.11
3	0.03

5. $y = 10 \cdot 3^x$

x	y
-3	0.3
-2	1.1
-1	3.3
0	1
1	30
2	90
3	270

7. $y = 10 \cdot 2^{2x}$

x	y
-3	0.15
-2	0.62
-1	2.5
0	10
1	40
2	160
3	640

9. $y = e^x$

x	y
-3	0.0497
-2	0.135
-1	0.386
0	1
1	2.71
2	7.3891
3	20.086

11. $y = 10e^{0.2x}$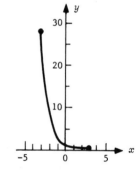

x	$e^{0.2x}$	$10e^{0.2x}$
-3	0.548	5.5
-2	0.670	5.7
-1	0.818	8.2
0	1	10
1	1.22	12.2
2	1.49	14.9
3	1.82	18.2

13. $y = 100e^{-0.1x}$

x	$e^{-0.1x}$	$100e^{-0.1x}$
-3	1.35	135
-2	1.22	122
-1	1.10	110
0	1	100
1	0.90	90
2	0.82	82
3	0.74	74

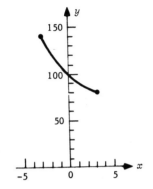

15. $y = e^{-x^2}$

x	x^2	e^{-x^2}
-1.5	2.25	0.105
-1	1	0.368
-0.5	0.25	0.779
0	0	1
0.5	0.25	0.779
1	1	0.368
1.5	2.25	0.105

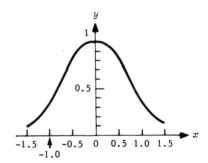

17. $y = 2^x$ $x = 2^y$

x	y
-3	0.125
-2	0.25
-1	0.5
0	1
1	2
2	4
3	8

y	x
-3	0.125
-2	0.25
-1	0.5
0	1
1	2
2	4
3	8

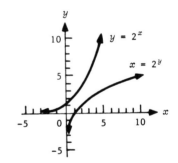

19. Growth function: $f(n) = 2^n$

n	$f(n) = 2^n$
1	2
4	16
6	64
8	256
10	1024

21. $A = 100 \cdot 2^{2t}$

t	$A = 100 \cdot 2^{2t}$
0	100
1	400
2	1,600
3	6,400
4	25,600
5	102,400

23. $N = 100(1 - e^{-0.1t})$

t	$e^{-0.1t}$	$1 - e^{-0.1t}$	$100(1 - e^{-0.1t})$
0	1	0	0
5	0.61	0.39	39
10	0.38	0.62	62
20	0.14	0.86	86
30	0.05	0.95	95
40	0.02	0.98	98

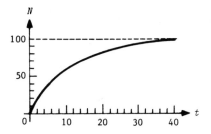

EXERCISE 0-7

Things to remember:

1. Let $b > 0$, $b \neq 1$. The LOGARITHMIC FUNCTION with base b is defined by

   $$y = \log_b x \text{ if and only if } x = b^y.$$

   In words, the logarithm of a number x to the base b is the exponent to which b must be raised to equal x.

   The domain of a logarithm function is the set of positive real numbers, and the range is the set of all real numbers.

2. Properties of logarithmic functions: let $b > 0$, $b \neq 1$, $M > 0$, and $N > 0$.

   (a) $\log_b b^x = x$

   (b) $\log_b M \cdot N = \log_b M + \log_b N$

   (c) $\log_b \dfrac{M}{N} = \log_b M - \log_b N$

   (d) $\log_b M^p = p \log_b M$

   (e) $\log_b M = \log_b N$ if and only if $M = N$

   (f) $\log_b 1 = 0$

3. $\log_{10} x$ is denoted by $\log x$, and is called the COMMON LOGARITHMIC FUNCTION. $\log x = y$ is equivalent to $x = 10^y$.

   $\log_e x$ is denoted by $\ln x$, and is called the NATURAL LOGARITHMIC FUNCTION. $\ln x = y$ is equivalent to $x = e^y$.

1. $27 = 3^3$ (using 1)

3. $1 = 10^0$

5. $8 = 4^{3/2}$

7. $\log_7 49 = 2$

9. $\log_4 8 = \dfrac{3}{2}$

11. $\log_b A = u$

13. $\log_{10} 10^3 = 3$
[using 2(a)]

15. $\log_2 2^{-3} = -3$

17. $\log_{10} 1000 = \log_{10} 10^3$
$= 3$

19. $\log_b \dfrac{P}{Q} = \log_b P - \log_b Q$ [using 2(c)]

21. $\log_b L^5 = 5 \log_b L$ [using 2(d)]

23. $\log_b \dfrac{p}{qrs} = \log_b p - \log_b qrs$ \qquad [using 2(c)]
$= \log_b p - (\log_b q + \log_b r + \log_b s)$ \quad [using 2(b)]
$= \log_b p - \log_b q - \log_b r - \log_b s$

25. $\log_3 x = 2$
$x = 3^2$ (using 1)
$x = 9$

27. $\log_7 49 = y$
$\log_7 7^2 = y$
$2 = y$
Thus, $y = 2$.

29. $\log_b 10^{-4} = -4$
$10^{-4} = b^{-4}$
This equality implies
$b = 10$
(since the exponents are the same).

31. $\log_4 x = \dfrac{1}{2}$
$x = 4^{1/2}$
$x = 2$

33. $\log_{1/3} 9 = y$
$9 = \left(\dfrac{1}{3}\right)^y$
$3^2 = (3^{-1})^y$
$3^2 = 3^{-y}$
This equality implies that
$2 = -y$
or
$y = -2$.

35. $\log_b 1000 = \dfrac{3}{2}$
$\log_b 10^3 = \dfrac{3}{2}$
$3 \log_b 10 = \dfrac{3}{2}$
$\log_b 10 = \dfrac{1}{2}$
$10 = b^{1/2}$
Square both sides:
$100 = b$
i.e., $b = 100$.

37. $\log_b \dfrac{x^5}{y^3}$
$= \log_b x^5 - \log_b y^3$
$= 5 \log_b x - 3 \log_b y$

39. $\log_b \sqrt[3]{N} = \log_b N^{1/3}$
$= \dfrac{1}{3} \log_b N$

41. $\log_b x^2 \sqrt[3]{y} = \log_b x^2 + \log_b y^{1/3}$
$= 2 \log_b x + \dfrac{1}{3} \log_b y$

43. $\log_b 50 \cdot 2^{-0.2t} = \log_b 50 + \log_b 2^{-0.2t}$
$= \log_b 50 - 0.2t \log_b 2$

45. $\log_b P(1 + r)^t = \log_b P + \log_b (1 + r)^t$
$= \log_b P + t \log_b (1 + r)$

47. $\log_e 100 e^{-0.01t} = \log_e 100 + \log_e e^{-0.01t}$
$= \log_e 100 - 0.01t \log_e e = \log_e 100 - 0.01t$

49. $\log_b x = \frac{2}{3} \log_b 8 + \frac{1}{2} \log_b 9 - \log_b 6$

$\quad = \log_b 8^{2/3} + \log_b 9^{1/2} - \log_b 6$

$\quad = \log_b 4 + \log_b 3 - \log_b 6$

$\quad = \log_b \frac{4 \cdot 3}{6}$

$\log_b x = \log_b 2$

$\quad x = 2 \text{ [using } \underline{2}(e)]$

51. $\log_b x = \frac{3}{2} \log_b 4 - \frac{2}{3} \log_b 8 + 2 \log_b 2$

$\quad = \log_b 4^{3/2} - \log_b 8^{2/3} + \log_b 2^2$

$\quad = \log_b 8 - \log_b 4 + \log_b 4$

$\quad = \log_b 8$

$\log_b x = \log_b 8$

$\quad x = 8 \text{ [using } \underline{2}(e)]$

53. $\log_b x + \log_b (x - 4) = \log_b 21$

$\quad \log_b x(x - 4) = \log_b 21$

Therefore, $x(x - 4) = 21$

$\quad x^2 - 4x - 21 = 0$

$\quad (x - 7)(x + 3) = 0$

Thus, $x = 7$.

[Note: $x = -3$ is not a solution since $\log_b (-3)$ is not defined.]

55. $\log_{10}(x - 1) - \log_{10}(x + 1) = 1$

$$\log_{10}\left(\frac{x - 1}{x + 1}\right) = 1$$

Therefore, $\dfrac{x - 1}{x + 1} = 10^1 = 10$

$\quad x - 1 = 10(x + 1)$

$\quad x - 1 = 10x + 10$

$\quad -9x = 11$

$$x = -\frac{11}{9}$$

There is *no solution*, since
$\log_{10}\left(-\dfrac{11}{9} - 1\right) = \log_{10}\left(-\dfrac{20}{9}\right)$
is not defined. Similarly,
$\log_{10}\left(-\dfrac{11}{9} + 1\right) = \log_{10}\left(-\dfrac{2}{9}\right)$
is not defined.

57. $y = \log_2(x - 2)$

$\quad x - 2 = 2^y$

$\quad x = 2^y + 2$

x	y
3	0
4	1
6	2
18	4
5/2	-1
9/4	-2

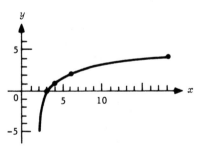

59.   (A) 3.54743   (B) -2.16032

     (C) 5.62629   (D) -3.19704

61.   (A) 1344   (B) .008919

     (C) 6479   (D) .002773

63. Let $\log_b 1 = y$, $b > 0$, $b \neq 1$.

Then $b^y = 1$, which implies $y = 0$ [see $\underline{2}(f)$]. Thus, $\log_b 1 = 0$.

65. $\log_{10} y - \log_{10} c = 0.8x$

$$\log_{10}\frac{y}{c} = 0.8x$$

Therefore, $\dfrac{y}{c} = 10^{0.8x}$ (using $\underline{1}$)

and $y = c \cdot 10^{0.8x}$.

67. From the compound interest formula $A = P(1 + i)^n$, we have

$$2P = P(1 + .06)^n \quad \text{or} \quad (1.06)^n = 2.$$

Take the natural log of both sides of this equation:

$\ln(1.06)^n = \ln 2$ [Note: The common log could have been used instead of the natural log.]

$n \ln(1.06) = \ln 2$

$$n = \frac{\ln 2}{\ln(1.06)}$$

$$\approx \frac{.69315}{.05827} = 11.90 \approx 12 \text{ years}$$

69. From the compound interest formula $A = P(1 + i)^n$, we have

$$3P = P(1 + i)^n \quad \text{or} \quad (1 + i)^n = 3.$$

Taking the natural log of both sides of this equation gives

$\ln(1 + i)^n = \ln 3 \quad \text{or} \quad n \ln(1 + i) = \ln 3.$

Thus, $n = \dfrac{\ln 3}{\ln(1 + i)}.$

71. $I = I_0 10^{N/10}$

Take the common log of both sides of this equation. Then,

$$\log I = \log(I_0 10^{N/10})$$

$$= \log I_0 + \log 10^{N/10}$$

$$= \log I_0 + \frac{N}{10} \log 10 = \log I_0 + \frac{N}{10} \quad \text{(since } \log 10 = 1\text{)}$$

Thus, $\dfrac{N}{10} = \log I - \log I_0 = \log\left(\dfrac{I}{I_0}\right)$

and $N = 10 \log\left(\dfrac{I}{I_0}\right).$

73. From the compound interest formula $A = P(1 + i)^n$, we have:

$$1.68 \times 10^{14} = 4 \times 10^9 (1 + .02)^n \quad \text{or} \quad (1.02)^n = \frac{1.68 \times 10^{14}}{4 \times 10^9}$$

$$= .42 \times 10^5$$

$$= 42,000$$

Taking the natural log of both sides of this equation gives:

$n \ln(1.02) = \ln(42,000) \quad \text{and} \quad n = \dfrac{\ln(42,000)}{\ln(1.02)} \approx \dfrac{10.6454}{.01980} \approx 537.65$

Thus, there will be one square yard of land per person in approximately 538 years.

1. (A) $7 \notin \{4, 6, 8\}$ is true (T)
    (B) $\{8\} \subset \{4, 6, 8\}$ is true (T)
    (C) $\emptyset \in \{4, 6, 8\}$ is false (F)
    (D) $\emptyset \subset \{4, 6, 8\}$ is true (T)

2. $\dfrac{u}{5} = \dfrac{u}{6} = \dfrac{6}{5}$

    Multiply each term by 30.

    $$6u = 5u + 36$$
    $$6u - 5u = 36$$
    $$u = 36$$

3. $2(x + 4) > 5x - 4$
    $2x + 8 > 5x - 4$
    $2x - 5x > -4 - 8$
       $-3x > -12$ (divide both sides
                by -3 and reverse
                the inequality)

    $x < 4$ or $(-\infty, 4)$

    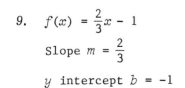

4. $x^2 = 5x$
       $x^2 - 5x = 0$ solve by factoring
       $x(x - 5) = 0$

       $x = 0$ or $x - 5 = 0$
                      $x = 5$

5. $y = \dfrac{x}{2} - 2 = \dfrac{1}{2}x - 2$

    Slope $m = \dfrac{1}{2}$

    y intercept $b = -2$

    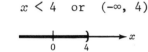

x	y
0	-2
2	-1

    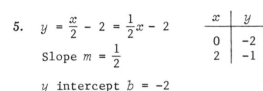

    Slope: $\dfrac{1}{2}$

    y intercept: -2

6. Using the point-slope form with $m = 1/2$ and $(x_1, y_1) = (4, 3)$, we have:

    $y - 3 = \dfrac{1}{2}(x - 4)$ or $y - 3 = \dfrac{1}{2}x - 2$ and $y = \dfrac{1}{2}x + 1$

7. $x - y = 2$. Solving for y, we have

    $-y = -x + 2$ or $y = x - 2$

    Slope $m = 1$

    y intercept $b = -2$

x	y
0	-2
2	0

    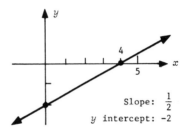

    Slope: 1
    y intercept: -2

8. $f(x) = 2x - 1$, $g(x) = x^2 - 2x$
    $f(-2) + g(-1) = [2(-2) - 1] + [(-1)^2 - 2(-1)]$
    $\qquad\qquad\quad = [-4 - 1] + [1 + 2]$
    $\qquad\qquad\quad = -5 + 3 = -2$

9. $f(x) = \dfrac{2}{3}x - 1$

    Slope $m = \dfrac{2}{3}$

    y intercept $b = -1$

x	$f(x)$
0	-1
3	1

    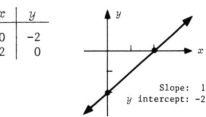
    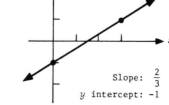

    Slope: $\dfrac{2}{3}$
    y intercept: -1

PRELIMINARIES

10. $\log_{10} y = x$ is the same as
    $y = 10^x$.

11. $\log_b \dfrac{wx}{y} = \log_b wx - \log_b y$
    $= \log_b w + \log_b x - \log_b y$

12. (A) $A \cup B = \{1, 2, 3\} \cup \{2, 3, 4\} = \{1, 2, 3, 4\}$

    (B) $\{x \mid x \in A \text{ and } x \in B\} = A \cap B$
    $= \{1, 2, 3\} \cap \{2, 3, 4\} = \{2, 3\}$

13. $u = \{2, 4, 5, 6, 8\}$, $M = \{2, 4, 5\}$, and $N = \{5, 6\}$

    (A) $M \cup N = \{2, 4, 5, 6\}$ (B) $M \cap N = \{5\}$

    (C) $(M \cup N)' = \{8\}$ (D) $M \cap N' = \{2, 4, 5\} \cap \{2, 4, 8\}$
    $= \{2, 4\}$

14. (A) $N \subset M$ is false (F)
    (B) $\emptyset \subset u$ is true (T)
    (C) $6 \notin M$ is true (T)
    (D) $5 \in N$ is true (T)

15. From the Venn diagram:

    (A) $M \cup N$ has $10 + 5 + 13 = 28$ elements
    (B) $M \cap N$ has 5 elements
    (C) $(M \cup N)'$ has 4 elements
    (D) $M \cap N'$ has 10 elements

16. Let u = the set of students in the sample (100),
    E = the set of students taking English (70),
    M = the set of students taking Math (45), and
    $E \cap M$ = the set of students taking English and Math (25).

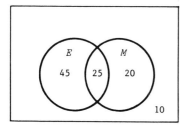

    (A) The number of students taking Engoish or Math is the number of
        elements in $E \cup M$, which is $45 + 25 + 20 = 90$.

    (B) The number of students taking English and not Math is the number of
        elements in $E \cap M'$, which is 45.

17. $\dfrac{x}{12} - \dfrac{x - 3}{3} = \dfrac{1}{2}$

    Multiply each term by 12: $x - 4(x - 3) = 6$
    $x - 4x + 12 = 6$
    $-3x = 6 - 12$
    $-3x = -6$
    $x = 2$

18. $1 - \dfrac{x-3}{3} \leqslant \dfrac{1}{2}$

Multiply both sides of the inequality by 6. We do not reverse the direction of the inequality, since $6 > 0$.

$$6 - 2(x - 3) \leqslant 3$$
$$6 - 2x + 6 \leqslant 3$$
$$-2x \leqslant 3 - 12$$
$$-2x \leqslant -9$$

Divide both sides by -2 and reverse the direction of the inequality, since $-2 < 0$.

$$x \geqslant \dfrac{9}{2} \quad \text{or} \quad \left[\dfrac{9}{2}, \infty\right)$$

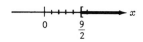

19. $-2 \leqslant \dfrac{x}{2} - 3 < 3$

$$-2 + 3 \leqslant \dfrac{x}{2} < 3 + 3$$

$$1 \leqslant \dfrac{x}{2} < 6$$

$$2 \leqslant x < 12 \quad \text{or} \quad [2, 12)$$

20. $2x - 3y = 6$
$$-3y = -2x + 6$$
$$y = \dfrac{2}{3}x - 2$$

21. $xy - y = 3$
$$y(x - 1) = 3$$
$$y = \dfrac{3}{x - 1}$$

22. $3x^2 - 21 = 0$
$x^2 - 7 = 0$ (solve by the
 square root method)
$$x^2 = 7$$
$$x = \pm\sqrt{7}$$

23. $x^2 - x - 20 = 0$ (solve by
 factoring)
$$(x - 5)(x + 4) = 0$$
$$x - 5 = 0 \quad \text{or} \quad x + 4 = 0$$
$$x = 5 \quad \text{or} \quad x = -4$$

24. $2x^2 = 3x + 1$
$2x^2 - 3x - 1 = 0$ (use the quadratic formula with $a = 2$, $b = -3$, $c = -1$)
$$x = \dfrac{-b \pm \sqrt{b^2 - 4ac}}{2a} = \dfrac{-(-3) \pm \sqrt{(-3)^2 - 4(2)(-1)}}{2(2)}$$
$$= \dfrac{3 \pm \sqrt{9 + 8}}{4} = \dfrac{3 \pm \sqrt{17}}{4}$$

25. $3x + 6y = 18$

To find the x intercept, set $y = 0$:

$$3x + 6(0) = 18$$
$$x = 6$$

To find the slope and the y intercept, rewrite the equation in the slope-intercept form:

$$6y = -3x + 18$$

$$y = -\frac{1}{2}x + 3$$

Thus, the slope $m = -1/2$ and the y intercept $b = 3$.

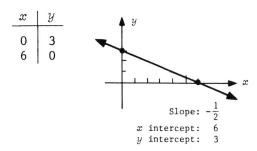

x	y
0	3
6	0

Slope: $-\frac{1}{2}$

x intercept: 6

y intercept: 3

26. Let $(x_1, y_1) = (-2, 3)$ and $(x_2, y_2) = (6, -1)$. The slope of the line is given by:

$$m = \frac{y_2 - y_1}{x_2 - x_1} = \frac{-1 - 3}{6 - (-2)} = -\frac{4}{8} = -\frac{1}{2}$$

Using the point-slope form, we have:

$$y - 3 = -\frac{1}{2}[x - (-2)]$$

$$y - 3 = -\frac{1}{2}(x + 2)$$

$$y - 3 = -\frac{1}{2}x - 1$$

$$y = -\frac{1}{2}x + 2$$

Rewriting this equation in the form $Ax + By = C$, we have:

$$2y = -x + 4 \quad \text{or} \quad x + 2y = 4$$

The slope of this line is $m = -\frac{1}{2}$.

27. Given the point P: $(-5, 2)$. The vertical line through P has equation $x = -5$. The horizontal line through P has equation $y = 2$.

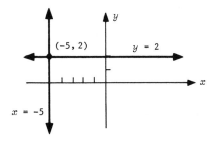

$(-5, 2)$ $y = 2$

$x = -5$

28. Let $(x_1, y_1) = (-2, 5)$ and $(x_2, y_2) = (2, -1)$. The slope of the line is given by:

$$m = \frac{y_2 - y_1}{x_2 - x_1} = \frac{-1 - 5}{2 - (-2)} = -\frac{6}{4} = -\frac{3}{2}$$

Using the point-slope form, we have:

$$y - 5 = -\frac{3}{2}[x - (-2)]$$

$$y - 5 = -\frac{3}{2}(x + 2)$$

$$y - 5 = -\frac{3}{2}x - 3$$

$$y = -\frac{3}{2}x + 2$$

29. $f(x) = 10x - 7$, $g(t) = 6 - 2t$, $F(u) = 3u^2$, and $G(v) = v - v^2$.

    (A) $\begin{aligned}[t] 2g(-1) - 3G(-1) &= 2[6 - 2(-1)] - 3[-1 - (-1)^2] \\ &= 2[6 + 2] - 3[-1 - 1] \\ &= 16 + 6 \\ &= 22 \end{aligned}$

    (B) $\begin{aligned}[t] 4G(-2) - g(-3) &= 4[-2 - (-2)^2] - [6 - 2(-3)] \\ &= 4[-6] - [12] \\ &= -24 - 12 \\ &= -36 \end{aligned}$

    (C) $\dfrac{f(2) \cdot g(-4)}{G(-1)} = \dfrac{[10(2) - 7] \cdot [6 - 2(-4)]}{-1 - (-1)^2} = \dfrac{(13)(14)}{-2} = -91$

    (D) $\dfrac{F(-1) \cdot G(2)}{g(-1)} = \dfrac{[3(-1)^2] \cdot [2 - (2)^2]}{6 - 2(-1)} = \dfrac{(3)(-2)}{8} = \dfrac{-6}{8} = \dfrac{-3}{4}$

30. $f(x) = \sqrt{x}$ and $g(x) = x^2 + 2x$.

    (A) $f[g(2)] = f[2^2 + 2(2)] = f[8] = \sqrt{8} = 2\sqrt{2}$

    (B) $g[f(a)] = g[\sqrt{a}] = (\sqrt{a})^2 + 2\sqrt{a} = a + 2\sqrt{a}$ $(a \geqslant 0)$

31. $f(x) = 2x - x^2$, $g(x) = \dfrac{1}{x - 2}$.

The domain of f is R—the set of real numbers.

The domain of g is all real numbers except $x = 2$; g is not defined at $x = 2$.

32. $g(x) = 8x - 2x^2$, $a = -2$, $b = 8$, $c = 0$.
The axis of symmetry is:

$$x = \frac{-b}{2a} = \frac{-8}{2(-2)} = 2$$

Since $a = -2 < 0$, the maximum value of g is:

$$g\left(\frac{-b}{2a}\right) = g(2) = 8(2) - 2(2)^2 = 8$$

The vertex is:

$$\left(\frac{-b}{2a},\ g\left(\frac{-b}{2a}\right)\right) = (2,\ 8)$$

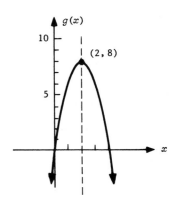

33. (A) $y = 10 \cdot 2^{3x}$, $-2 \leqslant x \leqslant 2$

x	y
-2	0.156
-1	1.25
0	10
1	80
2	640

(B) $y = 10 \cdot 2^{-3x}$, $-2 \leqslant x \leqslant 2$

x	y
-2	640
-1	80
0	10
1	1.25
2	0.156

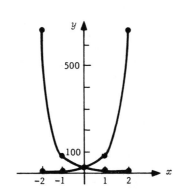

34. $y = 100e^{-0.1x}$

$0 \leqslant x \leqslant 10$

x	y
0	100
2	81.87
4	67.03
6	54.88
8	44.93
10	36.79

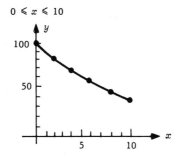

35. (A) $\log_b 9 = 2$

Therefore, $b^2 = 9$
and $b = 3$.

(B) $\log_4 x = -3$

Therefore, $x = 4^{-3} = 1/4^3$
or $x = 1/64$.

36. $\log_b(100 \cdot 1.06^t) = \log_b 100 + \log_b 1.06^t = \log_b 100 + t \log_b 1.06$

37. $\log_b x = 3\log_b 2 - \frac{3}{2}\log_b 4 - \frac{1}{2}\log_b 36 = \log_b 2^3 - \log_b 4^{3/2} - \log_b 36^{1/2}$
$= \log_b 8 - \log_b 8 - \log_b 6 = -\log_b 6 = \log_b 6^{-1}$

Therefore, $x = 6^{-1}$ or $x = 1/6$.

38. (A) $\log 0.0091085 = -2.04055$ (B) $\ln 9843.3 = 9.91455$

39. (A) $\log x = -3.8055$ (B) $\ln x = 12.8143$
       $x = 0.000156$ $x = 367,400$

40. $\ln x + \ln(x - 3) = \ln 28$
      $\ln x(x - 3) = \ln 28$

Therefore, $x(x - 3) = 28$ or $x^2 - 3x - 28 = 0$.

$(x - 7)(x + 4) = 0$

Thus, $x - 7 = 0$ or $x + 4 = 0$
        $x = 7$ or $x = -4$.

The solution is $x = 7$; -4 is not a solution since $\ln(-4)$ and $\ln(-7)$ are not defined.

41. Yes. If $A \not\subset B$, then there is at least one $x \in A$ such that $x \notin B$. Since $x \notin B$, $x \notin A \cap B$. Thus, we have $x \in A$ and $x \notin A \cap B$, and so $A \neq A \cap B$.

42. $x^2 + jx + k = 0$. Using the quadratic formula with $a = 1$, $b = j$, $c = k$, we have:

$$x = \frac{-j \pm \sqrt{j^2 - 4(1)(k)}}{2} = \frac{-j \pm \sqrt{j^2 - 4k}}{2}$$

43. Since both points have the same x-coordinate, the line is vertical. Therefore, the equation is $x = 4$.

44. Given the line L with equation $2x - 4y = 5$. Rewriting this equation in the slope-intercept form, we have:

$$-4y = -2x + 5$$
$$y = \frac{1}{2}x - \frac{5}{4}$$

Therefore, the slope of L is $m = 1/2$.

(A) Any line parallel to L has slope $m = 1/2$. Using the point-slope form, an equation for the line which is parallel to L and passes through $(2, -3)$ is:

$$y - (-3) = \frac{1}{2}(x - 2)$$
$$y + 3 = \frac{1}{2}x - 1$$
$$y = \frac{1}{2}x - 4$$
$$2y = x - 8$$
    or
$$x - 2y = 8$$

(B) Any line perpendicular to L has slope $m = (-1)/(1/2) = -2$. Using the point-slope form, an equation for the line which is perpendicular to L and passes through $(2, -3)$ is:

$$y + 3 = -2(x - 2)$$
$$y + 3 = -2x + 4$$
or
$$2x + y = 1$$

45. $f(x) = \dfrac{5}{x - 3}$ and $g(x) = \sqrt{x - 1}$.

The domain of f is all real numbers except $x = 3$; f is not defined at $x = 3$.

The domain of g is all real numbers such that $x - 1 \geqslant 0$, that is, all real numbers x such that $x \geqslant 1$.

46. $f(x) = 2x - 1$.

$$\frac{f(3 + h) - f(3)}{h} = \frac{[2(3 + h) - 1] - [2(3) - 1]}{h}$$

$$= \frac{[6 + 2h - 1] - [6 - 1]}{h} = \frac{5 + 2h - 5}{h} = \frac{2h}{h} = 2$$

47. Given $240 = 80e^{0.12t}$.

Then $e^{0.12t} = \dfrac{240}{80} = 3$

and $\quad 0.12t = \ln 3$

$$t = \frac{\ln 3}{0.12} \approx 9.15$$

48. $\ln y - \ln c = -0.2x$

$$\ln\left(\frac{y}{c}\right) = -0.2x$$

$$\frac{y}{c} = e^{-0.2x}$$

$$y = ce^{-0.2x}$$

49. Let C = the number of students who smoked (550)
and A = the number of students who drank alcoholic beverages (820).

Then, $C \cap A = 470$ students who did both.

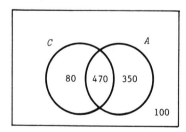

(A) The number of students who smoked or drank is the number of elements in $C \cup A$, which is $80 + 470 + 350 = 900$.

(B) The number of students who drank but did not smoke is the number of elements in $A \cap C'$, which is 350.

50. Let x = the amount invested at 8%. Then $60,000 - x$ = amount invested at 14%. The interest on \$60,000 at 12% for one year is:

$$0.12 \cdot 60,000 = 7200$$

Thus, we want

$$
\begin{aligned}
0.08x + 0.14(60,000 - x) &= 7200 \\
0.08x + 8400 - 0.14x &= 7200 \\
-0.06x &= -1200 \\
x &= 20,000.
\end{aligned}
$$

Therefore, \$20,000 should be invested at 8% and \$40,000 should be invested at 14%.

51. $\dfrac{x}{800} = \dfrac{247}{89}$. Thus, $89x = (247)(800) = 197,600$ and $x = \$2,220.22$.

52. In the formula $A = P(1 + r)^2$, set $A = 1210$ and $P = 1000$. This yields

$$1000(1 + r)^2 = 1210.$$

Therefore, $(1 + r)^2 = \dfrac{1210}{1000} = 1.21$. Thus, $1 + r = \pm\sqrt{1.21} = \pm 1.1$
and $r = 0.1$ or -2.1.

Since the interest rate r cannot be negative, $r = 0.1$ or $r = 10\%$.

53. We have $V = 12,000$ when $t = 0$ and $V = 2000$ when $t = 8$.

(A) We are looking for an equation for the line determined by the two points $(0, 12,000)$, $(8, 2000)$. The slope of this line is given by:

$$m = \frac{2000 - 12,000}{8 - 0} = \frac{-10,000}{8} = -1250.$$

Since $V = 12,000$ is the V intercept, the linear equation is $V(t) = -1250t + 12,000$.

(B) The value of the system after five years is:

$$V(5) = -1250(5) + 12,000 = -6250 + 12,000 = \$5750.$$

54. (A) We are looking for an equation for the line determined by the two points $(20, 32)$ and $(30, 48)$. The slope of this line is given by:

$$m = \frac{48 - 32}{30 - 20} = \frac{16}{10} = \frac{8}{5}.$$

Using the point-slope form with $(R_1, C_1) = (20, 32)$, we have:

$$R - 32 = \frac{8}{5}(C - 20) = \frac{8}{5}C - 32.$$

Thus, $R = \dfrac{8}{5} C$.

(B) For $C = 105$, we have: $R = \dfrac{8}{5}(105) = 8(21) = \$168$.

55.

Since $\ell + 2x = 20$, we have $\ell = 20 - 2x$ for the length of the rectangle.

(A) The area A of the rectangle is given by:

$A = \ell \cdot w = (20 - 2x)x$.

Thus, $A(x) = x(20 - 2x)$.

(B) Since the length and the width of the rectangle must be positive, we have:

$x > 0$ and $20 - 2x > 0$

$-2x > -20$ (divide by -2 and reverse the direction

$x < 10$ of the inequality)

Thus, $0 < x < 10$ or $(0, 10)$.

(C)

x	$A(x)$
2	32
4	48
5	50
6	48
8	32

56. $A = P(1 + r)^t$.

To find the tripling time, set $A = 3P$. Then, for $r = 0.15$, we have:

$3P = P(1 + 0.15)^t$ or $(1.15)^t = 3$.

Thus, $\ln(1.15) = \ln 3$ or $t \ln(1.15) = \ln 3$ and

$t = \dfrac{\ln 3}{\ln 1.15} \approx \dfrac{1.0986}{0.1398} = 7.9$.

Therefore, the tripling time is eight years.

57. $A = Pe^{rt}$.

To find the doubling time, set $A = 2P$. Then, for $r = 0.1$, we have:

$2P = Pe^{0.1t}$ or $e^{0.1t} = 2$.

Thus, $0.1t = \ln 2$ and

$t = \dfrac{\ln 2}{0.1} \approx 6.93$.

The doubling time is approximately 6.93 years.

CHAPTER 1   SYSTEMS OF LINEAR EQUATIONS; MATRICES

Things to remember:

1.   The system of two linear equations in two unknowns

$$ax + by = h$$
$$cx + dy = k$$

can be solved by:

(a)   graphing;
(b)   substitution;
(c)   elimination by addition.

2.   In general, a system of linear equations has either:

(a)   a unique solution;
(b)   infinitely many solutions;
(c)   no solutions.

In case (c), the system is said to be INCONSISTENT; in case (b), the system is said to be DEPENDENT.

3.   Two systems of linear equations are EQUIVALENT if they have exactly the same solution set. A system of linear equations is transformed into an equivalent system if:

(a)   two equations are interchanged;
(b)   an equation is multiplied by a nonzero constant;
(c)   a constant multiple of one equation is added to another equation.

$(4.)$ A linear system in three variables such as

$$a_1 x + b_1 y + c_1 z = k_1$$
$$a_2 x + b_2 y + c_2 z = k_2$$
$$a_3 x + b_3 y + c_3 z = k_3$$

may be solved by using Steps 1-4.

STEP 1. Choose two equations from the system and eliminate one of the three variables using elimination by addition. The result is generally one equation in two unknowns.

STEP 2. Now eliminate the same variable from the unused equation and one of those used in Step 1. We generally obtain another equation in two unknowns.

STEP 3. The two equations from Steps 1 and 2 form a system of two equations and two unknowns. Solve using one of the methods in 1.

STEP 4. Substitute the solution from Step 3 into any of the three original equations and solve for the third variable to complete the solution of the original system.

---

1. $x + y = 5$
    $x - y = 1$

    Point of intersection: $(3, 2)$

    Solution: $x = 3$
    $y = 2$

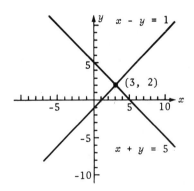

3. $3x - y = 2$
    $x + 2y = 10$

    Point of intersection: $(2, 4)$

    Solution: $x = 2$
    $y = 4$

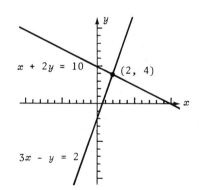

5. $m + 2n = 4$
    $2m + 4n = -8$

Since the graphs of the given equations are parallel lines, there is no solution.

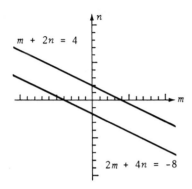

7. $y = 2x - 3$ (1)

    $y = -\dfrac{x}{2} + 7$ (2)

By substituting y from (1) into (2), we get:

$$2x - 3 = -\frac{x}{2} + 7$$

$$2x + \frac{x}{2} = 10$$

$$\frac{5}{2}x = 10$$

$$x = 4$$

Now, substituting $x = 4$ into (1), we have:

$y = 2(4) - 3$
$y = 5$

Solution: $x = 4$
           $y = 5$

9. $2x + y = 6$ (1)
    $x - y = -3$ (2)

Solve (2) for y to obtain the system

$2x + y = 6$ (3)
$\quad y = x + 3$ (4)

Substitute y from (4) into (3):

$2x + x + 3 = 6$
$\quad\quad 3x = 3$
$\quad\quad\; x = 1$

Now, substituting $x = 1$ into (4), we get:

$y = 1 + 3$
$y = 4$

Solution: $x = 1$
           $y = 4$

11. $3u - 2v = 12$ (1)
     $7u + 2v = 8$ (2)

Add (1) and (2):

$10u = 20$
$\;\; u = 2$

Substituting $u = 2$ into (2), we get:

$7(2) + 2v = 8$
$\quad\quad 2v = -6$
$\quad\quad\; v = -3$

Solution: $u = 2$
           $v = -3$

13. $2m - n = 10$ (1)
$m - 2n = -4$ (2)

Multiply (1) by -2 and add to
(1) to obtain:

$-3m = -24$
$m = 8$

Substituting $m = 8$ into (1),
we get:

$8 - 2n = -4$
$-2n = -12$
$n = 6$

Solution: $m = 8$
$n = 6$

15. $9x - 3y = 24$ (1)
$11x + 2y = 1$ (2)

Solve (1) for y to obtain

$y = 3x - 8$ (3)

and substitute into (2):

$11x + 2(3x - 8) = 1$
$11x + 6x - 16 = 1$
$17x = 17$
$x = 1$

Now, substitute $x = 1$ into (3):

$y = 3(1) - 8$
$y = -5$

Solution: $x = 1$
$y = -5$

17. $2x - 3y = -2$ (1)
$-4x + 6y = 7$ (2)

Multiply (1) by 2 and add to
(2) to get:

$0 = 3$

This implies that the system
is inconsistent, and thus there
is no solution.

19. $3x + 8y = 4$ (1)
$15x + 10y = -10$ (2)

Multiply (1) by -5 and add to (2)
to get:

$-30y = -30$
$y = 1$

Substituting $y = 1$ into (1), we
get:

$3x + 8(1) = 4$
$3x = -4$
$x = -\dfrac{4}{3}$

Solution: $x = -\dfrac{4}{3}$
$y = 1$

21. $-6x + 10y = -30$ (1)
$3x - 5y = 15$ (2)

Multiply (2) by 2 and add to (1). This yields

$0 = 0$

which implies that (1) and (2) are equivalent equations and there are
infinitely many solutions. Geometrically, the two lines are coincident.
The system is dependent.

44

23. $y = 0.07x$ (1)
$y = 80 + 0.05x$ (2)

Substitute y from (1) into (2):

$0.07x = 80 + 0.05x$
$0.02x = 80$
$x = \dfrac{80}{0.02}$
$x = 4000$

Next, by substituting $x = 4000$ into (1), we get:

$y = 0.07(4000) = 280$

Solution: $x = 4000$; $y = 280$

25. $0.2x - 0.5y = 0.07$ (1)
$0.8x - 0.3y = 0.79$ (2)

Clear the decimals from (1) and (2) by multiplying each equation by 10.

$20x - 50y = 7$ (3)
$80x - 30y = 79$ (4)

Multiply (3) by -4 and add to (4) to get:

$-170y = -51$
$y = \dfrac{-51}{-170}$
$y = 0.3$

Now, substitute $y = 0.3$ into (1):

$0.2x - 0.5(0.3) = 0.7$
$0.2x - 0.15 = 0.7$
$0.2x = 0.22$
$x = 1.1$

Solution: $x = 1.1$
$y = 0.3$

27. $4y - z = -13$ (1)
$3y + 2z = 4$ (2)
$6x - 5y - 2z = 0$ (3)

First, solve (1) and (2) for y and z. Multiply (1) by 2 and add to (2) to get:

$11y = -22$
$y = -2$

By substituting $y = -2$ in (2), we obtain:

$-6 + 2z = 4$
$z = 5$

Now substitute $y = -2$ and $z = 5$ in (3):

$6x - 5(-2) - 2(5) = 0$
$6x + 10 - 10 = 0$
$6x = 0$
$x = 0$

Thus, the solution is: $x = 0$
$y = -2$
$z = 5$

29. $2x + y - z = 5$ (1)
$x - 2y - 2z = 4$ (2)
$3x + 4y + 3z = 3$ (3)

First, eliminate z from (1) and (2). Multiply (1) by -2 and add to (2) to get:

$-3x - 4y = -6$

or

$3x + 4y = 6$ (4)

Next, eliminate z from (1) and (3). Multiply (1) by 3 and add to (3) to get:

$9x + 7y = 18$ (5)

Finally, eliminate x from (4) and (5). Multiply (4) by -3 and add to (5) to get:

$-5y = 0$
$y = 0$

Substitute $y = 0$ in (4): $3x = 6$
$x = 2$

Substitute $y = 0$ and $x = 2$ in (1): $2(2) + 0 - z = 5$
$4 - z = 5$
$-z = 1$
$z = -1$

Thus, the solution is: $x = 2$; $y = 0$; $z = -1$

31. $2a + 4b + 3c = 6$ (1)
     $a - 3b + 2c = -7$ (2)
  $-a + 2b - c = 5$ (3)

First, eliminate c from (1) and (3). Multiply (3) by 3 and add to (1) to get:

$-a + 10b = 21$ (4)

Next, eliminate c from (2) and (3). Multiply (3) by 2 and add to (2) to get:

$-a + b = 3$ (5)

Finally, eliminate a from (4) and (5). Multiply (5) by -1 and add to (4) to get:

$9b = 18$
$b = 2$

Substitute $b = 2$ in (4);

$-a + 20 = 21$
$a = -1$

Substitute $b = 2$ and $a = -1$ in (1):

$-2 + 8 + 3c = 6$
$3c = 0$
$c = 0$

Thus, the solution is: $a = -1$; $b = 2$; $c = 0$

33. $2x - 3y + 3z = -15$ (1)
     $3x + 2y - 5z = 19$ (2)
     $5x - 4y - 2z = -2$ (3)

First, eliminate x from (1) and (2). Multiply (1) by 3 and (2) by -2 and add to get:

$$3(2x - 3y + 3z) - 2(3x + 2y - 5z) = -45 - 38$$

or

$$-13y + 19z = -83 \qquad (4)$$

Then eliminate x from (1) and (3). Multiply (1) by 5 and (3) by -2 and add to get:

$$5(2x - 3y + 3z) - 2(5x - 4y - 2z) = -75 + 4$$

or

$$-7y + 19z = -71 \qquad (5)$$

Now, eliminate z from (4) and (5). Multiply (5) by -1 and add to (4) to get:

$$-6y = -12$$
$$y = 2$$

Substitute $y = 2$ in (4):

$$-26 + 19z = -83$$
$$19z = -57$$
$$z = -3$$

Substitute $y = 2$ and $z = -3$ in (1):

$$2x - 6 - 9 = -15$$
$$2x = 0$$
$$x = 0$$

Thus, the solution is: $x = 0$; $y = 2$; $z = -3$

35. $x - 8y + 2z = -1$ (1)
     $x - 3y + z = 1$ (2)
     $2x - 11y + 3z = 2$ (3)

Eliminate x from (1) and (2). Multiply (1) by -1 and add to (2) to get:

$$5y - z = 2 \qquad (4)$$

Eliminate x from (1) and (3). Multiply (1) by -2 and add to (3) to get:

$$5y - z = 4 \qquad (5)$$

Eliminate z from (4) and (5). Multiply (4) by -1 and add to (5) to get:

$$0 = 2$$

This implies that the given system is inconsistent and, hence, there is no solution.

37. (A)
$$p = 0.7q + 3 \quad (1)$$
$$p = -1.7q + 15 \quad (2)$$

Solve the above system for equilibrium price p and the equilibrium quantity q.

$$0.7q + 3 = -1.7q + 15$$
$$0.7q + 1.7q = 15 - 3$$
$$2.4q = 12$$
$$q = \frac{12}{2.4}$$
$$q = 5 \quad \text{(5 hundreds or 500)}$$

Equilibrium quantity $q = 5$.

Substitute $q = 5$ in (1):

$$p = 0.7(5) + 3$$
$$p = 3.5 + 3$$
$$p = 6.50$$

Equilibrium price $p = \$6.50$.

(B)

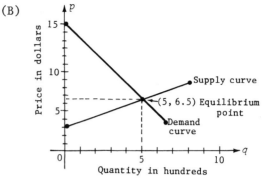

39. (A) The company breaks even when:

$$\text{Cost} = \text{Revenue}$$

$$48{,}000 + 1400x = 1800x$$
$$48{,}000 = 1800x - 1400x$$
or
$$400x = 48{,}000$$
$$x = \frac{48{,}000}{400}$$
$$x = 120$$

Thus, 120 units must be manufactured and sold to break even.

$$\text{Cost} = 48{,}000 + 1400(120)$$
$$= \$216{,}000$$

(B)

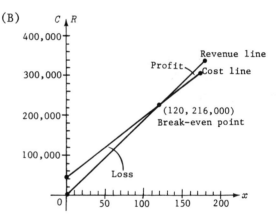

41. Let x = number of one-person boats;
y = number of two-person boats;
z = number of three-person boats.

We wish to solve the following system of linear equations:

$$0.6x + \quad y + 1.5z = 380$$
$$0.6x + 0.9y + 1.2z = 330$$
$$0.2x + 0.3y + 0.5z = 120$$

Clear the system of decimals by multiplying each side of each equation by 10. This produces the equivalent system:

$$6x + 10y + 15z = 3800 \quad (1)$$
$$6x + 9y + 12z = 3300 \quad (2)$$
$$2x + 3y + 5z = 1200 \quad (3)$$

Eliminate x from (1) and (2). Multiply (2) by -1 and add to (1) to get:

$y + 3z = 500$ (4)

Eliminate x from (1) and (3). Multiply (3) by -3 and add to (1) to get:

$y = 200$

Substituting $y = 200$ in (4), we get: $200 + 3z = 500$

$$3z = 300$$
$$z = 100$$

Finally, substituting $y = 200$ and $z = 100$ in (1), we get:

$6x + 10(200) + 15(100) = 3800$

$$6x = 300$$
$$x = 50$$

Thus, the solution is: $x = 50$ one-person boats
$y = 200$ two-person boats
$z = 100$ three-person boats

43. Let x = amount of mix A, and
y = amount of mix B.

We wish to solve the following system of equations:

$0.1x + 0.2y = 20$ (1)
$0.06x + 0.02y = 6$ (2)

Clear the decimals from (1) and (2) by multiplying both sides of (1) by 10 and both sides of (2) by 100.

$x + 2y = 200$ (3)
$6x + 2y = 600$ (4)

Multiply (3) by -1 and add to (4):

$5x = 400$
$x = 80$

Now substitute $x = 80$ into (3): $80 + 2y = 200$

$$2y = 120$$
$$y = 60$$

Solution: x = mix A = 80 grams
y = mix B = 60 grams

45. $p = -\dfrac{1}{5}d + 70$ (1)

$30 \leqslant d \leqslant 175$

$a = -\dfrac{4}{3}d + 230$ (2)

(A) The figure shows the graphs of equations (1) and (2).

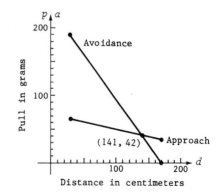

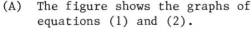
Distance in centimeters

(B) When $p = a$, we have:

$$-\frac{1}{5}d + 70 = -\frac{4}{3}d + 230$$

$$-\frac{1}{5}d + \frac{4}{3}d = 230 - 70$$

$$\frac{17}{15}d = 160$$

$$d = 141 \text{ cm (approx.)}$$

(C) The rat is very confused (!) and vascillates between the two boxes when they are placed 141 cm away.

EXERCISE 1-2

Things to remember:

1. A system of linear equations is transformed into an equivalent system if:

    (a) two equations are interchanged;
    (b) an equation is multiplied by a nonzero constant;
    (c) a constant multiple of one equation is added to another equation.

2. Associated with the linear system

$$\begin{array}{l} a_1 x_1 + b_1 y_1 = k_1 \\ a_2 x_1 + b_2 y_1 = k_2 \end{array} \qquad \text{(I)}$$

2 variable 2 equation system

    is the AUGMENTED MATRIX of the system

$$\begin{bmatrix} a_1 & b_1 & \Big| & k_1 \\ a_2 & b_2 & \Big| & k_2 \end{bmatrix}. \qquad \text{(II)}$$

3. An augmented matrix is transformed into a row-equivalent matrix if:

    (a) two rows are interchanged ($R_i \leftrightarrow R_j$);
    (b) a row is multiplied by a nonzero constant ($kR_i \rightarrow R_i$);
    (c) a constant multiple of one row is added to another row ($R_i + kR_j \rightarrow R_i$).

    (Note: The arrow $\rightarrow$ means "replaces.")

4. Given the system of linear equations (I) and its associated augmented matrix (II). If (II) is row equivalent to a matrix of the form:

$$(1) \begin{bmatrix} 1 & 0 & | & m \\ 0 & 1 & | & n \end{bmatrix}, \text{ then (I) has a unique solution;}$$

$$(2) \begin{bmatrix} 1 & m & | & n \\ 0 & 0 & | & 0 \end{bmatrix}, \text{ then (I) has infinitely many solutions (dependent);}$$

$$(3) \begin{bmatrix} 1 & m & | & n \\ 0 & 0 & | & p \end{bmatrix}, p \neq 0, \text{ then (I) has no solution (inconsistent).}$$

---

1. Interchange row 1 and row 2.

$$\begin{bmatrix} 4 & -6 & | & -8 \\ 1 & -3 & | & 2 \end{bmatrix}$$

3. Multiply row 1 by -4.

$$\begin{bmatrix} -4 & 12 & | & -8 \\ 4 & -6 & | & -8 \end{bmatrix}$$

5. Multiply row 2 by 2.

$$\begin{bmatrix} 1 & -3 & | & 2 \\ 8 & -12 & | & -16 \end{bmatrix}$$

7. Replace row 2 by the sum of row 2 and -4 times row 1.

$$\begin{bmatrix} 1 & -3 & | & 2 \\ 0 & 6 & | & -16 \end{bmatrix}$$

9. Replace row 2 by the sum of row 2 and -2 times row 1.

$$\begin{bmatrix} 1 & -3 & | & 2 \\ 2 & 0 & | & -12 \end{bmatrix}$$

11. Replace row 2 by the sum of row 2 and -1 times row 1.

$$\begin{bmatrix} 1 & -3 & | & 2 \\ 3 & -3 & | & -10 \end{bmatrix}$$

13. The corresponding augmented matrix is:

$$\begin{bmatrix} 1 & 1 & | & 5 \\ 1 & -1 & | & 1 \end{bmatrix} \sim \begin{bmatrix} 1 & 1 & | & 5 \\ 0 & -2 & | & -4 \end{bmatrix} \sim \begin{bmatrix} 1 & 1 & | & 5 \\ 0 & 1 & | & 2 \end{bmatrix} \sim \begin{bmatrix} 1 & 0 & | & 3 \\ 0 & 1 & | & 2 \end{bmatrix}$$

Thus, $x_1 = 3$ and $x_2 = 2$.

$$R_2 + (-1)R_1 \rightarrow R_2 \quad -\frac{1}{2}R_2 \rightarrow R_2 \quad R_1 + (-1)R_2 \rightarrow R_1$$

15.

$$\begin{bmatrix} 1 & -2 & | & 1 \\ 2 & -1 & | & 5 \end{bmatrix} \sim \begin{bmatrix} 1 & -2 & | & 1 \\ 0 & 3 & | & 3 \end{bmatrix} \sim \begin{bmatrix} 1 & -2 & | & 1 \\ 0 & 1 & | & 1 \end{bmatrix} \sim \begin{bmatrix} 1 & 0 & | & 3 \\ 0 & 1 & | & 1 \end{bmatrix}$$

Thus, $x_1 = 3$ and $x_2 = 1$.

$$R_2 + (-2)R_1 \rightarrow R_2 \quad \frac{1}{3}R_2 \rightarrow R_2 \quad R_1 + 2R_2 \rightarrow R_1$$

17.

$$\begin{bmatrix} 1 & -4 & | & -2 \\ -2 & 1 & | & -3 \end{bmatrix} \sim \begin{bmatrix} 1 & -4 & | & -2 \\ 0 & -7 & | & -7 \end{bmatrix} \sim \begin{bmatrix} 1 & -4 & | & -2 \\ 0 & 1 & | & 1 \end{bmatrix} \sim \begin{bmatrix} 1 & 0 & | & 2 \\ 0 & 1 & | & 1 \end{bmatrix}$$

Thus, $x_1 = 2$ and $x_2 = 1$.

$$R_2 + 2R_1 \rightarrow R_2 \quad -\frac{1}{7}R_2 \rightarrow R_2 \quad R_1 + 4R_2 \rightarrow R_1$$

19.
$$\begin{bmatrix} 3 & -1 & | & 2 \\ 1 & 2 & | & 10 \end{bmatrix} \sim \begin{bmatrix} 1 & 2 & | & 10 \\ 3 & -1 & | & 2 \end{bmatrix} \sim \begin{bmatrix} 1 & 2 & | & 10 \\ 0 & -7 & | & -28 \end{bmatrix} \sim \begin{bmatrix} 1 & 2 & | & 10 \\ 0 & 1 & | & 4 \end{bmatrix}$$

$\quad R_1 \leftrightarrow R_2 \qquad R_2 + (-3)R_1 \rightarrow R_2 \quad -\frac{1}{7}R_2 \rightarrow R_2 \quad R_1 + (-2)R_2 \rightarrow R_1$

$$\sim \begin{bmatrix} 1 & 0 & | & 2 \\ 0 & 1 & | & 4 \end{bmatrix} \qquad \text{Thus, } x_1 = 2 \text{ and } x_2 = 4.$$

21.
$$\begin{bmatrix} 1 & 2 & | & 4 \\ 2 & 4 & | & -8 \end{bmatrix} \sim \begin{bmatrix} 1 & 2 & | & 4 \\ 0 & 0 & | & -16 \end{bmatrix} \qquad \text{From } \underline{4}, \text{ Form (3), the system is inconsistent; there is no solution.}$$

$\quad R_2 + (-2)R_1 \rightarrow R_2$

23.
$$\begin{bmatrix} 2 & 1 & | & 6 \\ 1 & -1 & | & -3 \end{bmatrix} \sim \begin{bmatrix} 1 & -1 & | & -3 \\ 2 & 1 & | & 6 \end{bmatrix} \sim \begin{bmatrix} 1 & -1 & | & -3 \\ 0 & 3 & | & 12 \end{bmatrix} \sim \begin{bmatrix} 1 & -1 & | & -3 \\ 0 & 1 & | & 4 \end{bmatrix}$$

$\quad R_1 \leftrightarrow R_2 \quad R_2 + (-2)R_1 \rightarrow R_2 \quad \frac{1}{3}R_2 \rightarrow R_2 \qquad R_1 + R_2 \rightarrow R_1$

$$\sim \begin{bmatrix} 1 & 0 & | & 1 \\ 0 & 1 & | & 4 \end{bmatrix} \qquad \text{Thus, } x_1 = 1 \text{ and } x_2 = 4.$$

25.
$$\begin{bmatrix} 3 & -6 & | & -9 \\ -2 & 4 & | & 6 \end{bmatrix} \sim \begin{bmatrix} 1 & -2 & | & -3 \\ -2 & 4 & | & 6 \end{bmatrix} \sim \begin{bmatrix} 1 & -2 & | & -3 \\ 0 & 0 & | & 0 \end{bmatrix}$$

$\quad \frac{1}{3}R_1 \rightarrow R_1 \qquad R_2 + 2R_1 \rightarrow R_1$

From $\underline{4}$, Form (2), the system has infinitely many solutions (dependent). If $x_2 = s$, then $x_1 - 2s = -3$ or $x_1 = 2s - 3$. Thus, $x_2 = s$, $x_1 = 2s - 3$, for any real number s, are the solutions.

27.
$$\begin{bmatrix} 4 & -2 & | & 2 \\ -6 & 3 & | & -3 \end{bmatrix} \sim \begin{bmatrix} 1 & -\frac{1}{2} & | & \frac{1}{2} \\ -6 & 3 & | & -3 \end{bmatrix} \sim \begin{bmatrix} 1 & -\frac{1}{2} & | & \frac{1}{2} \\ 0 & 0 & | & 0 \end{bmatrix}$$

$\quad \frac{1}{4}R_1 \rightarrow R_1 \qquad R_2 + 6R_1 \rightarrow R_1$

Thus, the system has infinitely many solutions (dependent). Let $x_2 = s$. Then

$$x_1 - \frac{1}{2}s = \frac{1}{2} \quad \text{or} \quad x_1 = \frac{1}{2}s + \frac{1}{2}.$$

The set of solutions is $x_1 = \frac{1}{2}s + \frac{1}{2}$, $x_2 = s$ for any real number s.

29.
$$\begin{bmatrix} 3 & -1 & | & 7 \\ 2 & 3 & | & 1 \end{bmatrix} \sim \begin{bmatrix} 1 & -\dfrac{1}{3} & | & \dfrac{7}{3} \\ 2 & 3 & | & 1 \end{bmatrix} \sim \begin{bmatrix} 1 & -\dfrac{1}{3} & | & \dfrac{7}{3} \\ 0 & \dfrac{11}{3} & | & -\dfrac{11}{3} \end{bmatrix} \sim \begin{bmatrix} 1 & -\dfrac{1}{3} & | & \dfrac{7}{3} \\ 0 & 1 & | & -1 \end{bmatrix}$$

$\dfrac{1}{3}R_1 \to R_1 \qquad R_2 + (-2)R_1 \to R_2 \qquad \dfrac{3}{11}R_2 \to R_2 \qquad R_1 + \dfrac{1}{3}R_2 \to R_1$

$$\sim \begin{bmatrix} 1 & 0 & | & 2 \\ 0 & 1 & | & -1 \end{bmatrix} \qquad \text{Thus, } x_1 = 2 \text{ and } x_2 = -1.$$

31.
$$\begin{bmatrix} 3 & 2 & | & 4 \\ 2 & -1 & | & 5 \end{bmatrix} \sim \begin{bmatrix} 1 & \dfrac{2}{3} & | & \dfrac{4}{3} \\ 2 & -1 & | & 5 \end{bmatrix} \sim \begin{bmatrix} 1 & \dfrac{2}{3} & | & \dfrac{4}{3} \\ 0 & -\dfrac{7}{3} & | & \dfrac{7}{3} \end{bmatrix} \sim \begin{bmatrix} 1 & \dfrac{2}{3} & | & \dfrac{4}{3} \\ 0 & 1 & | & -1 \end{bmatrix}$$

$\dfrac{1}{3}R_1 \to R_1 \qquad R_2 + (-2)R_1 \to R_2 \qquad -\dfrac{3}{7}R_2 \to R_2 \qquad R_1 + \left(-\dfrac{2}{3}\right)R_2 \to R_1$

$$\sim \begin{bmatrix} 1 & 0 & | & 2 \\ 0 & 1 & | & -1 \end{bmatrix} \qquad \text{Thus, } x_1 = 2 \text{ and } x_2 = -1.$$

33.
$$\begin{bmatrix} 0.2 & -0.5 & | & 0.07 \\ 0.8 & -0.3 & | & 0.79 \end{bmatrix} \sim \begin{bmatrix} 1 & -2.5 & | & 0.35 \\ 0.8 & -0.3 & | & 0.79 \end{bmatrix} \sim \begin{bmatrix} 1 & -2.5 & | & 0.35 \\ 0 & 1.7 & | & 0.51 \end{bmatrix}$$

$\dfrac{1}{0.2}R_1 \to R_1 \qquad\qquad R_2 + (-0.8)R_1 \to R_2 \qquad \dfrac{1}{1.7}R_2 \to R_2$

$$\sim \begin{bmatrix} 1 & -2.5 & | & 0.35 \\ 0 & 1 & | & 0.3 \end{bmatrix} \sim \begin{bmatrix} 1 & 0 & | & 1.1 \\ 0 & 1 & | & 0.3 \end{bmatrix} \qquad \text{Thus, } x_1 = 1.1 \text{ and } x_2 = 0.3.$$

$R_1 + 2.5R_2 \to R_1$

EXERCISE 1-3

Things to remember:

1. A matrix is in REDUCED FORM if

   (a) each row consisting entirely of zeros is below any row having at least one nonzero element;

   (b) the left-most nonzero element in each row is 1;

   (c) the column containing the left-most 1 of a given row has zeros above and below the 1;

   (d) the left-most 1 in any row is to the right of the left-most 1 in the row above.

2. GAUSS–JORDAN ELIMINATION

(a) Choose the left-most nonzero column and use appropriate row operations to get a 1 at the top.

(b) Use multiples of the first row to get zeros in all places below the 1 obtained in part (a).

(c) Delete (mentally) the top row and first nonzero column of the matrix. Repeat parts (a)-(c) with the submatrix (the matrix remaining after deleting the top row and first nonzero column). Continue the process given above until it is not possible to go further.

(d) Consider the whole matrix that is obtained after returning all of the rows mentally deleted in the process given above. Begin with the bottom nonzero row and use appropriate multiples of it to get zeros above the left-most 1. Continue this process, moving up row by row until the matrix is finally in reduced form.

Note: If at any point in this process we obtain a row with all zeros to the left of the vertical line and a nonzero number to the right, then we can stop, since we will have a contradiction ($0 = n$, $n \neq 0$). We can conclude that the system has no solution.

---

1. $\begin{bmatrix} 1 & 0 & | & 2 \\ 0 & 1 & | & -1 \end{bmatrix}$

Is in reduced form. Use $\underline{1}$.

3. $\begin{bmatrix} 1 & 0 & 2 & | & 3 \\ 0 & 0 & 0 & | & 0 \\ 0 & 1 & -1 & | & 4 \end{bmatrix}$

is not in reduced form. Condition (a) has been violated. The second row should be at the bottom.

5. $\begin{bmatrix} 0 & 1 & 0 & | & 2 \\ 0 & 0 & 3 & | & -1 \\ 0 & 0 & 0 & | & 0 \end{bmatrix}$

is not in reduced form. Condition (b) has been violated. The left-most nonzero element in the second row should be 1, not 3.

7. $\begin{bmatrix} 1 & 2 & 0 & 3 & | & 1 \\ 0 & 0 & 1 & -1 & | & 0 \end{bmatrix}$

is in reduced form.

9.
$$x_1 \quad\quad = -2$$
$$x_2 \quad\ = 3$$
$$x_3 = 0$$

11.
$$x_1 \quad - 2x_3 = 3 \quad (1)$$
$$x_2 + \ x_3 = -5 \quad (2)$$

Let $x_3 = t$. From (2), $x_2 = -5 - t$. From (1), $x_1 = 3 + 2t$. Thus, the solution is

$$x_1 = 2t + 3$$
$$x_2 = -t - 5$$
$$x_3 = t$$

t any real number.

13.
$$x_1 \quad\ = 0$$
$$x_2 \ = 0$$
$$0 = 1$$

Inconsistent; no solution.

15.
$$x_1 - 2x_2 \quad - 3x_4 = -5$$
$$x_3 + 3x_4 = 2$$

Let $x_2 = s$ and $x_4 = t$. Then

$$x_1 = 2s + 3t - 5$$
$$x_2 = s$$
$$x_3 = -3t + 2$$
$$x_4 = t$$

s and t any real numbers.

17.
$$\begin{bmatrix} 1 & 2 & | & -1 \\ 0 & 1 & | & 3 \end{bmatrix} \sim \begin{bmatrix} 1 & 0 & | & -7 \\ 0 & 1 & | & 3 \end{bmatrix}$$

$R_1 + (-2)R_2 \to R_1$

19.
$$\begin{bmatrix} 1 & 0 & -3 & | & 1 \\ 0 & 1 & 2 & | & 0 \\ 0 & 0 & 3 & | & -6 \end{bmatrix} \sim \begin{bmatrix} 1 & 0 & -3 & | & 1 \\ 0 & 1 & 2 & | & 0 \\ 0 & 0 & 1 & | & -2 \end{bmatrix} \sim \begin{bmatrix} 1 & 0 & 0 & | & -5 \\ 0 & 1 & 0 & | & 4 \\ 0 & 0 & 1 & | & -2 \end{bmatrix}$$

$\frac{1}{3}R_3 \to R_3$

$R_1 + 3R_3 \to R_1$
$R_2 + (-2)R_3 \to R_2$

21.
$$\begin{bmatrix} 1 & 2 & -2 & | & -1 \\ 0 & 3 & -6 & | & 1 \\ 0 & -1 & 2 & | & -\frac{1}{3} \end{bmatrix} \sim \begin{bmatrix} 1 & 2 & -2 & | & -1 \\ 0 & 1 & -2 & | & \frac{1}{3} \\ 0 & -1 & 2 & | & -\frac{1}{3} \end{bmatrix} \sim \begin{bmatrix} 1 & 2 & -2 & | & -1 \\ 0 & 1 & -2 & | & \frac{1}{3} \\ 0 & 0 & 0 & | & 0 \end{bmatrix} \sim \begin{bmatrix} 1 & 0 & 2 & | & -\frac{5}{3} \\ 0 & 1 & -2 & | & \frac{1}{3} \\ 0 & 0 & 0 & | & 0 \end{bmatrix}$$

$\frac{1}{3}R_2 \to R_2$

$R_3 + R_2 \to R_3$

$R_1 + (-2)R_2 \to R_1$

23. The corresponding augmented matrix is:

$$\begin{bmatrix} 2 & 4 & -10 & | & -2 \\ 3 & 9 & -21 & | & 0 \\ 1 & 5 & -12 & | & 1 \end{bmatrix} \sim \begin{bmatrix} 1 & 2 & -5 & | & -1 \\ 3 & 9 & -21 & | & 0 \\ 1 & 5 & -12 & | & 1 \end{bmatrix} \sim \begin{bmatrix} 1 & 2 & -5 & | & -1 \\ 0 & 3 & -6 & | & 3 \\ 0 & 3 & -7 & | & 2 \end{bmatrix} \sim \begin{bmatrix} 1 & 2 & -5 & | & -1 \\ 0 & 1 & -2 & | & 1 \\ 0 & 3 & -7 & | & 2 \end{bmatrix}$$

$\frac{1}{2}R_1 \to R_1$

$R_2 + (-3)R_1 \to R_2$
$R_3 + (-1)R_1 \to R_3$

$\frac{1}{3}R_2 \to R_2$

$R_3 + (-3)R_2 \to R_3$

(continued)

$$\sim \begin{bmatrix} 1 & 2 & -5 & | & -1 \\ 0 & 1 & -2 & | & 1 \\ 0 & 0 & -1 & | & -1 \end{bmatrix} \sim \begin{bmatrix} 1 & 2 & -5 & | & -1 \\ 0 & 1 & -2 & | & 1 \\ 0 & 0 & 1 & | & 1 \end{bmatrix} \sim \begin{bmatrix} 1 & 2 & 0 & | & 4 \\ 0 & 1 & 0 & | & 3 \\ 0 & 0 & 1 & | & 1 \end{bmatrix} \sim \begin{bmatrix} 1 & 0 & 0 & | & -2 \\ 0 & 1 & 0 & | & 3 \\ 0 & 0 & 1 & | & 1 \end{bmatrix}$$

$(-1)R_3 \rightarrow R_3$ $R_2 + 2R_3 \rightarrow R_2$ $R_1 + (-2)R_2 \rightarrow R_1$
                             $R_1 + 5R_3 \rightarrow R_1$

Thus, $x_1 = -2$; $x_2 = 3$; $x_3 = 1$.

25. The corresponding augmented matrix is:

$$\begin{bmatrix} 3 & 8 & -1 & | & -18 \\ 2 & 1 & 5 & | & 8 \\ 2 & 4 & 2 & | & -4 \end{bmatrix} \sim \begin{bmatrix} 2 & 4 & 2 & | & -4 \\ 2 & 1 & 5 & | & 8 \\ 3 & 8 & -1 & | & -18 \end{bmatrix} \sim \begin{bmatrix} 1 & 2 & 1 & | & -2 \\ 2 & 1 & 5 & | & 8 \\ 3 & 8 & -1 & | & -18 \end{bmatrix}$$

$R_1 \leftrightarrow R_3$ $\frac{1}{2}R_1 \rightarrow R_1$ $R_2 + (-2)R_1 \rightarrow R_2$
                                 $R_3 + (-3)R_1 \rightarrow R_3$

$$\sim \begin{bmatrix} 1 & 2 & 1 & | & -2 \\ 0 & -3 & 3 & | & 12 \\ 0 & 2 & -4 & | & -12 \end{bmatrix} \sim \begin{bmatrix} 1 & 2 & 1 & | & -2 \\ 0 & 1 & -1 & | & -4 \\ 0 & 2 & -4 & | & -12 \end{bmatrix} \sim \begin{bmatrix} 1 & 2 & 1 & | & -2 \\ 0 & 1 & -1 & | & -4 \\ 0 & 0 & -2 & | & -4 \end{bmatrix}$$

$-\frac{1}{3}R_2 \rightarrow R_2$ $R_3 + (-2)R_2 \rightarrow R_3$ $-\frac{1}{2}R_3 \rightarrow R_3$

$$\sim \begin{bmatrix} 1 & 2 & 1 & | & -2 \\ 0 & 1 & -1 & | & -4 \\ 0 & 0 & 1 & | & 2 \end{bmatrix} \sim \begin{bmatrix} 1 & 2 & 0 & | & -4 \\ 0 & 1 & 0 & | & -2 \\ 0 & 0 & 1 & | & 2 \end{bmatrix} \sim \begin{bmatrix} 1 & 0 & 0 & | & 0 \\ 0 & 1 & 0 & | & -2 \\ 0 & 0 & 1 & | & 2 \end{bmatrix}$$

Thus, $x_1 = 0$
$x_2 = -2$
$x_3 = 2$.

$R_2 + R_3 \rightarrow R_2$ $R_1 + (-2)R_2 \rightarrow R_2$
$R_1 + (-1)R_3 \rightarrow R_1$

27. $$\begin{bmatrix} 2 & -1 & -3 & | & 8 \\ 1 & -2 & 0 & | & 7 \end{bmatrix} \sim \begin{bmatrix} 1 & -2 & 0 & | & 7 \\ 2 & -1 & -3 & | & 8 \end{bmatrix} \sim \begin{bmatrix} 1 & -2 & 0 & | & 7 \\ 0 & 3 & -3 & | & -6 \end{bmatrix} \sim \begin{bmatrix} 1 & -2 & 0 & | & 7 \\ 0 & 1 & -1 & | & -2 \end{bmatrix}$$

$R_1 \leftrightarrow R_2$ $R_2 + (-2)R_1 \rightarrow R_2$ $\frac{1}{3}R_2 \rightarrow R_2$ $R_1 + 2R_2 \rightarrow R_1$

$$\sim \begin{bmatrix} 1 & 0 & -2 & | & 3 \\ 0 & 1 & -1 & | & -2 \end{bmatrix}$$

Thus, $x_1 \quad - 2x_3 = 3$ (1)
$x_2 - \quad x_3 = -2$ (2)

Let $x_3 = t$, where t is any real number. Then:

$x_1 = 2t + 3$
$x_2 = t - 2$
$x_3 = t$

29.

$$\begin{bmatrix} 2 & 3 & -1 & | & 1 \\ 1 & -2 & 2 & | & -2 \end{bmatrix} \sim \begin{bmatrix} 1 & -2 & 2 & | & -2 \\ 2 & 3 & -1 & | & 1 \end{bmatrix} \sim \begin{bmatrix} 1 & -2 & 2 & | & -2 \\ 0 & 7 & -5 & | & 5 \end{bmatrix} \sim \begin{bmatrix} 1 & -2 & 2 & | & -2 \\ 0 & 1 & -\frac{5}{7} & | & \frac{5}{7} \end{bmatrix}$$

$\quad R_1 \leftrightarrow R_2 \qquad\qquad R_2 + (-2)R_1 \rightarrow R_2 \qquad \frac{1}{7}R_2 \rightarrow R_2 \qquad\qquad R_1 + 2R_2 \rightarrow R_1$

$$\sim \begin{bmatrix} 1 & 0 & \frac{4}{7} & | & -\frac{4}{7} \\ 0 & 1 & -\frac{5}{7} & | & \frac{5}{7} \end{bmatrix} \quad \text{Thus,} \quad \begin{aligned} x_1 \qquad + \frac{4}{7}x_3 &= -\frac{4}{7} \qquad (1) \\ x_2 - \frac{5}{7}x_3 &= \frac{5}{7} \qquad (2) \end{aligned}$$

Let $x_3 = t$, where t is any real number. Then:

$$x_1 = \frac{(-4t - 4)}{7}$$

$$x_2 = \frac{(5t + 5)}{7}$$

$$x_3 = t$$

31.

$$\begin{bmatrix} 2 & 2 & | & 2 \\ 1 & 2 & | & 3 \\ 0 & -3 & | & -6 \end{bmatrix} \sim \begin{bmatrix} 1 & 2 & | & 3 \\ 2 & 2 & | & 2 \\ 0 & -3 & | & -6 \end{bmatrix} \sim \begin{bmatrix} 1 & 2 & | & 3 \\ 0 & -2 & | & -4 \\ 0 & -3 & | & -6 \end{bmatrix} \sim \begin{bmatrix} 1 & 2 & | & 3 \\ 0 & 1 & | & 2 \\ 0 & -3 & | & -6 \end{bmatrix}$$

$\quad R_1 \leftrightarrow R_2 \qquad\quad R_2 + (-2)R_1 \rightarrow R_2 \qquad -\frac{1}{2}R_2 \rightarrow R_2 \qquad R_3 + 3R_2 \rightarrow R_2$

$$\sim \begin{bmatrix} 1 & 2 & | & 3 \\ 0 & 1 & | & 2 \\ 0 & 0 & | & 0 \end{bmatrix} \sim \begin{bmatrix} 1 & 0 & | & -1 \\ 0 & 1 & | & 2 \\ 0 & 0 & | & 0 \end{bmatrix} \quad \text{Thus,} \quad \begin{aligned} x_1 &= -1 \\ x_2 &= 2. \end{aligned}$$

$\quad R_1 + (-2)R_2 \rightarrow R_2$

33.

$$\begin{bmatrix} 2 & -1 & | & 0 \\ 3 & 2 & | & 7 \\ 1 & -1 & | & -2 \end{bmatrix} \sim \begin{bmatrix} 1 & -1 & | & -2 \\ 3 & 2 & | & 7 \\ 2 & -1 & | & 0 \end{bmatrix} \sim \begin{bmatrix} 1 & -1 & | & -2 \\ 0 & 5 & | & 13 \\ 0 & 1 & | & 4 \end{bmatrix} \sim \begin{bmatrix} 1 & -1 & | & -2 \\ 0 & 1 & | & 4 \\ 0 & 5 & | & 13 \end{bmatrix}$$

$\quad R_1 \leftrightarrow R_3 \qquad\quad R_2 + (-3)R_1 \rightarrow R_2 \qquad R_2 \leftrightarrow R_3 \qquad R_3 + (-5)R_2 \rightarrow R_3$

$\qquad\qquad\qquad\quad R_3 + (-2)R_1 \rightarrow R_3$

$$\sim \begin{bmatrix} 1 & -1 & | & -2 \\ 0 & 1 & | & 4 \\ 0 & 0 & | & -7 \end{bmatrix}$$

From the last row, we conclude that there is no solution; the system is inconsistent.

35.
$$\begin{bmatrix} 3 & -4 & -1 & | & 1 \\ 2 & -3 & 1 & | & 1 \\ 1 & -2 & 3 & | & 2 \end{bmatrix} \sim \begin{bmatrix} 1 & -2 & 3 & | & 2 \\ 2 & -3 & 1 & | & 1 \\ 3 & -4 & -1 & | & 1 \end{bmatrix} \sim \begin{bmatrix} 1 & -2 & 3 & | & 2 \\ 0 & 1 & -5 & | & -3 \\ 0 & 2 & -10 & | & -5 \end{bmatrix}$$

$R_1 \leftrightarrow R_3$ 　　　　　$R_2 + (-2)R_1 \rightarrow R_2$ 　　$R_3 + (-2)R_2 \rightarrow R_3$
　　　　　　　　　　　　　　　　$R_3 + (-3)R_1 \rightarrow R_3$

$$\sim \begin{bmatrix} 1 & -2 & 3 & | & 2 \\ 0 & 1 & -5 & | & -3 \\ 0 & 0 & 0 & | & 1 \end{bmatrix}$$

From the last row, we conclude that there is no solution; the system is inconsistent.

37.
$$\begin{bmatrix} 3 & -2 & 1 & | & -7 \\ 2 & 1 & -4 & | & 0 \\ 1 & 1 & -3 & | & 1 \end{bmatrix} \sim \begin{bmatrix} 1 & 1 & -3 & | & 1 \\ 2 & 1 & -4 & | & 0 \\ 3 & -2 & 1 & | & -7 \end{bmatrix} \sim \begin{bmatrix} 1 & 1 & -3 & | & 1 \\ 0 & -1 & 2 & | & -2 \\ 0 & -5 & 10 & | & -10 \end{bmatrix}$$

$R_1 \leftrightarrow R_3$ 　　　　　$R_2 + (-2)R_1 \rightarrow R_2$ 　　$(-1)R_2 \rightarrow R_2$
　　　　　　　　　　　　　　　　$R_3 + (-3)R_1 \rightarrow R_3$

$$\sim \begin{bmatrix} 1 & 1 & -3 & | & 1 \\ 0 & 1 & -2 & | & 2 \\ 0 & -5 & 10 & | & -10 \end{bmatrix} \sim \begin{bmatrix} 1 & 1 & -3 & | & 1 \\ 0 & 1 & -2 & | & 2 \\ 0 & 0 & 0 & | & 0 \end{bmatrix} \sim \begin{bmatrix} 1 & 0 & -1 & | & -1 \\ 0 & 1 & -2 & | & 2 \\ 0 & 0 & 0 & | & 0 \end{bmatrix}$$

$R_3 + 5R_2 \rightarrow R_3$ 　　　$R_1 + (-1)R_2 \rightarrow R_1$

From this matrix, $x_1 - x_3 = -1$ and $x_2 - 2x_3 = 2$. Let $x_3 = t$ be any real number, then $x_1 = t - 1$, $x_2 = 2t + 2$, and $x_3 = t$.

39.
$$\begin{bmatrix} 2 & 4 & -2 & | & 2 \\ -3 & -6 & 3 & | & -3 \end{bmatrix} \sim \begin{bmatrix} 1 & 2 & -1 & | & 1 \\ -3 & -6 & 3 & | & -3 \end{bmatrix} \sim \begin{bmatrix} 1 & 2 & -1 & | & 1 \\ 0 & 0 & 0 & | & 0 \end{bmatrix}$$

$\frac{1}{2}R_1 \rightarrow R_1$ 　　　　$R_2 + 3R_1 \rightarrow R_2$

From this matrix, $x_1 + 2x_2 - x_3 = 1$. Let $x_2 = s$ and $x_3 = t$. Then $x_1 = -2s + t + 1$, $x_2 = s$, and $x_3 = t$, s and t any real numbers.

41.
$$\begin{bmatrix} 2 & -3 & 3 & | & -15 \\ 3 & 2 & -5 & | & 19 \\ 5 & -4 & -2 & | & -2 \end{bmatrix} \sim \begin{bmatrix} 1 & -3/2 & 3/2 & | & -15/2 \\ 3 & 2 & -5 & | & 19 \\ 5 & -4 & -2 & | & -2 \end{bmatrix} \sim \begin{bmatrix} 1 & -3/2 & 3/2 & | & -15/2 \\ 0 & 13/2 & -19/2 & | & 83/2 \\ 0 & 7/2 & -19/2 & | & 71/2 \end{bmatrix}$$

$\frac{1}{2}R_1 \rightarrow R_1$ 　　　　$R_2 + (-3)R_1 \rightarrow R_2$ 　　$\frac{2}{13}R_2 \rightarrow R_2$
　　　　　　　　　　　　$R_3 + (-5)R_1 \rightarrow R_3$

(continued)

$$\sim \begin{bmatrix} 1 & -3/2 & 3/2 & | & -15/2 \\ 0 & 1 & -19/13 & | & 83/13 \\ 0 & 7/2 & -19/2 & | & 71/2 \end{bmatrix} \sim \begin{bmatrix} 1 & -3/2 & 3/2 & | & -15/2 \\ 0 & 1 & -19/13 & | & 83/13 \\ 0 & 0 & -114/26 & | & 342/26 \end{bmatrix}$$

$$R_3 + \left(-\frac{7}{2}\right)R_2 \to R_3 \qquad\qquad \frac{-26}{114}R_3 \to R_3$$

$$\sim \begin{bmatrix} 1 & -3/2 & 3/2 & | & -15/2 \\ 0 & 1 & -19/13 & | & 83/13 \\ 0 & 0 & 1 & | & -3 \end{bmatrix} \sim \begin{bmatrix} 1 & -3/2 & 0 & | & -3 \\ 0 & 1 & 0 & | & 2 \\ 0 & 0 & 1 & | & -3 \end{bmatrix} \sim \begin{bmatrix} 1 & 0 & 0 & | & 0 \\ 0 & 1 & 0 & | & 2 \\ 0 & 0 & 1 & | & -3 \end{bmatrix}$$

$$R_2 + \frac{19}{13}R_3 \to R_2 \qquad\qquad R_1 + \frac{3}{2}R_2 \to R_1$$

$$R_1 + \left(-\frac{3}{2}\right)R_2 \to R_1$$

Thus, $x_1 = 0$, $x_2 = 2$, and $x_3 = -3$.

43. $$\begin{bmatrix} 5 & -3 & 2 & | & 13 \\ 2 & 4 & -3 & | & -9 \\ 4 & -2 & 5 & | & 13 \end{bmatrix} \sim \begin{bmatrix} 2 & 4 & -3 & | & -9 \\ 5 & -3 & 2 & | & 13 \\ 4 & -2 & 5 & | & 13 \end{bmatrix} \sim \begin{bmatrix} 1 & 2 & -3/2 & | & -9/2 \\ 5 & -3 & 2 & | & 13 \\ 4 & -2 & 5 & | & 13 \end{bmatrix}$$

$$R_2 \leftrightarrow R_1 \qquad\qquad \frac{1}{2}R_1 \to R_1 \qquad\qquad \begin{aligned} R_2 + (-5)R_1 &\to R_2 \\ R_3 + (-4)R_1 &\to R_3 \end{aligned}$$

$$\sim \begin{bmatrix} 1 & 2 & -3/2 & | & -9/2 \\ 0 & -13 & 19/2 & | & 71/2 \\ 0 & -10 & 11 & | & 31 \end{bmatrix} \sim \begin{bmatrix} 1 & 2 & -3/2 & | & -9/2 \\ 0 & 1 & -19/26 & | & -71/26 \\ 0 & -10 & 11 & | & 31 \end{bmatrix} \sim \begin{bmatrix} 1 & 2 & -3/2 & | & -9/2 \\ 0 & 1 & -19/26 & | & -71/26 \\ 0 & 0 & 48/13 & | & 48/13 \end{bmatrix}$$

$$-\frac{1}{13}R_2 \to R_2 \qquad\qquad R_3 + 10R_2 \to R_3 \qquad\qquad \frac{13}{48}R_3 \to R_3$$

$$\sim \begin{bmatrix} 1 & 2 & -3/2 & | & -9/2 \\ 0 & 1 & -19/26 & | & -71/26 \\ 0 & 0 & 1 & | & 1 \end{bmatrix} \sim \begin{bmatrix} 1 & 2 & 0 & | & -3 \\ 0 & 1 & 0 & | & -2 \\ 0 & 0 & 1 & | & 1 \end{bmatrix} \sim \begin{bmatrix} 1 & 0 & 0 & | & 1 \\ 0 & 1 & 0 & | & -2 \\ 0 & 0 & 1 & | & 1 \end{bmatrix}$$

$$R_2 + \frac{19}{26}R_3 \to R_2 \qquad\qquad R_1 + (-2)R_2 \to R_1$$

$$R_1 + \frac{3}{2}R_3 \to R_1$$

Thus, $x_1 = 1$, $x_2 = -2$, and $x_3 = 1$.

45.
$$\begin{bmatrix} 1 & 2 & -4 & -1 & | & 7 \\ 2 & 5 & -9 & -4 & | & 16 \\ 1 & 5 & -7 & -7 & | & 13 \end{bmatrix} \sim \begin{bmatrix} 1 & 2 & -4 & -1 & | & 7 \\ 0 & 1 & -1 & -2 & | & 2 \\ 0 & 3 & -3 & -6 & | & 6 \end{bmatrix} \sim \begin{bmatrix} 1 & 2 & -4 & -1 & | & 7 \\ 0 & 1 & -1 & -2 & | & 2 \\ 0 & 0 & 0 & 0 & | & 0 \end{bmatrix}$$

$R_2 + (-2)R_1 \to R_2$ $R_3 + (-3)R_2 \to R_3$ $R_1 + (-2)R_2 \to R_1$
$R_3 + (-1)R_1 \to R_3$

$$\sim \begin{bmatrix} 1 & 0 & -2 & 3 & | & 3 \\ 0 & 1 & -1 & -2 & | & 2 \\ 0 & 0 & 0 & 0 & | & 0 \end{bmatrix}$$

Thus, $x_1 - 2x_3 + 3x_4 = 3$ and $x_2 - x_3 - 2x_4 = 2$. Let $x_3 = s$ and $x_4 = t$.
Then $x_1 = 2s - 3t + 3$, $x_2 = s + 2t + 2$, $x_3 = s$, and $x_4 = t$, s, t any real
numbers.

47. Let x_1 = number of one-person boats,
       x_2 = number of two-person boats,
and x_3 = number of four-person boats.

We have the following system of linear equations:

$0.5x_1 + \quad x_2 + 1.5x_3 = 380$
$0.6x_1 + 0.9x_2 + 1.2x_3 = 330$
$0.2x_1 + 0.3x_2 + 0.5x_3 = 120$

$$\begin{bmatrix} 0.5 & 1 & 1.5 & | & 380 \\ 0.6 & 0.9 & 1.2 & | & 330 \\ 0.2 & 0.3 & 0.5 & | & 120 \end{bmatrix} \sim \begin{bmatrix} 1 & 2 & 3 & | & 760 \\ 0.6 & 0.9 & 1.2 & | & 330 \\ 0.2 & 0.3 & 0.5 & | & 120 \end{bmatrix} \sim \begin{bmatrix} 1 & 2 & 3 & | & 760 \\ 0 & -0.3 & -0.6 & | & -126 \\ 0 & -0.1 & -0.1 & | & -32 \end{bmatrix}$$

$2R_1 \to R_1$ $R_2 + (-0.6)R_1 \to R_2$ $-\dfrac{1}{0.3}R_2 \to R_2$
                     $R_3 + (-0.2)R_1 \to R_3$

$$\sim \begin{bmatrix} 1 & 2 & 3 & | & 760 \\ 0 & 1 & 2 & | & 420 \\ 0 & -0.1 & -0.1 & | & -32 \end{bmatrix} \sim \begin{bmatrix} 1 & 2 & 3 & | & 760 \\ 0 & 1 & 2 & | & 420 \\ 0 & 0 & 0.1 & | & 10 \end{bmatrix} \sim \begin{bmatrix} 1 & 2 & 3 & | & 760 \\ 0 & 1 & 2 & | & 420 \\ 0 & 0 & 1 & | & 100 \end{bmatrix}$$

$R_3 + (0.1)R_2 \to R_3$ $10R_3 \to R_3$ $R_1 + (-3)R_3 \to R_1$
                                      $R_2 + (-2)R_3 \to R_2$

$$\sim \begin{bmatrix} 1 & 2 & 0 & | & 460 \\ 0 & 1 & 0 & | & 220 \\ 0 & 0 & 1 & | & 100 \end{bmatrix} \sim \begin{bmatrix} 1 & 0 & 0 & | & 20 \\ 0 & 1 & 0 & | & 220 \\ 0 & 0 & 1 & | & 100 \end{bmatrix}$$

$R_1 + (-2)R_2 \to R_1$

Thus, $x_1 = 20$, $x_2 = 220$, and $x_3 = 100$, or 20 one-person boats, 220 two-person boats, and 100 four-person boats.

              CHAPTER 1

49. Referring to Problem 43, we now have the following system of equations to solve:

$$0.5x_1 + x_2 + 1.5x_3 = 380$$
$$0.6x_1 + 0.9x_2 + 1.2x_3 = 330$$

$$\begin{bmatrix} 0.5 & 1 & 1.5 & | & 380 \\ 0.6 & 0.9 & 1.2 & | & 330 \end{bmatrix} \sim \begin{bmatrix} 1 & 2 & 3 & | & 760 \\ 0.6 & 0.9 & 1.2 & | & 330 \end{bmatrix} \sim \begin{bmatrix} 1 & 2 & 3 & | & 760 \\ 0 & -0.3 & -0.6 & | & -126 \end{bmatrix}$$

$$\frac{1}{0.5}R_1 \rightarrow R_1 \qquad\qquad R_2 + (-0.6)R_1 \rightarrow R_2 \qquad\qquad -\frac{1}{0.3}R_2 \rightarrow R_2$$

$$\sim \begin{bmatrix} 1 & 2 & 3 & | & 760 \\ 0 & 1 & 2 & | & 420 \end{bmatrix} \sim \begin{bmatrix} 1 & 0 & -1 & | & -80 \\ 0 & 1 & 2 & | & 420 \end{bmatrix}$$

$$R_1 + (-2)R_2 \rightarrow R_1$$

Thus, $x_1 - x_3 = -80 \qquad$ (1)
$$x_2 + 2x_3 = 420 \qquad (2)$$

Let $x_3 = t \qquad\qquad$ (t any real number)

Then, $x_2 = 420 - 2t \quad$ [from (2)]
$$x_1 = t - 80 \quad \text{[from (1)]}$$

In order to keep x_1 and x_2 positive, $t \leqslant 210$ and $t \geqslant 80$.

Thus, $x_1 = t - 80 \quad$ (one-person boats)
$$x_2 = 420 - 2t \quad \text{(two-person boats)}$$
$$x_3 = t \quad\quad\;\; \text{(four-person boats)}$$

where $80 \leqslant t \leqslant 210$.

51. Again referring to Problem 43, we now have the following system:

$$0.5x_1 + x_2 = 380$$
$$0.6x_1 + 0.9x_2 = 330$$
$$0.2x_1 + 0.3x_2 = 120$$

$$\begin{bmatrix} 0.5 & 1 & | & 380 \\ 0.6 & 0.9 & | & 330 \\ 0.2 & 0.3 & | & 120 \end{bmatrix} \sim \begin{bmatrix} 1 & 2 & | & 760 \\ 0.6 & 0.9 & | & 330 \\ 0.2 & 0.3 & | & 120 \end{bmatrix} \sim \begin{bmatrix} 1 & 2 & | & 760 \\ 0 & -0.3 & | & -126 \\ 0 & -0.1 & | & -32 \end{bmatrix} \sim \begin{bmatrix} 1 & 2 & | & 760 \\ 0 & 1 & | & 420 \\ 0 & -0.1 & | & -32 \end{bmatrix}$$

$$\frac{1}{0.5}R_1 \rightarrow R_1 \qquad R_2 - 0.6R_1 \rightarrow R_2 \qquad -\frac{1}{0.3}R_2 \rightarrow R_2 \qquad R_3 + 0.1R_2 \rightarrow R_3$$
$$R_3 - 0.2R_1 \rightarrow R_3$$

$$\begin{bmatrix} 1 & 2 & | & 760 \\ 0 & 1 & | & 420 \\ 0 & 0 & | & 10 \end{bmatrix}$$ From this matrix, we conclude that there is no solution; there is no production schedule that will use all the labor-hours in all departments.

53. Let x_1 = amount of federal income tax (in thousands of dollars),
x_2 = amount of state income tax (in thousands of dollars),
and x_3 = amount of local income tax (in thousands of dollars).

Then,

$x_1 = 0.25(1664 - x_2 - x_3)$
$x_2 = 0.10(1664 - x_1 - x_3)$
$x_3 = 0.05(1664 - x_1 - x_2)$

We rewrite this system in the standard form:

$$x_1 + 0.25x_2 + 0.25x_3 = 416 \quad (1)$$
$$0.10x_1 + x_2 + 0.10x_3 = 166.4 \quad (2)$$
$$0.05x_1 + 0.05x_2 + x_3 = 83.2 \quad (3)$$

Multiply (1) by 100, (2) by 10, and (3) by 100 to obtain:

$$100x_1 + 25x_2 + 25x_3 = 41,600$$
$$x_1 + 10x_2 + x_3 = 1,664$$
$$5x_1 + 5x_2 + 100x_3 = 8,320$$

The augmented matrix corresponding to this system is:

$$\left[\begin{array}{ccc|c} 100 & 25 & 25 & 41,600 \\ 1 & 10 & 1 & 1,664 \\ 5 & 5 & 100 & 8,320 \end{array}\right] \sim \left[\begin{array}{ccc|c} 1 & 10 & 1 & 1,664 \\ 100 & 25 & 25 & 41,600 \\ 5 & 5 & 100 & 8,320 \end{array}\right]$$

$R_1 \leftrightarrow R_2$
$\qquad\qquad R_2 + (-100)R_1 \rightarrow R_2$
$\qquad\qquad R_3 + (-5)R_1 \rightarrow R_3$

$$\sim \left[\begin{array}{ccc|c} 1 & 10 & 1 & 1,664 \\ 0 & -975 & -75 & 124,800 \\ 0 & -45 & 95 & 0 \end{array}\right] \sim \left[\begin{array}{ccc|c} 1 & 10 & 1 & 1,664 \\ 0 & -45 & 95 & 0 \\ 0 & -975 & -75 & 124,800 \end{array}\right]$$

$R_2 \leftrightarrow R_3$
$\qquad\qquad -\dfrac{1}{45}R_2 \rightarrow R_2$

$$\sim \left[\begin{array}{ccc|c} 1 & 10 & 1 & 1,664 \\ 0 & 1 & -2.11 & 0 \\ 0 & -975 & -75 & 124,800 \end{array}\right] \sim \left[\begin{array}{ccc|c} 1 & 10 & 1 & 1,664 \\ 0 & 1 & -2.11 & 0 \\ 0 & 0 & 2132.25 & 124,800 \end{array}\right]$$

$R_3 + 975R_2 \rightarrow R_3$
$\qquad\qquad \dfrac{1}{2132.25}R_3 \rightarrow R_3$

$$\sim \left[\begin{array}{ccc|c} 1 & 10 & 1 & 1,664 \\ 0 & 1 & -2.11 & 0 \\ 0 & 0 & 1 & 58.5 \end{array}\right] \sim \left[\begin{array}{ccc|c} 1 & 10 & 0 & 1,605.5 \\ 0 & 1 & 0 & 123.5 \\ 0 & 0 & 1 & 58.5 \end{array}\right]$$

$R_2 + 2.11R_3 \rightarrow R_2$
$\qquad\qquad R_1 + (-10)R_2 \rightarrow R_1$
$R_1 + (-1)R_3 \rightarrow R_1$

(continued)

$$\sim \begin{bmatrix} 1 & 0 & 0 & | & 370.5 \\ 0 & 1 & 0 & | & 123.5 \\ 0 & 0 & 1 & | & 58.5 \end{bmatrix}$$

Thus, $x_1 = \$370,500$, $x_2 = \$123,500$, and $x_3 = \$58,500$.

55. Let x_1 = number of ounces of food A,
x_2 = number of ounces of food B,
and x_3 = number of ounces of food C.

We have the following system of equations to solve:

$$30x_1 + 10x_2 + 20x_3 = 340$$
$$10x_1 + 10x_2 + 20x_3 = 180$$
$$10x_1 + 30x_2 + 20x_3 = 220$$

$$\begin{bmatrix} 30 & 10 & 20 & | & 340 \\ 10 & 10 & 20 & | & 180 \\ 10 & 30 & 20 & | & 220 \end{bmatrix} \sim \begin{bmatrix} 10 & 10 & 20 & | & 180 \\ 30 & 10 & 20 & | & 340 \\ 10 & 30 & 20 & | & 220 \end{bmatrix} \sim \begin{bmatrix} 1 & 1 & 2 & | & 18 \\ 3 & 1 & 2 & | & 34 \\ 1 & 3 & 2 & | & 22 \end{bmatrix}$$

$\quad\quad R_1 \leftrightarrow R_2 \quad\quad\quad\quad\quad (1/10)R_1 \rightarrow R_1 \quad\quad R_2 + (-3)R_1 \rightarrow R_2$
$\quad\quad\quad\quad\quad\quad\quad\quad\quad\quad (1/10)R_2 \rightarrow R_2 \quad\quad R_3 + (-1)R_1 \rightarrow R_3$
$\quad\quad\quad\quad\quad\quad\quad\quad\quad\quad (1/10)R_3 \rightarrow R_3$

$$\sim \begin{bmatrix} 1 & 1 & 2 & | & 18 \\ 0 & -2 & -4 & | & -20 \\ 0 & 2 & 0 & | & 4 \end{bmatrix} \sim \begin{bmatrix} 1 & 1 & 2 & | & 18 \\ 0 & 1 & 2 & | & 10 \\ 0 & 2 & 0 & | & 4 \end{bmatrix} \sim \begin{bmatrix} 1 & 1 & 2 & | & 18 \\ 0 & 1 & 2 & | & 10 \\ 0 & 0 & -4 & | & -16 \end{bmatrix}$$

$\quad\quad -\dfrac{1}{2}R_2 \rightarrow R_2 \quad\quad\quad R_3 + (-2)R_2 \rightarrow R_3 \quad \dfrac{1}{4}R_3 \rightarrow R_3$

$$\sim \begin{bmatrix} 1 & 1 & 2 & | & 18 \\ 0 & 1 & 2 & | & 10 \\ 0 & 0 & 1 & | & 4 \end{bmatrix} \sim \begin{bmatrix} 1 & 1 & 0 & | & 10 \\ 0 & 1 & 0 & | & 2 \\ 0 & 0 & 1 & | & 4 \end{bmatrix} \sim \begin{bmatrix} 1 & 0 & 0 & | & 8 \\ 0 & 1 & 0 & | & 2 \\ 0 & 0 & 1 & | & 4 \end{bmatrix}$$

$\quad\quad R_2 + (-2)R_3 \rightarrow R_2 \quad R_1 + (-1)R_2 \rightarrow R_1$
$\quad\quad R_1 + (-2)R_3 \rightarrow R_1$

Thus, $x_1 = 8$, $x_2 = 2$, and $x_3 = 4$ or 8 ounces of food A, 2 ounces of food B, and 4 ounces of food C.

57. Referring to Problem 55, we have:

$$30x_1 + 10x_2 = 340$$
$$10x_1 + 10x_2 = 180$$
$$10x_1 + 30x_2 = 220$$

$$\begin{bmatrix} 30 & 10 & | & 340 \\ 10 & 10 & | & 180 \\ 10 & 30 & | & 220 \end{bmatrix} \sim \begin{bmatrix} 3 & 1 & | & 34 \\ 1 & 1 & | & 18 \\ 1 & 3 & | & 22 \end{bmatrix} \sim \begin{bmatrix} 1 & 1 & | & 18 \\ 3 & 1 & | & 34 \\ 1 & 3 & | & 22 \end{bmatrix} \sim \begin{bmatrix} 1 & 1 & | & 18 \\ 0 & -2 & | & -20 \\ 0 & 2 & | & 4 \end{bmatrix}$$

$(1/10)R_1 \rightarrow R_1$ $R_1 \leftrightarrow R_2$ $R_2 + (-3)R_1 \rightarrow R_2$ $-\dfrac{1}{2}R_2 \rightarrow R_2$
$(1/10)R_2 \rightarrow R_2$ $R_3 + (-1)R_1 \rightarrow R_3$
$(1/10)R_3 \rightarrow R_3$

$$\sim \begin{bmatrix} 1 & 1 & | & 18 \\ 0 & 1 & | & 10 \\ 0 & 2 & | & 4 \end{bmatrix} \sim \begin{bmatrix} 1 & 1 & | & 18 \\ 0 & 1 & | & 10 \\ 0 & 0 & | & -16 \end{bmatrix}$$

From this matrix, we conclude that there is no solution.

$R_3 + (-2)R_2 \rightarrow R_3$

59. Referring to Problem 55, we have the following system of equations to solve:

$$30x_1 + 10x_2 + 20x_3 = 340$$
$$10x_1 + 10x_2 + 20x_3 = 180$$

$$\begin{bmatrix} 30 & 10 & 20 & | & 340 \\ 10 & 10 & 20 & | & 180 \end{bmatrix} \sim \begin{bmatrix} 10 & 10 & 20 & | & 180 \\ 30 & 10 & 20 & | & 340 \end{bmatrix} \sim \begin{bmatrix} 1 & 1 & 2 & | & 18 \\ 3 & 1 & 2 & | & 34 \end{bmatrix}$$

$R_1 \leftrightarrow R_2$ $(1/10)R_1 \rightarrow R_1$ $R_2 + (-3)R_1 \rightarrow R_2$
  $(1/10)R_2 \rightarrow R_2$

$$\sim \begin{bmatrix} 1 & 1 & 2 & | & 18 \\ 0 & -2 & -4 & | & -20 \end{bmatrix} \sim \begin{bmatrix} 1 & 1 & 2 & | & 18 \\ 0 & 1 & 2 & | & 10 \end{bmatrix} \sim \begin{bmatrix} 1 & 0 & 0 & | & 8 \\ 0 & 1 & 2 & | & 10 \end{bmatrix}$$

$-\dfrac{1}{2}R_2 \rightarrow R_2$ $R_1 + (-1)R_2 \rightarrow R_1$

Thus, $x_1 \qquad = 8$
$\qquad x_2 + 2x_3 = 10$

Let $x_3 = t$ (t any real number). Then, $x_2 = 10 - 2t$, $0 \leqslant t \leqslant 5$, for x_2 to be positive.

The solution is: $x_1 = 8$ ounces of food A; $x_2 = 10 - 2t$ ounces of food B; $x_3 = t$ ounces of food C, $0 \leqslant t \leqslant 5$.

61. Let x_1 = number of barrels of mix A,
$\qquad x_2$ = number of barrels of mix B,
$\qquad x_3$ = number of barrels of mix C,
and x_4 = number of barrels of mix D.

Then,

$$30x_1 + 30x_2 + 30x_3 + 60x_4 = 900 \qquad (1)$$
$$50x_1 + 75x_2 + 25x_3 + 25x_4 = 750 \qquad (2)$$
$$30x_1 + 20x_2 + 20x_3 + 50x_4 = 700 \qquad (3)$$

Divide each side of equation (1) by 30, each side of equation (2) by 25, and each side of equation (3) by 10. This yields the system of linear equations:

$$x_1 + x_2 + x_3 + 2x_4 = 30$$
$$2x_1 + 3x_2 + x_3 + x_4 = 30$$
$$3x_1 + 2x_2 + 2x_3 + 5x_4 = 70$$

$$\begin{bmatrix} 1 & 1 & 1 & 2 & | & 30 \\ 2 & 3 & 1 & 1 & | & 30 \\ 3 & 2 & 2 & 5 & | & 70 \end{bmatrix} \sim \begin{bmatrix} 1 & 1 & 1 & 2 & | & 30 \\ 0 & 1 & -1 & -3 & | & -30 \\ 0 & -1 & -1 & -1 & | & -20 \end{bmatrix} \sim \begin{bmatrix} 1 & 1 & 1 & 2 & | & 30 \\ 0 & 1 & -1 & -3 & | & -30 \\ 0 & 0 & -2 & -4 & | & -50 \end{bmatrix}$$

$$R_2 + (-1)R_1 \rightarrow R_2 \qquad R_3 + R_2 \rightarrow R_3 \qquad -\frac{1}{2}R_3 \rightarrow R_3$$
$$R_3 + (-3)R_1 \rightarrow R_3$$

$$\sim \begin{bmatrix} 1 & 1 & 1 & 2 & | & 30 \\ 0 & 1 & -1 & -3 & | & -30 \\ 0 & 0 & 1 & 2 & | & 25 \end{bmatrix} \sim \begin{bmatrix} 1 & 1 & 0 & 0 & | & 5 \\ 0 & 1 & 0 & -1 & | & -5 \\ 0 & 0 & 1 & 2 & | & 25 \end{bmatrix} \sim \begin{bmatrix} 1 & 0 & 0 & 1 & | & 10 \\ 0 & 1 & 0 & -1 & | & -5 \\ 0 & 0 & 1 & 2 & | & 25 \end{bmatrix}$$

$$R_2 + R_3 \rightarrow R_2 \qquad R_1 + (-1)R_2 \rightarrow R_1$$
$$R_1 + (-1)R_3 \rightarrow R_1$$

Thus,
$$x_1 \quad\quad + x_4 = 10$$
$$x_2 \quad - x_4 = -5$$
$$x_3 + 2x_4 = 25$$

Let $x_4 = t$ = number of barrels of mix D. Then $x_1 = 10 - t$ = number of barrels of mix A, $x_2 = t - 5$ = number of barrels of mix B, and $x_3 = 25 - 2t$ = number of barrels of mix C.

Since the number of barrels of each mix must be nonnegative, $5 \leqslant t \leqslant 10$.

63. Let x_1 = number of hours for Company A, and x_2 = number of hours for Company B.

Then,

$$30x_1 + 20x_2 = 600$$
$$10x_1 + 20x_2 = 400$$

Divide each side of each equation by 10. This yields the system of linear equations:

$$3x_1 + 2x_2 = 60$$
$$x_1 + 2x_2 = 40$$

$$\begin{bmatrix} 3 & 2 & | & 60 \\ 1 & 2 & | & 40 \end{bmatrix} \sim \begin{bmatrix} 1 & 2 & | & 40 \\ 3 & 2 & | & 60 \end{bmatrix} \sim \begin{bmatrix} 1 & 2 & | & 40 \\ 0 & -4 & | & -60 \end{bmatrix} \sim \begin{bmatrix} 1 & 2 & | & 40 \\ 0 & 1 & | & 15 \end{bmatrix}$$

$$R_1 \leftrightarrow R_2 \qquad R_2 + (-3)R_1 \rightarrow R_2 \qquad -\frac{1}{4}R_2 \rightarrow R_2 \qquad R_1 + (-2)R_2 \rightarrow R_1$$

$$\sim \begin{bmatrix} 1 & 0 & | & 10 \\ 0 & 1 & | & 15 \end{bmatrix}$$

Thus, $x_1 = 10$ and $x_2 = 15$, or 10 hours for Company A and 15 hours for Company B.

Things to remember:

1. A matrix with m rows and n columns is said to have SIZE or DIMENSION $m \times n$. If a matrix has the same number of rows and columns, then it is called a SQUARE MATRIX. A matrix with only one column is a COLUMN MATRIX, and a matrix with only one row is a ROW MATRIX.

2. Two matrices are EQUAL if they have the same dimension and their corresponding elements are equal.

3. The SUM of two matrices of the same dimension, $m \times n$, is an $m \times n$ matrix whose elements are the sum of the corresponding elements of the two given matrices. Addition is not defined for matrices with different dimensions. Matrix addition is commutative: $A + B = B + A$, and associative: $(A + B) + C = A + (B + C)$.

4. A matrix with all elements equal to zero is called a ZERO MATRIX.

5. The NEGATIVE OF A MATRIX M, denoted by $-M$, is the matrix whose elements are the negatives of the elements of M.

6. If A and B are matrices of the same dimension, then subtraction is defined by $A - B = A + (-B)$. Thus, to subtract B from A, simply subtract corresponding elements.

7. If M is a matrix and k is a number, then kM is the matrix formed by multiplying each element of M by k.

---

1. Dimension of B is 2×2 (2 rows $\times$ 2 columns)   *3.* 2   *5.* $\begin{bmatrix} 0 & 0 \\ 0 & 0 \end{bmatrix}$
Dimension of E is 1×4 (1 row $\times$ 4 columns)

7. C and D are column matrices.   *9.* A and B are square matrices. [Note: Number of rows = number of columns.]

11.

$$A + B = \begin{bmatrix} 2 & -1 \\ 3 & 0 \end{bmatrix} + \begin{bmatrix} -3 & 1 \\ 2 & -3 \end{bmatrix}$$

$$= \begin{bmatrix} 2 - 3 & -1 + 1 \\ 3 + 2 & 0 - 3 \end{bmatrix} = \begin{bmatrix} -1 & 0 \\ 5 & -3 \end{bmatrix}$$

13.

$$-C = \begin{bmatrix} -2 \\ -(-3) \\ 0 \end{bmatrix} = \begin{bmatrix} -2 \\ 3 \\ 0 \end{bmatrix}$$

15.

$$D - C = \begin{bmatrix} 1 \\ 3 \\ 5 \end{bmatrix} - \begin{bmatrix} 2 \\ -3 \\ 0 \end{bmatrix} = \begin{bmatrix} 1 \\ 3 \\ 5 \end{bmatrix} + \begin{bmatrix} -2 \\ 3 \\ 0 \end{bmatrix}$$

$$= \begin{bmatrix} 1 - 2 \\ 3 + 3 \\ 5 + 0 \end{bmatrix} = \begin{bmatrix} -1 \\ 6 \\ 5 \end{bmatrix}$$

17.

$$5B = 5 \begin{bmatrix} -3 & 1 \\ 2 & -3 \end{bmatrix} = \begin{bmatrix} -15 & 5 \\ 10 & -15 \end{bmatrix}$$

19.

$$\begin{bmatrix} 3 & -2 & 0 & 1 \\ 2 & -3 & -1 & 4 \\ 0 & 2 & -1 & 6 \end{bmatrix} + \begin{bmatrix} -2 & 5 & -1 & 0 \\ -3 & -2 & 8 & -2 \\ 4 & 6 & 1 & -8 \end{bmatrix} = \begin{bmatrix} 3 - 2 & -2 + 5 & 0 - 1 & 1 + 0 \\ 2 - 3 & -3 - 2 & -1 + 8 & 4 - 2 \\ 0 + 4 & 2 + 6 & -1 + 1 & 6 - 8 \end{bmatrix}$$

$$= \begin{bmatrix} 1 & 3 & -1 & 1 \\ -1 & -5 & 7 & 2 \\ 4 & 8 & 0 & -2 \end{bmatrix}$$

21.

$$\begin{bmatrix} 1.3 & 2.5 & -6.1 \\ 8.3 & -1.4 & 6.7 \end{bmatrix} - \begin{bmatrix} -4.1 & 1.8 & -4.3 \\ 0.7 & 2.6 & -1.2 \end{bmatrix} = \begin{bmatrix} 1.3 + 4.1 & 2.5 - 1.8 & -6.1 + 4.3 \\ 8.3 - 0.7 & -1.4 - 2.6 & 6.7 + 1.2 \end{bmatrix}$$

$$= \begin{bmatrix} 5.4 & 0.7 & -1.8 \\ 7.6 & -4.0 & 7.9 \end{bmatrix}$$

23.

$$1000 \begin{bmatrix} 0.25 & 0.36 \\ 0.04 & 0.35 \end{bmatrix} = \begin{bmatrix} 250 & 360 \\ 40 & 350 \end{bmatrix}$$

25.

$$0.08 \begin{bmatrix} 24,000 & 35,000 \\ 12,000 & 24,000 \end{bmatrix} + 0.03 \begin{bmatrix} 12,000 & 22,000 \\ 14,000 & 13,000 \end{bmatrix} = \begin{bmatrix} 1920 & 2800 \\ 960 & 1920 \end{bmatrix} + \begin{bmatrix} 360 & 660 \\ 420 & 390 \end{bmatrix}$$

$$= \begin{bmatrix} 1920 + 360 & 2800 + 660 \\ 960 + 420 & 1920 + 390 \end{bmatrix}$$

$$= \begin{bmatrix} 2280 & 3460 \\ 1380 & 2310 \end{bmatrix}$$

27. $\begin{bmatrix} a & b \\ c & d \end{bmatrix} + \begin{bmatrix} 2 & -3 \\ 0 & 1 \end{bmatrix} = \begin{bmatrix} a+2 & b-3 \\ c+0 & d+1 \end{bmatrix} = \begin{bmatrix} 1 & -2 \\ 3 & -4 \end{bmatrix}$ Thus, $a+2=1$, $a=-1$
$$b-3=-2, \; b=1$$
$$c+0=3, \; c=3$$
$$d+1=-4, \; d=-5$$

29. $\begin{bmatrix} 2x & 4 \\ -3 & 5x \end{bmatrix} + \begin{bmatrix} 3y & -2 \\ -2 & -y \end{bmatrix} = \begin{bmatrix} -5 & 2 \\ -5 & 13 \end{bmatrix}$

$\begin{bmatrix} 2x+3y & 4-2 \\ -3-2 & 5x-y \end{bmatrix} = \begin{bmatrix} -5 & 2 \\ -5 & 13 \end{bmatrix}$

$\begin{bmatrix} 2x+3y & 2 \\ -5 & 5x-y \end{bmatrix} = \begin{bmatrix} -5 & 2 \\ -5 & 13 \end{bmatrix}$ Thus, $2x+3y=-5$ (1)
$$5x-y=13 \qquad (2)$$
Solve the above system for x, y.

From (2), $y = 5x - 13$.   Substitute $y = 5x - 13$ in (1):

$2x + 3(5x - 13) = -5$
$2x + 15x - 39 = -5$
$17x = -5 + 39$
$17x = 34$
$x = 2$

Substitute $x = 2$ in (1): $2(2) + 3y = -5$
$4 + 3y = -5$
$3y = -9$
$y = -3$

Thus, the solution is $x = 2$ and $y = -3$.

31.
$A + B = \begin{bmatrix} \$30 & \$25 \\ \$60 & \$80 \end{bmatrix} + \begin{bmatrix} \$36 & \$27 \\ \$54 & \$74 \end{bmatrix} = \begin{bmatrix} \$66 & \$52 \\ \$114 & \$154 \end{bmatrix}$

Guitar   Banjo

$\frac{1}{2}(A + B) = \frac{1}{2}\begin{bmatrix} \$66 & \$52 \\ \$114 & \$154 \end{bmatrix} = \begin{bmatrix} \$33 & \$26 \\ \$57 & \$77 \end{bmatrix}$ Materials
Labor

33.
$A + B = \begin{bmatrix} 70 & 122 & 20 \\ 30 & 118 & 80 \end{bmatrix} + \begin{bmatrix} 65 & 160 & 30 \\ 25 & 140 & 75 \end{bmatrix} = \begin{bmatrix} 135 & 282 & 50 \\ 55 & 258 & 155 \end{bmatrix}$

Total sample size $= 135 + 282 + 50 + 55 + 258 + 155 = 935$.   Percent of total sample in each category is given by:

$\frac{1}{935}\begin{bmatrix} 135 & 282 & 50 \\ 55 & 285 & 155 \end{bmatrix} = \begin{bmatrix} 0.14 & 0.30 & 0.05 \\ 0.06 & 0.28 & 0.17 \end{bmatrix}$

(continued)

$$\begin{array}{ccc}
\text{Under} & \text{5 ft to} & \text{Over} \\
\text{5 ft} & \text{5 ft 6 in.} & \text{5 ft 6 in.}
\end{array}$$

$$= \begin{bmatrix} 14\% & 30\% & 5\% \\ 6\% & 28\% & 17\% \end{bmatrix} \begin{array}{l} \text{Passive} \\ \text{Aggressive} \end{array}$$

EXERCISE 1-5

Things to remember:

<u>1</u>. Let

$$A = [a_1 \quad a_2 \quad \cdots \quad a_n]$$

be a $1 \times n$ row vector and

$$B = \begin{bmatrix} b_1 \\ b_2 \\ \vdots \\ b_n \end{bmatrix}$$

be an $n \times 1$ column vector. The DOT PRODUCT $A \cdot B$ of A and B, in this order, is given by

$$[a_1 \quad a_2 \quad \cdots \quad a_n] \cdot \begin{bmatrix} b_1 \\ b_2 \\ \vdots \\ b_n \end{bmatrix} = a_1 b_1 + a_2 b_2 + \cdots + a_n b_n$$

<u>2</u>. Let A be an $m \times p$ matrix and B be a $p \times n$ matrix. The MATRIX PRODUCT AB of A and B, in this order, is the $m \times n$ matrix whose element in the ith row and jth column is the dot product of the ith row of A and the jth column of B.

1.

$$[2 \quad 4] \cdot \begin{bmatrix} 3 \\ 1 \end{bmatrix} = 2 \cdot 3 + 4 \cdot 1 \text{ (using } \underline{1}) $$
$$= 10$$

3.

$$[-3 \quad 2] \cdot \begin{bmatrix} -1 \\ -2 \end{bmatrix} = (-3)(-1) + 2(-2)$$
$$= 3 - 4 = -1$$

5.

$$[2 \quad 5] \begin{bmatrix} 1 & -1 \\ 2 & 3 \end{bmatrix} = \begin{bmatrix} [2 \quad 5] \cdot \begin{bmatrix} 1 \\ 2 \end{bmatrix} & [2 \quad 5] \cdot \begin{bmatrix} -1 \\ 3 \end{bmatrix} \end{bmatrix} = [2 + 10 \quad -2 + 15] = [12 \quad 13]$$

7.

$$\begin{bmatrix} 3 & 4 \\ -1 & -2 \end{bmatrix} \begin{bmatrix} -1 \\ 2 \end{bmatrix} = \begin{bmatrix} [3 \quad 4] \cdot \begin{bmatrix} -1 \\ 2 \end{bmatrix} \\ [-1 \quad -2] \cdot \begin{bmatrix} -1 \\ 2 \end{bmatrix} \end{bmatrix} = \begin{bmatrix} -3 + 8 \\ 1 - 4 \end{bmatrix} = \begin{bmatrix} 5 \\ -3 \end{bmatrix}$$

9.

$$\begin{bmatrix} 2 & -3 \\ 1 & 2 \end{bmatrix} \begin{bmatrix} 1 & -1 \\ 0 & -2 \end{bmatrix} = \begin{bmatrix} [2 \quad -3] \cdot \begin{bmatrix} 1 \\ 0 \end{bmatrix} & [2 \quad -3] \cdot \begin{bmatrix} -1 \\ -2 \end{bmatrix} \\ [1 \quad 2] \cdot \begin{bmatrix} 1 \\ 0 \end{bmatrix} & [1 \quad 2] \cdot \begin{bmatrix} -1 \\ -2 \end{bmatrix} \end{bmatrix} = \begin{bmatrix} 2 + 0 & -2 + 6 \\ 1 + 0 & -1 - 4 \end{bmatrix} = \begin{bmatrix} 2 & 4 \\ 1 & -5 \end{bmatrix}$$

11.

$$\begin{bmatrix} 1 & -1 \\ 0 & -2 \end{bmatrix} \begin{bmatrix} 2 & -3 \\ 1 & 2 \end{bmatrix} = \begin{bmatrix} [1 \quad -1] \cdot \begin{bmatrix} 2 \\ 1 \end{bmatrix} & [1 \quad -1] \cdot \begin{bmatrix} -3 \\ 2 \end{bmatrix} \\ [0 \quad -2] \cdot \begin{bmatrix} 2 \\ 1 \end{bmatrix} & [0 \quad -2] \cdot \begin{bmatrix} -2 \\ 2 \end{bmatrix} \end{bmatrix} = \begin{bmatrix} 2 - 1 & -3 - 2 \\ 0 - 2 & 0 - 4 \end{bmatrix} = \begin{bmatrix} 1 & -5 \\ -2 & -4 \end{bmatrix}$$

13.

$$[5 \quad -2] \begin{bmatrix} -3 \\ -4 \end{bmatrix} = [-15 + 8] = [-7]$$

(<u>Note</u>: This is a 1 × 1 matrix.)

15. $\begin{bmatrix} -3 \\ -4 \end{bmatrix} \begin{bmatrix} 5 & -2 \end{bmatrix} = \begin{bmatrix} [-3] \cdot [5] & [-3] \cdot [-2] \\ [-4] \cdot [5] & [-4] \cdot [-2] \end{bmatrix} = \begin{bmatrix} -15 & 6 \\ -20 & 8 \end{bmatrix}$

17. $\begin{bmatrix} -1 & -2 & 2 \end{bmatrix} \cdot \begin{bmatrix} 2 \\ -1 \\ 3 \end{bmatrix} = (-1)2 + (-2)(-1) + 2 \cdot 3 = 6$

19. $\begin{bmatrix} -1 & -3 & 0 & 5 \end{bmatrix} \cdot \begin{bmatrix} 4 \\ -3 \\ -1 \\ 2 \end{bmatrix} = (-1)4 + (-3)(-3) + 0(-1) + 5 \cdot 2 = 15$

21.

$\begin{bmatrix} 2 & -1 & 1 \\ 1 & 3 & -2 \end{bmatrix} \begin{bmatrix} 1 & 3 \\ 0 & -1 \\ -2 & 2 \end{bmatrix} = \begin{bmatrix} \begin{bmatrix} 2 & -1 & 1 \end{bmatrix} \cdot \begin{bmatrix} 1 \\ 0 \\ -2 \end{bmatrix} & \begin{bmatrix} 2 & -1 & 1 \end{bmatrix} \cdot \begin{bmatrix} 3 \\ -1 \\ 2 \end{bmatrix} \\ \begin{bmatrix} 1 & 3 & -2 \end{bmatrix} \cdot \begin{bmatrix} 1 \\ 0 \\ -2 \end{bmatrix} & \begin{bmatrix} 1 & 3 & -2 \end{bmatrix} \cdot \begin{bmatrix} 3 \\ -1 \\ 2 \end{bmatrix} \end{bmatrix}$

$= \begin{bmatrix} 2 + 0 - 2 & 6 + 1 + 2 \\ 1 + 0 + 4 & 3 - 3 - 4 \end{bmatrix} = \begin{bmatrix} 0 & 9 \\ 5 & -4 \end{bmatrix}$

23.

$\begin{bmatrix} 1 & 3 \\ 0 & -1 \\ -2 & 2 \end{bmatrix} \begin{bmatrix} 2 & -1 & 1 \\ 1 & 3 & -2 \end{bmatrix} = \begin{bmatrix} \begin{bmatrix} 1 & 3 \end{bmatrix} \cdot \begin{bmatrix} 2 \\ 1 \end{bmatrix} & \begin{bmatrix} 1 & 3 \end{bmatrix} \cdot \begin{bmatrix} -1 \\ 3 \end{bmatrix} & \begin{bmatrix} 1 & 3 \end{bmatrix} \cdot \begin{bmatrix} 1 \\ -2 \end{bmatrix} \\ \begin{bmatrix} 0 & -1 \end{bmatrix} \cdot \begin{bmatrix} 2 \\ 1 \end{bmatrix} & \begin{bmatrix} 0 & -1 \end{bmatrix} \cdot \begin{bmatrix} -1 \\ 3 \end{bmatrix} & \begin{bmatrix} 0 & -1 \end{bmatrix} \cdot \begin{bmatrix} 1 \\ -2 \end{bmatrix} \\ \begin{bmatrix} -2 & 2 \end{bmatrix} \cdot \begin{bmatrix} 2 \\ 1 \end{bmatrix} & \begin{bmatrix} -2 & 2 \end{bmatrix} \cdot \begin{bmatrix} -1 \\ 3 \end{bmatrix} & \begin{bmatrix} -2 & 2 \end{bmatrix} \cdot \begin{bmatrix} 1 \\ -2 \end{bmatrix} \end{bmatrix}$

$= \begin{bmatrix} 2 + 3 & -1 + 9 & 1 - 6 \\ 0 - 1 & 0 - 3 & 0 + 2 \\ -4 + 2 & 2 + 6 & -2 - 4 \end{bmatrix} = \begin{bmatrix} 5 & 8 & -5 \\ -1 & -3 & 2 \\ -2 & 8 & -6 \end{bmatrix}$

25.

$$[3 \quad -2 \quad -4] \begin{bmatrix} 1 \\ 2 \\ -3 \end{bmatrix} = [(3 - 4 + 12)] = [11]$$

27.

$$\begin{bmatrix} 1 \\ 2 \\ -3 \end{bmatrix} [3 \quad -2 \quad -4] = \begin{bmatrix} [1] \cdot [3] & [1] \cdot [(-2)] & [1] \cdot [(-4)] \\ [2] \cdot [3] & [2] \cdot [(-2)] & [2] \cdot [(-4)] \\ [-3] \cdot [3] & [-3] \cdot [(-2)] & [-3] \cdot [(-4)] \end{bmatrix} = \begin{bmatrix} 3 & -2 & -4 \\ 6 & -4 & -8 \\ -9 & 6 & 12 \end{bmatrix}$$

29.

$$\begin{bmatrix} 2 & -1 & 3 & 0 \\ -3 & 4 & 2 & -1 \\ 0 & -2 & 1 & 4 \end{bmatrix} \begin{bmatrix} 2 & -3 & -2 \\ 1 & 0 & 1 \\ -1 & 2 & 0 \\ 2 & -2 & -3 \end{bmatrix}$$

$$= \begin{bmatrix} [2 \ -1 \ 3 \ 0] \cdot \begin{bmatrix} 2 \\ 1 \\ -1 \\ 2 \end{bmatrix} & [2 \ -1 \ 3 \ 0] \cdot \begin{bmatrix} -3 \\ 0 \\ 2 \\ -2 \end{bmatrix} & [2 \ -1 \ 3 \ 0] \cdot \begin{bmatrix} -2 \\ 1 \\ 0 \\ -3 \end{bmatrix} \\[6pt] [-3 \ 4 \ 2 \ -1] \cdot \begin{bmatrix} 2 \\ 1 \\ -1 \\ 2 \end{bmatrix} & [-3 \ 4 \ 2 \ -1] \cdot \begin{bmatrix} -3 \\ 0 \\ 2 \\ -2 \end{bmatrix} & [-3 \ 4 \ 2 \ -1] \cdot \begin{bmatrix} -2 \\ 1 \\ 0 \\ -3 \end{bmatrix} \\[6pt] [0 \ -2 \ 1 \ 4] \cdot \begin{bmatrix} 2 \\ 1 \\ -1 \\ 2 \end{bmatrix} & [0 \ -2 \ 1 \ 4] \cdot \begin{bmatrix} -3 \\ 0 \\ 2 \\ -2 \end{bmatrix} & [0 \ -2 \ 1 \ 4] \cdot \begin{bmatrix} -2 \\ 1 \\ 0 \\ -3 \end{bmatrix} \end{bmatrix}$$

$$= \begin{bmatrix} 4 - 1 - 3 + 0 & -6 + 0 + 6 + 0 & -4 - 1 + 0 + 0 \\ -6 + 4 - 2 - 2 & 9 + 0 + 4 + 2 & 6 + 4 + 0 + 3 \\ 0 - 2 - 1 + 8 & 0 + 0 + 2 - 8 & 0 - 2 + 0 - 12 \end{bmatrix}$$

$$= \begin{bmatrix} 0 & 0 & -5 \\ -6 & 15 & 13 \\ 5 & -6 & -14 \end{bmatrix}$$

31.

$$\begin{bmatrix} 2.1 & 3.2 & -1.1 \\ -0.8 & 5.7 & -4.3 \end{bmatrix} \begin{bmatrix} -4.5 & 3.7 \\ 1.1 & -2.6 \\ -2.0 & 4.3 \end{bmatrix}$$

$$\begin{bmatrix} [2.1 \quad 3.2 \quad -1.1] \cdot \begin{bmatrix} -4.5 \\ 1.1 \\ -2.0 \end{bmatrix} & [2.1 \quad 3.2 \quad -1.1] \cdot \begin{bmatrix} 3.7 \\ -2.6 \\ 4.3 \end{bmatrix} \\ [-0.8 \quad 5.7 \quad -4.3] \cdot \begin{bmatrix} -4.5 \\ 1.1 \\ -2.0 \end{bmatrix} & [-0.8 \quad 5.7 \quad -4.3] \cdot \begin{bmatrix} 3.7 \\ -2.6 \\ 4.3 \end{bmatrix} \end{bmatrix} = \begin{bmatrix} -3.73 & -5.28 \\ 18.47 & 36.27 \end{bmatrix}$$

33.

$$AB = \begin{bmatrix} 1 & 2 \\ 0 & 1 \end{bmatrix} \begin{bmatrix} 1 & 1 \\ 2 & 3 \end{bmatrix} = \begin{bmatrix} [1 \quad 2] \cdot \begin{bmatrix} 1 \\ 2 \end{bmatrix} & [1 \quad 2] \cdot \begin{bmatrix} 1 \\ 3 \end{bmatrix} \\ [0 \quad 1] \cdot \begin{bmatrix} 1 \\ 2 \end{bmatrix} & [0 \quad 1] \cdot \begin{bmatrix} 1 \\ 3 \end{bmatrix} \end{bmatrix} = \begin{bmatrix} 5 & 7 \\ 2 & 3 \end{bmatrix}$$

$$BA = \begin{bmatrix} 1 & 1 \\ 2 & 3 \end{bmatrix} \begin{bmatrix} 1 & 2 \\ 0 & 1 \end{bmatrix} = \begin{bmatrix} [1 \quad 1] \cdot \begin{bmatrix} 1 \\ 0 \end{bmatrix} & [1 \quad 1] \cdot \begin{bmatrix} 2 \\ 1 \end{bmatrix} \\ [2 \quad 3] \cdot \begin{bmatrix} 1 \\ 0 \end{bmatrix} & [2 \quad 3] \cdot \begin{bmatrix} 2 \\ 1 \end{bmatrix} \end{bmatrix} = \begin{bmatrix} 1 & 3 \\ 2 & 7 \end{bmatrix}$$

35.

$$A(B + C) = \begin{bmatrix} 1 & 2 \\ 0 & 1 \end{bmatrix} \left(\begin{bmatrix} 1 & 1 \\ 2 & 3 \end{bmatrix} + \begin{bmatrix} -3 & 1 \\ -1 & 2 \end{bmatrix} \right) = \begin{bmatrix} 1 & 2 \\ 0 & 1 \end{bmatrix} \cdot \begin{bmatrix} -2 & 2 \\ 1 & 5 \end{bmatrix}$$

$$\begin{bmatrix} [1 \quad 2] \cdot \begin{bmatrix} -2 \\ 1 \end{bmatrix} & [1 \quad 2] \cdot \begin{bmatrix} 2 \\ 5 \end{bmatrix} \\ [0 \quad 1] \cdot \begin{bmatrix} -2 \\ 1 \end{bmatrix} & [0 \quad 1] \cdot \begin{bmatrix} 2 \\ 5 \end{bmatrix} \end{bmatrix} = \begin{bmatrix} 0 & 12 \\ 1 & 5 \end{bmatrix}$$

$$AB + AC = \begin{bmatrix} 1 & 2 \\ 0 & 1 \end{bmatrix} \begin{bmatrix} 1 & 2 \\ 2 & 3 \end{bmatrix} + \begin{bmatrix} 1 & 2 \\ 0 & 1 \end{bmatrix} \begin{bmatrix} -3 & 1 \\ -1 & 2 \end{bmatrix}$$

$$= \begin{bmatrix} [1 \quad 2] \cdot \begin{bmatrix} 1 \\ 2 \end{bmatrix} & [1 \quad 2] \cdot \begin{bmatrix} 1 \\ 3 \end{bmatrix} \\ [0 \quad 1] \cdot \begin{bmatrix} 1 \\ 2 \end{bmatrix} & [0 \quad 1] \cdot \begin{bmatrix} 1 \\ 3 \end{bmatrix} \end{bmatrix} + \begin{bmatrix} [1 \quad 2] \cdot \begin{bmatrix} -3 \\ -1 \end{bmatrix} & [1 \quad 2] \cdot \begin{bmatrix} 1 \\ 2 \end{bmatrix} \\ [0 \quad 1] \cdot \begin{bmatrix} -3 \\ -1 \end{bmatrix} & [0 \quad 1] \cdot \begin{bmatrix} 1 \\ 2 \end{bmatrix} \end{bmatrix}$$

$$= \begin{bmatrix} 5 & 7 \\ 2 & 3 \end{bmatrix} + \begin{bmatrix} -5 & 5 \\ -1 & 2 \end{bmatrix} = \begin{bmatrix} 0 & 12 \\ 1 & 5 \end{bmatrix} \qquad \text{Thus, } A(B+C) = AB + AC.$$

37. (A)

$$[0.6 \quad 0.6 \quad 0.2] \cdot \begin{bmatrix} 6 \\ 8 \\ 3 \end{bmatrix} = 3.6 + 4.8 + 0.6 = 9$$

Thus, the labor cost per boat for 1-person boats at plant I = \$9.00.

(B)

$$[1.5 \quad 1.2 \quad 0.4] \cdot \begin{bmatrix} 7 \\ 10 \\ 4 \end{bmatrix} = 10.5 + 12 + 1.6 = 24.1$$

Thus, the labor cost per boat for 4-person boats at plant II = \$24.10.

(C) Dimension of $M = 3 \times 3$
Dimension of $N = 3 \times 2$ Thus, the dimension of $MN = 3 \times 2$.

(D)

$$MN = \begin{bmatrix} 0.6 & 0.6 & 0.2 \\ 1 & 0.9 & 0.3 \\ 1.5 & 1.2 & 0.4 \end{bmatrix} \begin{bmatrix} 6 & 7 \\ 8 & 10 \\ 3 & 4 \end{bmatrix}$$

$$= \begin{bmatrix} [0.6 \quad 0.6 \quad 0.2] \cdot \begin{bmatrix} 6 \\ 8 \\ 3 \end{bmatrix} & [0.6 \quad 0.6 \quad 0.2] \cdot \begin{bmatrix} 7 \\ 10 \\ 4 \end{bmatrix} \\ [1 \quad 0.9 \quad 0.3] \cdot \begin{bmatrix} 6 \\ 8 \\ 3 \end{bmatrix} & [1 \quad 0.9 \quad 0.3] \cdot \begin{bmatrix} 7 \\ 10 \\ 4 \end{bmatrix} \\ [1.5 \quad 1.2 \quad 0.4] \cdot \begin{bmatrix} 6 \\ 8 \\ 3 \end{bmatrix} & [1.5 \quad 1.2 \quad 0.4] \cdot \begin{bmatrix} 7 \\ 10 \\ 4 \end{bmatrix} \end{bmatrix}$$

(continued)

$$= \begin{bmatrix} \$ 9.00 & \$11.00 \\ \$14.10 & \$17.20 \\ \$19.80 & \$24.10 \end{bmatrix} \begin{matrix} \text{one-person} \\ \text{two-person} \\ \text{four-person} \end{matrix}$$

This matrix represents labor costs per boat for each kind of boat at each plant. For example, $19.80 represents labor costs per boat for four-person boats at plant I.

39. (A)

$$[1 \quad 1 \quad 1] \begin{bmatrix} 4 & 2 & 3 & 7 & 1 \\ 2 & 3 & 5 & 0 & 6 \\ 10 & 4 & 3 & 4 & 3 \end{bmatrix}$$

$$= \begin{bmatrix} [1 & 1 & 1] \cdot \begin{bmatrix} 4 \\ 2 \\ 10 \end{bmatrix} & [1 & 1 & 1] \cdot \begin{bmatrix} 2 \\ 3 \\ 4 \end{bmatrix} & [1 & 1 & 1] \cdot \begin{bmatrix} 3 \\ 5 \\ 3 \end{bmatrix} \\ & [1 & 1 & 1] \cdot \begin{bmatrix} 7 \\ 0 \\ 4 \end{bmatrix} & [1 & 1 & 1] \cdot \begin{bmatrix} 1 \\ 6 \\ 3 \end{bmatrix} \end{bmatrix}$$

$$= [4 + 2 + 10 \quad 2 + 3 + 4 \quad 3 + 5 + 3 \quad 7 + 0 + 4 \quad 1 + 6 + 3]$$

$$= [16 \quad 9 \quad 11 \quad 11 \quad 10], \text{ which is the combined inventory of models}$$
A, B, C, D, and E in all three stores.

(B)

$$MN = \begin{bmatrix} 4 & 2 & 3 & 7 & 1 \\ 2 & 3 & 5 & 0 & 6 \\ 10 & 4 & 3 & 4 & 3 \end{bmatrix} \begin{bmatrix} \$ 700 & \$ 840 \\ \$1400 & \$1800 \\ \$1800 & \$2400 \\ \$2700 & \$3300 \\ \$3500 & \$4900 \end{bmatrix}$$

$$= \begin{bmatrix} [4 & 2 & 3 & 7 & 1] \cdot \begin{bmatrix} 700 \\ 1400 \\ 1800 \\ 2700 \\ 3500 \end{bmatrix} & [4 & 2 & 3 & 7 & 1] \cdot \begin{bmatrix} 840 \\ 1800 \\ 2400 \\ 3300 \\ 4900 \end{bmatrix} \\ [2 & 3 & 5 & 0 & 6] \cdot \begin{bmatrix} 700 \\ 1400 \\ 1800 \\ 2700 \\ 3500 \end{bmatrix} & [2 & 3 & 5 & 0 & 6] \cdot \begin{bmatrix} 840 \\ 1800 \\ 2400 \\ 3300 \\ 4900 \end{bmatrix} \\ [10 & 4 & 3 & 4 & 3] \cdot \begin{bmatrix} 700 \\ 1400 \\ 1800 \\ 2700 \\ 3500 \end{bmatrix} & [10 & 4 & 3 & 4 & 3] \cdot \begin{bmatrix} 840 \\ 1800 \\ 2400 \\ 3300 \\ 4900 \end{bmatrix} \end{bmatrix}$$

(continued)

$$= \begin{bmatrix} 2800 + 2800 + 5400 + 18,900 + 3500 & 3360 + 3600 + 7200 + 23,100 + 4900 \\ 1400 + 4200 + 9000 + 0 + 21,000 & 1680 + 5400 + 12,000 + 0 + 29,400 \\ 7000 + 5600 + 5400 + 10,800 + 10,500 & 8400 + 7200 + 7200 + 13,200 + 14,700 \end{bmatrix}$$

$$= \begin{bmatrix} 33,400 & 42,160 \\ 35,600 & 48,480 \\ 39,300 & 50,700 \end{bmatrix}$$

$$\begin{bmatrix} 1 & 1 & 1 \end{bmatrix} \begin{bmatrix} 33,400 & 42,160 \\ 35,600 & 48,480 \\ 39,300 & 50,700 \end{bmatrix} \qquad \text{(Note: } \begin{bmatrix} 1 & 1 & 1 \end{bmatrix} \cdot MN)$$

$$= \begin{bmatrix} 33,400 + 35,600 + 39,300 & 42,160 + 48,480 + 50,700 \end{bmatrix}$$

$= \begin{bmatrix} 108,300 & 141,340 \end{bmatrix}$, which is the total wholesale and retail values of the total inventory in all three stores.

41. (A)

$$\begin{bmatrix} 1000 & 500 & 5000 \end{bmatrix} \cdot \begin{bmatrix} 0.4 \\ 0.75 \\ 0.25 \end{bmatrix} = 1000(0.4) + 500(0.75) + 5000(0.25) = 2025$$

Thus, the total amount spent in Berkeley = \$2025.

(B)

$$\begin{bmatrix} 2000 & 800 & 8000 \end{bmatrix} \cdot \begin{bmatrix} 0.40 \\ 0.75 \\ 0.25 \end{bmatrix} = 2000(0.4) + 800(0.75) + 8000(0.25) = 3400$$

Thus, the total amount spent in Oakland = \$3400.

(C)

$$NM = \begin{bmatrix} 1000 & 500 & 5000 \\ 2000 & 800 & 8000 \end{bmatrix} \begin{bmatrix} 0.4 \\ 0.75 \\ 0.25 \end{bmatrix} = \begin{bmatrix} \begin{bmatrix} 1000 & 500 & 5000 \end{bmatrix} \cdot \begin{bmatrix} 0.4 \\ 0.75 \\ 0.25 \end{bmatrix} \\ \begin{bmatrix} 2000 & 800 & 8000 \end{bmatrix} \cdot \begin{bmatrix} 0.4 \\ 0.75 \\ 0.25 \end{bmatrix} \end{bmatrix}$$

This matrix represents cost per town.

$$= \begin{bmatrix} \$2025 \\ \$3400 \end{bmatrix} \begin{matrix} \text{Berkeley} \\ \text{Oakland} \end{matrix}$$

(D)

$$[1 \quad 1] \begin{bmatrix} 1000 & 500 & 5000 \\ 2000 & 800 & 8000 \end{bmatrix}$$

$$= \begin{bmatrix} [1 \quad 1] \cdot \begin{bmatrix} 1000 \\ 2000 \end{bmatrix} & [1 \quad 1] \cdot \begin{bmatrix} 500 \\ 800 \end{bmatrix} & [1 \quad 1] \cdot \begin{bmatrix} 5000 \\ 8000 \end{bmatrix} \end{bmatrix}$$

$$\begin{array}{ccc} \text{Phone} & \text{House} & \text{Letter} \end{array}$$

$$= [3000 \qquad 1300 \qquad 13{,}000]$$

This matrix indicates the number of each type of contact made in both towns.

EXERCISE 1-6

Things to remember:

1. The IDENTITY element for multiplication for the set of square matrices of order n (dimension $n \times n$) is the square matrix I of order n which has 1's on main diagonal (upper left corner to lower right corner) and 0's elseqhere. The identity matrices of order 2 and 3, respectively, are

$$I = \begin{bmatrix} 1 & 0 \\ 0 & 1 \end{bmatrix} \quad \text{and} \quad I = \begin{bmatrix} 1 & 0 & 0 \\ 0 & 1 & 0 \\ 0 & 0 & 1 \end{bmatrix}.$$

2. If M is any square matrix of order n and I is the identity matrix of order n, then

$$IM = MI = M.$$

3. Let M be a square matrix of order n. If there exists a square matrix B of order n such that

$$MB = BM = I,$$

where I is the identity matrix of order n, then B is called the INVERSE OF M, and is denoted by M^{-1}.

4. If the augmented matrix $[M|I]$ is transformed by row operations into $[I|B]$, then the resulting matrix B is M^{-1}. However, if all zeros are obtained in one or more rows to the left of the vertical line during the row transformation procedure, then M^{-1} does not exist.

A system of n linear equations in n unknowns has the matrix representation $AX = B$, where A is a square matrix of order n and B is an $n \times 1$ column matrix. If A^{-1} exists, then the solution to the system is $X = A^{-1}B$.

1. $M = \begin{bmatrix} 2 & -3 \\ 4 & 5 \end{bmatrix}$

$IM = \begin{bmatrix} 1 & 0 \\ 0 & 1 \end{bmatrix} \begin{bmatrix} 2 & -3 \\ 4 & 5 \end{bmatrix} = \begin{bmatrix} 1 \cdot 2 + 0 \cdot 4 & 1(-3) + 0 \cdot 5 \\ 0 \cdot 2 + 1 \cdot 4 & 0(-3) + 1 \cdot 5 \end{bmatrix} = \begin{bmatrix} 2 & -3 \\ 4 & 5 \end{bmatrix}$

$MI = \begin{bmatrix} 2 & -3 \\ 4 & 5 \end{bmatrix} \begin{bmatrix} 1 & 0 \\ 0 & 1 \end{bmatrix} = \begin{bmatrix} 2 \cdot 1 + (-3)0 & 2 \cdot 0 + (-3)1 \\ 4 \cdot 1 + 5 \cdot 0 & 4 \cdot 0 + 5 \cdot 1 \end{bmatrix} = \begin{bmatrix} 2 & -3 \\ 4 & 5 \end{bmatrix}$

3. $M = \begin{bmatrix} -2 & 1 & 3 \\ 2 & 4 & -2 \\ 5 & 1 & 0 \end{bmatrix}$

$IM = \begin{bmatrix} 1 & 0 & 0 \\ 0 & 1 & 0 \\ 0 & 0 & 1 \end{bmatrix} \begin{bmatrix} -2 & 1 & 3 \\ 2 & 4 & -2 \\ 5 & 1 & 0 \end{bmatrix}$

$= \begin{bmatrix} 1(-2) + 0 \cdot 2 + 0 \cdot 5 & 1 \cdot 1 + 0 \cdot 4 + 0 \cdot 1 & 1 \cdot 3 + 0(-2) + 0 \cdot 0 \\ 0(-2) + 1 \cdot 2 + 0 \cdot 5 & 0 \cdot 1 + 1 \cdot 4 + 0 \cdot 1 & 0 \cdot 3 + 1(-2) + 0 \cdot 0 \\ 0(-2) + 0 \cdot 2 + 1 \cdot 5 & 0 \cdot 1 + 0 \cdot 4 + 1 \cdot 1 & 0 \cdot 3 + 0(-2) + 1 \cdot 0 \end{bmatrix}$

$= \begin{bmatrix} -2 & 1 & 3 \\ 2 & 4 & -2 \\ 5 & 1 & 0 \end{bmatrix}$

$MI = \begin{bmatrix} -2 & 1 & 3 \\ 2 & 4 & -2 \\ 5 & 1 & 0 \end{bmatrix} \begin{bmatrix} 1 & 0 & 0 \\ 0 & 1 & 0 \\ 0 & 0 & 1 \end{bmatrix}$

$= \begin{bmatrix} (-2)1 + 1 \cdot 0 + 3 \cdot 0 & (-2)0 + 1 \cdot 1 + 3 \cdot 0 & (-2)0 + 1 \cdot 0 + 3 \cdot 1 \\ 2 \cdot 1 + 4 \cdot 0 + (-2)0 & 2 \cdot 0 + 4 \cdot 1 + (-2)0 & 2 \cdot 0 + 4 \cdot 0 + (-2)1 \\ 5 \cdot 1 + 1 \cdot 0 + 0 \cdot 0 & 5 \cdot 0 + 1 \cdot 1 + 0 \cdot 0 & 5 \cdot 0 + 1 \cdot 0 + 0 \cdot 1 \end{bmatrix}$

3. (continued)

$$= \begin{bmatrix} -2 & 1 & 3 \\ 2 & 4 & -2 \\ 5 & 1 & 0 \end{bmatrix}$$

5. $\begin{bmatrix} 3 & -4 \\ -2 & 3 \end{bmatrix} \begin{bmatrix} 3 & 4 \\ 2 & 3 \end{bmatrix} = \begin{bmatrix} 3 \cdot 3 + (-4)2 & 3 \cdot 4 + (-4)3 \\ (-2)3 + 3 \cdot 2 & (-2)4 + 3 \cdot 3 \end{bmatrix} = \begin{bmatrix} 1 & 0 \\ 0 & 1 \end{bmatrix}$

7. $\begin{bmatrix} 1 & -1 & 1 \\ 0 & 2 & -1 \\ 2 & 3 & 0 \end{bmatrix} \begin{bmatrix} 3 & 3 & -1 \\ -2 & -2 & 1 \\ -4 & -5 & 2 \end{bmatrix}$

$$= \begin{bmatrix} 1 \cdot 3 + (-1)(-2) + 1(-4) & 1 \cdot 3 + (-1)(-2) + 1(-5) & 1(-1) + (-1)1 + 1 \cdot 2 \\ 0 \cdot 3 + 2(-2) + (-1)(-4) & 0 \cdot 3 + 2(-2) + (-1)(-5) & 0(-1) + 2 \cdot 1 + (-1)2 \\ 2 \cdot 3 + 3(-2) + 0(-4) & 2 \cdot 3 + 3(-2) + 0(-5) & 2(-1) + 3 \cdot 1 + 0 \cdot 2 \end{bmatrix}$$

$$= \begin{bmatrix} 1 & 0 & 0 \\ 0 & 1 & 0 \\ 0 & 0 & 1 \end{bmatrix}$$

9. $\begin{bmatrix} x_1 \\ x_2 \end{bmatrix} = \begin{bmatrix} 3 & -2 \\ 1 & 3 \end{bmatrix} \begin{bmatrix} -2 \\ 1 \end{bmatrix} = \begin{bmatrix} 3(-2) + (-2)1 \\ 1(-2) + 3 \cdot 1 \end{bmatrix} = \begin{bmatrix} -8 \\ 2 \end{bmatrix}$ Thus, $x_1 = -8$ and $x_2 = 2$.

11. $\begin{bmatrix} x_1 \\ x_2 \end{bmatrix} = \begin{bmatrix} -2 & 3 \\ 2 & -1 \end{bmatrix} \begin{bmatrix} 3 \\ 2 \end{bmatrix} = \begin{bmatrix} (-2)3 + 3 \cdot 2 \\ 2 \cdot 3 + (-1)2 \end{bmatrix} = \begin{bmatrix} 0 \\ 4 \end{bmatrix}$ Thus, $x_1 = 0$ and $x_2 = 4$.

13. $\left[\begin{array}{cc|cc} 1 & 2 & 1 & 0 \\ 1 & 3 & 0 & 1 \end{array} \right] \sim \left[\begin{array}{cc|cc} 1 & 2 & 1 & 0 \\ 0 & 1 & -1 & 1 \end{array} \right] \sim \left[\begin{array}{cc|cc} 1 & 0 & 3 & -2 \\ 0 & 1 & -1 & 1 \end{array} \right]$

$\qquad R_2 + (-1)R_1 \to R_2 \qquad R_1 + (-1)R_2 \to R_1$

Thus, $M^{-1} = \begin{bmatrix} 3 & -2 \\ -1 & 1 \end{bmatrix}$.

Check:

$$M \cdot M^{-1} = \begin{bmatrix} 1 & 2 \\ 1 & 3 \end{bmatrix} \begin{bmatrix} 3 & -2 \\ -1 & 1 \end{bmatrix} = \begin{bmatrix} 1 \cdot 3 + 2(-1) & 1(-2) + 2 \cdot 1 \\ 1 \cdot 3 + 3(-1) & 1(-2) + 3 \cdot 1 \end{bmatrix} = \begin{bmatrix} 1 & 0 \\ 0 & 1 \end{bmatrix}$$

15.
$$\begin{bmatrix} 1 & 3 & | & 1 & 0 \\ 2 & 7 & | & 0 & 1 \end{bmatrix} \sim \begin{bmatrix} 1 & 3 & | & 1 & 0 \\ 0 & 1 & | & -2 & 1 \end{bmatrix} \sim \begin{bmatrix} 1 & 0 & | & 7 & -3 \\ 0 & 1 & | & -2 & 1 \end{bmatrix}$$

$R_2 + (-2)R_1 \to R_2 \qquad R_1 + (-3)R_2 \to R_1$

Thus, $M^{-1} = \begin{bmatrix} 7 & -3 \\ -2 & 1 \end{bmatrix}$.

Check:

$$\begin{bmatrix} 1 & 3 \\ 2 & 7 \end{bmatrix} \begin{bmatrix} 7 & -3 \\ -2 & 1 \end{bmatrix} = \begin{bmatrix} 1 \cdot 7 + 3(-2) & 1(-3) + 3 \cdot 1 \\ 2 \cdot 7 + 7(-2) & 2(-3) + 7 \cdot 1 \end{bmatrix} = \begin{bmatrix} 1 & 0 \\ 0 & 1 \end{bmatrix}$$

17.
$$\begin{bmatrix} 1 & -3 & 0 & | & 1 & 0 & 0 \\ 0 & 3 & 1 & | & 0 & 1 & 0 \\ 2 & -1 & 2 & | & 0 & 0 & 1 \end{bmatrix} \sim \begin{bmatrix} 1 & -3 & 0 & | & 1 & 0 & 0 \\ 0 & 3 & 1 & | & 0 & 1 & 0 \\ 0 & 5 & 2 & | & -2 & 0 & 1 \end{bmatrix} \sim \begin{bmatrix} 1 & -3 & 0 & | & 1 & 0 & 0 \\ 0 & 1 & 1/3 & | & 0 & 1/3 & 0 \\ 0 & 5 & 2 & | & -2 & 0 & 1 \end{bmatrix}$$

$R_3 + (-2)R_1 \to R_3 \qquad\qquad \frac{1}{3}R_2 \to R_2 \qquad\qquad R_3 + (-5)R_2 \to R_3$

$$\sim \begin{bmatrix} 1 & -3 & 0 & | & 1 & 0 & 0 \\ 0 & 1 & 1/3 & | & 0 & 1/3 & 0 \\ 0 & 0 & 1/3 & | & -2 & -5/3 & 1 \end{bmatrix} \sim \begin{bmatrix} 1 & -3 & 0 & | & 1 & 0 & 0 \\ 0 & 1 & 1/3 & | & 0 & 1/3 & 0 \\ 0 & 0 & 1 & | & -6 & -5 & 3 \end{bmatrix}$$

$3R_3 \to R_3 \qquad\qquad R_2 + \left(-\frac{1}{3}\right)R_3 \to R_2$

$$\sim \begin{bmatrix} 1 & -3 & 0 & | & 1 & 0 & 0 \\ 0 & 1 & 0 & | & 2 & 2 & -1 \\ 0 & 0 & 1 & | & -6 & -5 & 3 \end{bmatrix} \sim \begin{bmatrix} 1 & 0 & 0 & | & 7 & 6 & -3 \\ 0 & 1 & 0 & | & 2 & 2 & -1 \\ 0 & 0 & 1 & | & -6 & -5 & 3 \end{bmatrix}$$

$R_1 + 3R_2 \to R_1$

Thus, $M^{-1} = \begin{bmatrix} 7 & 6 & -3 \\ 2 & 2 & -1 \\ -6 & -5 & 3 \end{bmatrix}$.

Check:

$$
\begin{bmatrix} 1 & -3 & 0 \\ 0 & 3 & 1 \\ 2 & -1 & 2 \end{bmatrix}
\begin{bmatrix} 7 & 6 & -3 \\ 2 & 2 & -1 \\ -6 & -5 & 3 \end{bmatrix}
$$

$$
= \begin{bmatrix}
1 \cdot 7 + (-3)2 + 0 \cdot 6 & 1 \cdot 6 + (-3)2 + 0(-5) & 1(-3) + (-3)(-1) + 0 \cdot 3 \\
0 \cdot 7 + 3 \cdot 2 + 1(-6) & 0 \cdot 6 + 3 \cdot 2 + 1(-5) & 0(-3) + 3(-1) + 1 \cdot 3 \\
2 \cdot 7 + (-1)2 + 2(-6) & 2 \cdot 6 + (-1)2 + 2(-5) & 2(-3) + (-1)(-1) + 2 \cdot 3
\end{bmatrix}
$$

$$
= \begin{bmatrix} 1 & 0 & 0 \\ 0 & 1 & 0 \\ 0 & 0 & 1 \end{bmatrix}
$$

19.
$$
\left[\begin{array}{ccc|ccc}
1 & 1 & 0 & 1 & 0 & 0 \\
0 & 3 & -1 & 0 & 1 & 0 \\
1 & 0 & 1 & 0 & 0 & 1
\end{array}\right]
\sim
\left[\begin{array}{ccc|ccc}
1 & 1 & 0 & 1 & 0 & 0 \\
0 & 3 & -1 & 0 & 1 & 0 \\
0 & -1 & 1 & -1 & 0 & 1
\end{array}\right]
\sim
\left[\begin{array}{ccc|ccc}
1 & 1 & 0 & 1 & 0 & 0 \\
0 & -1 & 1 & -1 & 0 & 1 \\
0 & 3 & -1 & 0 & 1 & 0
\end{array}\right]
$$

$R_3 + (-1)R_1 \to R_1$ $R_2 \leftrightarrow R_3$ $(-1)R_2 \to R_2$

$$
\sim
\left[\begin{array}{ccc|ccc}
1 & 1 & 0 & 1 & 0 & 0 \\
0 & 1 & -1 & 1 & 0 & -1 \\
0 & 3 & -1 & 0 & 1 & 0
\end{array}\right]
\sim
\left[\begin{array}{ccc|ccc}
1 & 1 & 0 & 1 & 0 & 0 \\
0 & 1 & -1 & 1 & 0 & -1 \\
0 & 0 & 2 & -3 & 1 & 3
\end{array}\right]
$$

$R_3 + (-3)R_2 \to R_3$ $\frac{1}{2}R_3 \to R_3$

$$
\sim
\left[\begin{array}{ccc|ccc}
1 & 1 & 0 & 1 & 0 & 0 \\
0 & 1 & -1 & 1 & 0 & -1 \\
0 & 0 & 1 & -3/2 & 1/2 & 3/2
\end{array}\right]
\sim
\left[\begin{array}{ccc|ccc}
1 & 1 & 0 & 1 & 0 & 0 \\
0 & 1 & 0 & -1/2 & 1/2 & 1/2 \\
0 & 0 & 1 & -3/2 & 1/2 & 3/2
\end{array}\right]
$$

$R_2 + R_3 \to R_2$ $R_1 + (-1)R_2 \to R_1$

$$
\left[\begin{array}{ccc|ccc}
1 & 0 & 0 & 3/2 & -1/2 & -1/2 \\
0 & 1 & 0 & -1/2 & 1/2 & 1/2 \\
0 & 0 & 1 & -3/2 & 1/2 & 3/2
\end{array}\right]
$$

Thus, $M^{-1} = \begin{bmatrix} 3/2 & -1/2 & -1/2 \\ -1/2 & 1/2 & 1/2 \\ -3/2 & 1/2 & 3/2 \end{bmatrix} = \frac{1}{2} \begin{bmatrix} 3 & -1 & -1 \\ -1 & 1 & 1 \\ -3 & 1 & 3 \end{bmatrix}.$

$$
\begin{bmatrix} 1 & 1 & 0 \\ 0 & 3 & -1 \\ 1 & 0 & 1 \end{bmatrix} \begin{bmatrix} 3/2 & -1/2 & -1/2 \\ -1/2 & 1/2 & 1/2 \\ -3/2 & 1/2 & 3/2 \end{bmatrix} = \begin{bmatrix} 3/2 - 1/2 & -1/2 + 1/2 & -1/2 + 1/2 \\ -3/2 + 3/2 & 3/2 - 1/2 & 3/2 - 3/2 \\ 3/2 - 3/2 & -1/2 + 1/2 & -1/2 + 3/2 \end{bmatrix}
$$

$$
= \begin{bmatrix} 1 & 0 & 0 \\ 0 & 1 & 0 \\ 0 & 0 & 1 \end{bmatrix}
$$

21. The matrix equation for the given system is:

$$
\begin{bmatrix} 1 & 2 \\ 1 & 3 \end{bmatrix} \begin{bmatrix} x_1 \\ x_2 \end{bmatrix} = \begin{bmatrix} k_1 \\ k_2 \end{bmatrix}
$$

From Problem 13, the inverse of the coefficient matrix is $\begin{bmatrix} 3 & -2 \\ -1 & 1 \end{bmatrix}$. Thus,

$$
\begin{bmatrix} x_1 \\ x_2 \end{bmatrix} = \begin{bmatrix} 3 & -2 \\ -1 & 1 \end{bmatrix} \begin{bmatrix} k_1 \\ k_2 \end{bmatrix}.
$$

(A) $\begin{bmatrix} x_1 \\ x_2 \end{bmatrix} = \begin{bmatrix} 3 & -2 \\ -1 & 1 \end{bmatrix} \begin{bmatrix} 1 \\ 3 \end{bmatrix} = \begin{bmatrix} -3 \\ 2 \end{bmatrix}$ Thus, $x_1 = -3$ and $x_2 = 2$.

(B) $\begin{bmatrix} x_1 \\ x_2 \end{bmatrix} = \begin{bmatrix} 3 & -2 \\ -1 & 1 \end{bmatrix} \begin{bmatrix} 3 \\ 5 \end{bmatrix} = \begin{bmatrix} -1 \\ 2 \end{bmatrix}$ Thus, $x_1 = -1$ and $x_2 = 2$.

(C) $\begin{bmatrix} x_1 \\ x_2 \end{bmatrix} = \begin{bmatrix} 3 & -2 \\ -1 & 1 \end{bmatrix} \begin{bmatrix} -2 \\ 1 \end{bmatrix} = \begin{bmatrix} -8 \\ 3 \end{bmatrix}$ Thus, $x_1 = -8$ and $x_2 = 3$.

23. The matrix equation for the given system is:

$$
\begin{bmatrix} 1 & 3 \\ 2 & 7 \end{bmatrix} \begin{bmatrix} x_1 \\ x_2 \end{bmatrix} = \begin{bmatrix} k_1 \\ k_2 \end{bmatrix}
$$

From Problem 15, the inverse of the coefficient matrix is $\begin{bmatrix} 7 & -3 \\ -2 & 1 \end{bmatrix}$. Thus,

$$
\begin{bmatrix} x_1 \\ x_2 \end{bmatrix} = \begin{bmatrix} 7 & -3 \\ -2 & 1 \end{bmatrix} \begin{bmatrix} k_1 \\ k_2 \end{bmatrix}
$$

(A) $\begin{bmatrix} x_1 \\ x_2 \end{bmatrix} = \begin{bmatrix} 7 & -3 \\ -2 & 1 \end{bmatrix} \begin{bmatrix} 2 \\ -1 \end{bmatrix} = \begin{bmatrix} 17 \\ -5 \end{bmatrix}$ Thus, $x_1 = 17$ and $x_2 = -5$.

(B) $\begin{bmatrix} x_1 \\ x_2 \end{bmatrix} = \begin{bmatrix} 7 & -3 \\ -2 & 1 \end{bmatrix} \begin{bmatrix} 1 \\ 0 \end{bmatrix} = \begin{bmatrix} 7 \\ -2 \end{bmatrix}$ Thus, $x_1 = 7$ and $x_2 = -2$.

(C) $\begin{bmatrix} x_1 \\ x_2 \end{bmatrix} = \begin{bmatrix} 7 & -3 \\ -2 & 1 \end{bmatrix} \begin{bmatrix} 3 \\ -1 \end{bmatrix} = \begin{bmatrix} 24 \\ -7 \end{bmatrix}$ Thus, $x_1 = 24$ and $x_2 = -7$.

25. The matrix equation for the given system is:

$$\begin{bmatrix} 1 & -3 & 0 \\ 0 & 3 & 1 \\ 2 & -1 & 2 \end{bmatrix} \begin{bmatrix} x_1 \\ x_2 \\ x_3 \end{bmatrix} = \begin{bmatrix} k_1 \\ k_2 \\ k_3 \end{bmatrix}$$

From Problem 17, the inverse of the coefficient matrix is $\begin{bmatrix} 7 & 6 & -3 \\ 2 & 2 & -1 \\ -6 & -5 & 3 \end{bmatrix}$. Thus,

$$\begin{bmatrix} x_1 \\ x_2 \\ x_3 \end{bmatrix} = \begin{bmatrix} 7 & 6 & -3 \\ 2 & 2 & -1 \\ -6 & -5 & 3 \end{bmatrix} \begin{bmatrix} k_1 \\ k_2 \\ k_3 \end{bmatrix}$$

(A) $\begin{bmatrix} x_1 \\ x_2 \\ x_3 \end{bmatrix} = \begin{bmatrix} 7 & 6 & -3 \\ 2 & 2 & -1 \\ -6 & -5 & 3 \end{bmatrix} \begin{bmatrix} 1 \\ 0 \\ 2 \end{bmatrix} = \begin{bmatrix} 1 \\ 0 \\ 0 \end{bmatrix}$ Thus, $x_1 = 1$, $x_2 = 0$, $x_3 = 0$.

(B) $\begin{bmatrix} x_1 \\ x_2 \\ x_3 \end{bmatrix} = \begin{bmatrix} 7 & 6 & -3 \\ 2 & 2 & -1 \\ -6 & -5 & 3 \end{bmatrix} \begin{bmatrix} -1 \\ 1 \\ 0 \end{bmatrix} = \begin{bmatrix} -1 \\ 0 \\ 1 \end{bmatrix}$ Thus, $x_1 = -1$, $x_2 = 0$, $x_3 = 1$.

(C) $\begin{bmatrix} x_1 \\ x_2 \\ x_3 \end{bmatrix} = \begin{bmatrix} 7 & 6 & -3 \\ 2 & 2 & -1 \\ -6 & -5 & 3 \end{bmatrix} \begin{bmatrix} 2 \\ -2 \\ 1 \end{bmatrix} = \begin{bmatrix} -1 \\ -1 \\ 1 \end{bmatrix}$ Thus, $x_1 = -1$, $x_2 = -1$, $x_3 = 1$.

27. The matrix equation for the given system is:

$$\begin{bmatrix} 1 & 1 & 0 \\ 0 & 3 & -1 \\ 1 & 0 & 1 \end{bmatrix} \begin{bmatrix} x_1 \\ x_2 \\ x_3 \end{bmatrix} = \begin{bmatrix} k_1 \\ k_2 \\ k_3 \end{bmatrix}$$

From Problem 19, the inverse of the coefficient matrix is $\frac{1}{2}\begin{bmatrix} 3 & -1 & -1 \\ -1 & 1 & 1 \\ -3 & 1 & 3 \end{bmatrix}$.

Thus,

$$\begin{bmatrix} x_1 \\ x_2 \\ x_3 \end{bmatrix} = \frac{1}{2}\begin{bmatrix} 3 & -1 & -1 \\ -1 & 1 & 1 \\ -3 & 1 & 3 \end{bmatrix}\begin{bmatrix} k_1 \\ k_2 \\ k_3 \end{bmatrix}$$

(A) $\begin{bmatrix} x_1 \\ x_2 \\ x_3 \end{bmatrix} = \frac{1}{2}\begin{bmatrix} 3 & -1 & -1 \\ -1 & 1 & 1 \\ -3 & 1 & 3 \end{bmatrix}\begin{bmatrix} 2 \\ 0 \\ 4 \end{bmatrix} = \frac{1}{2}\begin{bmatrix} 2 \\ 2 \\ 6 \end{bmatrix} = \begin{bmatrix} 1 \\ 1 \\ 3 \end{bmatrix}$ Thus, $x_1 = 1$, $x_2 = 1$, and $x_3 = 3$.

(B) $\begin{bmatrix} x_1 \\ x_2 \\ x_3 \end{bmatrix} = \frac{1}{2}\begin{bmatrix} 3 & -1 & -1 \\ -1 & 1 & 1 \\ -3 & 1 & 3 \end{bmatrix}\begin{bmatrix} 0 \\ 4 \\ -2 \end{bmatrix} = \frac{1}{2}\begin{bmatrix} -2 \\ 2 \\ -2 \end{bmatrix} = \begin{bmatrix} -1 \\ 1 \\ -1 \end{bmatrix}$ Thus, $x_1 = -1$, $x_2 = 1$, and $x_3 = -1$.

(C) $\begin{bmatrix} x_1 \\ x_2 \\ x_3 \end{bmatrix} = \frac{1}{2}\begin{bmatrix} 3 & -1 & -1 \\ -1 & 1 & 1 \\ -3 & 1 & 3 \end{bmatrix}\begin{bmatrix} 4 \\ 2 \\ 0 \end{bmatrix} = \frac{1}{2}\begin{bmatrix} 10 \\ -2 \\ -10 \end{bmatrix} = \begin{bmatrix} 5 \\ -1 \\ -5 \end{bmatrix}$ Thus, $x_1 = 5$, $x_2 = -1$, and $x_3 = -5$.

29. $\begin{bmatrix} 3 & 9 & | & 1 & 0 \\ 2 & 6 & | & 0 & 1 \end{bmatrix} \sim \begin{bmatrix} 1 & 3 & | & 1/3 & 0 \\ 2 & 6 & | & 0 & 1 \end{bmatrix} \sim \begin{bmatrix} 1 & 3 & | & 1/3 & 0 \\ 0 & 0 & | & -2/3 & 1 \end{bmatrix}$

$\frac{1}{3}R_1 \to R_1$ $R_2 + (-2)R_1 \to R_2$

From this matrix, we conclude that the inverse does not exist. See $\underline{4}$. All entries to the left of the vertical line of row 2 (R_2) are zero.

31. $\begin{bmatrix} 3 & 1 & | & 1 & 0 \\ 4 & 2 & | & 0 & 1 \end{bmatrix} \sim \begin{bmatrix} 1 & 1/3 & | & 1/3 & 0 \\ 4 & 2 & | & 0 & 1 \end{bmatrix} \sim \begin{bmatrix} 1 & 1/3 & | & 1/3 & 0 \\ 0 & 2/3 & | & -4/3 & 1 \end{bmatrix}$

$\frac{1}{3}R_1 \to R_1$ $R_2 + (-4)R_1 \to R_2$ $\frac{3}{2}R_2 \to R_2$

$\sim \begin{bmatrix} 1 & 1/3 & | & 1/3 & 0 \\ 0 & 1 & | & -2 & 3/2 \end{bmatrix} \sim \begin{bmatrix} 1 & 0 & | & 1 & -1/2 \\ 0 & 1 & | & -2 & 3/2 \end{bmatrix}$

$R_1 + -\frac{1}{3}R_2 \to R_1$

Thus, the inverse is $\begin{bmatrix} 1 & -1/2 \\ -2 & 3/2 \end{bmatrix}$.

33.
$$\begin{bmatrix} -5 & -2 & -2 & | & 1 & 0 & 0 \\ 2 & 1 & 0 & | & 0 & 1 & 0 \\ 1 & 0 & 1 & | & 0 & 0 & 1 \end{bmatrix} \sim \begin{bmatrix} 1 & 0 & 1 & | & 0 & 0 & 1 \\ 2 & 1 & 0 & | & 0 & 1 & 0 \\ -5 & -2 & -2 & | & 1 & 0 & 0 \end{bmatrix}$$

$R_1 \leftrightarrow R_3$ $\qquad\qquad\qquad$ $R_2 + (-2)R_1 \to R_2$
$\qquad\qquad\qquad\qquad\qquad\qquad$ $R_3 + 5R_1 \to R_3$

$$\sim \begin{bmatrix} 1 & 0 & 1 & | & 0 & 0 & 1 \\ 0 & 1 & -2 & | & 0 & 1 & -2 \\ 0 & -2 & 3 & | & 1 & 0 & 5 \end{bmatrix} \sim \begin{bmatrix} 1 & 0 & 1 & | & 0 & 0 & 1 \\ 0 & 1 & -2 & | & 0 & 1 & -2 \\ 0 & 0 & -1 & | & 1 & 2 & 1 \end{bmatrix}$$

$R_3 + 2R_2 \to R_3$ $\qquad\qquad\qquad$ $(-1)R_3 \to R_3$

$$\sim \begin{bmatrix} 1 & 0 & 1 & | & 0 & 0 & 1 \\ 0 & 1 & -2 & | & 0 & 1 & -2 \\ 0 & 0 & 1 & | & -1 & -2 & -1 \end{bmatrix} \sim \begin{bmatrix} 1 & 0 & 0 & | & 1 & 2 & 2 \\ 0 & 1 & 0 & | & -2 & -3 & -4 \\ 0 & 0 & 1 & | & -1 & -2 & -1 \end{bmatrix}$$

$R_2 + 2R_3 \to R_2$
$R_1 + (-1)R_3 \to R_1$

Thus, the inverse is $\begin{bmatrix} 1 & 2 & 2 \\ -2 & -3 & -4 \\ -1 & -2 & -1 \end{bmatrix}$.

35.
$$\begin{bmatrix} 2 & 1 & 1 & | & 1 & 0 & 0 \\ 1 & 1 & 0 & | & 0 & 1 & 0 \\ -1 & -1 & 0 & | & 0 & 0 & 1 \end{bmatrix} \sim \begin{bmatrix} 1 & 1 & 0 & | & 0 & 1 & 0 \\ 2 & 1 & 1 & | & 1 & 0 & 0 \\ -1 & -1 & 0 & | & 0 & 0 & 1 \end{bmatrix} \sim \begin{bmatrix} 1 & 1 & 0 & | & 0 & 1 & 0 \\ 0 & -1 & 1 & | & 1 & -2 & 0 \\ 0 & 0 & 0 & | & 0 & 1 & 1 \end{bmatrix}$$

$R_1 \leftrightarrow R_2$ $\qquad\qquad\qquad$ $R_2 + (-2)R_1 \to R_2$
$\qquad\qquad\qquad\qquad\qquad\qquad$ $R_3 + R_1 \to R_3$

From this matrix, we conclude that the inverse does not exist.

37.
$$\begin{bmatrix} -1 & -2 & 2 & | & 1 & 0 & 0 \\ 4 & 2 & 0 & | & 0 & 1 & 0 \\ 4 & 0 & 4 & | & 0 & 0 & 1 \end{bmatrix} \sim \begin{bmatrix} 1 & 2 & -2 & | & -1 & 0 & 0 \\ 4 & 2 & 0 & | & 0 & 1 & 0 \\ 4 & 0 & 4 & | & 0 & 0 & 1 \end{bmatrix}$$

$(-1)R_1 \to R_1$ $\qquad\qquad\qquad$ $R_2 + (-4)R_1 \to R_2$
$\qquad\qquad\qquad\qquad\qquad\qquad$ $R_3 + (-4)R_1 \to R_3$

$$\sim \begin{bmatrix} 1 & 2 & -2 & | & -1 & 0 & 0 \\ 0 & -6 & 8 & | & 4 & 1 & 0 \\ 0 & -8 & 12 & | & 4 & 0 & 1 \end{bmatrix} \sim \begin{bmatrix} 1 & 2 & -2 & | & -1 & 0 & 0 \\ 0 & 1 & -4/3 & | & -2/3 & -1/6 & 0 \\ 0 & -8 & 12 & | & 4 & 0 & 1 \end{bmatrix}$$

$-\dfrac{1}{6}R_2 \to R_2$ $\qquad\qquad\qquad$ $R_3 + 8R_2 \to R_3$

(continued)

$$\sim \begin{bmatrix} 1 & 2 & -2 & | & -1 & 0 & 0 \\ 0 & 1 & -4/3 & | & -2/3 & -1/6 & 0 \\ 0 & 0 & 4/3 & | & -4/3 & -4/3 & 1 \end{bmatrix} \sim \begin{bmatrix} 1 & 2 & -2 & | & -1 & 0 & 0 \\ 0 & 1 & -4/3 & | & -2/3 & -1/6 & 0 \\ 0 & 0 & 1 & | & -1 & -1 & 3/4 \end{bmatrix}$$

$$\frac{3}{4}R_3 \rightarrow R_3 \qquad\qquad\qquad R_2 + \frac{4}{3}R_3 \rightarrow R_2$$
$$R_1 + 2R_3 \rightarrow R_1$$

$$\sim \begin{bmatrix} 1 & 2 & 0 & | & -3 & -2 & 3/2 \\ 0 & 1 & 0 & | & -2 & -3/2 & 1 \\ 0 & 0 & 1 & | & -1 & -1 & 3/4 \end{bmatrix} \sim \begin{bmatrix} 1 & 0 & 0 & | & 1 & 1 & -1/2 \\ 0 & 1 & 0 & | & -2 & -3/2 & 1 \\ 0 & 0 & 1 & | & -1 & -1 & 3/4 \end{bmatrix}$$

$$R_1 + (-2)R_2 \rightarrow R_1$$

Thus, the inverse is $\begin{bmatrix} 1 & 1 & -1/2 \\ -2 & -3/2 & 1 \\ -1 & -1 & 3/4 \end{bmatrix}$.

39. $A = \begin{bmatrix} 3 & 4 \\ 2 & 3 \end{bmatrix}$

$$\begin{bmatrix} 3 & 4 & | & 1 & 0 \\ 2 & 3 & | & 0 & 1 \end{bmatrix} \sim \begin{bmatrix} 1 & 4/3 & | & 1/3 & 0 \\ 2 & 3 & | & 0 & 1 \end{bmatrix} \sim \begin{bmatrix} 1 & 4/3 & | & 1/3 & 0 \\ 0 & 1/3 & | & -2/3 & 1 \end{bmatrix}$$

$$\frac{1}{3}R_1 \rightarrow R_1 \qquad R_2 + (-2)R_1 \rightarrow R_2 \qquad 3R_2 \rightarrow R_2$$

$$\sim \begin{bmatrix} 1 & 4/3 & | & 1/3 & 0 \\ 0 & 1 & | & -2 & 3 \end{bmatrix} \sim \begin{bmatrix} 1 & 0 & | & 3 & -4 \\ 0 & 1 & | & -2 & 3 \end{bmatrix}$$

$$R_1 + \left(-\frac{4}{3}\right)R_2 \rightarrow R_1$$

Thus, $A^{-1} = \begin{bmatrix} 3 & -4 \\ -2 & 3 \end{bmatrix}$.

$$\begin{bmatrix} 3 & -4 & | & 1 & 0 \\ -2 & 3 & | & 0 & 1 \end{bmatrix} \sim \begin{bmatrix} 1 & -4/3 & | & 1/3 & 0 \\ -2 & 3 & | & 0 & 1 \end{bmatrix} \sim \begin{bmatrix} 1 & -4/3 & | & 1/3 & 0 \\ 0 & 1/3 & | & 2/3 & 1 \end{bmatrix}$$

$$\frac{1}{3}R_1 \rightarrow R_1 \qquad R_2 + 2R_1 \rightarrow R_2 \qquad\qquad 3R_2 \rightarrow R_2$$

$$\sim \begin{bmatrix} 1 & -4/3 & | & 1/3 & 0 \\ 0 & 1 & | & 2 & 3 \end{bmatrix} \sim \begin{bmatrix} 1 & 0 & | & 3 & 4 \\ 0 & 1 & | & 2 & 3 \end{bmatrix}$$

$$R_1 + \frac{4}{3}R_2 \rightarrow R_1$$

Therefore, $(A^{-1})^{-1} = \begin{bmatrix} 3 & 4 \\ 2 & 3 \end{bmatrix} = A.$

41. Let x_1 = number of \$4 tickets sold
and x_2 = number of \$8 tickets sold.

For the first return of \$56,000 we have the following system to solve:

$x_1 + x_2 = 10,000$
$4x_1 + 8x_2 = 56,000$

The corresponding matrix equation is: $\begin{bmatrix} 1 & 1 \\ 4 & 8 \end{bmatrix}\begin{bmatrix} x_1 \\ x_2 \end{bmatrix} = \begin{bmatrix} 10,000 \\ 56,000 \end{bmatrix}.$

First, we compute the inverse of $\begin{bmatrix} 1 & 1 \\ 4 & 8 \end{bmatrix}.$

$$\begin{bmatrix} 1 & 1 & | & 1 & 0 \\ 4 & 8 & | & 0 & 1 \end{bmatrix} \sim \begin{bmatrix} 1 & 1 & | & 1 & 0 \\ 0 & 4 & | & -4 & 1 \end{bmatrix} \sim \begin{bmatrix} 1 & 1 & | & 1 & 0 \\ 0 & 1 & | & -1 & \frac{1}{4} \end{bmatrix} \sim \begin{bmatrix} 1 & 0 & | & 2 & -\frac{1}{4} \\ 0 & 1 & | & -1 & \frac{1}{4} \end{bmatrix}$$

$R_2 + (-4)R_1 \rightarrow R_2 \qquad \frac{1}{4}R_2 \rightarrow R_2 \qquad\qquad R_1 + (-1)R_2 \rightarrow R_1$

Thus, $\begin{bmatrix} x_1 \\ x_2 \end{bmatrix} = \begin{bmatrix} 2 & -\frac{1}{4} \\ -1 & \frac{1}{4} \end{bmatrix}\begin{bmatrix} 10,000 \\ 56,000 \end{bmatrix} = \begin{bmatrix} 20,000 - 14,000 \\ -10,000 + 14,000 \end{bmatrix} = \begin{bmatrix} 6000 \\ 4000 \end{bmatrix}.$

So, for Concert 1, x_1 = 6000 \$4 tickets
x_2 = 4000 \$8 tickets.

For a return of \$60,000:

$\begin{bmatrix} x_1 \\ x_2 \end{bmatrix} = \begin{bmatrix} 2 & -\frac{1}{4} \\ -1 & \frac{1}{4} \end{bmatrix}\begin{bmatrix} 10,000 \\ 60,000 \end{bmatrix} = \begin{bmatrix} 20,000 - 15,000 \\ -10,000 + 15,000 \end{bmatrix} = \begin{bmatrix} 5000 \\ 5000 \end{bmatrix}.$

For Concert 2, x_1 = 5000 \$4 tickets
x_2 = 5000 \$8 tickets.

Finally, for a return of \$68,000:

$\begin{bmatrix} x_1 \\ x_2 \end{bmatrix} = \begin{bmatrix} 2 & -\frac{1}{4} \\ -1 & \frac{1}{4} \end{bmatrix}\begin{bmatrix} 10,000 \\ 68,000 \end{bmatrix} = \begin{bmatrix} 20,000 - 17,000 \\ -10,000 + 17,000 \end{bmatrix} = \begin{bmatrix} 3000 \\ 7000 \end{bmatrix}.$

Thus, for Concert 3, x_1 = 3000 \$4 tickets
x_2 = 7000 \$8 tickets.

43. Let x_1 = number of ounces of mix A
and x_2 = number of ounces of mix B.

For Diet 1, we have the following system to solve:
$$0.2x_1 + 0.1x_2 = 20$$
$$0.02x_1 + 0.06x_2 = 6$$

or

$$\text{Diet 1} \left. \begin{array}{l} \text{(Diet 2)} \\[4pt] \end{array} \right. \text{(Diet 3)}$$

$$\left. \begin{array}{l} 2x_1 + x_2 = 200 \\ 2x_1 + 6x_2 = 600 \end{array} \right\} \begin{array}{l} = 100 \\ = 400 \end{array} \left. \begin{array}{l} \\ \end{array} \right\} \begin{array}{l} = 100 \\ = 600 \end{array} \left. \begin{array}{l} \\ \end{array} \right\}$$

First, compute the inverse matrix of $\begin{bmatrix} 2 & 1 \\ 2 & 6 \end{bmatrix}$.

$$\left[\begin{array}{cc|cc} 2 & 1 & 1 & 0 \\ 2 & 6 & 0 & 1 \end{array}\right] \sim \left[\begin{array}{cc|cc} 1 & \frac{1}{2} & \frac{1}{2} & 0 \\ 2 & 6 & 0 & 1 \end{array}\right] \sim \left[\begin{array}{cc|cc} 1 & \frac{1}{2} & \frac{1}{2} & 0 \\ 0 & 5 & -1 & 1 \end{array}\right] \sim \left[\begin{array}{cc|cc} 1 & \frac{1}{2} & \frac{1}{2} & 0 \\ 0 & 1 & -\frac{1}{5} & \frac{1}{5} \end{array}\right]$$

$$\frac{1}{2}R_1 \to R_1 \qquad\qquad R_2 + (-2)R_1 \to R_2 \qquad \frac{1}{5}R_2 \to R_2 \qquad\qquad R_1 + \left(-\frac{1}{2}\right)R_2 \to R_1$$

$$\sim \left[\begin{array}{cc|cc} 1 & 0 & \frac{6}{10} & -\frac{1}{10} \\ 0 & 1 & -\frac{1}{5} & \frac{1}{5} \end{array}\right]$$

Thus, $\begin{bmatrix} x_1 \\ x_2 \end{bmatrix} = \begin{bmatrix} \frac{3}{5} & -\frac{1}{10} \\ -\frac{1}{5} & \frac{1}{5} \end{bmatrix} \begin{bmatrix} 200 \\ 600 \end{bmatrix} = \begin{bmatrix} 120 - 60 \\ -40 + 120 \end{bmatrix} = \begin{bmatrix} 60 \\ 80 \end{bmatrix}$

So, for Diet 1, x_1 = 60 ounces of mix A
x_2 = 80 ounces of mix B.

For Diet 2, the solution is:

$$\begin{bmatrix} x_1 \\ x_2 \end{bmatrix} = \begin{bmatrix} \frac{3}{5} & -\frac{1}{10} \\ -\frac{1}{5} & \frac{1}{5} \end{bmatrix} \begin{bmatrix} 100 \\ 400 \end{bmatrix} = \begin{bmatrix} 60 - 40 \\ -20 + 80 \end{bmatrix} = \begin{bmatrix} 20 \\ 60 \end{bmatrix}$$

So, for Diet 2, x_1 = 20 ounces of mix A
x_2 = 60 ounces of mix B.

For Diet 3, we have:

$$\begin{bmatrix} x_1 \\ x_2 \end{bmatrix} = \begin{bmatrix} \frac{3}{5} & -\frac{1}{10} \\ -\frac{1}{5} & \frac{1}{5} \end{bmatrix} \begin{bmatrix} 100 \\ 600 \end{bmatrix} = \begin{bmatrix} 60 - 60 \\ -20 + 120 \end{bmatrix} = \begin{bmatrix} 0 \\ 100 \end{bmatrix}$$

Thus, for Diet 3, x_1 = 0 ounces of mix A
x_2 = 100 ounces of mix B.

Things to remember:

1. Given two companies C_1 and C_2, with

$$M = \begin{array}{c} \\ C_1 \\ C_2 \end{array} \overset{\begin{array}{cc} C_1 & C_2 \end{array}}{\begin{bmatrix} a_{11} & a_{12} \\ a_{21} & a_{22} \end{bmatrix}}, \quad X = \begin{bmatrix} x_1 \\ x_2 \end{bmatrix}, \quad D = \begin{bmatrix} d_1 \\ d_2 \end{bmatrix},$$

Technology   Output   Final Demand
Matrix   Matrix   Matrix

where a_{ij} is the input required from C_i to produce a dollar's worth of output for C_j. The solution to the input-output matrix equation

$$X = MX + D$$

is

$$X = (I - M)^{-1}D,$$

where I is the identity matrix, assuming $I - M$ has an inverse.

---

1. 40¢ from A and 20¢ from E are required to produce a dollar's worth of output for A.

3. $I - M = \begin{bmatrix} 1 & 0 \\ 0 & 1 \end{bmatrix} - \begin{bmatrix} 0.4 & 0.2 \\ 0.2 & 0.1 \end{bmatrix} = \begin{bmatrix} 0.6 & -0.2 \\ -0.2 & 0.9 \end{bmatrix}$

Converting the decimals to fractions to calculate the inverse, we have:

$$\left[\begin{array}{cc|cc} 3/5 & -1/5 & 1 & 0 \\ -1/5 & 9/10 & 0 & 1 \end{array}\right] \sim \left[\begin{array}{cc|cc} 1 & -1/3 & 5/3 & 0 \\ -1/5 & 9/10 & 0 & 1 \end{array}\right] \sim \left[\begin{array}{cc|cc} 1 & -1/3 & 5/3 & 0 \\ 0 & 5/6 & 1/3 & 1 \end{array}\right]$$

$$\frac{5}{3}R_1 \rightarrow R_1 \qquad\qquad R_2 + \frac{1}{5}R_1 \rightarrow R_2 \qquad\qquad \frac{6}{5}R_2 \rightarrow R_2$$

$$\sim \left[\begin{array}{cc|cc} 1 & -1/3 & 5/3 & 0 \\ 0 & 1 & 2/5 & 6/5 \end{array}\right] \sim \left[\begin{array}{cc|cc} 1 & 0 & 9/5 & 2/5 \\ 0 & 1 & 2/5 & 6/5 \end{array}\right]$$

$$R_1 + \frac{1}{3}R_2 \rightarrow R_1$$

Thus, $I - M = \begin{bmatrix} 0.6 & -0.2 \\ -0.2 & 0.9 \end{bmatrix}$ and $(I - M)^{-1} = \begin{bmatrix} 1.8 & 0.4 \\ 0.4 & 1.2 \end{bmatrix}$.

5. $X = (I - M)^{-1}D_2 = \begin{bmatrix} 1.8 & 0.4 \\ 0.4 & 1.2 \end{bmatrix} \begin{bmatrix} 8 \\ 5 \end{bmatrix}$

   Thus, $\begin{bmatrix} x_1 \\ x_2 \end{bmatrix} = \begin{bmatrix} 16.4 \\ 9.2 \end{bmatrix}$ and $x_1 = 16.4$, $x_2 = 9.2$.

7. 20¢ from A, 10¢ from B, and 10¢ from E are required to produce a dollar's worth of output for B.

9. $\begin{bmatrix} 1 & 0 & 0 \\ 0 & 1 & 0 \\ 0 & 0 & 1 \end{bmatrix} - \begin{bmatrix} 0.3 & 0.2 & 0.2 \\ 0.1 & 0.1 & 0.1 \\ 0.2 & 0.1 & 0.1 \end{bmatrix} = \begin{bmatrix} 0.7 & -0.2 & -0.2 \\ -0.1 & 0.9 & -0.1 \\ -0.2 & -0.1 & 0.9 \end{bmatrix}$

11. $X = (I - M)^{-1}D_1$

    Therefore, $\begin{bmatrix} x_1 \\ x_2 \\ x_3 \end{bmatrix} = \begin{bmatrix} 1.6 & 0.4 & 0.4 \\ 0.22 & 1.18 & 0.18 \\ 0.38 & 0.22 & 1.22 \end{bmatrix} \begin{bmatrix} 5 \\ 10 \\ 15 \end{bmatrix}$

    $= \begin{bmatrix} (1.6)5 + (0.4)10 + (0.4)15 \\ (0.22)5 + (1.18)10 + (0.18)15 \\ (0.38)5 + (0.22)10 + (1.22)15 \end{bmatrix}$

    $= \begin{bmatrix} 8 + 4 + 6 \\ 1.1 + 11.8 + 2.7 \\ 1.9 + 2.2 + 18.3 \end{bmatrix} = \begin{bmatrix} 18 \\ 15.6 \\ 22.4 \end{bmatrix}$

    Thus, agriculture, \$18 billion; building, \$15.6 billion; and energy, \$22.4 billion.

13. $I - M = \begin{bmatrix} 1 & 0 \\ 0 & 1 \end{bmatrix} - \begin{bmatrix} 0.2 & 0.2 \\ 0.3 & 0.3 \end{bmatrix} = \begin{bmatrix} 0.8 & -0.2 \\ -0.3 & 0.7 \end{bmatrix} = \begin{bmatrix} \dfrac{4}{5} & -\dfrac{1}{5} \\ -\dfrac{3}{10} & \dfrac{7}{10} \end{bmatrix}$,

    converting the decimals to fractions.

$$\begin{bmatrix} \dfrac{4}{5} & -\dfrac{1}{5} & \bigg| & 1 & 0 \\ -\dfrac{3}{10} & \dfrac{7}{10} & \bigg| & 0 & 1 \end{bmatrix} \sim \begin{bmatrix} 1 & -\dfrac{1}{4} & \bigg| & \dfrac{5}{4} & 0 \\ -\dfrac{3}{10} & \dfrac{7}{10} & \bigg| & 0 & 1 \end{bmatrix} \sim \begin{bmatrix} 1 & -\dfrac{1}{4} & \bigg| & \dfrac{5}{4} & 0 \\ 0 & \dfrac{5}{8} & \bigg| & \dfrac{3}{8} & 1 \end{bmatrix}$$

$$\dfrac{5}{4}R_1 \to R_1 \qquad\qquad R_2 + \dfrac{3}{10}R_1 \to R_2 \qquad\qquad \dfrac{8}{5}R_2 \to R_2$$

13. (continued)

$$\sim \begin{bmatrix} 1 & -\dfrac{1}{4} & \bigm| & \dfrac{5}{4} & 0 \\ 0 & 1 & \bigm| & \dfrac{3}{5} & \dfrac{8}{5} \end{bmatrix} \sim \begin{bmatrix} 1 & 0 & \bigm| & \dfrac{7}{5} & \dfrac{2}{5} \\ 0 & 1 & \bigm| & \dfrac{3}{5} & \dfrac{8}{5} \end{bmatrix}$$

$$R_1 + \dfrac{1}{4} R_2 \rightarrow R_1$$

Thus, $(I - M)^{-1} = \begin{bmatrix} 1.4 & 0.4 \\ 0.6 & 1.6 \end{bmatrix}$.

Now, $X = (I - M)^{-1}D = \begin{bmatrix} 1.4 & 0.4 \\ 0.6 & 1.6 \end{bmatrix} \begin{bmatrix} 10 \\ 25 \end{bmatrix} = \begin{bmatrix} 24 \\ 46 \end{bmatrix}$.

15. $I - M = \begin{bmatrix} 1 & 0 & 0 \\ 0 & 1 & 0 \\ 0 & 0 & 1 \end{bmatrix} - \begin{bmatrix} 0.3 & 0.1 & 0.3 \\ 0.2 & 0.1 & 0.2 \\ 0.1 & 0.1 & 0.1 \end{bmatrix} = \begin{bmatrix} 0.7 & -0.1 & -0.3 \\ -0.2 & 0.9 & -0.2 \\ -0.1 & -0.1 & 0.9 \end{bmatrix}$

$$\begin{bmatrix} 0.7 & -0.1 & -0.3 & \bigm| & 1 & 0 & 0 \\ -0.2 & 0.9 & -0.2 & \bigm| & 0 & 1 & 0 \\ -0.1 & -0.1 & 0.9 & \bigm| & 0 & 0 & 1 \end{bmatrix} \sim \begin{bmatrix} 7 & -1 & -3 & \bigm| & 10 & 0 & 0 \\ -2 & 9 & -2 & \bigm| & 0 & 10 & 0 \\ 1 & 1 & -9 & \bigm| & 0 & 0 & -10 \end{bmatrix}$$

$$\begin{array}{l} 10R_1 \rightarrow R_1 \\ 10R_2 \rightarrow R_2 \\ -10R_3 \rightarrow R_3 \end{array} \qquad\qquad\qquad R_1 \leftrightarrow R_3$$

$$\sim \begin{bmatrix} 1 & 1 & -9 & \bigm| & 0 & 0 & -10 \\ -2 & 9 & -2 & \bigm| & 0 & 10 & 0 \\ 7 & -1 & -3 & \bigm| & 10 & 0 & 0 \end{bmatrix} \sim \begin{bmatrix} 1 & 1 & -9 & \bigm| & 0 & 0 & -10 \\ 0 & 11 & -20 & \bigm| & 0 & 10 & -20 \\ 0 & -8 & 60 & \bigm| & 10 & 0 & 70 \end{bmatrix}$$

$$\begin{array}{l} R_2 + 2R_1 \rightarrow R_2 \\ R_3 + (-7)R_1 \rightarrow R_3 \end{array} \qquad\qquad \dfrac{1}{11} R_2 \rightarrow R_2$$

$$\sim \begin{bmatrix} 1 & 1 & -9 & \bigm| & 0 & 0 & -10 \\ 0 & 1 & -1.82 & \bigm| & 0 & 0.91 & -1.82 \\ 0 & -8 & 60 & \bigm| & 10 & 0 & 70 \end{bmatrix} \sim \begin{bmatrix} 1 & 1 & -9 & \bigm| & 0 & 0 & -10 \\ 0 & 1 & -1.82 & \bigm| & 0 & 0.91 & -1.82 \\ 0 & 0 & 45.44 & \bigm| & 10 & 7.28 & 55.44 \end{bmatrix}$$

$$R_3 + 8R_2 \rightarrow R_3 \qquad\qquad \dfrac{1}{45.44} R_3 \rightarrow R_3$$

(continued)

$$\sim \begin{bmatrix} 1 & 1 & -9 & | & 0 & 0 & -10 \\ 0 & 1 & -1.82 & | & 0 & 0.91 & -1.82 \\ 0 & 0 & 1 & | & 0.22 & 0.16 & 1.22 \end{bmatrix} \sim \begin{bmatrix} 1 & 1 & 0 & | & 1.98 & 1.44 & 0.98 \\ 0 & 1 & 0 & | & 0.4 & 1.2 & 0.4 \\ 0 & 0 & 1 & | & 0.22 & 0.16 & 1.22 \end{bmatrix}$$

$R_2 + 1.82R_3 \rightarrow R_2$ $\qquad\qquad\qquad\qquad$ $R_1 + (-1)R_2 \rightarrow R_1$
$R_1 + 9R_3 \rightarrow R_1$

$$\sim \begin{bmatrix} 1 & 0 & 0 & | & 1.58 & 0.24 & 0.58 \\ 0 & 1 & 0 & | & 0.4 & 1.2 & 0.4 \\ 0 & 0 & 1 & | & 0.22 & 0.16 & 1.22 \end{bmatrix} \qquad \text{Thus,}\ (I - M)^{-1} = \begin{bmatrix} 1.58 & 0.24 & 0.58 \\ 0.4 & 1.2 & 0.4 \\ 0.22 & 0.16 & 1.22 \end{bmatrix},$$

$$\text{and } X = (I - M)^{-1}D = \begin{bmatrix} 1.58 & 0.24 & 0.58 \\ 0.4 & 1.2 & 0.4 \\ 0.22 & 0.16 & 1.22 \end{bmatrix} \begin{bmatrix} 20 \\ 5 \\ 10 \end{bmatrix}$$

$$= \begin{bmatrix} (1.58)20 + (0.24)5 + (0.58)10 \\ (0.4)20 + (1.2)5 + (0.4)10 \\ (0.22)20 + (0.16)5 + (1.22)10 \end{bmatrix} = \begin{bmatrix} 38.6 \\ 18 \\ 17.4 \end{bmatrix}.$$

17. The technology matrix

$$M = \begin{bmatrix} 0.1 & 0.2 \\ 0.2 & 0.4 \end{bmatrix}$$

and the final demand matrix $D = \begin{bmatrix} 20 \\ 10 \end{bmatrix}$.

The input-output matrix equation is $X = MX + D$ or

$$X = \begin{bmatrix} 0.1 & 0.2 \\ 0.2 & 0.4 \end{bmatrix} X + \begin{bmatrix} 20 \\ 10 \end{bmatrix} \quad \text{where } X = \begin{bmatrix} x_1 \\ x_2 \end{bmatrix}.$$

The solution is $X = (I - M)^{-1}D$, provided $(I - M)$ has an inverse. Now,

$$I - M = \begin{bmatrix} 1 & 0 \\ 0 & 1 \end{bmatrix} - \begin{bmatrix} 0.1 & 0.2 \\ 0.2 & 0.4 \end{bmatrix} = \begin{bmatrix} 0.9 & -0.2 \\ -0.2 & 0.6 \end{bmatrix} = \begin{bmatrix} 9/10 & -1/5 \\ -1/5 & 3/5 \end{bmatrix}$$

$$\begin{bmatrix} 9/10 & -1/5 & | & 1 & 0 \\ -1/5 & 3/5 & | & 0 & 1 \end{bmatrix} \sim \begin{bmatrix} 1 & -2/9 & | & 10/9 & 0 \\ -1/5 & 3/5 & | & 0 & 1 \end{bmatrix} \sim \begin{bmatrix} 1 & -2/9 & | & 10/9 & 0 \\ 0 & 5/9 & | & 2/9 & 1 \end{bmatrix}$$

$\dfrac{10}{9} R_1 \rightarrow R_1$ $\qquad\qquad$ $R_2 + \dfrac{1}{5} R_1 \rightarrow R_2$ $\qquad\qquad$ $\dfrac{9}{5} R_2 \rightarrow R_2$

(continued)

$$\sim \begin{bmatrix} 1 & -2/9 & | & 10/9 & 0 \\ 0 & 1 & | & 2/5 & 9/5 \end{bmatrix} \sim \begin{bmatrix} 1 & 0 & | & 6/5 & 2/5 \\ 0 & 1 & | & 2/5 & 9/5 \end{bmatrix}$$

$$R_1 + \frac{2}{9}R_2 \rightarrow R_1$$

Thus, $(I - M)^{-1} = \begin{bmatrix} 6/5 & 2/5 \\ 2/5 & 9/5 \end{bmatrix} = \begin{bmatrix} 1.2 & 0.4 \\ 0.4 & 1.8 \end{bmatrix}$, and

$$X = \begin{bmatrix} 1.2 & 0.4 \\ 0.4 & 1.8 \end{bmatrix} \begin{bmatrix} 20 \\ 10 \end{bmatrix} = \begin{bmatrix} 28 \\ 26 \end{bmatrix}.$$

Therefore, the output for each sector is: coal, $28 billion; steel, $26 billion.

19. The technology matrix

$$M = \begin{bmatrix} 0.2 & 0.4 & 0.3 \\ 0.2 & 0.1 & 0.1 \\ 0.2 & 0.1 & 0.1 \end{bmatrix}$$

and the final demand matrix $D = \begin{bmatrix} 10 \\ 15 \\ 20 \end{bmatrix}$.

The input-output matrix equation is $X = MX + D$ or

$$X = \begin{bmatrix} 0.2 & 0.4 & 0.3 \\ 0.2 & 0.1 & 0.1 \\ 0.2 & 0.1 & 0.1 \end{bmatrix} X + \begin{bmatrix} 10 \\ 15 \\ 20 \end{bmatrix}.$$

The solution is $X = (I - M)^{-1}D$, provided $I - M$ has an inverse. Now,

$$I - M = \begin{bmatrix} 1 & 0 & 0 \\ 0 & 1 & 0 \\ 0 & 0 & 1 \end{bmatrix} - \begin{bmatrix} 0.2 & 0.4 & 0.3 \\ 0.2 & 0.1 & 0.1 \\ 0.2 & 0.1 & 0.1 \end{bmatrix} = \begin{bmatrix} 0.8 & -0.4 & -0.3 \\ -0.2 & 0.9 & -0.1 \\ -0.2 & -0.1 & 0.9 \end{bmatrix}.$$

$$\begin{bmatrix} 0.8 & -0.4 & -0.3 & | & 1 & 0 & 0 \\ -0.2 & 0.9 & -0.1 & | & 0 & 1 & 0 \\ -0.2 & -0.1 & 0.9 & | & 0 & 0 & 1 \end{bmatrix} \sim \begin{bmatrix} 8 & -4 & -3 & | & 10 & 0 & 0 \\ -2 & 9 & -1 & | & 0 & 10 & 0 \\ -2 & -1 & 9 & | & 0 & 0 & 10 \end{bmatrix}$$

$10R_1 \rightarrow R_1$
$10R_2 \rightarrow R_2$ $-\frac{1}{2}R_2 \rightarrow R_2$
$10R_3 \rightarrow R_3$

(continued)

$$\sim \begin{bmatrix} 8 & -4 & -3 & | & 10 & 0 & 0 \\ 1 & -9/2 & 1/2 & | & 0 & -5 & 0 \\ -2 & -1 & 9 & | & 0 & 0 & 10 \end{bmatrix} \sim \begin{bmatrix} 1 & -9/2 & 1/2 & | & 0 & -5 & 0 \\ 8 & -4 & -3 & | & 10 & 0 & 0 \\ -2 & -1 & 9 & | & 0 & 0 & 10 \end{bmatrix}$$

$$R_1 \leftrightarrow R_2 \qquad\qquad\qquad \begin{array}{l} R_2 + (-8)R_1 \to R_2 \\ R_3 + 2R_1 \to R_3 \end{array}$$

$$\sim \begin{bmatrix} 1 & -9/2 & 1/2 & | & 0 & -5 & 0 \\ 0 & 32 & -7 & | & 10 & 40 & 0 \\ 0 & -10 & 10 & | & 0 & -10 & 10 \end{bmatrix} \sim \begin{bmatrix} 1 & -9/2 & 1/2 & | & 0 & -5 & 0 \\ 0 & 32 & -7 & | & 10 & 40 & 0 \\ 0 & 1 & -1 & | & 0 & 1 & -1 \end{bmatrix}$$

$$-\frac{1}{10}R_3 \to R_3 \qquad\qquad\qquad R_2 \leftrightarrow R_3$$

$$\sim \begin{bmatrix} 1 & -9/2 & 1/2 & | & 0 & -5 & 0 \\ 0 & 1 & -1 & | & 0 & 1 & -1 \\ 0 & 32 & -7 & | & 10 & 40 & 0 \end{bmatrix} \sim \begin{bmatrix} 1 & -9/2 & 1/2 & | & 0 & -5 & 0 \\ 0 & 1 & -1 & | & 0 & 1 & -1 \\ 0 & 0 & 25 & | & 10 & 8 & 32 \end{bmatrix}$$

$$R_3 + (-32)R_2 \to R_3 \qquad\qquad\qquad \frac{1}{25}R_3 \to R_3$$

$$\sim \begin{bmatrix} 1 & -9/2 & 1/2 & | & 0 & -5 & 0 \\ 0 & 1 & -1 & | & 0 & 1 & -1 \\ 0 & 0 & 1 & | & 0.4 & 0.32 & 1.28 \end{bmatrix} \sim \begin{bmatrix} 1 & -9/2 & 0 & | & -0.2 & -5.16 & -0.64 \\ 0 & 1 & 0 & | & 0.4 & 1.32 & 0.28 \\ 0 & 0 & 1 & | & 0.4 & 0.32 & 1.28 \end{bmatrix}$$

$$\begin{array}{l} R_2 + R_3 \to R_2 \\ R_1 + \left(-\frac{1}{2}\right)R_3 \to R_1 \end{array} \qquad\qquad R_1 + \frac{9}{2}R_2 \to R_1$$

$$\sim \begin{bmatrix} 1 & 0 & 0 & | & 1.6 & 0.78 & 0.62 \\ 0 & 1 & 0 & | & 0.4 & 1.32 & 0.28 \\ 0 & 0 & 1 & | & 0.4 & 0.32 & 1.28 \end{bmatrix}$$

Thus, $(I - M)^{-1} = \begin{bmatrix} 1.6 & 0.78 & 0.62 \\ 0.4 & 1.32 & 0.28 \\ 0.4 & 0.32 & 1.28 \end{bmatrix}$, and

$$X = (I - M)^{-1}D = \begin{bmatrix} 1.6 & 0.78 & 0.62 \\ 0.4 & 1.32 & 0.28 \\ 0.4 & 0.32 & 1.28 \end{bmatrix} \begin{bmatrix} 10 \\ 15 \\ 20 \end{bmatrix}$$

$$= \begin{bmatrix} (1.6)10 + (0.78)15 + (0.62)20 \\ (0.4)10 + (1.32)15 + (0.28)20 \\ (0.4)10 + (0.32)15 + (1.28)20 \end{bmatrix} = \begin{bmatrix} 40.1 \\ 29.4 \\ 34.4 \end{bmatrix}.$$

Therefore, agriculture, \$40.1 billion; manufacturing, \$29.4 billion; and
energy, \$34.4 billion.

EXERCISE 1-8   CHAPTER REVIEW

1. $y = 2x - 4$ (1)

$y = \frac{1}{2}x + 2$ (2)

The point of intersection
is the solution. This is
$x = 4$, $y = 4$.

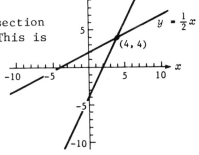

2. Substitute equation
(1) into (2):

$2x - 4 = \frac{1}{2}x + 2$

$\frac{3}{2}x = 6$

$x = 4$

Substitute $x = 4$
into (1):

$y = 2 \cdot 4 - 4 = 4$

Solution: $x = 4$
$y = 4$

3.

$A + B = \begin{bmatrix} 1 + 2 & 2 + 1 \\ 3 + 1 & 1 + 1 \end{bmatrix} = \begin{bmatrix} 3 & 3 \\ 4 & 2 \end{bmatrix}$

4.

$B + D = \begin{bmatrix} 2 & 1 \\ 1 & 1 \end{bmatrix} + \begin{bmatrix} 1 \\ 2 \end{bmatrix}$

The matrices B and D cannot be
added because their dimensions
are different.

5.

$A - 2B = \begin{bmatrix} 1 & 2 \\ 3 & 1 \end{bmatrix} - 2\begin{bmatrix} 2 & 1 \\ 1 & 1 \end{bmatrix} = \begin{bmatrix} 1 & 2 \\ 3 & 1 \end{bmatrix} + \begin{bmatrix} -4 & -2 \\ -2 & -2 \end{bmatrix} = \begin{bmatrix} -3 & 0 \\ 1 & -1 \end{bmatrix}$

6.

$AB = \begin{bmatrix} 1 & 2 \\ 3 & 1 \end{bmatrix}\begin{bmatrix} 2 & 1 \\ 1 & 1 \end{bmatrix} = \begin{bmatrix} [1 \quad 2] \cdot \begin{bmatrix} 2 \\ 1 \end{bmatrix} & [1 \quad 2] \cdot \begin{bmatrix} 1 \\ 1 \end{bmatrix} \\ [3 \quad 1] \cdot \begin{bmatrix} 2 \\ 1 \end{bmatrix} & [3 \quad 1] \cdot \begin{bmatrix} 1 \\ 1 \end{bmatrix} \end{bmatrix} = \begin{bmatrix} 4 & 3 \\ 7 & 4 \end{bmatrix}$

7. AC is *not defined* because the
dimension of A is 2×2 and the
dimension of C is 1×2. So,
the number of columns in A is
not equal to the number of rows
in B.

8.

$AD = \begin{bmatrix} 1 & 2 \\ 3 & 1 \end{bmatrix}\begin{bmatrix} 1 \\ 2 \end{bmatrix} = \begin{bmatrix} [1 \quad 2] \cdot \begin{bmatrix} 1 \\ 2 \end{bmatrix} \\ [3 \quad 1] \cdot \begin{bmatrix} 1 \\ 2 \end{bmatrix} \end{bmatrix}$

$= \begin{bmatrix} 5 \\ 5 \end{bmatrix}$

9.

$$DC = \begin{bmatrix} 1 \\ 2 \end{bmatrix} \begin{bmatrix} 2 & 3 \end{bmatrix} = \begin{bmatrix} [1] \cdot [2] & [1] \cdot [3] \\ [2] \cdot [2] & [2] \cdot [3] \end{bmatrix} = \begin{bmatrix} 2 & 3 \\ 4 & 6 \end{bmatrix}$$

10.

$$C \cdot D = \begin{bmatrix} 2 & 3 \end{bmatrix} \cdot \begin{bmatrix} 1 \\ 2 \end{bmatrix} = 2 + 6 = 8$$

[Note: $C \cdot D$ is a dot product.]

11.

$$C + D = \begin{bmatrix} 2 & 3 \end{bmatrix} + \begin{bmatrix} 1 \\ 2 \end{bmatrix}$$

Not defined because the dimensions of C and D are different.

12.

$$\begin{bmatrix} 3 & 2 & | & 1 & 0 \\ 4 & 3 & | & 0 & 1 \end{bmatrix} \sim \begin{bmatrix} 1 & \frac{2}{3} & | & \frac{1}{3} & 0 \\ 4 & 3 & | & 0 & 1 \end{bmatrix} \sim \begin{bmatrix} 1 & \frac{2}{3} & | & \frac{1}{3} & 0 \\ 0 & \frac{1}{3} & | & -\frac{4}{3} & 1 \end{bmatrix} \sim \begin{bmatrix} 1 & \frac{2}{3} & | & \frac{1}{3} & 0 \\ 0 & 1 & | & -4 & 3 \end{bmatrix}$$

$\frac{1}{3} R_1 \to R_1 \qquad\qquad R_2 + (-4)R_1 \to R_2 \qquad 3R_2 \to R_2 \qquad\qquad R_1 + \left(-\frac{2}{3}\right)R_2 \to R_1$

$$\sim \begin{bmatrix} 1 & 0 & | & 3 & -2 \\ 0 & 1 & | & -4 & 3 \end{bmatrix} \qquad \text{Thus, } A^{-1} = \begin{bmatrix} 3 & -2 \\ -4 & 3 \end{bmatrix} \text{ and}$$

$$A^{-1}A = \begin{bmatrix} 3 & -2 \\ -4 & 3 \end{bmatrix} \begin{bmatrix} 3 & 2 \\ 4 & 3 \end{bmatrix} = \begin{bmatrix} [3 \ -2] \cdot \begin{bmatrix} 3 \\ 4 \end{bmatrix} & [3 \ -2] \cdot \begin{bmatrix} 2 \\ 3 \end{bmatrix} \\ [-4 \ 3] \cdot \begin{bmatrix} 3 \\ 4 \end{bmatrix} & [-4 \ 3] \cdot \begin{bmatrix} 2 \\ 3 \end{bmatrix} \end{bmatrix} = \begin{bmatrix} 1 & 0 \\ 0 & 1 \end{bmatrix}$$

13.

$3x_1 + 2x_2 = 3 \qquad (1)$
$4x_1 + 3x_2 = 5 \qquad (2)$

Multiply (1) by 4 and (2) by −3, then add:

$0 - x_2 = -3$
$\qquad x_2 = 3$

Substitute $x_2 = 3$ into (1) to get:

$3x_1 + 2(3) = 3$
$\quad 3x_1 + 6 = 3$
$\qquad\quad 3x_1 = -3$
$\qquad\quad x_1 = -1$

Solution: $x_1 = -1$, $x_2 = 3$.

14. The augmented matrix of the system is:

$$\begin{bmatrix} 3 & 2 & | & 3 \\ 4 & 3 & | & 4 \end{bmatrix} \sim \begin{bmatrix} 1 & \frac{2}{3} & | & 1 \\ 4 & 3 & | & 5 \end{bmatrix} \sim \begin{bmatrix} 1 & \frac{2}{3} & | & 1 \\ 0 & \frac{1}{3} & | & 1 \end{bmatrix} \sim \begin{bmatrix} 1 & \frac{2}{3} & | & 1 \\ 0 & 1 & | & 3 \end{bmatrix} \sim \begin{bmatrix} 1 & 0 & | & -1 \\ 0 & 1 & | & 3 \end{bmatrix}$$

$\frac{1}{3}R_1 \to R_1$ $\quad$ $R_2 + (-4)R_1 \to R_2$ $\quad$ $3R_2 \to R_2$ $\quad$ $R_1 + \left(-\frac{2}{3}\right)R_2 \to R_1$

Thus, the solution is: $x_1 = -1$, $x_2 = 3$.

15. (A) The matrix equation of the given system is: $\begin{bmatrix} 3 & 2 \\ 4 & 3 \end{bmatrix}\begin{bmatrix} x_1 \\ x_2 \end{bmatrix} = \begin{bmatrix} 3 \\ 5 \end{bmatrix}$.

The inverse of $\begin{bmatrix} 3 & 2 \\ 4 & 3 \end{bmatrix}$, by Problem 12, is: $\begin{bmatrix} 3 & -2 \\ -4 & 3 \end{bmatrix}$.

Thus, $\begin{bmatrix} x_1 \\ x_2 \end{bmatrix} = \begin{bmatrix} 3 & -2 \\ -4 & 3 \end{bmatrix}\begin{bmatrix} 3 \\ 5 \end{bmatrix} = \begin{bmatrix} -1 \\ 3 \end{bmatrix}$. Solution: $x_1 = -1$, $x_2 = 3$.

(B) $\begin{bmatrix} 3 & 2 \\ 4 & 3 \end{bmatrix}\begin{bmatrix} x_1 \\ x_2 \end{bmatrix} = \begin{bmatrix} 7 \\ 10 \end{bmatrix}$

$\begin{bmatrix} x_1 \\ x_2 \end{bmatrix} = \begin{bmatrix} 3 & -2 \\ -4 & 3 \end{bmatrix}\begin{bmatrix} 7 \\ 10 \end{bmatrix} = \begin{bmatrix} 1 \\ 2 \end{bmatrix}$. Thus, $x_1 = 1$ and $x_2 = 2$.

(C) $\begin{bmatrix} 3 & 2 \\ 4 & 3 \end{bmatrix}\begin{bmatrix} x_1 \\ x_2 \end{bmatrix} = \begin{bmatrix} 4 \\ 2 \end{bmatrix}$

$\begin{bmatrix} x_1 \\ x_2 \end{bmatrix} = \begin{bmatrix} 3 & -2 \\ -4 & 3 \end{bmatrix}\begin{bmatrix} 4 \\ 2 \end{bmatrix} = \begin{bmatrix} 8 \\ -10 \end{bmatrix}$. Thus, $x_1 = 8$ and $x_2 = -10$.

16. $A + D = \begin{bmatrix} 2 & -2 \\ 1 & 0 \\ 3 & 2 \end{bmatrix} + \begin{bmatrix} 3 & -2 & 1 \\ -1 & 1 & 2 \end{bmatrix}$ $\quad$ Not defined, because the dimensions of A and D are different.

17. $E + DA = \begin{bmatrix} 3 & -4 \\ -1 & 0 \end{bmatrix} + \begin{bmatrix} 3 & -2 & 1 \\ -1 & 1 & 2 \end{bmatrix}\begin{bmatrix} 2 & -2 \\ 1 & 0 \\ 3 & 2 \end{bmatrix} = \begin{bmatrix} 3 & -4 \\ -1 & 0 \end{bmatrix} + \begin{bmatrix} 7 & -4 \\ 5 & 6 \end{bmatrix} = \begin{bmatrix} 10 & -8 \\ 4 & 6 \end{bmatrix}$

(continued)

18. From Problem 17,

$$DA = \begin{bmatrix} 7 & -4 \\ 5 & 6 \end{bmatrix}$$

Thus,

$$DA - 3E = \begin{bmatrix} 7 & -4 \\ 5 & 6 \end{bmatrix} - 3\begin{bmatrix} 3 & -4 \\ -1 & 0 \end{bmatrix}$$

$$= \begin{bmatrix} 7 & -4 \\ 5 & 6 \end{bmatrix} + \begin{bmatrix} -9 & 12 \\ 3 & 0 \end{bmatrix} = \begin{bmatrix} -2 & 8 \\ 8 & 6 \end{bmatrix}$$

19. $C \cdot B =$ Dot product of C and B

$$= \begin{bmatrix} 2 & 1 & 3 \end{bmatrix} \cdot \begin{bmatrix} -1 \\ 2 \\ 3 \end{bmatrix}$$

$$= -2 + 2 + 9$$

$$= 9 \quad \text{(a real number)}$$

20.

$$CB = \begin{bmatrix} 2 & 1 & 3 \end{bmatrix}\begin{bmatrix} -1 \\ 2 \\ 3 \end{bmatrix} = [-2 + 2 + 9] = [9] \quad \text{(a } 1 \times 1 \text{ matrix)}$$

21. $AD - BC$

$$AD = \begin{bmatrix} 2 & -2 \\ 1 & 0 \\ 3 & 2 \end{bmatrix}\begin{bmatrix} 3 & -2 & 1 \\ -1 & 1 & 2 \end{bmatrix} = \begin{bmatrix} [2 \ -2]\cdot\begin{bmatrix}3\\-1\end{bmatrix} & [2 \ -2]\cdot\begin{bmatrix}-2\\1\end{bmatrix} & [2 \ -2]\cdot\begin{bmatrix}1\\2\end{bmatrix} \\ [1 \ \ \ 0]\cdot\begin{bmatrix}3\\-1\end{bmatrix} & [1 \ \ \ 0]\cdot\begin{bmatrix}-2\\1\end{bmatrix} & [1 \ \ \ 0]\cdot\begin{bmatrix}1\\2\end{bmatrix} \\ [3 \ \ \ 2]\cdot\begin{bmatrix}3\\-1\end{bmatrix} & [3 \ \ \ 2]\cdot\begin{bmatrix}-2\\1\end{bmatrix} & [3 \ \ \ 2]\cdot\begin{bmatrix}1\\2\end{bmatrix} \end{bmatrix}$$

$$= \begin{bmatrix} 8 & -6 & -2 \\ 3 & -2 & 1 \\ 7 & -4 & 7 \end{bmatrix}$$

$$BC = \begin{bmatrix} -1 \\ 2 \\ 3 \end{bmatrix}\begin{bmatrix} 2 & 1 & 3 \end{bmatrix} = \begin{bmatrix} -2 & -1 & -3 \\ 4 & 2 & 6 \\ 6 & 3 & 9 \end{bmatrix}$$

$$AD - BC = \begin{bmatrix} 8 & -6 & -2 \\ 3 & -2 & 1 \\ 7 & -4 & 7 \end{bmatrix} - \begin{bmatrix} -2 & -1 & -3 \\ -4 & -2 & -6 \\ 6 & 3 & 9 \end{bmatrix} = \begin{bmatrix} 8-(-2) & -6-(-1) & -2-(-3) \\ 3-4 & -2-2 & 1-6 \\ 7-6 & -4-3 & 7-9 \end{bmatrix} = \begin{bmatrix} 10 & -5 & 1 \\ -1 & -4 & -5 \\ 1 & -7 & -2 \end{bmatrix}$$

22.

$$\left[\begin{array}{ccc|ccc} 1 & 2 & 3 & 1 & 0 & 0 \\ 2 & 3 & 4 & 0 & 1 & 0 \\ 1 & 2 & 1 & 0 & 0 & 1 \end{array}\right] \sim \left[\begin{array}{ccc|ccc} 1 & 2 & 3 & 1 & 0 & 0 \\ 0 & -1 & -2 & -2 & 1 & 0 \\ 0 & 0 & -2 & -1 & 0 & 1 \end{array}\right] \sim \left[\begin{array}{ccc|ccc} 1 & 0 & -1 & -3 & 2 & 0 \\ 0 & 1 & 2 & 2 & -1 & 0 \\ 0 & 0 & 1 & \frac{1}{2} & 0 & -\frac{1}{2} \end{array}\right]$$

$R_2 + (-1)R_1 \rightarrow R_2$ $\quad\quad -R_2 \rightarrow R_2$ $\quad\quad\quad\quad R_1 + R_3 \rightarrow R_1$
$R_3 + (-1)R_1 \rightarrow R_3$ $\quad\quad -\frac{1}{2}R_3 \rightarrow R_3$ $\quad\quad\quad R_2 + (-2)R_3 \rightarrow R_2$

$$\sim \left[\begin{array}{ccc|ccc} 1 & 0 & 0 & -\frac{5}{2} & 2 & -\frac{1}{2} \\ 0 & 1 & 0 & 1 & -1 & 1 \\ 0 & 0 & 1 & \frac{1}{2} & 0 & -\frac{1}{2} \end{array}\right] \quad \text{Thus, } A^{-1} = \left[\begin{array}{ccc} -\frac{5}{2} & 2 & -\frac{1}{2} \\ 1 & -1 & 1 \\ \frac{1}{2} & 0 & -\frac{1}{2} \end{array}\right].$$

Check:

$$A^{-1}A = \left[\begin{array}{ccc} -\frac{5}{2} & 2 & -\frac{1}{2} \\ 1 & -1 & 1 \\ \frac{1}{2} & 0 & -\frac{1}{2} \end{array}\right]\left[\begin{array}{ccc} 1 & 2 & 3 \\ 2 & 3 & 4 \\ 1 & 2 & 1 \end{array}\right] = \left[\begin{array}{ccc} -\frac{5}{2} + 4 - \frac{1}{2} & -5 + 6 - 1 & -\frac{15}{2} + 8 - \frac{1}{2} \\ 1 - 2 + 1 & 2 - 3 + 2 & 3 - 4 + 1 \\ \frac{1}{2} + 0 - \frac{1}{2} & 1 + 0 - 1 & \frac{3}{2} + 0 - \frac{1}{2} \end{array}\right]$$

$$= \left[\begin{array}{ccc} 1 & 0 & 0 \\ 0 & 1 & 0 \\ 0 & 0 & 1 \end{array}\right]$$

23. **(A)** The augmented matrix corresponding to the given system is:

$$\left[\begin{array}{ccc|c} 1 & 2 & 3 & 1 \\ 2 & 3 & 4 & 3 \\ 1 & 2 & 1 & 3 \end{array}\right] \sim \left[\begin{array}{ccc|c} 1 & 2 & 3 & 1 \\ 0 & -1 & -2 & 1 \\ 0 & 0 & -2 & 2 \end{array}\right] \sim \left[\begin{array}{ccc|c} 1 & 2 & 3 & 1 \\ 0 & 1 & 2 & -1 \\ 0 & 0 & 1 & -1 \end{array}\right]$$

$R_2 + (-2)R_1 \rightarrow R_2$ $\quad -R_2 \rightarrow R_2$ $\quad\quad R_2 + (-2)R_3 \rightarrow R_2$
$R_3 + (-1)R_1 \rightarrow R_3$ $\quad (-1/2)R_3 \rightarrow R_3$ $\quad R_1 + (-3)R_3 \rightarrow R_1$

$$\sim \left[\begin{array}{ccc|c} 1 & 2 & 0 & 4 \\ 0 & 1 & 0 & 1 \\ 0 & 0 & 1 & -1 \end{array}\right] \sim \left[\begin{array}{ccc|c} 1 & 0 & 0 & 2 \\ 0 & 1 & 0 & 1 \\ 0 & 0 & 1 & -1 \end{array}\right] \quad \begin{array}{l} \text{Thus, the solution is: } x_1 = 2 \\ \quad\quad\quad\quad\quad\quad\quad\quad\quad x_2 = 1 \\ \quad\quad\quad\quad\quad\quad\quad\quad\quad x_3 = -1. \end{array}$$

$R_1 + (-2)R_2 \rightarrow R_1$

(B) The augmented matrix corresponding to the given system is:

$$\begin{bmatrix} 1 & 2 & -1 & | & 2 \\ 2 & 3 & 1 & | & -3 \\ 3 & 5 & 0 & | & -1 \end{bmatrix} \sim \begin{bmatrix} 1 & 2 & -1 & | & 2 \\ 0 & -1 & 3 & | & -7 \\ 0 & -1 & 3 & | & -7 \end{bmatrix} \sim \begin{bmatrix} 1 & 2 & -1 & | & 2 \\ 0 & 1 & -3 & | & 7 \\ 0 & -1 & 3 & | & -7 \end{bmatrix}$$

$R_2 + (-2)R_1 \rightarrow R_2$ $(-1)R_2 \rightarrow R_2$ $R_3 + R_2 \rightarrow R_3$
$R_3 + (-3)R_1 \rightarrow R_3$

$$\sim \begin{bmatrix} 1 & 2 & -1 & | & 2 \\ 0 & 1 & -3 & | & 7 \\ 0 & 0 & 0 & | & 0 \end{bmatrix} \sim \begin{bmatrix} 1 & 0 & 5 & | & -12 \\ 0 & 1 & -3 & | & 7 \\ 0 & 0 & 0 & | & 0 \end{bmatrix}$$

$R_1 + (-2)R_2 \rightarrow R_1$

Thus, $x_1 \quad + 5x_3 = -12$ (1)
$\qquad\quad x_2 - 3x_3 = 7$ (2)

Let $x_3 = t$ (t any real number). Then, from (1),

$x_1 = -5t - 12$

and, from (2),

$x_2 = 3t + 7$.

Thus, the solution is $x_1 = -5t - 12$, $x_2 = 3t + 7$, $x_3 = t$.

24. (A) The matrix equation for the given system is:

$$\begin{bmatrix} 1 & 2 & 3 \\ 2 & 3 & 4 \\ 1 & 2 & 1 \end{bmatrix} \begin{bmatrix} x_1 \\ x_2 \\ x_3 \end{bmatrix} = \begin{bmatrix} 1 \\ 3 \\ 3 \end{bmatrix}$$

The inverse matrix of the coefficient matrix of the system, from Problem 22, is:

$$\begin{bmatrix} -\dfrac{5}{2} & 2 & -\dfrac{1}{2} \\ 1 & -1 & 1 \\ \dfrac{1}{2} & 0 & -\dfrac{1}{2} \end{bmatrix}$$

Thus, $\begin{bmatrix} x_1 \\ x_2 \\ x_3 \end{bmatrix} = \begin{bmatrix} -\dfrac{5}{2} & 2 & -\dfrac{1}{2} \\ 1 & -1 & 1 \\ \dfrac{1}{2} & 0 & -\dfrac{1}{2} \end{bmatrix} \begin{bmatrix} 1 \\ 3 \\ 3 \end{bmatrix} = \begin{bmatrix} \dfrac{-5 + 12 - 3}{2} \\ 1 - 3 + 3 \\ \dfrac{1 + 0 - 3}{2} \end{bmatrix} = \begin{bmatrix} 2 \\ 1 \\ -1 \end{bmatrix}$

Solution: $x_1 = 2$, $x_2 = 1$, $x_3 = -1$.

(B) $\begin{bmatrix} x_1 \\ x_2 \\ x_3 \end{bmatrix} = \begin{bmatrix} -\frac{5}{2} & 2 & -\frac{1}{2} \\ 1 & -1 & 1 \\ \frac{1}{2} & 0 & -\frac{1}{2} \end{bmatrix} \begin{bmatrix} 0 \\ 0 \\ -2 \end{bmatrix} = \begin{bmatrix} 1 \\ -2 \\ 1 \end{bmatrix}$ Solution: $x_1 = 1$, $x_2 = -2$, $x_3 = 1$.

(C) $\begin{bmatrix} x_1 \\ x_2 \\ x_3 \end{bmatrix} = \begin{bmatrix} -\frac{5}{2} & 2 & -\frac{1}{2} \\ 1 & -1 & 1 \\ \frac{1}{2} & 0 & -\frac{1}{2} \end{bmatrix} \begin{bmatrix} -3 \\ -4 \\ 1 \end{bmatrix} = \begin{bmatrix} \frac{15 - 16 - 1}{2} \\ -3 + 4 + 1 \\ \frac{-3 + 0 - 1}{2} \end{bmatrix} = \begin{bmatrix} -1 \\ 2 \\ -2 \end{bmatrix}$ Solution: $\begin{aligned} x_1 &= -1 \\ x_2 &= 2 \\ x_3 &= -2. \end{aligned}$

25. $\begin{bmatrix} 4 & 5 & 6 & | & 1 & 0 & 0 \\ 4 & 5 & -6 & | & 0 & 1 & 0 \\ 1 & 1 & 1 & | & 0 & 0 & 1 \end{bmatrix} \sim \begin{bmatrix} 1 & 1 & 1 & | & 0 & 0 & 1 \\ 4 & 5 & -6 & | & 0 & 1 & 0 \\ 4 & 5 & 6 & | & 1 & 0 & 0 \end{bmatrix} \sim \begin{bmatrix} 1 & 1 & 1 & | & 0 & 0 & 1 \\ 0 & 1 & -10 & | & 0 & 1 & -4 \\ 0 & 1 & 2 & | & 1 & 0 & -4 \end{bmatrix}$

$R_1 \leftrightarrow R_3$ $\qquad\qquad\qquad$ $\begin{aligned} R_2 &+ (-4)R_1 \rightarrow R_2 \\ R_3 &+ (-4)R_1 \rightarrow R_3 \end{aligned}$ $\qquad\qquad$ $R_3 + (-1)R_2 \rightarrow R_3$

$\sim \begin{bmatrix} 1 & 1 & 1 & | & 0 & 0 & 1 \\ 0 & 1 & -10 & | & 0 & 1 & -4 \\ 0 & 0 & 12 & | & 1 & -1 & 0 \end{bmatrix} \sim \begin{bmatrix} 1 & 1 & 1 & | & 0 & 0 & 1 \\ 0 & 1 & -10 & | & 0 & 1 & -4 \\ 0 & 0 & 1 & | & \frac{1}{12} & -\frac{1}{12} & 0 \end{bmatrix}$

$\frac{1}{12} R_3 \rightarrow R_3$ $\qquad\qquad\qquad\qquad$ $\begin{aligned} R_2 &+ 10R_3 \rightarrow R_2 \\ R_1 &+ (-1)R_3 \rightarrow R_1 \end{aligned}$

$\sim \begin{bmatrix} 1 & 1 & 0 & | & -\frac{1}{12} & \frac{1}{12} & 1 \\ 0 & 1 & 0 & | & \frac{10}{12} & \frac{2}{12} & -4 \\ 0 & 0 & 1 & | & \frac{1}{12} & -\frac{1}{12} & 0 \end{bmatrix} \sim \begin{bmatrix} 1 & 0 & 0 & | & -\frac{11}{12} & -\frac{1}{12} & 5 \\ 0 & 1 & 0 & | & \frac{10}{12} & \frac{2}{12} & -4 \\ 0 & 0 & 1 & | & \frac{1}{12} & -\frac{1}{12} & 0 \end{bmatrix}$

$R_1 + (-1)R_2 \rightarrow R_1$

Thus, $A^{-1} = \begin{bmatrix} -\frac{11}{12} & -\frac{1}{12} & 5 \\ \frac{10}{12} & \frac{2}{12} & -4 \\ \frac{1}{12} & -\frac{1}{12} & 0 \end{bmatrix}$;

$$A^{-1}A = \begin{bmatrix} -\dfrac{11}{12} & -\dfrac{1}{12} & 5 \\ \dfrac{10}{12} & \dfrac{2}{12} & -4 \\ \dfrac{1}{12} & -\dfrac{1}{12} & 0 \end{bmatrix} \begin{bmatrix} 4 & 5 & 6 \\ 4 & 5 & -6 \\ 1 & 1 & 1 \end{bmatrix}$$

$$= \begin{bmatrix} \dfrac{-44-4+60}{12} & \dfrac{-55-5+60}{12} & \dfrac{-66+6+60}{12} \\ \dfrac{40+8-48}{12} & \dfrac{50+10-48}{12} & \dfrac{60-12-48}{12} \\ \dfrac{4-4+0}{12} & \dfrac{5-5+0}{12} & \dfrac{6+6+0}{12} \end{bmatrix} = \begin{bmatrix} 1 & 0 & 0 \\ 0 & 1 & 0 \\ 0 & 0 & 1 \end{bmatrix}$$

26. Multiply by 100 to eliminate the decimals from the first two equations. We get the following system:

$$4x_1 + 5x_2 + 6x_3 = 36,000$$
$$4x_1 + 5x_2 - 6x_3 = 12,000$$
$$x_1 + x_2 + x_3 = 7,000$$

The matrix equation of the above system is: $\begin{bmatrix} 4 & 5 & 6 \\ 4 & 5 & -6 \\ 1 & 1 & 1 \end{bmatrix} \begin{bmatrix} x_1 \\ x_2 \\ x_3 \end{bmatrix} = \begin{bmatrix} 36,000 \\ 12,000 \\ 7,000 \end{bmatrix}$

The inverse of the coefficient matrix has been computed in Problem 25. It follows that:

$$\begin{bmatrix} x_1 \\ x_2 \\ x_3 \end{bmatrix} = \begin{bmatrix} -\dfrac{11}{12} & -\dfrac{1}{12} & 5 \\ \dfrac{10}{12} & \dfrac{2}{12} & -4 \\ \dfrac{1}{12} & -\dfrac{1}{12} & 0 \end{bmatrix} \begin{bmatrix} 36,000 \\ 12,000 \\ 7,000 \end{bmatrix} = \begin{bmatrix} -33,000 - 1,000 + 35,000 \\ 30,000 + 2,000 - 28,000 \\ 3,000 - 1,000 + 0 \end{bmatrix} = \begin{bmatrix} 1,000 \\ 4,000 \\ 2,000 \end{bmatrix}$$

Solution: $x_1 = 1,000$, $x_2 = 4,000$, $x_3 = 2,000$.

27. The augmented matrix corresponding to the given system is:

$$\begin{bmatrix} 0.04 & 0.05 & 0.06 & | & 360 \\ 0.04 & 0.05 & -0.06 & | & 120 \\ 1 & 1 & 1 & | & 7,000 \end{bmatrix} \sim \begin{bmatrix} 4 & 5 & 6 & | & 36,000 \\ 4 & 5 & -6 & | & 12,000 \\ 1 & 1 & 1 & | & 7,000 \end{bmatrix}$$

$100R_1 \rightarrow R_1$ $\qquad\qquad\qquad\qquad$ $R_1 \leftrightarrow R_3$
$100R_2 \rightarrow R_2$

$$\sim \begin{bmatrix} 1 & 1 & 1 & | & 7,000 \\ 4 & 5 & -6 & | & 12,000 \\ 4 & 5 & 6 & | & 36,000 \end{bmatrix} \sim \begin{bmatrix} 1 & 1 & 1 & | & 7,000 \\ 0 & 1 & -10 & | & -16,000 \\ 0 & 1 & 2 & | & 9,000 \end{bmatrix} \sim \begin{bmatrix} 1 & 1 & 1 & | & 7,000 \\ 0 & 1 & -10 & | & -16,000 \\ 0 & 0 & 12 & | & 24,000 \end{bmatrix}$$

$R_2 + (-4)R_1 \rightarrow R_2$ $\qquad$ $R_3 + (-1)R_1 \rightarrow R_3$ $\qquad$ $\dfrac{1}{12}R_3 \rightarrow R_3$
$R_3 + (-4)R_1 \rightarrow R_3$

$$\sim \begin{bmatrix} 1 & 1 & 1 & | & 7{,}000 \\ 0 & 1 & -10 & | & -16{,}000 \\ 0 & 0 & 1 & | & 2{,}000 \end{bmatrix} \sim \begin{bmatrix} 1 & 1 & 0 & | & 5{,}000 \\ 0 & 1 & 0 & | & 4{,}000 \\ 0 & 0 & 1 & | & 2{,}000 \end{bmatrix} \sim \begin{bmatrix} 1 & 0 & 0 & | & 1{,}000 \\ 0 & 1 & 0 & | & 4{,}000 \\ 0 & 0 & 1 & | & 2{,}000 \end{bmatrix}$$

$R_2 + 10R_3 \rightarrow R_2$ $\qquad\qquad R_1 + (-1)R_2 \rightarrow R_1$
$R_1 + (-1)R_3 \rightarrow R_1$

Thus, $x_1 = 1000$, $x_2 = 4{,}000$, $x_3 = 2{,}000$.

28. Let x_1 = number of tons of ore A
and x_2 = number of tons of ore B.

Then, we have the following system of equations:

$0.01x_1 + 0.02x_2 = 4.5$
$0.02x_1 + 0.05x_2 = 10$

Multiply each equation by 100. This yields

$x_1 + 2x_2 = 450$
$2x_1 + 5x_2 = 1000$

The augmented matrix corresponding to this system is:

$$\begin{bmatrix} 1 & 2 & | & 450 \\ 2 & 5 & | & 1000 \end{bmatrix} \sim \begin{bmatrix} 1 & 2 & | & 450 \\ 0 & 1 & | & 100 \end{bmatrix} \sim \begin{bmatrix} 1 & 0 & | & 250 \\ 0 & 1 & | & 100 \end{bmatrix}$$

$R_2 + (-2)R_1 \rightarrow R_2$ $\qquad R_1 + (-2)R_2 \rightarrow R_1$

Thus, the solution is: $x_1 = 250$ tons of ore A, $x_2 = 100$ tons of ore B.

29. (A) The matrix equation for Problem 28 is:

$$\begin{bmatrix} 0.01 & 0.02 \\ 0.02 & 0.05 \end{bmatrix} \begin{bmatrix} x_1 \\ x_2 \end{bmatrix} = \begin{bmatrix} 4.5 \\ 10 \end{bmatrix}$$

First, compute the inverse of $\begin{bmatrix} 0.01 & 0.02 \\ 0.02 & 0.05 \end{bmatrix}$:

$$\begin{bmatrix} 0.01 & 0.02 & | & 1 & 0 \\ 0.02 & 0.05 & | & 0 & 1 \end{bmatrix} \sim \begin{bmatrix} 1 & 2 & | & 100 & 0 \\ 0.02 & 0.05 & | & 0 & 1 \end{bmatrix} \sim \begin{bmatrix} 1 & 2 & | & 100 & 0 \\ 0 & 0.01 & | & -2 & 1 \end{bmatrix}$$

$100R_1 \rightarrow R_1$ $\qquad R_2 + (-0.02)R_1 \rightarrow R_2$ $\qquad 100R_2 \rightarrow R_2$

$$\sim \begin{bmatrix} 1 & 2 & | & 100 & 0 \\ 0 & 1 & | & -200 & 100 \end{bmatrix} \sim \begin{bmatrix} 1 & 0 & | & 500 & -200 \\ 0 & 1 & | & -200 & 100 \end{bmatrix}$$

$R_1 + (-2)R_2 \rightarrow R_1$

Thus, the inverse matrix is $\begin{bmatrix} 500 & -200 \\ -200 & 100 \end{bmatrix}$.

Hence, $\begin{bmatrix} x_1 \\ x_2 \end{bmatrix} = \begin{bmatrix} 500 & -200 \\ -200 & 100 \end{bmatrix} \begin{bmatrix} 4.5 \\ 10 \end{bmatrix} = \begin{bmatrix} 2250 - 2000 \\ -900 + 1000 \end{bmatrix} = \begin{bmatrix} 250 \\ 100 \end{bmatrix}$.

Again the solution is: $x_1 = 250$ tons of ore A
$x_2 = 100$ tons of ore B.

(B) $\begin{bmatrix} x_1 \\ x_2 \end{bmatrix} = \begin{bmatrix} 500 & -200 \\ -200 & 100 \end{bmatrix} \begin{bmatrix} 2.3 \\ 5 \end{bmatrix} = \begin{bmatrix} 1150 - 1000 \\ -460 + 500 \end{bmatrix} = \begin{bmatrix} 150 \\ 40 \end{bmatrix}$

Now the solution is: $x_1 = 150$ tons of ore A
$x_2 = 40$ tons of ore B.

30. (A) $MN = \begin{bmatrix} 4800 & 600 & 300 \\ 6000 & 1400 & 700 \end{bmatrix} \begin{bmatrix} 0.75 & 0.70 \\ 6.50 & 6.70 \\ 0.40 & 0.50 \end{bmatrix}$

$= \begin{bmatrix} 4800(0.75) + 600(6.50) + 300(0.40) & 4800(0.70) + 600(6.70) + 300(0.50) \\ 6000(0.75) + 1400(6.50) + 700(0.40) & 6000(0.70) + 1400(6.70) + 700(0.50) \end{bmatrix}$

	Supplier A	Supplier B	
$=$	$ 7,620	$ 7,530	Alloy 1
	$13,880	$13,930	Alloy 2

This matrix represents the cost of each allow from each supplier.

(B) $[1 \quad 1]MN = [1 \quad 1] \begin{bmatrix} 7,620 & 7,530 \\ 13,800 & 13,930 \end{bmatrix}$

$= [7,620 + 13,880 \quad 7,530 + 13,930]$

$= [\$21,500 \quad \$21,460]$

This matrix represents the total cost of both alloys from each supplier.

31. (A) The labor cost for producing one Model B calculator in California is:

$$[0.25 \text{ hr} \quad 0.20 \text{ hr} \quad 0.05 \text{ hr}] \cdot \begin{bmatrix} \$15 \\ \$12 \\ \$4 \end{bmatrix}$$

$$= (0.25)(15) + (0.20)(12) + (0.05)(4)$$
$$= 3.75 + 2.40 + 0.20$$
$$= \$6.35$$

(B) $MN = \begin{bmatrix} 0.15 \text{ hr} & 0.10 \text{ hr} & 0.05 \text{ hr} \\ 0.25 \text{ hr} & 0.20 \text{ hr} & 0.05 \text{ hr} \end{bmatrix} \begin{bmatrix} \$15 & \$12 \\ \$12 & \$10 \\ \$4 & \$4 \end{bmatrix}$

$$= \begin{bmatrix} (0.15)15 + (0.10)12 + (0.05)4 & (0.15)12 + (0.10)10 + (0.05)4 \\ (0.25)15 + (0.20)12 + (0.05)4 & (0.25)12 + (0.20)10 + (0.05)4 \end{bmatrix}$$

$$= \begin{array}{cc} & \text{Calif.} \quad \text{Texas} \\ & \begin{bmatrix} \$3.65 & \$3.00 \\ \$6.35 & \$5.20 \end{bmatrix} \begin{array}{l} \text{Model A} \\ \text{Model B} \end{array} \end{array}$$

This matrix represents the total labor costs for each model at each plant.

32. Let x_1 = amount invested at 5% and x_2 = amount invested at 10%.

Then,
$$x_1 + x_2 = 5000$$
$$0.05x_1 + 0.1x_2 = 400$$

The augmented matrix for the system given above is:

$$\begin{bmatrix} 1 & 1 & | & 5000 \\ 0.05 & 0.1 & | & 400 \end{bmatrix} \sim \begin{bmatrix} 1 & 1 & | & 5000 \\ 0 & 0.05 & | & 150 \end{bmatrix} \sim \begin{bmatrix} 1 & 1 & | & 5000 \\ 0 & 1 & | & 3000 \end{bmatrix} \sim \begin{bmatrix} 1 & 0 & | & 2000 \\ 0 & 1 & | & 3000 \end{bmatrix}$$

$$R_2 + (-0.05)R_1 \rightarrow R_2 \qquad \frac{1}{0.05}R_2 \rightarrow R_2 \qquad R_1 + (-1)R_2 \rightarrow R_1$$

Hence, $x_1 = \$2000$ at 5% $x_2 = \$3000$ at 10%.

33. The matrix equation corresponding to the system in Problem 32 is:

$$\begin{bmatrix} 1 & 1 \\ 0.05 & 0.1 \end{bmatrix} \begin{bmatrix} x_1 \\ x_2 \end{bmatrix} = \begin{bmatrix} 5000 \\ 400 \end{bmatrix}$$

SYSTEMS OF LINEAR EQUATIONS; MATRICES

Now we compute the inverse matrix of $\begin{bmatrix} 1 & 1 \\ 0.05 & 0.1 \end{bmatrix}$.

$$\left[\begin{array}{cc|cc} 1 & 1 & 1 & 0 \\ 0.05 & 0.1 & 0 & 1 \end{array}\right] \sim \left[\begin{array}{cc|cc} 1 & 1 & 1 & 0 \\ 0 & 0.05 & -0.05 & 1 \end{array}\right] \sim \left[\begin{array}{cc|cc} 1 & 1 & 1 & 0 \\ 0 & 1 & -1 & 20 \end{array}\right]$$

$$R_2 + (-0.05)R_1 \to R_2 \qquad \frac{1}{0.05}R_2 \to R_2 \qquad\qquad R_1 + (-1)R_2 \to R_1$$

$$\sim \left[\begin{array}{cc|cc} 1 & 0 & 2 & -20 \\ 0 & 1 & -1 & 20 \end{array}\right]$$

Thus, the inverse of the coefficient matrix is $\begin{bmatrix} 2 & -20 \\ -1 & 20 \end{bmatrix}$, and

$$\begin{bmatrix} x_1 \\ x_2 \end{bmatrix} = \begin{bmatrix} 2 & -20 \\ -1 & 20 \end{bmatrix} \begin{bmatrix} 5000 \\ 400 \end{bmatrix} = \begin{bmatrix} 10{,}000 - 8000 \\ -5000 + 8000 \end{bmatrix} = \begin{bmatrix} 2000 \\ 3000 \end{bmatrix}.$$

So, $x_1 = \$2000$ at 5%
$x_2 = \$3000$ at 10%.

CHAPTER 2   LINEAR INEQUALITIES
AND LINEAR PROGRAMMING

EXERCISE 2-1

Things to remember:

1. The graph of the linear inequality

    $$Ax + By < C \quad \text{or} \quad Ax + By > C$$

    with $B \neq 0$ is either the <u>upper half-plane</u> or the <u>lower half-plane</u> (but not both) determined by the line $Ax + By = C$. If $B = 0$, the graph of

    $$Ax < C \quad \text{or} \quad Ax > C$$

    is either the right half-plane or the left half-plane (but not both) determined by the vertical line $Ax = C$.

2. For strict inequalities ("$<$" or "$>$"), the line is not included in the graph. For weak inequalities ("$\leqslant$" or "$\geqslant$"), the line is included in the graph.

3. PROCEDURE FOR GRAPHING LINEAR INEQUALITIES

    (a) First graph $Ax + By = C$ as a broken line if equality is not included in the original statement or as a solid line if equality is included.

    (b) Choose a test point anywhere in the plane not on the line [the origin $(0, 0)$ often requires the least computation] and substitute the coordinates into the inequality.

    (c) The graph of the original inequality includes the half-plane containing the test point if the inequality is satisfied by that point or

the half-plane not containing the test point
if the inequality is not satisfied by that
point.

4. To solve a system of linear inequalities graphi-
cally, graph each inequality in the system and
then take the intersection of all the graphs.
The resulting graph is called the SOLUTION REGION,
or FEASIBLE REGION.

5. The solution region of a system of linear
inequalities is BOUNDED if it can be enclosed
within a circle; if it cannot be enclosed within
a circle, then it is UNBOUNDED.

6. A CORNER POINT of a solution region is a point in
the solution region which is the intersection of
two boundary lines.

---

1. $y \leqslant x - 1$

Graph $y = x - 1$ as a solid line.

Test point $(0, 0)$:

$0 \leqslant 0 - 1$
$0 \leqslant -1$

The inequality is false. Thus,
the graph is below the line
$y = x - 1$, including the line.

x	y
0	-1
1	0

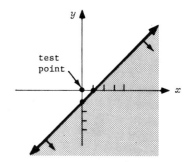

3. $3x - 2y > 6$

Graph $3x - 2y = 6$ as a broken line.

Test point $(0, 0)$:

$3 \cdot 0 - 2 \cdot 0 > 6$
$0 > 6$

The inequality is false. Thus,
the graph is below the line
$3x - 2y = 6$, not including the line.

x	y
0	-3
2	0

5. $x \geqslant -4$

Graph $x = -4$ [the vertical line
through $(-4, 0)$] as a solid line.

Test point $(0, 0)$:

$0 \geqslant -4$

The inequality is true. Thus, the
graph is to the right of the line
$x = -4$, including the line.

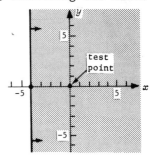

CHAPTER 2

7. $-4 \leqslant y < 4$

Graph $y = -4$ as a solid line and
$y = 4$ as a broken line [hori-
zontal lines through $(0, -4)$ and
$(0, 4)$, respectively].

Test point $(0, 0)$:

$4 \leqslant 0$ and $0 < 4$
i.e., $-4 \leqslant 0 < 4$

Both inequalities are true. Thus,
the graph is between the lines
$y = -4$ and $y = 4$, including the
line $y = -4$ but not including the
line $y = 4$.

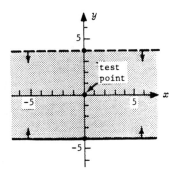

9. $10x + 2y \geqslant 84$

Graph the line
$10x + 2y = 84$ as a
solid line.

x	y
0	42
8.4	0

Test point $(0, 0)$:

$10 \cdot 0 + 2 \cdot 0 \geqslant 84$
$0 \geqslant 85$

The inequality is false. Thus,
the graph is above the line
$10x + 2y = 84$, including the
line.

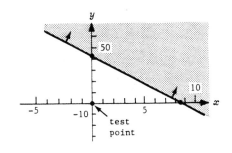

11. $0.9x + 1.8y \leqslant 864$

Graph the line $0.9x + 1.8y = 864$ or $9x + 18y = 8640$ as a solid line.

Test point $(0, 0)$:

$9(0) + 18(0) \leqslant 8640$
$0 \leqslant 8640$

x	y
0	480
960	0

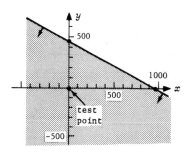

The inequality is true. Thus,
the graph is below the line
$0.9x + 1.8y = 864$, including
the line.

13. The graphs of the inequalities are shown
at the right. The solution is indicated
by the shaded region.

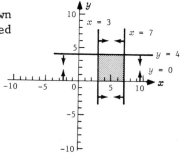

15. The graphs of the inequalities are shown at the right. The solution is indicated by the shaded region.

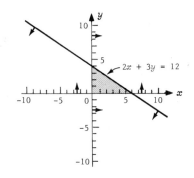

17. The graphs of the inequalities are shown below. The solution is indicated by the shaded region.

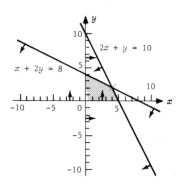

19. The graphs of the inequalities are shown below. The solution is indicated by the shaded region.

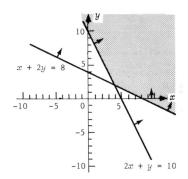

21. The graphs of the inequalities are shown at the right. The solution is indicated by the shaded region. The solution region is *bounded*.

The corner points of the solution region are:

$(0, 0)$, the intersection of $x = 0$, $y = 0$;
$(0, 6)$, the intersection of $x = 0$, $x + 2y = 12$;
$(2, 5)$, the intersection of $x + 2y = 12$,
$\qquad\qquad x + y = 7$;
$(3, 4)$, the intersection of $x + y = 7$,
$\qquad\qquad 2x + y = 10$;
$(5, 0)$, the intersection of $y = 0$, $2x + y = 10$.

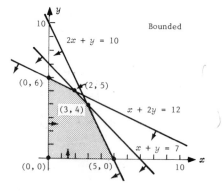

Note that the point of intersection of the lines $2x + y = 10$, $x + 2y = 12$ is not a corner point because it is not in the solution region.

23. The graphs of the inequalities are shown at the right. The solution is indicated by the shaded region, which is *unbounded*.

The corner points are:

(0, 16), the intersection of $x = 0$,
$\qquad\qquad 2x + y = 16$;
(4, 8), the intersection of $2x + y = 16$,
$\qquad\qquad x + y = 12$;
(10, 2), the intersection of $x + y = 12$,
$\qquad\qquad\quad x + 2y = 14$;
(14, 0), the intersection of $x = 0$,
$\qquad\qquad\quad x + 2y = 14$.

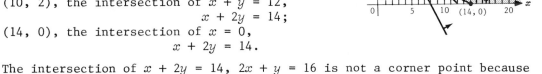

The intersection of $x + 2y = 14$, $2x + y = 16$ is not a corner point because it is not in the solution region.

25. The graphs of the inequalities are shown below. The solution is indicated by the shaded region, which is *bounded*.

The corner points are (8, 6), (4, 7), and (9, 3).

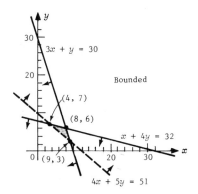

27. The graphs of the inequalities are shown below. The system of inequalities does not have a solution because the intersection of the graphs is empty.

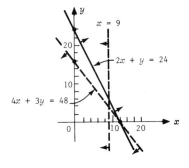

29. The graphs of the inequalities are shown at the right. The solution is indicated by the shaded region, which is *unbounded*.

The corner points are (0, 0), (4, 4), and (8, 12).

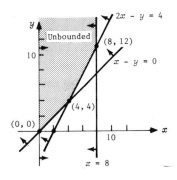

31. The graphs of the inequalities are shown below. The solution is indicated by the shaded region, which is *bounded*.

The corner points are (2, 1), (3, 6), (5, 4), and (5, 2).

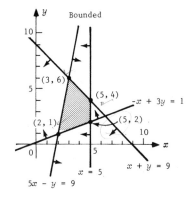

33. The graphs of the inequalities are shown below. The solution is indicated by the shaded region, which is *bounded*.

The corner points are (0, 0), (0, 800), (400, 600), (600, 450), and (900, 0).

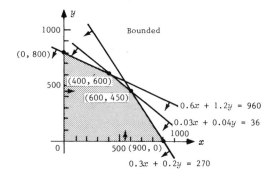

35. Let x = the number of trick skis and y = the number of slalom skis produced per day. We have the following inequalities:

$6x + 4y \leq 104$ for fabrication
$x + y \leq 24$ for finishing

Also, $x \geq 0$ and $y \geq 0$.

The graphs of these inequalities are shown below. The shaded region indicates the set of feasible solutions.

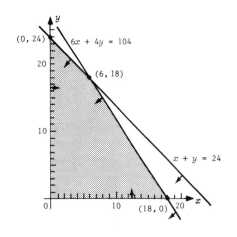

37. Let x = the number of mice used and y = the number of rats used. We have the following inequalities:

$10x + 20y \leq 800$ for box A
$20x + 10y \leq 640$ for box B

Also, $x \geq 0$ and $y \geq 0$.

The graphs of these inequalities are shown below. The shaded region indicates the set of feasible solutions.

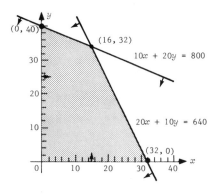

Things *to* remember:

1. A LINEAR PROGRAMMING PROBLEM is one that is concerned with finding the maximum or minimum value of a linear OBJECTIVE FUNCTION of the form

$$z = c_1 x_1 + c_2 x_2 + \cdots + c_n x_n,$$

where the DECISION VARIABLES x_1, x_2, ..., x_n are subject to PROBLEM CONSTRAINTS in the form of linear inequalities and equations. In addition, the decision variables must satisfy the NON-NEGATIVE CONSTRAINTS $x_i \geq 0, 1, 2, ..., n$. The set of points satisfying both the problem constraints and the nonnegative constraints is called the FEASIBLE REGION for the problem.

2. FUNDAMENTAL THEOREM OF LINEAR PROGRAMMING

If a linear programming problem has an optimal solution, then this solution must occur at one (or more) of the corner points of the feasible region.

3. EXISTENCE OF SOLUTIONS

Given a linear programming problem with feasible region S and objective function $z = ax_1 + bx_2$:

(A) If S is bounded, then z has both a maximum and a minimum value on S. That is, both

maximize z over S

and

minimize z over S

have solutions.

(B) If S is unbounded and $a > 0$, $b > 0$, then z has a minimum value over S, but no maximum value over S. That is,

minimize z over S

has a solution, but

maximize z over S

does not have a solution.

(C) If S is the empty set (that is, there are no points that satisfy all the constraints),

Handwritten margin notes:

① Decide on the objective,

② Set up constraints, called the problem constraints,

③ Seek the solution

Best solutions lay at the corner points.

then z has neither a maximum value nor a minimum value over S.

<u>4.</u> GEOMETRICAL SOLUTION OF A LINEAR PROGRAMMING PROBLEM

  (A) Form a mathematical model for the problem:

   (i) Introduce decision variables and write a linear objective function.
   (ii) Write problem constraints using linear inequalities and/or equations.
   (iii) Write nonnegative constraints.

  (B) Graph the feasible region and find the corner points.

  (C) Use <u>3</u> to determine if an optimal solution exists.

  (D) If an optimal solution exists, evaluate the objective function at each corner point to determine the optimal solution.

---

1. The feasible region S is the solution set of the given inequalities. This region is indicated by the shading in the graph at the right.

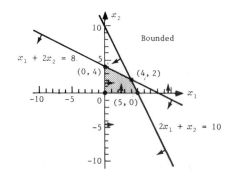

The corner points are $(0, 0)$, $(0, 4)$, $(4, 2)$, and $(5, 0)$.

Since S is bounded, it follows from <u>3</u>(A) that P has a maximum value.

The value of P at each corner point is given in the following table.

Corner Point	$P = 5x_1 + 5x_2$
$(0, 0)$	$P = 5(0) + 5(0) = 0$
$(0, 4)$	$P = 5(0) + 5(4) = 20$
$(4, 2)$	$P = 5(4) + 5(2) = 30$
$(5, 0)$	$P = 5(5) + 5(0) = 25$

Thus, the maximum occurs at $x_1 = 4$, $x_2 = 2$, and the maximum value is $P = 30$.

3. The feasible region S is the solution set of the given inequalities. This region is indicated by the shading in the graph at the top of the following page.

The corner points are $(0, 10)$, $(4, 2)$, and $(8, 0)$.

Since S is unbounded and $a = 2 > 0$, $b = 3 > 0$, it follows from <u>3</u>(B) that P has a minimum value but not a maximum value.

The value of P at each corner point is given in the following table:

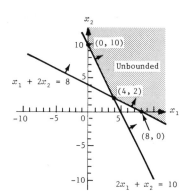

Corner Point	$P = 2x_1 + 3x_2$
$(0,10)$	$P = 2(0) + 3(10) = 30$
$(4,2)$	$P = 2(4) + 3(2) = 14$
$(8,0)$	$P = 2(8) + 3(0) = 16$

The minimum occurs at $x_1 = 4$, $x_2 = 2$, and the minimum value is $P = 14$; P does not have a maximum value.

5. The feasible region S is the solution set of the given inequalities. This region is indicated by the shading in the graph at the right.

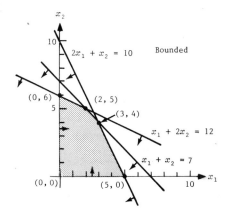

The corner points are $(0, 0)$, $(0, 6)$, $(2, 5)$, $(3, 4)$, and $(5, 0)$.

Since S is bounded, it follows from $\underline{3}$(A) that P has a maximum value.

The value of P at each corner point is:

Corner Point	$P = 30x_1 + 40x_2$
$(0, 0)$	$P = 30(0) + 30(0) = 0$
$(0, 6)$	$P = 30(0) + 40(6) = 240$
$(2, 5)$	$P = 30(2) + 40(5) = 260$
$(3, 4)$	$P = 30(3) + 40(4) = 250$
$(5, 0)$	$P = 30(5) + 40(0) = 150$

Thus, the maximum occurs at $x_1 = 2$, $x_2 = 5$, and the maximum value is $P = 260$.

7. The feasible region S is the solution set of the given inequalities, and is indicated by the shading in the graph at the right.

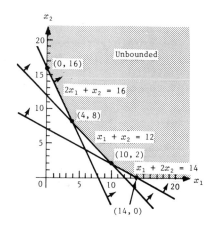

The corner points are $(0, 16)$, $(4, 8)$, $(10, 2)$, and $(14, 0)$.

Since S is unbounded and $a = 10 > 0$, $b = 30 > 0$, it follows from $\underline{3}$(B) that P has a minimum value but not a maximum value.

Corner Point	$P = 10x_1 + 30x_2$
$(0, 16)$	$P = 10(0) + 30(16) = 480$
$(4, 8)$	$P = 10(4) + 30(8) = 280$
$(10, 2)$	$P = 10(10) + 30(2) = 160$
$(14, 0)$	$P = 10(14) + 30(0) = 140$

The minimum occurs at $x_1 = 14$, $x_2 = 0$, and the minimum value is $P = 140$; P does not have a maximum value.

9. The feasible region S is the solution set of the given inequalities, and is indicated by the shading in the graph at the right.

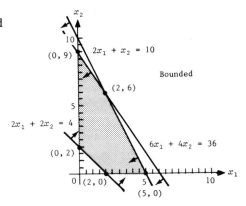

The corner points are $(0, 2)$, $(0, 9)$, $(2, 6)$, $(5, 0)$, and $(2, 0)$.

Since S is bounded, it follows from $\underline{3}(A)$ that P has a maximum value and a minimum value.

The value of P at each corner point is:

Corner Point	$P = 30x_1 + 10x_2$
$(0, 2)$	$P = 30(0) + 10(2) = 20$
$(0, 9)$	$P = 30(0) + 10(9) = 90$
$(2, 6)$	$P = 30(2) + 10(6) = 120$
$(5, 0)$	$P = 30(5) + 10(0) = 150$
$(2, 0)$	$P = 30(2) + 0(0) = 60$

Thus, the maximum occurs at $x_1 = 5$, $x_2 = 0$, and the maximum value is $P = 150$; the minimum occurs at $x_1 = 0$, $x_2 = 2$, and the minimum value is $P = 20$.

11. The feasible region S is the solution set of the given inequalities. As indicated, the feasible region is empty. Thus, by $\underline{3}(C)$, there are no optimal solutions.

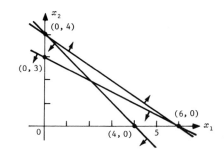

13. The feasible region S is the solution set of the given inequalities, and is indicated by the shading in the graph at the right.

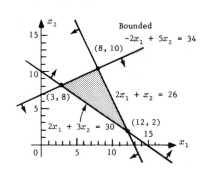

The corner points are $(3, 8)$, $(8, 10)$, and $(12, 2)$.

Since S is bounded, it follows from $\underline{3}(A)$ that P has a maximum value and a minimum value.

The value of P at each corner point is:

Corner Point	$P = 20x_1 + 10x_2$
$(3, 8)$	$P = 20(3) + 10(8) = 140$
$(8, 10)$	$P = 20(8) + 10(10) = 260$
$(12, 2)$	$P = 20(12) + 10(2) = 260$

The minimum occurs at $x_1 = 3$, $x_2 = 8$ and the minimum value is $P = 140$; the maximum occurs at $x_1 = 8$, $x_2 = 10$, at $x_1 = 12$, $x_2 = 2$, and at any point along the line segment joining $(8, 10)$ and $(12, 2)$. The maximum value is $P = 260$.

15. The feasible region S is the set of solutions of the given inequalities and is indicated by the shading in the graph at the right.

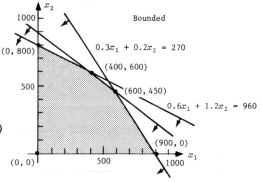

The corner points are $(0, 0)$, $(0, 800)$, $(400, 600)$, $(600, 450)$, and $(900, 0)$.

Since S is bounded, it follows from **3**(A) that P has a maximum value.

The value of P at each corner point is:

Corner Point	$P = 20x_1 + 30x_2$
$(0, 0)$	$P = 20(0) + 30(0) = 0$
$(0, 800)$	$P = 20(0) + 30(800) = 24,000$
$(400, 600)$	$P = 20(400) + 30(600) = 26,000$
$(600, 450)$	$P = 20(600) + 30(450) = 25,500$
$(900, 0)$	$P = 20(900) + 30(0) = 18,000$

The maximum occurs at $x_1 = 400$, $x_2 = 600$, and the maximum value is $P = 26,000$.

17. The value of $P = ax_1 + bx_2$, $a > 0$, $b > 0$, at each corner point is:

Corner Point	P
$(0, 0)$	$P = a(0) + b(0) = 0$
A: $(0, 5)$	$P = a(0) + b(5) = 5b$
B: $(4, 3)$	$P = a(4) + b(3) = 4a + 3b$
C: $(5, 0)$	$P = a(5) + b(0) = 5a$

(A) For the maximum value of P to occur at A only, we must have $5b > 4a + 3b$ and $5b > 5a$. Solving the first inequality, we get $2b > 4a$ or $b > 2a$; from the second inequality, we get $b > a$. Therefore, we must have $b > 2a$ or $2a < b$ in order for P to have its maximum value at A only.

(B) For the maximum value of P to occur at B only, we must have $4a + 3b > 5b$ and $4a + 3b > 5a$. Solving this pair of inequalities, we get $4a > 2b$ and $3b > a$, which is the same as $(a/3) < b < 2a$.

(C) For the maximum value of P to occur at C only, we must have $5a > 4a + 3b$ and $5a > 5b$. This pair of inequalities implies that $a > 3b$ or $b < (a/3)$.

(D) For the maximum value of P to occur at both A and B, we must have $5b = 4a + 3b$ or $b = 2a$.

(E) For the maximum value of P to occur at both B and C, we must have $4a + 3b = 5a$ or $b = a/3$.

19. Let x_1 = the number of trick skis
and x_2 = the number of slalom skis
produced per day. The mathematical
model for this problem is:

Maximize $P = 40x_1 + 30x_2$

Subject to: $6x_1 + 4x_2 \leqslant 108$
$x_1 + x_2 \leqslant 24$
$x_1 \geqslant 0, \ x_2 \geqslant 0$

The feasible region S is the solution set
of the given system of inequalities, and
is indicated by the shading in the graph
at the right.

The corner points are $(0, 0)$, $(0, 24)$,
$(6, 18)$, and $(18, 0)$.

Since S is bounded, P has a maximum value by $\underline{3}$(A).

The value of P at each corner point is:

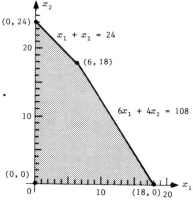

Corner Point	$P = 40x_1 + 30x_2$
$(0, 0)$	$P = 40(0) + 30(0) = 0$
$(0, 24)$	$P = 40(0) + 30(24) = 720$
$(6, 18)$	$P = 40(6) + 30(18) = 780$
$(18, 0)$	$P = 40(18) + 30(0) = 720$

Thus, the maximum occurs when $x_1 = 6$ (trick skis) and $x_2 = 18$ (slalom skis)
are produced. The maximum profit is $P = \$780$.

21. Let x_1 = the number of days to operate Plant A
and x_2 = the number of days to operate Plant B.

(A) The mathematical model for this problem is:

Minimize $C = 1000x_1 + 900x_2$

Subject to: $20x_1 + 25x_2 \geqslant 200$
$60x_1 + 50x_2 \geqslant 500$
$x_1 \geqslant 0, \ x_2 \geqslant 0$

The feasible region S is the solution
set of the system of inequalities,
and is indicated by the shading in
the graph at the right.

The corner points are $(0, 10)$, $(5, 4)$,
and $(10, 0)$.

Since S is unbounded and $a = 1000 > 0$,
$b = 900 > 0$, C has a minimum value by $\underline{3}$(B).

The value of C at each corner point is
shown in the following table.

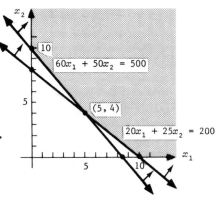

Corner Point	$C = 100x_1 + 900x_2$
(0, 10)	$C = 1000(0) + 900(10) = 9000$
(5, 4)	$C = 1000(5) + 900(4) = 8600$
(10, 0)	$C = 1000(10) + 900(0) = 10000$

Thus, the minimum occurs when $x_1 = 5$ and $x_2 = 4$. That is, Plant A should be operated five days and Plant B should be operated four days. The minimum cost is $C = \$8600$.

(B) The mathematical model for this problem is:

Minimize $C = 600x_1 + 900x_2$

Subject to: $20x_1 + 25x_2 \geqslant 200$
$60x_1 + 50x_2 \geqslant 500$
$x_1 \geqslant 0, \ x_2 \geqslant 0$

The feasible region S and the corner points are the same as in part (A), and C has a minimum value.

The value of C at each corner point is:

Corner point	$C = 600x_1 + 900x_2$
(0, 10)	$C = 600(0) + 900(10) = 9000$
(5, 4)	$C = 600(5) + 900(4) = 6600$
(10, 0)	$C = 600(10) + 900(0) = 6000$

Thus, the minimum occurs when $x_1 = 10$ and $x_2 = 0$. That is, Plant A should be operated 10 days and Plant B should not be operated at all. The minimum cost is $C = \$6000$.

(C) The mathematical model for this problem is:

Minimize $C = 1000x_1 + 800x_2$

Subject to: $20x_1 + 25x_2 \geqslant 200$
$60x_1 + 50x_2 \geqslant 500$
$x_1 \geqslant 0, \ x_2 \geqslant 0$

The feasible region S and the corner points are the same as in Part (A) and C has a minimum value.

The value of C at each corner point is:

Corner Point	$C = 1000x_1 + 800x_2$
(0, 10)	$C = 1000(0) + 800(10) = 8000$
(5, 4)	$C = 1000(5) + 800(4) = 8200$
(10, 0)	$C = 1000(10) + 800(0) = 10000$

Thus, the minimum occurs when $x_1 = 0$ and $x_2 = 10$. That is, Plant A should not be operated and Plant B should be operated 10 days. The minimum cost is $C = \$8000$.

23. Let x_1 = the number of buses
and x_2 = the number of vans.

The mathematical model for this problem is:

Minimize $C = 1200x_1 + 100x_2$

Subject to: $40x_1 + 8x_2 \geqslant 400$
$3x_1 + x_2 \leqslant 36$
$x_1 \geqslant 0,\ x_2 \geqslant 0$

The feasible region S is the solution
set of the system of inequalities,
and is indicated by the shading in
the graph at the right.

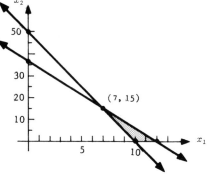

The corner points are $(10, 0)$,
$(7, 15)$, and $(12, 0)$.

Since S is bounded, C has a minimum
value by $\underline{3}$(A).

The value of C at each corner point is:

Corner point	$C = 1200x_1 + 100x_2$
$(10, 0)$	$C = 1200(10) + 100(0)\ \ = 12{,}000$
$(7, 15)$	$C = 1200(7)\ + 100(15) = 9{,}900$
$(12, 0)$	$C = 1200(12) + 100(0)\ \ = 14{,}400$

Thus, the minimum occurs when $x_1 = 7$ and $x_2 = 15$. That is, the officers
should rent 7 buses and 15 vans at the minimum cost of $9900.

25. Let x_1 = the number of gallons produced by the old process
and x_2 = the number of gallons produced by the new process.
The mathematical model for this problem is:

Maximize $P = 30x_1 + 20x_2$

Subject to: $15x_1 + 5x_2 \leqslant 10{,}500$
$40x_1 + 20x_2 \leqslant 30{,}000$
$x_1 \geqslant 0,\ x_2 \geqslant 0$

The feasible region S is the solution set
of the given inequalities, and is indicated by the shading in the graph at the
right.

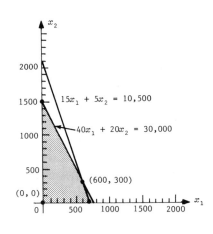

The corner points are $(0, 0)$, $(0, 1500)$,
$(600, 300)$, and $(700, 0)$.

Since S is bounded, P has a maximum value
by $\underline{3}$(A).

The value of P at each corner point is
shown in the table at the top of the
following page.

Corner Point	$P = 30x_1 + 20x_2$
$(0, 0)$	$P = 30(0) + 20(0) = 0$
$(0, 1500)$	$P = 30(0) + 20(1500) = 30,000$
$(600, 300)$	$P = 30(600) + 20(300) = 24,000$
$(700, 0)$	$P = 30(700) + 20(0) = 21,000$

Thus, the maximum occurs when the chemical produced by the old process is zero and that produced by the new process is 1500 gallons. The maximum profit is $P = 30,000$¢, i.e., $P = \$300$.

27. Let x_1 = the number of bags of Brand A
and x_2 = the number of bags of Brand B.

(A) The mathematical model for this problem is:

Maximize $N = 8x_1 + 3x_2$

Subject to: $4x_1 + 4x_2 \geqslant 1000$
$2x_1 + x_2 \leqslant 400$
$x_1 \geqslant 0, \; x_2 \geqslant 0$

The feasible region S is the solution set of the system of inequalities, and is indicated by the shading in the graph below.

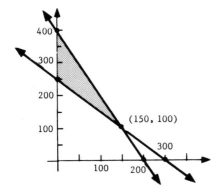

The corner points are $(0, 250)$, $(0, 400)$, and $(150, 100)$.

Since S is bounded, N has a maximum value by $\underline{3}$(A).

The value of N at each corner point is given in the table below:

Corner Point	$N = 8x_1 + 3x_2$
$(0, 250)$	$N = 8(0) + 3(250) = 750$
$(150, 100)$	$N = 8(150) + 3(100) = 1500$
$(0, 400)$	$N = 8(0) + 3(400) = 1200$

Thus, the maximum occurs when $x_1 = 150$ and $x_2 = 100$. That is, the grower should use 150 bags of Brand A and 100 bags of Brand B. The maximum number of pounds of nitrogen is 1500.

(B) The mathematical model for this problem is:

$$\text{Minimize } N = 8x_1 + 3x_2$$

$$\text{Subject to: } \begin{aligned} 4x_1 + 4x_2 &\geqslant 1000 \\ 2x_1 + x_2 &\leqslant 400 \\ x_1 \geqslant 0, \; x_2 &\geqslant 0 \end{aligned}$$

The feasible region S and the corner points are the same as in part (A). Thus, the minimum occurs when $x_1 = 0$ and $x_2 = 250$. That is, the grower should use 0 bags of Brand A and 250 bags of Brand B. The minimum number of pounds of nitrogen is 750.

29. Let x_1 = the number of cubic yards of mix A and x_2 = the number of cubic yards of mix B. The mathematical model for this problem is:

$$\text{Minimize } C = 30x_1 + 35x_2$$

$$\text{Subject to: } \begin{aligned} 20x_1 + 10x_2 &\geqslant 460 \\ 30x_1 + 30x_2 &\geqslant 960 \\ 5x_1 + 10x_2 &\geqslant 220 \\ x_1 \geqslant 0, \; x_2 &\geqslant 0 \end{aligned}$$

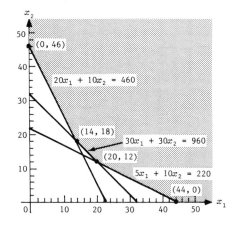

The feasible region S is the solution set of the given inequalities and is indicated by the shading in the graph at the right.

The corner points are $(0, 46)$, $(14, 18)$, $(20, 12)$, and $(44, 0)$.

Since S is unbounded and $a = 30 > 0$, $b = 35 > 0$, C has a minimum value by $\underline{3}$(B).

The value of C at each corner point is:

Corner Point	$C = 30x_1 + 35x_2$
$(0, 46)$	$C = 30(0) + 35(46) = 1610$
$(14, 8)$	$C = 30(14) + 35(18) = 1050$
$(20, 12)$	$C = 30(20) + 35(12) = 1020$
$(44, 0)$	$C = 30(44) + 35(0) = 1320$

Thus, the minimum occurs when the amount of mix A used is 20 cubic yards and the amount of mix B used is 12 cubic yards. The minimum cost is $C = \$1020$.

31. Let x_1 = the number of mice used and x_2 = the number of rats used. The mathematical model for this problem is:

$$\text{Maximize } P = x_1 + x_2$$

$$\text{Subject to: } \begin{aligned} 10x_1 + 20x_2 &\leqslant 800 \\ 20x_1 + 10x_2 &\leqslant 640 \\ x_1 \geqslant 0, \; x_2 &\geqslant 0 \end{aligned}$$

The feasible region S is the solution set of the given inequalities, and is indicated by the shading in the graph at the right.

The corner points are $(0, 0)$, $(0, 40)$ $(16, 32)$, and $(32, 0)$.

Since S is bounded, P has a maximum value by $\underline{3}$(A).

The value of P at each corner point is:

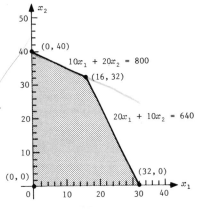

Corner Point	$P = x_1 + x_2$
$(0, 0)$	$P = 0 + 0 = 0$
$(0, 40)$	$P = 0 + 40 = 40$
$(16, 32)$	$P = 16 + 32 = 48$
$(32, 0)$	$P = 32 + 0 = 32$

Thus, the maximum occurs when the number of mice used is 16 and the number of rats used is 32. The maximum number of mice and rats that can be used is 48.

EXERCISE 2-3

Things to remember:

$\underline{1}$. Given a linear programming problem. SLACK VARIABLES are nonnegative quantities which are introduced to convert the problem constraint inequalities into equations.

$\underline{2}$. Given a system of m linear equations with n variables, $n > m$, associated with a linear programming problem. A solution obtained by setting $n - m$ variables equal to zero and solving for the remaining m variables is called a BASIC SOLUTION. A basic solution in which all values are nonnegative is called a BASIC FEASIBLE SOLUTION. The $n - m$ variables set equal to zero are called NONBASIC VARIABLES; the remaining variables are called BASIC VARIABLES.

$\underline{3}$. FUNDAMENTAL THEOREM OF LINEAR PROGRAMMING

If a linear programming problem has an optimal solution, then it must be one (or more) of the basic feasible solutions.

1.

	Nonbasic	Basic	Feasible?
(A)	x_1, x_2	s_1, s_2	Yes, all values are nonnegative.
(B)	x_1, s_1	x_2, s_2	Yes, all values are nonnegative.
(C)	x_1, s_2	x_2, s_1	No, $s_1 = -12 < 0.$
(D)	x_2, s_1	x_1, s_2	No, $s_2 = -12 < 0.$
(E)	x_2, s_2	x_1, s_1	Yes, all values are nonnegative.
(F)	s_1, s_2	x_1, x_2	Yes, all values are nonnegative.

3.

	x_1	x_2	s_1	s_2	Feasible?
(A)	0	0	50	40	Yes, all values are nonnegative.
(B)	0	50	0	-60	No, $s_2 = -60 < 0.$
(C)	0	20	30	0	Yes, all values are nonnegative.
(D)	25	0	0	15	Yes, all values are nonnegative.
(E)	40	0	-30	0	No, $s_1 = -30 < 0$
(F)	20	10	0	0	Yes, all values are nonnegative.

5.

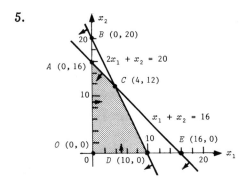

Introduce slack variables s_1 and s_2 to obtain the system of equations:

$$\begin{aligned} x_1 + x_2 + s_1 \quad\quad &= 16 \\ 2x_1 + x_2 \quad\quad + s_2 &= 20 \end{aligned}$$

x_1	x_2	s_1	s_2	Intersection Point	Feasible?
0	0	16	20	O	Yes
0	16	0	4	A	Yes
0	20	-4	0	B	No, $s_1 = -4 < 0$
16	0	0	-12	E	No, $s_2 = -16 < 0$
10	0	6	0	D	Yes
4	12	0	0	C	Yes

7.

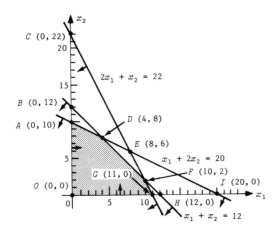

Introduce slack variables s_1, s_2, and s_3 to obtain the system of equations:

$$2x_1 + x_2 + s_1 \qquad\qquad = 22$$
$$x_1 + x_2 \qquad + s_2 \qquad = 12$$
$$x_1 + 2x_2 \qquad\qquad + s_3 = 20$$

x_1	x_2	s_1	s_2	s_3	Intersection Point	Feasible?
0	0	22	12	20	O	Yes
0	22	0	-10	-24	C	No
0	12	10	0	-4	B	No
0	10	12	2	0	A	Yes
11	0	0	1	9	G	Yes
12	0	-2	0	8	H	No
20	0	-18	-8	0	I	No
10	2	0	0	6	F	Yes
8	6	0	-2	0	E	No
4	8	6	0	0	D	Yes

EXERCISE 2-4

Things to remember:

1. A linear programming problem is said to be a STANDARD MAXIMIZATION PROBLEM if the objective function is to be maximized and each problem constraint can be written in the form:

$$a_1x_1 + a_2x_2 + \cdots + a_nx_n \leqslant b, \ b \geqslant 0.$$

2. THE SIMPLEX METHOD (Standard Maximization Problems)

(a) Introduce slack variables and write the initial form.

(b) Write the simplex tableau associated with the initial form.

(c) Determine the pivot element as follows:

(i) Locate the most negative indicator in the bottom row of the tableau. The column containing this element is the PIVOT COLUMN. If there is a tie for the most negative, choose either.

(ii) Divide each POSITIVE element in the pivot column above the dashed line into the corresponding element in the last column. The PIVOT ROW is the row corresponding to the smallest quotient. If there is a tie for the smallest quotient, choose either. If the pivot column above the dashed line has no positive elements, then there is no solution to the problem.

(iii) The PIVOT (or PIVOT ELEMENT) is the element in the pivot row and pivot column. (Note: The pivot element is always positive and is never in the bottom row.)

(d) Perform the pivot operation as follows:

(i) Multiply the pivot row by the reciprocal of the pivot element to transform the pivot element into a 1. (If the pivot element is already a 1, omit this step.)

(ii) Add multiples of the pivot row to other rows in the tableau to transform all other nonzero elements in the pivot column into zeros. (Note: Rows cannot be interchanged when performing a pivot operation.)

(e) Repeat steps (c) and (d) until all indicators in the bottom row are nonnegative. When this occurs, stop the process and read the optimal solution.

---

1. Given the simplex tableau

$$
\begin{array}{ccccc}
x_1 & x_2 & s_1 & s_2 & P \\
\end{array}
$$

$$
\left[
\begin{array}{ccccc|c}
2 & 1 & 0 & 3 & 0 & 12 \\
3 & 0 & 1 & -2 & 0 & 15 \\
\hline
-4 & 0 & 0 & 4 & 1 & 20
\end{array}
\right]
$$

which corresponds to the system of equations:

$$\text{(I)} \quad \begin{cases} 2x_1 + x_2 & + 3s_2 & = 12 \\ 3x_1 & + s_1 - 2s_2 & = 15 \\ -4x_1 & + 4s_2 + P & = 20 \end{cases}$$

(A) The basic variables are x_2, s_1, and P, and the nonbasic variables are x_1 and s_2.

(B) The obvious basic solution is found by setting the nonbasic variables equal to 0 in system (I). This yields:

$$x_1 = 0, \ x_2 = 12, \ s_1 = 15, \ s_2 = 0, \ P = 20$$

(C) An additional pivot is required, since the last row of the tableau has a negative indicator, the -4 in the first column.

3. Given the simplex tableau

$$\begin{array}{ccccccc} x_1 & x_2 & x_3 & s_1 & s_2 & s_3 & P \end{array}$$

$$\left[\begin{array}{ccccccc|c} -2 & 0 & 1 & 3 & 1 & 0 & 0 & 5 \\ 0 & 1 & 0 & -2 & 0 & 0 & 0 & 15 \\ -1 & 0 & 0 & 4 & 1 & 1 & 0 & 12 \\ \hline -4 & 0 & 0 & 2 & 4 & 0 & 1 & 45 \end{array}\right]$$

which corresponds to the system of equations:

$$\text{(I)} \quad \begin{cases} -2x_1 & + x_3 + 3s_1 + s_2 & = 5 \\ x_2 & - 2s_1 & = 15 \\ -x_1 & + 4s_1 + s_2 + s_3 & = 12 \\ -4x_1 & + 2s_1 + 4s_2 & + P = 45 \end{cases}$$

(A) The basic variables are x_2, x_3, s_3, and P, and the nonbasic variables are x_1, s_1, and s_2.

(B) The obvious basic solution is found by setting the nonbasic variables equal to 0 in system (I). This yields:

$$x_1 = 0, \ x_2 = 15, \ x_3 = 5, \ s_1 = 0, \ s_2 = 0, \ s_3 = 12, \ P = 20$$

(C) Since the last row of the tableau has a negative indicator, the -4 in the first column, an additional pivot should be required. However, since there are no positive elements in the pivot column (the first column), the problem has *no solution*.

5. Given the simplex tableau

$$
\begin{array}{ccccc}
x_1 & x_2 & s_1 & s_2 & P
\end{array}
$$

$$
\left[\begin{array}{ccccc|c}
1 & 4 & 1 & 0 & 0 & 4 \\
3 & 5 & 0 & 1 & 0 & 24 \\
\hline
-8 & -5 & 0 & 0 & 1 & 0
\end{array}\right]
$$

The most negative indicator is -8 in the first column. Thus, the first column is the pivot column. Now $4/1 = 4$ and $24/3 = 8$. Thus, the first row is the pivot row and the pivot element is the element in the first row, first column. These are indicated in the following tableau.

$$
\begin{array}{c}
\text{pivot} \\
\text{row}
\end{array} \rightarrow
\left[\begin{array}{ccccc|c}
\textcircled{1} & 4 & 1 & 0 & 0 & 4 \\
3 & 5 & 0 & 1 & 0 & 24 \\
\hline
-8 & -5 & 0 & 0 & 1 & 0
\end{array}\right]
\begin{array}{l}
\dfrac{4}{1} = 4 \ (\text{minimum}) \\[2mm]
\dfrac{24}{3} = 8
\end{array}
$$

$$
\begin{array}{c}
\uparrow \\
\text{pivot} \\
\text{column}
\end{array}
$$

$$
\left[\begin{array}{ccccc|c}
\textcircled{1} & 4 & 1 & 0 & 0 & 4 \\
3 & 5 & 0 & 1 & 0 & 24 \\
\hline
-8 & -5 & 0 & 0 & 1 & 0
\end{array}\right]
\sim
\left[\begin{array}{ccccc|c}
1 & 4 & 1 & 0 & 0 & 4 \\
0 & -7 & -3 & 1 & 0 & 12 \\
\hline
0 & 27 & 8 & 0 & 1 & 32
\end{array}\right]
$$

$$R_2 + (-3)R_1 \rightarrow R_2$$
$$R_3 + 8R_1 \rightarrow R_3$$

7. Given the simplex tableau

$$
\begin{array}{cccccc}
x_1 & x_2 & s_1 & s_2 & s_3 & P
\end{array}
$$

$$
\left[\begin{array}{cccccc|c}
2 & 1 & 1 & 0 & 0 & 0 & 4 \\
3 & 0 & 1 & 1 & 0 & 0 & 8 \\
0 & 0 & 2 & 0 & 1 & 0 & 2 \\
\hline
-4 & 0 & -3 & 0 & 0 & 1 & 5
\end{array}\right]
$$

The most negative indicator is -4. Thus, the first column is the pivot column. Now, $4/2 = 2$, $8/3 = 2\frac{2}{3}$. Thus, the first row is the pivot row, and the pivot element is the element in the first row, first column. These are indicated in the tableau.

pivot row →
$$\begin{bmatrix} 2 & 1 & 1 & 0 & 0 & 0 & | & 4 \\ 3 & 0 & 1 & 1 & 0 & 0 & | & 8 \\ 0 & 0 & 2 & 0 & 1 & 0 & | & 2 \\ -4 & 0 & -3 & 0 & 0 & 1 & | & 5 \end{bmatrix}$$

$\dfrac{4}{2} = 2$ (minimum)

$\dfrac{8}{3} = 2\dfrac{2}{3}$

↑
pivot column

$$\begin{bmatrix} \circled{2} & 1 & 1 & 0 & 0 & 0 & | & 4 \\ 3 & 0 & 1 & 1 & 0 & 0 & | & 8 \\ 0 & 0 & 2 & 0 & 1 & 0 & | & 2 \\ -4 & 0 & -3 & 0 & 0 & 1 & | & 5 \end{bmatrix} \sim \begin{bmatrix} 1 & \frac{1}{2} & \frac{1}{2} & 0 & 0 & 0 & | & 2 \\ 3 & 0 & 1 & 1 & 0 & 0 & | & 8 \\ 0 & 0 & 2 & 0 & 1 & 0 & | & 2 \\ -4 & 0 & -3 & 0 & 0 & 1 & | & 5 \end{bmatrix}$$

$\dfrac{1}{2}R_1 \to R_1$

$R_2 + (-3)R_1 \to R_2$
$R_4 + 4R_1 \to R_4$

$$\sim \begin{bmatrix} 1 & \frac{1}{2} & \frac{1}{2} & 0 & 0 & 0 & | & 2 \\ 0 & -\frac{3}{2} & -\frac{1}{2} & 1 & 0 & 0 & | & 2 \\ 0 & 0 & 2 & 0 & 1 & 0 & | & 2 \\ 0 & 2 & -1 & 0 & 0 & 1 & | & 13 \end{bmatrix}$$

9. (A) Introduce slack variables s_1 and s_2 to obtain:

Maximize $P = 15x_1 + 10x_2$

Subject to:
$$2x_1 + x_2 + s_1 \qquad = 10$$
$$x_1 + 2x_2 \qquad + s_2 = 8$$
$$x_1,\ x_2,\ s_1,\ s_2 \geqslant 0$$

This system can be written in initial form:

$$2x_1 + x_2 + s_1 \qquad\qquad = 10$$
$$x_1 + 2x_2 \qquad + s_2 \qquad = 8$$
$$-15x_1 - 10x_2 \qquad\qquad + P = 0$$
$$x_1,\ x_2,\ s_1,\ s_2 \geqslant 0$$

(B) The simplex tableau for this problem is:

$$
\begin{array}{ccccc}
x_1 & x_2 & s_1 & s_2 & P \\
\end{array}
$$

$$
\left[
\begin{array}{ccccc|c}
②& 1 & 1 & 0 & 0 & 10 \\
1 & 2 & 0 & 1 & 0 & 8 \\
\hline
-15 & -10 & 0 & 0 & 1 & 0
\end{array}
\right]
\quad
\begin{array}{l}
\dfrac{10}{2} = 5 \ (\text{minimum}) \\[2mm]
\dfrac{8}{1} = 8
\end{array}
$$

Column 1 is the pivot column (-15 is the most negative indicator). Row 1 is the pivot row (5 is the smallest positive quotient). Thus, the pivot element is the circled 2.

(C) We use the simplex method as outlined above. The pivot elements are circled.

$$
\begin{array}{ccccc}
x_1 & x_2 & s_1 & s_2 & P \\
\end{array}
$$

$$
\left[
\begin{array}{ccccc|c}
②& 1 & 1 & 0 & 0 & 10 \\
1 & 2 & 0 & 1 & 0 & 8 \\
\hline
-15 & -10 & 0 & 0 & 1 & 0
\end{array}
\right]
\sim
\left[
\begin{array}{ccccc|c}
1 & \frac{1}{2} & \frac{1}{2} & 0 & 0 & 5 \\
1 & 2 & 0 & 1 & 0 & 8 \\
\hline
-15 & -10 & 0 & 0 & 1 & 0
\end{array}
\right]
$$

$$\frac{1}{2}R_1 \to R_1$$

$$R_2 + (-1)R_1 \to R_2 \text{ and}$$
$$R_3 + 15R_1 \to R_3$$

$$
\sim
\left[
\begin{array}{ccccc|c}
1 & \frac{1}{2} & \frac{1}{2} & 0 & 0 & 5 \\
0 & ③\!\!\!\frac{3}{2} & -\frac{1}{2} & 1 & 0 & 3 \\
\hline
0 & -\frac{5}{2} & \frac{15}{2} & 0 & 1 & 75
\end{array}
\right]
\quad
\begin{array}{l}
\dfrac{5}{1/2} = 10 \\[2mm]
\dfrac{3}{3/2} = 2 \leftarrow \text{pivot row}
\end{array}
$$

pivot column $\dfrac{2}{3}R_2 \to R_2$

$$
\sim
\left[
\begin{array}{ccccc|c}
1 & \frac{1}{2} & \frac{1}{2} & 0 & 0 & 5 \\
0 & 1 & -\frac{1}{3} & \frac{2}{3} & 0 & 2 \\
\hline
0 & -\frac{5}{2} & \frac{15}{2} & 0 & 1 & 75
\end{array}
\right]
$$

$$
\begin{array}{ccccc}
x_1 & x_2 & s_1 & s_2 & P \\
\end{array}
$$

$$
\sim
\left[
\begin{array}{ccccc|c}
1 & 0 & \frac{2}{3} & -\frac{1}{3} & 0 & 4 \\
0 & 1 & -\frac{1}{3} & \frac{2}{3} & 0 & 2 \\
\hline
0 & 0 & \frac{40}{6} & \frac{5}{3} & 1 & 80
\end{array}
\right]
$$

$$R_1 + \left(-\frac{1}{2}\right)R_2 \to R_1 \text{ and}$$

$$R_3 + \frac{5}{2}R_2 \to R_3$$

All the elements in the last row are nonnegative. Thus, max $P = 80$ at $x_1 = 4$, $x_2 = 2$, $s_1 = 0$, $s_2 = 0$.

11. **(A)** Introduce slack variables s_1 and s_2 to obtain:

Maximize $P = 30x_1 + x_2$

Subject to:
$$2x_1 + x_2 + s_1 \qquad\quad = 10$$
$$x_1 + 2x_2 \qquad\; + s_2 = 8$$
$$x_1,\, x_2,\, s_1,\, s_2 \geqslant 0$$

This system can be written in the initial form:

$$2x_1 + x_2 + s_1 \qquad\qquad\quad = 10$$
$$x_1 + 2x_2 \qquad + s_2 \qquad = 8$$
$$-30x_1 - x_2 \qquad\qquad + P = 0$$

(B) The simplex tableau for this problem is:

$$
\begin{array}{c}
\\
\text{pivot} \rightarrow \\
\text{row} \\
\\
\\
\end{array}
\begin{array}{ccccc}
x_1 & x_2 & s_1 & s_2 & P \\
\end{array}
$$

$$
\begin{bmatrix}
\,\textcircled{2} & 1 & 1 & 0 & 0 & 10\, \\
1 & 2 & 0 & 1 & 0 & 8 \\
\hline
-30 & -1 & 0 & 0 & 1 & 0
\end{bmatrix}
\begin{array}{l}
\dfrac{10}{2} = 5 \text{ (minimum)} \\[2mm]
\dfrac{8}{1} = 8
\end{array}
$$

pivot column

(C)

$$
\begin{array}{ccccc}
x_1 & x_2 & s_1 & s_2 & P
\end{array}
$$

$$
\begin{bmatrix}
\textcircled{2} & 1 & 1 & 0 & 0 & 10 \\
1 & 2 & 0 & 1 & 0 & 8 \\
\hline
-30 & -1 & 0 & 0 & 1 & 0
\end{bmatrix}
\sim
\begin{bmatrix}
1 & \frac{1}{2} & \frac{1}{2} & 0 & 0 & 5 \\
1 & 2 & 0 & 1 & 0 & 8 \\
\hline
-30 & -1 & 0 & 0 & 1 & 0
\end{bmatrix}
$$

$\frac{1}{2}R_1 \rightarrow R_2$

$R_2 + (-1)R_1 \rightarrow R_2$ and
$R_3 + 30R_1 \rightarrow R_3$

$$
\sim
\begin{bmatrix}
1 & \frac{1}{2} & \frac{1}{2} & 0 & 0 & 5 \\
0 & \frac{3}{2} & -\frac{1}{2} & 1 & 0 & 3 \\
\hline
0 & 14 & 15 & 0 & 1 & 150
\end{bmatrix}
$$

All elements in the last row are nonnegative.

Thus, max $P = 150$ at $x_1 = 5$, $x_2 = 0$, $s_1 = 0$, $s_2 = 3$.

13. The simplex tableau for this problem is:

$$
\begin{array}{cccccc}
x_1 & x_2 & s_1 & s_2 & s_3 & P
\end{array}
$$

$$
\begin{bmatrix}
2 & 1 & 1 & 0 & 0 & 0 & | & 10 \\
1 & 1 & 0 & 1 & 0 & 0 & | & 7 \\
1 & \boxed{2} & 0 & 0 & 1 & 0 & | & 12 \\
\hline
-30 & -40 & 0 & 0 & 0 & 1 & | & 0
\end{bmatrix}
$$

pivot row →

$$10$$
$$7$$
$$\frac{12}{2} = 6 \text{ (minimum)}$$

[Note: The pivot elements have been circled.]

pivot column ↑ $\frac{1}{2}R_3 \to R_3$

$$
\sim
\begin{bmatrix}
2 & 1 & 1 & 0 & 0 & 0 & | & 10 \\
1 & 1 & 0 & 1 & 0 & 0 & | & 7 \\
\frac{1}{2} & 1 & 0 & 0 & \frac{1}{2} & 0 & | & 6 \\
\hline
-30 & -40 & 0 & 0 & 0 & 1 & | & 0
\end{bmatrix}
$$

$R_1 + (-1)R_3 \to R_1$, $R_2 + (-1)R_3 \to R_2$, and $R_4 + 40R_3 \to R_4$

$$
\sim
\begin{bmatrix}
\frac{3}{2} & 0 & 1 & 0 & -\frac{1}{2} & 0 & | & 4 \\
\boxed{\frac{1}{2}} & 0 & 0 & 1 & -\frac{1}{2} & 0 & | & 1 \\
\frac{1}{2} & 1 & 0 & 0 & \frac{1}{2} & 0 & | & 6 \\
\hline
-10 & 0 & 0 & 0 & 20 & 1 & | & 240
\end{bmatrix}
$$

pivot row →

$$\frac{4}{3/2} = \frac{8}{3}$$
$$\frac{1}{1/2} = 2 \text{ (minimum)}$$
$$\frac{6}{1/2} = 12$$

pivot column ↑ $2R_2 \to R_2$

$$
\sim
\begin{bmatrix}
\frac{3}{2} & 0 & 1 & 0 & -\frac{1}{2} & 0 & | & 4 \\
1 & 0 & 0 & 2 & -1 & 0 & | & 2 \\
\frac{1}{2} & 1 & 0 & 0 & \frac{1}{2} & 0 & | & 6 \\
\hline
-10 & 0 & 0 & 0 & 20 & 1 & | & 240
\end{bmatrix}
\sim
$$

$R_1 + \left(-\frac{3}{2}\right)R_2 \to R_1$, $R_3 + \left(-\frac{1}{2}\right)R_2 \to R_3$,

and $R_4 + 10R_2 \to R_4$

(continued)

$$
\begin{array}{cccccc}
x_1 & x_2 & s_1 & s_2 & s_3 & P
\end{array}
$$

$$
\sim
\left[
\begin{array}{cccccc|c}
0 & 0 & 1 & -3 & 1 & 0 & 1 \\
1 & 0 & 0 & 2 & -1 & 0 & 2 \\
0 & 1 & 0 & -1 & 1 & 0 & 5 \\
\hline
0 & 0 & 0 & 20 & 10 & 1 & 260
\end{array}
\right]
$$

Optimal solution: max $P = 260$ at
$x_1 = 2$, $x_2 = 5$, $s_1 = 1$, $s_2 = 0$,
$s_3 = 0$.

15. The simplex tableau for this problem is:

$$
\begin{array}{cccccc}
x_1 & x_2 & s_1 & s_2 & s_3 & P
\end{array}
$$

pivot →
row
$$
\left[
\begin{array}{cccccc|c}
-2 & \boxed{1} & 1 & 0 & 0 & 0 & 2 \\
-1 & 1 & 0 & 1 & 0 & 0 & 5 \\
0 & 1 & 0 & 0 & 0 & 0 & 6 \\
\hline
-2 & -3 & 0 & 0 & 0 & 1 & 0
\end{array}
\right]
\quad
\begin{array}{l}
\frac{2}{1} = 2 \text{ (minimum)} \\[4pt]
\frac{5}{1} = 5 \\[4pt]
\frac{6}{1} = 6
\end{array}
$$

↑
pivot
column

$R_2 + (-1)R_1 \rightarrow R_2$, $R_3 + (-1)R_1 \rightarrow R_3$, and $R_4 + 3R_1 \rightarrow R_4$

pivot →
row
$$
\sim
\left[
\begin{array}{cccccc|c}
-2 & 1 & 1 & 0 & 0 & 0 & 2 \\
1 & 0 & -1 & 1 & 0 & 0 & 3 \\
\boxed{2} & 0 & -1 & 0 & 0 & 0 & 4 \\
\hline
-8 & 0 & 3 & 0 & 0 & 1 & 6
\end{array}
\right]
\quad
\begin{array}{l}
\frac{3}{1} = 3 \\[4pt]
\frac{4}{2} = 2 \text{ (minimum)}
\end{array}
$$

↑
pivot
column

$\frac{1}{2} R_3 \rightarrow R_3$

$$
\sim
\left[
\begin{array}{cccccc|c}
-2 & 1 & 1 & 0 & 0 & 0 & 2 \\
1 & 0 & -1 & 1 & 0 & 0 & 3 \\
1 & 0 & -\frac{1}{2} & 0 & 0 & 0 & 2 \\
\hline
-8 & 0 & 3 & 0 & 0 & 1 & 6
\end{array}
\right]
\quad
\sim
\begin{array}{c}
\begin{array}{cccccc}
x_1 & x_2 & s_1 & s_2 & s_3 & P
\end{array} \\
\left[
\begin{array}{cccccc|c}
0 & 1 & 0 & 0 & 0 & 0 & 6 \\
0 & 0 & -\frac{1}{2} & 1 & 0 & 0 & 1 \\
1 & 0 & -\frac{1}{2} & 0 & 0 & 0 & 2 \\
\hline
0 & 0 & -1 & 0 & 0 & 0 & 22
\end{array}
\right]
\end{array}
$$

$R_1 + 2R_3 \rightarrow R_1$, $R_2 + (-1)R_3 \rightarrow R_2$,
and $R_4 + 8R_3 \rightarrow R_4$

↑
pivot
column

Since there are no positive elements in the pivot column (above the dashed
line), we conclude that there is no solution.

LINEAR INEQUALITIES AND LINEAR PROGRAMMING

17. The simplex tableau for this problem is:

$$
\begin{array}{cccccc}
 & x_1 & x_2 & s_1 & s_2 & s_3 & P
\end{array}
$$

$\text{pivot} \rightarrow$
row
$$
\left[
\begin{array}{cccccc|c}
-1 & \boxed{1} & 1 & 0 & 0 & 0 & 2 \\
-1 & 3 & 0 & 1 & 0 & 0 & 12 \\
1 & -4 & 0 & 0 & 1 & 0 & 4 \\
\hline
1 & -2 & 0 & 0 & 0 & 1 & 0
\end{array}
\right]
\begin{array}{l}
\frac{2}{1} = 2 \ \text{(minimum)} \\[4pt]
\frac{12}{3} = 4 \\[30pt]
\end{array}
$$

$$\uparrow$$
$$\text{pivot column} \quad R_2 + (-3)R_1 \rightarrow R_2, \ R_3 + 4R_1 \rightarrow R_3, \ \text{and} \ R_4 + 2R_1 \rightarrow R_4$$

$\text{pivot} \rightarrow$
row
$\sim$
$$
\left[
\begin{array}{cccccc|c}
-1 & 1 & 1 & 0 & 0 & 0 & 2 \\
\boxed{2} & 0 & -3 & 1 & 0 & 0 & 6 \\
-3 & 0 & 4 & 0 & 1 & 0 & 12 \\
\hline
-1 & 0 & 2 & 0 & 0 & 1 & 4
\end{array}
\right]
\begin{array}{l}
\frac{6}{2} = 3 \leftarrow \text{pivot row} \\[6pt]
\text{[Note: We only use the} \\
\textit{positive} \text{ elements above} \\
\text{the dashed line in the} \\
\text{pivot column.]}
\end{array}
$$

$$\uparrow$$
$$\text{pivot column} \quad \tfrac{1}{2}R_2 \rightarrow R_2$$

$$
\sim
\left[
\begin{array}{cccccc|c}
-1 & 1 & 1 & 0 & 0 & 0 & 2 \\
1 & 0 & -\frac{3}{2} & \frac{1}{2} & 0 & 0 & 3 \\
-3 & 0 & 4 & 0 & 1 & 0 & 12 \\
\hline
-1 & 0 & 2 & 0 & 0 & 1 & 4
\end{array}
\right]
\sim
\begin{array}{cccccc}
x_1 & x_2 & s_1 & s_2 & s_3 & P
\end{array}
\left[
\begin{array}{cccccc|c}
0 & 1 & -\frac{1}{2} & \frac{1}{2} & 0 & 0 & 5 \\
1 & 0 & -\frac{3}{2} & \frac{1}{2} & 0 & 0 & 3 \\
0 & 0 & -\frac{1}{2} & \frac{3}{2} & 1 & 0 & 21 \\
\hline
0 & 0 & \frac{1}{2} & \frac{1}{2} & 0 & 1 & 7
\end{array}
\right]
$$

$R_1 + R_2 \rightarrow R_1, \ R_3 + 3R_2 \rightarrow R_3,$
and $R_4 + R_2 \rightarrow R_4$

Optimal solution: max $P = 7$ at
$x_1 = 3, \ x_2 = 5, \ s_1 = 0, \ s_2 = 0,$
$s_3 = 21.$

19. The simplex tableau for this problem is:

$$
\begin{array}{cccccc}
 & x_1 & x_2 & x_3 & s_1 & s_2 & P
\end{array}
$$

$\text{pivot} \rightarrow$
row
$$
\left[
\begin{array}{cccccc|c}
\boxed{1} & 1 & -1 & 1 & 0 & 0 & 10 \\
2 & 4 & 1 & 0 & 1 & 0 & 30 \\
\hline
-5 & -2 & 1 & 0 & 0 & 1 & 0
\end{array}
\right]
\begin{array}{l}
\frac{10}{1} = 10 \ \text{(minimum)} \\[6pt]
\frac{30}{2} = 15
\end{array}
$$

$$\uparrow$$
$$\text{pivot column} \quad R_2 + (-2)R_1 \rightarrow R_2 \ \text{and} \ R_3 + 5R_1 \rightarrow R_3$$

(continued)

CHAPTER 2

$$\sim \begin{bmatrix} 1 & 1 & -1 & 1 & 0 & 0 & | & 10 \\ 0 & 2 & ③ & -2 & 1 & 0 & | & 10 \\ \hline 0 & 3 & -4 & 5 & 0 & 1 & | & 50 \end{bmatrix} \sim \begin{bmatrix} 1 & 1 & -1 & 1 & 0 & 0 & | & 10 \\ 0 & \frac{2}{3} & 1 & -\frac{2}{3} & \frac{1}{3} & 0 & | & \frac{10}{3} \\ \hline 0 & 3 & -4 & 5 & 0 & 1 & | & 50 \end{bmatrix}$$

$$\frac{1}{3}R_2 \to R_2 \qquad\qquad\qquad R_2 + R_1 \to R_2 \text{ and } R_3 + 4R_2 \to R_3$$

$$\begin{array}{cccccc} x_1 & x_2 & x_3 & s_1 & s_2 & P \end{array}$$

$$\sim \begin{bmatrix} 1 & \frac{5}{3} & 0 & \frac{1}{3} & \frac{1}{3} & 0 & | & \frac{40}{3} \\ 0 & \frac{2}{3} & 1 & -\frac{2}{3} & \frac{1}{3} & 0 & | & \frac{10}{3} \\ \hline 0 & \frac{17}{3} & 0 & \frac{7}{3} & \frac{4}{3} & 1 & | & \frac{190}{3} \end{bmatrix}$$

Optimal solution: max $P = 190/3$ at $x_1 = 40/3$, $x_2 = 0$, $x_3 = 10/3$, $s_1 = 0$, $s_2 = 0$.

21. The simplex tableau for this problem is:

$$\begin{array}{cccccc} x_1 & x_2 & x_3 & s_1 & s_2 & P \end{array}$$

$$\text{pivot} \to \atop \text{row} \begin{bmatrix} 1 & 0 & 1 & 1 & 0 & 0 & | & 4 \\ 0 & 1 & ① & 0 & 1 & 0 & | & 3 \\ \hline -2 & -3 & -4 & 0 & 0 & 1 & | & 0 \end{bmatrix} \begin{array}{l} \frac{4}{1} = 4 \\ \frac{3}{1} = 3 \ (\text{minimum}) \end{array}$$

$$\underset{\substack{\text{pivot} \\ \text{column}}}{\uparrow} \qquad \begin{array}{l} R_1 + (-1)R_2 \to R_1 \\ R_3 + 4R_2 \to R_3 \end{array}$$

$$\sim \begin{bmatrix} ① & -1 & 0 & 1 & -1 & 0 & | & 1 \\ 0 & 1 & 1 & 0 & 1 & 0 & | & 3 \\ \hline -2 & 1 & 0 & 0 & 4 & 1 & | & 12 \end{bmatrix} \sim \begin{bmatrix} 1 & -1 & 0 & 1 & -1 & 0 & | & 1 \\ 0 & ① & 1 & 0 & 1 & 0 & | & 3 \\ \hline 0 & -1 & 0 & 2 & 2 & 1 & | & 14 \end{bmatrix}$$

$$R_3 + 2R_1 \to R_3 \qquad\qquad \begin{array}{l} R_1 + R_2 \to R_1 \\ R_3 + R_2 \to R_3 \end{array}$$

$$\begin{array}{cccccc} x_1 & x_2 & x_3 & s_1 & s_2 & P \end{array}$$

$$\sim \begin{bmatrix} 1 & 0 & 1 & 1 & 0 & 0 & | & 4 \\ 0 & 1 & 1 & 0 & 1 & 0 & | & 3 \\ \hline 0 & 0 & 1 & 2 & 3 & 1 & | & 17 \end{bmatrix}$$

Optimal solution: max $P = 17$ at $x_1 = 4$, $x_2 = 3$, $x_3 = 0$, $s_1 = 0$, $s_2 = 0$.

23. The simplex tableau for this problem is:

$$
\begin{array}{ccccccc}
x_1 & x_2 & x_3 & s_1 & s_2 & s_3 & P
\end{array}
$$

$$
\begin{array}{l}
\text{pivot} \\
\text{row} \rightarrow
\end{array}
\left[
\begin{array}{ccccccc|c}
3 & 2 & 5 & 1 & 0 & 0 & 0 & 23 \\
\textcircled{2} & 1 & 1 & 0 & 1 & 0 & 0 & 8 \\
1 & 1 & 2 & 0 & 0 & 1 & 0 & 7 \\
\hline
-4 & -3 & -2 & 0 & 0 & 0 & 1 & 0
\end{array}
\right]
\begin{array}{l}
\dfrac{23}{3} = 7\dfrac{2}{3} \\[2mm]
\dfrac{8}{2} = 4 \ (\text{minimum}) \\[2mm]
\dfrac{7}{1} = 7
\end{array}
$$

$$
\begin{array}{c}
\text{pivot} \\
\text{column}
\end{array}
\qquad \frac{1}{2}R_2 \rightarrow R_2
$$

$$
\sim
\left[
\begin{array}{ccccccc|c}
3 & 2 & 5 & 1 & 0 & 0 & 0 & 23 \\
1 & \frac{1}{2} & \frac{1}{2} & 0 & \frac{1}{2} & 0 & 0 & 4 \\
1 & 1 & 2 & 0 & 0 & 1 & 0 & 7 \\
\hline
-4 & -3 & -2 & 0 & 0 & 0 & 1 & 0
\end{array}
\right]
\sim
\left[
\begin{array}{ccccccc|c}
0 & \frac{1}{2} & \frac{7}{2} & 1 & -\frac{3}{2} & 0 & 0 & 11 \\
1 & \frac{1}{2} & \frac{1}{2} & 0 & \frac{1}{2} & 0 & 0 & 4 \\
0 & \textcircled{$\frac{1}{2}$} & \frac{3}{2} & 0 & -\frac{1}{2} & 1 & 0 & 3 \\
\hline
0 & -1 & 0 & 0 & 2 & 0 & 1 & 16
\end{array}
\right]
$$

$$
\begin{array}{l}
R_1 + (-3)R_2 \rightarrow R_1 \\
R_3 + (-1)R_2 \rightarrow R_3 \\
R_4 + 4R_2 \rightarrow R_4
\end{array}
\qquad\qquad
2R_3 \rightarrow R_3
$$

$$
\begin{array}{ccccccc}
x_1 & x_2 & x_3 & s_1 & s_2 & s_3 & P
\end{array}
$$

$$
\sim
\left[
\begin{array}{ccccccc|c}
0 & \frac{1}{2} & \frac{7}{2} & 1 & -\frac{3}{2} & 0 & 0 & 11 \\
1 & \frac{1}{2} & \frac{1}{2} & 0 & \frac{1}{2} & 0 & 0 & 4 \\
0 & 1 & 3 & 0 & -1 & 2 & 0 & 6 \\
\hline
0 & -1 & 0 & 0 & 2 & 0 & 1 & 16
\end{array}
\right]
\sim
\left[
\begin{array}{ccccccc|c}
0 & 0 & 2 & 1 & -1 & -1 & 0 & 8 \\
1 & 0 & -1 & 0 & 1 & -1 & 0 & 1 \\
0 & 1 & 3 & 0 & -1 & 2 & 0 & 6 \\
\hline
0 & 0 & 3 & 0 & 1 & 2 & 1 & 22
\end{array}
\right]
$$

$$
R_1 + \left(-\frac{1}{2}\right)R_3 \rightarrow R_1
$$

$$
R_2 + \left(-\frac{1}{2}\right)R_3 \rightarrow R_2
$$

$$
R_4 + R_3 \rightarrow R_4
$$

Optimal solution: max $P = 22$ at $x_1 = 1$, $x_2 = 6$, $x_3 = 0$, $s_1 = 8$, $s_2 = 0$, $s_3 = 0$.

25. Multiply the first problem constraint by 10, the second by 100, and the third by 10 to clear the fractions. Then, the simplex tableau for this problem is:

$$\begin{array}{cccccc}
x_1 & x_2 & s_1 & s_2 & s_3 & P
\end{array}$$

$$\left[\begin{array}{cccccc|c}
1 & ② & 1 & 0 & 0 & 0 & 1{,}600 \\
3 & 4 & 0 & 1 & 0 & 0 & 3{,}600 \\
3 & 2 & 0 & 0 & 1 & 0 & 2{,}700 \\
\hline
-20 & -30 & 0 & 0 & 0 & 1 & 0
\end{array}\right]$$

$\dfrac{1{,}600}{2} = 800$

$\dfrac{3{,}600}{4} = 900$

$\dfrac{2{,}700}{2} = 1{,}350$

$\frac{1}{2}R_1 \to R_1$

$$\sim \left[\begin{array}{cccccc|c}
\frac{1}{2} & 1 & \frac{1}{2} & 0 & 0 & 0 & 800 \\
3 & 4 & 0 & 1 & 0 & 0 & 3{,}600 \\
3 & 2 & 0 & 0 & 1 & 0 & 2{,}700 \\
\hline
-20 & -30 & 0 & 0 & 0 & 1 & 0
\end{array}\right]$$

$R_2 + (-4)R_1 \to R_2$, $R_3 + (-2)R_1 \to R_3$, and $R_4 + 30R_1 \to R_4$

$$\sim \left[\begin{array}{cccccc|c}
\frac{1}{2} & 1 & \frac{1}{2} & 0 & 0 & 0 & 800 \\
① & 0 & -2 & 1 & 0 & 0 & 400 \\
2 & 0 & -1 & 0 & 1 & 0 & 1{,}100 \\
\hline
-5 & 0 & 15 & 0 & 0 & 1 & 24{,}000
\end{array}\right]$$

$\dfrac{800}{1/2} = 1{,}600$

$\dfrac{400}{1} = 400$

$\dfrac{1{,}100}{2} = 550$

$R_1 + \left(-\frac{1}{2}\right)R_2 \to R_1$, $R_3 + (-2)R_2 \to R_3$, and $R_4 + 5R_2 \to R_4$

$$\begin{array}{cccccc}
x_1 & x_2 & s_1 & s_2 & s_3 & P
\end{array}$$

$$\sim \left[\begin{array}{cccccc|c}
0 & 1 & \frac{3}{2} & -\frac{1}{2} & 0 & 0 & 600 \\
1 & 0 & -2 & 1 & 0 & 0 & 400 \\
0 & 0 & 3 & -2 & 1 & 0 & 300 \\
\hline
0 & 0 & 5 & 5 & 0 & 1 & 26{,}000
\end{array}\right]$$

Optimal solution: max $P = 26{,}000$ at $x_1 = 400$, $x_2 = 600$, $s_1 = 0$, $s_2 = 0$, $s_3 = 300$.

27. The simplex tableau for this problem is:

$$
\begin{array}{ccccccc}
x_1 & x_2 & x_3 & s_1 & s_2 & s_3 & P
\end{array}
$$

$$
\left[\begin{array}{ccccccc|c}
2 & 2 & \boxed{8} & 1 & 0 & 0 & 0 & 600 \\
1 & 3 & 2 & 0 & 1 & 0 & 0 & 600 \\
3 & 2 & 1 & 0 & 0 & 1 & 0 & 400 \\
\hline
-1 & -2 & -3 & 0 & 0 & 0 & 1 & 0
\end{array}\right]
\qquad
\begin{array}{l}
\dfrac{600}{8} = 75 \\[6pt]
\dfrac{600}{2} = 300 \\[6pt]
\dfrac{400}{1} = 400
\end{array}
$$

$$\tfrac{1}{8}R_1 \to R_1$$

$$
\sim
\left[\begin{array}{ccccccc|c}
\frac{1}{4} & \frac{1}{4} & 1 & \frac{1}{8} & 0 & 0 & 0 & 75 \\
1 & 3 & 2 & 0 & 1 & 0 & 0 & 600 \\
3 & 2 & 1 & 0 & 0 & 1 & 0 & 400 \\
\hline
-1 & -2 & -3 & 0 & 0 & 0 & 1 & 0
\end{array}\right]
$$

$$R_2 + (-2)R_1 \to R_2, \quad R_3 + (-1)R_1 \to R_3, \quad \text{and } R_4 + 3R_1 \to R_4$$

$$
\sim
\left[\begin{array}{ccccccc|c}
\frac{1}{4} & \frac{1}{4} & 1 & \frac{1}{8} & 0 & 0 & 0 & 75 \\
\frac{1}{2} & \boxed{\frac{5}{2}} & 0 & -\frac{1}{4} & 1 & 0 & 0 & 450 \\
\frac{11}{4} & \frac{7}{4} & 0 & -\frac{1}{8} & 0 & 1 & 0 & 325 \\
\hline
-\frac{1}{4} & -\frac{5}{4} & 0 & \frac{3}{8} & 0 & 0 & 1 & 225
\end{array}\right]
\qquad
\begin{array}{l}
\dfrac{75}{1/4} = 300 \\[6pt]
\dfrac{450}{5/2} = 180 \\[6pt]
\dfrac{325}{7/4} = 185.71
\end{array}
$$

$$\tfrac{2}{5}R_2 \to R_2$$

$$
\sim
\left[\begin{array}{ccccccc|c}
\frac{1}{4} & \frac{1}{4} & 1 & \frac{1}{8} & 0 & 0 & 0 & 75 \\
\frac{1}{5} & 1 & 0 & -\frac{1}{10} & \frac{2}{5} & 0 & 0 & 180 \\
\frac{11}{4} & \frac{7}{4} & 0 & -\frac{1}{8} & 0 & 1 & 0 & 325 \\
\hline
-\frac{1}{4} & -\frac{5}{4} & 0 & \frac{3}{8} & 0 & 0 & 1 & 225
\end{array}\right]
\quad \sim \quad
\begin{array}{ccccccc}
x_1 & x_2 & x_3 & s_1 & s_2 & s_3 & P
\end{array}
$$

$$
\left[\begin{array}{ccccccc|c}
\frac{1}{5} & 0 & 1 & \frac{3}{20} & -\frac{1}{10} & 0 & 0 & 30 \\
\frac{1}{5} & 1 & 0 & -\frac{1}{10} & \frac{2}{5} & 0 & 0 & 180 \\
\frac{12}{5} & 0 & 0 & \frac{3}{40} & -\frac{7}{12} & 1 & 0 & 10 \\
\hline
0 & 0 & 0 & \frac{1}{2} & \frac{1}{2} & 0 & 1 & 450
\end{array}\right]
$$

$$R_1 + \left(-\tfrac{1}{4}\right)R_2 \to R_1, \quad R_3 + \left(-\tfrac{7}{4}\right)R_2 \to R_3,$$

$$\text{and } R_4 + \tfrac{5}{4}R_2 \to R_4$$

Optimal solution: max $P = 450$ at $x_1 = 0$, $x_2 = 180$, $x_3 = 30$, $s_1 = 0$, $s_2 = 0$, $s_3 = 10$.

29. The simplex tableau for this problem is:

$$
\begin{array}{ccccccc}
x_1 & x_2 & s_1 & s_2 & s_3 & s_4 & P
\end{array}
$$

$$
\left[\begin{array}{ccccccc|c}
1 & 2 & 1 & 0 & 0 & 0 & 0 & 40 \\
1 & 3 & 0 & 1 & 0 & 0 & 0 & 48 \\
1 & 4 & 0 & 0 & 1 & 0 & 0 & 60 \\
0 & \boxed{1} & 0 & 0 & 0 & 1 & 0 & 14 \\
\hline
-2 & -5 & 0 & 0 & 0 & 0 & 1 & 0
\end{array}\right]
\begin{array}{l}
\frac{40}{2} = 20 \\[4pt]
\frac{48}{3} = 16 \\[4pt]
\frac{60}{4} = 15 \\[4pt]
\frac{14}{1} = 14 \\[4pt]

\end{array}
$$

$R_1 + (-2)R_4 \to R_1$, $R_2 + (-3)R_4 \to R_2$, $R_3 + (-4)R_4 \to R_3$, and $R_5 + 5R_4 \to R_5$

$$
\sim
\left[\begin{array}{ccccccc|c}
1 & 0 & 1 & 0 & 0 & -2 & 0 & 12 \\
1 & 0 & 0 & 1 & 0 & -3 & 0 & 6 \\
\boxed{1} & 0 & 0 & 0 & 1 & -4 & 0 & 4 \\
0 & 1 & 0 & 0 & 0 & 1 & 0 & 14 \\
\hline
-2 & 0 & 0 & 0 & 0 & 5 & 1 & 70
\end{array}\right]
\begin{array}{l}
\frac{12}{1} = 12 \\[4pt]
\frac{6}{1} = 6 \\[4pt]
\frac{4}{1} = 4 \\[4pt]
 \\[4pt]

\end{array}
$$

$R_1 + (-1)R_3 \to R_1$, $R_2 + (-1)R_3 \to R_2$, and $R_5 + 2R_3 \to R_5$

$$
\sim
\left[\begin{array}{ccccccc|c}
0 & 0 & 1 & 0 & -1 & 2 & 0 & 8 \\
0 & 0 & 0 & 1 & -1 & \boxed{1} & 0 & 2 \\
1 & 0 & 0 & 0 & 1 & -4 & 0 & 4 \\
0 & 1 & 0 & 0 & 0 & 1 & 0 & 14 \\
\hline
0 & 0 & 0 & 0 & 2 & -3 & 1 & 78
\end{array}\right]
\begin{array}{l}
\frac{8}{2} = 4 \\[4pt]
\frac{2}{1} = 2 \\[4pt]
 \\[4pt]
\frac{14}{1} = 14 \\[4pt]

\end{array}
$$

$R_1 + (-2)R_2 \to R_1$, $R_3 + 4R_2 \to R_3$, $R_4 + (-1)R_2 \to R_4$, and $R_5 + 3R_2 \to R_5$

$$
\sim
\left[\begin{array}{ccccccc|c}
0 & 0 & 1 & -2 & \boxed{1} & 0 & 0 & 4 \\
0 & 0 & 0 & 1 & -1 & 1 & 0 & 2 \\
1 & 0 & 0 & 4 & -3 & 0 & 0 & 12 \\
0 & 1 & 0 & -1 & 1 & 0 & 0 & 12 \\
\hline
0 & 0 & 0 & 3 & -1 & 0 & 1 & 84
\end{array}\right]
\begin{array}{l}
\frac{4}{1} = 4 \\[4pt]
 \\[4pt]
 \\[4pt]
\frac{12}{1} = 12 \\[4pt]

\end{array}
$$

$R_2 + R_1 \to R_2$, $R_3 + 3R_1 \to R_3$, $R_4 + (-1)R_1 \to R_4$, and $R_5 + R_1 \to R_5$

(continued)

$$\sim \begin{bmatrix} x_1 & x_2 & s_1 & s_2 & s_3 & s_4 & P \\ 0 & 0 & 1 & -2 & 1 & 0 & 0 & 4 \\ 0 & 0 & 1 & -1 & 0 & 1 & 0 & 6 \\ 1 & 0 & 3 & -2 & 0 & 0 & 0 & 24 \\ 0 & 1 & -1 & 1 & 0 & 0 & 0 & 8 \\ \hline 0 & 0 & 1 & 1 & 0 & 0 & 1 & 88 \end{bmatrix}$$

Optimal solution: max $P = 88$ at $x_1 = 24$, $x_2 = 8$, $s_1 = 0$, $s_2 = 0$, $s_3 = 4$, $s_4 = 6$.

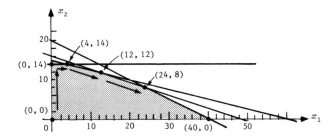

31.   Let x_1 = the number of A components,
   x_2 = the number of B components,
and x_3 = the number of C components.

The mathematical model for this problem is:

Maximize $P = 7x_1 + 9x_2 + 10x_3$

Subject to: $2x_1 + x_2 + 2x_3 \leqslant 1000$
   $x_1 + 2x_2 + 2x_3 \leqslant 800$
   $x_1, x_2, x_3 \geqslant 0$

We introduce slack variables s_1 and s_2 and write this problem in the initial form:

$$\begin{aligned} 2x_1 + x_2 + 2x_3 + s_1 &= 1000 \\ x_1 + 2x_2 + 2x_3 + s_2 &= 800 \\ -7x_1 - 9x_2 - 10x_3 + P &= 0 \end{aligned}$$

The simplex tableau for this problem is:

$$\begin{bmatrix} x_1 & x_2 & x_3 & s_1 & s_2 & P \\ 2 & 1 & 2 & 1 & 0 & 0 & 1000 \\ 1 & 2 & \textcircled{2} & 0 & 1 & 0 & 800 \\ \hline -7 & -9 & -10 & 0 & 0 & 1 & 0 \end{bmatrix} \begin{array}{l} \dfrac{1000}{2} = 500 \\[2mm] \dfrac{800}{2} = 400 \end{array}$$

$\dfrac{1}{2}R_2 \rightarrow R_2$

(continued)

$$\sim \begin{bmatrix} 2 & 1 & 2 & 1 & 0 & 0 & | & 1000 \\ \frac{1}{2} & 1 & 1 & 0 & \frac{1}{2} & 0 & | & 400 \\ \hline -7 & -9 & -10 & 0 & 0 & 1 & | & 0 \end{bmatrix} \sim \begin{bmatrix} \boxed{1} & -1 & 0 & 1 & -1 & 0 & | & 200 \\ \frac{1}{2} & 1 & 1 & 0 & \frac{1}{2} & 0 & | & 400 \\ \hline -2 & 1 & 0 & 0 & 5 & 1 & | & 4000 \end{bmatrix}$$

$$R_1 + (-2)R_2 \rightarrow R_1 \qquad\qquad\qquad R_2 + \left(-\frac{1}{2}\right)R_1 \rightarrow R_2$$
$$R_3 + 10R_2 \rightarrow R_3 \qquad\qquad\qquad R_3 + 2R_1 \rightarrow R_3$$

$$\sim \begin{bmatrix} 1 & -1 & 0 & 1 & -1 & 0 & | & 200 \\ 0 & \boxed{\frac{3}{2}} & 1 & -\frac{1}{2} & 1 & 0 & | & 300 \\ \hline 0 & -1 & 0 & 2 & 3 & 1 & | & 4400 \end{bmatrix} \sim \begin{bmatrix} 1 & -1 & 0 & 1 & -1 & 0 & | & 200 \\ 0 & 1 & \frac{2}{3} & -\frac{1}{3} & \frac{2}{3} & 0 & | & 200 \\ \hline 0 & -1 & 0 & 2 & 3 & 1 & | & 4400 \end{bmatrix}$$

$$\frac{2}{3}R_2 \rightarrow R_2 \qquad\qquad\qquad R_1 + R_2 \rightarrow R_1, \; R_3 + R_2 \rightarrow R_3$$

$$\begin{array}{cccccc} x_1 & x_2 & x_3 & s_1 & s_2 & P \end{array}$$
$$\sim \begin{bmatrix} 1 & 0 & \frac{2}{3} & \frac{2}{3} & -\frac{1}{3} & 0 & | & 400 \\ 0 & 1 & \frac{2}{3} & -\frac{1}{3} & \frac{2}{3} & 0 & | & 200 \\ \hline 0 & 0 & \frac{2}{3} & \frac{5}{3} & \frac{8}{3} & 1 & | & 4600 \end{bmatrix}$$

Optimal solution: the maximum profit is $4600 when 400 A components, 200 B components, and 0 C components are manufactured.

33. Let x_1 = the amount invested in government bonds,
x_2 = the amount invested in mutual funds,
and x_3 = the amount invested in money market funds.
The mathematical model for this problem is:

Maximize $P = .08x_1 + .13x_2 + .15x_3$

Subject to: $x_1 + x_2 + x_3 \leq 100{,}000$
$$x_2 + x_3 \leq x_1$$
$$x_1, \; x_2, \; x_3 \geq 0$$

We introduce slack variables s_1 and s_2 to obtain the initial form:

$$\begin{aligned} x_1 + x_2 + x_3 + s_1 &= 100{,}000 \\ -x_1 + x_2 + x_3 + s_2 &= 0 \\ -.08x_1 - .13x_2 - .15x_3 + P &= 0 \end{aligned}$$

The simplex tableau for this problem is:

$$
\begin{array}{cccccc}
x_1 & x_2 & x_3 & s_1 & s_2 & P \\
\end{array}
$$

$$
\left[
\begin{array}{cccccc|c}
1 & 1 & 1 & 1 & 0 & 0 & 100,000 \\
-1 & 1 & ① & 0 & 1 & 0 & 0 \\
\hline
-.08 & -.13 & -.15 & 0 & 0 & 1 & 0
\end{array}
\right]
\quad \dfrac{100,000}{1} = 100,000
$$

$$R_1 + (-1)R_2 \to R_1 \text{ and } R_3 + .15R_2 \to R_3$$

$$
\sim
\left[
\begin{array}{cccccc|c}
② & 0 & 0 & 1 & -1 & 0 & 100,000 \\
-1 & 1 & 1 & 0 & 1 & 0 & 0 \\
\hline
-.23 & .02 & 0 & 0 & .15 & 1 & 0
\end{array}
\right]
$$

$$\tfrac{1}{2}R_2 \to R_2$$

$$
\sim
\left[
\begin{array}{cccccc|c}
1 & 0 & 0 & \frac{1}{2} & -\frac{1}{2} & 0 & 50,000 \\
-1 & 1 & 1 & 0 & 1 & 0 & 0 \\
\hline
-.23 & .02 & 0 & 0 & .15 & 1 & 0
\end{array}
\right]
$$

$$R_2 + R_1 \to R_2 \text{ and } R_3 + .23R_1 \to R_3$$

$$
\begin{array}{cccccc}
x_1 & x_2 & x_3 & s_1 & s_2 & P \\
\end{array}
$$

$$
\sim
\left[
\begin{array}{cccccc|c}
1 & 0 & 0 & \frac{1}{2} & -\frac{1}{2} & 0 & 50,000 \\
0 & 1 & 1 & \frac{1}{2} & -\frac{1}{2} & 0 & 50,000 \\
\hline
0 & .02 & 0 & .115 & .035 & 1 & 11,500
\end{array}
\right]
$$

Optimal solution: the maximum return is \$11,500 when $x_1 = \$50,000$ is invested in government bonds, $x_2 = \$0$ is invested in mutual funds, and $x_3 = \$50,000$ is invested in money market funds.

35. Let x_1 = the number of daytime ads,
  x_2 = the number of prime-time ads,
and x_3 = the number of late-night ads.

The mathematical model for this problem is:

$$\text{Maximize } P = 14,000x_1 + 24,000x_2 + 18,000x_3$$

$$
\begin{aligned}
\text{Subject to: } \quad 1000x_1 + 2000x_2 + 1500x_3 &\leq 20,000 \\
x_1 + x_2 + x_3 &\leq 15 \\
x_1, x_2, x_3 &\geq 0
\end{aligned}
$$

We introduce slack variables to obtain the following initial form:

$$1000x_1 + 2000x_2 + 1500x_3 + s_1 \qquad = 20{,}000$$
$$x_1 + x_2 + x_3 \qquad + s_2 \qquad = 15$$
$$-14{,}000x_1 - 24{,}000x_2 - 18{,}000x_3 \qquad + P = 0$$

The simplex tableau for this problem is:

$$
\begin{array}{cccccc}
x_1 & x_2 & x_3 & s_1 & s_2 & P
\end{array}
$$

$$
\left[
\begin{array}{cccccc|c}
1000 & \boxed{2000} & 1500 & 1 & 0 & 0 & 20{,}000 \\
1 & 1 & 1 & 0 & 1 & 0 & 15 \\
\hline
-14{,}000 & -24{,}000 & -18{,}000 & 0 & 0 & 1 & 0
\end{array}
\right]
\begin{array}{l}
\dfrac{20{,}000}{2000} = 10 \\[6pt]
\dfrac{15}{1} = 15
\end{array}
$$

$\dfrac{1}{2000}R_1 \rightarrow R_1$

$$
\sim
\left[
\begin{array}{cccccc|c}
\dfrac{1}{2} & 1 & \dfrac{3}{4} & \dfrac{1}{2000} & 0 & 0 & 10 \\[6pt]
1 & 1 & 1 & 0 & 1 & 0 & 15 \\
\hline
-14{,}000 & -24{,}000 & -18{,}000 & 0 & 0 & 1 & 0
\end{array}
\right]
$$

$R_2 + (-1)R_1 \rightarrow R_2,\ R_3 + 24{,}000R_1 \rightarrow R_3$

$$
\sim
\left[
\begin{array}{cccccc|c}
\dfrac{1}{2} & 1 & \dfrac{3}{4} & \dfrac{1}{2000} & 0 & 0 & 10 \\[6pt]
\boxed{\dfrac{1}{2}} & 0 & \dfrac{1}{4} & -\dfrac{1}{2000} & 1 & 0 & 5 \\[6pt]
\hline
-2000 & 0 & 0 & 12 & 0 & 1 & 240{,}000
\end{array}
\right]
$$

$2R_2 \rightarrow R_2$

$$
\sim
\left[
\begin{array}{cccccc|c}
\dfrac{1}{2} & 1 & \dfrac{3}{4} & \dfrac{1}{2000} & 0 & 0 & 10 \\[6pt]
1 & 0 & \dfrac{1}{2} & -\dfrac{1}{1000} & 2 & 0 & 10 \\[6pt]
\hline
-2000 & 0 & 0 & 12 & 0 & 1 & 240{,}000
\end{array}
\right]
$$

$R_1 + \left(-\dfrac{1}{2}\right)R_2 \rightarrow R_1,\ R_3 + 2000R_2 \rightarrow R_3$

$$
\begin{array}{cccccc}
x_1 & x_2 & x_3 & s_1 & s_2 & P
\end{array}
$$

$$
\sim
\left[
\begin{array}{cccccc|c}
0 & 1 & \dfrac{1}{2} & \dfrac{1}{1000} & -1 & 0 & 5 \\[6pt]
1 & 0 & \dfrac{1}{2} & -\dfrac{1}{1000} & 2 & 0 & 10 \\[6pt]
\hline
0 & 0 & 1000 & 10 & 4000 & 1 & 260{,}000
\end{array}
\right]
$$

Optimal solution: maximum number of potential customers is 260,000 when x_1 = 10 daytime ads, x_2 = 5 prime-time ads, and x_3 = 0 late-night ads are placed.

37. Let x_1 = the number of colonial houses,
    x_2 = the number of split-level houses,
and x_3 = the number of ranch-style houses.

The mathematical model for this problem is:

Maximize $P = 20{,}000x_1 + 18{,}000x_2 + 24{,}000x_3$

Subject to:
$$\frac{1}{2}x_1 + \frac{1}{2}x_2 + x_3 \leqslant 30$$
$$60{,}000x_1 + 60{,}000x_2 + 80{,}000x_3 \leqslant 3{,}200{,}000$$
$$4000x_1 + 3000x_2 + 4000x_3 \leqslant 180{,}000$$
$$x_1,\ x_2,\ x_3 \geqslant 0$$

We simplify these inequalities and then introduce slack variables to obtain the initial form:

$$\frac{1}{2}x_1 \quad \frac{1}{2}x_2 \quad x_3 + s_1 \qquad\qquad = \quad 30$$
$$6x_1 \quad 6x_2 \quad 8x_3 \quad + s_2 \qquad = \quad 320$$
$$4x_1 \quad 3x_2 \quad 4x_3 \qquad + s_3 \quad = \quad 180$$
$$-20{,}000x_1 - 18{,}000x_2 - 24{,}000x_3 \qquad\qquad + P = \quad 0$$

[<u>Note</u>: This simplification will change the interpretation of the slack variables.]

The simplex tableau for this problem is:

x_1	x_2	x_3	s_1	s_2	s_3	P		
$\frac{1}{2}$	$\frac{1}{2}$	①	1	0	0	0	30	$\frac{30}{1} = 30$
6	6	8	0	1	0	0	320	$\frac{320}{8} = 40$
4	3	4	0	0	1	0	180	$\frac{180}{4} = 45$
−20,000	−18,000	−24,000	0	0	0	1	0	

$$R_2 + (-8)R_1 \rightarrow R_2,\ R_3 + (-4)R_1 \rightarrow R_3,\ R_4 + 24{,}000R_1 \rightarrow R_4$$

	$\frac{1}{2}$	$\frac{1}{2}$	1	1	0	0	0	30
	2	2	0	−8	1	0	0	80
~	②	1	0	−4	0	1	0	60
	−8000	−6000	0	24,000	0	0	1	720,000

$$\frac{1}{2}R_3 \rightarrow R_3$$

(continued)

$$\sim \begin{bmatrix} \frac{1}{2} & \frac{1}{2} & 1 & 1 & 0 & 0 & 0 & \bigm| & 30 \\ 2 & 2 & 0 & -8 & 1 & 0 & 0 & \bigm| & 80 \\ 1 & \frac{1}{2} & 0 & -2 & 0 & \frac{1}{2} & 0 & \bigm| & 30 \\ \hline -8000 & -6000 & 0 & 24{,}000 & 0 & 0 & 1 & \bigm| & 720{,}000 \end{bmatrix}$$

$$R_1 + \left(-\tfrac{1}{2}\right)R_3 \to R_1, \quad R_2 + (-2)R_3 \to R_2, \quad R_4 + 8000R_3 \to R_4$$

$$\sim \begin{bmatrix} 0 & \frac{1}{4} & 1 & 2 & 0 & -\frac{1}{4} & 0 & \bigm| & 15 \\ 0 & \boxed{1} & 0 & -4 & 1 & -1 & 0 & \bigm| & 20 \\ 1 & \frac{1}{2} & 0 & -2 & 0 & \frac{1}{2} & 0 & \bigm| & 30 \\ \hline 0 & -2000 & 0 & 8000 & 0 & 4000 & 1 & \bigm| & 960{,}000 \end{bmatrix}$$

$$R_1 + \left(-\tfrac{1}{4}\right)R_2 \to R_1, \quad R_3 + \left(-\tfrac{1}{2}\right)R_2 \to R_3, \quad R_4 + 2000R_2 \to R_4$$

$$\begin{array}{ccccccc} x_1 & x_2 & x_3 & s_1 & s_2 & s_3 & P \end{array}$$
$$\sim \begin{bmatrix} 0 & 0 & 1 & 1 & -\frac{1}{4} & 0 & 0 & \bigm| & 10 \\ 0 & 1 & 0 & -4 & 1 & -1 & 0 & \bigm| & 20 \\ 1 & 0 & 0 & 0 & -\frac{1}{2} & 1 & 0 & \bigm| & 20 \\ \hline 0 & 0 & 0 & 0 & 2000 & 2000 & 1 & \bigm| & 1{,}000{,}000 \end{bmatrix}$$

Optimal solution: maximum profit is \$1,000,000 when $x_1 = 20$ colonial houses, $x_2 = 20$ split-level houses, and $x_3 = 10$ ranch-style houses are built.

39. Let x_1 = the number of boxes of Assortment I,
  x_2 = the number of boxes of Assortment II,
and x_3 = the number of boxes of Assortment III.

The profit per box of Assortment I is:

  $9.40 - [4(0.20) + 4(0.25) + 12(0.30)] = \$4.00$

The profit per box of Assortment II is:

  $7.60 - [12(0.20) + 4(0.25) + 4(0.30)] = \$3.00$

The profit per box of Assortment III is:

  $11.00 - [8(0.20) + 8(0.25) + 8(0.30)] = \$5.00$

The mathematical model for this problem is:

Maximize $P = 4x_1 + 3x_2 + 5x_3$

Subject to:
$$4x_1 + 12x_2 + 8x_3 \leqslant 4800$$
$$4x_1 + 4x_2 + 8x_3 \leqslant 4000$$
$$12x_1 + 4x_2 + 8x_3 \leqslant 5600$$
$$x_1, \; x_2, \; x_3 \geqslant 0$$

We introduce slack variables to obtain the initial form:

$$4x_1 + 12x_2 + 8x_3 + s_1 \qquad\qquad = 4800$$
$$4x_1 + 4x_2 + 8x_3 \qquad + s_2 \qquad = 4000$$
$$12x_1 + 4x_2 + 8x_3 \qquad\quad + s_3 \quad = 5600$$
$$-4x_1 - 3x_2 - 5x_3 \qquad\qquad + P = 0$$

$$\left[\begin{array}{ccccccc|c}
4 & 12 & 8 & 1 & 0 & 0 & 0 & 4800 \\
4 & 4 & \boxed{8} & 0 & 1 & 0 & 0 & 4000 \\
12 & 4 & 8 & 0 & 0 & 1 & 0 & 5600 \\
\hline
-4 & -3 & -5 & 0 & 0 & 0 & 1 & 0
\end{array}\right]
\qquad
\begin{array}{l}
\dfrac{4800}{8} = 600 \\[2mm]
\dfrac{4000}{8} = 500 \\[2mm]
\dfrac{5600}{8} = 700
\end{array}$$

$\dfrac{1}{8} R_2 \rightarrow R_2$

$$\sim \left[\begin{array}{ccccccc|c}
4 & 12 & 8 & 1 & 0 & 0 & 0 & 4800 \\
\frac{1}{2} & \frac{1}{2} & 1 & 0 & \frac{1}{8} & 0 & 0 & 500 \\
12 & 4 & 8 & 0 & 0 & 1 & 0 & 5600 \\
\hline
-4 & -3 & -5 & 0 & 0 & 0 & 1 & 0
\end{array}\right]$$

$R_1 + (-8)R_2 \rightarrow R_1, \; R_3 + (-8)R_2 \rightarrow R_3, \; R_4 + 5R_2 \rightarrow R_4$

$$\sim \left[\begin{array}{ccccccc|c}
0 & 8 & 0 & 1 & -1 & 0 & 0 & 800 \\
\frac{1}{2} & \frac{1}{2} & 1 & 0 & \frac{1}{8} & 0 & 0 & 500 \\
\boxed{8} & 0 & 0 & 0 & -1 & 1 & 0 & 1600 \\
\hline
-\frac{3}{2} & -\frac{1}{2} & 0 & 0 & \frac{5}{8} & 0 & 1 & 2500
\end{array}\right]$$

$\dfrac{1}{8} R_3 \rightarrow R_3$

(continued)

$$\sim \begin{bmatrix} 0 & 8 & 0 & 1 & -1 & 0 & 0 & | & 800 \\ \frac{1}{2} & \frac{1}{2} & 1 & 0 & \frac{1}{8} & 0 & 0 & | & 500 \\ 1 & 0 & 0 & 0 & -\frac{1}{8} & \frac{1}{8} & 0 & | & 200 \\ \hline -\frac{3}{2} & -\frac{1}{2} & 0 & 0 & \frac{5}{8} & 0 & 1 & | & 2500 \end{bmatrix}$$

$$R_2 + \left(-\frac{1}{2}\right)R_3 \to R_2, \quad R_4 + \frac{3}{2}R_3 \to R_4$$

$$\sim \begin{bmatrix} 0 & \boxed{8} & 0 & 1 & -1 & 0 & 0 & | & 800 \\ 0 & \frac{1}{2} & 1 & 0 & \frac{3}{16} & 0 & 0 & | & 400 \\ 1 & 0 & 0 & 0 & -\frac{1}{8} & \frac{1}{8} & 0 & | & 200 \\ \hline 0 & -\frac{1}{2} & 0 & 0 & \frac{7}{16} & \frac{3}{16} & 1 & | & 2800 \end{bmatrix}$$

$$\frac{1}{8}R_1 \to R_1$$

$$\sim \begin{bmatrix} 0 & 1 & 0 & \frac{1}{8} & -\frac{1}{8} & 0 & 0 & | & 100 \\ 0 & \frac{1}{2} & 1 & 0 & \frac{3}{16} & 0 & 0 & | & 400 \\ 1 & 0 & 0 & 0 & -\frac{1}{8} & \frac{1}{8} & 0 & | & 200 \\ \hline 0 & -\frac{1}{2} & 0 & 0 & \frac{7}{16} & \frac{3}{16} & 1 & | & 2800 \end{bmatrix}$$

$$R_2 + \left(-\frac{1}{2}\right)R_1 \to R_2, \quad R_4 + \frac{1}{2}R_1 \to R_4$$

$$\sim \begin{bmatrix} 0 & 1 & 0 & \frac{1}{8} & -\frac{1}{8} & 0 & 0 & | & 100 \\ 0 & 0 & 1 & -\frac{1}{16} & \frac{1}{4} & 0 & 0 & | & 350 \\ 1 & 0 & 0 & 0 & -\frac{1}{8} & \frac{1}{8} & 0 & | & 200 \\ \hline 0 & 0 & 0 & \frac{1}{16} & \frac{3}{8} & \frac{3}{16} & 1 & | & 2850 \end{bmatrix}$$

Optimal solution: maximum profit is $2850 when 200 boxes of Assortment I, 100 boxes of Assortment II, and 350 boxes of Assortment III are made.

41. Let x_1 = the number of grams of food A,
x_2 = the number of grams of food B,
and x_3 = the number of grams of food C.
The mathematical model for this problem is:

Maximize $P = 3x_1 + 3x_2 + 5x_3$

Subject to:
$$x_1 + 3x_2 + 2x_3 \leqslant 30$$
$$2x_1 + x_2 + x_3 \leqslant 24$$
$$x_1, \; x_2, \; x_3 \geqslant 0$$

We introduce slack variables s_1 and s_2 to obtain the initial form:

$$x_1 + 3x_2 + 2x_3 + s_1 \qquad\qquad = 30$$
$$2x_1 + x_2 + x_3 \qquad + s_2 \qquad = 24$$
$$-3x_1 - 3x_2 - 5x_3 \qquad\qquad + P = 0$$

The simplex tableau for this problem is:

$$
\begin{array}{cccccc}
x_1 & x_2 & x_3 & s_1 & s_2 & P \\
\end{array}
$$

$$
\left[\begin{array}{cccccc|c}
1 & 3 & ② & 1 & 0 & 0 & 30 \\
2 & 1 & 1 & 0 & 1 & 0 & 24 \\
\hline
-3 & -3 & -5 & 0 & 0 & 1 & 0
\end{array}\right]
\qquad
\begin{array}{l}
\dfrac{30}{2} = 15 \\[2mm]
\dfrac{24}{1} = 24
\end{array}
$$

$$\tfrac{1}{2}R_1 \rightarrow R_1$$

$$
\sim
\left[\begin{array}{cccccc|c}
\frac{1}{2} & \frac{3}{2} & 1 & \frac{1}{2} & 0 & 0 & 15 \\
2 & 1 & 1 & 0 & 1 & 0 & 24 \\
\hline
-3 & -3 & -5 & 0 & 0 & 1 & 0
\end{array}\right]
\quad
\sim
\left[\begin{array}{cccccc|c}
\frac{1}{2} & \frac{3}{2} & 1 & \frac{1}{2} & 0 & 0 & 15 \\
③\frac{3}{2} & -\frac{1}{2} & 0 & -\frac{1}{2} & 1 & 0 & 9 \\
\hline
-\frac{1}{2} & \frac{9}{2} & 0 & \frac{5}{2} & 0 & 1 & 75
\end{array}\right]
\quad
\begin{array}{l}
\dfrac{15}{1/2} = 30 \\[2mm]
\dfrac{9}{3/2} = 6
\end{array}
$$

$$R_2 + (-1)R_1 \rightarrow R_2 \text{ and} \qquad\qquad \tfrac{2}{3}R_2 \rightarrow R_2$$
$$R_3 + 5R_1 \rightarrow R_3$$

$$
\begin{array}{cccccc}
& & & & & \\
\end{array}
$$

$$
\sim
\left[\begin{array}{cccccc|c}
\frac{1}{2} & \frac{3}{2} & 1 & \frac{1}{2} & 0 & 0 & 15 \\
1 & -\frac{1}{3} & 0 & -\frac{1}{3} & \frac{2}{3} & 0 & 6 \\
\hline
-\frac{1}{2} & \frac{9}{2} & 0 & \frac{5}{2} & 0 & 1 & 75
\end{array}\right]
\quad
\sim
\begin{array}{cccccc}
x_1 & x_2 & x_3 & s_1 & s_2 & P \\
\end{array}
$$

$$
\left[\begin{array}{cccccc|c}
0 & \frac{5}{3} & 1 & \frac{2}{3} & -\frac{1}{3} & 0 & 12 \\
1 & -\frac{1}{3} & 0 & -\frac{1}{3} & \frac{2}{3} & 0 & 6 \\
\hline
0 & \frac{13}{3} & 0 & \frac{7}{3} & \frac{1}{3} & 0 & 78
\end{array}\right]
$$

$$R_1 + \left(-\tfrac{1}{2}\right)R_2 \rightarrow R_1 \text{ and}$$

$$R_3 + \tfrac{1}{2}R_2 \rightarrow R_3$$

Optimal solution: the maximum amount of protein is 78 units when $x_1 = 6$ grams of food A, $x_2 = 0$ grams of food B, and $x_3 = 12$ grams of food C.

43. Let x_1 = the number of undergraduate students,
x_2 = the number of graduate students,
and x_3 = the number of faculty members.
The mathematical model for this problem is:

Maximize $P = 18x_1 + 25x_2 + 30x_3$

Subject to:
$$x_1 + x_2 + x_3 \leqslant 20$$
$$60x_1 + 90x_2 + 120x_3 \leqslant 1620$$
$$x_1, x_2, x_3 \geqslant 0$$

We introduce slack variables s_1 and s_2 to obtain the initial form:

$$x_1 + x_2 + x_3 + s_1 \qquad\qquad = 20$$
$$60x_1 + 90x_2 + 120x_3 \qquad + s_2 \qquad = 1620$$
$$-18x_1 - 25x_2 - 30x_3 \qquad\qquad\quad + P = 0$$

The simplex tableau for this problem is:

$$
\begin{array}{cccccc|c}
x_1 & x_2 & x_3 & s_1 & s_2 & P & \\
\end{array}
$$

$$
\left[\begin{array}{cccccc|c}
1 & 1 & 1 & 1 & 0 & 0 & 20 \\
60 & 90 & \boxed{120} & 0 & 1 & 0 & 1620 \\
\hline
-18 & -25 & -30 & 0 & 0 & 1 & 0
\end{array}\right]
\qquad
\begin{array}{l}
\dfrac{20}{1} = 20 \\[2mm]
\dfrac{1620}{120} = \dfrac{27}{2}
\end{array}
$$

$$\frac{1}{120}R_2 \to R_2$$

$$
\sim
\left[\begin{array}{cccccc|c}
1 & 1 & 1 & 1 & 0 & 0 & 20 \\
\frac{1}{2} & \frac{3}{4} & 1 & 0 & \frac{1}{120} & 0 & \frac{27}{2} \\
\hline
-18 & -25 & -30 & 0 & 0 & 1 & 0
\end{array}\right]
$$

$$R_1 + (-1)R_2 \to R_1 \text{ and } R_3 + 30R_2 \to R_3$$

$$
\sim
\left[\begin{array}{cccccc|c}
\boxed{\frac{1}{2}} & \frac{1}{4} & 0 & 1 & -\frac{1}{120} & 0 & \frac{13}{2} \\
\frac{1}{2} & \frac{3}{4} & 1 & 0 & \frac{1}{120} & 0 & \frac{27}{2} \\
\hline
-3 & -\frac{5}{2} & 0 & 0 & \frac{3}{4} & 1 & 405
\end{array}\right]
\qquad
\begin{array}{l}
\dfrac{13/2}{1/2} = 13 \\[2mm]
\dfrac{27/2}{1/2} = 27
\end{array}
$$

$$2R_1 \to R_1$$

$$
\sim
\left[\begin{array}{cccccc|c}
1 & \frac{1}{2} & 0 & 2 & -\frac{1}{20} & 0 & 13 \\
\frac{1}{2} & \frac{3}{4} & 1 & 0 & \frac{1}{40} & 0 & \frac{27}{2} \\
\hline
-3 & -\frac{5}{2} & 0 & 0 & \frac{3}{4} & 1 & 405
\end{array}\right]
$$

$$R_2 + \left(-\frac{1}{2}\right)R_1 \to R_2 \text{ and } R_3 + 3R_1 \to R_3$$

(continued)

$$\sim \begin{bmatrix} 1 & \frac{1}{2} & 0 & 2 & -\frac{1}{20} & 0 & 13 \\ 0 & \boxed{\frac{1}{2}} & 1 & -1 & \frac{1}{20} & 0 & 7 \\ \hline 0 & -1 & 0 & 6 & \frac{3}{5} & 1 & 444 \end{bmatrix} \quad \begin{array}{l} \frac{13}{1/2} = 26 \\ \frac{7}{1/2} = 14 \end{array}$$

$2R_2 \rightarrow R_2$

$$\sim \begin{bmatrix} 1 & \frac{1}{2} & 0 & 2 & -\frac{1}{20} & 0 & 13 \\ 0 & 1 & 2 & -2 & \frac{1}{10} & 0 & 14 \\ \hline 0 & -1 & 0 & 6 & \frac{3}{5} & 1 & 444 \end{bmatrix} \quad \sim \quad \begin{array}{cccccc} x_1 & x_2 & x_3 & s_1 & s_2 & P \end{array}$$

$$\begin{bmatrix} 1 & 0 & -1 & 3 & -\frac{1}{10} & 0 & 6 \\ 0 & 1 & 2 & -2 & \frac{1}{10} & 0 & 14 \\ \hline 0 & 0 & 2 & 4 & \frac{7}{10} & 1 & 458 \end{bmatrix}$$

$R_1 + \left(-\frac{1}{2}\right)R_2 \rightarrow R_1$ and

$R_3 + R_2 \rightarrow R_3$

Optimal solution: the maximum number of interviews is 458 when $x_1 = 6$ undergraduate students, $x_2 = 14$ graduate students, and $x_3 = 0$ faculty members are hired.

EXERCISE 2-5

Things to remember:

1. FORMULATION OF THE DUAL PROBLEM

   Given a minimization problem with $\geqslant$ problem constraints:

   (i) Use the coefficients of the problem constraints and the objective function to form a matrix A with the coefficients of the objective function in the last row.

   (ii) Let B be the transpose of A, i.e., the rows of A are the columns of B (in order).

   (iii) Use the rows of B to form a maximization problem with $\leqslant$ problem constraints.

2. A minimization problem has a solution if and only if its dual problem has a solution. If a solution exists, then the optimal value of the minimization problem is the same as the optimal value of the dual problem.

3. SOLUTION OF A MINIMIZATION PROBLEM

(i) Write all problem constraints as $\geqslant$ inequalities. (This may introduce negative numbers on the right side of the problem constraints.)

(ii) Form the dual problem.

(iii) Write the initial form of the dual problem, using the variables from the minimization problem as the slack variables.

(iv) Use the simplex method to solve the dual problem.

(v) Read the solution of the minimization problem from the bottom row of the final simplex tableau in Step (iv).

[Note: If the dual problem has no solution, then the minimization problem has no solution.]

---

1. (A) Given the minimization problem:

Minimize $C = 8x_1 + 9x_2$

Subject to: $\quad x_1 + 3x_2 \geqslant 4$
$\quad\quad\quad\quad 2x_1 + x_2 \geqslant 5$
$\quad\quad\quad\quad x_1, x_2 \geqslant 0$

The matrix A corresponding to this problem is:

$$A = \begin{bmatrix} 1 & 3 & | & 4 \\ 2 & 1 & | & 5 \\ \hline 8 & 9 & | & 1 \end{bmatrix}$$

The matrix B corresponding to the dual problem has the rows of A as its columns. Thus:

$$B = \begin{bmatrix} 1 & 2 & | & 8 \\ 3 & 1 & | & 9 \\ \hline 4 & 5 & | & 1 \end{bmatrix}$$

The dual problem is:

Maximize $P = 4y_1 + 5y_2$

Subject to: $\quad y_1 + 2y_2 \leqslant 8$
$\quad\quad\quad\quad 3y_1 + y_2 \leqslant 9$
$\quad\quad\quad\quad y_1, y_2 \geqslant 0$

(B) Letting x_1 and x_2 be slack variables, the initial form for the dual problem is:

$$\begin{aligned}
y_1 + 2y_2 + x_1 \qquad\qquad &= 8 \\
3y_1 + y_2 \qquad + x_2 \qquad &= 9 \\
-4y_1 - 5y_2 \qquad\qquad + P &= 0
\end{aligned}$$

(C) The simplex tableau for this problem is:

$$
\begin{array}{ccccc}
y_1 & y_2 & x_1 & x_2 & P
\end{array}
$$

$$
\left[\begin{array}{ccccc|c}
1 & 2 & 1 & 0 & 0 & 8 \\
3 & 1 & 0 & 1 & 0 & 9 \\
\hline
-4 & -5 & 0 & 0 & 1 & 0
\end{array}\right]
$$

3. From the final simplex tableau,

$$
\begin{array}{ccccc}
y_1 & y_2 & x_1 & x_2 & P
\end{array}
$$

$$
\left[\begin{array}{ccccc|c}
0 & 1 & 5 & -2 & 0 & 5 \\
1 & 0 & -7 & 3 & 0 & 3 \\
\hline
0 & 0 & 1 & 2 & 1 & 121
\end{array}\right]:
$$

(A) the optimal solution of the dual problem is:

maximum value of $P = 121$ at $y_1 = 3$ and $y_2 = 5$;

(B) the optimal solution of the minimization problem is:

minimum value of $C = 121$ at $x_1 = 1$, $x_2 = 2$.

5. (A) The matrix corresponding to the given problem is: $A = \begin{bmatrix} 4 & 1 & 13 \\ 3 & 1 & 12 \\ 9 & 2 & 1 \end{bmatrix}$

The matrix B corresponding to the dual problem has the rows of A as its columns, that is:

$$
B = \left[\begin{array}{cc|c}
4 & 3 & 9 \\
1 & 1 & 2 \\
\hline
13 & 12 & 1
\end{array}\right]
$$

Thus, the dual problem is: Maximize $P = 13y_1 + 12y_2$

Subject to: $4y_1 + 3y_2 \leqslant 9$

$y_1 + y_2 \leqslant 2$

$y_1, \ y_2 \geqslant 0$

(B) We introduce slack variables x_1 and x_2 to obtain the initial form for the dual problem:

$$
\begin{aligned}
4y_1 + 3y_2 + x_1 \qquad\qquad &= 9 \\
y_1 + y_2 \qquad + x_2 \qquad &= 2 \\
-13y_1 - 12y_2 \qquad\qquad + P &= 0
\end{aligned}
$$

The simplex tableau for this problem is:

$$
\begin{array}{ccccc}
y_1 & y_2 & x_1 & x_2 & P
\end{array}
$$

$$
\left[\begin{array}{ccccc|c}
4 & 3 & 1 & 0 & 0 & 9 \\
\boxed{1} & 1 & 0 & 1 & 0 & 2 \\
\hline
-13 & -12 & 0 & 0 & 1 & 0
\end{array}\right]
\quad
\begin{array}{c}
\frac{9}{4} = 2.25 \\[4pt]
\frac{2}{1} = 2
\end{array}
\quad \sim \quad
\begin{array}{ccccc}
y_1 & y_2 & x_1 & x_2 & P
\end{array}
\left[\begin{array}{ccccc|c}
0 & -1 & 1 & -4 & 0 & 1 \\
1 & 1 & 0 & 1 & 0 & 2 \\
\hline
0 & 1 & 0 & 13 & 1 & 26
\end{array}\right]
$$

$$
R_1 + (-4)R_2 \rightarrow R_1 \text{ and } R_3 + 13R_2 \rightarrow R_3
$$

Optimal solution: min $C = 26$ at $x_1 = 0$, $x_2 = 13$.

7. (A) The matrix corresponding to the given problem is: $A = \begin{bmatrix} 2 & 3 & 15 \\ 1 & 2 & 8 \\ 7 & 12 & 1 \end{bmatrix}$

The matrix B corresponding to the dual problem has the rows of A as its columns, that is:

$$
B = \begin{bmatrix} 2 & 1 & 7 \\ 3 & 2 & 12 \\ 15 & 8 & 1 \end{bmatrix}
$$

The dual problem is: Maximize $P = 15y_1 + 8y_2$

$$
\begin{aligned}
\text{Subject to:} \quad 2y_1 + y_2 &\leqslant 7 \\
3y_1 + 2y_2 &\leqslant 12 \\
y_1, \ y_2 &\geqslant 0
\end{aligned}
$$

(B) We introduce slack variables x_1 and x_2 to obtain the initial form for the dual problem:

$$
\begin{aligned}
2y_1 + y_2 + x_1 \qquad\qquad &= 7 \\
3y_1 + 2y_2 \qquad + x_2 \qquad &= 12 \\
-15y_1 - 8y_2 \qquad\qquad + P &= 0
\end{aligned}
$$

The simplex tableau for this problem is:

$$\begin{array}{ccccc} y_1 & y_2 & x_1 & x_2 & P \end{array}$$

$$\left[\begin{array}{ccccc|c} \textcircled{2} & 1 & 1 & 0 & 0 & 7 \\ 3 & 2 & 0 & 1 & 0 & 12 \\ \hline -15 & -8 & 0 & 0 & 1 & 0 \end{array}\right] \quad \begin{array}{l} \frac{7}{2} = 3.5 \\[4pt] \frac{12}{3} = 4 \end{array} \quad \sim \quad \left[\begin{array}{ccccc|c} 1 & \frac{1}{2} & \frac{1}{2} & 0 & 0 & \frac{7}{2} \\ 3 & 2 & 0 & 1 & 0 & 12 \\ \hline -15 & -8 & 0 & 0 & 1 & 0 \end{array}\right]$$

$$\frac{1}{2}R_1 \to R_1 \qquad\qquad\qquad\qquad\qquad\qquad\qquad \begin{array}{l} R_2 + (-3)R_1 \to R_2 \text{ and} \\ R_3 + 15R_1 \to R_3 \end{array}$$

$$\sim \left[\begin{array}{ccccc|c} 1 & \frac{1}{2} & \frac{1}{2} & 0 & 0 & \frac{7}{2} \\ 0 & \textcircled{$\frac{1}{2}$} & -\frac{3}{2} & 1 & 0 & \frac{3}{2} \\ \hline 0 & -\frac{1}{2} & \frac{15}{2} & 0 & 1 & \frac{105}{2} \end{array}\right] \quad \begin{array}{l} \frac{7/2}{1/2} = 7 \\[4pt] \frac{3/2}{1/2} = 3 \end{array} \sim \left[\begin{array}{ccccc|c} 1 & \frac{1}{2} & \frac{1}{2} & 0 & 0 & \frac{7}{2} \\ 0 & 1 & -3 & 2 & 0 & 3 \\ \hline 0 & -\frac{1}{2} & \frac{15}{2} & 0 & 1 & \frac{105}{2} \end{array}\right]$$

$$2R_2 \to R_2 \qquad\qquad\qquad\qquad\qquad\qquad R_1 + \left(-\frac{1}{2}\right)R_2 \to R_1 \text{ and}$$
$$R_3 + \frac{1}{2}R_2 \to R_3$$

$$\begin{array}{ccccc} y_1 & y_2 & x_1 & x_2 & P \end{array}$$

$$\sim \left[\begin{array}{ccccc|c} 1 & 0 & 2 & -1 & 0 & 2 \\ 0 & 1 & -3 & 2 & 0 & 3 \\ \hline 0 & 0 & 6 & 1 & 1 & 54 \end{array}\right]$$

Optimal solution: min $C = 54$ at $x_1 = 6$, $x_2 = 1$.

9. (A) The matrices corresponding to the given problem and to the dual problem are:

$$A = \left[\begin{array}{cc|c} 2 & 1 & 8 \\ -2 & 3 & 4 \\ \hline 11 & 4 & 1 \end{array}\right] \quad \text{and} \quad B = \left[\begin{array}{cc|c} 2 & -2 & 11 \\ 1 & 3 & 4 \\ \hline 8 & 4 & 1 \end{array}\right]$$

respectively. Thus, the dual problem is: Maximize $P = 8y_1 + 4y_2$

$$\begin{array}{ll} \text{Subject to:} & 2y_1 - 2y_2 \leqslant 11 \\ & y_1 + 3y_2 \leqslant 4 \\ & y_1, \ y_2 \geqslant 0 \end{array}$$

(B) We introduce slack variables x_1 and x_2 to obtain the initial form for the dual problem:

$$\begin{array}{rcl} 2y_1 - 2y_2 + x_1 & = & 11 \\ y_1 + 3y_2 \qquad\ + x_2 & = & 4 \\ -8y_1 - 4y_2 \qquad\qquad + P & = & 0 \end{array}$$

The simplex tableau for this problem is:

$$
\begin{array}{ccccc}
y_1 & y_2 & x_1 & x_2 & P \\
\end{array}
$$

$$
\left[\begin{array}{ccccc|c}
2 & -2 & 1 & 0 & 0 & 11 \\
\boxed{1} & 3 & 0 & 1 & 0 & 4 \\
\hline
-8 & -4 & 0 & 0 & 1 & 0
\end{array}\right]
\quad
\begin{array}{l}
\frac{11}{2} = 5.5 \\[4pt]
\frac{4}{1} = 4
\end{array}
\quad \sim \quad
\left[\begin{array}{ccccc|c}
0 & -8 & 1 & -2 & 0 & 3 \\
1 & 3 & 0 & 1 & 0 & 4 \\
\hline
0 & 20 & 0 & 8 & 1 & 32
\end{array}\right]
$$

$$
\begin{array}{ccccc}
y_1 & y_2 & x_1 & x_2 & P
\end{array}
$$

$R_1 + (-2)R_2 \rightarrow R_1$ and
$R_3 + 8R_2 \rightarrow R_3$

Optimal solution: min $C = 32$ at $x_1 = 0$, $x_2 = 8$.

11. (A) The matrices corresponding to the given problem and the dual problem are:

$$
A = \left[\begin{array}{cc|c}
-3 & 1 & 6 \\
1 & -2 & 4 \\
\hline
7 & 9 & 1
\end{array}\right]
\quad \text{and} \quad
B = \left[\begin{array}{cc|c}
-3 & 1 & 7 \\
1 & -2 & 9 \\
\hline
6 & 4 & 1
\end{array}\right]
$$

respectively. Thus, the dual problem is: Maximize $P = 6y_1 + 4y_2$

Subject to: $-3y_1 + y_2 \leqslant 7$
$y_1 - 2y_2 \leqslant 9$
$y_1, y_2 \geqslant 0$

(B) We introduce slack variables x_1 and x_2 to obtain the initial form for the dual problem:

$$
\begin{array}{rcl}
-3y_1 + y_2 + x_1 & = & 7 \\
y_1 - 2y_2 \quad + x_2 & = & 9 \\
-6y_1 - 4y_2 \quad\quad + P & = & 0
\end{array}
$$

The simplex tableau for this problem is:

$$
\begin{array}{ccccc}
y_1 & y_2 & x_1 & x_2 & P
\end{array}
$$

$$
\left[\begin{array}{ccccc|c}
-3 & 1 & 1 & 0 & 0 & 7 \\
\boxed{1} & -2 & 0 & 1 & 0 & 9 \\
\hline
-6 & -4 & 0 & 0 & 1 & 0
\end{array}\right]
\quad \sim \quad
\left[\begin{array}{ccccc|c}
0 & -5 & 1 & 3 & 0 & 34 \\
1 & -2 & 0 & 1 & 0 & 9 \\
\hline
0 & -16 & 0 & 6 & 1 & 54
\end{array}\right]
$$

$$
\begin{array}{ccccc}
y_1 & y_2 & x_1 & x_2 & P
\end{array}
$$

$R_1 + 3R_2 \rightarrow R_1$ and
$R_3 + 6R_2 \rightarrow R_3$

The negative elements in the second column above the dashed line indicate that the problem does not have a solution.

13. The matrices corresponding to the given problem and the dual problem are:

$$A = \begin{bmatrix} 2 & 1 & | & 8 \\ 1 & 2 & | & 8 \\ 3 & 9 & | & 1 \end{bmatrix} \quad \text{and} \quad B = \begin{bmatrix} 2 & 1 & | & 3 \\ 1 & 2 & | & 9 \\ 8 & 8 & | & 1 \end{bmatrix}$$

respectively.

Thus, the dual problem is: Maximize $P = 8y_1 + 8y_2$

Subject to: $\quad 2y_1 + y_2 \leqslant 3$
$\quad\quad\quad\quad y_1 + 2y_2 \leqslant 9$
$\quad\quad\quad\quad\quad y_1, y_2 \geqslant 0$

We introduce slack variables x_1 and x_2 to obtain the initial form:

$$\begin{aligned} 2y_1 + y_2 + x_1 \quad\quad\quad &= 3 \\ y_1 + 2y_2 \quad + x_2 \quad &= 9 \\ -8y_1 - 8y_2 \quad\quad\quad + P &= 0 \end{aligned}$$

The simplex tableau for this problem is:

$$\begin{array}{ccccc} y_1 & y_2 & x_1 & x_2 & P \\ \begin{bmatrix} 2 & 1 & 1 & 0 & 0 & | & 3 \\ 1 & 2 & 0 & 1 & 0 & | & 9 \\ \hline -8 & -8 & 0 & 0 & 1 & | & 0 \end{bmatrix} \end{array} \begin{array}{l} \frac{3}{1} = 3 \\ \frac{9}{2} = 4.5 \end{array} \sim \begin{array}{ccccc} y_1 & y_2 & x_1 & x_2 & P \\ \begin{bmatrix} 2 & 1 & 1 & 0 & 0 & | & 3 \\ -3 & 0 & -2 & 1 & 0 & | & 3 \\ \hline 8 & 0 & 8 & 0 & 1 & | & 24 \end{bmatrix} \end{array}$$

$R_2 + (-2)R_1 \rightarrow R_2$ and
$R_3 + 8R_1 \rightarrow R_3$

Optimal solution: min $C = 24$ at $x_1 = 8$, $x_2 = 0$.

[Note: We could use either column 1 or column 2 as the pivot column. Column 2 involves slightly simpler calculations.]

15. The matrices corresponding to the given problem and the dual problem are:

$$A = \begin{bmatrix} 1 & 1 & | & 4 \\ 1 & -2 & | & -8 \\ -2 & 1 & | & -8 \\ \hline 7 & 5 & | & 1 \end{bmatrix} \quad \text{and} \quad B = \begin{bmatrix} 1 & 1 & -2 & | & 7 \\ 1 & -2 & 1 & | & 5 \\ 4 & -8 & -8 & | & 1 \end{bmatrix}$$

respectively. Thus, the dual problem is: Maximize $P = 4y_1 - 8y_2 - 8y_3$

Subject to: $\quad y_1 + y_2 - 2y_3 \leqslant 7$
$\quad\quad\quad\quad y_1 - 2y_2 + y_3 \leqslant 5$
$\quad\quad\quad\quad\quad y_1, y_2, y_3 \geqslant 0$

We introduce slack variables x_1 and x_2 to obtain the initial form:

$$\begin{aligned} y_1 + y_2 - 2y_3 + x_1 \quad\quad\quad &= 7 \\ y_1 - 2y_2 + y_3 \quad + x_2 \quad &= 5 \\ -4y_1 + 8y_2 + 8y_3 \quad\quad\quad + P &= 0 \end{aligned}$$

The simplex tableau for this problem is:

$$
\begin{array}{cccccc}
y_1 & y_2 & y_3 & x_1 & x_2 & P \\
\end{array}
$$

$$
\left[\begin{array}{cccccc|c}
1 & 1 & -2 & 1 & 0 & 0 & 7 \\
\boxed{1} & -2 & 1 & 0 & 1 & 0 & 5 \\
\hline
-4 & 8 & 8 & 0 & 0 & 1 & 0
\end{array}\right]
\quad
\begin{array}{l}
\frac{7}{1} = 7 \\[4pt]
\frac{5}{1} = 5
\end{array}
\quad \sim \quad
\begin{array}{cccccc}
y_1 & y_2 & y_3 & x_1 & x_2 & P \\
\end{array}
\left[\begin{array}{cccccc|c}
0 & 3 & -3 & 1 & -1 & 0 & 2 \\
1 & -2 & 1 & 0 & 1 & 0 & 5 \\
\hline
0 & 0 & 12 & 0 & 4 & 1 & 20
\end{array}\right]
$$

$R_1 + (-1)R_2 \to R_1$ and
$R_3 + 4R_2 \to R_3$

Optimal solution: min C = 20 at
$x_1 = 0,\ x_2 = 4$.

17. The matrices corresponding to the given problem and the dual problem are

$$
A = \left[\begin{array}{cc|c}
2 & 1 & 16 \\
1 & 1 & 12 \\
1 & 2 & 14 \\
\hline
10 & 30 & 1
\end{array}\right]
\qquad \text{and} \qquad
B = \left[\begin{array}{ccc|c}
2 & 1 & 1 & 10 \\
1 & 1 & 2 & 30 \\
\hline
16 & 12 & 14 & 1
\end{array}\right]
$$

respectively. Thus, the dual problem is: Maximize $P = 16y_1 + 12y_2 + 14y_3$

Subject to: $2y_1 + y_2 + y_3 \leqslant 10$
$y_1 + y_2 + 2y_3 \leqslant 30$
$y_1,\ y_2,\ y_3 \geqslant 0$

We introduce slack variables x_1 and x_2 to obtain the initial form:

$$
\begin{aligned}
2y_1 + y_2 + y_3 + x_1 \qquad\qquad &= 10 \\
y_1 + y_2 + 2y_3 \qquad + x_2 \qquad &= 30 \\
-16y_1 - 12y_2 - 14y_3 \qquad\qquad + P &= 0
\end{aligned}
$$

The simplex tableau for this problem is:

$$
\begin{array}{cccccc}
y_1 & y_2 & y_3 & x_1 & x_2 & P \\
\end{array}
\left[\begin{array}{cccccc|c}
\boxed{2} & 1 & 1 & 1 & 0 & 0 & 10 \\
1 & 1 & 2 & 0 & 1 & 0 & 30 \\
\hline
-16 & -12 & -14 & 0 & 0 & 1 & 0
\end{array}\right]
\quad
\begin{array}{l}
\frac{10}{2} = 5 \\[6pt]
\frac{30}{1} = 30
\end{array}
\ \sim
\left[\begin{array}{cccccc|c}
1 & \frac{1}{2} & \frac{1}{2} & \frac{1}{2} & 0 & 0 & 5 \\
1 & 1 & 2 & 0 & 1 & 0 & 30 \\
\hline
-16 & -12 & -14 & 0 & 0 & 1 & 0
\end{array}\right]
$$

$\frac{1}{2}R_1 \to R_1$

$R_2 + (-1)R_1 \to R_2$ and
$R_3 + 16R_1 \to R_3$

$$
\sim
\left[\begin{array}{cccccc|c}
1 & \frac{1}{2} & \boxed{\frac{1}{2}} & \frac{1}{2} & 0 & 0 & 5 \\
0 & \frac{1}{2} & \frac{3}{2} & -\frac{1}{2} & 1 & 0 & 25 \\
\hline
0 & -4 & -6 & 8 & 0 & 1 & 80
\end{array}\right]
\quad
\begin{array}{l}
\frac{5}{1/2} = 10 \\[6pt]
\frac{25}{3/2} = 16.66
\end{array}
\ \sim
\left[\begin{array}{cccccc|c}
2 & 1 & 1 & 1 & 0 & 0 & 10 \\
0 & \frac{1}{2} & \frac{3}{2} & -\frac{1}{2} & 1 & 0 & 25 \\
\hline
0 & -4 & -6 & 8 & 0 & 1 & 80
\end{array}\right]
$$

$2R_1 \to R_1$

$R_2 + \left(-\frac{3}{2}\right)R_1 \to R_2$ and
$R_3 + 6R_1 \to R_3$

(continued)

$$\begin{array}{cccccc} y_1 & y_2 & y_3 & x_1 & x_2 & P \end{array}$$

$$\sim \begin{bmatrix} 2 & 1 & 1 & 1 & 0 & 0 & | & 10 \\ -3 & -1 & 0 & -2 & 1 & 0 & | & 10 \\ \hline 12 & 2 & 0 & 14 & 0 & 1 & | & 140 \end{bmatrix}$$

Optimal solution: $\min C = 140$ at $x_1 = 14$, $x_2 = 0$.

19. The matrices corresponding to the given problem and the dual problem are:

$$A = \begin{bmatrix} 1 & 0 & | & 4 \\ 1 & 1 & | & 8 \\ 1 & 2 & | & 10 \\ 5 & 7 & | & 1 \end{bmatrix} \quad \text{and} \quad B = \begin{bmatrix} 1 & 1 & 1 & | & 5 \\ 0 & 1 & 2 & | & 7 \\ 4 & 8 & 10 & | & 1 \end{bmatrix}$$

respectively. Thus, the dual problem is: Maximize $P = 4y_1 + 8y_2 + 10y_3$

Subject to: $y_1 + y_2 + y_3 \leqslant 5$
$\qquad\qquad y_2 + 2y_3 \leqslant 7$
$\qquad\qquad y_1, \ y_2, \ y_3 \geqslant 0$

We introduce slack variables x_1 and x_2 to obtain the initial form:

$$\begin{aligned} y_1 + y_2 + y_3 + x_1 & & = 5 \\ y_2 + 2y_3 & + x_2 & = 7 \\ -4y_1 - 8y_2 - 10y_3 & + P & = 0 \end{aligned}$$

The simplex tableau for this problem is:

$$\begin{array}{cccccc} y_1 & y_2 & y_3 & x_1 & x_2 & P \end{array}$$

$$\begin{bmatrix} 1 & 1 & 1 & 1 & 0 & 0 & | & 5 \\ 0 & 1 & \boxed{2} & 0 & 1 & 0 & | & 7 \\ \hline -4 & -8 & -10 & 0 & 0 & 1 & | & 0 \end{bmatrix} \begin{array}{l} \frac{5}{1} = 5 \\ \frac{7}{2} = 3.5 \end{array} \sim \begin{bmatrix} 1 & 1 & 1 & 1 & 0 & 0 & | & 5 \\ 0 & \frac{1}{2} & 1 & 0 & \frac{1}{2} & 0 & | & \frac{7}{2} \\ \hline -4 & -8 & -10 & 0 & 0 & 1 & | & 0 \end{bmatrix}$$

$$\tfrac{1}{2} R_2 \to R_2$$

$$\begin{array}{l} R_1 + (-1)R_2 \to R_1 \text{ and} \\ R_3 + 10R_2 \to R_3 \end{array}$$

$$\sim \begin{bmatrix} \boxed{1} & \frac{1}{2} & 0 & 1 & -\frac{1}{2} & 0 & | & \frac{3}{2} \\ 0 & \frac{1}{2} & 1 & 0 & \frac{1}{2} & 0 & | & \frac{7}{2} \\ \hline -4 & -3 & 0 & 0 & 5 & 1 & | & 35 \end{bmatrix} \sim \begin{bmatrix} 1 & \boxed{\frac{1}{2}} & 0 & 1 & -\frac{1}{2} & 0 & | & \frac{3}{2} \\ 0 & \frac{1}{2} & 1 & 0 & \frac{1}{2} & 0 & | & \frac{7}{2} \\ \hline 0 & -1 & 0 & 4 & 3 & 1 & | & 41 \end{bmatrix} \begin{array}{l} \frac{3/2}{1/2} = 3 \\ \frac{7/2}{1/2} = 7 \end{array}$$

$$R_3 + 4R_1 \to R_3 \qquad\qquad\qquad\qquad 2R_1 \to R_1$$

(continued)

$$\sim \begin{bmatrix} 2 & 1 & 0 & 2 & -1 & 0 & | & 3 \\ 0 & \frac{1}{2} & 1 & 0 & \frac{1}{2} & 0 & | & \frac{7}{2} \\ \hline 0 & -1 & 0 & 4 & 3 & 1 & | & 41 \end{bmatrix} \sim \begin{bmatrix} 2 & 1 & 0 & 2 & -1 & 0 & | & 3 \\ -1 & 0 & 1 & -1 & 1 & 0 & | & 2 \\ \hline 2 & 0 & 0 & 6 & 2 & 1 & | & 44 \end{bmatrix}$$

$R_2 + \left(-\frac{1}{2}\right)R_1 \to R_2$ and

$R_3 + R_1 \to R_3$

Optimal solution: min $C = 44$ at $x_1 = 6$, $x_2 = 2$.

17. The matrices corresponding to the given problem and the dual problem are:

$$A = \begin{bmatrix} 1 & 1 & 2 & | & 7 \\ 2 & 1 & 1 & | & 4 \\ 10 & 7 & 12 & | & 1 \end{bmatrix} \quad \text{and} \quad B = \begin{bmatrix} 1 & 2 & | & 10 \\ 1 & 1 & | & 7 \\ 2 & 1 & | & 12 \\ 7 & 4 & | & 1 \end{bmatrix}$$

respectively. Thus, the dual problem is:

Maximize $P = 7y_1 + 4y_2$

Subject to: $\quad y_1 + 2y_2 \leq 10$

$\qquad\qquad\quad y_1 + \ y_2 \leq 7$

$\qquad\qquad 2y_1 + \ y_2 \leq 12$

$\qquad\qquad\qquad y_1, \ y_2 \leq 0$

We introduce slack variables x_1, x_2, and x_3 to obtain the initial form:

$$\begin{aligned} y_1 + 2y_2 + x_1 \qquad\qquad\qquad &= 10 \\ y_1 + \ y_2 \qquad + x_2 \qquad\qquad &= 7 \\ 2y_1 + \ y_2 \qquad\qquad + x_3 \qquad &= 12 \\ -7y_1 - 4y_2 \qquad\qquad\qquad + P &= 0 \end{aligned}$$

The simplex tableau for this problem is:

$$\begin{array}{cccccc} y_1 & y_2 & x_1 & x_2 & x_3 & P \end{array}$$

$$\begin{bmatrix} 1 & 2 & 1 & 0 & 0 & 0 & | & 10 \\ 1 & 1 & 0 & 1 & 0 & 0 & | & 7 \\ ② & 1 & 0 & 0 & 1 & 0 & | & 12 \\ \hline -7 & -4 & 0 & 0 & 0 & 1 & | & 0 \end{bmatrix} \begin{array}{l} \frac{10}{1} = 10 \\ \frac{7}{1} = 7 \\ \frac{12}{2} = 6 \end{array} \sim \begin{bmatrix} 1 & 2 & 1 & 0 & 0 & 0 & | & 10 \\ 1 & 1 & 0 & 1 & 0 & 0 & | & 7 \\ 1 & \frac{1}{2} & 0 & 0 & \frac{1}{2} & 0 & | & 6 \\ \hline -7 & -4 & 0 & 0 & 0 & 1 & | & 0 \end{bmatrix}$$

$\frac{1}{2}R_3 \to R_3$

$R_1 + (-1)R_3 \to R_1$,

$R_2 + (-1)R_3 \to R_2$, and

$R_4 + 7R_3 \to R_4$

(continued)

$$\sim \begin{bmatrix} 0 & \frac{3}{2} & 1 & 0 & -\frac{1}{2} & 0 & 4 \\ 0 & \boxed{\frac{1}{2}} & 0 & 1 & -\frac{1}{2} & 0 & 1 \\ 1 & \frac{1}{2} & 0 & 0 & \frac{1}{2} & 0 & 6 \\ \hline 0 & -\frac{1}{2} & 0 & 0 & \frac{7}{2} & 1 & 42 \end{bmatrix} \quad \begin{array}{l} \frac{4}{3/2} = \frac{8}{3} \\ \frac{1}{1/2} = 2 \\ \frac{6}{1/2} = 12 \end{array} \quad \sim \begin{bmatrix} 0 & \frac{3}{2} & 1 & 0 & -\frac{1}{2} & 0 & 4 \\ 0 & 1 & 0 & 2 & -1 & 0 & 2 \\ 1 & \frac{1}{2} & 0 & 0 & \frac{1}{2} & 0 & 6 \\ \hline 0 & -\frac{1}{2} & 0 & 0 & \frac{7}{2} & 1 & 42 \end{bmatrix}$$

$$2R_2 \rightarrow R_2$$

$$R_1 + \left(-\frac{3}{2}\right)R_2 \rightarrow R_1,$$

$$R_3 + \left(-\frac{1}{2}\right)R_2 \rightarrow R_3, \text{ and}$$

$$R_4 + \frac{1}{2}R_2 \rightarrow R_4$$

$$\begin{array}{cccccc} y_1 & y_2 & x_1 & x_2 & x_3 & P \end{array}$$
$$\sim \begin{bmatrix} 0 & 0 & 1 & -3 & 1 & 0 & 1 \\ 0 & 1 & 0 & 2 & -1 & 0 & 2 \\ 1 & 0 & 0 & -1 & 1 & 0 & 5 \\ \hline 0 & 0 & 0 & 1 & 3 & 1 & 43 \end{bmatrix}$$

Optimal solution: min $C = 43$ at $x_1 = 0$, $x_2 = 1$, $x_3 = 3$.

23. The matrices corresponding to the given problem and the dual problem are

$$A = \begin{bmatrix} 1 & -4 & 1 & 6 \\ -1 & 1 & -2 & 4 \\ 5 & 2 & 2 & 1 \end{bmatrix} \quad \text{and} \quad B = \begin{bmatrix} 1 & -1 & 5 \\ -4 & 1 & 2 \\ 1 & -2 & 2 \\ 6 & 4 & 1 \end{bmatrix}$$

respectively. Thus, the dual problem is:

Maximize $P = 6y_1 + 4y_2$

Subject to:
$$\begin{aligned} y_1 - y_2 &\leqslant 5 \\ -4y_1 + y_2 &\leqslant 2 \\ y_1 - 2y_2 &\leqslant 2 \\ y_1, \; y_2 &\geqslant 0 \end{aligned}$$

We introduce the slack variables x_1, x_2, and x_3 to obtain the initial form:

$$\begin{aligned} y_1 - y_2 + x_1 &= 5 \\ -4y_1 + y_2 \qquad + x_2 &= 2 \\ y_1 - 2y_2 \qquad\quad + x_3 &= 2 \\ -6y_1 - 4y_2 \qquad\qquad\quad + P &= 0 \end{aligned}$$

The simplex tableau for this problem is:

$$
\begin{array}{cccccc}
y_1 & y_2 & x_1 & x_2 & x_3 & P \\
\end{array}
$$

$$
\left[\begin{array}{cccccc|c}
1 & -1 & 1 & 0 & 0 & 0 & 5 \\
-4 & 1 & 0 & 1 & 0 & 0 & 2 \\
\boxed{1} & -2 & 0 & 0 & 1 & 0 & 2 \\
\hline
-6 & -4 & 0 & 0 & 0 & 1 & 0
\end{array}\right]
\quad
\begin{array}{l}
\frac{5}{1} = 5 \\[20pt]
\frac{2}{1} = 2
\end{array}
\quad \sim \quad
\left[\begin{array}{cccccc|c}
0 & \boxed{1} & 1 & 0 & -1 & 0 & 3 \\
0 & -7 & 0 & 1 & 4 & 0 & 10 \\
1 & -2 & 0 & 0 & 1 & 0 & 2 \\
\hline
0 & -16 & 0 & 0 & 6 & 1 & 12
\end{array}\right]
$$

$R_1 + (-1)R_3 \to R_1, \ R_2 + 4R_3 \to R_2,$
and $R_4 + 6R_3 \to R_4$

$R_2 + 7R_1 \to R_2, \ R_3 + 2R_1 \to R_3,$
and $R_4 + 16R_1 \to R_4$

$$
\begin{array}{cccccc}
y_1 & y_2 & x_1 & x_2 & x_3 & P \\
\end{array}
$$

$$
\sim \quad
\left[\begin{array}{cccccc|c}
0 & 1 & 1 & 0 & -1 & 0 & 3 \\
0 & 0 & 7 & 1 & -3 & 0 & 31 \\
1 & 0 & 2 & 0 & -1 & 0 & 8 \\
\hline
0 & 0 & 16 & 0 & -10 & 1 & 60
\end{array}\right]
$$

Since all the entries above the dashed line in the pivot column, the x_3 column, are negative, the problem does not have an optimal solution.

25. The matrices corresponding to the given problem and the dual problem are:

$$
A = \left[\begin{array}{ccc|c}
3 & 2 & 2 & 16 \\
4 & 3 & 1 & 14 \\
5 & 3 & 1 & 12 \\
\hline
16 & 8 & 4 & 1
\end{array}\right]
\quad \text{and} \quad
B = \left[\begin{array}{ccc|c}
3 & 4 & 5 & 16 \\
2 & 3 & 3 & 8 \\
2 & 1 & 1 & 4 \\
\hline
16 & 14 & 12 & 1
\end{array}\right]
$$

respectively. Thus, the dual problem is: Maximize $P = 16y_1 + 14y_2 + 12y_3$

Subject to: $3y_1 + 4y_2 + 5y_3 \leqslant 16$
$2y_1 + 3y_2 + 3y_3 \leqslant 8$
$2y_1 + y_2 + y_3 \leqslant 4$
$y_1, y_2, y_3 \geqslant 0$

We introduce the slack variables x_1, x_2, and x_3 to obtain the initial form:

$$
\begin{array}{rcl}
3y_1 + 4y_2 + 5y_3 + x_1 & = & 16 \\
2y_1 + 3y_2 + 3y_3 \quad + x_2 & = & 8 \\
2y_1 + y_2 + y_3 \quad\quad + x_3 & = & 4 \\
-16y_1 - 14y_2 - 12y_3 \quad\quad\quad + P & = & 0
\end{array}
$$

The simplex tableau for this problem is:

$$
\begin{array}{ccccccc|c}
y_1 & y_2 & y_3 & x_1 & x_2 & x_3 & P & \\
3 & 4 & 5 & 1 & 0 & 0 & 0 & 16 \\
2 & 3 & 3 & 0 & 1 & 0 & 0 & 8 \\
② & 1 & 1 & 0 & 0 & 1 & 0 & 4 \\
\hline
-16 & -14 & -12 & 0 & 0 & 0 & 1 & 0
\end{array}
\qquad
\begin{array}{l}
\frac{16}{3} = 5.33 \\[4pt]
\frac{8}{2} = 4 \\[4pt]
\frac{4}{2} = 2 \\[4pt]
\end{array}
$$

$\frac{1}{2}R_3 \to R_3$

$$
\sim
\begin{bmatrix}
3 & 4 & 5 & 1 & 0 & 0 & 0 & 16 \\
2 & 3 & 3 & 0 & 1 & 0 & 0 & 8 \\
1 & \frac{1}{2} & \frac{1}{2} & 0 & 0 & \frac{1}{2} & 0 & 2 \\
\hline
-16 & -14 & -12 & 0 & 0 & 0 & 1 & 0
\end{bmatrix}
$$

$R_1 + (-3)R_3 \to R_1$, $R_2 + (-2)R_3 \to R_2$, and $R_4 + 16R_3 \to R_4$

$$
\sim
\begin{bmatrix}
0 & \frac{5}{2} & \frac{7}{2} & 1 & 0 & -\frac{3}{2} & 0 & 10 \\
0 & ② & 2 & 0 & 1 & -1 & 0 & 4 \\
1 & \frac{1}{2} & \frac{1}{2} & 0 & 0 & \frac{1}{2} & 0 & 2 \\
\hline
0 & -6 & -4 & 0 & 0 & 8 & 1 & 32
\end{bmatrix}
\begin{array}{l}
\frac{10}{5/2} = 4 \\[4pt]
\frac{4}{2} = 2 \\[4pt]
\frac{2}{1/2} = 4 \\[4pt]
\end{array}
\sim
\begin{bmatrix}
0 & \frac{5}{2} & \frac{7}{2} & 1 & 0 & -\frac{3}{2} & 0 & 10 \\
0 & 1 & 1 & 0 & \frac{1}{2} & -\frac{1}{2} & 0 & 2 \\
1 & \frac{1}{2} & \frac{1}{2} & 0 & 0 & \frac{1}{2} & 0 & 2 \\
\hline
0 & -6 & -4 & 0 & 0 & 8 & 1 & 32
\end{bmatrix}
$$

$\frac{1}{2}R_2 \to R_2$

$$
\begin{array}{ccccccc|c}
y_1 & y_2 & y_3 & x_1 & x_2 & x_3 & P & \\
0 & 0 & 1 & 1 & -\frac{5}{4} & -\frac{1}{4} & 0 & 5 \\
0 & 1 & 1 & 0 & \frac{1}{2} & -\frac{1}{2} & 0 & 2 \\
1 & 0 & 0 & 0 & -\frac{1}{4} & \frac{3}{4} & 0 & 1 \\
\hline
0 & 0 & 2 & 0 & 3 & 5 & 1 & 44
\end{array}
$$

$R_1 + \left(-\frac{5}{2}\right)R_2 \to R_1$,

$R_3 + \left(-\frac{1}{2}\right)R_2 \to R_3$,

and $R_4 + 6R_2 \to R_4$

Optimal solution: min $C = 44$ at $x_1 = 0$, $x_2 = 3$, $x_3 = 5$.

27. The matrices corresponding to the given problem and the dual problem are:

$$
A =
\begin{bmatrix}
1 & 1 & 0 & 0 & 12 \\
0 & 0 & 1 & 1 & 25 \\
1 & 0 & 1 & 0 & 20 \\
0 & 1 & 0 & 1 & 15 \\
\hline
5 & 4 & 5 & 6 & 1
\end{bmatrix}
\quad\text{and}\quad
B =
\begin{bmatrix}
1 & 0 & 1 & 0 & 5 \\
1 & 0 & 0 & 1 & 4 \\
0 & 1 & 1 & 0 & 5 \\
0 & 1 & 0 & 1 & 6 \\
\hline
12 & 25 & 20 & 15 & 1
\end{bmatrix}
$$

The dual problem is: Maximize $P = 12y_1 + 25y_2 + 20y_3 + 15y_4$

$$\text{Subject to: } \begin{array}{l} y_1 \qquad\; + y_3 \qquad\;\; \leqslant 5 \\ y_1 \qquad\qquad\; + y_4 \leqslant 4 \\ \quad y_2 + y_3 \qquad\;\; \leqslant 5 \\ \quad y_2 \qquad\; + y_4 \leqslant 6 \\ y_1, \; y_2, \; y_3, \; y_4 \;\geqslant 0 \end{array}$$

We introduce the slack variables x_1, x_2, x_3, and x_4 to obtain the initial form:

$$\begin{array}{l} y_1 \qquad\; + \; y_3 \qquad\qquad + x_1 \qquad\qquad\qquad\qquad\quad = 5 \\ y_1 \qquad\qquad\quad + y_4 \qquad\quad + x_2 \qquad\qquad\qquad\quad = 4 \\ \quad y_2 + \; y_3 \qquad\qquad\qquad\qquad + x_3 \qquad\qquad = 5 \\ \quad y_2 \qquad\quad + y_4 \qquad\qquad\qquad\qquad + x_4 \qquad = 6 \\ -12y_1 - 25y_2 - 20y_3 - 15y_4 \qquad\qquad\qquad\qquad + P = 0 \end{array}$$

The simplex tableau for this problem is:

$$
\begin{array}{ccccccccc}
y_1 & y_2 & y_3 & y_4 & x_1 & x_2 & x_3 & x_4 & P \\
\end{array}
$$

$$
\left[
\begin{array}{ccccccccc|c}
1 & 0 & 1 & 0 & 1 & 0 & 0 & 0 & 0 & 5 \\
1 & 0 & 0 & 1 & 0 & 1 & 0 & 0 & 0 & 4 \\
0 & \boxed{1} & 1 & 0 & 0 & 0 & 1 & 0 & 0 & 5 \\
0 & 1 & 0 & 1 & 0 & 0 & 0 & 1 & 0 & 6 \\
\hline
-12 & -25 & -20 & -15 & 0 & 0 & 0 & 0 & 1 & 0
\end{array}
\right]
\begin{array}{l}
\\
\\
\frac{5}{1} = 5 \\
\frac{6}{1} = 6 \\
\\
\end{array}
$$

$R_4 + (-1)R_3 \to R_4$ and $R_5 + 25R_3 \to R_5$

$$
\sim \left[
\begin{array}{ccccccccc|c}
0 & 0 & 1 & 0 & 1 & 0 & 0 & 0 & 0 & 5 \\
1 & 0 & 0 & 1 & 0 & 1 & 0 & 0 & 0 & 4 \\
0 & 1 & 1 & 0 & 0 & 0 & 1 & 0 & 0 & 5 \\
0 & 0 & -1 & \boxed{1} & 0 & 0 & -1 & 1 & 0 & 1 \\
\hline
-12 & 0 & 5 & -15 & 0 & 0 & 25 & 0 & 1 & 125
\end{array}
\right]
\begin{array}{l}
\\
\frac{4}{1} = 4 \\
\\
\frac{1}{1} = 1 \\
\\
\end{array}
$$

$R_2 + (-1)R_4 \to R_2$ and $R_5 + 15R_4 \to R_5$

$$
\sim \left[
\begin{array}{ccccccccc|c}
1 & 0 & 1 & 0 & 1 & 0 & 0 & 0 & 0 & 5 \\
\boxed{1} & 0 & 1 & 0 & 0 & 1 & 1 & -1 & 0 & 3 \\
0 & 1 & 1 & 0 & 0 & 0 & 1 & 0 & 0 & 5 \\
0 & 0 & -1 & 1 & 0 & 0 & -1 & 1 & 0 & 1 \\
\hline
-12 & 0 & -10 & 0 & 0 & 0 & 10 & 15 & 0 & 140
\end{array}
\right]
\begin{array}{l}
\frac{5}{1} = 5 \\
\frac{3}{1} = 3 \\
\\
\\
\\
\end{array}
$$

$R_1 + (-1)R_2 \to R_1$ and $R_5 + 12R_2 \to R_5$

(continued)

$$\begin{array}{c}\begin{array}{ccccccccc}y_1 & y_2 & y_3 & y_4 & x_1 & x_2 & x_3 & x_4 & P\end{array}\\ \sim \left[\begin{array}{ccccccccc|c}0 & 0 & 0 & 0 & 1 & -1 & -1 & 1 & 0 & 2\\ 1 & 0 & 1 & 0 & 0 & 1 & 1 & -1 & 0 & 3\\ 0 & 1 & 1 & 0 & 0 & 0 & 1 & 0 & 0 & 5\\ 0 & 0 & -1 & 1 & 0 & 0 & -1 & 1 & 0 & 1\\ \hline 0 & 0 & 2 & 0 & 0 & 12 & 22 & 3 & 1 & 176\end{array}\right]\end{array}$$

Optimal solution: min $C = 176$ at $x_1 = 0$, $x_2 = 12$, $x_3 = 22$, $x_4 = 3$.

29. Let x_1 = the number of hours the Cedarburg plant is operated,
    x_2 = the number of hours the Grafton plant is operated,
and x_3 = the number of hours the West Bend plant is operated.
The mathematical model for this problem is:

$$\text{Minimize } C = 70x_1 + 75x_2 + 90x_3$$

$$\begin{aligned}\text{Subject to: } \quad 20x_1 + 10x_2 + 20x_3 &\geqslant 300\\ 10x_1 + 20x_2 + 20x_3 &\geqslant 200\\ x_1, x_2, x_3 &\geqslant 0\end{aligned}$$

Divide each of the problem constraint inequalities by 10 to simplify the calculations. The matrices corresponding to the given problem and the dual problem are:

$$A = \left[\begin{array}{ccc|c}2 & 1 & 2 & 30\\ 1 & 2 & 2 & 20\\ 70 & 75 & 90 & 1\end{array}\right] \quad \text{and} \quad B = \left[\begin{array}{cc|c}2 & 1 & 70\\ 1 & 2 & 75\\ 2 & 2 & 90\\ 31 & 20 & 1\end{array}\right]$$

respectively. Thus, the dual problem is: Maximize $P = 30y_1 + 20y_2$

$$\begin{aligned}\text{Subject to: } \quad 2y_1 + y_2 &\leqslant 70\\ y_1 + 2y_2 &\leqslant 75\\ 2y_1 + 2y_2 &\leqslant 90\\ y_1, y_2 &\geqslant 0\end{aligned}$$

We introduce the slack variables x_1, x_2, and x_3 to obtain the initial form:

$$\begin{aligned}2y_1 + y_2 + x_1 \qquad\qquad\qquad &= 70\\ y_1 + 2y_2 \qquad + x_2 \qquad\qquad &= 75\\ 2y_1 + 2y_2 \qquad\qquad + x_3 \qquad &= 90\\ -30y_1 - 20y_2 \qquad\qquad\qquad + P &= 0\end{aligned}$$

The simplex tableau for this problem is:

$$
\begin{array}{cccccc}
y_1 & y_2 & x_1 & x_2 & x_3 & P
\end{array}
$$

$$
\left[
\begin{array}{cccccc|c}
\boxed{2} & 1 & 1 & 0 & 0 & 0 & 70 \\
1 & 2 & 0 & 1 & 0 & 0 & 75 \\
2 & 2 & 0 & 0 & 1 & 0 & 90 \\
\hline
-30 & -20 & 0 & 0 & 0 & 1 & 0
\end{array}
\right]
\quad
\begin{array}{l}
\frac{70}{2} = 35 \\[4pt]
\frac{75}{1} = 75 \\[4pt]
\frac{90}{2} = 45
\end{array}
\sim
\left[
\begin{array}{cccccc|c}
1 & \frac{1}{2} & \frac{1}{2} & 0 & 0 & 0 & 35 \\
1 & 2 & 0 & 1 & 0 & 0 & 75 \\
2 & 2 & 0 & 0 & 1 & 0 & 90 \\
\hline
-30 & -20 & 0 & 0 & 0 & 1 & 0
\end{array}
\right]
$$

$\frac{1}{2}R_1 \rightarrow R_1$

$R_2 + (-1)R_1 \rightarrow R_2,$
$R_3 + (-2)R_1 \rightarrow R_3,$ and
$R_4 + 30R_1 \rightarrow R_4$

$$
\sim
\left[
\begin{array}{cccccc|c}
1 & \frac{1}{2} & \frac{1}{2} & 0 & 0 & 0 & 35 \\
0 & \frac{3}{2} & -\frac{1}{2} & 1 & 0 & 0 & 40 \\
0 & \boxed{1} & -1 & 0 & 1 & 0 & 20 \\
\hline
0 & -5 & 15 & 0 & 0 & 1 & 1050
\end{array}
\right]
\quad
\begin{array}{l}
\frac{35}{1/2} = 70 \\[4pt]
\frac{40}{3/2} = \frac{80}{3} \approx 26.67 \\[4pt]
\frac{20}{1} = 20
\end{array}
$$

$R_1 + \left(-\frac{1}{2}\right)R_3 \rightarrow R_1, \quad R_2 + \left(-\frac{3}{2}\right)R_3 \rightarrow R_2,$ and $R_4 + 5R_3 \rightarrow R_4$

$$
\begin{array}{cccccc}
y_1 & y_2 & x_1 & x_2 & x_3 & P
\end{array}
$$

$$
\sim
\left[
\begin{array}{cccccc|c}
1 & 0 & 1 & 0 & -\frac{1}{2} & 0 & 25 \\
0 & 0 & 1 & 1 & -\frac{3}{2} & 0 & 10 \\
0 & 1 & -1 & 0 & 1 & 0 & 20 \\
\hline
0 & 0 & 10 & 0 & 5 & 1 & 1150
\end{array}
\right]
$$

The minimal production cost is $1150 when the Cedarburg plant is operated 10 hours per day, the West Bend plant is operated 5 hours per day, and the Grafton plant is not used.

31. Let x_1 = the number of single-sided drives from Associated Electronics,
x_2 = the number of double-sided drives from Associated Electronics,
x_3 = the number of single-sided drives from Digital Drives
and x_4 = the number of double-sided drives from Digital Drives.

The mathematical model for this problem is:

Minimize $C = 250x_1 + 350x_2 + 290x_3 + 320x_4$

Subject to:
$$
\begin{aligned}
x_1 + x_2 \quad\quad\quad &\leqslant 1000 \\
x_3 + x_4 &\leqslant 2000 \\
x_1 \quad\quad + x_3 \quad\quad &\geqslant 1200 \\
x_2 \quad\quad + x_4 &\geqslant 1600 \\
x_1,\ x_2,\ x_3,\ x_4 &\geqslant 0
\end{aligned}
$$

We multiply the first two problem constraints by -1 to obtain inequalities of the $\geqslant$ type. The model becomes:

Minimize $C = 250x_1 + 350x_2 + 290x_3 + 320x_4$

Subject to:
$$-x_1 - x_2 \qquad\qquad \geqslant -1000$$
$$- x_3 - x_4 \geqslant -1200$$
$$x_1 \qquad + x_3 \qquad \geqslant 1200$$
$$x_2 \qquad + x_4 \geqslant 1600$$
$$x_1, x_2, x_3, x_4 \geqslant 0$$

The matrices for this problem and the dual problem are:

$$A = \begin{bmatrix} -1 & -1 & 0 & 0 & -1000 \\ 0 & 0 & -1 & -1 & -2000 \\ 1 & 0 & 1 & 0 & 1200 \\ 0 & 1 & 0 & 1 & 1600 \\ \hline 250 & 350 & 290 & 320 & 1 \end{bmatrix} \quad \text{and} \quad B = \begin{bmatrix} -1 & 0 & 1 & 0 & 250 \\ -1 & 0 & 0 & 1 & 350 \\ 0 & -1 & 1 & 0 & 290 \\ 0 & -1 & 0 & 1 & 320 \\ \hline -1000 & -2000 & 1200 & 1600 & 1 \end{bmatrix}$$

Thus, the dual problem is: Maximize $P = -1000y_1 - 2000y_2 + 1200y_3 + 1600y_4$

Subject to:
$$-y_1 \qquad + y_3 \qquad \leqslant 250$$
$$-y_1 \qquad\qquad + y_4 \leqslant 350$$
$$-y_2 + y_3 \qquad \leqslant 290$$
$$-y_2 \qquad + y_4 \leqslant 320$$
$$y_1, y_2, y_3, y_4 \geqslant 0$$

We introduce the slack variables x_1, x_2, x_3, and x_4 to obtain the initial form:

$$-y_1 \qquad + y_3 \qquad + x_1 \qquad\qquad\qquad = 250$$
$$-y_1 \qquad\qquad + y_4 \qquad + x_2 \qquad\qquad = 350$$
$$-y_2 + y_3 \qquad\qquad\qquad + x_3 \qquad = 290$$
$$-y_2 \qquad + y_4 \qquad\qquad\qquad + x_4 = 320$$
$$1000y_1 + 2000y_2 - 1200y_3 - 1600y_4 \qquad\qquad\qquad + P = 0$$

The simplex tableau for this problem is:

y_1	y_2	y_3	y_4	x_1	x_2	x_3	x_4	P	
-1	0	1	0	1	0	0	0	0	250
-1	0	0	1	0	1	0	0	0	350
0	-1	1	0	0	0	1	0	0	290
0	-1	0	①	0	0	0	1	0	320
1000	2000	-1200	-1600	0	0	0	0	1	0

$$\frac{350}{1} = 350$$
$$\frac{320}{1} = 320$$

$R_2 + (-1)R_4 \to R_2$ and $R_5 + 1600R_4 \to R_5$

(continued)

$$\sim \begin{bmatrix} -1 & 0 & \boxed{1} & 0 & 1 & 0 & 0 & 0 & 0 & 250 \\ -1 & 1 & 0 & 0 & 0 & 1 & 0 & -1 & 0 & 30 \\ 0 & -1 & 1 & 0 & 0 & 0 & 1 & 0 & 0 & 290 \\ 0 & -1 & 0 & 1 & 0 & 0 & 0 & 1 & 0 & 320 \\ \hline 1000 & 400 & -1200 & 0 & 0 & 0 & 0 & 1600 & 1 & 512{,}000 \end{bmatrix} \quad \begin{array}{l} \frac{250}{1} = 250 \\[12pt] \frac{290}{1} = 290 \end{array}$$

$R_3 + (-1)R_1 \to R_3$ and $R_5 + 1200R_1 \to R_5$

$$\sim \begin{bmatrix} -1 & 0 & 1 & 0 & 1 & 0 & 0 & 0 & 0 & 250 \\ -1 & 1 & 0 & 0 & 0 & 1 & 0 & -1 & 0 & 30 \\ \boxed{1} & -1 & 0 & 0 & -1 & 0 & 1 & 0 & 0 & 40 \\ 0 & -1 & 0 & 1 & 0 & 0 & 0 & 1 & 0 & 320 \\ \hline -200 & 400 & 0 & 0 & 1200 & 0 & 0 & 1600 & 1 & 812{,}000 \end{bmatrix}$$

$R_1 + R_3 \to R_1$, $R_2 + R_3 \to R_2$, and $R_5 + 200R_3 \to R_5$

$$\begin{array}{ccccccccc} y_1 & y_2 & y_3 & y_4 & x_1 & x_2 & x_3 & x_4 & P \end{array}$$

$$\sim \begin{bmatrix} 0 & -1 & 1 & 0 & 0 & 0 & 1 & 0 & 0 & 290 \\ 0 & 0 & 0 & 0 & -1 & 1 & 1 & -1 & 0 & 70 \\ 1 & -1 & 0 & 0 & -1 & 0 & 1 & 0 & 0 & 40 \\ 0 & -1 & 0 & 1 & 0 & 0 & 0 & 1 & 0 & 320 \\ \hline 0 & 200 & 0 & 0 & 1000 & 0 & 200 & 1600 & 1 & 820{,}000 \end{bmatrix}$$

The minimal purchase cost is $820,000 when 1000 single-sided and no double-sided drives are ordered from Associated Electronics, and 200 single-sided and 1600 double-sided drives are ordered from Digital Drives.

33. Let x_1 = the number of ounces of food L,
    x_2 = the number of ounces of food M,
    and x_3 = the number of ounces of food N.
    The mathematical model for this problem is: Minimize

$$\text{Minimize } C = 20x_1 + 24x_2 + 18x_3$$

$$\text{Subject to: } \begin{aligned} 20x_1 + 10x_2 + 10x_3 &\geqslant 300 \\ 10x_1 + 10x_2 + 10x_3 &\geqslant 200 \\ 10x_1 + 20x_2 + 10x_3 &\geqslant 240 \\ x_1, \; x_2, \; x_3 &\geqslant 0 \end{aligned}$$

We divide each of the problem constraint inequalities by 10 to simplify the calculations. The matrices for this problem and the dual problem are:

$$A = \begin{bmatrix} 2 & 1 & 1 & 30 \\ 1 & 1 & 1 & 20 \\ 1 & 2 & 1 & 24 \\ 20 & 24 & 18 & 1 \end{bmatrix} \quad \text{and} \quad B = \begin{bmatrix} 2 & 1 & 1 & 20 \\ 1 & 1 & 2 & 24 \\ 1 & 1 & 1 & 18 \\ 30 & 20 & 24 & 1 \end{bmatrix}$$

The dual problem is: Maximize $P = 30y_1 + 20y_2 + 24y_3$

Subject to:
$$2y_1 + y_2 + y_3 \leqslant 20$$
$$y_1 + y_2 + 2y_3 \leqslant 24$$
$$y_1 + y_2 + y_3 \leqslant 18$$
$$y_1, y_2, y_3 \geqslant 0$$

We introduce the slack variables x_1, x_2, and x_3 to obtain the initial form:

$$2y_1 + y_2 + y_3 + x_1 \qquad\qquad = 20$$
$$y_1 + y_2 + 2y_3 \quad + x_2 \qquad = 24$$
$$y_1 + y_2 + y_3 \qquad\quad + x_3 = 18$$
$$-30y_1 - 20y_2 - 24y_3 \qquad\qquad\quad + P = 0$$

The simplex tableau for this problem is:

$$
\begin{array}{ccccccc}
y_1 & y_2 & y_3 & x_1 & x_2 & x_3 & P
\end{array}
$$

$$
\left[\begin{array}{ccccccc|c}
\boxed{2} & 1 & 1 & 1 & 0 & 0 & 0 & 20 \\
1 & 1 & 2 & 0 & 1 & 0 & 0 & 24 \\
1 & 1 & 1 & 0 & 0 & 1 & 0 & 18 \\
\hline
-30 & -20 & -24 & 0 & 0 & 0 & 1 & 0
\end{array}\right]
\quad
\begin{array}{l}
\frac{20}{2} = 10 \\[6pt]
\frac{24}{1} = 24 \\[6pt]
\frac{18}{1} = 18
\end{array}
$$

$$\tfrac{1}{2}R_1 \to R_1$$

$$
\sim
\left[\begin{array}{ccccccc|c}
1 & \frac{1}{2} & \frac{1}{2} & \frac{1}{2} & 0 & 0 & 0 & 10 \\
1 & 1 & 2 & 0 & 1 & 0 & 0 & 24 \\
1 & 1 & 1 & 0 & 0 & 1 & 0 & 18 \\
\hline
-30 & -20 & -24 & 0 & 0 & 0 & 1 & 0
\end{array}\right]
$$

$$R_2 + (-1)R_1 \to R_2, \quad R_3 + (-1)R_1 \to R_3, \quad \text{and} \quad R_4 + 30R_1 \to R_4$$

$$
\sim
\left[\begin{array}{ccccccc|c}
1 & \frac{1}{2} & \frac{1}{2} & \frac{1}{2} & 0 & 0 & 0 & 10 \\
0 & \frac{1}{2} & \boxed{\tfrac{3}{2}} & -\frac{1}{2} & 1 & 0 & 0 & 14 \\
0 & \frac{1}{2} & \frac{1}{2} & -\frac{1}{2} & 0 & 1 & 0 & 8 \\
\hline
0 & -5 & -9 & 15 & 0 & 0 & 1 & 300
\end{array}\right]
\quad
\begin{array}{l}
\frac{10}{1/2} = 20 \\[6pt]
\frac{14}{3/2} = \frac{28}{3} \approx 9.33 \\[6pt]
\frac{8}{1/2} = 16
\end{array}
$$

$$\tfrac{2}{3}R_2 \to R_2$$

(continued)

$$\sim \begin{bmatrix} 1 & \frac{1}{2} & \frac{1}{2} & \frac{1}{2} & 0 & 0 & 0 & 10 \\ 0 & \frac{1}{3} & 1 & -\frac{1}{3} & \frac{2}{3} & 0 & 0 & \frac{28}{3} \\ 0 & \frac{1}{2} & \frac{1}{2} & -\frac{1}{2} & 0 & 1 & 0 & 8 \\ \hline 0 & -5 & -9 & 15 & 0 & 0 & 1 & 300 \end{bmatrix}$$

$$R_1 + \left(-\frac{1}{2}\right)R_2 \to R_1, \quad R_3 + \left(-\frac{1}{2}\right)R_2 \to R_3, \quad \text{and } R_4 + 9R_2 \to R_4$$

$$\sim \begin{bmatrix} 1 & \frac{1}{3} & 0 & \frac{2}{3} & -\frac{1}{3} & 0 & 0 & \frac{16}{3} \\ 0 & \frac{1}{3} & 1 & -\frac{1}{3} & \frac{2}{3} & 0 & 0 & \frac{28}{3} \\ 0 & \boxed{\frac{1}{3}} & 0 & -\frac{1}{3} & -\frac{1}{3} & 1 & 0 & \frac{10}{3} \\ \hline 0 & -2 & 0 & 12 & 6 & 0 & 1 & 384 \end{bmatrix} \quad \begin{array}{l} \frac{16/3}{1/3} = 16 \\[4pt] \frac{28/3}{1/3} = 28 \\[4pt] \frac{10/3}{1/3} = 10 \end{array}$$

$$3R_3 \to R_3$$

$$\sim \begin{bmatrix} 1 & \frac{1}{3} & 0 & \frac{2}{3} & -\frac{1}{3} & 0 & 0 & \frac{16}{3} \\ 0 & \frac{1}{3} & 1 & -\frac{1}{3} & \frac{2}{3} & 0 & 0 & \frac{28}{3} \\ 0 & 1 & 0 & -1 & -1 & 3 & 0 & 10 \\ \hline 0 & -2 & 0 & 12 & 6 & 0 & 1 & 384 \end{bmatrix}$$

$$\sim \begin{array}{ccccccc} y_1 & y_2 & y_3 & x_1 & x_2 & x_3 & P \end{array}$$
$$\begin{bmatrix} 1 & 0 & 0 & 1 & 0 & -1 & 0 & \frac{26}{3} \\ 0 & 0 & 1 & 0 & 1 & -1 & 0 & \frac{38}{3} \\ 0 & 1 & 0 & -1 & -1 & 3 & 0 & 10 \\ \hline 0 & 0 & 0 & 10 & 4 & 6 & 1 & 404 \end{bmatrix}$$

$$R_1 + \left(-\frac{1}{3}\right)R_3 \to R_1,$$

$$R_2 + \left(-\frac{1}{3}\right)R_3 \to R_2,$$

and $R_4 + 2R_3 \to R_4$

The minimal cholesterol intake is 404 units when 10 ounces of food L, 4 ounces of food M, and 6 ounces of food N are used.

35. Let x_1 = the number of students bused from North Division to Central,
x_2 = the number of students bused from North Division to Washington,
x_3 = the number of students bused from South Division to Central,
x_4 = the number of students bused from South Division to Washington.
The mathematical model for this problem is:

Minimize $C = 5x_1 + 2x_2 + 3x_3 + 4x_4$

Subject to:
$$\begin{aligned} x_1 + x_2 &\geq 300 \\ x_3 + x_4 &\geq 500 \\ x_1 \quad\;\; + x_3 &\leq 400 \\ x_2 \quad\;\; + x_4 &\leq 500 \\ x_1, x_2, x_3, x_4 &\geq 0 \end{aligned}$$

We multiply the last two problem constraints by -1 so that all the constraints are of the $\geq$ type. The model becomes:

Minimize $C = 5x_1 + 2x_2 + 3x_3 + 4x_4$

Subject to:
$$x_1 + x_2 \quad\qquad\geqslant 300$$
$$x_3 + x_4 \geqslant 500$$
$$-x_1 \quad\;\; - x_3 \qquad\geqslant -400$$
$$-x_2 \quad\qquad - x_4 \geqslant -500$$
$$x_1, \, x_2, \, x_3, \, x_4 \geqslant 0$$

The matrices for this problem and the dual problem are:

$$A = \begin{bmatrix} 1 & 1 & 0 & 0 & | & 300 \\ 0 & 0 & 1 & 1 & | & 500 \\ -1 & 0 & -1 & 0 & | & -400 \\ 0 & -1 & 0 & -1 & | & -500 \\ \hline 5 & 2 & 3 & 4 & | & 1 \end{bmatrix} \quad \text{and} \quad B = \begin{bmatrix} 1 & 0 & -1 & 0 & | & 5 \\ 1 & 0 & 0 & 1 & | & 2 \\ 0 & 1 & -1 & 0 & | & 3 \\ 0 & 1 & 0 & -1 & | & 4 \\ \hline 300 & 500 & -400 & -500 & | & 1 \end{bmatrix}$$

The dual problem is: Maximize $P = 300y_1 + 500y_2 - 400y_3 - 500y_4$

Subject to:
$$y_1 \quad\;\; - y_3 \qquad\qquad \leqslant 5$$
$$y_1 \quad\qquad + y_4 \leqslant 2$$
$$y_2 - y_3 \qquad\qquad \leqslant 3$$
$$y_2 \quad\;\; - y_4 \leqslant 4$$
$$y_1, \, y_2, \, y_3, \, y_4 \geqslant 0$$

We introduce the slack variables x_1, x_2, x_3, and x_4 to obtain the initial form:

$$y_1 \quad\quad - y_3 \quad\quad + x_1 \quad\qquad\qquad\qquad = 5$$
$$y_1 \quad\quad\quad\; + y_4 \quad\quad + x_2 \qquad\qquad\qquad = 2$$
$$y_2 - y_3 \qquad\qquad\quad + x_3 \qquad\qquad = 3$$
$$y_2 \quad\; + y_4 \qquad\qquad\qquad + x_4 \quad = 4$$
$$-300y_1 - 500y_2 + 400y_3 + 500y_4 \qquad\qquad\qquad\qquad + P = 0$$

The simplex tableau for this problem is:

y_1	y_2	y_3	y_4	x_1	x_2	x_3	x_4	P		
1	0	-1	0	1	0	0	0	0	5	
1	0	0	1	0	1	0	0	0	2	
0	①	-1	0	0	0	1	0	0	3	$\frac{3}{1} = 3$
0	1	0	1	0	0	0	1	0	4	$\frac{4}{1} = 4$
-300	-500	400	500	0	0	0	0	1	0	

$R_4 + (-1)R_3 \rightarrow R_4$ and $R_5 + 500R_4 \rightarrow R_5$

(continued)

$$\sim \begin{bmatrix} 1 & 0 & -1 & 0 & 1 & 0 & 0 & 0 & 0 & 5 \\ \textcircled{1} & 0 & 0 & 1 & 0 & 1 & 0 & 0 & 0 & 2 \\ 0 & 1 & -1 & 0 & 0 & 0 & 1 & 0 & 0 & 3 \\ 0 & 0 & 1 & 1 & 0 & 0 & -1 & 1 & 0 & 1 \\ \hline -300 & 0 & -100 & 500 & 0 & 0 & 500 & 0 & 1 & 1500 \end{bmatrix} \begin{matrix} \frac{5}{1} = 5 \\ \frac{2}{1} = 2 \\ \\ \\ \\ \end{matrix}$$

$$R_1 + (-1)R_2 \rightarrow R_1 \text{ and } R_5 + 300R_2 \rightarrow R_5$$

$$\sim \begin{bmatrix} 0 & 0 & -1 & -1 & 1 & -1 & 0 & 0 & 0 & 3 \\ 1 & 0 & 0 & 1 & 0 & 1 & 0 & 0 & 0 & 2 \\ 0 & 1 & -1 & 0 & 0 & 0 & 1 & 0 & 0 & 3 \\ 0 & 0 & \textcircled{1} & 1 & 0 & 0 & -1 & 1 & 0 & 1 \\ \hline 0 & 0 & -100 & 800 & 0 & 300 & 500 & 0 & 1 & 2100 \end{bmatrix}$$

$$R_1 + R_4 \rightarrow R_1, \quad R_3 + R_4 \rightarrow R_3, \text{ and } R_5 + 100R_4 \rightarrow R_5$$

$$\begin{matrix} y_1 & y_2 & y_3 & y_4 & x_1 & x_2 & x_3 & x_4 & P \end{matrix}$$
$$\sim \begin{bmatrix} 0 & 0 & 0 & 0 & 1 & -1 & -1 & 1 & 0 & 4 \\ 1 & 0 & 0 & 1 & 0 & 1 & 0 & 0 & 0 & 2 \\ 0 & 1 & 0 & 1 & 0 & 0 & 0 & 1 & 0 & 4 \\ 0 & 0 & 1 & 1 & 0 & 0 & -1 & 1 & 0 & 1 \\ \hline 0 & 0 & 0 & 900 & 0 & 300 & 400 & 100 & 1 & 2200 \end{bmatrix}$$

The minimal cost is $2200 when 300 students are bused from North Division to Washington, 400 students are bused from South Division to Central, and 100 students are bused from South Division to Washington. No students are bused from North Division to Central.

EXERCISE 2-6

Things to remember:

Given a linear programming problem with an objective function to be maximized and problem constraints that are a combination of $\geq$ and $\leq$ inequalities as well as equations. The solution method is called the BIG M method and it involves the following nine steps.

STEP 1. Insure that the problem constraints have nonnegative constants on the right-hand side. If a constraint has a negative quantity on the right side, multiply both sides of the constraint by -1 (and reverse the direction of the inequality).

STEP 2. Introduce a SLACK VARIABLE in each $\leqslant$ constraint.

STEP 3. Introduce a SURPLUS VARIABLE and an ARTIFICIAL VARIABLE in each $\geqslant$ constraint.

STEP 4. Introduce an artificial variable in each = constraint.

STEP 5. For each artificial variable a_i, add $-Ma_i$ to the objective function. Use the same constant for all artificial variables.

STEP 6. Form the preliminary simplex tableau for the modified problem.

STEP 7. Use row operations to eliminate the M's in the bottom row of the preliminary simplex tableau in the columns corresponding to the artificial variables. The resulting tableau is the initial simplex tableau.

STEP 8. Solve the modified problem by applying the simplex method to the initial simplex tableau found in Step 7.

STEP 9. Relate the solution of the modified problem to the original problem.

(a) If the modified problem has no solution, then the original problem has no solution.

(b) If all artificial variables are zero in the solution to the modified problem, then delete the artificial variables to find a solution to the original problem.

(c) If any artificial variables are nonzero in the solution to the modified problem, then the original problem has no solution.

---

1. (A) We introduce a slack variable s_1 to convert the first inequality ($\leqslant$) into an equation, and we use a surplus variable s_2 and an artificial variable a_1 to convert the second inequality ($\geqslant$) into an equation. Then, the modified problem is:

Maximize $P = 5x_1 + 2x_2 - Ma_1$

Subject to:
$$x_1 + 2x_2 + s_1 \qquad\qquad = 12$$
$$x_1 + x_2 \qquad - s_2 + a_1 = 4$$
$$x_1,\ x_2,\ s_1,\ s_2,\ a_1 \geqslant 0$$

(B) The preliminary simplex tableau for the modified problem is:

$$
\begin{array}{cccccc}
x_1 & x_2 & s_1 & s_2 & a_1 & P \\
\end{array}
$$

$$
\left[\begin{array}{cccccc|c}
1 & 2 & 1 & 0 & 0 & 0 & 12 \\
1 & 1 & 0 & -1 & 1 & 0 & 4 \\
\hline
-5 & -2 & 0 & 0 & M & 1 & 0
\end{array}\right]
\sim
\left[\begin{array}{cccccc|c}
1 & 2 & 1 & 0 & 0 & 0 & 12 \\
1 & 1 & 0 & -1 & 1 & 0 & 4 \\
\hline
-M-5 & -M-2 & 0 & M & 0 & 1 & -4M
\end{array}\right]
$$

$$R_3 + (-M)R_2 \rightarrow R_3$$

Thus, the initial simplex tableau is:

$$
\begin{array}{cccccc}
x_1 & x_2 & s_1 & s_2 & a_1 & P \\
\end{array}
$$

$$
\left[\begin{array}{cccccc|c}
1 & 2 & 1 & 0 & 0 & 0 & 12 \\
1 & 1 & 0 & -1 & 1 & 0 & 4 \\
\hline
-M-5 & -M-2 & 0 & M & 0 & 1 & -4M
\end{array}\right]
$$

(C) We use the simplex method to solve the modified problem.

$$
\left[\begin{array}{cccccc|c}
1 & 2 & 1 & 0 & 0 & 0 & 12 \\
\textcircled{1} & 1 & 0 & -1 & 1 & 0 & 4 \\
\hline
-M-5 & -M-2 & 0 & M & 0 & 1 & -4M
\end{array}\right]
\begin{array}{l}
\frac{12}{1} = 12 \\[4pt]
\frac{4}{1} = 4
\end{array}
$$

$$R_1 + (-1)R_2 \rightarrow R_1 \text{ and } R_3 + (M+5)R_2 \rightarrow R_3$$

$$
\begin{array}{cccccc}
 & & & & & \\
\end{array}
$$

$$
\sim
\left[\begin{array}{cccccc|c}
0 & 1 & 1 & \textcircled{1} & -1 & 0 & 8 \\
1 & 1 & 0 & -1 & 1 & 0 & 4 \\
\hline
0 & 3 & 0 & -5 & M+5 & 1 & 20
\end{array}\right]
\sim
\begin{array}{cccccc}
x_1 & x_2 & s_1 & s_2 & a_1 & P \\
\end{array}
$$

$$
\left[\begin{array}{cccccc|c}
0 & 1 & 1 & 1 & -1 & 0 & 8 \\
1 & 2 & 1 & 0 & 0 & 0 & 12 \\
\hline
0 & 8 & 5 & 0 & M & 1 & 60
\end{array}\right]
$$

$$R_2 + R_1 \rightarrow R_2 \text{ and } R_3 + 5R_1 \rightarrow R_3$$

Thus, the optimal solution of the modified problem is: max $P = 60$ at $x_1 = 12$, $x_2 = 0$, $s_1 = 0$, $s_2 = 8$, $a_1 = 0$.

(D) The optimal solution of the original problem is: max $P = 60$ at $x_1 = 12$, $x_2 = 0$.

3. **(A)** We introduce the slack variable s_1 and the artificial variable a_1 to obtain the modified problem:

$$\text{Maximize } P = 3x_1 + 5x_2 - Ma_1$$

$$\text{Subject to: } \begin{array}{l} 2x_1 + x_2 + s_1 \hphantom{+ a_1} = 8 \\ x_1 + x_2 \hphantom{+ s_1} + a_1 = 6 \\ x_1,\ x_2,\ s_1,\ a_1 \geq 0 \end{array}$$

(B) The preliminary simplex tableau for the modified problem is:

$$\begin{array}{ccccc} x_1 & x_2 & s_1 & a_1 & P \end{array}$$

$$\left[\begin{array}{ccccc|c} 2 & 1 & 1 & 0 & 0 & 8 \\ 1 & 1 & 0 & 1 & 0 & 6 \\ \hline -3 & -5 & 0 & M & 1 & 0 \end{array}\right] \sim \left[\begin{array}{ccccc|c} 2 & 1 & 1 & 0 & 0 & 8 \\ 1 & 1 & 0 & 1 & 0 & 6 \\ \hline -M-3 & -M-5 & 0 & 0 & 1 & -6M \end{array}\right]$$

$$R_3 + (-M)R_2 \rightarrow R_3$$

Thus, the initial simplex tableau is:

$$\begin{array}{ccccc} x_1 & x_2 & s_1 & a_1 & P \end{array}$$

$$\left[\begin{array}{ccccc|c} 2 & 1 & 1 & 0 & 0 & 8 \\ 1 & 1 & 0 & 1 & 0 & 6 \\ \hline -M-3 & -M-5 & 0 & 0 & 1 & -6M \end{array}\right]$$

(C) We use the simplex method to solve the modified problem.

$$\begin{array}{ccccc} & & & x_1 & x_2 & s_1 & a_1 & P \end{array}$$

$$\left[\begin{array}{ccccc|c} 2 & 1 & 1 & 0 & 0 & 8 \\ 1 & \textcircled{1} & 0 & 1 & 0 & 6 \\ \hline -M-3 & -M-5 & 0 & 0 & 1 & -6M \end{array}\right] \begin{array}{l} \frac{8}{1} = 8 \\[4pt] \frac{6}{1} = 6 \end{array} \sim \left[\begin{array}{ccccc|c} 1 & 0 & 1 & -1 & 0 & 2 \\ 1 & 1 & 0 & 1 & 0 & 6 \\ \hline 2 & 0 & 0 & M+5 & 1 & 30 \end{array}\right]$$

$$R_1 + (-1)R_2 \rightarrow R_1 \text{ and}$$
$$R_3 + (M+5)R_2 \rightarrow R_3$$

Thus, the optimal solution of the modified problem is: max $P = 30$ at $x_1 = 0$, $x_2 = 6$, $s_1 = 2$, $a_1 = 0$.

(D) The optimal solution of the original problem is: max $P = 30$ at $x_1 = 0$, $x_2 = 6$.

5. (A) We introduce slack, surplus, and artificial variables to obtain the modified problem:

$$\text{Maximize } P = 4x_1 + 3x_2 - Ma_1$$

Subject to:
$$-x_1 + 2x_2 + s_1 \qquad\qquad = 2$$
$$x_1 + x_2 \qquad - s_2 + a_1 = 4$$
$$x_1, \; x_2, \; s_1, \; s_2, \; a_1 \geqslant 0$$

(B) The preliminary simplex tableau for the modified problem is:

$$\begin{array}{cccccc} x_1 & x_2 & s_1 & s_2 & a_1 & P \end{array}$$

$$\left[\begin{array}{cccccc|c} -1 & 2 & 1 & 0 & 0 & 0 & 2 \\ 1 & 1 & 0 & -1 & 1 & 0 & 4 \\ \hline -4 & -3 & 0 & 0 & M & 1 & 0 \end{array}\right] \sim \left[\begin{array}{cccccc|c} -1 & 2 & 1 & 0 & 0 & 0 & 2 \\ 1 & 1 & 0 & -1 & 1 & 0 & 4 \\ \hline -M-4 & -M-3 & 0 & M & 0 & 1 & -4M \end{array}\right]$$

$$R_3 + (-M)R_2 \to R_3$$

Thus, the initial simplex tableau is:

$$\left[\begin{array}{cccccc|c} -1 & 2 & 1 & 0 & 0 & 0 & 2 \\ 1 & 1 & 0 & -1 & 1 & 0 & 4 \\ \hline -M-4 & -M-3 & 0 & M & 0 & 1 & -4M \end{array}\right]$$

(C) We use the simplex method to solve the modified problem:

$$\begin{array}{cccccc} & & & & x_1 & x_2 & s_1 & s_2 & a_1 & P \end{array}$$

$$\left[\begin{array}{cccccc|c} -1 & 2 & 1 & 0 & 0 & 0 & 2 \\ \boxed{1} & 1 & 0 & -1 & 1 & 0 & 4 \\ \hline -M-4 & -M-3 & 0 & M & 0 & 1 & -4M \end{array}\right] \sim \left[\begin{array}{cccccc|c} 0 & 3 & 1 & -1 & 1 & 0 & 6 \\ 1 & 1 & 0 & -1 & 1 & 0 & 4 \\ \hline 0 & 1 & 0 & -4 & M+4 & 0 & 16 \end{array}\right]$$

$$R_1 + R_2 \to R_1, \; R_3 + (M+4)R_2 \to R_3$$

No optimal solution exists because the elements in the pivot column (the s_2 column) above the dashed line are negative.

7. (A) We introduce slack, surplus, and artificial variables to obtain the modified problem:

$$\text{Maximize } P = 5x_1 + 10x_2 - Ma_1$$

Subject to:
$$x_1 + x_2 + s_1 \qquad\qquad = 3$$
$$2x_1 + 3x_2 \qquad - s_2 + a_1 = 12$$
$$x_1, \; x_2, \; s_1, \; s_2, \; a_1 \geqslant 0$$

(B) The preliminary simplex tableau for the modified problem is:

$$
\begin{array}{cccccc}
x_1 & x_2 & s_1 & s_2 & a_1 & P \\
\end{array}
$$

$$
\left[
\begin{array}{cccccc|c}
1 & 1 & 1 & 0 & 0 & 0 & 3 \\
2 & 3 & 0 & -1 & 1 & 0 & 12 \\
\hline
-5 & -10 & 0 & 0 & M & 0 & 0 \\
\end{array}
\right]
$$

$R_3 + (-M)R_2 \rightarrow R_3$

$$
\sim
\left[
\begin{array}{cccccc|c}
1 & 1 & 1 & 0 & 0 & 0 & 3 \\
2 & 3 & 0 & -1 & 1 & 0 & 12 \\
\hline
-2M-5 & -3M-10 & 0 & M & 0 & 1 & -12M \\
\end{array}
\right]
$$

Thus, the initial simplex tableau is:

$$
\begin{array}{cccccc}
x_1 & x_2 & s_1 & s_2 & a_1 & P \\
\end{array}
$$

$$
\left[
\begin{array}{cccccc|c}
1 & 1 & 1 & 0 & 0 & 0 & 3 \\
2 & 3 & 0 & -1 & 1 & 0 & 12 \\
\hline
-2M-5 & -3M-10 & 0 & M & 0 & 1 & -12M \\
\end{array}
\right]
$$

(C) Applying the simplex method to the initial tableau, we have:

$$
\left[
\begin{array}{cccccc|c}
1 & \boxed{1} & 1 & 0 & 0 & 0 & 3 \\
2 & 3 & 0 & -1 & 1 & 0 & 12 \\
\hline
-2M-5 & -3M-10 & 0 & M & 0 & 1 & -12M \\
\end{array}
\right]
$$

$R_2 + (-3)R_1 \rightarrow R_2$, $R_3 + (3M+10)R_1 \rightarrow R_3$

$$
\begin{array}{cccccc}
x_1 & x_2 & s_1 & s_2 & a_1 & P \\
\end{array}
$$

$$
\sim
\left[
\begin{array}{cccccc|c}
1 & 1 & 1 & 0 & 0 & 0 & 3 \\
-1 & 0 & -3 & -1 & 1 & 0 & 3 \\
\hline
M+5 & 0 & 3M+10 & M & 0 & 1 & -3M+30 \\
\end{array}
\right]
$$

The optimal solution of the modified problem is: max $P = -3M + 30$ at $x_1 = 0$, $x_2 = 3$, $s_1 = 0$, $s_2 = 0$, and $a_1 = 3$.

(D) The original problem does not have an optimal solution, since the artificial variable a_1 in the solution of the modified problem has a nonzero value.

9. To minimize $P = 6x_1 - 2x_2$, we maximize $T = -P = -6x_1 + 2x_2$. Introducing slack, surplus, and artificial variables, we obtain the modified problem:

Maximize $T = -6x_1 + 2x_2 - Ma_1$

Subject to:
$$\begin{aligned}
x_1 + x_2 + s_1 &= 10 \\
3x_1 + 2x_2 \quad - s_2 + a_1 &= 24 \\
x_1, x_2, s_1, s_2, a_1 &\geqslant 0
\end{aligned}$$

The preliminary simplex tableau for this problem is:

$$\begin{array}{cccccc|c}
x_1 & x_2 & s_1 & s_2 & a_1 & P & \\
\hline
1 & 1 & 1 & 0 & 0 & 0 & 10 \\
3 & 2 & 0 & -1 & 1 & 0 & 24 \\
\hline
6 & -2 & 0 & 0 & M & 1 & 0
\end{array}$$

$R_3 + (-M)R_2 \rightarrow R_3$

$$\sim \begin{array}{cccccc|c}
1 & 1 & 1 & 0 & 0 & 0 & 10 \\
\boxed{3} & 2 & 0 & -1 & 1 & 0 & 24 \\
\hline
-3M+6 & -2M-2 & 0 & M & 0 & 1 & -24M
\end{array}$$

$\dfrac{10}{1} = 10$

$\dfrac{24}{3} = 8$

(This is the initial simplex tableau.)

$\frac{1}{3}R_2 \rightarrow R_2$

$$\sim \begin{array}{cccccc|c}
1 & 1 & 1 & 0 & 0 & 0 & 10 \\
1 & \frac{2}{3} & 0 & -\frac{1}{3} & \frac{1}{3} & 0 & 8 \\
\hline
-3M+6 & -2M-2 & 0 & M & 0 & 1 & -24M
\end{array}$$

$R_1 + (-1)R_2 \rightarrow R_1$ and $R_3 + (3M-6)R_2 \rightarrow R_3$

$$\sim \begin{array}{cccccc|c}
0 & 1 & 3 & 1 & -1 & 0 & 6 \\
1 & \frac{2}{3} & 0 & -\frac{1}{3} & \frac{1}{3} & 0 & 8 \\
\hline
0 & -6 & 0 & 2 & M-2 & 1 & -48
\end{array}$$

$$\sim \begin{array}{cccccc|c}
x_1 & x_2 & s_1 & s_2 & a_1 & P & \\
\hline
0 & 1 & 3 & 1 & -1 & 0 & 6 \\
1 & 0 & -2 & -1 & 1 & 0 & 4 \\
\hline
0 & 0 & 18 & 8 & M-6 & 1 & -12
\end{array}$$

$R_1 + \left(-\frac{2}{3}\right)R_1 \rightarrow R_2$

$R_3 + 6R_1 \rightarrow R_3$

LINEAR INEQUALITIES AND LINEAR PROGRAMMING

Thus, the optimal solution is: max $T = -12$ at $x_1 = 4$, $x_2 = 6$, and min $P = -\max T = 12$.

The modified problem for maximizing $P = 6x_1 - 2x_2$ subject to given constraints is:

Maximize $P = 6x_1 - 2x_2 - Ma_1$

Subject to: $\begin{array}{l} x_1 + x_2 + s_1 \qquad\qquad = 10 \\ 3x_1 + 2x_2 \qquad - s_2 + a_1 = 24 \\ x_1,\ x_2,\ s_1,\ s_2,\ a_1 \geqslant 0 \end{array}$

The preliminary simplex tableau for the modified problem is:

$$
\begin{array}{cccccc}
x_1 & x_2 & s_1 & s_2 & a_1 & P \\
\end{array}
$$

$$
\left[\begin{array}{cccccc|c}
1 & 1 & 1 & 0 & 0 & 0 & 10 \\
3 & 2 & 0 & -1 & 1 & 0 & 24 \\
\hline
-6 & 2 & 0 & 0 & M & 1 & 0
\end{array}\right]
$$

$R_3 + (-M)R_2 \rightarrow R_3$

$$
\sim \left[\begin{array}{cccccc|c}
1 & 1 & 1 & 0 & 0 & 0 & 10 \\
\boxed{3} & 2 & 0 & -1 & 1 & 0 & 24 \\
\hline
-3M-6 & -2M+2 & 0 & M & 0 & 1 & -24M
\end{array}\right]
\begin{array}{l} \dfrac{10}{1} = 10 \\[2mm] \dfrac{24}{3} = 8 \end{array}
$$

(This is the initial simplex tableau.)

$\frac{1}{3}R_2 \rightarrow R_2$

$$
\sim \left[\begin{array}{cccccc|c}
1 & 1 & 1 & 0 & 0 & 0 & 10 \\
1 & \frac{2}{3} & 0 & -\frac{1}{3} & \frac{1}{3} & 0 & 8 \\
\hline
-3M-6 & -2M+2 & 0 & M & 0 & 1 & -24M
\end{array}\right]
$$

$R_1 + (-1)R_2 \rightarrow R_1$ and $R_3 + (3M+6)R_2 \rightarrow R_3$

$$
\sim \left[\begin{array}{cccccc|c}
0 & \frac{1}{3} & 1 & \boxed{\frac{1}{3}} & -\frac{1}{3} & 0 & 2 \\
1 & \frac{2}{3} & 0 & -\frac{1}{3} & \frac{1}{3} & 0 & 8 \\
\hline
0 & 6 & 0 & -2 & M+2 & 1 & 48
\end{array}\right]
\sim \left[\begin{array}{cccccc|c}
0 & 1 & 3 & 1 & -1 & 0 & 6 \\
1 & \frac{2}{3} & 0 & -\frac{1}{3} & \frac{1}{3} & 0 & 8 \\
\hline
0 & 6 & 0 & -2 & M+2 & 1 & 48
\end{array}\right]
$$

$3R_1 \rightarrow R_1$ $\qquad\qquad\qquad\qquad R_2 + \frac{1}{3}R_1 \rightarrow R_2$ and $R_3 + 2R_1 \rightarrow R_3$

$$
\begin{array}{cccccc}
x_1 & x_2 & s_1 & s_2 & a_1 & P \\
\end{array}
$$

$$
\sim \left[\begin{array}{cccccc|c}
0 & 1 & 3 & 1 & -1 & 0 & 6 \\
1 & 1 & 1 & 0 & 0 & 0 & 10 \\
\hline
0 & 8 & 6 & 0 & M & 1 & 60
\end{array}\right]
$$

Optimal solution: max $P = 60$ at $x_1 = 10$, $x_2 = 0$.

11. We introduce slack, surplus, and artificial variables to obtain the modified problem.

$$\text{Maximize } P = 2x_1 + 5x_2 - Ma_1$$

Subject to:
$$
\begin{aligned}
x_1 + 2x_2 + s_1 &= 18 \\
2x_1 + x_2 + s_2 &= 21 \\
x_1 + x_2 - s_3 + a_1 &= 10 \\
x_1, x_2, s_1, s_2, s_3, a_1 &\geq 0
\end{aligned}
$$

The preliminary simplex tableau for the modified problem is:

$$
\begin{array}{ccccccc}
x_1 & x_2 & s_1 & s_2 & s_3 & a_1 & P
\end{array}
$$

$$
\left[
\begin{array}{ccccccc|c}
1 & 2 & 1 & 0 & 0 & 0 & 0 & 18 \\
2 & 1 & 0 & 1 & 0 & 0 & 0 & 21 \\
1 & 1 & 0 & 0 & -1 & 1 & 0 & 10 \\
\hline
-2 & -5 & 0 & 0 & 0 & M & 1 & 0
\end{array}
\right]
$$

$$R_4 + (-M)R_3 \rightarrow R_4$$

$$
\sim
\left[
\begin{array}{ccccccc|c}
1 & \boxed{2} & 1 & 0 & 0 & 0 & 0 & 18 \\
2 & 1 & 0 & 1 & 0 & 0 & 0 & 21 \\
1 & 1 & 0 & 0 & -1 & 1 & 0 & 10 \\
\hline
-M-2 & -M-5 & 0 & 0 & M & 0 & 1 & -10M
\end{array}
\right]
\begin{array}{l}
\frac{18}{2} = 9 \\[4pt]
\frac{21}{1} = 21 \quad \text{(This is the initial}\\
\hspace{2.2cm}\text{simplex tableau.)}\\[4pt]
\frac{10}{1} = 10
\end{array}
$$

$$\tfrac{1}{2}R_1 \rightarrow R_1$$

$$
\sim
\left[
\begin{array}{ccccccc|c}
\frac{1}{2} & 1 & \frac{1}{2} & 0 & 0 & 0 & 0 & 9 \\
2 & 1 & 0 & 1 & 0 & 0 & 0 & 21 \\
1 & 1 & 0 & 0 & -1 & 1 & 0 & 10 \\
\hline
-M-2 & -M-5 & 0 & 0 & M & 0 & 1 & -10M
\end{array}
\right]
$$

$$R_2 + (-1)R_1 \rightarrow R_2, \quad R_3 + (-1)R_1 \rightarrow R_3, \quad \text{and } R_4 + (M+5)R_1 \rightarrow R_4$$

$$
\sim
\left[
\begin{array}{ccccccc|c}
\frac{1}{2} & 1 & \frac{1}{2} & 0 & 0 & 0 & 0 & 9 \\
\frac{3}{2} & 0 & -\frac{1}{2} & 1 & 0 & 0 & 0 & 12 \\
\boxed{\frac{1}{2}} & 0 & -\frac{1}{2} & 0 & -1 & 1 & 0 & 1 \\
\hline
-\frac{1}{2}M+\frac{1}{2} & 0 & \frac{1}{2}M+\frac{5}{2} & 0 & M & 0 & 1 & -M+45
\end{array}
\right]
\begin{array}{l}
\frac{9}{1/2} = 18 \\[4pt]
\frac{12}{3/2} = 8 \\[4pt]
\frac{1}{1/2} = 2
\end{array}
$$

$$2R_3 \rightarrow R_3$$

(continued)

$$\sim \begin{bmatrix} \frac{1}{2} & 1 & \frac{1}{2} & 0 & 0 & 0 & 0 & 9 \\ \frac{3}{2} & 0 & -\frac{1}{2} & 1 & 0 & 0 & 0 & 12 \\ 1 & 0 & -1 & 0 & -2 & 2 & 0 & 2 \\ \hline -\frac{1}{2}M + \frac{1}{2} & 0 & \frac{1}{2}M + \frac{5}{2} & 0 & M & 0 & 1 & -M + 45 \end{bmatrix}$$

$$R_1 + \left(-\frac{1}{2}\right)R_3 \to R_1, \quad R_2 + \left(-\frac{3}{2}\right)R_3 \to R_2, \text{ and } R_4 + \left(\frac{1}{2}M - \frac{1}{2}\right)R_3 \to R_4$$

$$\begin{array}{ccccccc} x_1 & x_2 & s_1 & s_2 & s_3 & a_1 & P \end{array}$$

$$\sim \begin{bmatrix} 0 & 1 & 1 & 0 & 1 & -1 & 0 & 8 \\ 0 & 0 & 1 & 1 & 3 & -3 & 0 & 9 \\ 1 & 0 & -1 & 0 & -2 & 2 & 0 & 2 \\ \hline 0 & 0 & 3 & 0 & 1 & M-1 & 1 & 44 \end{bmatrix}$$

Optimal solution: max $P = 44$ at $x_1 = 2$, $x_2 = 8$.

13. We introduce surplus and artificial variables to obtain the modified problem:

Maximize $P = 10x_1 + 12x_2 + 20x_3 - Ma_1 - Ma_2$

Subject to:
$$\begin{aligned} 3x_1 + x_2 + 2x_3 - s_1 + a_1 \quad &= 12 \\ x_1 - x_2 + 2x_3 \qquad\qquad + a_2 &= 6 \\ x_1, x_2, x_3, s_1, a_1, a_2 &\geqslant 0 \end{aligned}$$

The preliminary simplex tableau for the modified problem is:

$$\begin{array}{ccccccc} x_1 & x_2 & x_3 & s_1 & a_1 & a_2 & P \end{array}$$

$$\begin{bmatrix} 3 & 1 & 2 & -1 & 1 & 0 & 0 & 12 \\ 1 & -1 & 2 & 0 & 0 & 1 & 0 & 6 \\ \hline -10 & -12 & -20 & 0 & M & M & 1 & 0 \end{bmatrix}$$

$$R_3 + (-M)R_1 \to R_3$$

$$\sim \begin{bmatrix} 3 & 1 & 2 & -1 & 1 & 0 & 0 & 12 \\ 1 & -1 & 2 & 0 & 0 & 1 & 0 & 6 \\ \hline -3M-10 & -M-12 & -2M-20 & M & 0 & M & 1 & -12M \end{bmatrix}$$

$$R_3 + (-M)R_2 \to R_3$$

(continued)

$$\sim \begin{bmatrix} 3 & 1 & 2 & -1 & 1 & 0 & 0 & 12 \\ 1 & -1 & \textcircled{2} & 0 & 0 & 1 & 0 & 6 \\ \hline -4M-10 & -12 & -4M-20 & M & 0 & 0 & 1 & -18M \end{bmatrix} \begin{matrix} \frac{12}{2}=6 \\ \frac{6}{2}=3 \\ \\ \end{matrix}$$

$\frac{1}{2}R_2 \rightarrow R_2$

$$\sim \begin{bmatrix} 3 & 1 & 2 & -1 & 1 & 0 & 0 & 12 \\ \frac{1}{2} & -\frac{1}{2} & 1 & 0 & 0 & \frac{1}{2} & 0 & 3 \\ \hline -4M-10 & -12 & -4M-20 & M & 0 & 0 & 1 & -18M \end{bmatrix}$$

$R_1 + (-2)R_2 \rightarrow R_1$ and $R_3 + (4M+20)R_2 \rightarrow R_3$

$$\sim \begin{bmatrix} 2 & 0 & 0 & -1 & 1 & -1 & 0 & 6 \\ \frac{1}{2} & \textcircled{$\frac{1}{2}$} & 1 & 0 & 0 & \frac{1}{2} & 0 & 3 \\ \hline -2M & -2M-22 & 0 & M & 0 & 2M+10 & 1 & -6M+60 \end{bmatrix}$$

$2R_2 \rightarrow R_2$

$$\sim \begin{bmatrix} 2 & 0 & 0 & -1 & 1 & -1 & 0 & 6 \\ 1 & 1 & 2 & 0 & 0 & 1 & 0 & 6 \\ \hline -2M & -2M-22 & 0 & M & 0 & 2M+10 & 1 & -6M+60 \end{bmatrix}$$

$R_3 + (2M+22)R_2 \rightarrow R_3$

$$\sim \begin{matrix} x_1 & x_2 & x_3 & s_1 & a_1 & a_2 & P & \\ \begin{bmatrix} 2 & 0 & 0 & -1 & 1 & -1 & 0 & 6 \\ 1 & 1 & 2 & 0 & 0 & 1 & 0 & 6 \\ \hline 22 & 0 & 4M+44 & M & 0 & 4M+32 & 1 & 6M+192 \end{bmatrix} \end{matrix}$$

No optimal solution exists because the value of the artificial variable $a_1 = 6 \neq 0$.

15. We will maximize $P = -C = 5x_1 + 12x_2 - 16x_3$ subject to the given constraints. Introduce slack, surplus, and artificial variables to obtain the modified problem:

Maximize $P = 5x_1 + 12x_2 - 16x_3 - Ma_1 - Ma_2$

Subject to:
$$\begin{aligned} x_1 + 2x_2 + x_3 + s_1 \qquad\qquad\qquad &= 10 \\ 2x_1 + 3x_2 + x_3 \qquad - s_2 + a_1 \qquad &= 6 \\ 2x_1 + x_2 - x_3 \qquad\qquad\qquad + a_2 &= 1 \\ x_1, \ x_2, \ x_3, \ s_1, \ s_2, \ a_1, \ a_2 &\geqslant 0 \end{aligned}$$

The preliminary simplex tableau for the modified problem is:

$$
\begin{array}{cccccccc}
x_1 & x_2 & x_3 & s_1 & s_2 & a_1 & a_2 & P \\
\end{array}
$$

$$
\left[
\begin{array}{cccccccc|c}
1 & 2 & 1 & 1 & 0 & 0 & 0 & 0 & 10 \\
2 & 3 & 1 & 0 & -1 & 1 & 0 & 0 & 6 \\
2 & 1 & -1 & 0 & 0 & 0 & 1 & 0 & 1 \\
\hline
-5 & -12 & 16 & 0 & 0 & M & M & 1 & 0 \\
\end{array}
\right]
$$

$R_4 + (-M)R_2 \to R_4$

$$
\sim
\left[
\begin{array}{cccccccc|c}
1 & 2 & 1 & 1 & 0 & 0 & 0 & 0 & 10 \\
2 & 3 & 1 & 0 & -1 & 1 & 0 & 0 & 6 \\
2 & 1 & -1 & 0 & 0 & 0 & 1 & 0 & 1 \\
\hline
-2M-5 & -3M-12 & -M+16 & 0 & M & 0 & M & 1 & -6M \\
\end{array}
\right]
$$

$R_4 + (-M)R_3 \to R_4$

$$
\sim
\left[
\begin{array}{cccccccc|c}
1 & 2 & 1 & 1 & 0 & 0 & 0 & 0 & 10 \\
2 & 3 & 1 & 0 & -1 & 1 & 0 & 0 & 6 \\
2 & \textcircled{1} & -1 & 0 & 0 & 0 & 1 & 0 & 1 \\
\hline
-4M-5 & -4M-12 & 16 & 0 & M & 0 & 0 & 1 & -7M \\
\end{array}
\right]
\begin{array}{l}
\frac{10}{2}=5 \\[4pt]
\frac{6}{3}=2 \\[4pt]
\frac{1}{1}=1
\end{array}
$$

$R_1 + (-2)R_3 \to R_1,\ R_2 + (-3)R_3 \to R_2,\ \text{and}\ R_4 + (4M+12)R_3 \to R_4$

$$
\sim
\left[
\begin{array}{cccccccc|c}
-3 & 0 & 3 & 1 & 0 & 0 & -2 & 0 & 8 \\
-4 & 0 & \textcircled{4} & 0 & -1 & 1 & -3 & 0 & 3 \\
2 & 1 & -1 & 0 & 0 & 0 & 1 & 0 & 1 \\
\hline
4M+19 & 0 & -4M+4 & 0 & M & 0 & 4M+12 & 1 & -3M+12 \\
\end{array}
\right]
\begin{array}{l}
\frac{8}{3}\approx 2.67 \\[4pt]
\frac{3}{4}=.75
\end{array}
$$

$\frac{1}{4}R_2 \to R_2$

$$
\sim
\left[
\begin{array}{cccccccc|c}
-3 & 0 & 3 & 1 & 0 & 0 & -2 & 0 & 8 \\
-1 & 0 & 1 & 0 & -\frac{1}{4} & \frac{1}{4} & -\frac{3}{4} & 0 & \frac{3}{4} \\
2 & 1 & -1 & 0 & 0 & 0 & 1 & 0 & 1 \\
\hline
4M+19 & 0 & -4M+4 & 0 & M & 0 & 4M+12 & 1 & -3M+12 \\
\end{array}
\right]
$$

$R_1 + (-3)R_2 \to R_1,\ R_3 + R_2 \to R_3,\ \text{and}\ R_4 + (4M-4)R_2 \to R_4$

(continued)

$$\sim \begin{bmatrix} x_1 & x_2 & x_3 & s_1 & s_2 & a_1 & a_2 & P & \\ 0 & 0 & 0 & 1 & \frac{3}{4} & -\frac{3}{4} & \frac{1}{4} & 0 & \frac{23}{4} \\ -1 & 0 & 1 & 0 & -\frac{1}{4} & \frac{1}{4} & -\frac{3}{4} & 0 & \frac{3}{4} \\ 1 & 1 & 0 & 0 & -\frac{1}{4} & \frac{1}{4} & \frac{1}{4} & 0 & \frac{7}{4} \\ \hline 23 & 0 & 0 & 0 & 1 & M-1 & M+15 & 1 & 9 \end{bmatrix}$$

Optimal solution: min $C = -9$ at $x_1 = 0$, $x_2 = 7/4$, and $x_3 = 3/4$.

17. We introduce a slack and an artificial variable to obtain the modified problem:

Maximize $P = 3x_1 + 5x_2 + 6x_3 - Ma_1$

Subject to:
$$\begin{aligned} 2x_1 + x_2 + 2x_3 + s_1 \quad\quad &= 8 \\ 2x_1 + x_2 - 2x_3 \quad\quad + a_1 &= 0 \\ x_1, \ x_2, \ x_3, \ s_1, \ a_1 &\geqslant 0 \end{aligned}$$

The preliminary simplex tableau for the modified problem is:

$$\begin{bmatrix} 2 & 1 & 2 & 1 & 0 & 0 & 8 \\ 2 & 1 & -2 & 0 & 1 & 0 & 0 \\ \hline -3 & -5 & -6 & 0 & M & 1 & 0 \end{bmatrix} \sim \begin{bmatrix} 2 & 1 & 2 & 1 & 0 & 0 & 8 \\ \boxed{2} & 1 & -2 & 0 & 1 & 0 & 0 \\ \hline -3-2M & -5-M & -6+2M & 0 & 0 & 1 & 0 \end{bmatrix}$$

$$R_3 + (-M)R_2 \to R_3 \qquad\qquad \tfrac{1}{2}R_2 \to R_2$$

$$\sim \begin{bmatrix} 2 & 1 & 2 & 1 & 0 & 0 & 8 \\ 1 & \frac{1}{2} & -1 & 0 & \frac{1}{2} & 0 & 0 \\ \hline -3-2M & -5-M & -6+2M & 0 & 0 & 1 & 0 \end{bmatrix} \sim \begin{bmatrix} 0 & 0 & \boxed{4} & 1 & -1 & 0 & 8 \\ 1 & \frac{1}{2} & -1 & 0 & \frac{1}{2} & 0 & 0 \\ \hline 0 & -\frac{7}{2} & -9 & 0 & \frac{3}{2}+M & 1 & 0 \end{bmatrix}$$

$$R_1 + (-2)R_2 \to R_1, \ R_3 + (3+2M)R_2 \to R_3 \qquad\qquad \tfrac{1}{4}R_1 \to R_1$$

$$\sim \begin{bmatrix} 0 & 0 & 1 & \frac{1}{4} & -\frac{1}{4} & 0 & 2 \\ 1 & \frac{1}{2} & -1 & 0 & \frac{1}{2} & 0 & 0 \\ \hline 0 & -\frac{7}{2} & -9 & 0 & \frac{3}{2}+M & 1 & 0 \end{bmatrix} \sim \begin{bmatrix} 0 & 0 & 1 & \frac{1}{4} & -\frac{1}{4} & 0 & 2 \\ 1 & \boxed{\frac{1}{2}} & 0 & \frac{1}{4} & \frac{1}{4} & 0 & 2 \\ \hline 0 & -\frac{7}{2} & 0 & \frac{9}{4} & -\frac{3}{4}+M & 1 & 18 \end{bmatrix}$$

$$R_2 + R_1 \to R_2, \ R_3 + 9R_1 \to R_3 \qquad\qquad 2R_2 \to R_2$$

$$\sim \begin{bmatrix} 0 & 0 & 1 & \frac{1}{4} & -\frac{1}{4} & 0 & 2 \\ 2 & 1 & 0 & \frac{1}{2} & \frac{1}{2} & 0 & 4 \\ \hline 0 & -\frac{7}{2} & 0 & \frac{9}{4} & -\frac{3}{4}+M & 1 & 18 \end{bmatrix}$$

$$R_3 + \frac{7}{2}R_2 \to R_3$$

(continued)

$$\begin{array}{cccccc}
x_1 & x_2 & x_3 & s_1 & a_1 & P
\end{array}$$

$$\sim \left[\begin{array}{ccccc|c}
0 & 0 & 1 & \frac{1}{4} & -\frac{1}{4} & 0 \\
2 & 1 & 0 & \frac{1}{2} & \frac{1}{2} & 0 \\
\hline
7 & 0 & 0 & 4 & 1+M & 1
\end{array}\middle|\begin{array}{c} 2 \\ 4 \\ \hline 32 \end{array}\right]$$

Optimal solution: max $P = 32$ at $x_1 = 0$, $x_2 = 4$, $x_3 = 2$.

19. We introduce slack, surplus, and artificial variables to obtain the modified problem:

Maximize $P = 2x_1 + 3x_2 + 4x_3 - Ma_1$

Subject to:
$$\begin{aligned}
x_1 + 2x_2 + x_3 + s_1 &= 25 \\
2x_1 + x_2 + 2x_3 + s_2 &= 60 \\
x_1 + 2x_2 - x_3 - s_3 + a_1 &= 10 \\
x_1, x_2, x_3, s_1, s_2, s_3, a_1 &\geqslant 0
\end{aligned}$$

The preliminary simplex tableau for the modified problem is:

$$\begin{array}{cccccccc}
x_1 & x_2 & x_3 & s_1 & s_2 & s_3 & a_1 & P
\end{array}$$

$$\left[\begin{array}{cccccccc|c}
1 & 2 & 1 & 1 & 0 & 0 & 0 & 0 & 25 \\
2 & 1 & 2 & 0 & 1 & 0 & 0 & 0 & 60 \\
1 & 2 & -1 & 0 & 0 & -1 & 1 & 0 & 10 \\
\hline
-2 & -3 & -4 & 0 & 0 & 0 & M & 1 & 0
\end{array}\right]$$

$R_4 + (-M)R_3 \rightarrow R_4$

$$\sim \left[\begin{array}{cccccccc|c}
1 & 2 & 1 & 1 & 0 & 0 & 0 & 0 & 25 \\
2 & 1 & 2 & 0 & 1 & 0 & 0 & 0 & 60 \\
1 & ② & -1 & 0 & 0 & -1 & 1 & 0 & 10 \\
\hline
-2-M & -3-2M & -4+M & 0 & 0 & M & 0 & 0 & -10M
\end{array}\right]$$

$\frac{1}{2}R_3 \rightarrow R_3$

$$\sim \left[\begin{array}{cccccccc|c}
1 & 2 & 1 & 1 & 0 & 0 & 0 & 0 & 25 \\
2 & 1 & 2 & 0 & 1 & 0 & 0 & 0 & 60 \\
\frac{1}{2} & 1 & -\frac{1}{2} & 0 & 0 & -\frac{1}{2} & \frac{1}{2} & 0 & 5 \\
\hline
-2-M & -3-2M & -4+M & 0 & 0 & M & 0 & 1 & -10M
\end{array}\right]$$

$R_1 + (-2)R_3 \rightarrow R_1,\ R_2 + (-1)R_3 \rightarrow R_2,\ R_4 + (3+2M)R_3 \rightarrow R_4$

(continued)

$$\sim \begin{bmatrix} 0 & 0 & \boxed{2} & 1 & 0 & 1 & -1 & 0 & 15 \\ \frac{3}{2} & 0 & \frac{5}{2} & 0 & 1 & \frac{1}{2} & -\frac{1}{2} & 0 & 55 \\ \frac{1}{2} & 1 & -\frac{1}{2} & 0 & 0 & -\frac{1}{2} & \frac{1}{2} & 0 & 5 \\ \hdashline -\frac{1}{2} & 0 & -\frac{11}{2} & 0 & 0 & -\frac{3}{2} & \frac{3}{2}+M & 1 & 15 \end{bmatrix}$$

$$\tfrac{1}{2}R_1 \to R_1$$

$$\sim \begin{bmatrix} 0 & 0 & 1 & \frac{1}{2} & 0 & \frac{1}{2} & -\frac{1}{2} & 0 & \frac{15}{2} \\ \frac{3}{2} & 0 & \frac{5}{2} & 0 & 1 & \frac{1}{2} & -\frac{1}{2} & 0 & 55 \\ \frac{1}{2} & 1 & -\frac{1}{2} & 0 & 0 & -\frac{1}{2} & \frac{1}{2} & 0 & 5 \\ \hdashline -\frac{1}{2} & 0 & -\frac{11}{2} & 0 & 0 & -\frac{3}{2} & \frac{3}{2}+M & 1 & 15 \end{bmatrix}$$

$$R_2 + \left(-\tfrac{5}{2}\right)R_1 \to R_2, \quad R_3 + \tfrac{1}{2}R_1 \to R_3, \quad R_4 + \tfrac{11}{2}R_1 \to R_4$$

$$\sim \begin{bmatrix} 0 & 0 & 1 & \frac{1}{2} & 0 & \frac{1}{2} & -\frac{1}{2} & 0 & \frac{15}{2} \\ \frac{3}{2} & 0 & 0 & -\frac{5}{4} & 1 & -\frac{3}{4} & \frac{3}{4} & 0 & \frac{145}{4} \\ \boxed{\frac{1}{2}} & 1 & 0 & \frac{1}{4} & 0 & -\frac{1}{4} & \frac{1}{4} & 0 & \frac{35}{4} \\ \hdashline -\frac{1}{2} & 0 & 0 & \frac{11}{4} & 0 & \frac{5}{4} & -\frac{5}{4}+M & 1 & \frac{225}{4} \end{bmatrix}$$

$$2R_3 \to R_3$$

$$\sim \begin{bmatrix} 0 & 0 & 1 & \frac{1}{2} & 0 & \frac{1}{2} & -\frac{1}{2} & 0 & \frac{15}{2} \\ \frac{3}{2} & 0 & 0 & -\frac{5}{4} & 1 & -\frac{3}{4} & \frac{3}{4} & 0 & \frac{145}{4} \\ 1 & 2 & 0 & \frac{1}{2} & 0 & -\frac{1}{2} & \frac{1}{2} & 0 & \frac{35}{2} \\ \hdashline -\frac{1}{2} & 0 & 0 & \frac{11}{4} & 0 & \frac{5}{4} & -\frac{5}{4}+M & 1 & \frac{225}{4} \end{bmatrix}$$

$$R_2 + \left(-\tfrac{3}{2}\right)R_3 \to R_2, \quad R_4 + \tfrac{1}{2}R_3 \to R_4$$

(continued)

$$\begin{array}{ccccccccc}
 & x_1 & x_2 & x_3 & s_1 & s_2 & s_3 & a_1 & P \\
\sim \left[\begin{array}{c} \\ \\ \\ \hline \\ \end{array}\right.
\end{array}$$

	x_1	x_2	x_3	s_1	s_2	s_3	a_1	P	
	0	0	1	$\frac{1}{2}$	0	$\frac{1}{2}$	$-\frac{1}{2}$	0	$\frac{15}{2}$
	0	-3	0	-2	1	0	0	0	10
$\sim$	1	2	0	$\frac{1}{2}$	0	$-\frac{1}{2}$	$\frac{1}{2}$	0	$\frac{35}{2}$
	0	1	0	3	0	1	$-1+M$	0	65

Optimal solution: max $P = 65$ at $x_1 = 35/2$, $x_2 = 0$, $x_3 = 15/2$.

21. We introduce slack, surplus, and artificial variables to obtain the modified problem:

Maximize $P = x_1 + 2x_2 + 5x_3 - Ma_1 - Ma_2$

Subject to:
$$\begin{aligned}
x_1 + 3x_2 + 2x_3 + s_1 &= 60 \\
2x_1 + 4x_2 + x_3 \qquad\quad - s_2 \qquad\quad + a_1 &= 50 \\
x_1 - 2x_2 + x_3 \qquad\qquad\quad - s_2 \qquad\quad + a_2 &= 40 \\
x_1, \; x_2, \; x_3, \; s_1, \; s_2, \; s_3, \; a_1, \; a_2 &\geqslant 0
\end{aligned}$$

The preliminary simplex tableau for the modified problem is:

x_1	x_2	x_3	s_1	s_2	s_3	a_1	a_2	P	
1	3	2	1	0	0	0	0	0	60
2	4	1	0	-1	0	1	0	0	50
1	-2	1	0	0	-1	0	1	0	40
-1	-2	-5	0	0	0	M	M	1	0

$R_4 + (-M)R_2 \rightarrow R_4$

	x_1	x_2	x_3	s_1	s_2	s_3	a_1	a_2	P	
	1	3	2	1	0	0	0	0	0	60
$\sim$	2	4	1	0	-1	0	1	0	0	50
	1	-2	1	0	0	-1	0	1	0	40
	$-1-2M$	$-2-4M$	$-5-M$	0	M	0	0	M	1	$-50M$

$R_4 + (-M)R_3 \rightarrow R_4$

(continued)

$$\sim \begin{bmatrix} 1 & 3 & 2 & 1 & 0 & 0 & 0 & 0 & 0 & 60 \\ ② & 4 & 1 & 0 & -1 & 0 & 1 & 0 & 0 & 50 \\ 1 & -2 & 1 & 0 & 0 & -1 & 0 & 1 & 0 & 40 \\ \hline -1-3M & -2-2M & -5-2M & 0 & M & M & 0 & 0 & 1 & -90M \end{bmatrix}$$

$$\tfrac{1}{2}R_2 \to R_2$$

$$\sim \begin{bmatrix} 1 & 3 & 2 & 1 & 0 & 0 & 0 & 0 & 0 & 60 \\ 1 & 2 & \tfrac{1}{2} & 0 & -\tfrac{1}{2} & 0 & \tfrac{1}{2} & 0 & 0 & 25 \\ 1 & -2 & 1 & 0 & 0 & -1 & 0 & 1 & 0 & 40 \\ \hline -1-3M & -2-2M & -5-2M & 0 & M & M & 0 & 0 & 1 & -90M \end{bmatrix}$$

$$R_1 + (-1)R_2 \to R_1, \ R_3 + (-1)R_2 \to R_3, \ R_4 + (1+3M)R_2 \to R_4$$

$$\sim \begin{bmatrix} 0 & 1 & ③/② & 1 & \tfrac{1}{2} & 0 & -\tfrac{1}{2} & 0 & 0 & 35 \\ 1 & 2 & \tfrac{1}{2} & 0 & -\tfrac{1}{2} & 0 & \tfrac{1}{2} & 0 & 0 & 25 \\ 0 & -4 & \tfrac{1}{2} & 0 & \tfrac{1}{2} & -1 & -\tfrac{1}{2} & 1 & 0 & 15 \\ \hline 0 & 4M & -\tfrac{9}{2}-\tfrac{1}{2}M & 0 & -\tfrac{1}{2}-\tfrac{1}{2}M & M & \tfrac{1}{2}+\tfrac{3}{2}M & 0 & 1 & 25-15M \end{bmatrix}$$

$$\tfrac{2}{3}R_1 \to R_1$$

$$\sim \begin{bmatrix} 0 & \tfrac{2}{3} & 1 & \tfrac{2}{3} & \tfrac{1}{3} & 0 & -\tfrac{1}{3} & 0 & 0 & \tfrac{70}{3} \\ 1 & 2 & \tfrac{1}{2} & 0 & -\tfrac{1}{2} & 0 & \tfrac{1}{2} & 0 & 0 & 25 \\ 0 & -4 & \tfrac{1}{2} & 0 & \tfrac{1}{2} & -1 & -\tfrac{1}{2} & 1 & 0 & 15 \\ \hline 0 & 4M & -\tfrac{9}{2}-\tfrac{1}{2}M & 0 & -\tfrac{1}{2}-\tfrac{1}{2}M & M & \tfrac{1}{2}+\tfrac{3}{2}M & 0 & 1 & 25-15M \end{bmatrix}$$

$$R_2 + \left(-\tfrac{1}{2}\right)R_1 \to R_2, \ R_3 + \left(-\tfrac{1}{2}\right)R_1 \to R_3, \ R_4 + \left(\tfrac{9}{2}+\tfrac{1}{2}M\right)R_1 \to R_4$$

(continued)

$$\sim \begin{bmatrix} 0 & \frac{2}{3} & 1 & \frac{2}{3} & \frac{1}{3} & 0 & -\frac{1}{3} & 0 & 0 & \Big| & \frac{70}{3} \\ 1 & \frac{5}{3} & 0 & -\frac{1}{3} & -\frac{2}{3} & 0 & \frac{2}{3} & 0 & 0 & \Big| & \frac{40}{3} \\ 0 & -\frac{13}{3} & 0 & -\frac{1}{3} & \boxed{\tfrac{1}{3}} & -1 & -\frac{1}{3} & 1 & 0 & \Big| & \frac{10}{3} \\ \hline 0 & 3+\frac{13}{3}M & 0 & 3+\frac{1}{3}M & 1-\frac{1}{3}M & M & -1+\frac{4}{3}M & 0 & 1 & \Big| & 130-\frac{10}{3}M \end{bmatrix}$$

$3R_3 \to R_3$

$$\sim \begin{bmatrix} 0 & \frac{2}{3} & 1 & \frac{2}{3} & \frac{1}{3} & 0 & -\frac{1}{3} & 0 & 0 & \Big| & \frac{70}{3} \\ 1 & \frac{5}{3} & 0 & -\frac{1}{3} & -\frac{2}{3} & 0 & \frac{2}{3} & 0 & 0 & \Big| & \frac{40}{3} \\ 0 & -13 & 0 & -1 & 1 & -3 & -1 & 3 & 0 & \Big| & 10 \\ \hline 0 & 3+\frac{13}{3}M & 0 & 3+\frac{1}{3}M & 1-\frac{1}{3}M & M & -1+\frac{4}{3}M & 0 & 1 & \Big| & 130-\frac{10}{3}M \end{bmatrix}$$

$R_1 + \left(-\frac{1}{3}\right)R_3 \to R_1,\; R_2 + \frac{2}{3}R_1 \to R_2,\; R_4 + \left(-1+\frac{1}{3}M\right)R_3 \to R_4$

$$\begin{array}{cccccccc} x_1 & x_2 & x_3 & s_1 & s_2 & s_3 & a_1 & a_2 & P \end{array}$$
$$\sim \begin{bmatrix} 0 & 5 & 1 & 1 & 0 & 1 & 0 & -1 & 0 & \Big| & 20 \\ 1 & -7 & 0 & -1 & 0 & -2 & 0 & 2 & 0 & \Big| & 20 \\ 0 & -13 & 0 & -1 & 1 & -3 & -1 & 3 & 0 & \Big| & 10 \\ \hline 0 & 16 & 0 & 4 & 0 & 3 & M & -3+M & 1 & \Big| & 120 \end{bmatrix}$$

Optimal solution: max $P = 120$ at $x_1 = 20$, $x_2 = 0$, $x_3 = 20$.

23. We will maximize $P = -C = -10x_1 + 40x_2 + 5x_3$

Subject to:
$$\begin{aligned} x_1 + 3x_2 \qquad\; + s_1 \qquad &= 6 \\ 4x_2 + x_3 \qquad\; + s_2 &= 3 \\ x_1,\, x_2,\, x_3,\, s_1,\, s_2 &\geqslant 0 \end{aligned}$$

where s_1, s_2 are slack variables. The simplex tableau for this problem is:

$$\begin{array}{cccccc} x_1 & x_2 & x_3 & s_1 & s_2 & P \end{array}$$
$$\begin{bmatrix} 1 & 3 & 0 & 1 & 0 & 0 & \Big| & 6 \\ 0 & \boxed{4} & 1 & 0 & 1 & 0 & \Big| & 3 \\ \hline 10 & -40 & -5 & 0 & 0 & 1 & \Big| & 0 \end{bmatrix} \begin{array}{l} \frac{6}{3} = 2 \\[8pt] \frac{3}{4} = .75 \end{array}$$

$\frac{1}{4}R_2 \to R_2$

(continued)

$$\sim \begin{bmatrix} 1 & 3 & 0 & 1 & 0 & 0 & | & 6 \\ 0 & 1 & \frac{1}{4} & 0 & \frac{1}{4} & 0 & | & \frac{3}{4} \\ \hline 10 & -40 & -5 & 0 & 0 & 1 & | & 0 \end{bmatrix}$$

$R_1 + (-3)R_2 \to R_1$ and $R_3 + 40R_2 \to R_3$

$$\sim \begin{bmatrix} x_1 & x_2 & x_3 & s_1 & s_2 & P & \\ 1 & 0 & -\frac{3}{4} & 1 & -\frac{3}{4} & 0 & | & \frac{15}{4} \\ 0 & 1 & \frac{1}{4} & 0 & \frac{1}{4} & 0 & | & \frac{3}{4} \\ \hline 10 & 0 & 5 & 0 & 10 & 1 & | & 30 \end{bmatrix}$$

Optimal solution: min $C = -30$ at $x_1 = 0$, $x_2 = 3/4$, $x_3 = 0$.

25. Introduce slack, surplus, and artificial variables to obtain the modified problem:

Maximize $P = -5x_1 + 10x_2 + 15x_3 - Ma_1$

Subject to:
$$\begin{aligned} 2x_1 + 3x_2 + x_3 + s_1 &= 24 \\ x_1 - 2x_2 - 2x_3 \quad\quad - s_2 + a_1 &= 1 \\ x_1, \ x_2, \ x_3, \ s_1, \ s_2, \ a_1 &\geqslant 0 \end{aligned}$$

The preliminary simplex tableau for the modified problem is:

$$\begin{array}{ccccccc} x_1 & x_2 & x_3 & s_1 & s_2 & a_1 & P \\ \end{array}$$
$$\begin{bmatrix} 2 & 3 & 1 & 1 & 0 & 0 & 0 & | & 24 \\ 1 & -2 & -2 & 0 & -1 & 1 & 0 & | & 1 \\ \hline 5 & -10 & -15 & 0 & 0 & M & 1 & | & 0 \end{bmatrix}$$

$R_3 + (-M)R_2 \to R_3$

$$\sim \begin{bmatrix} 2 & 3 & 1 & 1 & 0 & 0 & 0 & | & 24 \\ \textcircled{1} & -2 & -2 & 0 & -1 & 1 & 0 & | & 1 \\ \hline -M+5 & 2M-10 & 2M-15 & 0 & M & 0 & 1 & | & -M \end{bmatrix} \begin{array}{l} \frac{24}{2} = 12 \\ \\ \frac{1}{1} = 1 \end{array}$$

$R_1 + (-2)R_2 \to R_1$ and $R_3 + (M-5)R_2 \to R_3$

$$\sim \begin{bmatrix} 0 & 7 & \textcircled{5} & 1 & 2 & -2 & 0 & | & 22 \\ 1 & -2 & -2 & 0 & -1 & 1 & 0 & | & 1 \\ \hline 0 & 0 & -5 & 0 & 5 & M-5 & 1 & | & -5 \end{bmatrix}$$

$\frac{1}{5}R_1 \to R_1$

$$\sim \begin{bmatrix} 0 & \frac{7}{5} & 1 & \frac{1}{5} & \frac{2}{5} & -\frac{2}{5} & 0 & | & \frac{22}{5} \\ 1 & -2 & -2 & 0 & -1 & 1 & 0 & | & 1 \\ \hline 0 & 0 & -5 & 0 & 5 & M-5 & 1 & | & -5 \end{bmatrix}$$

$R_2 + 2R_1 \to R_2$ and $R_3 + 5R_1 \to R_3$

$$\begin{array}{ccccccc} x_1 & x_2 & x_3 & s_1 & s_2 & a_1 & P \\ \end{array}$$
$$\sim \begin{bmatrix} 0 & \frac{7}{5} & 1 & \frac{1}{5} & \frac{2}{5} & -\frac{2}{5} & 0 & | & \frac{22}{5} \\ 1 & \frac{4}{5} & 0 & \frac{2}{5} & -\frac{1}{5} & \frac{1}{5} & 0 & | & \frac{49}{5} \\ \hline 0 & 7 & 0 & 1 & 7 & M-7 & 1 & | & 17 \end{bmatrix}$$

Optimal solution: max $P = 17$ at $x_1 = 49/5$, $x_2 = 0$, $x_3 = 22/5$.

LINEAR INEQUALITIES AND LINEAR PROGRAMMING

27. The matrices corresponding to the given problem and the dual problem are:

$$A = \begin{bmatrix} 1 & 3 & 0 & 6 \\ 0 & 4 & 1 & 3 \\ \hline 10 & 40 & 5 & 1 \end{bmatrix} \quad \text{and} \quad B = \begin{bmatrix} 1 & 0 & 10 \\ 3 & 4 & 40 \\ 0 & 1 & 5 \\ \hline 6 & 3 & 1 \end{bmatrix}$$

Thus, the dual problem is: Maximize $P = 6y_1 + 3y_2$

$$\begin{aligned}
\text{Subject to:} \quad y_1 &\leqslant 10 \\
3y_1 + 4y_2 &\leqslant 40 \\
y_2 &\leqslant 5 \\
y_1, \ y_2 &\geqslant 0
\end{aligned}$$

We introduce the slack variables x_1, x_2, and x_3 to obtain the initial form:

$$\begin{aligned}
y_1 \qquad\quad + x_1 \qquad\qquad\qquad &= 10 \\
3y_1 + 4y_2 \qquad\quad + x_2 \qquad\qquad &= 40 \\
y_2 \qquad\qquad\quad + x_3 \qquad &= 5 \\
-6y_1 - 3y_2 \qquad\qquad\qquad + P &= 0
\end{aligned}$$

The simplex tableau for this problem is:

$$\begin{array}{cccccc}
y_1 & y_2 & x_1 & x_2 & x_3 & P \\
\end{array}$$
$$\begin{bmatrix}
① & 0 & 1 & 0 & 0 & 0 & 10 \\
3 & 4 & 0 & 1 & 0 & 0 & 40 \\
0 & 1 & 0 & 0 & 1 & 0 & 5 \\
\hline
-6 & -3 & 0 & 0 & 0 & 1 & 0
\end{bmatrix}
\begin{array}{l}
\frac{10}{1} = 10 \\[6pt]
\frac{40}{3} \approx 13.33
\end{array}$$

$R_2 + (-3)R_1 \to R_2$ and $R_4 + 6R_1 \to R_4$

$$\sim \begin{bmatrix}
1 & 0 & 1 & 0 & 0 & 0 & 10 \\
0 & ④ & -3 & 1 & 0 & 0 & 10 \\
0 & 1 & 0 & 0 & 1 & 0 & 5 \\
\hline
0 & -3 & 6 & 0 & 0 & 1 & 60
\end{bmatrix}
\begin{array}{l}
\frac{10}{4} = 2.5 \\[6pt]
\frac{5}{1} = 5
\end{array}
\quad \sim \begin{bmatrix}
1 & 0 & 1 & 0 & 0 & 0 & 10 \\
0 & 1 & -\frac{3}{4} & \frac{1}{4} & 0 & 0 & \frac{5}{2} \\
0 & 1 & 0 & 0 & 1 & 0 & 5 \\
\hline
0 & -3 & 6 & 0 & 0 & 1 & 60
\end{bmatrix}$$

$\frac{1}{4}R_2 \to R_2$

$\begin{aligned} R_3 + (-1)R_2 &\to R_3 \text{ and} \\ R_4 + 3R_2 &\to R_4 \end{aligned}$

$$\begin{array}{cccccc}
y_1 & y_2 & x_1 & x_2 & x_3 & P \\
\end{array}$$
$$\sim \begin{bmatrix}
1 & 0 & 1 & 0 & 0 & 0 & 10 \\
0 & 1 & -\frac{3}{4} & \frac{1}{4} & 0 & 0 & \frac{5}{2} \\
0 & 0 & \frac{3}{4} & -\frac{1}{4} & 1 & 0 & \frac{5}{2} \\
\hline
0 & 0 & \frac{15}{4} & \frac{3}{4} & 0 & 1 & \frac{135}{2}
\end{bmatrix}$$

Optimal solution: min $C = 135/2$, $x_1 = 15/4$, $x_2 = 3/4$, $x_3 = 0$.

29. We introduce the slack variables s_1 and s_2 to obtain the initial form:

$$x_1 + 2x_2 + x_3 + s_1 \qquad\qquad = 40$$
$$2x_1 \quad\ x_2 + 3x_3 \qquad + s_2 \qquad = 60$$
$$-12x_1 - 9x_2 - 5x_3 \qquad\qquad + P = 0$$

The simplex tableau for this problem is:

$$
\begin{array}{cccccc}
x_1 & x_2 & x_3 & s_1 & s_2 & P
\end{array}
$$

$$
\left[\begin{array}{cccccc|c}
1 & 2 & 1 & 1 & 0 & 0 & 40 \\
② & 1 & 3 & 0 & 1 & 0 & 60 \\
\hline
-12 & -9 & -5 & 0 & 0 & 1 & 0
\end{array}\right]
\quad
\begin{array}{l}
\frac{40}{1} = 40 \\[4pt]
\frac{60}{2} = 30
\end{array}
\ \sim\
\left[\begin{array}{cccccc|c}
1 & 2 & 1 & 1 & 0 & 0 & 40 \\
1 & \frac{1}{2} & \frac{3}{2} & 0 & \frac{1}{2} & 0 & 30 \\
\hline
-12 & -9 & -5 & 0 & 0 & 1 & 0
\end{array}\right]
$$

$$\frac{1}{2}R_2 \to R_2$$

$$R_1 + (-1)R_2 \to R_1 \text{ and}$$
$$R_3 + 12R_2 \to R_3$$

$$
\sim
\left[\begin{array}{cccccc|c}
0 & ③\!\!/\!\!② & -\frac{1}{2} & 1 & -\frac{1}{2} & 0 & 10 \\
1 & \frac{1}{2} & \frac{3}{2} & 0 & \frac{1}{2} & 0 & 30 \\
\hline
0 & -3 & 13 & 0 & 6 & 1 & 360
\end{array}\right]
\quad
\begin{array}{l}
\frac{10}{3/2} \approx 6.67 \\[4pt]
\frac{30}{1/2} = 60
\end{array}
\ \sim\
\left[\begin{array}{cccccc|c}
0 & 1 & -\frac{1}{3} & \frac{2}{3} & -\frac{1}{3} & 0 & \frac{20}{3} \\
1 & \frac{1}{2} & \frac{3}{2} & 0 & \frac{1}{2} & 0 & 30 \\
\hline
0 & -3 & 13 & 0 & 6 & 1 & 360
\end{array}\right]
$$

$$\frac{2}{3}R_1 \to R_1$$

$$R_2 + \left(-\frac{1}{2}\right)R_1 \to R_2 \text{ and}$$
$$R_3 + 3R_1 \to R_3$$

$$
\begin{array}{cccccc}
x_1 & x_2 & x_3 & s_1 & s_2 & P
\end{array}
$$

$$
\sim
\left[\begin{array}{cccccc|c}
0 & 1 & -\frac{1}{3} & \frac{2}{3} & -\frac{1}{3} & 0 & \frac{20}{3} \\
1 & 0 & \frac{5}{3} & -\frac{1}{3} & \frac{2}{3} & 0 & \frac{80}{3} \\
\hline
0 & 0 & 12 & 2 & 5 & 1 & 380
\end{array}\right]
$$

Optimal solution: max $P = 380$ at $x_1 = 80/3$, $x_2 = 20/3$, $x_3 = 0$.

31. Let x_1 = the number of 16K modules
and x_2 = the number of 64K modules.

The mathematical model for this problem is:

Maximize $P = 18x_1 + 30x_2$

Subject to:
$$10x_1 + 15x_2 \leqslant 1500$$
$$2x_1 + 4x_2 \leqslant 400$$
$$x_1 \qquad\qquad \geqslant 50$$
$$x_1,\ x_2 \geqslant 0$$

We introduce slack, surplus, and artificial variables to obtain the modified problem.

Maximize $P = 18x_1 + 30x_2 - Ma_1$

Subject to:
$$10x_1 + 15x_2 + s_1 \qquad\qquad\qquad = 1500$$
$$2x_1 + 4x_2 \qquad + s_2 \qquad\qquad = 400$$
$$x_1 \qquad\qquad\qquad\qquad - s_3 + a_1 = 50$$
$$x_1,\ x_2,\ s_1,\ s_2,\ s_3,\ a_1 \geqslant 0$$

The preliminary simplex tableau for the modified problem is:

$$\begin{array}{ccccccc}
x_1 & x_2 & s_1 & s_2 & s_3 & a_1 & P
\end{array}$$

$$\left[\begin{array}{ccccccc|c}
10 & 15 & 1 & 0 & 0 & 0 & 0 & 1500 \\
2 & 4 & 0 & 1 & 0 & 0 & 0 & 400 \\
1 & 0 & 0 & 0 & -1 & 1 & 0 & 50 \\
\hline
-18 & -30 & 0 & 0 & 0 & M & 1 & 0
\end{array}\right]$$

$R_4 + (-M)R_3 \to R_4$

$$\sim \left[\begin{array}{ccccccc|c}
10 & 15 & 1 & 0 & 0 & 0 & 0 & 1500 \\
2 & 4 & 0 & 1 & 0 & 0 & 0 & 400 \\
① & 0 & 0 & 0 & -1 & 1 & 0 & 50 \\
\hline
-M-18 & -30 & 0 & 0 & M & 0 & 1 & -50M
\end{array}\right]$$

$\dfrac{1500}{10} = 150$

$\dfrac{400}{2} = 200$

$\dfrac{50}{1} = 50$

$R_1 + (-10)R_3 \to R_1$, $R_2 + (-2)R_3 \to R_2$, and $R_4 + (M+18)R_3 \to R_3$

$$\sim \left[\begin{array}{ccccccc|c}
0 & ⑮ & 1 & 0 & 10 & -10 & 0 & 1000 \\
0 & 4 & 0 & 1 & 2 & -2 & 0 & 300 \\
1 & 0 & 0 & 0 & -1 & 1 & 0 & 50 \\
\hline
0 & -30 & 0 & 0 & -18 & M+18 & 1 & 900
\end{array}\right]$$

$\dfrac{1000}{15} \approx 66.67$

$\dfrac{300}{4} = 75$

$\dfrac{1}{15}R_1 \to R_1$

$$\sim \left[\begin{array}{ccccccc|c}
0 & 1 & \frac{1}{15} & 0 & \frac{2}{3} & -\frac{2}{3} & 0 & \frac{200}{3} \\
0 & 4 & 0 & 1 & 2 & -2 & 0 & 300 \\
1 & 0 & 0 & 0 & -1 & 1 & 0 & 50 \\
\hline
0 & -30 & 0 & 0 & -18 & M+18 & 1 & 900
\end{array}\right]$$

$R_2 + (-4)R_1 \to R_2$ and $R_4 + 30R_1 \to R_4$

$$\begin{array}{ccccccc}
x_1 & x_2 & s_1 & s_2 & s_3 & a_1 & P
\end{array}$$

$$\sim \left[\begin{array}{ccccccc|c}
0 & 1 & \frac{1}{15} & 0 & \frac{2}{3} & -\frac{2}{3} & 0 & \frac{200}{3} \\
0 & 0 & -\frac{4}{15} & 1 & -\frac{2}{3} & \frac{2}{3} & 0 & \frac{100}{3} \\
1 & 0 & 0 & 0 & -1 & 1 & 0 & 50 \\
\hline
0 & 0 & 2 & 0 & 20 & M-2 & 1 & 2900
\end{array}\right]$$

The maximum profit is $2900 when 50 16K modules and $\dfrac{200}{3} = 66\frac{2}{3}$ 64K modules are manufactured each day.

33. Let x_1 = the number of ads placed in the *Sentinel*,
    x_2 = the number of ads placed in the *Journal*
    and x_3 = the number of ads placed in the *Tribune*.
    The mathematical model for this problem is:

   Minimize $C = 200x_1 + 200x_2 + 100x_3$

   Subject to:
   $$x_1 + x_2 + x_3 \leqslant 10$$
   $$2000x_1 + 500x_2 + 1500x_3 \geqslant 16,000$$
   $$x_1,\ x_2,\ x_3 \geqslant 0$$

Divide the second constraint inequality by 100 to simplify the calculations, and introduce slack, surplus, and artificial variables to obtain the modified problem:

   Maximize $P = -C - 200x_1 - 200x_2 - 100x_3 - Ma_1$

   Subject to:
   $$x_1 + x_2 + x_3 + s_1 = 10$$
   $$20x_1 + 5x_2 + 15x_3 - s_2 + a_1 = 160$$
   $$x_1\ \ x_2,\ x_3,\ s_1,\ s_2,\ a_1 \geqslant 0$$

The preliminary simplex tableau for the modified problem is:

x_1	x_2	x_3	s_1	s_2	a_1	P	
1	1	1	1	0	0	0	10
20	5	15	0	-1	1	0	160
200	200	100	0	0	M	1	0

$R_4 + (-M)R_3 \to R_4$

1	1	1	1	0	0	0	10	$\frac{10}{1} = 10$
(20)	5	15	0	-1	1	0	160	$\frac{160}{20} = 8$
$-20M+200$	$-5M+200$	$-15M+100$	0	M	0	1	$-160M$	

$\frac{1}{20}R_2 \to R_2$

1	1	1	1	0	0	0	10
1	$\frac{1}{4}$	$\frac{3}{4}$	0	$-\frac{1}{20}$	$\frac{1}{20}$	0	8
$-20M+200$	$-5M+200$	$-15M+100$	0	M	0	1	$-160M$

$R_1 + (-1)R_2 \to R_1$ and $R_3 + (20M-200)R_2 \to R_3$

0	$\frac{3}{4}$	($\frac{1}{4}$)	1	$\frac{1}{20}$	$-\frac{1}{20}$	0	2	$\frac{2}{1/4} = 8$
1	$\frac{1}{4}$	$\frac{3}{4}$	0	$-\frac{1}{20}$	$\frac{1}{20}$	0	8	$\frac{8}{3/4} = \frac{32}{3} \approx 10.67$
0	150	-50	0	10	$M-10$	1	-1600	

$4R_1 \to R_1$

(continued)

$$\sim \begin{bmatrix} 0 & 3 & 1 & 4 & \frac{1}{5} & -\frac{1}{5} & 0 & 8 \\ 1 & \frac{1}{4} & \frac{3}{4} & 0 & -\frac{1}{20} & \frac{1}{20} & 0 & 8 \\ \hline 0 & 150 & -50 & 0 & 10 & M-10 & 1 & -1600 \end{bmatrix}$$

$$R_2 + \left(-\frac{3}{4}\right)R_1 \to R_2 \text{ and } R_3 + 50R_1 \to R_3$$

$$\begin{array}{ccccccc} x_1 & x_2 & x_3 & s_1 & s_2 & a_1 & P \end{array}$$

$$\sim \begin{bmatrix} 0 & 3 & 1 & 4 & \frac{1}{5} & -\frac{1}{5} & 0 & 8 \\ 1 & -2 & 0 & -3 & -\frac{1}{5} & \frac{1}{5} & 0 & 2 \\ \hline 0 & 300 & 0 & 200 & 20 & M-20 & 1 & -1200 \end{bmatrix}$$

The minimal cost is $1200 when two ads are placed in the *Sentinel*, no ads are placed in the *Journal*, and eight ads are placed in the *Tribune*.

35. Let x_1 = the number of bottles of brand A,
    x_2 = the number of bottles of brand B,
    and x_3 = the number of bottles of brand C.
    The mathematical model for this problem is:

    Minimize $C = 0.6x_1 + 0.4x_2 + 0.9x_3$

    Subject to: $\quad 10x_1 + 10x_2 + 20x_3 \geqslant 100$
    $$2x_1 + 3x_2 + 4x_3 \leqslant 24$$
    $$x_1, \; x_2, \; x_3 \geqslant 0$$

    Divide the first inequality by 10, and introduce slack, surplus, and artificial variables to obtain the modified problem:

    Maximize $P = -10C = -6x_1 - 4x_2 - 9x_3 - Ma_1$

    Subject to: $\quad x_1 + x_2 + 2x_3 - s_1 \qquad + a_1 = 10$
    $$2x_1 + 3x_2 + 4x_3 \qquad + s_2 \qquad = 24$$
    $$x_1, \; x_2, \; x_3, \; s_1, \; s_2, \; a_1 \geqslant 0$$

    The preliminary simplex tableau for the modified problem is:

$$\begin{array}{ccccccc} x_1 & x_2 & x_3 & s_1 & s_2 & a_1 & P \end{array}$$

$$\begin{bmatrix} 1 & 1 & 2 & -1 & 0 & 1 & 0 & 10 \\ 2 & 3 & 4 & 0 & 1 & 0 & 0 & 24 \\ \hline 6 & 4 & 9 & 0 & 0 & M & 1 & 0 \end{bmatrix}$$

$$R_3 + (-M)R_1 \to R_3$$

(continued)

$$\begin{bmatrix} 1 & 1 & ② & -1 & 0 & 1 & 0 & 10 \\ 2 & 3 & 4 & 0 & 1 & 0 & 0 & 24 \\ \hline -M+6 & -M+4 & -2M+9 & M & 0 & 0 & 1 & -10M \end{bmatrix} \begin{matrix} \frac{10}{2}=5 \\ \frac{24}{4}=6 \\ \\ \end{matrix}$$

$\frac{1}{2}R_1 \rightarrow R_1$

$$\begin{bmatrix} \frac{1}{2} & \frac{1}{2} & 1 & -\frac{1}{2} & 0 & \frac{1}{2} & 0 & 5 \\ 2 & 3 & 4 & 0 & 1 & 0 & 0 & 24 \\ \hline -M+6 & -M+4 & -2M+9 & M & 0 & 0 & 1 & -10M \end{bmatrix}$$

$R_2 + (-4)R_1 \rightarrow R_2$ and $R_3 + (2M-9)R_1 \rightarrow R_3$

$$\begin{bmatrix} \frac{1}{2} & \frac{1}{2} & 1 & -\frac{1}{2} & 0 & \frac{1}{2} & 0 & 5 \\ 0 & ① & 0 & 2 & 1 & -2 & 0 & 4 \\ \hline \frac{3}{2} & -\frac{1}{2} & 0 & \frac{9}{2} & 0 & M-\frac{9}{2} & 1 & -45 \end{bmatrix} \begin{matrix} \frac{5}{1/2}=10 \\ \frac{4}{1}=4 \\ \\ \end{matrix}$$

$R_1 + \left(-\frac{1}{2}\right)R_2 \rightarrow R_1$ and $R_3 + \frac{1}{2}R_2 \rightarrow R_3$

$$\begin{array}{ccccccc} x_1 & x_2 & x_3 & s_1 & s_2 & a_1 & P \end{array}$$
$$\begin{bmatrix} \frac{1}{2} & 0 & 1 & -\frac{3}{2} & -1 & \frac{3}{2} & 0 & 3 \\ 0 & 1 & 0 & 2 & 1 & -2 & 0 & 4 \\ \hline \frac{3}{2} & 0 & 0 & \frac{11}{2} & \frac{1}{2} & -\frac{11}{2} & 1 & -43 \end{bmatrix}$$

The minimal cost is $4.30 when 0 bottles of brand A, 4 bottles of brand B and 3 bottles of brand C are consumed.

37. Let x_1 = the number of cubic yards of mix A,
         x_2 = the number of cubic yards of mix B,
     and x_3 = the number of cubic yards of mix C.
     The mathematical model for this problem is:

Maximize $P = 12x_1 + 16x_2 + 8x_3$

Subject to: $16x_1 + 8x_2 + 16x_3 \geqslant 800$
$12x_1 + 8x_2 + 16x_3 \leqslant 700$
$x_1, x_2, x_3 \geqslant 0$

We simplify the inequalities, and introduce slack, surplus, and artificial variables to obtain the modified problem:

Maximize $P = 12x_1 + 16x_2 + 8x_3 - Ma_1$

Subject to: $4x_1 + 2x_2 + 4x_3 - s_1 + a_1 = 200$
$3x_1 + 2x_2 + 4x_3 + s_2 = 175$
$x_1, x_2, x_3, s_1, s_2, a_1 \geqslant 0$

The simplex tableau for the modified problem is:

$$
\begin{array}{ccccccc}
x_1 & x_2 & x_3 & s_1 & s_2 & a_1 & P \\
\end{array}
$$

$$
\left[
\begin{array}{ccccccc|c}
4 & 2 & 4 & -1 & 0 & 1 & 0 & 200 \\
3 & 2 & 4 & 0 & 1 & 0 & 0 & 175 \\
\hline
-12 & -16 & -8 & 0 & 0 & M & 1 & 0
\end{array}
\right]
$$

$R_3 + (-M)R_1 \rightarrow R_3$

$$
\sim
\left[
\begin{array}{ccccccc|c}
④ & 2 & 4 & -1 & 0 & 1 & 0 & 200 \\
3 & 2 & 4 & 0 & 1 & 0 & 0 & 175 \\
\hline
-4M-12 & -2M-16 & -4M-8 & M & 0 & 0 & 1 & -200M
\end{array}
\right]
\quad
\begin{array}{l}
\frac{200}{4} = 50 \\[4pt]
\frac{175}{3} \approx 58.33
\end{array}
$$

$\frac{1}{4}R_1 \rightarrow R_1$

$$
\sim
\left[
\begin{array}{ccccccc|c}
1 & \frac{1}{2} & 1 & -\frac{1}{4} & 0 & \frac{1}{4} & 0 & 50 \\
3 & 2 & 4 & 0 & 1 & 0 & 0 & 175 \\
\hline
-4M-12 & -2M-16 & -4M-8 & M & 0 & 0 & 1 & -200M
\end{array}
\right]
$$

$R_2 + (-3)R_1 \rightarrow R_2$ and $R_3 + (4M+12)R_1 \rightarrow R_3$

$$
\sim
\left[
\begin{array}{ccccccc|c}
1 & \frac{1}{2} & 1 & -\frac{1}{4} & 0 & \frac{1}{4} & 0 & 50 \\
0 & ⓵/2 & 1 & \frac{3}{4} & 1 & -\frac{3}{4} & 0 & 25 \\
\hline
0 & -10 & 4 & -3 & 0 & M+3 & 1 & 600
\end{array}
\right]
\quad
\begin{array}{l}
\frac{50}{1/2} = 100 \\[4pt]
\frac{25}{1/2} = 50
\end{array}
$$

$2R_2 \rightarrow R_2$

$$
\sim
\left[
\begin{array}{ccccccc|c}
1 & \frac{1}{2} & 1 & -\frac{1}{4} & 0 & \frac{1}{4} & 0 & 50 \\
0 & 1 & 2 & \frac{3}{2} & 2 & -\frac{3}{2} & 0 & 50 \\
\hline
0 & -10 & 4 & -3 & 0 & M+3 & 1 & 600
\end{array}
\right]
$$

$R_1 + \left(-\frac{1}{2}\right)R_2 \rightarrow R_1$ and $R_3 + 10R_2 \rightarrow R_3$

$$
\begin{array}{ccccccc}
x_1 & x_2 & x_3 & s_1 & s_2 & a_1 & P \\
\end{array}
$$

$$
\sim
\left[
\begin{array}{ccccccc|c}
1 & 0 & 0 & -1 & -1 & 1 & 0 & 25 \\
0 & 1 & 2 & \frac{3}{2} & 2 & -\frac{3}{2} & 0 & 50 \\
\hline
0 & 0 & 24 & 12 & 20 & M-12 & 1 & 1100
\end{array}
\right]
$$

The maximum amount of nitrogen is 1100 pounds when 25 cubic yards of mix A, 50 cubic yards of mix B, and 0 cubic yards of mix C are used.

39. Let x_1 = the number of car frames produced in Milwaukee,
   x_2 = the number of truck frames produced in Milwaukee,
   x_3 = the number of car frames produced in Racine,
   and x_4 = the number of truck frames produced in Racine.
   The mathematical model for this problem is:

Maximize $P = 50x_1 + 70x_2 + 50x_3 + 70x_4$

Subject to:
$$
\begin{aligned}
x_1 + x_3 &\leq 250 \\
x_2 + x_4 &\leq 350 \\
x_1 + x_2 &\leq 300 \\
x_3 + x_4 &\leq 200 \\
150x_1 + 200x_2 &\leq 50{,}000 \\
135x_3 + 180x_4 &\leq 35{,}000 \\
x_1, \; x_2, \; x_3, \; x_4 &\geq 0
\end{aligned}
$$

41. Let x_1 = the number of barrels of A used in regular gasoline,
   x_2 = the number of barrels of A used in premium gasoline,
   x_3 = the number of barrels of B used in regular gasoline,
   x_4 = the number of barrels of B used in premium gasoline,
   x_5 = the number of barrels of C used in regular gasoline,
   x_6 = the number of barrels of C used in premium gasoline.

Cost $C = 28(x_1 + x_2) + 30(x_3 + x_4) + 34(x_5 + x_6)$
Revenue $R = 38(x_1 + x_3 + x_5) + 46(x_2 + x_4 + x_6)$
Profit $P = R - C = 10x_1 + 18x_2 + 8x_3 + 16x_4 + 4x_5 + 12x_6$

Thus, the mathematical model for this problem is:

Maximize $P = 10x_1 + 18x_2 + 8x_3 + 16x_4 + 4x_5 + 12x_6$

Subject to:
$$
\begin{aligned}
x_1 + x_2 &\leq 40{,}000 \\
x_3 + x_4 &\leq 25{,}000 \\
x_5 + x_6 &\leq 15{,}000 \\
x_1 + x_3 + x_5 &\geq 30{,}000 \\
x_2 + x_4 + x_6 &\geq 25{,}000 \\
-5x_1 + 5x_3 + 15x_5 &\geq 0 \\
-15x_2 - 5x_4 + 5x_6 &\geq 0 \\
x_1, \; x_2, \; x_3, \; x_4, \; x_5, \; x_6 &\geq 0
\end{aligned}
$$

43. Let x_1 = the number of ounces of food L,
   x_2 = the number of ounces of food M,
   x_3 = the number of ounces of food N.
   The mathematical model for this problem is:

Minimize $C = 0.4x_1 + 0.6x_2 + 0.8x_3$

Subject to:
$$
\begin{aligned}
30x_1 + 10x_2 + 30x_3 &\geq 400 \\
10x_1 + 10x_2 + 10x_3 &\geq 200 \\
10x_1 + 30x_2 + 20x_3 &\geq 300 \\
8x_1 + 4x_2 + 6x_3 &\leq 150 \\
60x_1 + 40x_2 + 50x_3 &\leq 900 \\
x_1, \; x_2, \; x_3 &\geq 0
\end{aligned}
$$

45. Let x_1 = the number of students from A enrolled in school I,
x_2 = the number of students from A enrolled in school II,
x_3 = the number of students from B enrolled in school I,
x_4 = the number of students from B enrolled in school II,
x_5 = the number of students from C enrolled in school I,
x_6 = the number of students from C enrolled in school II.
The mathematical model for this problem is:

Minimize $C = 4x_1 + 8x_2 + 6x_3 + 4x_4 + 3x_5 + 9x_6$

Subject to:
$$\begin{aligned}
x_1 + x_2 &= 500 \\
x_3 + x_4 &= 1200 \\
x_5 + x_6 &= 1800 \\
x_1 + x_3 + x_5 &\geqslant 1400 \\
x_2 + x_4 + x_6 &\geqslant 1400 \\
x_1 + x_3 + x_5 &\leqslant 2000 \\
x_2 + x_4 + x_6 &\leqslant 2000 \\
x_1 &\leqslant 300 \\
x_2 &\leqslant 300 \\
x_3 &\leqslant 720 \\
x_4 &\leqslant 720 \\
x_5 &\leqslant 1080 \\
x_6 &\leqslant 1080 \\
x_1, \ x_2, \ x_3, \ x_4, \ x_5, \ x_6 &\geqslant 0
\end{aligned}$$

EXERCISE 2-7   CHAPTER REVIEW

1. The graphs of the inequalities are shown below; the solution is indicated by the shaded region.

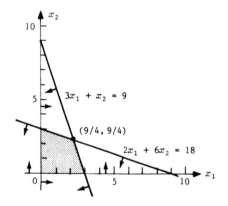

2. The feasible region is the solution set of the given inequalities, and is indicated by the shaded region in the graph at the right.

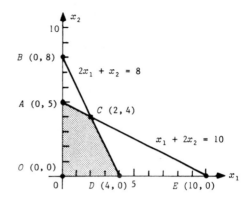

The corner points are $(0, 0, (0, 5),$ $(2, 4),$ and $(4, 0).$

The value of P at each corner point is:

Corner Point	$P = 6x_1 + 2x_2$
$(0, 0)$	$P = 6(0) + 2(0) = 0$
$(0, 5)$	$P = 6(0) + 2(5) = 10$
$(2, 4)$	$P = 6(2) + 2(4) = 20$
$(4, 0)$	$P = 6(4) + 2(0) = 24$

Thus, the maximum occurs at $x_1 = 4$, $x_2 = 0$, and the maximum value is $P = 24$.

3. We introduce the slack variables s_1 and s_2 to obtain the system of equations:

$$2x_1 + x_2 + s_1 \qquad\quad = 8$$
$$x_1 + 2x_2 \qquad + s_2 = 10$$

4. The basic solutions are given in the following table.

x_1	x_2	s_1	s_2	Intersection Point	Feasible?
0	0	8	10	O	Yes
0	8	0	-6	B	No
0	5	3	0	A	Yes
4	0	0	6	D	Yes
10	0	-12	0	E	No
2	4	0	0	C	Yes

5. The simplex tableau for Problem 2 is:

$$
\begin{array}{ccccc}
x_1 & x_2 & s_1 & s_2 & P
\end{array}
$$

$$
\left[
\begin{array}{ccccc|c}
\boxed{2} & 1 & 1 & 0 & 0 & 8 \\
1 & 2 & 0 & 1 & 0 & 10 \\
\hline
-6 & -2 & 0 & 0 & 1 & 0
\end{array}
\right]
\quad
\begin{array}{l}
\dfrac{8}{2} = 4 \\[2mm]
\dfrac{10}{1} = 10
\end{array}
$$

6.

$$\sim \begin{bmatrix} \fbox{2} & 1 & 1 & 0 & 0 & 8 \\ 1 & 2 & 0 & 1 & 0 & 10 \\ \hline -6 & -2 & 0 & 0 & 1 & 0 \end{bmatrix} \quad \sim \begin{bmatrix} 1 & \frac{1}{2} & \frac{1}{2} & 0 & 0 & 4 \\ 1 & 2 & 0 & 1 & 0 & 10 \\ \hline -6 & -2 & 0 & 0 & 1 & 0 \end{bmatrix}$$

$\frac{1}{2} R_1 \to R_1$ $\qquad\qquad R_2 + (-1)R_1 \to R_2$ and $R_3 + 6R_1 \to R_3$

$$\sim \begin{array}{c} \begin{matrix} x_1 & x_2 & s_1 & s_2 & P \end{matrix} \\ \begin{bmatrix} 1 & \frac{1}{2} & \frac{1}{2} & 0 & 0 & 4 \\ 0 & \frac{3}{2} & -\frac{1}{2} & 1 & 0 & 6 \\ \hline 0 & 1 & 3 & 0 & 1 & 24 \end{bmatrix} \end{array}$$

Optimal solution: max $P = 24$ at $x_1 = 4$, $x_2 = 0$.

7.

$$\begin{array}{c} \begin{matrix} x_1 & x_2 & x_3 & s_1 & s_2 & s_3 & P \end{matrix} \\ \begin{bmatrix} 2 & 1 & 3 & -1 & 0 & 0 & 0 & 20 \\ 3 & 0 & 4 & 1 & 1 & 0 & 0 & 30 \\ \fbox{2} & 0 & 5 & 2 & 0 & 1 & 0 & 10 \\ \hline -8 & 0 & -5 & 3 & 0 & 0 & 1 & 50 \end{bmatrix} \end{array} \begin{matrix} \frac{20}{2} = 10 \\ \frac{30}{3} = 10 \\ \frac{10}{2} = 5 \\ \; \end{matrix}$$

pivot row → (third row)
↑
pivot column

The basic variables are x_2, s_2, and s_3, and the nonbasic variables are x_1, x_3, and s_1.

The first column is the pivot column and the third row is the pivot row. The pivot element is circled.

$$\sim \begin{bmatrix} 2 & 1 & 3 & -1 & 0 & 0 & 0 & 20 \\ 3 & 0 & 4 & 1 & 1 & 0 & 0 & 30 \\ 1 & 0 & \frac{5}{2} & 1 & 0 & \frac{1}{2} & 0 & 5 \\ \hline -8 & 0 & -5 & 3 & 0 & 0 & 1 & 50 \end{bmatrix}$$

$R_1 + (-2)R_3 \to R_1$, $R_2 + (-3)R_3 \to R_2$, $R_4 + 8R_3 \to R_4$

$$\sim \begin{bmatrix} 0 & 1 & -2 & -3 & 0 & -1 & 0 & 10 \\ 0 & 0 & -\frac{7}{2} & -2 & 1 & -\frac{3}{2} & 0 & 15 \\ 1 & 0 & \frac{5}{2} & 1 & 0 & \frac{1}{2} & 0 & 5 \\ \hline 0 & 0 & 15 & 11 & 0 & 4 & 1 & 90 \end{bmatrix}$$

8. (A) The obvious basic solution is: $x_1 = 0$, $x_2 = 2$, $s_1 = 0$, $s_2 = 5$, $P = 12$.
         Additional pivoting is required because the last row contains a nega-
         tive indicator.

    (B) The obvious basic solution is: $x_1 = 0$, $x_2 = 0$, $s_1 = 0$, $s_2 = 7$, $P = 22$.
         There is no optimal solution because there are no positive elements
         above the dashed line in the pivot column, column 1.

    (C) The obvious basic solution is: $x_1 = 6$, $x_2 = 0$, $s_1 = 15$, $s_2 = 0$, $P = 10$.
         This is the optimal solution.

9. The feasible region is the solution
    set of the given inequalities and is
    indicated by the shaded region in
    the graph at the right.

    The corner points are $(0, 20)$, $(9, 2)$,
    and $(15, 0)$.

    The value of C at each corner point is:

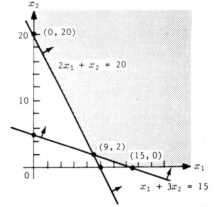

Corner Point	$C = 5x_1 + 2x_2$
$(0, 20)$	$C = 5(0) + 2(20) = 40$
$(9, 2)$	$C = 5(9) + 2(2) = 49$
$(15, 0)$	$C = 5(15) + 2(0) = 75$

The minimum occurs at $x_1 = 0$, $x_2 = 20$, and the minimum value is $C = 40$.

10. The matrices corresponding to the given problem and the dual problem are:

$$A = \begin{bmatrix} 1 & 3 & | & 15 \\ 2 & 1 & | & 20 \\ \hline 5 & 2 & | & 1 \end{bmatrix} \quad \text{and} \quad B = \begin{bmatrix} 1 & 2 & | & 5 \\ 3 & 1 & | & 2 \\ \hline 15 & 20 & | & 1 \end{bmatrix}$$

Thus, the dual problem is: Maximize $P = 15y_1 + 20y_2$

Subject to: $y_1 + 2y_2 \le 5$
             $3y_1 + y_2 \le 2$
             $y_1, y_2 \ge 0$

11. Introduce the slack variables x_1 and x_2 to obtain the initial form:

$$\begin{aligned} y_1 + 2y_2 + x_1 &= 5 \\ 3y_1 + y_2 + x_2 &= 2 \\ -15y_1 - 20y_2 + P &= 0 \end{aligned}$$

12. The first simplex tableau for the dual problem, Problem 10, is:

$$
\begin{array}{ccccc}
y_1 & y_2 & x_1 & x_2 & P \\
\end{array}
$$
$$
\left[
\begin{array}{ccccc|c}
1 & 2 & 1 & 0 & 0 & 5 \\
3 & 1 & 0 & 1 & 0 & 2 \\
\hline
-15 & -20 & 0 & 0 & 1 & 0 \\
\end{array}
\right]
$$

13. Using the simplex method, we have:

$$
\left[
\begin{array}{ccccc|c}
1 & 2 & 1 & 0 & 0 & 5 \\
3 & \boxed{1} & 0 & 1 & 0 & 2 \\
\hline
-15 & -20 & 0 & 0 & 1 & 0 \\
\end{array}
\right]
\begin{array}{l}
\frac{5}{2} = 2.5 \\
\\
\frac{2}{1} = 2 \\
\end{array}
\sim
$$

$$
\begin{array}{ccccc}
y_1 & y_2 & x_1 & x_2 & P \\
\end{array}
$$
$$
\left[
\begin{array}{ccccc|c}
-5 & 0 & 1 & -2 & 0 & 1 \\
3 & 1 & 0 & 1 & 0 & 2 \\
\hline
45 & 0 & 0 & 20 & 1 & 40 \\
\end{array}
\right]
$$

$R_1 + (-2)R_2 \rightarrow R_1$, $R_3 + 20R_2 \rightarrow R_3$

Optimal solution: max $P = 40$ at $y_1 = 0$ and $y_2 = 2$.

14. Minimum $C = 40$ at $x_1 = 0$ and $x_2 = 20$.

15. The feasible region is the solution set of the given inequalities and is indicated by the shading in the graph at the right.

The corner points are $(0, 0)$, $(0, 6)$, $(2, 5)$, $(3, 4)$, and $(5, 0)$.

The value of P at each corner point is:

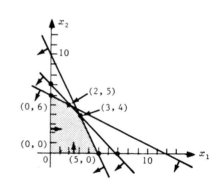

Corner Point	$P = 3x_1 + 4x_2$
$(0, 0)$	$P = 3(0) + 4(0) = 0$
$(0, 6)$	$P = 3(0) + 4(6) = 24$
$(2, 5)$	$P = 3(2) + 4(5) = 26$
$(3, 4)$	$P = 3(3) + 4(4) = 25$
$(5, 0)$	$P = 3(5) + 4(0) = 15$

Thus, the maximum occurs at $x_1 = 2$, $x_2 = 5$, and the maximum value is $P = 26$.

16. We simplify the inequalities and introduce the slack variables s_1, s_2, and s_3 to obtain the equivalent form:

$$
\begin{array}{rrrrrrl}
x_1 & + & 2x_2 & + & s_1 & & = 12 \\
x_1 & + & x_2 & & & + s_2 & = 7 \\
2x_1 & + & x_2 & & & + s_3 & = 10 \\
-3x_1 & - & 4x_2 & & & + P & = 0 \\
\end{array}
$$

The simplex tableau for this problem is:

$$
\begin{array}{cccccc}
x_1 & x_2 & s_1 & s_2 & s_3 & P \\
\end{array}
$$

$$
\left[\begin{array}{cccccc|c}
1 & ② & 1 & 0 & 0 & 0 & 12 \\
1 & 1 & 0 & 1 & 0 & 0 & 7 \\
2 & 1 & 0 & 0 & 1 & 0 & 10 \\
\hline
-3 & -4 & 0 & 0 & 0 & 1 & 0
\end{array}\right]
\quad
\begin{array}{l}
\frac{12}{2} = 6 \\[4pt]
\frac{7}{1} = 7 \\[4pt]
\frac{10}{1} = 10
\end{array}
$$

$\frac{1}{2}R_1 \to R_1$

$$
\left[\begin{array}{cccccc|c}
\frac{1}{2} & 1 & \frac{1}{2} & 0 & 0 & 0 & 6 \\
1 & 1 & 0 & 1 & 0 & 0 & 7 \\
2 & 1 & 0 & 0 & 1 & 0 & 10 \\
\hline
-3 & -4 & 0 & 0 & 0 & 1 & 0
\end{array}\right]
\sim
\left[\begin{array}{cccccc|c}
\frac{1}{2} & 1 & \frac{1}{2} & 0 & 0 & 0 & 6 \\
①/② & 0 & -\frac{1}{2} & 1 & 0 & 0 & 1 \\
\frac{3}{2} & 0 & -\frac{1}{2} & 0 & 1 & 0 & 4 \\
\hline
-1 & 0 & 2 & 0 & 0 & 1 & 24
\end{array}\right]
\quad
\begin{array}{l}
\frac{6}{1/2} = 12 \\[4pt]
\frac{1}{1/2} = 2 \\[4pt]
\frac{4}{3/2} \approx 2.67
\end{array}
$$

$R_2 + (-1)R_1 \to R_2,$
$R_3 + (-1)R_1 \to R_3,$ and
$R_4 + 4R_1 \to R_4$

$2R_2 \to R_2$

$$
\begin{array}{cccccc}
x_1 & x_2 & s_1 & s_2 & s_3 & P \\
\end{array}
$$

$$
\left[\begin{array}{cccccc|c}
\frac{1}{2} & 1 & \frac{1}{2} & 0 & 0 & 0 & 6 \\
① & 0 & -1 & 2 & 0 & 0 & 2 \\
\frac{3}{2} & 0 & -\frac{1}{2} & 0 & 1 & 0 & 4 \\
\hline
-1 & 0 & 2 & 0 & 0 & 1 & 24
\end{array}\right]
\sim
\left[\begin{array}{cccccc|c}
0 & 1 & 1 & -1 & 0 & 0 & 5 \\
1 & 0 & -1 & 2 & 0 & 0 & 2 \\
0 & 0 & 1 & -3 & 1 & 0 & 1 \\
\hline
0 & 0 & 1 & 2 & 0 & 1 & 26
\end{array}\right]
$$

$R_1 + \left(-\frac{1}{2}\right)R_2 \to R_1,$

$R_3 + \left(-\frac{3}{2}\right)R_2 \to R_3,$ and $R_4 + R_2 \to R_4$

Optimal solution: max $P = 26$ at
$x_1 = 2,\ x_2 = 5.$

17. The feasible region is the solution
set of the given inequalities and
is indicated by the shaded region
in the graph at the right.

The corner points are $(0, 10)$, $(5, 5)$,
and $(9, 3)$.

The value of C at each corner point is:

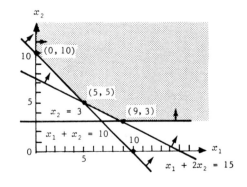

Corner Point	$C = 3x_1 + 8x_2$
$(0, 10)$	$C = 3(0) + 8(10) = 80$
$(5, 5)$	$C = 3(5) + 8(5) = 55$
$(9, 3)$	$C = 3(9) + 8(3) = 51$

Thus, the minimum occurs at $x_1 = 9$, $x_2 = 3$, and the minimum value is $C = 51$.

18. The matrices corresponding to the given problem and the dual problem are:

$$A = \begin{bmatrix} 1 & 1 & 10 \\ 1 & 2 & 15 \\ 0 & 1 & 3 \\ 3 & 8 & 1 \end{bmatrix} \quad \text{and} \quad B = \begin{bmatrix} 1 & 1 & 0 & 3 \\ 1 & 2 & 1 & 8 \\ 10 & 15 & 3 & 1 \end{bmatrix}$$

Thus, the dual problem is:

Maximize $P = 10y_1 + 15y_2 + 3y_3$

Subject to:
$$y_1 + y_2 \leqslant 3$$
$$y_1 + 2y_2 + y_3 \leqslant 8$$
$$y_1, y_2, y_3 \geqslant 0$$

19. Introduce the slack variables x_1 and x_2 to obtain the initial form:

$$y_1 + y_2 + x_1 = 3$$
$$y_1 + 2y_2 + y_3 + x_2 = 8$$
$$-10y_1 - 15y_2 - 3y_3 + P = 0$$

The simplex tableau for this problem is:

$$\begin{bmatrix} y_1 & y_2 & y_3 & x_1 & x_2 & P & \\ 1 & \textcircled{1} & 0 & 1 & 0 & 0 & 3 \\ 1 & 2 & 1 & 0 & 1 & 0 & 8 \\ \hline -10 & -15 & -3 & 0 & 0 & 1 & 0 \end{bmatrix} \quad \begin{array}{l} \frac{3}{1} = 3 \\[4pt] \frac{8}{2} = 4 \end{array}$$

$R_2 + (-2)R_1 \to R_2$ and $R_3 + 15R_1 \to R_3$

$$\sim \begin{bmatrix} 1 & 1 & 0 & 1 & 0 & 0 & 3 \\ -1 & 0 & \textcircled{1} & -2 & 1 & 0 & 2 \\ \hline 5 & 0 & -3 & 15 & 0 & 1 & 45 \end{bmatrix} \sim \begin{bmatrix} y_1 & y_2 & y_3 & x_1 & x_2 & P & \\ 1 & 1 & 0 & 1 & 0 & 0 & 3 \\ -1 & 0 & 1 & -2 & 1 & 0 & 2 \\ \hline 2 & 0 & 0 & 9 & 3 & 1 & 51 \end{bmatrix}$$

$R_3 + 3R_2 \to R_3$

Optimal solution: min $C = 51$ at $x_1 = 9$, $x_2 = 3$.

20. Introduce slack variables s_1 and s_2 to obtain the initial form:

$$x_1 - x_2 - 2x_3 + s_1 = 3$$
$$2x_1 + 2x_2 - 5x_3 + s_2 = 10$$
$$-5x_1 - 3x_2 + 3x_3 + P = 0$$

The simplex tableau for this problem is:

$$
\begin{array}{cccccc}
x_1 & x_2 & x_3 & s_1 & s_2 & P \\
\end{array}
$$

$$
\left[\begin{array}{cccccc|c}
\boxed{1} & -1 & -2 & 1 & 0 & 0 & 3 \\
2 & 2 & -5 & 0 & 1 & 0 & 10 \\
\hline
-5 & -3 & 3 & 0 & 0 & 1 & 0
\end{array}\right]
\quad
\begin{array}{l}
\frac{3}{1} = 3 \\[4pt]
\frac{10}{2} = 5
\end{array}
\sim
\left[\begin{array}{cccccc|c}
1 & -1 & -2 & 1 & 0 & 0 & 3 \\
0 & \boxed{4} & -1 & -2 & 1 & 0 & 4 \\
\hline
0 & -8 & -7 & 5 & 0 & 1 & 15
\end{array}\right]
$$

$R_2 + (-2)R_1 \rightarrow R_2$ and
$R_3 + 5R_1 \rightarrow R_3$

$\frac{1}{4}R_2 \rightarrow R_2$

$$
\begin{array}{cccccc}
 & & & & & \\
\end{array}
$$

$$
\sim
\left[\begin{array}{cccccc|c}
1 & -1 & -2 & 1 & 0 & 0 & 3 \\
0 & \boxed{1} & -\frac{1}{4} & -\frac{1}{2} & \frac{1}{4} & 0 & 1 \\
\hline
0 & -8 & -7 & 5 & 0 & 1 & 15
\end{array}\right]
\sim
\begin{array}{cccccc}
x_1 & x_2 & x_3 & s_1 & s_2 & P \\
\end{array}
$$

$$
\left[\begin{array}{cccccc|c}
1 & 0 & -\frac{9}{4} & \frac{1}{2} & \frac{1}{4} & 0 & 4 \\
0 & 1 & -\frac{1}{4} & -\frac{1}{2} & \frac{1}{4} & 0 & 1 \\
\hline
0 & 0 & -9 & 1 & 2 & 1 & 23
\end{array}\right]
$$

$R_1 + R_2 \rightarrow R_1$ and $R_3 + 8R_2 \rightarrow R_3$

No optimal solution exists; the elements in the pivot column (the x_3 column) above the dashed line are negative.

21. Introduce slack variables s_1 and s_2 to obtain the equivalent form:

$$
\begin{array}{rcl}
x_1 - x_2 - 2x_3 + s_1 & = & 3 \\
x_1 + x_2 \qquad\quad + s_2 & = & 10 \\
-5x_1 - 3x_2 + 3x_3 \qquad\quad + P & = & 0
\end{array}
$$

The simplex tableau for this problem is:

$$
\begin{array}{cccccc}
x_1 & x_2 & x_3 & s_1 & s_2 & P \\
\end{array}
$$

$$
\left[\begin{array}{cccccc|c}
\boxed{1} & -1 & -2 & 1 & 0 & 0 & 3 \\
1 & 1 & 0 & 0 & 1 & 0 & 5 \\
\hline
-5 & -3 & 3 & 0 & 0 & 1 & 0
\end{array}\right]
\quad
\begin{array}{l}
\frac{3}{1} = 3 \\[4pt]
\frac{10}{1} = 10
\end{array}
\sim
\left[\begin{array}{cccccc|c}
1 & -1 & -2 & 1 & 0 & 0 & 3 \\
0 & \boxed{2} & 2 & -1 & 1 & 0 & 2 \\
\hline
0 & -8 & -7 & 5 & 0 & 1 & 15
\end{array}\right]
$$

$R_2 + (-1)R_1 \rightarrow R_2$ and $R_3 + 5R_1 \rightarrow R_3$

$\frac{1}{2}R_2 \rightarrow R_2$

$$
\sim
\left[\begin{array}{cccccc|c}
1 & -1 & -2 & 1 & 0 & 0 & 3 \\
0 & 1 & 1 & -\frac{1}{2} & \frac{1}{2} & 0 & 1 \\
\hline
0 & -8 & -7 & 5 & 0 & 1 & 15
\end{array}\right]
\sim
\begin{array}{cccccc}
x_1 & x_2 & x_3 & s_1 & s_2 & P \\
\end{array}
$$

$$
\left[\begin{array}{cccccc|c}
1 & 0 & -1 & \frac{1}{2} & \frac{1}{2} & 0 & 4 \\
0 & 1 & 1 & -\frac{1}{2} & \frac{1}{2} & 0 & 1 \\
\hline
0 & 0 & 1 & 1 & 4 & 1 & 23
\end{array}\right]
$$

$R_1 + R_2 \rightarrow R_1$ and
$R_3 + 8R_2 \rightarrow R_3$

Optimal solution: max $P = 23$ at $x_1 = 4$, $x_2 = 1$, $x_3 = 0$.

22. Multiply the first constraint inequality by −1 to transform it into a ⩾ inequality. The problem now is:

Minimize $C = 2x_1 + 3x_2$

Subject to:
$$-2x_1 - x_2 \geqslant -20$$
$$2x_1 + x_2 \geqslant 10$$
$$x_1 + 2x_2 \geqslant 8$$
$$x_1, x_2 \geqslant 0$$

The matrices corresponding to this problem and its dual are, respectively:

$$A = \left[\begin{array}{cc|c} -2 & -1 & -20 \\ 2 & 1 & 10 \\ 1 & 2 & 8 \\ \hline 2 & 3 & 1 \end{array}\right] \quad \text{and} \quad B = \left[\begin{array}{ccc|c} -2 & 2 & 1 & 2 \\ -1 & 1 & 2 & 3 \\ \hline -20 & 10 & 8 & 1 \end{array}\right]$$

Thus, the dual problem is:

Maximize $P = -20y_1 + 10y_2 + 8y_3$

Subject to:
$$-2y_1 + 2y_2 + y_3 \leqslant 2$$
$$-y_1 + y_2 + 2y_3 \leqslant 3$$
$$y_1, y_2, y_3 \geqslant 0$$

We introduce the slack variables x_1 and x_2 to obtain the initial form for the dual problem:

$$-2y_1 + 2y_2 + y_3 + x_1 \qquad = 2$$
$$-y_1 + y_2 + 2y_3 \qquad + x_2 \qquad = 3$$
$$20y_1 - 10y_2 - 8y_3 \qquad\qquad + P = 0$$

The simplex tableau for this problem is:

$$\begin{array}{cccccc} y_1 & y_2 & y_3 & x_1 & x_2 & P \end{array}$$

$$\left[\begin{array}{cccccc|c} -2 & ② & 1 & 1 & 0 & 0 & 2 \\ -1 & 1 & 2 & 0 & 1 & 0 & 3 \\ \hline 20 & -10 & -8 & 0 & 0 & 1 & 0 \end{array}\right] \begin{array}{l} \frac{2}{2} = 1 \\ \frac{3}{1} = 3 \end{array} \sim \left[\begin{array}{cccccc|c} -1 & 1 & \frac{1}{2} & \frac{1}{2} & 0 & 0 & 1 \\ -1 & 1 & 2 & 0 & 1 & 0 & 3 \\ \hline 20 & -10 & -8 & 0 & 0 & 1 & 0 \end{array}\right]$$

$$\tfrac{1}{2}R_1 \to R_1 \qquad\qquad\qquad\qquad\qquad\qquad R_2 + (-1)R_1 \to R_2$$
$$R_3 + 10R_1 \to R_3$$

$$\sim \left[\begin{array}{cccccc|c} -1 & 1 & \frac{1}{2} & \frac{1}{2} & 0 & 0 & 1 \\ 0 & 0 & ③\!\!/\!\!② & -\frac{1}{2} & 1 & 0 & 2 \\ \hline 10 & 0 & -3 & 5 & 0 & 1 & 10 \end{array}\right] \sim \left[\begin{array}{cccccc|c} -1 & 1 & \frac{1}{2} & \frac{1}{2} & 0 & 0 & 1 \\ 0 & 0 & ① & -\frac{1}{3} & \frac{2}{3} & 0 & \frac{4}{3} \\ \hline 10 & 0 & -3 & 5 & 0 & 1 & 10 \end{array}\right]$$

$$\tfrac{2}{3}R_2 \to R_2 \qquad\qquad\qquad R_1 + \left(-\tfrac{1}{2}\right)R_2 \to R_1, \ R_3 + 3R_2 \to R_3$$

(continued)

$$\begin{array}{cccccc|c}
y_1 & y_2 & y_3 & x_1 & x_2 & P & \\
\hline
-1 & 1 & 0 & \dfrac{2}{3} & -\dfrac{1}{3} & 0 & \dfrac{1}{3} \\
0 & 0 & 1 & -\dfrac{1}{3} & \dfrac{2}{3} & 0 & \dfrac{4}{3} \\
\hline
10 & 0 & 0 & 4 & 2 & 1 & 14
\end{array}$$

Optimal solution: min $C = 14$ at $x = 4$ and $x = 2$.

23. Multiply the first two constraint inequalities by -1 to transform them into $\geqslant$ inequalities. The problem now is:

$$\text{Minimize } C = 15x_1 + 12x_2 + 15x_3 + 18x_4$$

Subject to:
$$\begin{aligned}
-x_1 - x_2 && \geqslant -240 \\
- x_3 - x_4 & \geqslant -500 \\
x_1 \quad + x_3 && \geqslant 400 \\
x_2 \quad + x_4 & \geqslant 300 \\
x_1, \ x_2, \ x_3, \ x_4 & \geqslant 0
\end{aligned}$$

The matrices corresponding to this problem and its dual are, respectively:

$$A = \begin{bmatrix}
-1 & -1 & 0 & 0 & -240 \\
0 & 0 & -1 & -1 & -500 \\
1 & 0 & 1 & 0 & 400 \\
0 & 1 & 0 & 1 & 300 \\
15 & 12 & 15 & 18 & 1
\end{bmatrix}
\quad \text{and} \quad
B = \begin{bmatrix}
-1 & 0 & 1 & 0 & 15 \\
-1 & 0 & 0 & 1 & 12 \\
0 & -1 & 1 & 0 & 15 \\
0 & -1 & 0 & 1 & 18 \\
-240 & -500 & 400 & 300 & 1
\end{bmatrix}$$

Thus, the dual problem is:

$$\text{Maximize } P = -240y_1 - 500y_2 + 400y_3 + 300y_4$$

Subject to:
$$\begin{aligned}
-y_1 \quad + y_3 && \leqslant 15 \\
-y_1 \quad + y_4 & \leqslant 12 \\
- y_2 + y_3 && \leqslant 15 \\
- y_2 \quad + y_4 & \leqslant 18 \\
y_1, \ y_2, \ y_3, \ y_4 & \geqslant 0
\end{aligned}$$

We introduce the slack variables x_1, x_2, x_3, and x_4 to obtain the initial form for the dual problem:

$$\begin{aligned}
-y_1 \quad + y_3 \quad + x_1 \qquad\qquad\qquad\qquad &= 15 \\
-y_1 \qquad + y_4 \qquad + x_2 \qquad\qquad &= 12 \\
- y_2 + y_3 \qquad\qquad + x_3 \qquad &= 15 \\
- y_2 \qquad + y_4 \qquad\qquad + x_4 &= 18 \\
240y_1 + 500y_2 - 400y_3 - 300y_4 \qquad\qquad + P &= 0
\end{aligned}$$

The simplex tableau for this problem is:

$$
\begin{array}{ccccccccc|c}
y_1 & y_2 & y_3 & y_4 & x_1 & x_2 & x_3 & x_4 & P & \\
-1 & 0 & \boxed{1} & 0 & 1 & 0 & 0 & 0 & 0 & 15 \\
-1 & 0 & 0 & 1 & 0 & 1 & 0 & 0 & 0 & 12 \\
0 & .-1 & 1 & 0 & 0 & 0 & 1 & 0 & 0 & 15 \\
0 & -1 & 0 & 1 & 0 & 0 & 0 & 1 & 0 & 18 \\
\hline
240 & 500 & -400 & -300 & 0 & 0 & 0 & 0 & 1 & 0
\end{array}
$$

$\dfrac{15}{1} = 15$ (row 1)

$\dfrac{15}{1} = 15$ (row 3)

$R_3 + (-1)R_1 \rightarrow R_3$
$R_5 + 400\, R_1 \rightarrow R_5$

[Note: Either element can be chosen as the pivot; we choose the element in the first row.]

$$
\sim
\begin{array}{ccccccccc|c}
-1 & 0 & 1 & 0 & 1 & 0 & 0 & 0 & 0 & 15 \\
-1 & 0 & 0 & \boxed{1} & 0 & 1 & 0 & 0 & 0 & 12 \\
1 & -1 & 0 & 0 & -1 & 0 & 1 & 0 & 0 & 0 \\
0 & -1 & 0 & 1 & 0 & 0 & 0 & 1 & 0 & 18 \\
\hline
-160 & 500 & 0 & -300 & 400 & 0 & 0 & 0 & 1 & 6000
\end{array}
$$

$R_4 + (-1)R_2 \rightarrow R_4, \quad R_5 + 300R_2 \rightarrow R_5$

$$
\sim
\begin{array}{ccccccccc|c}
-1 & 0 & 1 & 0 & 1 & 0 & 0 & 0 & 0 & 15 \\
-1 & 0 & 0 & 1 & 0 & 1 & 0 & 0 & 0 & 12 \\
\boxed{1} & -1 & 0 & 0 & -1 & 0 & 1 & 0 & 0 & 0 \\
1 & -1 & 0 & 0 & 0 & -1 & 0 & 1 & 0 & 6 \\
\hline
-460 & 500 & 0 & 0 & 400 & 300 & 0 & 0 & 1 & 9600
\end{array}
$$

$R_1 + R_3 \rightarrow R_1, \quad R_2 + R_3 \rightarrow R_2$
$R_4 + (-1)R_3 \rightarrow R_4, \quad R_5 + 460R_3 \rightarrow R_5$

(continued)

$$\sim \begin{bmatrix} -1 & 0 & 1 & 0 & 0 & 0 & 0 & 0 & 0 & | & 15 \\ -1 & 0 & 0 & 1 & 0 & 1 & 0 & 0 & 0 & | & 12 \\ 1 & -1 & 0 & 0 & -1 & 0 & 1 & 0 & 0 & | & 0 \\ 1 & -1 & 0 & 0 & 0 & -1 & 0 & 1 & 0 & | & 6 \\ \hline -460 & 500 & 0 & 0 & 400 & 300 & 0 & 0 & 1 & | & 9600 \end{bmatrix}$$

$$\sim \begin{bmatrix} 0 & -1 & 1 & 0 & 0 & 0 & 1 & 0 & 0 & | & 15 \\ 0 & -1 & 0 & 1 & -1 & 1 & 1 & 0 & 0 & | & 12 \\ 1 & -1 & 0 & 0 & -1 & 0 & 1 & 0 & 0 & | & 0 \\ 0 & 0 & 0 & 0 & \boxed{1} & -1 & -1 & 1 & 0 & | & 6 \\ \hline 0 & 40 & 0 & 0 & -60 & 300 & 460 & 0 & 1 & | & 9600 \end{bmatrix}$$

$R_5 + 60R_4 \rightarrow R_5$

$$\sim \begin{matrix} y_1 & y_2 & y_3 & y_4 & x_1 & x_2 & x_3 & x_4 & P & & \\ \begin{bmatrix} 0 & -1 & 1 & 0 & 0 & 0 & 1 & 0 & 0 & | & 15 \\ 0 & -1 & 0 & 1 & -1 & 1 & 1 & 0 & 0 & | & 12 \\ 1 & -1 & 0 & 0 & -1 & 0 & 1 & 0 & 0 & | & 0 \\ 0 & 0 & 0 & 0 & 1 & -1 & -1 & 1 & 0 & | & 6 \\ \hline 0 & 40 & 0 & 0 & 0 & 240 & 400 & 60 & 1 & | & 9960 \end{bmatrix} \end{matrix}$$

Optimal solution: min $C = 9960$ at $x_1 = 0$, $x_2 = 240$, $x_3 = 400$, $x_4 = 60$.

24. Let x_1 = the number of regular sails
and x_2 = the number of competition sails.
The mathematical model for this problem is: Maximize $P = 100x_1 + 200x_2$

Subject to: $2x_1 + 3x_2 \leqslant 150$
$4x_1 + 9x_2 \leqslant 360$
$x_1, \ x_2 \geqslant 0$

25. Let x_1 = the number of motors from A to X,
x_2 = the number of motors from A to Y,
x_3 = the number of motors from A to Z,
x_4 = the number of motors from B to X,
x_5 = the number of motors from B to Y,
x_6 = the number of motors from B to Z.

The mathematical model for this problem is:

Minimize $C = 5x_1 + 8x_2 + 12x_3 + 9x_4 + 7x_5 + 6x_6$

Subject to:
$$
\begin{aligned}
x_1 + x_2 + x_3 &\leqslant 1500 \\
x_4 + x_5 + x_6 &\leqslant 1000 \\
x_1 \qquad\qquad + x_4 &\geqslant 500 \\
x_2 \qquad\qquad + x_5 &\geqslant 700 \\
x_3 \qquad\qquad + x_6 &\geqslant 800 \\
x_1, \; x_2, \; x_3, \; x_4, \; x_5, \; x_6 &\geqslant 0
\end{aligned}
$$

26. Let x_1 = the number of grams of mix A
and x_2 = the number of grams of mix B.

The mathematical model for this problem is:

Minimize $C = 0.02x_1 + 0.04x_2$

Subject to:
$$
\begin{aligned}
3x_1 + 4x_2 &\geqslant 300 \\
2x_1 + 5x_2 &\geqslant 200 \\
6x_1 + 10x_2 &\geqslant 900 \\
x_1, \; x_2 &\geqslant 0
\end{aligned}
$$

CHAPTER 3   MATHEMATICS OF FINANCE

Things to remember:

1. SIMPLE INTEREST

$I = Prt$

where P = Principal
r = Annual simple interest rate expressed
     as a decimal
t = Time in years

2. AMOUNT—SIMPLE INTEREST

$A = P + Prt = P(1 + rt)$

where P = Principal or *present value*
r = Annual simple interest rate expressed
     as a decimal
t = Time in years
A = Amount or *future value*

---

1. $P = \$500$, $r = 8\% = 0.08$, $t = 6$ months $= \dfrac{1}{2}$ year

$I = Prt$ (using **1**)

$= 500(0.08)\left(\dfrac{1}{2}\right) = \$20$

3. $I = \$80$, $P = \$500$, $t = 2$ years

$I = Prt$

$r = \dfrac{I}{Pt} = \dfrac{80}{500(2)} = 0.08$ or 8%

5. $P = \$100$, $r = 8\% = 0.08$,

   $t = 18$ months $= 1.5$ years

   $A = P(1 + rt)$

      $= 100(1 + 0.08 \cdot 1.5) = \$112$

7. $A = \$1000$, $r = 10\% = 0.1$

   $t = 15$ months $= \dfrac{15}{12}$ years

   $A = P(1 + rt)$

   $P = \dfrac{A}{1 + rt} = \dfrac{1000}{1 + (0.1)\left(\dfrac{15}{12}\right)} = \$888.89$

9. $I = Prt$

   Divide both sides by Pt.

   $\dfrac{I}{Pt} = \dfrac{Prt}{Pt}$

   $\dfrac{I}{Pt} = r$ or $r = \dfrac{I}{Pt}$.

11. $A = P + Prt = P(1 + rt)$

   Divide both sides by $(1 + rt)$.

   $\dfrac{A}{1 + rt} = \dfrac{P(1 + rt)}{1 + rt}$

   $\dfrac{A}{1 + rt} = P$ or $P = \dfrac{A}{1 + rt}$

13. $P = \$3000$, $r = 14\% = 0.14$,

   $t = 4$ months $= \dfrac{1}{3}$ year

   $I = Prt$

      $= 3000(0.14)\left(\dfrac{1}{3}\right) = \$140$

15. $P = \$554$, $r = 20\% = 0.2$,

   $t = 1$ month $= \dfrac{1}{12}$ year

   $I = Prt$

      $= 554(0.2)\left(\dfrac{1}{12}\right) = \$9.23$

17. $P = \$7250$, $r = 9\% = 0.09$, $t = 8$ months $= \dfrac{2}{3}$ year

   $A = 7250\left[1 + 0.09\left(\dfrac{2}{3}\right)\right] = 7250[1.06] = \$7685.00$

19. $P = \$4000$, $A = \$4270$, $t = 8$ months $= \dfrac{2}{3}$ year

   The interest on the loan is $I = A - P = \$270$. From Problem 9,

   $r = \dfrac{I}{Pt} = \dfrac{270}{4000\left(\dfrac{2}{3}\right)} = 0.10125$. Thus, $r = 10.125\%$.

21. $P = \$1000$, $I = \$30$, $t = 60$ days $= \dfrac{1}{6}$ year

   $r = \dfrac{I}{Pt} = \dfrac{30}{1000\left(\dfrac{1}{6}\right)} = 0.18$

   Thus, $r = 18\%$.

23. $P = \$1500$, $I = (0.5)(3)(120) = \$180$, $t = 120$ days $= \dfrac{1}{3}$ year

   $r = \dfrac{I}{Pt} = \dfrac{180}{1500\left(\dfrac{1}{3}\right)} = 0.36$

   Thus, $r = 36\%$.

25. $P = \$9776.94$, $A = \$10,000$, $t = 13$ weeks $= \dfrac{1}{4}$ year

   The interest is $I = A - P = \$223.06$.

(continued)

$$r = \frac{I}{Pt} = \frac{223.06}{9776.94\left(\frac{1}{4}\right)} = 0.09126$$

Thus, $r = 9.126\%$.

27. $A = \$10,000$, $r = 12.63\% = 0.1263$, $t = 13$ weeks $= \frac{1}{4}$ year.

From Problem 11, $P = \dfrac{A}{1 + rt} = \dfrac{10,000}{1 + (0.1263)\frac{1}{4}} = \dfrac{10,000}{1.03158} = \$9693.91$.

29. The interest I on a principal $P = \$5500$ at an interest rate $r = 12\% = 0.12$ for $t = 90$ days $= 1/4$ year is:

$$I = Prt = 5500(0.12)\left(\frac{1}{4}\right) = \$165$$

The third party will receive \$165 in interest on a principal of \$5500 for $t = 60$ days $= 1/6$ year. Thus,

$$r = \frac{I}{Pt} = \frac{165}{5500\left(\frac{1}{6}\right)} = 0.18 \text{ or } r = 18\%.$$

31. The principal P is the cost of the stock plus the broker's commission. The cost of the stock is $500(14.20) = \$7,100$ and the commission on this is $62 + (0.003)7100 = \$83.30$. Thus, $P = \$7183.30$. The investor sells the stock for $500(16.84) = \$8420$, and the commission on this amount is $62 + (0.003)8420 = 87.26$. Thus, the investor has $8420 - 87.26 = \$8332.74$ after selling the stock. We can now conclude that the investor has earned $8332.74 - 7183.30 = \$1149.44$.

Now, $P = \$7183.30$, $I = \$1149.44$, $t = 39$ weeks $= \frac{3}{4}$ year. Therefore,

$$r = \frac{I}{Pt} = \frac{1149.44}{7183.30\left(\frac{3}{4}\right)} = 0.21335 \text{ or } r = 21.335\%.$$

EXERCISE 3-2

Things to remember:

1. AMOUNT—COMPOUND INTEREST

$$A = P(1 + i)^n, \text{ where } i = \frac{r}{m} \text{ and}$$

r = Annual (quoted) rate
m = Number of compounding periods per year
n = Total number of compounding periods
i = Rate per compounding period
P = Principal (present value)
A = Amount (future value) at end of n periods

2. EFFECTIVE RATE

If principal P is invested at the (nominal) rate r, compounded m times per year, then the effective rate, r_e, is given by

$$r_e = \left(1 + \frac{r}{m}\right)^m - 1.$$

---

1. $P = \$100$, $i = 0.01$, $n = 12$

Using 1,

$$\begin{aligned} A = P(1 + i)^n &= 100(1 + 0.01)^{12} \\ &= 100(1.01)^{12} \\ &= \$112.68 \end{aligned}$$

3. $P = \$800$, $i = 0.06$, $n = 25$

Using 1,

$$\begin{aligned} A &= 800(1 + 0.06)^{25} \\ &= 800(1.06)^{25} \\ &= \$3433.50 \end{aligned}$$

5. $A = \$10,000$, $i = 0.03$, $n = 48$

Using 1,

$$A = P(1 + i)^n$$

$$P = \frac{A}{(1 + i)^n} = \frac{10,000}{(1 + 0.03)^{48}}$$

$$= \frac{10,000}{(1.03)^{48}} = \$2419.99$$

7. $A = \$18,000$, $i = 0.01$, $n = 90$

Refer to Problem 5:

$$P = \frac{A}{(1 + i)^n} = \frac{18,000}{(1 + 0.01)^{90}}$$

$$= \frac{18,000}{(1.01)^{90}} = \$7351.04$$

9. $P = \$100$, $r = 6\% = 0.06$

(A) $m = 1$, $i = 0.06$, $n = 4$

$$\begin{aligned} A &= (1 + i)^n \\ &= 100(1 + 0.06)^4 \\ &= 100(1.06)^4 = \$126.25 \end{aligned}$$

Interest $= 126.25 - 100$
$ = \$26.25$

(B) $m = 4$, $i = \dfrac{0.06}{4} = 0.015$,

$n = 4(4) = 16$

$$A = 100(1 + 0.015)^{16} = 100(1.015)^{16}$$
$$= \$126.90$$

Interest $= 126.90 - 100$
$ = \$26.90$

(C) $m = 12$, $i = \dfrac{0.06}{12} = 0.005$, $n = 4(12) = 48$

$$\begin{aligned} A = 100(1 + 0.005)^{48} &= 100(1.005)^{48} \\ &= \$127.05 \end{aligned}$$

Interest $= 127.05 - 100$
$ = \$27.05$

11. $P = \$5000$, $r = 18\% = 0.18$, $m = 12$

(A) $n = 2(12) = 24$

$$i = \frac{0.18}{12} = 0.015$$

$$\begin{aligned} A &= 5000(1 + 0.015)^{24} \\ &= 5000(1.015)^{24} = \$7147.51 \end{aligned}$$

(B) $n = 4(12) = 48$

$$i = \frac{0.18}{12} = 0.015$$

$$\begin{aligned} A &= 5000(1 + 0.015)^{48} \\ &= 5000(1.015)^{48} \\ &= \$10,217.39 \end{aligned}$$

13. $A = \$10,000,\ r = 8\% = 0.08,\ i = \dfrac{0.08}{2} = 0.04$

(A) $n = 2(5) = 10$

$$A = P(1 + i)^n$$
$$10,000 = P(1 + 0.04)^{10}$$
$$= P(1.04)^{10}$$
$$P = \frac{10,000}{(1.04)^{10}} = \$6755.64$$

(B) $n = 2(10) = 20$

$$P = \frac{A}{(1 + i)^n} = \frac{10,000}{(1 + 0.04)^{20}}$$
$$= \frac{10,000}{(1.04)^{20}} = \$4563.87$$

15. Use the formula for r_e in $\underline{2}$.

(A) $r = 10\% = 0.1,\ m = 4$

$$r_e = \left(1 + \frac{0.1}{4}\right)^4 - 1 = 0.1038$$
$$\text{or } 10.38\%$$

(B) $r = 12\% = 0.12,\ m = 12$

$$r_e = \left(1 + \frac{0.12}{12}\right)^{12} - 1 = 0.1268$$
$$\text{or } 12.68\%$$

17. We have $P = \$4000,\ A = \$9000,\ r = 15\% = 0.15,\ m = 12,$ and $i = \dfrac{0.15}{12} = 0.0125.$ Since $A = P(1 + i)^n$, we have:

$$9000 = 4000(1 + 0.0125)^n \text{ or } (1.0125)^n = 2.25$$

<u>Method 1</u>: Use Table V. Look down the $(1 + i)^n$ column on the page that has $i = 0.0125$. Find the value of n in this column that is closest to and greater than 2.25. In this case, $n = 66$ months or 5 years and 6 months.

<u>Method 2</u>: Use logarithms and a calculator.

$$\ln(1.0125)^n = \ln 2.25$$
$$n \ln 1.0125 = \ln 2.25$$
$$n = \frac{\ln 2.25}{\ln 1.0125} \approx \frac{0.8109}{0.01242} \approx 65.29$$

Thus, $n = 66$ months or 5 years and 6 months.

19. $A = 2P,\ i = 0.06$

$$A = P(1 + i)^n$$
$$2P = P(1 + 0.06)^n$$
$$(1.06)^n = 2$$
$$\ln(1.06)^n = \ln 2$$
$$n \ln(1.06) = \ln 2$$
$$n = \frac{\ln 2}{\ln 1.06} \approx \frac{0.6931}{0.0583} \approx 11.9$$

MATHEMATICS OF FINANCE

21. We have $A = P(1 + i)^n$. To find the doubling time, set $A = 2P$. This yields:

$2P = P(1 + i)^n$ or $(1 + i)^n = 2$

Taking the natural logarithm of both sides, we obtain:

$\ln(1 + i)^n = \ln 2$
$n \ln(1 + i) = \ln 2$

and

$$n = \frac{\ln 2}{\ln(1 + i)} \approx \frac{0.6931}{\ln(1 + i)}$$

(A) $r = 10\% = 0.1$, $m = 4$. Thus,

$$i = \frac{0.1}{4} = 0.025 \quad \text{and} \quad n = \frac{0.6931}{\ln(1.025)} \approx 28.07 \text{ quarters or 7 years}$$

(B) $r = 12\% = 0.12$, $m = 4$. Thus,

$$i = \frac{0.12}{4} = 0.03 \quad \text{and} \quad n = \frac{0.6931}{\ln(1.03)} \approx 23.44 \text{ quarters}$$

That is, 24 quarters or 6 years.

23. $P = \$5000$, $r = 9\% = 0.09$, $m = 4$, $i = \dfrac{0.09}{4} = 0.0225$, $n = 17(4) = 68$

Thus, $A = P(1 + i)^n$
$= 5000(1 + 0.0225)^{68}$
$= 5000(1.0225)^{68}$
$= \$22,702.60$

25. $P = \$110,000$, $r = 6\%$ or 0.06, $m = 1$, $i = 0.06$, $n = 10$

Thus, $A = P(1 + i)^n$
$= 110,000(1 + 0.06)^{10}$
$= 110,000(1.06)^{10}$
$\approx \$196,993.25$

27. $A = \$20$, $r = 7\% = 0.07$, $m = 1$, $i = 0.07$, $n = 5$

$A = P(1 + i)^n$

$$P = \frac{A}{(1 + i)^n} = \frac{20}{(1.07)^5} \approx \$14.26 \text{ per square foot per month}$$

29. From Problem 21, the doubling time is:

$$n = \frac{\ln 2}{\ln(1 + i)} \approx \frac{0.6931}{\ln(1 + i)}$$

Here $r = i = 0.04$. Thus,

$$n = \frac{0.6931}{\ln(1.04)} \approx 17.67 \text{ or 18 years}$$

31. The effective rate, r_e, of $r = 9\% = 0.09$ compounded monthly is:

$$r_e = \left(1 + \frac{0.09}{12}\right)^{12} - 1 = .0938 \text{ or } 9.38\%$$

The effective rate of 9.3% compounded annually is 9.3%. Thus, 9% compounded monthly is better than 9.3% compounded annually.

33. $P = \$7000$, $A = \$9000$, $r = 9\% = 0.09$, $m = 12$, $i = \frac{0.09}{12} = 0.0075$

Since $A = P(1 + i)^n$, we have:

$$9000 = 7000(1 + 0.0075)^n \text{ or } (1.0075)^n = \frac{9}{7}$$

Therefore, $\ln(1.0075)^n = \ln\left(\frac{9}{7}\right)$

$$n \ln(1.0075) = \ln\left(\frac{9}{7}\right)$$

$$n = \frac{\ln\left(\frac{9}{7}\right)}{\ln(1.0075)} \approx \frac{0.2513}{0.0075} \approx 33.6$$

Thus, it will take 34 months or 2 years and 10 months.

35. $P = \$20,000$, $r = 8\% = 0.08$, $m = 365$, $i = \frac{0.08}{365} \approx 0.0002192$, $n = (365)35 = 12,775$

Since $A = P(1 + i)^n$, we have:

$$A = 20,000(1.000219)^{12,775} \approx \$328,791.70$$

37. From Problem 21, the doubling time is:

$$n = \frac{\ln 2}{\ln(1 + i)} \approx \frac{0.6931}{\ln(1 + i)}$$

(A) $r = 14\% = 0.14$, $m = 365$, $i = \frac{0.14}{365}$ 0.0003836

Thus, $n = \dfrac{0.6931}{\ln(1.0003836)} \approx 1807.18$ days or 4.952 years.

(B) $r = 15\% = 0.15$, $m = 1$, $i = 0.15$

Thus, $n = \dfrac{0.6931}{\ln(1.15)} \approx 4.959$ years.

39. $A = \$30,000$, $r = 10\% = 0.1$, $m = 1$, $i = 0.1$, $n = 17$

From $A = P(1 + i)^n$, we have:

$$P = \frac{A}{(1+i)^n} = \frac{30,000}{(1.1)^{17}} \approx \$5935.34$$

41. $A = \$30,000$, $P = \$6844.79$, $r = i$, $n = 17$

Using $A = P(1 + r)^n$, we have:

$$30,000 = 6844.79(1 + r)^{17}$$

$$(1 + r)^{17} = \frac{30,000}{6844.79} \approx 4.3829$$

Therefore,

$$\ln(1 + r)^{17} = \ln(4.3829)$$
$$17 \ln(1 + r) \approx 1.4777$$
$$\ln(1 + r) = 0.08692$$
$$1 + r = 1.0908$$

and $\qquad r = 0.908$ or $r = 9.08\%$

43. From 2, $r_e = \left(1 + \dfrac{r}{m}\right)^m - 1$.

(A) $r = 8.28\% = 0.0828$, $m = 12$

$$r_e = \left(1 + \frac{0.0828}{12}\right)^{12} - 1 \approx 0.0860 \text{ or } 8.60\%$$

(B) $r = 8.25\% = 0.0825$, $m = 365$

$$r_e = \left(1 + \frac{0.0825}{365}\right)^{365} - 1 \approx 0.0860 \text{ or } 8.60\%$$

(C) $r = 8.25\% = 0.0825$, $m = 12$

$$r_e = \left(1 + \frac{0.0825}{12}\right)^{12} - 1 \approx 0.0857 \text{ or } 8.57\%$$

45. $A = \$32,456.32$, $P = \$24,766.81$, $m = 1$, $n = 2$

$$A = P(1 + r)^n$$
$$32,456.32 = 24,766.81(1 + r)^2$$

$$(1 + r)^2 = \frac{32,456.32}{24,766.81} \approx 1.3105$$

Therefore, $1 + r = \sqrt{1.3105} \approx 1.1448$ and $r \approx 0.1448$ or 14.48%.

EXERCISE 3-3

Things to remember:

1. FUTURE VALUE OF AN ORDINARY ANNUITY

$$FV = PMT\,\frac{(1 + i)^n - 1}{i} = PMT\,s_{\overline{n}|i}$$

where PMT = Periodic payment
i = Rate per period
n = Number of payments (periods)
FV = Future value (amount)

(Payments are made at the end of each period.)

2. SINKING FUND PAYMENT

$$PMT = FV \frac{i}{(1 + i)^n - 1} = \frac{FV}{s_{\overline{n}|i}}$$

where PMT = Sinking fund payment
FV = Value of annuity after n payments (future value)
n = Number of payments (periods)
i = Rate per period

(Payments are made at the end of each period.)

---

1. $n = 20$, $i = 0.03$, $PMT = \$500$

$$FV = PMT \frac{(1 + i)^n - 1}{i}$$

$$= PMTs_{\overline{n}|i} \quad (\text{using } \underline{1})$$

$$= 500 \frac{(1 + 0.03)^{20} - 1}{0.03} = 500s_{\overline{20}|0.03}$$

$$= 500(26.87037449) = \$13,435.19$$

3. $n = 40$, $i = 0.02$, $PMT = \$1000$

$$FV = 1000 \frac{(1 + 0.02)^{40} - 1}{0.02}$$

$$= 1000s_{\overline{40}|0.02}$$

$$= 1000(60.40198318) = \$60,401.98$$

5. $FV = \$3000$, $n = 20$, $i = 0.02$

$$3000 = PMT \frac{(1 + 0.02)^{20} - 1}{0.02}$$

$$= PMTs_{\overline{20}|0.02} \quad (\text{using } \underline{1} \text{ or } \underline{2})$$

$$= PMT(24.29736980)$$

$$PMT = \frac{3000}{24.29736980} = \$123.47$$

7. $FV = \$5000$, $n = 15$, $i = 0.01$

$$PMT = FV \frac{i}{(1 + i)^n - 1}$$

$$= \frac{FV}{s_{\overline{n}|i}} \quad (\text{using } \underline{2})$$

$$= 5000 \frac{0.01}{(1 + 0.01)^{15} - 1}$$

$$= \frac{5000}{16.09689554} = \$310.62$$

9. $FV = \$4000$, $i = 0.02$, $PMT = 200$, $n = ?$

$$FV = PMT \frac{(1 + i)^n - 1}{i}$$

$$\frac{FVi}{PMT} = (1 + i)^n - 1$$

$$(1 + i)^n = \frac{FVi}{PMT} + 1$$

$$\ln(1 + i)^n = \ln\left[\frac{FVi}{PMT} + 1\right]$$

$$n \ln(1 + i) = \ln\left[\frac{FVi}{PMT} + 1\right]$$

(continued)

$$n = \frac{\ln\left[\frac{FVi}{PMT} + 1\right]}{\ln(1 + i)} = \frac{\ln\left[\frac{4000(0.02)}{200} + 1\right]}{\ln(1.02)}$$

$$= \frac{\ln(1.4)}{\ln(1.02)} \approx \frac{0.3365}{0.01980} = 16.99 \text{ or } 17 \text{ years}$$

11. $PMT = \$500$, $n = 10(4) = 40$, $i = \dfrac{0.08}{4} = 0.02$

$$FV = 500 \frac{(1 + 0.02)^{40} - 1}{0.02} = 500s_{\overline{40}|0.02}$$

$$= 500(60.40198318) = \$30,200.99$$

Total deposits = $500(40) = \$20,000$.

Interest = $FV - 20,000 = 30,200.99 - 20,000 = \$10,200.99$.

13. $PMT = \$300$, $i = \dfrac{0.06}{12} = 0.005$, $n = 5(12) = 60$

$$FV = 300 \frac{(1 + 0.005)^{60} - 1}{0.005} = 300s_{\overline{60}|0.005} \quad \text{(using } \underline{1}\text{)}$$

$$= 300(69.77003051) = \$20,931.01$$

After five years, $\$20,931.01$ will be in the account.

15. $FV = \$25,000$, $i = \dfrac{0.09}{12} = 0.0075$, $n = 12(5) = 60$

$$PMT = \frac{FV}{s_{\overline{60}|0.0075}} = \frac{25,000}{75.42413693} \quad \text{(using the table)}$$

$$= \$331.46 \text{ per month}$$

17. $FV = \$100,000$, $i = \dfrac{0.12}{12} = 0.01$, $n = 8(12) = 96$

$$PMT = \frac{FV}{s_{\overline{96}|0.01}} = \frac{100,000}{159.92729236} = \$625.28 \text{ per month}$$

19. $FV = PMT \dfrac{(1 + i)^{n} - 1}{i} = 100 \dfrac{(1 + 0.0075)^{12} - 1}{0.0075}$ (after one year)

$$= 100 \frac{(1.0075)^{12} - 1}{0.0075} \quad \left[\underline{\text{Note:}} \; PMT = \$100, \; P = \frac{0.09}{12} = 0.0075\right]$$

$$= \$1250.76 \tag{1}$$

Total deposits in one year = $12(100) = \$1200$.

Interest earned in first year = $FV - 1200 = 1250.76 - 1200 = \$50.76$.

At the end of the second year,

$$FV = 100 \frac{(1 + 0.0075)^{24} - 1}{0.0075} \quad [\underline{\text{Note:}} \; n = 24]$$

$$= 100 \frac{(1.0075)^{24} - 1}{0.0075} = \$2618.85 \tag{2}$$

Total deposits plus interest in the second year = (2) – (1)
$$= 2618.85 - 1250.76$$
$$= \$1368.09 \tag{3}$$

Interest earned in the second year = (3) – 1200
$$= 1368.09 - 1200$$
$$= \$168.09$$

At the end of the third year,

$$FV = 100 \, \frac{(1 + 0.0075)^{36} - 1}{0.0075} \qquad [\underline{\text{Note}}: n = 36]$$

$$= 100 \, \frac{(1.0075)^{36} - 1}{0.0075}$$

$$= \$4115.27 \tag{4}$$

Total deposits plus interest in the third year = (4) – (2)
$$= 4115.27 - 2618.85$$
$$= \$1496.42 \tag{5}$$

Interest earned in the third year = (5) – 1200
$$= 1496.42 - 1200$$
$$= \$296.42$$

Thus,

Year	Interest earned
1	$ 50.76
2	$168.09
3	$296.42

21. (A) $P = \$2000$, $n = 8$, $i = 9\% = 0.09$

$$FV = 2000 \, \frac{(1 + 0.09)^{8} - 1}{0.09} = \frac{2000(0.99256)}{0.09} \approx 22{,}056.95$$

Thus, Jane will have $22,056.95 in her account on her 31st birthday. On her 65th birthday, she will have:

$$A = 22{,}056.95(1.09)^{34} \approx \$413{,}092$$

(B) $P = \$2000$, $n = 34$, $i = 9\% = 0.09$

$$FV = 2000 \, \frac{(1 + 0.09)^{34} - 1}{0.09} \approx \frac{2000(17.7284)}{0.09} \approx \$393{,}965$$

23. $FV = \$10{,}000$, $n = 48$, $i = \dfrac{8\%}{12} = \dfrac{0.08}{12} \approx 0.00667$

From 2, $PMT = \dfrac{10{,}000(0.00667)}{(1 + 0.00667)^{48} - 1} = \dfrac{66.7}{0.3759} \approx \$177.46$

25. $PMT = \$150$, $FV = \$7000$, $i = \dfrac{8.5\%}{12} = \dfrac{0.085}{12} \approx 0.00708$. From Problem 9:

$$n = \frac{\ln\left[\dfrac{FVi}{PMT} + 1\right]}{\ln(1 + i)} \approx \frac{\ln\left[\dfrac{7000(0.00708)}{150} + 1\right]}{\ln(1.00708)} \approx \frac{0.2855}{0.00706} \approx 40.46$$

Thus, $n = 41$ months or 3 years and 5 months.

EXERCISE 3-4

Things to remember:

$\underline{1.}$ PRESENT VALUE OF AN ORDINARY ANNUITY

$$PV = PMT \frac{1 - (1 + i)^{-n}}{i} = PMTa_{\overline{n}|i}$$

where PMT = Periodic payment
   i = Rate per period
   n = Number of periods
   PV = Present value of all payments

(Payments are made at the end of each period.)

$\underline{2.}$ AMORTIZATION FORMULA

$$PMT = PV \frac{i}{1 - (1 + i)^{-n}} = PV \frac{1}{a_{\overline{n}|i}}$$

where PV = Amount of loan (present value)
   i = Rate per period
   n = Number of payments (periods)
   PMT = Periodic payment

(Payments are made at the end of each period.)

---

1. $PV = 200 \dfrac{1 - (1 + 0.04)^{-30}}{0.04}$

$= PMTa_{\overline{30}|0.04}$

$= 200(17.29203330)$
   (using the table)

$= \$3458.41$

3. $PV = 250 \dfrac{1 - (1 + 0.025)^{-25}}{0.025}$

$= 250a_{\overline{25}|0.025}$

$= 250(18.42437642)$

$= \$4606.09$

5. $PMT = 6000 \dfrac{0.01}{1 - (1 + 0.01)^{-36}}$

$= \dfrac{PV}{a_{\overline{36}|0.01}}$

$= \dfrac{6000}{30.10750504} = \$199.29$

7. $PMT = 40{,}000 \dfrac{0.0075}{1 - (1 + 0.0075)^{-96}}$

$= \dfrac{40{,}000}{a_{\overline{96}|0.0075}}$

$= \dfrac{40{,}000}{68.25843856} = \$586.01$

9. $PV = \$5000$, $i = 0.01$, $\dot{P}MT = 200$

We have, $PV = PMT \dfrac{1 - (1 + i)^{-n}}{i}$

$5000 = 200 \dfrac{1 - (1 + 0.01)^{-n}}{0.01}$

$\qquad = 20{,}000(1 - (1.01)^{-n})$

$\dfrac{1}{4} = 1 - (1.01)^{-n}$

$(1.01)^{-n} = \dfrac{3}{4} = 0.75$

$\ln(1.01)^{-n} = \ln(0.75)$

$-n \ln(1.01) = \ln(0.75)$

$n = \dfrac{-\ln(0.75)}{\ln(1.01)} \approx 29$

11. $PMT = \$4000$, $n = 10(4) = 40$

$i = \dfrac{0.08}{4} = 0.02$

$PV =$ Present value

$\qquad = PMT \dfrac{1 - (1 + i)^{-n}}{i}$

$\qquad = PMTa_{\overline{n}|i}$

$\qquad = 4000a_{\overline{40}|0.02}$

$\qquad = 4000(27.35547924)$

$\qquad = \$109{,}421.92$

13. This is a present value problem.

$PMT = \$350$, $n = 4(12) = 48$, $i = \dfrac{0.09}{12} = 0.0075$

Hence, $PV = PMTa_{\overline{n}|i} = 350a_{\overline{48}|0.0075}$

$\qquad\qquad = 350(40.18478189) = \$14{,}064.67$

They should deposit $\$14{,}064.67$. The child will receive $350(48) = \$16{,}800.00$.

15. (A) $PV = \$600$, $n = 18$, $i = 0.01$

Monthly payment $= PMT = PV \dfrac{i}{1 - (1 + i)^{-n}}$

$\qquad = \dfrac{PV}{a_{\overline{n}|i}} = \dfrac{600}{a_{\overline{18}|0.01}} = \dfrac{600}{16.39826858}$

$\qquad = \$36.59$ per month

The amount paid in 18 payments $= 36.59(18) = \$658.62$.

Thus, the interest paid $= 658.62 - 600 = \$58.62$.

(B) $PMT = \dfrac{600}{a_{\overline{18}|0.015}}$ $\qquad (i = 0.015)$

$\qquad = \dfrac{600}{15.67256089} = \$38.28$ per month

For 18 payments, the total amount $= 38.28(18) = \$689.04$.

Thus, the interest paid $= 689.04 - 600 = \$89.04$.

17. Amortized amount = $16,000 - (16,000)(0.25) = \$12,000$

Thus, $P = \$12,000$, $n = 6(12) = 72$, $i = 0.015$

PMT = monthly payment $= \dfrac{PV}{a_{\overline{n}|i}} = \dfrac{12,000}{a_{\overline{72}|0.015}} = \dfrac{12,000}{43.84466677} = \$273.69$ per month

The total amount paid in 72 months $= 273.69(72) = \$19,705.68$.

Thus, the interest paid $= 19,705.68 - 12,000 = \$7705.68$.

19. First, we compute the required quarterly payment for $PV = \$5000$, $i = 0.045$, and $n = 8$, as follows:

$PMT = PV \dfrac{i}{1 - (1 + i)^{-n}} = 5000 \dfrac{0.045}{1 - (1 + 0.045)^{-8}} = \dfrac{225}{1 - (1.045)^{-8}} = \$758.05$ per quarter

The amortization schedule is as follows:

Payment number	Payment	Interest	Unpaid balance reduction	Unpaid balance
0				$5000.00
1	$785.05	$225.00	$533.05	4466.95
2	758.05	201.01	557.04	3909.91
3	758.05	175.95	582.10	3327.81
4	758.05	149.75	608.30	2719.51
5	758.05	122.38	635.67	2083.84
6	758.05	93.77	664.28	1419.56
7	758.05	63.88	694.17	725.39
8	758.05	32.64	725.39	0.00
Totals	$6064.38	$1064.38	$5000.00	

21. First, we compute the required monthly payment for $PV = \$6000$,

$i = \dfrac{12}{12(100)} = 0.01$, $n = 3(12) = 36$.

$PMT = PV \dfrac{i}{1 - (1 + i)^{-n}} = 6000 \dfrac{0.01}{1 - (1 + 0.01)^{-36}} = \dfrac{60}{1 - (1.01)^{-36}} = \$199.29$

Now, compute the unpaid balance after 12 payments by considering 24 unpaid payments: $PMT = \$199.29$, $i = 0.01$, and $n = 24$.

$PV = PMT \dfrac{1 - (1 + i)^{-n}}{i} = 199.29 \dfrac{1 - (1 + 0.01)^{-24}}{0.01} = 19,929(1 - (1.01)^{-24})$

$= \$4233.59$

Thus, the amount of the loan paid in 12 months $= 6000 - 4233.59 = \$1766.41$, and the amount of total payment made during 12 months $= 12(199.29) = \$2391.48$. The interest paid during the first 12 months (first year) is:

2391.48 - 1766.41 = $625.07

Similarly, the unpaid balance after two years can be computed by considering 12 unpaid payments: $PMT = \$199.29$, $i = 0.01$, and $n = 12$.

$$PV = 199.29 \frac{1 - (1 + 0.01)^{-12}}{0.01} = 19,929(1 - (1.01)^{-12}) = \$2243$$

Thus, the amount of the loan paid during 24 months = 6000 - 2243.02 = $3756.98, and the amount of the loan paid during the second year = 3756.98 - 1766.41 = $1990.57. The amount of total payment during the second year = 12(199.29) = $2391.48. The interest paid during the second year is:

2391.48 - 1990.57 = $400.91

The amount of the loan paid during the third year = 6000 - 3756.98 = $2243.02, and the amount of total payment during the third year = 12(199.29) = $2391.48. The interest paid during the third year is:

2391.48 - 2243.02 = $148.46

23. PMT = monthly payment = $525, $n = 30(12) = 360$, $i = \frac{0.098}{12} \approx 0.008167$. Thus, the present value of all payments is:

$$PV = PMT \frac{1 - (1 + i)^{-n}}{i} = 525 \frac{1 - (1 + 0.008167)^{-360}}{0.008167} = \$60,846.38$$

Hence, selling price = loan + down payment
$$= 60,846.38 + 25,000$$
$$= \$85,846.38$$

The total amount paid in 30 years (360 months) = 525(360) = $189,000. The interest paid is:

189,000 - 60,846.38 = $128,153.62

25. $PV = \$6000$, $n = 2(12) = 24$, $i = \frac{0.035}{12} = 0.0029167$

The total amount at the end of the two years is:

$$P = (1 + i)^n = 6000(1 + 0.0029167)^{24} = 6000(1.0029167)^{24}$$
$$= 6000(1.07) = \$6420$$

Now, the monthly payment is:

$$PMT = PV \frac{i}{1 - (1 + i)^{-n}}$$

where $n = 4(12) = 48$, $PV = \$6420$, $i = \frac{3.5}{12} = 0.0029167$. Thus,

$$PMT = 6420 \frac{0.0029167}{1 - (1 + 0.0029167)^{-48}} = \$143.85 \text{ per month}$$

The total amount paid in 48 payments = 143.85(48) = $6904.80. Thus, the interest paid is:

6904.80 - 6000 = $904.80

27. First, compute the monthly payment: $PV = \$75,000$, $i = \dfrac{0.132}{12} = 0.011$, $n = 30(12) = 360$.

$$\text{Monthly payment} = PV\,\frac{i}{1 - (1 + i)^{-n}} = 75{,}000\,\frac{0.011}{1 - (1 + 0.011)^{-360}}$$

$$= 75{,}000\,\frac{0.011}{1 - (1.011)^{-360}} = \$841.39$$

(A) Now, to compute the balance after 10 years (with balance of loan to be paid in 20 years), use $PMT = \$841.39$, $i = 0.011$, $n = 20(12) = 240$.

$$\text{Balance after 10 years} = PMT\,\frac{1 - (1 + i)^{-n}}{i}$$

$$= 841.39\,\frac{1 - (1 + 0.011)^{-240}}{0.011}$$

$$= 941.39\,\frac{1 - (1.011)^{-240}}{0.011}$$

$$= \$70{,}952.33$$

(B) Similarly, the balance of the loan after 20 years (with remainder of loan to be paid in 10 years) is:

$$841.39\,\frac{1 - (1 + 0.011)^{-120}}{0.011} \qquad [\underline{\text{Note}}:\ n = 12(10) = 120]$$

$$= 841.39\,\frac{1 - (1.011)^{-120}}{0.011} = \$55{,}909.02$$

(C) The balance of the loan after 25 years (with remainder of loan to be paid in 5 years) is:

$$841.39\,\frac{1 - (1 + 0.011)^{-60}}{0.011} \qquad [\underline{\text{Note}}:\ n = 12(5) = 60]$$

$$= 841.39\,\frac{1 - (1.011)^{-60}}{0.011} = \$36{,}813.32$$

29. (A) $PV = \$30,000$, $i = \dfrac{0.15}{12} = 0.0125$, $n = 20(12) = 240$.

$$\text{Monthly payment } PMT = PV\,\frac{i}{1 - (1 + i)^{-n}} = 30{,}000\,\frac{0.0125}{1 - (1 + 0.0125)^{-240}}$$

$$= 30{,}000\,\frac{0.0125}{1 - (1.0125)^{-240}}$$

$$= \$395.04$$

The total amount paid in 240 payments is:

$395.04(240) = \$94,809.60$

Thus, the interest paid is:

$\$94,809.60 - \$30,000 = \$64,809.60$

(B)   New payment = $PMT = \$395.04 + \$100.00 = \$495.04.$ $PV = \$30,000,$
$i = 0.0125.$

$$PMT = PV \, \frac{i}{1 - (1 + i)^{-n}}$$

$$495.04 = 30,000 \, \frac{0.0125}{1 - (1 + 0.0125)^{-n}} = \frac{375}{1 - (1.0125)^{-n}}$$

Therefore,

$$1 - (1.0125)^{-n} = \frac{375}{495.04} = 0.7575$$

$$(1.0125)^{-n} = 1 - 0.7575 = 0.2425$$

$$\ln(1.0125)^{-n} = \ln(0.2425)$$

$$-n \ln(1.0125) = \ln(0.2425)$$

$$= \frac{-\ln(0.2425)}{\ln(1.0125)} \approx 114.047 \approx 114 \text{ months or } 9.5 \text{ years}$$

The total amount paid in 114 payments of \$495.04 is:

495.04(114) = \$56,434.56

Thus, the interest paid is:

\$56,434.56 - \$30,000 = \$26,434.56

The savings on interest is:

\$64,809.60 - \$26,434.56 = \$38,375.04

31. $PV = (\$79,000)(0.80) = \$63.200,$ $i = \dfrac{0.12}{12} = 0.01,$ $n = 12(30) = 360.$

Monthly payment $PMT = PV \, \dfrac{i}{1 - (1 + i)^{-n}} = 63,200 \, \dfrac{0.01}{1 - (1 + 0.01)^{-360}}$

$$= \frac{632}{1 - (1.01)^{-360}} = \$650.08$$

Next, we find the present value of a \$650.08 per month, 18-year annuity.
$PMT = \$650.08,$ $i = 0.01,$ and $n = 12(18) = 216.$

$$PV = PMT \, \frac{1 - (1 + i)^{-n}}{i} = 650.08 \, \frac{1 - (1.01)^{-216}}{0.01}$$

$$= \frac{650.08(0.8834309)}{0.01} = \$57,430.08$$

Finally,

Equity = (current market value) - (unpaid loan balance)

$= \$100,000 - \$57,430.08 = \$42,569.92$

The couple can borrow (\$42,569.92)(0.70) = \$29,799.

1. $A = 100\left(1 + 0.09 \cdot \frac{1}{2}\right)$

    $= 100(1.045) = \$104.50$

2. $808 = P\left(1 + 0.12 \cdot \frac{1}{12}\right)$

    $P = \frac{808}{1.01} = \$800$

3. $212 = 200(1 + 0.08 \cdot t)$

    $1 + 0.08t = \frac{212}{200}$

    $0.08t = \frac{212}{200} - 1 = \frac{12}{200} = 0.06$

    $t = \frac{0.06}{0.08} = 0.75$ year
            or 9 months

4. $4120 = 4000\left(1 + r \cdot \frac{1}{2}\right)$

    $1 + \frac{r}{2} = \frac{4120}{4000}$

    $\frac{r}{2} = \frac{4120}{4000} - 1 = \frac{120}{4000} = 0.03$

    $r = 0.06$ or 6%

5. $A = 1200(1 + 0.005)^{30}$

    $= 1200(1.005)^{30} = \$1393.68$

6. $P = \dfrac{5000}{(1 + 0.0075)^{60}} = \dfrac{5000}{(1.0075)^{60}}$

    $= \$3193.50$

7. $FV = 1000s_{\overline{60}|0.005}$

    $= 1000 \cdot 69.77003051$

    $= \$69,770.03$

8. $PMT = \dfrac{FV}{s_{\overline{n}|i}} = \dfrac{8000}{s_{\overline{48}|0.015}}$

    $= \dfrac{8000}{69.56321929} = \$115.00$

9. $PV = PMTa_{\overline{n}|i} = 2500a_{\overline{16}|0.02}$

    $= 2500 \cdot 13.57770931$

    $= \$33,944.27$

10. $PMT = \dfrac{PV}{a_{\overline{n}|i}} = \dfrac{8000}{a_{\overline{60}|0.0075}}$

    $= \dfrac{8000}{48.17337352} = \$166.07$

11. $2500 = 1000(1.06)^n$

    $(1.06)^n = \frac{2500}{1000}$

    $n = \dfrac{\ln 2.5}{\ln 1.06} \approx 16$

12. $5000 = 100\,\dfrac{(1.01)^n - 1}{0.01}$

    $= 10,000[(1.01)^n - 1]$

    $(1.01)^n - 1 = \dfrac{5000}{10,000}$

    $(1.01)^n = \frac{1}{2} + 1$

    $n = \dfrac{\ln 1.5}{\ln 1.01} \approx 41$

13. $P = \$3000,\ r = 0.14,\ t = \frac{10}{12}$

    $A = 3000\left(1 + 0.14 \cdot \frac{10}{12}\right)$ [using $A = P(1 + rt)$]

    $= \$3350$

    Interest $= 3350 - 3000 = \$350$

14. $P = \$635$, $r = 22\% = 0.22$, $t = \dfrac{1}{12}$

$$I = Prt = 635(0.22)\dfrac{1}{12}$$
$$= \$11.64$$

15. The interest paid was
$\$2812.50 - \$2500 = \$312.50$.

$P = \$2500$, $t = \dfrac{10}{12} = \dfrac{5}{6}$

Solving $I = Prt$ for r, we have:

$$r = \dfrac{I}{Pt} = \dfrac{312.50}{2500\left(\dfrac{5}{6}\right)} = 0.15 \text{ or } 15\%$$

16. $P = \$1500$, $I = \$100$,

$t = \dfrac{120}{360} = \dfrac{1}{3}$ year

From Problem 15,

$$r = \dfrac{I}{Pt} = \dfrac{100}{1500\left(\dfrac{1}{3}\right)} = 0.20 \text{ or } 20\%$$

17. $P = \$100$, $I = \$0.08$, $t = \dfrac{1}{360}$

From Problem 15,

$$r = \dfrac{I}{Pt} = \dfrac{0.08}{100\left(\dfrac{1}{360}\right)} = 0.288 \text{ or } 28.8\%$$

18. $A = \$5000$, $P = \$4899.08$, $t = \dfrac{13}{52} = 0.25$

The interest earned is $I = \$5000.00 - \$4899.08 = \$100.92$. Thus,

$$r = \dfrac{I}{Pt} = \dfrac{100.92}{(4899.08)(0.25)} \quad 0.0824 \text{ or } 8.24\%$$

19. $A = \$5000$, $r = 10.76\% = 0.1076$, $t = \dfrac{26}{52} = 0.5$

$$P = \dfrac{A}{1 + rt} = \dfrac{5000}{1 + (0.1076)(0.5)} = \$4744.73$$

20. $P = \$6000$, $r = 9\% = 0.09$, $m = 12$, $i = \dfrac{0.09}{12} = 0.0075$, $n = 12(17) = 204$

$$A = P(1 + i)^n = 6000(1 + 0.0075)^{204} = 6000(1.0075)^{204} \approx \$27,551$$

21. $A = \$25,000$, $r = 10\% = 0.10$, $m = 2$, $i = \dfrac{0.10}{2} = 0.05$, $n = 2(10) = 20$

$$P = \dfrac{A}{(1 + i)^n} = \dfrac{25,000}{(1 + 0.05)^{20}} = \dfrac{25,000}{(1.05)^{20}} \approx \$9422.24$$

22. $P = \$8000$, $r = 5\% = 0.05$, $m = 1$, $i = \dfrac{0.05}{1} = 0.05$, $n = 5$

$$A = P(1 + i)^n = 8000(1 + 0.05)^5 = 8000(1.05)^5 \approx \$10,210$$

23. $P = \$8000$, $r = 5\% = 0.05$, $m = 1$, $i = \dfrac{0.05}{1} = 0.05$, $n = 5$

$$P = \dfrac{A}{(1 + i)^n} = \dfrac{8000}{(1 + 0.05)^5} = \dfrac{8000}{(1.05)^5} \approx \$6268$$

24. $P = \$2500$, $r = 9\% = 0.09$, $m = 4$, $i = \dfrac{0.09}{4} = 0.0225$, $A = \$3000$

$$A = P(1 + i)^n$$
$$3000 = 2500(1 + 0.0225)^n$$
$$(1.0225)^n = \frac{3000}{2500} = 1.2$$
$$\ln(1.0225)^n = \ln 1.2$$
$$n \ln 1.0225 = \ln 1.2$$
$$n = \frac{\ln 1.2}{\ln 1.0225} \approx 8.19$$

Thus, it will take 9 quarters, or 2 years and 3 months.

25. (A) $r = 12\% = 0.12$, $m = 12$, $i = \dfrac{0.12}{12} = 0.01$

If we invest P dollars, then we want to know how long it will take to have $2P$ dollars:

$$A = P(1 + i)^n$$
$$2P = P(1 + 0.01)^n$$
$$(1.01)^n = 2$$
$$\ln(1.01)^n = \ln 2$$
$$n \ln 1.01 = \ln 2$$
$$n = \frac{\ln 2}{\ln 1.01} \approx 69.66$$

Thus, it will take 70 months, or 5 years and 10 months, for an investment to double at 12% interest compounded monthly.

(B) $r = 18\% = 0.18$, $m = 12$, $i = \dfrac{0.18}{12} = 0.015$

$$2P = P(1 + 0.015)^n$$
$$(1.015)^n = 2$$
$$\ln(1.015)^n = \ln 2$$
$$n = \frac{\ln 2}{\ln 1.015} \approx 46.56$$

Thus, it will take 47 months, or 3 years and 11 months, for an investment to double at 18% compounded monthly.

26. $r = 9\% = 0.09$, $m = 12$

$$r_e = \left(1 + \frac{r}{m}\right)^m - 1$$
$$= \left(1 + \frac{0.09}{12}\right)^{12} - 1 = (1.0075)^{12} - 1 \approx 0.0938 \text{ or } 9.38\%$$

27. The effective rate for 9% compounded quarterly is:

$$r_e = \left(1 + \frac{r}{m}\right)^m - 1, \ r = 0.09, \ m = 4$$

$$= \left(1 + \frac{0.09}{4}\right)^4 - 1 = (1.0225)^4 - 1 \approx 0.0931 \text{ or } 9.31\%$$

The effective rate for 9.25% compounded annually is 9.25%. Thus, 9% compounded quarterly is the better investment.

28. $PMT = \$200, \ r = 9\% = 0.09, \ m = 12, \ i = \dfrac{0.09}{12} = 0.0075, \ n = 12(8) = 96$

$$FV = PMT \frac{(1 + i)^n - 1}{i}$$

$$= 200 \frac{(1 + 0.0075)^{96} - 1}{0.0075} = 200 \frac{(1.0075)^{96} - 1}{0.0075} \approx \$27,971.23$$

The total amount invested with 96 payments of $200 is:

$96(200) = \$19,200$

Thus, the interest earned with this annuity is:

$I = \$27,971.23 - \$19,200 = \$8771.23$

29. $FV = \$50,000, \ r = 9\% = 0.09, \ m = 12, \ i = \dfrac{0.09}{12} = 0.0075, \ n = 12(6) = 72$

$$PMT = FV \frac{i}{(1 + i)^n - 1} = \frac{FV}{s_{\overline{n}|i}}$$

$$= \frac{50,000}{s_{\overline{72}|0.0075}} = \frac{50,000}{95.007028} \quad \text{(from Table V)}$$

$$= \$526.28 \text{ per month}$$

30. Using the sinking fund formula

$$PMT = FV \frac{i}{(1 + i)^n - 1}$$

with $PMT = \$200, \ FV = \$10,000,$ and $i = \dfrac{0.09}{12} = 0.0075$, we have:

$$200 = 10,000 \frac{0.0075}{(1 + 0.0075)^n - 1} = \frac{75}{(1.0075)^n - 1}$$

Therefore,

$$(1.0075)^n - 1 = \frac{75}{200} = 0.375$$

$$(1.0075)^n = 0.375 + 1 = 1.375$$

$$\ln(1.0075)^n = \ln 1.375$$

$$n = \frac{\ln 1.375}{\ln 1.0075} \approx 42.62$$

Thus, the couple will have to make 43 deposits.

31. $PMT = \$1500$, $r = 8\% = 0.08$, $m = 4$, $i = \dfrac{0.08}{4} = 0.02$, $n = 2(4) = 8$

We want to find the present value, PV, of this annuity.

$$PV = PMT\ \frac{1 - (1 + i)^{-n}}{i}$$

$$= 1500\ \frac{1 - (1 + 0.02)^{-8}}{0.02} = 1500\ \frac{1 - (1.02)^{-8}}{0.02} = \$10,988.22$$

The student will receive $8(\$1500) = \$12,000$.

32. The amount of the loan is $\$3000(2/3) = \$2000$. The monthly interest rate is $i = 1.5\% = 0.015$ and $n = 2(12) = 24$.

$$PMT = PV\ \frac{i}{1 - (1 + i)^{-n}}$$

$$= 2000\ \frac{0.015}{1 - (1 + 0.015)^{-24}} = \frac{30}{1 - (1.015)^{-24}} = \$99.85 \text{ per month}$$

33. $PV = \$1000$, $i = 0.025$, $n = 4$

The quarterly payment is:

$$PMT = PV\ \frac{i}{1 - (1 + i)^{-n}}$$

$$= 1000\ \frac{0.025}{1 - (1 + 0.025)^{-4}} = \frac{25}{1 - (1.025)^{-4}} \approx \$265.82$$

The amortization table is shown below.

Payment number	Payment	Interest	Unpaid balance reduction	Unpaid balance
0				$1000.00
1	$265.82	$25.00	$240.82	759.18
2	265.82	18.98	246.84	512.34
3	265.82	12.81	253.01	259.33
4	265.82	6.48	259.33	0.00
Totals	$1063.27	$63.27	$1000.00	

34. We first compute the monthly payment using $PV = \$10,000$, $i = \dfrac{0.12}{12} = 0.01$, and $n = 5(12) = 60$.

$$PMT = PV\ \frac{i}{1 - (1 + i)^{-n}}$$

$$= 10,000\ \frac{0.01}{1 - (1 + 0.01)^{-60}} = \frac{100}{1 - (1.01)^{-60}} = \$222.44 \text{ per month}$$

Now, we calculate the unpaid balance after 24 payments by using $PMT = \$222.44$, $i = 0.01$, and $n = 60 - 24 = 36$.

$$PV = PMT \frac{1 - (1 + i)^{-n}}{i}$$

$$= 222.44 \frac{1 - (1 + 0.01)^{-36}}{0.01} = 22244[1 - (1.01)^{-36}] = \$6697.11$$

Thus, the unpaid balance after 2 years is $6697.11.

35. $PV = \$80,000$, $i = \dfrac{0.15}{12} = 0.0125$, $n = 8(12) = 96$

(A) $PMT = PV \dfrac{i}{1 - (1 + i)^{-n}}$

$$= 80,000 \frac{0.0125}{1 - (1 + 0.0125)^{-96}} = \frac{1000}{1 - (1.0125)^{-96}}$$

$$= \$1435.63 \text{ monthly payment}$$

(B) Now use $PMT = \$1435.63$, $i = 0.0125$, and $n = 96 - 12 = 84$ to calculate the unpaid balance.

$$PV = PMT \frac{1 - (1 + i)^{-n}}{i}$$

$$= 1435.63 \frac{1 - (1 + 0.0125)^{-84}}{0.0125} = 114,850.40[1 - (1.0125)^{-84}]$$

$$= \$74,397.48 \text{ unpaid balance after the first year}$$

(C) Amount of loan paid during the first year:

$80,000 - $74,397.48 = $5602.52

Amount of payments during the first year:

12($1435.63) = $17,227.56

Thus, the interest paid during the first year is:

$17,227.56 - $5602.52 = $11,625.04

36. (A) The present value of annuity which provides for quarterly withdrawals of $5000 for 10 years at 12% interest compounded quarterly is given by:

$$PV = PMT \frac{1 - (1 + i)^{-n}}{i} \qquad \begin{array}{l} \text{with } PMT = \$5000, \ i = \dfrac{0.12}{4} = 0.03, \\ \text{and } n = 10(4) = 40 \end{array}$$

$$= 5000 \frac{1 - (1 + 0.03)^{-40}}{0.03}$$

$$= 166,666.67[1 - (1.03)^{-40}] = \$115,573.86$$

This is the amount which will have to be in the account when he retires.

(B) To determine the quarterly deposit to accumulate the amount in part (A), we use the formula:

$$PMT = FV \frac{i}{(1 + i)^n - 1} \qquad \text{where } FV = \$115{,}573.86, \ i = 0.03,$$
$$\text{and } n = 4(20) = 80$$

$$= 115{,}573.86 \frac{0.03}{(1 + 0.03)^{80} - 1}$$

$$= \frac{3467.22}{(1.03)^{80} - 1} = \$359.64 \text{ quarterly payment}$$

(C) The amount collected during the 10-year period is:

($5000)40 = $200,000

The amount deposited during the 20-year period is:

($359.64)80 = $28,771.20

Thus, the interest earned during the 30-year period is:

$200,000 - $28,771.20 = $171,228.80

37. $P = \$10{,}000, \ r = 7\% = 0.07, \ m = 365, \ i = \dfrac{0.07}{365} = 0.000192,$ and $n = 40(365) = 14{,}600$

$$A = P(1 + i)^n = 10{,}000(1 + 0.0001918)^{14{,}600}$$
$$= 10{,}000(1.0001918)^{14{,}600}$$
$$= \$164{,}402$$

38. To determine how long it will take money to double, we need to solve the equation $2P = P(1 + i)^n$ for n. From this equation, we obtain:

$$(1 + i)^n = 2$$
$$\ln(1 + i)^n = \ln 2$$
$$n \ln(1 + i) = \ln 2$$
$$n = \frac{\ln 2}{\ln(1 + i)}$$

(A) $i = \dfrac{0.10}{365} = 0.00274$

Thus, $n = \dfrac{\ln 2}{\ln(1.000274)} \approx 2530.08$ days or 6.93 years.

(B) $i = 0.10$

Thus, $n = \dfrac{\ln 2}{\ln(1.1)} \approx 7.27$ years.

39. The effective rate for Security S & L is:

$$r_e = \left(1 + \frac{r}{m}\right)^m - 1 \quad \text{where } r = 9.38\% = 0.0938 \text{ and } m = 12$$

$$= \left(1 + \frac{0.0938}{12}\right)^{12} - 1 \approx 0.09794 \text{ or } 9.794\%$$

The effective rate for West Lake S & L is:

$$r_e = \left(1 + \frac{r}{m}\right)^m - 1 \quad \text{where } r = 9.35\% = 0.0935 \text{ and } m = 365$$

$$= \left(1 + \frac{0.0935}{365}\right)^{365} - 1 \approx 0.09799 \text{ or } 9.8\%$$

Thus, West Lake S & L is a better investment.

40. $A = \$5000$, $r = i = 9.5\% = 0.095$, $n = 5$

$$P = \frac{A}{(1 + i)^n} = \frac{5000}{(1 + 0.095)^5} = \frac{5000}{(1.095)^5} \approx \$3176.14$$

41. $P = \$4476.20$, $A = \$10,000$, $m = 1$, $r = i$, $n = 10$

$$A = P(1 + i)^n$$

$$10,000 = 4476.20(1 + i)^{10}$$

$$(1 + i)^{10} = \frac{10,000}{4476.20} \approx 2.23404$$

$$10 \ln(1 + i) = \ln(2.23404)$$

$$\ln(1 + i) = \frac{\ln(2.23404)}{10} \approx 0.8038106 \div 10 =$$

$$1 + i \approx 1.0837$$

$$i = 0.0837 \text{ or } 8.37\%$$

42. $A = \$17,388.17$, $P = \$12,903.28$, $m = 1$, $r = i$, $n = 3$

$$A = P(1 + i)^n$$

$$17,388.17 = 12,903.28(1 + i)^3$$

$$(1 + i)^3 = \frac{17,388.17}{12,903.28} \approx 1.3475775$$

$$3 \ln(1 + i) = \ln(1.3475775)$$

$$\ln(1 + i) \approx \frac{0.2983085}{3} \approx 0.0994362$$

$$1 + i \approx 1.1045$$

$$i = 0.1045 \text{ or } 10.45\%$$

43. (A) $PMT = \$2000$, $m = 1$, $r = i = 7\% = 0.07$, $n = 45$

$$FV = PMT\,\frac{(1 + i)^n - 1}{i}$$

$$= 2000\,\frac{(1 + 0.07)^{45} - 1}{0.07} = 2000\,\frac{(1.07)^{45} - 1}{0.07} \approx \$571{,}499$$

(B) $PMT = \$2000$, $m = 1$, $r = i = 11\% = 0.11$, $n = 45$

$$FV = PMT\,\frac{(1 + i)^n - 1}{i}$$

$$= 2000\,\frac{(1 + 0.11)^{45} - 1}{0.11} = 2000\,\frac{(1.11)^{45} - 1}{0.11} \approx \$1{,}973{,}277$$

44. $FV = \$850{,}000$, $r = 8.76\% = 0.0876$, $m = 2$, $i = \dfrac{0.0876}{2} = 0.0438$, $n = 2(6) = 12$

$$PMT = FV\,\frac{i}{(1 + i)^n - 1}$$

$$= 850{,}000\,\frac{0.0438}{(1 + 0.0438)^{12} - 1} = \frac{37{,}230}{(1.0438)^{12} - 1} \approx \$55{,}347.48$$

The total amount invested is:

$12(55{,}347.48) = \$664{,}169.76$

Thus, the interest earned with this annuity is:

$I = \$850{,}000 - \$664{,}169.76 = \$185{,}830.24$

45. $PMT = \$200$, $FV = \$2500$, $i = \dfrac{0.0798}{12} = 0.00665$

$$FV = PMT\,\frac{(1 + i)^n - 1}{i}$$

$$2500 = 200\,\frac{(1 + 0.00665)^n - 1}{0.00665} = 30{,}075.188[(1.00665)^n - 1]$$

$$(1.00665)^n - 1 = \frac{2500}{30{,}075.188} \approx 0.083125$$

$$(1.0065)^n = 1.083125$$

$$n\,\ln 1.0065 = \ln 1.083125$$

$$n = \frac{\ln 1.083125}{\ln 1.0065} \approx 12.32 \text{ months}$$

Thus, it will take 13 months, or 1 year and 1 month.

46. The present value, PV, of an annuity of $200 per month for 48 months at 14% interest compounded monthly is given by:

$$PV = PMT \frac{1 - (1 + i)^{-n}}{i} \quad \text{where } PMT = \$200, \ i = \frac{0.14}{12} = 0.0116667$$
$$\text{and } n = 48$$

$$= 200 \frac{1 - (1 + 0.0117)^{-48}}{0.0117}$$

$$= 17,094.017[1 - (1.0117)^{-48}] = \$7318.91$$

With the \$3000 down payment, the selling price of the car is \$10,318.91.

The total amount paid is:

$3000 + 48(\$200) = \$12,600$

Thus, the interest paid is:

$I = \$12,600 - \$10,318.91 = \$2281.09$

47. First, we must calculate the future value of \$8000 at 5.5% interest compounded monthly for 2.5 years.

$$A = P(1 + i)^n \quad \text{where } P = \$8000, \ i = \frac{0.055}{12}, \text{ and } n = 30$$

$$= 8000\left(1 + \frac{0.055}{12}\right)^{30} = \$9176.33$$

Now, we calculate the monthly payment to amortize this debt at 5.5% interest compounded monthly over 5 years.

$$PMT = PV \frac{i}{1 - (1 + i)^{-n}} \quad \text{where } PV = \$9176.33, \ i = \frac{0.055}{12} \approx 0.00458,$$
$$\text{and } n = 12(5) = 60$$

$$= 9176.33 \frac{0.00458}{1 - (1 + 0.00458)^{-60}} = \frac{42.058179}{1 - (1.00458)^{-60}} \approx \$175.28$$

The total amount paid on the loan is:

$\$175.28(60) = \$10,516.80$

Thus, the interest paid is:

$I = \$10,516.80 - \$8000 = \$2516.80$

48. (A) We first calculate the future value of an annuity of \$2000 at 8% compounded annually for 9 years.

$$FV = PMT \frac{(1 + i)^n - 1}{i} \quad \text{where } PMT = \$2000, \ i = 0.08, \text{ and } n = 9$$

$$= 2000 \frac{(1 + 0.08)^9 - 1}{0.08} = 25,000[(1.08)^9 - 1] \approx \$24,975.12$$

Now, we calculate the future value of this amount at 8% compounded annually for 36 years.

$A = P(1 + i)^n$ where $P = \$24,975.12$, $i = 0.08$, and $n = 36$

$\qquad = 24,975.12(1 + 0.08)^{36} = 24,975.12(1.08)^{36} \approx \$398,807$

(B) This is the future value of a \$2000 annuity at 8% compounded annually for 35 years.

$FV = PMT \dfrac{(1 + i)^n - 1}{i}$ where $PMT = \$2000$, $i = 0.08$, and $n = 36$

$\qquad = 2000 \dfrac{(1 + 0.08)^{36} - 1}{0.08} = 25,000[(1.08)^{36} - 1] \approx \$374,204$

49. The amount of the loan is $(\$100,000)(0.8) = \$80,000$ and

$PMT = PV \dfrac{i}{1 - (1 + i)^{-n}}.$

(A) First, let $i = \dfrac{0.1075}{12} = 0.0089583$, $n = 12(30) = 360$. Then,

$PMT = 80,000 \dfrac{0.0089583}{1 - (1 + 0.0089583)^{-360}} = \dfrac{716.66667}{0.9596687}$

$\qquad \approx \$746.79$ monthly payment for 30 years.

Next, let $i = \dfrac{0.1075}{12} = 0.0089583$, $n = 12(15) = 180$. Then,

$PMT = 80,000 \dfrac{0.0089583}{1 - (1 + 0.0089583)^{-180}} = \dfrac{716.66667}{0.7991735}$

$\qquad \approx \$896.76$ monthly payment for 15 years.

(B) To find the unpaid balance after 10 years, we use

$PV = PMT \dfrac{1 - (1 + i)^{-n}}{i}$

First, for the 30-year mortgage:

$PMT = \$746.79$, $i = \dfrac{0.1075}{12} = 0.0089583$, $n = 12(20) = 240$

$PV = 746.79 \dfrac{1 - (1 + 0.0089583)^{-240}}{0.0089583} = 83,362.915[1 - (1.0089583)^{-240}]$

$\qquad \$73,558.78$ unpaid balance for the 30-year mortgage

Next, for the 15-year mortgage:

$PMT = \$896.76$, $i = 0.0089583$, $n = 5(12) = 60$

(continued)

CHAPTER 3

$$= 896.76 \, \frac{1 - (1.0089583)^{-60}}{0.0089583} = 100,103.81[1 - (1.0089583)^{-60}]$$

$$\approx \$41,482.22 \text{ unpaid balance for the 15-year mortgage}$$

50. The amount of the mortgage is:

($83,000)(0.8) = $66,400

The monthly payment is given by:

$$PMT = PV \, \frac{i}{1 - (1 + i)^{-n}} \qquad \text{where } PV = \$66,400, \; i = \frac{0.1125}{12} = 0.009375,$$
$$\text{and } n = 12(30) = 360$$

$$= 66,400 \, \frac{0.009375}{1 - (1 + 0.009375)^{-360}}$$

$$= \frac{622.50}{1 - (1.009375)^{-360}} \approx \$644.92$$

Next, we find the present value of a $644.92 per month, 22-year annuity:

$$PV = PMT \, \frac{1 - (1 + i)^{-n}}{i} \qquad \text{where } PMT = \$644.92, \; i = 0.009375,$$
$$\text{and } n = 12(22) = 264$$

$$= 644.92 \, \frac{1 - (1 + 0.009375)^{-264}}{0.009375}$$

$$= 68,791.467[1 - (1.009375)^{-264}] = \$62,934.63$$

Finally,

Equity = (current market value) − (unpaid loan balance)

$$= \$95,000 - \$62,934.63 = \$32,065.67$$

The family can borrow up to ($32,065.67)(0.60) = $19,239.

CHAPTER 4   PROBABILITY

Things to remember:

1. MULTIPLICATION PRINCIPLE

    (a) If two operations O_1 and O_2 are performed
         in order, with N_1 possible outcomes for the
         first operation and N_2 possible outcomes
         for the second operation, then there are

         $$N_1 \cdot N_2$$

         possible combined outcomes of the first
         operation followed by the second.

    (b) In general, if n operations O_1, O_2, ..., O_n
         are performed in order, with possible
         number of outcomes N_1, N_2, ..., N_n, respec-
         tively, then there are

         $$N_1 \cdot N_2 \cdot \cdots \cdot N_n$$

         possible combined outcomes of the operations
         performed in the given order.

2. FACTORIAL

    For n a natural number,
    $$n! = n(n - 1)(n - 2) \cdots \cdot 2 \cdot 1$$
    $$0! = 1$$
    $$n! = n(n - 1)!$$

3. PERMUTATIONS OF n OBJECTS TAKEN r AT A TIME

    The number of permutations of n objects taken r
    at a time is given by:

$$P_{n,r} = n(n-1)(n-2) \cdots (n-r+1)$$

$$\text{(r factors)}$$

or

$$P_{n,r} = \frac{n!}{(n-r)!} \qquad 0 \leqslant r \leqslant n$$

$$\left[\underline{\text{Note:}} \quad P_{n,n} = \frac{n!}{(n-n)!} = \frac{n!}{0!} = n!, \right.$$
$$\left. \text{the number of permutations of } n \text{ objects.}\right]$$

<u>**4.**</u>   COMBINATIONS OF n OBJECTS TAKEN r AT A TIME

The number of combinations of n objects taken r at a time is given by:

$$C_{n,r} = \binom{n}{r} = \frac{P_{n,r}}{r!} = \frac{n!}{r!(n-r)!} \qquad 0 \leqslant r \leqslant n$$

<u>**5.**</u>   <u>NOTE:</u>   In a permutation, the <u>ORDER</u> of the objects counts. In a combination, order does not count.

---

1. $4! = 4 \cdot 3 \cdot 2 \cdot 1 = 24$

3. $\dfrac{9!}{8!} = \dfrac{9 \cdot 8!}{8!} = 9$

5. $\dfrac{11!}{8!} = \dfrac{11 \cdot 10 \cdot 9 \cdot 8!}{8!} = 990$

7. $\dfrac{5!}{2!\,3!} = \dfrac{5 \cdot 4 \cdot 3!}{2 \cdot 1 \cdot 3!} = 10$

9. $\dfrac{7!}{4!(7-4)!} = \dfrac{7!}{4!\,3!}$
$$= \dfrac{7 \cdot 6 \cdot 5 \cdot 4!}{4! \cdot 3 \cdot 2 \cdot 1} = 35$$

11. $\dfrac{7!}{7!(7-7)!} = \dfrac{7!}{7!\,0!} = \dfrac{1}{1} = 1$

13. $P_{5,3} = \dfrac{5!}{(5-3)!} = \dfrac{5!}{2!}$
$$= \dfrac{5 \cdot 4 \cdot 3 \cdot 2!}{2!} = 60$$

15. $P_{52,4} = \dfrac{52!}{(52-4)!} = \dfrac{52!}{48!}$
$$= \dfrac{52 \cdot 51 \cdot 50 \cdot 49 \cdot 48!}{48!}$$
$$= 6{,}497{,}400$$

17. $C_{5,3} = \dfrac{5!}{3!(5-3)!} = \dfrac{5!}{3!\,2!}$
$$= \dfrac{5 \cdot 4 \cdot 3!}{3! \cdot 2 \cdot 1} = 10$$

19. $C_{52,4} = \dfrac{52!}{4!(52-4)!} = \dfrac{52!}{4!\,48!}$
$$= \dfrac{52 \cdot 51 \cdot 50 \cdot 49 \cdot 48!}{4 \cdot 3 \cdot 2 \cdot 1 \cdot 48!}$$
$$= 270{,}725$$

21. Using the Multiplication Principle 1:

O_1: Choose the color　　　　　　　　O_3: Choose the interior
N_1: 5 ways　　　　　　　　　　　　　N_3: 4 ways

O_2: Choose the transmission　　　　　O_4: Choose the engine
N_2: 3 ways　　　　　　　　　　　　　N_4: 2 ways

Thus, there are

$$N_1 \cdot N_2 \cdot N_3 \cdot N_4 = 5 \cdot 3 \cdot 4 \cdot 2 = 120$$

different variations of this model car.

23. The number of different finishes (win, place, show) for the ten horses is the number of permutations of 10 objects 3 at a time. This is:

$$P_{10,3} = \frac{10!}{(10-3)!} = \frac{10!}{7!} = \frac{10 \cdot 9 \cdot 8 \cdot 7!}{7!} = 720$$

25. (A) The number of ways that a three-person subcommittee can be selected from a seven-member committee is the number of combinations (since order *is not* important in selecting a subcomittee) of 7 objects 3 at a time. This is:

$$C_{7,3} = \frac{7!}{3!(7-3)!} = \frac{7!}{3!4!} = \frac{7 \cdot 6 \cdot 5 \cdot 4!}{3 \cdot 2 \cdot 1 \cdot 4!} = 35$$

(B) The number of ways a president, vice-president, and secretary can be chosen from a committee of 7 people is the number of permutations (since order *is* important in choosing 3 people for the positions) of 7 objects 3 at a time. This is:

$$P_{7,3} = \frac{7!}{(7-3)!} = \frac{7!}{4!} = \frac{7 \cdot 6 \cdot 5 \cdot 4!}{4!} = 7 \cdot 6 \cdot 5 = 210$$

27. This is a "combinations" problem; we want the number of different ways of selecting two teams from the ten teams.

$$C_{10,2} = \frac{10!}{2!(10-2)!} = \frac{10!}{2!8!} = \frac{10 \cdot 9 \cdot 8!}{2 \cdot 1 \cdot 8!} = 45$$

29. (A) Number of four-letter code words, no letter repeated.

O_1: Selecting the first letter　　　O_3: Selecting the third letter
N_1: 6 ways　　　　　　　　　　　　　N_3: 4 ways

O_2: Selecting the second letter　　O_4: Selecting the fourth letter
N_2: 2 ways　　　　　　　　　　　　　N_4: 3 ways

Thus, there are

$$N_1 \cdot N_2 \cdot N_3 \cdot N_4 = 6 \cdot 5 \cdot 4 \cdot 3 = 360$$

possible code words. Note that this is the number of permutations of 6 objects taken 4 at a time:

$$P_{6,4} = \frac{6!}{(6-4)!} = \frac{6 \cdot 5 \cdot 4 \cdot 3 \cdot 2!}{2!} = 360$$

(B) Number of four-letter code words, allowing repetition.

O_1: Selecting the first letter
N_1: 6 ways

O_3: Selecting the third letter
N_3: 6 ways

O_2: Selecting the second letter
N_2: 6 ways

O_4: Selecting the fourth letter
N_4: 6 ways

Thus, there are

$$N_1 \cdot N_2 \cdot N_3 \cdot N_4 = 6 \cdot 6 \cdot 6 \cdot 6 = 6^4 = 1296$$

possible code words.

31. (A) The number of possible opening combinations, assuming no digits are repeated, is:

$$P_{10,5} = \frac{10!}{(10-5)!} = \frac{10 \cdot 9 \cdot 8 \cdot 7 \cdot 6 \cdot 5!}{5!} = 10 \cdot 9 \cdot 8 \cdot 7 \cdot 6 = 30,240$$

(B) The number of possible opening combinations, assuming that digits can be repeated is:

$$10^5 = 100,000$$

33. This is a "combinations" problem. We want the number of ways to select 5 objects from 13 objects with order not counting. This is:

$$C_{13,5} = \frac{13!}{5!(13-5)!} = \frac{13!}{5!8!} = \frac{13 \cdot 12 \cdot 11 \cdot 10 \cdot 9 \cdot 8!}{5 \cdot 4 \cdot 3 \cdot 2 \cdot 1 \cdot 8!} = 1287$$

35. (A) Letters and/or digits may be repeated.

O_1: Selecting the first letter
N_1: 26 ways

O_4: Selecting the first digit
N_4: 10 ways

O_2: Selecting the second letter
N_2: 26 ways

O_5: Selecting the second digit
N_5: 10 ways

O_3: Selecting the third letter
N_3: 26 ways

O_6: Selecting the third digit
N_6: 10 ways

Thus, there are

$$N_1 \cdot N_2 \cdot N_3 \cdot N_4 \cdot N_5 \cdot N_6 = 26 \cdot 26 \cdot 26 \cdot 10 \cdot 10 \cdot 10 = 17,576,000$$

different license plates.

(B) No repeated letters and no repeated digits are allowed.

O_1: Select the three letters, no letter repeated

$$N_1: P_{26,3} = \frac{26!}{(26-3)!} = \frac{26!}{23!} = \frac{26 \cdot 25 \cdot 24 \cdot 23!}{23!} = 26 \cdot 25 \cdot 24$$

O_2: Select the three numbers, no number repeated

$$N_2: P_{10,3} = \frac{10!}{(10-3)!} = \frac{10!}{7!} = \frac{10 \cdot 9 \cdot 8 \cdot 7!}{7!} = 10 \cdot 9 \cdot 8$$

Thus, there are

$$N_1 \cdot N_2 = 26 \cdot 25 \cdot 24 \cdot 10 \cdot 9 \cdot 8 = 11,232,000$$

different license plates with no letter or digit repeated.

37. The five spades can be selected in $C_{13,5}$ ways and the two hearts can be selected in $C_{13,2}$ ways. Applying the Multiplication Principle, we have:

$$\text{Total number of hands} = C_{13,5} \cdot C_{13,2} = \frac{13!}{5!(13-5)!} \cdot \frac{13!}{2!(13-2)!}$$

$$= \frac{13!}{5!8!} \cdot \frac{13!}{2!11!} = 100,386$$

39. The three appetizers can be selected in $C_{8,3}$ ways. The four main courses can be selected in $C_{10,4}$ ways. The two desserts can be selected in $C_{7,2}$ ways. Now, applying the Multiplication Principle, the total number of ways in which the above can be selected is given by:

$$C_{8,3} \cdot C_{10,4} \cdot C_{7,2} = \frac{8!}{3!(8-3)!} \cdot \frac{10!}{4!(10-4)!} \cdot \frac{7!}{2!(7-2)!} = 246,960$$

41. O_1: Select the left-hand glove
N_1: 12 ways

O_2: Select the right-hand glove, different brand from the left-hand glove
N_2: 11 ways

Thus, there are

$$N_1 \cdot N_2 = 12 \cdot 11 = 132$$

pairs of gloves that do not match.

43. (A) A chord joins two distinct points. Thus, the total number of chords is given by:

$$C_{8,2} = \frac{8!}{2!(8-2)!} = \frac{8!}{2!6!} = \frac{8 \cdot 7 \cdot 6!}{2 \cdot 1 \cdot 6!} = 28$$

(B) Each triangle requires three distinct points. Thus, there are

$$C_{8,3} = \frac{8!}{3!(8-3)!} = \frac{8!}{3!5!} = \frac{8 \cdot 7 \cdot 6 \cdot 5!}{3 \cdot 2 \cdot 1 \cdot 5!} = 56$$

triangles.

(C) Each quadrilateral requires four distinct points. Thus, there are

$$C_{8,4} = \frac{8!}{4!(8-4)!} = \frac{8!}{4!4!} = \frac{8 \cdot 7 \cdot 6 \cdot 5 \cdot 4!}{4 \cdot 3 \cdot 2 \cdot 1 \cdot 4!} = 70$$

quadrilaterals.

45. (A) Two people.

O_1: First person selects a chair O_2: Second person selects a chair
N_1: 5 ways N_2: 4 ways

Thus, there are

$$N_1 \cdot N_2 = 5 \cdot 4 = 20$$

ways to seat two people in a row of 5 chairs. Note that this is $P_{5,2}$.

(B) Three people. There will be $P_{5,3}$ ways to seat 3 people in a row of 5 chairs:

$$P_{5,3} = \frac{5!}{(5-3)!} = \frac{5!}{2!} = \frac{5 \cdot 4 \cdot 3 \cdot 2!}{2!} = 60$$

(C) Four people. The number of ways to seat 4 people in a row of 5 chairs is given by:

$$P_{5,4} = \frac{5!}{(5-4)!} = \frac{5!}{1!} = 5 \cdot 4 \cdot 3 \cdot 2 = 120$$

(D) Five people. The number of ways to seat 5 people in a row of 5 chairs is given by:

$$P_{5,5} = \frac{5!}{(5-1)!} = \frac{5!}{0!} = 5! = 120$$

47. (A) The distinct positions are taken into consideration. The number of starting teams is given by:

$$P_{8,5} = \frac{8!}{(8-5)!} = \frac{8!}{3!} = \frac{8 \cdot 7 \cdot 6 \cdot 5 \cdot 4 \cdot 3!}{3!} = 6720$$

(B) The distinct positions are not taken into consideration. The number of starting teams is given by:

$$C_{8,5} = \frac{8!}{5!(8-5)!} = \frac{8!}{5!3!} = \frac{8 \cdot 7 \cdot 6 \cdot 5!}{5! \cdot 3 \cdot 2 \cdot 1} = 56$$

(C) Either Mike or Ken, but not both, must start; distinct positions are not taken into consideration.

O_1: Select either Mike or Ken
N_1: 2 ways

O_2: Select 4 players from the remaining 6
N_2: $C_{6,4}$

Thus, the number of starting teams is given by:

$$N_1 \cdot N_2 = 2 \cdot C_{6,4}$$

$$= 2 \cdot \frac{6!}{4!(6-4)!}$$

$$= 2 \cdot \frac{6 \cdot 5 \cdot 4!}{4! \cdot 2 \cdot 1} = 30$$

49. **(A)**

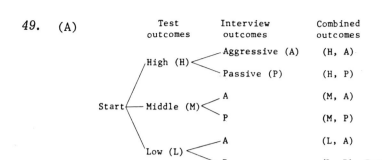

(B) Operation 1: Test scores can be classified into three groups, high, middle, or low:

$$N_1 = 3$$

Operation 2: Interviews can be classified into two groups, aggressive or passive:

$$N_2 = 2$$

The total possible combined classifications is:

$$N_1 \cdot N_2 = 3 \cdot 2 = 6$$

51. O_1: Travel from home to airport and back O_3: Fly to second city
N_1: 2 ways N_3: 2 ways

O_2: Fly to first city O_4: Fly to third city
N_2: 3 ways N_4: 1 way

Thus, there are

$$N_1 \cdot N_2 \cdot N_3 \cdot N_4 = 2 \cdot 3 \cdot 2 \cdot 1 = 12$$

different travel plans.

53. **(A)** Three females can be selected in $C_{6,3}$ ways. Two males can be selected in $C_{5,2}$ ways. Applying the Multiplication Principle, we have:

$$\text{Total number of ways} = C_{6,3} \cdot C_{5,2} = \frac{6!}{3!\,(6-3)!} \cdot \frac{5!}{2!\,(5-2)!} = 200$$

(B) Four females and one male can be selected in $C_{6,4} \cdot C_{5,1}$ ways. Thus,

$$C_{6,4} \cdot C_{5,1} = \frac{6!}{4!\,(6-4)!} \cdot \frac{5!}{1!\,(5-1)!} = 75$$

(C) Number of ways in which 5 females can be selected is:

$$C_{6,5} = \frac{6!}{5!\,(6-5)!} = 6$$

(D) Number of ways in which 5 people can be selected is:

$$C_{6+5,5} = C_{11,5} = \frac{11!}{5!(11-5)!} = 462$$

(E) At least four females includes four females and five females. Four females and one male can be selected in 75 ways [see part (B)]. Five females can be selected in 6 ways [see part (C)]. Thus,

Total number of ways $= C_{6,4} \cdot C_{5,1} + C_{6,5} = 75 + 6 = 81$

55. (A)

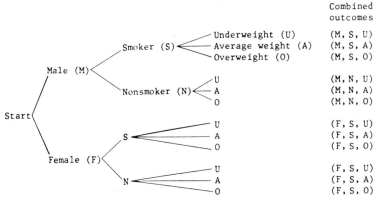

(B) Operation 1: Two classifications, male and female; $N_1 = 2$.
Operation 2: Two classifications, smoker and nonsmoker; $N_2 = 2$.
Operation 3: Three classifications, underweight, average weight, and overweight; $N_3 = 3$.

Using <u>2</u>, the total possible combined classifications $= N_1 \cdot N_2 \cdot N_3$
$= 2 \cdot 2 \cdot 3$
$= 12$

57. (A) Select 3 samples from 8 blood tyes, no two samples having the same type. This is a permutation problem. The number of different examinations is:

$$P_{8,3} = \frac{8!}{(8-3)!} = \frac{8!}{5!} = \frac{8 \cdot 7 \cdot 6 \cdot 5!}{5!} = 336$$

(B) Select 3 samples from 8 blood types, repetition is allowed.

O_1: Select the first sample
N_1: 8 ways

O_2: Select the second sample
N_2: 8 ways

O_3: Select the third sample
N_3: 8 ways

Thus, the number of different examinations in this case is:

$$N_1 \cdot N_2 \cdot N_3 = 8 \cdot 8 \cdot 8 = 8^3 = 512$$

59. This is a permutation problem. The number of buttons is given by:

$$P_{4,2} = \frac{4!}{(4-2)!} = \frac{4!}{2!} = \frac{4 \cdot 3 \cdot 2!}{2!} = 12$$

EXERCISE 4-2

Things to remember:

1. SAMPLE SPACE

A set S is a SAMPLE SPACE for an experiment if:

(a) Each element of S is an outcome of the experiment.

(b) Each outcome of the experiment corresponds to one and only one element of S.

Each element in the sample space is called a SAMPLE POINT or SIMPLE OUTCOME.

2. EVENT

Given a sample space S. An EVENT E is a subset of S. Event E OCCURS if any of the simple outcomes in E occurs. An event with only one element is called a SIMPLE EVENT; an event with more than one element is a COMPOUND EVENT.

3. PROBABILITIES FOR SIMPLE EVENTS

Given a sample space

$$S = \{e_1, e_2, \ldots, e_n\}.$$

To each simple event e_i assign a real number $P(e_i)$, called the PROBABILITY OF THE EVENT e_i, such that the following conditions are satisfied:

(a) $0 \leqslant P(e_i) \leqslant 1$

(b) $P(e_1) + P(e_2) + \cdots + P(e_n) = 1$

Any probability assignment that meets these two conditions is called an ACCEPTABLE PROBABILITY ASSIGNMENT.

4. PROBABILITY OF AN EVENT E

Given an acceptable probability assignment for the simple events in a sample space S, the probability of an arbitrary event E, denoted $P(E)$, is defined as follows:

(a) $P(E) = 0$ if E is the empty set.

(b) If E is a simple event, then $P(E)$ has already been assigned.

(c) If E is the union of two or more simple events, then $P(E)$ is the sum of the probabilities of the simple events whose union is E.

(d) If $E = S$, then $P(E) = P(S) = 1$.

5. PROBABILITIES UNDER AN EQUALLY LIKELY ASSUMPTION

If, in a sample space

$$S = \{e_1, e_2, \ldots, e_n\},$$

each simple event is as likely to occur as any other, then $P(e_i) = 1/n$, $i = 1, 2, \ldots, n$. The probability of an arbitrary event E in this case is:

$$P(E) = \frac{\text{Number of elements in } E}{\text{Number of elements in } S} = \frac{n(E)}{n(S)}$$

---

1. $P(E) = 1$ means that the occurrence of E is certain.

3. Let H = heads and T = tails. Then,

$$S = \{(H, H, H), (H, H, T), (H, T, H), (H, T, T), (T, H, H),$$
$$(T, H, T), (T, T, H), (T, T, T)\},$$

where (H, H, T) means that heads appears first, heads second, and tails third, and so on.

5. $E = \{(H, H, T), (H, T, H), (T, H, H), (H, H, H)\}$

$$P(E) = \frac{n(E)}{n(S)} = \frac{4}{8} = \frac{1}{2}$$

7. We reject (A) because $P(G) = -0.35$, and probability cannot be negative.

We reject (B) because $P(R) + P(G) + P(Y) + P(B) = .32 + .28 + .24 + .30 = 1.14 \neq 1$.

9. $E = \{R, Y\}$

$$P(E) = P(R) + P(Y)$$
$$= .26 + .30 = .56$$

11. The number of three-digit sequences with no digit repeated is $P_{10,3}$. Since the possible opening combinations are equally likely, the probability of guessing the right combination is:

$$\frac{1}{P_{10,3}} = \frac{1}{10 \cdot 9 \cdot 8} = \frac{1}{720} \approx 0.0014$$

13. Let S = the set of five-card hands. Then $n(S) = C_{52,5}$.
Let A = "five black cards." Then $n(A) = C_{26,5}$.

Since individual hands are equally likely to occur:

$$P(A) = \frac{n(A)}{n(S)} = \frac{C_{26,5}}{C_{52,5}} = \frac{\frac{26!}{5!21!}}{\frac{52!}{5!47!}} = \frac{26 \cdot 25 \cdot 24 \cdot 23 \cdot 22}{52 \cdot 51 \cdot 50 \cdot 49 \cdot 48} \approx 0.025$$

15. S = set of five-card hands; $n(S) = C_{52,5}$.
B = "five face cards, including aces"; $n(B) = C_{16,5}$.

Since individual hands are equally likely to occur:

$$P(B) = \frac{n(B)}{n(S)} = \frac{C_{16,5}}{C_{52,5}} = \frac{\frac{16!}{5!11!}}{\frac{52!}{5!47!}} = \frac{16 \cdot 15 \cdot 14 \cdot 13 \cdot 12}{52 \cdot 51 \cdot 50 \cdot 49 \cdot 48} \approx 0.00168$$

17. The thousands digit can be selected in 2 ways (1 and 3).
The hundreds digit can be selected in 5 ways.
The tens digit can be selected in 5 ways.
The ones digit can be selected in 5 ways.

Thus, $n(S) = 2 \cdot 5 \cdot 5 \cdot 5 = 250$, where S is the set of five-digit numbers less than 5000 formed from 1, 3, 5, 7, and 9.

To form a number that is divisible by 5, the last digit (the ones digit) must be a 5. Thus, $n(A) = 2 \cdot 5 \cdot 5 \cdot 1 = 50$, where A is the elements of S which are divisible by 5.

Since the simple events are equally likely:

$$P(A) = \frac{n(A)}{n(S)} = \frac{50}{250} = .2$$

19. $n(S) = P_{5,5} = 5! = 120$

Let A = all notes inserted into the correct envelopes. Then $n(A) = 1$ and

$$P(A) = \frac{n(A)}{n(S)} = \frac{1}{120} \approx 0.008.$$

21. Using the sample space shown in Figure 1, we have

$n(S) = 36$, $n(A) = 1$,

where Event A = "Sum being 2":

$$P(A) = \frac{n(A)}{n(S)} = \frac{1}{16}$$

23. Let E = "Sum being 6." Then $n(E) = 5$. Thus, $P(E) = \dfrac{n(E)}{n(S)} = \dfrac{5}{36}$.

25. Let E = "Sum being less than 5." Then $n(E) = 6$. Thus, $P(E) = \dfrac{n(E)}{n(S)} = \dfrac{6}{36}$
$$= \dfrac{1}{6}.$$

27. Let E = "Sum not 7 or 11." Then $n(E) = 28$. Thus, $P(E) = \dfrac{n(E)}{n(S)} = \dfrac{28}{36} = \dfrac{7}{9}$.

29. E = "Sum being 1" is not possible. Thus, $P(E) = 0$.

31. Let E = "Sum is divisible by 3" = "Sum is 3, 6, 9, or 12." Then $n(E) = 12$

and $P(E) = \dfrac{n(E)}{n(S)} = \dfrac{12}{36} = \dfrac{1}{3}$.

33. Let E = "Sum is 7 or 11." Then $n(E) = 8$. Thus, $P(E) = \dfrac{n(E)}{n(S)} = \dfrac{8}{36} = \dfrac{2}{9}$.

35. Let E = "Sum is divisible by 2 or 3" = "Sum is 2, 3, 4, 6, 8, 9, 10, 12."

Then $n(E) = 24$, and $P(E) = \dfrac{n(E)}{n(S)} = \dfrac{24}{36} = \dfrac{2}{3}$.

For Problems 37–41, the sample space S is given by:
$$S = \{(H, H, H), (H, H, T), (H, T, H), (H, T, T)\}$$
The outcomes are equally likely and $n(S) = 4$.

37. Let E = "1 head." Then $n(E) = 1$ and $P(E) = \dfrac{n(E)}{n(S)} = \dfrac{1}{4}$.

39. Let E = "3 heads." Then $n(E) = 1$ and $P(E) = \dfrac{n(E)}{n(S)} = \dfrac{1}{4}$.

41. Let E = "More than 1 head." Then $n(E) = 3$ and $P(E) = \dfrac{n(E)}{n(S)} = \dfrac{3}{4}$.

For Problems 43–49, the sample space S is given by:
$$S = \begin{Bmatrix} (1, 1), (1, 2), (1, 3) \\ (2, 1), (2, 2), (2, 3) \\ (3, 1), (3, 2), (3, 3) \end{Bmatrix}$$
The outcomes are equally likely and $n(S) = 9$.

43. Let E = "Sum is 2." Then $n(E) = 1$ and $P(E) = \dfrac{n(E)}{n(S)} = \dfrac{1}{9}$.

45. Let E = "Sum is 4." Then $n(E) = 3$ and $P(E) = \dfrac{n(E)}{n(S)} = \dfrac{3}{9} = \dfrac{1}{3}$.

47. Let E = "Sum is 6." Then $n(E) = 1$ and $P(E) = \dfrac{n(E)}{n(S)} = \dfrac{1}{9}$.

49. Let E = "Sum is odd" = "Sum is 3 or 5." Then $n(E) = 4$ and

$P(E) = \dfrac{n(E)}{n(S)} = \dfrac{4}{9}$.

In Problems 51–57, the sample space S is the set of all 5-card hands. Then $n(S) = C_{52,5}$. The outcomes are equally likely.

51. Let E = "5 face cards, jacks through aces." Then $n(E) = C_{16,5}$. Thus,

$$P(E) = \frac{C_{16,5}}{C_{52,5}} = \frac{\dfrac{16!}{5!\,11!}}{\dfrac{52!}{5!\,47!}} = \frac{16 \cdot 15 \cdot 14 \cdot 13 \cdot 12}{52 \cdot 51 \cdot 50 \cdot 49 \cdot 48} \approx 0.00168.$$

53. Let E = "4 aces." Then $n(E) = 48$ (the remaining card can be any one of the 48 cards which are not aces). Thus,

$$P(E) = \frac{48}{C_{52,5}} = \frac{48}{\dfrac{52!}{5!\,47!}} = \frac{48}{52 \cdot 51 \cdot 50 \cdot 49 \cdot 48} \approx 0.000018.$$

55. Let E = "Straight flush, ace high." Then $n(E) = 4$ (one such hand in each suit). Thus,

$$P(E) = \frac{4}{C_{52,5}} = \frac{4}{52 \cdot 51 \cdot 50 \cdot 49 \cdot 48} \approx 0.000001.$$

57. Let E = "2 aces and 3 queens." The number of ways to get 2 aces is $C_{4,2}$ and the number of ways to get 3 queens is $C_{4,3}$. Thus,

$$n(E) = C_{4,2} \cdot C_{4,3} = \frac{4!}{2!\,2!} \cdot \frac{4!}{3!\,1!} = \frac{4 \cdot 3}{2} \cdot \frac{4}{1} = 24$$

and

$$P(E) = \frac{n(E)}{n(S)} = \frac{24}{C_{52,5}} = \frac{24}{52 \cdot 51 \cdot 50 \cdot 49 \cdot 48} \approx 0.000009.$$

59. (A) The sample space S is the set of all possible permutations of the 12 brands taken 4 at a time, and $n(S) = P_{12,4}$. Thus, the probability of selecting 4 brands and identifying them correctly, with no answer repeated, is:

$$P(E) = \frac{1}{P_{12,4}} = \frac{1}{\dfrac{12!}{(12-4)!}} = \frac{1}{12 \cdot 11 \cdot 10 \cdot 9} \approx 0.000084$$

(B) Allowing repetition, $n(S) = 12^4$ and the probability of identifying them correctly is:

$$P(F) = \frac{1}{12^4} \approx 0.00004$$

61. The sample space S consists of the set of all 6-element samples of the 100 cassettes, and $n(S) = C_{100,6}$. Let E be the event "At least one defective cassette." Then,

$$n(E) = C_{5,1} \cdot C_{95,5} + C_{5,2} \cdot C_{95,4} + C_{5,3} \cdot C_{95,3} + C_{5,4} \cdot C_{95,2} + C_{5,5} \cdot C_{95,1}$$

where $C_{5,i} \cdot C_{95,6-i}$, $1 \leqslant i \leqslant 5$, is the number of ways for a sample of 6 to have exactly i defective cassettes. The number of elements in E is also given by

$$n(E) = C_{100,6} - C_{95,6}$$

since $C_{95,6}$ is the total number of ways that a sample of 6 will have *no* defective cassettes. Thus,

$$P(E) = \frac{n(E)}{n(S)} = \frac{C_{100,6} - C_{95,6}}{C_{100,6}} = 1 - \frac{C_{95,6}}{C_{100,6}} \approx 0.27.$$

63. (A) Total number of applicants $= 6 + 5 = 11$.

$$n(S) = C_{11,5} = \frac{11!}{5!(11-5)!} = 462$$

The number of ways that three females and two males can be selected is:

$$C_{6,3} \cdot C_{5,2} = \frac{6!}{3!(6-3)!} \cdot \frac{5!}{2!(5-2)!} = 20 \cdot 10 = 200$$

Thus, $P(A) = \dfrac{C_{6,3} \cdot C_{5,2}}{C_{11,5}} = \dfrac{200}{462} = 0.433$

(B) $P(\text{4 females and 1 male}) = \dfrac{C_{6,4} \cdot C_{5,1}}{C_{11,5}} = 0.162$

(C) $P(\text{5 females}) = \dfrac{C_{6,5}}{C_{11,5}} = 0.013$

(D) $P(\text{at least four females}) = P(\text{4 females and 1 male}) + P(\text{5 females})$

$$= \frac{C_{6,5} \cdot C_{5,1}}{C_{11,5}} + \frac{C_{6,5}}{C_{11,5}}$$

$$= 0.162 + 0.013 \ [\text{refer to parts (B) and (C)}]$$

$$= 0.175$$

65. (A) The sample space S consists of the number of permutations of the 8 blood types chosen 3 at a time. Thus, $n(S) = P_{8,3}$ and the probability of guessing the three types in a sample correctly is:

$$P(E) = \frac{1}{P_{8,3}} = \frac{1}{\dfrac{8!}{(8-3)!}} = \frac{1}{8 \cdot 7 \cdot 6} \approx 0.0030$$

(B) Allowing repetition, $n(S) = 8^3$ and the probability of guessing the three types in a sample correctly is:

$$P(E) = \frac{1}{8^3} \approx 0.0020$$

67. **(A)** The total number of ways of selecting a president and a vice-president from the 11 members of the council is:

$P_{11,2}$, i.e., $n(S) = P_{11,2}$.

The total number of ways of selecting the president and the vice-president from the 6 Democrats is $P_{6,2}$. Thus, if E is the event "The president and vice-president are both Democrats," then

$$P(E) = \frac{P_{6,2}}{P_{11,2}} = \frac{\dfrac{6!}{(6-2)!}}{\dfrac{11!}{(11-2)!}} = \frac{6 \cdot 5}{11 \cdot 10} = \frac{30}{110} \approx 0.273.$$

(B) The total number of ways of selecting a committee of 3 from the 11 members of the council is:

$C_{11,3}$, i.e., $n(S) = C_{11,3} = \dfrac{11!}{3!(11-3)!} = \dfrac{11 \cdot 10 \cdot 9 \cdot 8!}{3 \cdot 2 \cdot 1 \cdot 8!} = 165$

If we let F be the event "The majority are Republicans," which is the same as having either 2 Republicans and 1 Democrat or all 3 Republicans, then

$$n(F) = C_{5,2} \cdot C_{6,1} + C_{5,3} = \frac{5!}{2!(5-2)!} \cdot \frac{6!}{1!(6-1)!} + \frac{5!}{3!(5-3)!}$$

$$= 10 \cdot 6 + 10 = 70.$$

Thus,

$$P(F) = \frac{n(F)}{n(S)} = \frac{70}{165} \approx 0.424.$$

Let E be an event and let n be the number of trials (or Expt). If E occurs k times in n trials, then the empirical probability of E $P(E) = \frac{k}{n}$

EXERCISE 4-3

Know This

Things to remember:

1. EMPIRICAL PROBABILITY OF EVENT E = $P(E) \approx \dfrac{f(E)}{n}$,

    where $f(E)$ = frequency of Event E, and n = total
    number of trials. *Empirical probability is different from theoretical probability, when n is large enough we expect the empirical probability to be close to the theoretical probability.*

1. Total number of trials: $n = 250$
    Frequency of event E: $f(E) = 25$

    Hence, $P(E) \approx \dfrac{25}{250} = .1$ (using 1)

3. $f(E) = 189$
    $n = 420$ ✓

    Hence, $P(E) \approx \dfrac{189}{420} = .45$

5. Event E_1 = "point down," $f(E_1) = 389$
Event E_2 = "point up," $f(E_2) = 611$
Total number of trials,

$n = 389 + 611 = 1000$

Thus, $P(E_1) \approx \dfrac{f(E_1)}{n} = \dfrac{389}{1000}$

and

$P(E_1) \approx .389$ (1)

$P(E_2) \approx \dfrac{f(E_2)}{n} = \dfrac{611}{1000}$

and

$P(E_2) \approx .611$ (2)

From (1) and (2), we conclude that the outcomes *do not* appear to be "equally likely."

9. (A)   Event E_1 = "3 heads," $f(E_1) = 132$
Event E_2 = "2 heads," $f(E_2) = 368$
Event E_3 = "1 head," $f(E_3) = 380$
Event E_4 = "0 heads," $f(E_4) = 120$
Total number of trials,

$n = 132 + 368 + 380 + 120 = 1000$

Thus, $P(E_1) \approx \dfrac{132}{1000} = .132$

$P(E_2) \approx \dfrac{368}{1000} = .368$

$P(E_3) \approx \dfrac{380}{1000} = .38$

$P(E_4) \approx \dfrac{120}{1000} = .12$

(C)   Using the results from part (B), the expected frequencies for each outcome are as follows:

3 heads = $1000 \cdot .125 = 125$

2 heads = $1000 \cdot .375 = 375$

1 head = $1000 \cdot .375 = 375$

0 heads = $1000 \cdot .125 = 125$

7. (A)   Empirical probabilities are as follows:

$P(2 \text{ girls}) \approx \dfrac{2351}{10,000} = .2351$

$P(1 \text{ girl}) \approx \dfrac{5435}{10,000} = .5435$

$P(0 \text{ girls}) \approx \dfrac{2214}{10,000} = .2214$

(B)   Theoretical probabilities are as follows:

$n(S) = 4$, $S = \{GG,\ GB,\ BG,\ BB\}$

$P(2 \text{ girls}) = \dfrac{1}{4} = .25$

$P(1 \text{ girl}) = \dfrac{2}{4} = .5$

$P(0 \text{ girls}) = \dfrac{1}{4} = .25$

(B)   Sample space $S = \{$HHH, HTH, THH, HHT, TTH, THT, HTT, TTT$\}$. Thus, the theoretical probabilities are as follows:

$P(3 \text{ heads}) = \dfrac{1}{8} = .125$

$P(2 \text{ heads}) = \dfrac{3}{8} = .375$

$P(1 \text{ heads}) = \dfrac{3}{8} = .375$

$P(0 \text{ heads}) = \dfrac{1}{8} = .125$

11. Sample space $S = \{$HHHH, THHH, HTHH, HHTH, HHHT, TTHH, THTH, HTTH, HTHT, HHTT, THHT, TTTH, TTHT, THTT, HTTT, TTTT$\}$. Thus, the theoretical probabilities are as follows:

$P(4 \text{ heads}) = \dfrac{1}{16}$

$P(3 \text{ heads}) = \dfrac{4}{16} = \dfrac{1}{4}$

$P(2 \text{ heads}) = \dfrac{6}{16} = \dfrac{3}{8}$

$P(1 \text{ head}) = \dfrac{4}{16} = \dfrac{1}{4}$

$P(0 \text{ heads}) = \dfrac{1}{16}$

The expected frequencies for each outcome are as follows:

$4 \text{ heads} = 80 \cdot \dfrac{1}{16} = 5$

$3 \text{ heads} = 80 \cdot \dfrac{1}{4} = 20$

$2 \text{ heads} = 80 \cdot \dfrac{3}{8} = 30$

$1 \text{ head} = 80 \cdot \dfrac{1}{4} = 20$

$0 \text{ heads} = 80 \cdot \dfrac{1}{16} = 5$

13. (A) $n(A) = 15$

$P(A) = \dfrac{15}{1000} = .015$

(B) $n(B) = 130 + 80 + 12 = 222$

$P(B) = \dfrac{222}{1000} = .222$

(C) Event $C = $ "Earning more than \$30,000 per year or owning more than three television sets."

$n(C) = 30 + 32 + 28 + 25 + 20 \\ \qquad\qquad + 1 + 12 + 21$

$\qquad = 169$

$P(C) = \dfrac{169}{1000} = .169$

(D) $n(D) = 1000 - (2 + 10 + 30)$

$\qquad = 958$

(958 families own at least one television set)

$P(D) = \dfrac{958}{1000} = .958$

15. (A) $P(\text{red}) \approx \dfrac{300}{1000} = .3$

$P(\text{pink}) \approx \dfrac{440}{1000} = .44$

$P(\text{white}) \approx \dfrac{260}{1000} = .260$

(B) $P(\text{red} = \dfrac{1}{4}$; $P(\text{pink}) = \dfrac{1}{2}$;

$P(\text{white}) = \dfrac{1}{4}$.

The expected frequencies for each color are as follows:

$P(\text{red}) = 1000 \cdot \dfrac{1}{4} = 250$

$P(\text{pink}) = 1000 \cdot \dfrac{1}{2} = 500$

$P(\text{white}) = 1000 \cdot \dfrac{1}{4} = 250$

Things to remember:

1. RANDOM VARIABLE

A random variable is a function that assigns a numerical value to each simple event in a sample space S.

2. PROBABILITY DISTRIBUTION OF A RANDOM VARIABLE X

A probability function $P(X = x) = p(x)$ is a PROBABILITY DISTRIBUTION OF THE RANDOM VARIABLE X if

(a) $0 \leqslant p(x) \leqslant 1$, $x \in \{x_1, x_2, \ldots, x_n\}$,

(b) $p(x_1) + p(x_2) + \cdots + p(x_n) = 1$,

where $\{x_1, x_2, \ldots, x_n\}$ are the values of X.

3. EXPECTED VALUE OF A RANDOM VARIABLE X

Given the probability distribution for the random variable X:

$$x_i: x_1, x_2, \cdots x_m$$
$$p_i: p_1, p_2, \cdots p_m \qquad p_i = p(x_i)$$

The expected value of X, denoted by $E(X)$, is given by the formula:

$$E(X) = x_1 p_1 + x_2 p_2 + \cdots + x_m p_m$$

4. Steps for computing the expected value of a random variable X.

(a) Form the probability distribution for the random variable X.

(b) Multiply each image value of X, x_i, by its corresponding probability of occurrence, p_i, then add the results.

---

1. Expected value of X:

$$E(X) = -3(.3) + 0(.5) + 4(.2) = -0.1$$

3. Assign the number 0 to the event of observing zero heads, the number 1 to the event of observing one head, and the number 2 to the event of observing two heads. The probability distribution for x, then, is:

x_i	0	1	2
p_i	$\frac{1}{4}$	$\frac{1}{2}$	$\frac{1}{4}$

[Note: One head can occur two ways out of a total of four different ways (HT, TH).]

Hence, $E(X) = 0 \cdot \frac{1}{4} + 1 \cdot \frac{1}{2} + 2 \cdot \frac{1}{4} = 1$.

5. Assign a payoff to $1 to the event of observing a head and -$1 to the event of observing a tail. Thus, the probability distribution for x is:

x_i	1	-1
p_i	$\frac{1}{2}$	$\frac{1}{2}$

Hence, $E(X) = 1 \cdot \frac{1}{2} + (-1) \cdot \frac{1}{2} = 0$. The game is fair.

7. The table shows a payoff or probability distribution for the game.

Net gain

x_i	-3	-2	-1	0	1	2
p_i	$\frac{1}{6}$	$\frac{1}{6}$	$\frac{1}{6}$	$\frac{1}{6}$	$\frac{1}{6}$	$\frac{1}{6}$

[Note: A payoff valued at -$3 is assigned to the event of observing a "1" on the die, resulting in a net gain of -$3, and so on.]

Hence, $E(X) = -3 \cdot \frac{1}{6} - 2 \cdot \frac{1}{6} - 1 \cdot \frac{1}{6} + 0 \cdot \frac{1}{6} + 1 \cdot \frac{1}{6} + 2 \cdot \frac{1}{6} = -\frac{1}{2}$ or -$0.50.

The game is not fair.

9. The probability distribution is:

Number of Heads	Gain, x_i	Probability, p_i
0	2	1/4
1	-3	1/2
2	2	1/4

The expected value is:

$$E(X) = 2 \cdot \frac{1}{4} + (-3) \cdot \frac{1}{2} + 2 \cdot \frac{1}{4} = 1 - \frac{3}{2} = -\frac{1}{2} \text{ or } -\$0.50.$$

11. In 4 rolls of a die, the total number of possible outcomes is $6 \cdot 6 \cdot 6 \cdot 6 = 6^4$. Thus, $n(S) = 6^4 = 1296$. The total number of outcomes that contain no 6's is $5 \cdot 5 \cdot 5 \cdot 5 = 5^4$. Thus, if E is the event "At least one 6," then $n(E) = 6^4 - 5^4 = 671$ and

$$P(E) = \frac{n(E)}{n(S)} = \frac{671}{1296} \approx 0.5178.$$

First, we compute the expected value to you.

The payoff table is:

x_i	-$1	$1
P_i	0.5178	0.4823

The expected value to you is:

$E(X) = (-1)(0.5178) + 1(0.4822) = -0.0356$ or $-\$0.036$

The expected value to her is:

$E(X) = 1(0.5178) + (-1)(0.4822) = 0.0356$ or $\$0.036$

13. $P(\text{sum} = 7) = \dfrac{6}{36} = \dfrac{1}{6}$

$P(\text{sum} = 11 \text{ or } 12) = P(\text{sum} = 11) + P(\text{sum} = 12)$

$$= \frac{2}{36} + \frac{1}{36} = \frac{3}{36} = \frac{1}{12}$$

$P(\text{sum other than 7, 11, or 12}) = 1 - P(\text{sum} = 7, 11, \text{ or } 12)$

$$= 1 - \frac{9}{36} = \frac{27}{36} = \frac{3}{4}$$

Let x_1 = sum is 7, x_2 = sum is 11 or 12, x_3 = sum is not 7, 11, or 12, and let t denote the amount you "win" if x_3 occurs. Then, the payoff table is:

x_i	-$10	$11	t
p_i	$\dfrac{1}{6}$	$\dfrac{1}{12}$	$\dfrac{3}{4}$

The expected value is:

$$E(X) = -10\left(\frac{1}{6}\right) + 11\left(\frac{1}{12}\right) + t\left(\frac{3}{4}\right) = \frac{-10}{6} + \frac{11}{12} + \frac{3t}{4}$$

The game is fair if $E(X) = 0$, i.e., if

$$\frac{-10}{6} + \frac{11}{12} + \frac{3}{4}t = 0 \quad \text{or} \quad \frac{3}{4}t = \frac{10}{6} - \frac{11}{12} = \frac{20}{12} - \frac{11}{12} = \frac{9}{12} = \frac{3}{4}$$

Therefore, $t = \$1$.

15. Course A_1: $E(X) = (-200)(.2) + 100(.2) + 400(.4) + 100(.3)$
$$= -20 + 20 + 160 + 30$$
$$= \$190$$

Course A_2: $E(X) = (-100)(.1) + 200(.1) + 300(.4) + 200(.3)$
$$= -10 + 40 + 120 + 60$$
$$= \$210$$

A_2 will produce the largest expected value, and that value is $210.

17. The probability of winning $35 is 1/38 and the probability of losing $1 is 37/38. Thus, the payoff table is:

x_i	$35	-$1
P_i	$\dfrac{1}{38}$	$\dfrac{37}{38}$

The expected value of the game is:

$$E(X) = 35\left(\frac{1}{38}\right) + (-1)\left(\frac{37}{38}\right) = \frac{35 - 37}{38} = \frac{-1}{19} \approx -0.0526 \text{ or } E(X) = -\$0.05$$

19.

p_i		x_i
$\dfrac{1}{5000}$	chance of winning	$499
$\dfrac{3}{5000}$	chance of winning	$99
$\dfrac{5}{5000}$	chance of winning	$19
$\dfrac{20}{5000}$	chance of winning	$4
$\dfrac{4971}{5000}$	chance of losing	$1 [Note: 5000 − (1 + 3 + 5 + 20) = 4971.]

The payoff table is:

x_i	$499	$99	$19	$4	-$1
P_i	0.0002	0.0006	0.001	0.004	0.9942

Thus,

$$E(X) = 499(0.0002) + 99(0.0006) + 19(0.001) + 4(0.004) - 1(0.9942)$$
$$= -0.80$$

or

$$E(X) = -\$0.80$$

21. (A) Total number of simple events $= n(S) = C_{10,2} = \dfrac{10!}{2!\,(10 - 2)!}$

$$= \frac{10!}{2!\,8!} = \frac{10 \cdot 9}{2} = 45$$

$P(\text{zero defective}) = P(0) = \dfrac{C_{7,2}}{45}$ [Note: None defective means 2 selected from 7 nondefective.]

$$= \frac{\dfrac{7!}{2!\,5!}}{45} = \frac{21}{45} = 0.46\overline{8} \approx 0.47$$

$$P(\text{one defective}) = P(1) = \frac{C_{3,1} \cdot C_{7,1}}{45} = \frac{21}{45} = 0.46\overline{8} \approx 0.47$$

$$P(\text{two defective}) = P(2) = \frac{C_{3,2}}{45} \quad \text{[\underline{Note}: Two defectives selected from 3 defectives.]}$$

$$= \frac{3}{45} = 0.0\overline{6} \approx 0.07$$

The probability distribution is as follows:

x_i	0	1	2
P_i	0.47	0.46	0.07

(B) $E(X) = 0(0.47) + 1(0.47) + 2(0.07) = 0.61 \approx 0.63$

23. (A) The total number of simple events = $n(S) = C_{1000,5}$.

$$P(\text{0 winning tickets}) = P(0) = \frac{C_{997,5}}{C_{1000,5}} = \frac{997 \cdot 996 \cdot 995 \cdot 994 \cdot 993}{1000 \cdot 999 \cdot 998 \cdot 997 \cdot 996}$$

$$\approx 0.985$$

$$P(\text{1 winning ticket}) = P(1) = \frac{C_{3,1} \cdot C_{997,4}}{C_{1000,5}} = \frac{3 \cdot \dfrac{997!}{4!(993)!}}{\dfrac{1000!}{5!(995)!}} \approx 0.0149$$

$$P(\text{2 winning tickets}) = P(2) = \frac{C_{3,2} \cdot C_{997,3}}{C_{1000,5}} = \frac{3 \cdot \dfrac{997!}{3!(994)!}}{\dfrac{1000!}{5!(995)!}} \approx 0.0000599$$

$$P(\text{3 winning tickets}) = P(3) = \frac{C_{3,3} \cdot C_{997,2}}{C_{1000,5}} = \frac{1 \cdot \dfrac{997!}{2!(995)!}}{\dfrac{1000!}{5!(995)!}} \approx 0.00000006$$

Thus, the payoff table is:

x_i	−$5	$195	$395	$595
P_i	0.985	0.0149	0.0000599	0.00000006

(B) The expected value to you is:

$$E(X) = (-5)(0.985) + 195(0.0149) + 395(0.0000599) + 595(0.00000006)$$

$$\approx -\$2.00$$

25. The payoff table is as follows:

Gain	x_i	\$4850	-\$150
	p_i	0.01	0.99

[Note: 5000 - 150 = 4850, the gain with a probability of 0.01 if stolen.]

Hence, $E(X) = 4850(0.01) - 150(0.99) = -\$100$

27. The payoff table for site A is as follows:

x_i	30 million	-3 million
p_i	0.2	0.8

Hence, $E(X) = 30(0.2) - 3(0.8)$
$= 6 - 2.4$
$= \$3.6$ million

The payoff table for site B is as follows:

x_i	70 million	-4 million
p_i	0.1	0.9

Hence, $E(X) = 70(0.1) + (-4)(0.9)$
$= 7 - 3.6$
$= \$3.4$ million

The company should choose site A with $E(X) = \$3.6$ million.

29. Determine the expected daily profit for 9, 10, 11, and 12 office suites made available for rental.

Choice 1: 9 office suites available for rental:

$$\text{Cost} = C(9) = (9)(140) = \$1260$$
$$\text{Revenue} = R(9) = (9)(200) = \$1800$$
$$\text{Profit} = P(9) = R(9) - C(9) = \$1800 - \$1260 = \$540$$

This is also the expected daily profit for this choice.

Choice 2: 10 office suites available for rental:

$$\text{Cost} = C(10) = (10)(140) = \$1400$$

The daily revenue and profit will now depend on the number of customers who want to rent the office suites.

If 9 customers want to rent:

$R(9) = (9)(200) = \$1800$
$P(9) = R(9) - C(10) = 1800 - 1400 = \$400$

If 10 customers want to rent:

$R(10) = (10)(200) = \$2000$
$P(10) = R(10) - C(10) = 2000 - 1400 = \$600$

The daily profit if 11 or 12 customers want to rent will remain \$600 for this choice. Thus, the probability distribution for this choice is:

	Ten office suites available for rental			
Daily demand	9	10	11	12
Probability p_i	0.2	0.3	0.4	0.1
Daily profit x_i	$400	$600	$600	$600

The expected daily profit is:

$E(X) = (0.2)(400) + (0.3)(600) + (0.4)(600) + (0.1)(600) = \$560$

Choice 3: 11 office suites available for rental:

$$C(11) = (11)(140) = \$1540$$

If 9 offices are rented:

$R(9) = (9)(200) = \$1800$
$P(9) = R(9) - C(11) = 1800 - 1540 = \$260$

If 10 offices are rented:

$R(10) = (10)(2000) = \$2000$
$P(10) = R(10) - C(11) = 2000 - 2540 = \$460$

If 11 offices are rented:

$R(11) = (11)(200) = \$2200$
$P(11) = R(11) - C(11) = 2200 = 1540 = \$660$

The probability distribution for this choice is given below.

	Eleven office suites available for rental			
Daily demand	9	10	11	12
Probability p_i	0.2	0.3	0.4	0.1
Daily profit x_i	$260	$460	$660	$660

The expected daily profit is:

$E(X) = (0.2)(260) + (0.3)(460) + (0.4)(660) + (0.1)(660)$
$= 52 + 138 + 264 + 66$
$= \$520$

Choice 4:   12 office suites available for rental:

$$C(12) = (12)(140) = \$1680$$

If 9 offices are rented:

$$R(9) = (9)(200) = \$1800$$
$$P(9) = R(9) - C(12) = 1800 - 1680 = \$120$$

If 10 offices are rented:

$$R(10) = (1)(200) = \$2000$$
$$P(10) = R(10) - C(12) = 2000 - 1680 = \$320$$

If 11 offices are rented:

$$R(11) = (11)(200) = \$2200$$
$$P(11) = R(11) - C(12) = 2200 - 1680 = \$520$$

If 12 offices are rented:

$$R(12) = (12)(200) = \$2400$$
$$P(12) = R(12) - C(12) = 2400 - 1680 = \$720$$

Thus, the probability distribution for this choice is:

	Twelve office suites available for rental			
Daily demand	9	10	11	12
Probability p_i	0.2	0.3	0.4	0.1
Daily profit x_i	\$120	\$320	\$520	\$720

The expected daily profit is:

$$E(X) = (0.2)(120) + (0.3)(320) + (0.4)(520) + (0.1)(720)$$
$$= 24 + 96 + 208 + 72$$
$$= \$400$$

Conclusion: The expected profits are shown in the following table.

Number of office suites available for rental	Expected daily profit	
9	\$540	
10	\$560	← Maximum expected profit
11	\$520	
12	\$400	

The maximum expected profit is $560, which occurs when the company makes ten office suites available for rental.

31. Using 4,

$E(X) = 0(0.12) + 1(0.36) + 2(0.38) + 3(0.14) = 1.54$

33. Action A_1: $E(X) = 10(0.3) + 5(0.2) + 0(0.5) = \$4.00$

Action A_2: $E(X) = 15(0.3) + 3(0.1) + 0(0.6) = \$4.80$

Action A_2 is the better choice.

EXERCISE 4-5   CHAPTER REVIEW

1. (A) We construct the following tree diagram for the experiment:

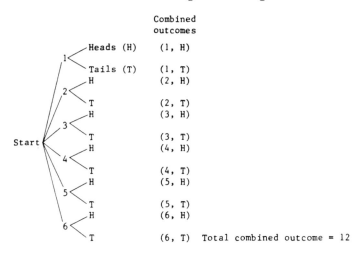

(B) Operation 1:   Six possible outcomes, 1, 2, 3, 4, 5, or 6; $N_1 = 6$.
Operation 2:   Two possible outcomes, heads (H) or tails (T); $N_2 = 2$.

Using the Multiplication Principle, the total combined outcomes = $N_1 \cdot N_2 = 6 \cdot 2 = 12$.

2. $C_{6,2} = \dfrac{6!}{2!(6-2)!} = \dfrac{6!}{2!4!}$ $P_{6,2} = \dfrac{6!}{(6-2)!} = \dfrac{6!}{4!}$

$= \dfrac{6 \cdot 5 \cdot 4!}{2 \cdot 1 \cdot 4!} = 15$ $= \dfrac{6 \cdot 5 \cdot 4!}{4!} = 30$

3. Operation 1:   First person can choose the seat in 6 different ways; $N_1 = 6$.
Operation 2:   Second person can choose the seat in 5 different ways; $N_2 = 5$.
Operation 3:   Third person can choose the seat in 4 different ways; $N_3 = 4$.
Operation 4:   Fourth person can choose the seat in 3 different ways; $N_4 = 3$.
Operation 5:   Fifth person can choose the seat in 2 different ways; $N_5 = 2$.
Operation 6:   Sixth person can choose the seat in 1 way; $N_6 = 1$.

(continued)

Using the Multiplication Principle, the total number of different arrangements that can be made is $6 \cdot 5 \cdot 4 \cdot 3 \cdot 2 \cdot 1 = 720$.

4. This is a permutations problem. The permutations of 6 objects taken 6 at a time is:

$$P_{6,6} = \frac{6!}{(6-6)!} = 6! = 720$$

5. First, we calculate the number of 5-card combinations that can be dealt out of 52 cards:

$$n(S) = C_{52,5} = \frac{52!}{5! \cdot 47!} = 2,598,960$$

We then calculate the number of 5-club combinations that can be obtained from 13 clubs:

$$n(E) = C_{13,5} = \frac{13!}{5! \cdot 8!} = 1287$$

Thus,

$$P(5 \text{ clubs}) = P(E) = \frac{n(E)}{n(S)} = \frac{1287}{2,598,960} \approx 0.0005$$

6. $n(S)$ is computed by using the permutation formula:

$$n(S) = P_{15,2} = \frac{15!}{(15-2)!} = 15 \cdot 14 = 210$$

Thus, the probability that Betty will be president and Bill will be treasurer is:

$$\frac{n(E)}{n(S)} = \frac{1}{210} \approx 0.0048$$

7. (A) The total number of ways of drawing 3 cards from 10 with order taken into account is given by:

$$P_{10,3} = \frac{10!}{(10-3)!} = \frac{10 \cdot 9 \cdot 8 \cdot 7!}{7!} = 720$$

Thus, the probability of drawing the code word "dig" is:

$$P(\text{"dig"}) = \frac{1}{720} \approx 0.0014$$

(B) The total number of ways of drawing 3 cards from 10 without regard to order is given by

$$C_{10,3} = \frac{10!}{3!(10-3)!} = \frac{10 \cdot 9 \cdot 8 \cdot 7!}{3!7!} = 120$$

Thus, the probability of drawing the 3 cards "d," "i," and "g" (in some order) is:

$$P(\text{"d," "i," "g"}) = \frac{1}{120} \approx 0.0083$$

8. $P(\text{person having side effects}) = \dfrac{f(E)}{n} = \dfrac{50}{1000} = 0.05$

9. The payoff table is as follows:

x_i	-\$2	-\$1	\$0	\$1	\$2
p_i	$\frac{1}{5}$	$\frac{1}{5}$	$\frac{1}{5}$	$\frac{1}{5}$	$\frac{1}{5}$

Hence,

$$E(X) = (-2) \cdot \frac{1}{5} + (-1) \cdot \frac{1}{5} + 0 \cdot \frac{1}{5} + 1 \cdot \frac{1}{5} + 2 \cdot \frac{1}{5} = 0$$

The game is fair.

10. The function P cannot be a probability function because:

   (a) P cannot be negative. [Note: $P(e_2) = -0.2$.]

   (b) P cannot have a value greater than 1. [Note: $P(e_4) = 2$.]

   (c) The sum of the values of P must equal 1. [Note: $P(e_1) + P(e_2) + P(e_3) + P(e_4) = 0.1 + (-0.2) + 0.6 + 2 = 2.5 \neq 1$.]

11. Each triangle requires 3 distinct points without regard to order. Thus, the total number of triangles that can be formed from the 6 points is:

$$C_{6,3} = \frac{6!}{3!(6-3)!} = \frac{6 \cdot 5 \cdot 4 \cdot 3!}{3 \cdot 2 \cdot 1 \cdot 3!} = 20$$

12.

	Number of ways of completing operation under condition:		
Operation	No letter repeated	Letters can be repeated	Adjacent letters not alike
O_1	8	8	8
O_2	7	8	7
O_3	6	8	7

Total outcomes, without repeating letters = $8 \cdot 7 \cdot 6 = 336$.
Total outcomes, with repeating letters = $8 \cdot 8 \cdot 8 = 512$.
Total outcomes, with adjacent letters not alike = $8 \cdot 7 \cdot 7 = 392$.

13. (A) This is a permutations problem.

$$P_{6,3} = \frac{6!}{(6-3)!} = \frac{6 \cdot 5 \cdot 4 \cdot 3!}{3!} = 120$$

   (B) This is a combinations problem.

$$C_{5,2} = \frac{5!}{2!(5-2)!} = \frac{5 \cdot 4 \cdot 3!}{2 \cdot 1 \cdot 3!} = 10$$

14. Event E_1 = 2 heads; $f(E_1)$ = 210.
    Event E_2 = 1 heads; $f(E_2)$ = 480.
    Event E_3 = 0 heads; $f(E_3)$ = 310.
    Total number of trials = 1000.

(A) The empirical probabilities for the events above are as follows:

$$P(E_1) = \frac{210}{1000} = 0.20 \qquad = .21$$

$$P(E_2) = \frac{480}{1000} = 0.48 \qquad .48$$

$$P(E_3) = \frac{310}{1000} = 0.31 \qquad .31$$

(B) Sample space S = {HH, HT, TH, TT}.

$$P(2 \text{ heads}) = \frac{1}{4} = 0.25$$

$$P(1 \text{ heads}) = \frac{2}{4} = 0.5$$

$$P(0 \text{ heads}) = \frac{1}{4} = 0.25$$

(C) Using part (B), the expected frequencies for each outcome are as follows:

$$2 \text{ heads} = 1000 \cdot \frac{1}{4} = 250$$

$$1 \text{ heads} = 1000 \cdot \frac{2}{4} = 500$$

$$0 \text{ heads} = 1000 \cdot \frac{1}{4} = 250$$

15. $n(S) = C_{52,5}$.

(A) Let A be the event "all diamonds." Then $n(A) = C_{13,5}$. Thus,

$$P(A) = \frac{n(A)}{n(S)} = \frac{C_{13,5}}{C_{52,5}} .$$

(B) Let B be the event "3 diamonds and 2 spades." Then
    $n(B) = C_{13,3} \cdot C_{13,2}$. Thus,

$$P(B) = \frac{n(B)}{n(S)} = \frac{C_{13,3} \cdot C_{13,2}}{C_{52,5}} .$$

16. $n(S) = C_{10,4} = \frac{10!}{4!(10-4)!} = \frac{10 \cdot 9 \cdot 8 \cdot 7 \cdot 6!}{4 \cdot 3 \cdot 2 \cdot 1 \cdot 6!} = 210$

Let A be the event "The married couple is in the group of 4 people."
Then

$$n(A) = C_{2,2} \cdot C_{8,2} = 1 \cdot \frac{8!}{2!(8-2)!} = \frac{8 \cdot 7 \cdot 6!}{2 \cdot 1 \cdot 6!} = 28.$$

Thus, $P(A) = \frac{n(A)}{n(S)} = \frac{28}{210} = \frac{2}{15} \approx 0.1333.$

PROBABILITY

17. $S = \{HH, HT, TH, TT\}$.

The probabilities for 2 "heads," 1 "head," and 0 "heads" are, respectively, 1/4, 1/2, and 1/4. Thus, the payoff table is:

x_i	\$5	-\$4	\$2
P_i	0.25	0.5	0.25

$E(X) = 0.25(5) + 0.5(-4) + 0.25(2) = -0.25$ or $-\$0.25$

The game is not fair.

18. $S = \{(1, 1), (2, 2), (3, 3), (1, 2), (2, 1), (1, 3), (3, 1), (2, 3), (3, 2)\}$

$n(S) = 3 \cdot 3 = 9$

(A) $P(A) = \dfrac{n(A)}{n(S)} = \dfrac{3}{9} = \dfrac{1}{3}$ $\quad [A = \{(1, 1), (2, 2), (3, 3)\}]$

(B) $P(B) = \dfrac{n(B)}{n(S)} = \dfrac{2}{9}$ $\quad [B = \{(2, 3), (3, 2)\}]$

19. (A) The sample space S is given by:

$S = \{(1, 1), (1, 2), (1, 3), (1, 4), (1, 5), (1, 6),$
Sum 2 $\quad (2, 1), (2, 2), (2, 3), (2, 4), (2, 5), (2, 6),$
Sum 3 $\quad (3, 1), (3, 2), (3, 3), (3, 4), (3, 5), (3, 6),$
Sum 4 $\quad (4, 1), (4, 2), (4, 3), (4, 4), (4, 5), (4, 6),$
Sum 5 $\quad (5, 1), (5, 2), (5, 3), (5, 4), (5, 5), (5, 6),$
$\quad (6, 1), (6, 2), (6, 3), (6, 4), (6, 5), (6, 6)\}$

[Note: Event $(2, 3)$ means 2 on the first die and 3 on the second die.]

The probability distribution corresponding to this sample space is:

Sum x_i	2	3	4	5	6	7	8	9	10	11	12
Probability p_i	$\dfrac{1}{36}$	$\dfrac{2}{36}$	$\dfrac{3}{36}$	$\dfrac{4}{36}$	$\dfrac{5}{36}$	$\dfrac{6}{36}$	$\dfrac{5}{36}$	$\dfrac{4}{36}$	$\dfrac{3}{36}$	$\dfrac{2}{36}$	$\dfrac{1}{36}$

(B) $E(X) = 2\left(\dfrac{1}{36}\right) + 3\left(\dfrac{2}{36}\right) + 4\left(\dfrac{3}{36}\right) + 5\left(\dfrac{4}{36}\right) + 6\left(\dfrac{5}{36}\right) + 7\left(\dfrac{6}{36}\right) + 8\left(\dfrac{5}{36}\right)$

$\qquad + 9\left(\dfrac{4}{36}\right) + 10\left(\dfrac{3}{36}\right) + 11\left(\dfrac{2}{36}\right) + 12\left(\dfrac{1}{36}\right) = 7$

20. Operation 1: Two possible outcomes, boy or girl, $N_1 = 2$.
    Operation 2: Two possible outcomes, boy or girl, $N_2 = 2$.
    Operation 3: Two possible outcomes, boy or girl, $N_3 = 2$.
    Operation 4: Two possible outcomes, boy or girl, $N_4 = 2$.
    Operation 5: Two possible outcomes, boy or girl, $N_5 = 2$.

    Using the Multiplication Principle, the total combined outcomes is:
    $N_1 \cdot N_2 \cdot N_3 \cdot N_4 \cdot N_5 = 2 \cdot 2 \cdot 2 \cdot 2 \cdot 2 = 32$.

    If order pattern is not taken into account, there would be only 6 possible outcomes: families with 0, 1, 2, 3, 4, or 5 boys.

21. The total number of ways that 3 people can be selected from a group of 10 is:

$$C_{10,3} = \frac{10!}{3!(10-3)!} = \frac{10 \cdot 9 \cdot 8 \cdot 7!}{3 \cdot 2 \cdot 1 \cdot 7!} = 120$$

The number of ways of selecting *no* women is:

$$C_{7,3} = \frac{7!}{3!(7-3)!} = \frac{7 \cdot 6 \cdot 5 \cdot 4!}{3 \cdot 2 \cdot 1 \cdot 4!} = 35$$

Thus, the number of samples of 3 people that contain at least one woman is $120 - 35 = 85$.

Therefore, if event A is "At least one woman is selected," then

$$P(A) = \frac{n(A)}{n(S)} = \frac{85}{120} = \frac{17}{24} \approx 0.708.$$

22. (A) This is a permutations problem.

$$P_{10,3} = \frac{10!}{(10-3)!} = \frac{10!}{7!} = 10 \cdot 9 \cdot 8 = 720$$

(B) The number of ways in which women are selected for all three positions is given by:

$$P_{6,3} = \frac{6!}{(6-3)!} = \frac{6!}{3!} = 6 \cdot 5 \cdot 4 = 120$$

Thus, $P(\text{three women are selected}) = \dfrac{P_{6,3}}{P_{10,3}} = \dfrac{120}{720} = \dfrac{1}{6}$

(C) This is a combinations problem.

$$C_{10,3} = \frac{10!}{3!(10-3)!} = \frac{10 \cdot 9 \cdot 8 \cdot 7!}{3 \cdot 2 \cdot 1 \cdot 7!} = 120$$

(D) Let Event D = majority of team members will be women. Then

$n(D)$ = team has 3 women + team has 2 women

$$= C_{6,3} + C_{6,2} \cdot C_{4,1}$$

$$= \frac{6!}{3!(6-3)!} + \frac{6!}{2!(6-2)!} \cdot \frac{4!}{1!(4-1)!}$$

$$= 20 + 15 \cdot 4 = 80$$

Thus,

$$P(D) = \frac{n(D)}{n(S)} = \frac{C_{6,3} + C_{6,2} \quad C_{4,1}}{C_{10,3}} = \frac{80}{120} = \frac{2}{3}$$

23. The number of ways the 2 people can be seated in a row of 4 chairs is:

$$P_{4,2} = \frac{4!}{(4-2)!} = \frac{4 \cdot 3 \cdot 2!}{2!} = 12$$

24. Let E_2 be the event "2 heads."

   (A) From the table, $f(E_2) = 350$. Thus, the approximate empirical probability of obtaining 2 heads is:

   $$P(E_2) \approx \frac{f(E_2)}{n} = \frac{350}{1000} = 0.350$$

   (B) $S = \{$HHH, HHT, HTH, HHT, THH, THT, TTH, TTT$\}$

   The theoretical probability of obtaining 2 heads is:

   $$P(E_2) = \frac{n(E_2)}{n(S)} = \frac{3}{8} = 0.375$$

   (C) The expected frequency of obtaining 2 heads in 1000 tosses of 3 fair coins is:

   $$f(E_2) = 1000(0.375) = 375$$

25. On one roll of the die, the probability of getting a double six is 1/36 and the probability of not getting a double six is 35/36.

   On two rolls of the die there are $(36)^2$ possible outcomes. There are 71 ways to get at least one double six, namely a double six on the first roll and any one of the 35 other outcomes on the second roll, or a double six on the second roll and any one of the 35 other outcomes on the first roll, or a double six on both rolls. Thus, the probability of at least one double six on two rolls is $71/(36)^2$ and the probability of no double sixes is:

   $$1 - \frac{71}{(36)^2} = \frac{(36)^2 - 2 \cdot 36 + 1}{(36)^2} = \frac{(36-1)^2}{(36)^2} = \left(\frac{35}{36}\right)^2$$

   Let E be the event "At least one double six." Then E' is the event "No double sixes." Continuing with the reasoning above, we conclude that, in 24 rolls of the die,

   $$P(E') = \left(\frac{35}{36}\right)^{24} \approx 0.509$$

   Therefore, $P(E) = 1 - 0.509 = 0.491$.

   The payoff table is shown on the following page:

x_i	1	-1
P_i	0.4914	0.5086

and $E(X) = 1(0.4914) + (-1)(0.5086)$
$$= 0.4914 - 0.5086$$
$$= -0.0172$$

Thus, your expectation is -$0.0172.

Your friend's expectation is $0.0172.

The game is not fair.

26. Since each die has 6 faces, there are $6 \cdot 6 = 36$ possible pairs for the two up faces.

A sum of 2 corresponds to having (1, 1) as the up faces. This sum can be obtained in $3 \cdot 3 = 9$ ways (3 faces on the first die, 3 faces on the second). Thus,

$$P(2) = \frac{9}{36} = \frac{1}{4} .$$

A sum of 3 corresponds to the two pairs (2, 1) and (1, 2). The number of such pairs is $2 \cdot 3 + 3 \cdot 2 = 12$. Thus,

$$P(3) = \frac{12}{36} = \frac{1}{3} .$$

A sum of 5 corresponds to the pairs (2, 3) and (3, 2). There are $2 \cdot 1 + 1 \cdot 2 = 4$ such pairs. Thus,

$$P(5) = \frac{4}{36} = \frac{1}{9} .$$

A sum of 6 corresponds to the pair (3, 3) and there is one such pair. Thus,

$$P(6) = \frac{1}{36} .$$

(A) The probability distribution for X is:

x_i	2	3	4	5	6
P_i	$\frac{9}{36}$	$\frac{12}{36}$	$\frac{10}{36}$	$\frac{4}{36}$	$\frac{1}{36}$

(B) The expected value is:

$$E(X) = 2\left(\frac{9}{36}\right) + 3\left(\frac{12}{36}\right) + 4\left(\frac{10}{36}\right) + 5\left(\frac{4}{36}\right) + 6\left(\frac{1}{36}\right)$$

$$= \frac{120}{36} = 3\frac{1}{3} \approx 3.33$$

27. The payoff table is:

x_i	-\$1.50	-\$0.50	\$0.50	\$1.50	\$2.50
P_i	$\dfrac{9}{36}$	$\dfrac{12}{36}$	$\dfrac{10}{36}$	$\dfrac{4}{36}$	$\dfrac{1}{36}$

and $E(X) = \dfrac{9}{36}(-1.50) + \dfrac{12}{36}(-0.50) + \dfrac{10}{36}(0.50) + \dfrac{4}{36}(1.50) + \dfrac{1}{36}(2.50)$

$\qquad\qquad = -0.375 - 0.167 + 0.139 + 0.167 + 0.069$

$\qquad\qquad = -0.167 \text{ or } -\$0.167$

The game is not fair.

28. The number of routes starting from A and visiting each of the 5 stores exactly once is the number of permutations of 5 objects taken 5 at a time, i.e.,

$$P_{5,5} = \frac{5!}{(5 - 5)!} = 120.$$

29. Venn diagram:

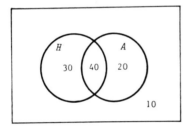

Event H = video games played at home.
Event A = video games played at arcades.

(A) $P(H \text{ or } A) = P(H \cup A) = \dfrac{90}{100}$ (from the Venn diagram)

$\qquad\qquad\qquad\qquad\qquad = 0.9$

$\qquad\qquad\text{or} = P(H) + P(A) - P(H \cap A)$

$\qquad\qquad\qquad = \dfrac{70}{100} + \dfrac{60}{100} - \dfrac{40}{100} = \dfrac{90}{100} = 0.9$

(B) $P(\text{played only at home}) = P(H \cap A')$

$\qquad\qquad\qquad\qquad\qquad = \dfrac{30}{100}$ (from the Venn diagram)

$\qquad\qquad\qquad\qquad\qquad = 0.3$

30.

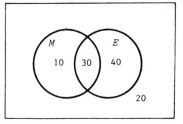

Event M = Reads the morning paper.
Event E = Reads the evening paper.

(A) P(reads a daily paper) = $P(M \text{ or } E)$ = $P(M \cup E)$
$$= P(M) + P(E) - P(M \cap E)$$
$$= \frac{40}{100} + \frac{70}{100} - \frac{30}{100} = 0.8$$

(B) P(does not read a daily paper) = $\frac{20}{100}$ (from the Venn diagram)
$$= 0.2$$
$$\text{or} = 1 - P(M \cup E) \quad [\text{i.e.,} \quad P((M \cup E)')]$$
$$= 1 - 0.8 = 0.2$$

(C) P(reads exactly one daily paper) = $\frac{10 + 40}{100}$ (from the Venn diagram)
$$= 0.5$$
$$\text{or} \quad P((M \cap E') \text{ or } (M' \cap E))$$
$$= P(M \cap E') + P(M' \cap E)$$
$$= \frac{10}{100} + \frac{40}{100} = 0.5$$

31. (A) From the table: $P(A) = \frac{40}{1000} = 0.04$

(B) From the table, the number of people between 12 and 18 who buy more than one album annually is $100 + 60 = 160$. Thus,
$$P(B) = \frac{160}{1000} = 0.16.$$

(C) The number of people who are either between 12 and 18 or buy more than one album annually is $290 + 290 + 120 - 100 - 60 = 540$. Thus,
$$P(C) = \frac{540}{1000} = 0.54.$$

32. The payoff table for plan A is:

x_i	10 million	-2 million
P_i	0.8	0.2

Hence, $E(X) = 10(0.8) - 2(0.2) = 8 - 0.4 = \$7.6$ million.

The payoff table for plan B is:

x_i	12 million	-2 million
P_i	0.7	0.3

Hence, $E(X) = 12(0.7) - 2(0.3) = 8.4 - 0.6 = \$7.8$ million.

Plan B should be chosen.

33. Determine the expected profit for one, two, and three truckloads of turkeys ordered.

Choice 1: One truckload of turkeys ordered.

$$\text{Cost} = C(1) = (1)(2000) = \$2000$$
$$\text{Revenue} = R(1) = (1)(6000) = \$6000$$
$$\text{Profit} = P(1) = R(1) - C(1) = 6000 - 2000 = \$4000$$

This is also the expected profit for this choice.

Choice 2: Two truckloads of turkeys ordered.

$$\text{Cost} = C(2) = (2)(2000) = \$4000$$

The revenue and profit will now depend on the number of truckloads of turkeys sold.

If one truckload is sold:

$$\text{Revenue} = R(1) = (1)(6000) = \$6000$$
$$\text{Profit} = P(1) = R(1) - C(2) = 6000 - 4000 = \$2000$$

If two truckloads are sold:

$$R(2) = (2)(6000) = \$12,000$$
$$P(2) = R(2) - C(2) = 12,000 - 4000 = \$8000$$

The probability distribution for this choice is:

	Two truckloads of turkeys ordered		
Number of truckloads sold	1	2	3
Probability p_i	0.2	0.4	0.4
Profit x_i	$2000	$8000	$8000

The expected profit is:

$$E(X) = (0.2)(2000) + (0.4)(8000) + (0.4)(8000)$$
$$= 400 + 3200 + 2200$$
$$= \$6800$$

Choice 3:   Three truckloads of turkeys ordered.

$C(3) = (3)(2000) = \$6000$

If one truckload is sold:

$R(1) = (1)(6000) = \$6000$
$P(1) = R(1) - C(3) = 6000 - 6000 = 0$

If two truckloads are sold:

$R(2) = (2)(6000) = \$12,000$
$P(2) = R(2) - C(3) = 12,000 = 6000 = \$6000$

If three truckloads are sold:

$R(3) = (3)(6000) = \$18,000$
$P(3) = R(3) - C(3) = 18,000 - 6000 = \$12,000$

The probability distribution for this choice is:

	Three truckloads of turkeys ordered		
Number of truckloads sold	1	2	3
Probability p_i	0.2	0.4	0.4
Profit x_i	0	$6000	$12,000

Thus, $E(X) = (0.2)(0) + (0.4)(6000) + (0.4)(12,000)$
$= 0 + 2400 + 4800$
$= \$7200$

Conclusion: The expected profits are:

Number of truckloads ordered	Expected profit
1	$4000
2	$6800
3	$7200 ← Maximum expected profit

The maximum expected profit is $7200, which occurs when three truckloads are ordered.

34. The payoff table is:

Gain	x_i	\$270	-\$30
	P_i	0.08	0.92

[Note: 300 – 30 = 270 is the "gain" if the bicycle is stolen.]

Hence, $E(X) = 270(0.08) - 30(0.92) = 21.6 - 27.6 = -\$6$.

35. $n(S) = C_{12,4} = \dfrac{12!}{4!(12-4)!} = \dfrac{12 \cdot 11 \cdot 10 \cdot 9 \cdot 8!}{4 \cdot 3 \cdot 2 \cdot 1 \cdot 8!} = 495$

The number of samples that contain *no* substandard parts is:

$C_{10,4} = \dfrac{10!}{4!(10-4)!} = \dfrac{10 \cdot 9 \cdot 8 \cdot 7 \cdot 6!}{4 \cdot 3 \cdot 2 \cdot 1 \cdot 6!} = 210$

Thus, the number of samples that have at least one defective part is 495 – 210 = 285. If E is the event "The shipment is returned," then

$P(E) = \dfrac{n(E)}{n(S)} = \dfrac{285}{495} \approx 0.576.$

36. $n(S) = C_{12,3} = \dfrac{12!}{3!(12-3)!} = \dfrac{12 \cdot 11 \cdot 10 \cdot 9!}{3 \cdot 2 \cdot 1 \cdot 9!} = 220$

A sample will either have 0, 1, or 2 defective circuit boards.

$P(0) = \dfrac{C_{10,3}}{C_{12,3}} = \dfrac{\dfrac{10!}{3!(10-3)!}}{220} = \dfrac{\dfrac{10 \cdot 9 \cdot 8 \cdot 7!}{3 \cdot 2 \cdot 1 \cdot 7!}}{220} = \dfrac{120}{220} = \dfrac{12}{22}$

$P(1) = \dfrac{C_{2,1} \cdot C_{10,2}}{C_{12,3}} = \dfrac{2 \cdot \dfrac{10!}{2!(10-2)!}}{220} = \dfrac{90}{220} = \dfrac{9}{22}$

$P(2) = \dfrac{C_{2,2} \cdot C_{10,1}}{220} = \dfrac{10}{220} = \dfrac{1}{22}$

(A) The probability distribution of X is:

x_i	0	1	2
P_i	$\dfrac{12}{22}$	$\dfrac{9}{22}$	$\dfrac{1}{22}$

(B) $E(X) = 0\left(\dfrac{12}{22}\right) + 1\left(\dfrac{9}{22}\right) + 2\left(\dfrac{1}{22}\right) = \dfrac{11}{22} = \dfrac{1}{2}$

CHAPTER 5   ADDITIONAL TOPICS IN PROBABILITY

EXERCISE 5-1

Things to remember:

1. PROBABILITY OF A UNION OF TWO EVENTS

For any events A and B,

(a) $P(A \cup B) = P(A) + P(B) - P(A \cap B)$.

If A and B are MUTUALLY EXCLUSIVE ($A \cap B = \emptyset$), then

(b) $P(A \cup B) = P(A) + P(B)$.

2. PROBABILITY OF COMPLEMENTS

For any event E, $E \cup E' = S$ and $E \cap E' = \emptyset$. Thus,

$$P(E) = 1 - P(E')$$
$$P(E') = 1 - P(E)$$

3. PROBABILITY TO ODDS

If $P(E)$ is the probability of the event E, then:

(a)   Odds for $E = \dfrac{P(E)}{1 - P(E)} = \dfrac{P(E)}{P(E')}$ $[P(E) \neq 1]$

(b)   Odds against $E = \dfrac{P(E')}{P(E)}$ $[P(E) \neq 0]$

4. ODDS TO PROBABILITY

If the odds for an event E are a/b, then the probability of E is:

$$P(E) = \frac{a}{a + b}$$

---

1. Let E be the event "failing within 90 days."
   Then $E' =$ "not failing within 90 days."

   $$\begin{aligned} P(E') &= 1 - P(E) \quad \text{(using } \underline{2}\text{)} \\ &= 1 - 0.003 \\ &= 0.997 \end{aligned}$$

3. Let Event $A =$ "a number less than 3" $= \{1, 2\}$.
   Let Event $B =$ "a number greater than 7" $= \{8, 9, 10\}$.

   Since $A \cap B = \emptyset$, A and B are mutually exclusive. So, using $\underline{1}$(b),

   $$P(A \cup B) = P(A) + P(B) = \frac{n(A)}{n(S)} + \frac{n(B)}{n(S)} = \frac{2}{10} + \frac{3}{10} = \frac{1}{2}$$

5. Let Event $A =$ "an even number" $= \{2, 4, 6, 8, 10\}$.
   Let Event $B =$ "a number divisible by 3" $= \{3, 6, 9\}$.

   Since $A \cap B = \{6\} \neq \emptyset$, A and B are not mutually exclusive. So, using $\underline{1}$(a),

   $$P(A \cup B) = P(A) + P(B) - P(A \cap B) = \frac{5}{10} + \frac{3}{10} - \frac{1}{10} = \frac{7}{10}$$

7. $$\begin{aligned} P(A) &= \frac{35 + 5}{35 + 5 + 20 + 40} \\ &= \frac{40}{100} = 0.4 \end{aligned}$$

9. $$\begin{aligned} P(B) &= \frac{5 + 20}{35 + 5 + 20 + 40} \\ &= \frac{25}{100} = 0.25 \end{aligned}$$

11. $$\begin{aligned} P(A \cap B) &= \frac{5}{35 + 5 + 20 + 40} \\ &= \frac{5}{100} = 0.05 \end{aligned}$$

13. $$\begin{aligned} P(A' \cap B) &= \frac{20}{35 + 5 + 20 + 40} \\ &= \frac{20}{100} = 0.2 \end{aligned}$$

15. $$\begin{aligned} P(A \cup B) &= \frac{35 + 5 + 20}{35 + 5 + 20 + 40} \\ &= \frac{60}{100} = 0.6 \end{aligned}$$

17. $$\begin{aligned} P(A' \cup B) &= \frac{20 + 40 + 5}{35 + 5 + 20 + 40} \\ &= \frac{65}{100} = 0.65 \end{aligned}$$

19. $$P(\text{sum of 5 or 6}) = P(\text{sum of 5}) + P(\text{sum of 6}) \quad [\text{using 1(b)}]$$

    $$= \frac{4}{36} + \frac{5}{36} = \frac{9}{36} = \frac{1}{4} \text{ or } 0.25$$

21. $P(1$ on first die or 1 on second die$)$ [using 1(a)]

= $P(1$ on first die + $P(1$ on second die$)$ − $P(1$ on both dice$)$

= $\dfrac{6}{36} + \dfrac{6}{36} - \dfrac{1}{36} = \dfrac{11}{36}$

23. Use 3 to find the odds for event E.

(A) $P(E) = \dfrac{3}{8}$, $P(E') = 1 - P(E) = \dfrac{5}{8}$

Odds for $E = \dfrac{P(E)}{P(E')} = \dfrac{3/8}{5/8} = \dfrac{3}{5}$ (3 to 5)

Odds against $E = \dfrac{P(E')}{P(E)} = \dfrac{5/8}{3/8} = \dfrac{5}{3}$ (5 to 3)

(B) $P(E) = \dfrac{1}{4}$, $P(E') = 1 - P(E) = \dfrac{3}{4}$

Odds for $E = \dfrac{P(E)}{P(E')} = \dfrac{1/4}{3/4} = \dfrac{1}{3}$ (1 to 3)

Odds against $E = \dfrac{P(E')}{P(E)} = \dfrac{3/4}{1/4} = \dfrac{3}{1}$ (3 to 1)

(C) $P(E) = 0.55$, $P(E') = 1 - P(E) = 0.45$

Odds for $E = \dfrac{P(E)}{P(E')} = \dfrac{0.55}{0.45} = \dfrac{11}{9}$ (11 to 9)

Odds against $E = \dfrac{P(E')}{P(E)} = \dfrac{0.45}{0.55} = \dfrac{9}{11}$ (9 to 11)

25. Use 4 to find the probability of event E.

(A) Odds for $E = \dfrac{3}{8}$

$P(E) = \dfrac{3}{3+8} = \dfrac{3}{11}$

(B) Odds for $E = \dfrac{11}{7}$

$P(E) = \dfrac{11}{11+7} = \dfrac{11}{18}$

(C) Odds for $E = \dfrac{4}{1}$

$P(E) = \dfrac{4}{4+1} = \dfrac{4}{5} = 0.8$

(D) Odds for $E = \dfrac{49}{51}$

$P(E) = \dfrac{49}{49+51} = \dfrac{49}{100} = 0.49$

27. Odds for $E = \dfrac{P(E)}{P(E')} = \dfrac{1/2}{1/2} = 1$.

The odds in favor of getting a head in a single toss of a coin are 1 to 1.

29. The sample space for this problem is:

$S = \{$HHH, HHT, THH, HTH, TTH, HTT, THT, TTT$\}$

Let Event $E = $ "getting at least 1 head."
Let Event $E' = $ "getting no heads."

ADDITIONAL TOPICS IN PROBABILITY

Thus, $\dfrac{P(E)}{P(E')} = \dfrac{7/8}{1/8} = \dfrac{7}{1}$

The odds in favor of getting at least 1 head are 7 to 1.

31. Let Event E = "getting a number greater than 4."
    Let Event E' = "not getting a number greater than 4."

    Thus, $\dfrac{P(E')}{P(E)} = \dfrac{4/6}{2/6} = \dfrac{2}{1}$

    The odds against getting a number greater than 4 in a single roll of a die are 2 to 1.

33. Let Event E = "getting 3 or an even number" = {2, 3, 4, 6}.
    Let Event E' = "not getting 3 or an even number" = {1, 5}.

    Thus, $\dfrac{P(E')}{P(E)} = \dfrac{2/6}{4/6} = \dfrac{1}{2}$

    The odds against getting 3 or an even number are 1 to 2.

35. Let E = "rolling a five." Then $P(E) = \dfrac{n(E)}{n(S)} = \dfrac{4}{36} = \dfrac{1}{9}$ and $P(E') = \dfrac{8}{9}$.

    (A) Odds for $D = \dfrac{1/9}{8/9} = \dfrac{1}{8}$ (1 to 8)

    (B) Let k be the amount the house should pay for the game to be fair. Then

    $$E(X) = k\left(\dfrac{1}{9}\right) + (-1)\left(\dfrac{8}{9}\right) = 0$$

    $$\dfrac{k}{9} = \dfrac{8}{9} \text{ and } k = 8$$

    The house should pay $8.

37. (A) Let E = "sum is less than 4 or greater than 9." Then

    $$P(E) = \dfrac{10 + 30 + 120 + 80 + 70}{1000} = \dfrac{310}{1000} = \dfrac{31}{100} = 0.31 \text{ and } P(E') = \dfrac{69}{100}.$$

    Thus,

    Odds for $E = \dfrac{31/100}{69/100} = \dfrac{31}{69}$

    (B) Let F = "sum is even or divisible by 5." Then

    $$P(F) = \dfrac{10 + 50 + 110 + 170 + 120 + 70 + 70}{1000} = \dfrac{600}{1000} = \dfrac{6}{10} = 0.6$$

    and $P(F') = \dfrac{4}{10}$. Thus,

    Odds for $F = \dfrac{6/10}{4/10} = \dfrac{6}{4} = \dfrac{3}{2}$

39. Let A = "drawing a face card" (Jack, Queen, King)
    and B = "drawing a club."

    Then $P(A \cup B) = P(A) + P(B) - P(A \cap B)$

    $$= \frac{12}{52} + \frac{13}{52} - \frac{3}{52} = \frac{22}{52} = \frac{11}{26}$$

    $P[(A \cup B)'] = \frac{15}{26}$

    Odds for $A \cup B = \dfrac{11/26}{15/26} = \dfrac{11}{15}$

41. Let A = "drawing a black card"
    and B = "drawing an ace."

    $P(A \cup B) = P(A) + P(B) - P(A \cap B) = \frac{26}{52} + \frac{4}{52} - \frac{2}{52} = \frac{28}{52} = \frac{7}{13}$

    $P[(A \cup B)'] = \frac{6}{13}$

    Odds for $A \cup B = \dfrac{7/13}{6/13} = \dfrac{7}{6}$

43. The sample space S is the set of all 5-card hands and $n(S) = C_{52,5}$

    Let E = "getting at least one diamond."
    Then E' = "no diamonds" and $n(E) = C_{39,5}$.

    Thus, $P(E') = \dfrac{C_{39,5}}{C_{52,5}}$, and

    $$P(E) = 1 - \frac{C_{39,5}}{C_{52,5}} = 1 - \frac{\frac{39!}{5!34!}}{\frac{52!}{5!47!}} = 1 - \frac{39 \cdot 38 \cdot 37 \cdot 36 \cdot 35}{52 \cdot 51 \cdot 50 \cdot 49 \cdot 48} \approx 1 - 0.22 = 0.78.$$

45. The number of numbers less than or equal to 1000 which are divisible by 6 is the largest integer in 1000/6 or 166.

    The number of numbers less than or equal to 1000 which are divisible by 8 is the largest integer in 1000/8 or 125.

    The number of numbers less than or equal to 1000 which are divisible by both 6 and 8 is the same as the number of numbers which are divisible by 24. This is the largest integer in 1000/24 or 41.

    Thus, if A is the event "selecting a number which is divisible by either 6 or 8," then

    $$n(A) = 166 + 125 - 41 = 250 \text{ and } P(A) = \frac{250}{1000} = 0.25.$$

47. Let S be the set of all lists of 5 integers selected from the first 50 integers. Then $n(S) = C_{50,5}$.

    Let E be the event "a list contains at least one number divisible by 3." Then E' is the event "a list contains no number divisible by 3." There are 16 integers less than 50 which are divisible by 3. Thus, 34 integers less than or equal to 50 are not divisible by 3 and $n(E') = C_{34,5}$.

Therefore,

$$P(E') = \frac{C_{34,5}}{C_{50,5}} = \frac{\dfrac{34!}{5!29!}}{\dfrac{50!}{5!45!}} = \frac{34 \cdot 33 \cdot 32 \cdot 31 \cdot 30}{50 \cdot 49 \cdot 48 \cdot 47 \cdot 46} \approx 0.13$$

and

$$P(E) = 1 - P(E') = 1 - 0.13 = 0.87.$$

49. Let R be the event "landing on red." Then

Odds for $R = \dfrac{9}{10}$ and $P(R) = \dfrac{9}{9 + 10} = \dfrac{9}{19}$ 0.4737

The payoff table is:

x_i	1	-1
P_i	0.4737	0.5263

$$E(X) = 1(0.4737) + (-1)(0.5263) = -0.0526 \text{ or } -\$0.0526$$

51. S = set of all lists of n birth months, $n \leqslant 12$. Then

$$n(S) = 12 \cdot 12 \cdot \cdots \cdot 12 \ (n \text{ times}) = 12^n.$$

Let E = "at least two people have the same birth month."
Then E' = "no two people have the same birth month."

$$n(E') = 12 \cdot 11 \cdot 10 \cdot \cdots \cdot [12 - (n - 1)]$$

$$= \frac{12 \cdot 11 \cdot 10 \cdot \cdots \cdot [12 - (n - 1)](12 - n)[12 - (n + 1)] \cdot \cdots \cdot 3 \cdot 2 \cdot 1}{(12 - n)[12 - (n + 1)] \cdot \cdots \cdot 3 \cdot 2 \cdot 1}$$

$$= \frac{12!}{(12 - n)!}$$

Thus, $P(E') = \dfrac{\dfrac{12!}{(12 - n)!}}{12^n} = \dfrac{12!}{12^n(12 - n)!}$ and $P(E) = 1 - \dfrac{12!}{12^n(12 - n)!}$.

53. Odds for $E = \dfrac{P(E)}{P(E')} = \dfrac{P(E)}{1 - P(E)} = \dfrac{a}{b}$. Therefore,

$$bP(E) = a[1 - P(E)] = a - aP(E).$$

Thus,

$$aP(E) + bP(E) = a$$
$$(a + b)P(E) = a$$
$$P(E) = \frac{a}{a + b}$$

55. Venn diagram:

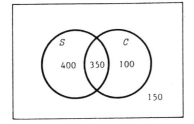

Let S be the event that the student owns a stereo and C be the event that the student owns a car.

The table corresponding to the given data is as follows:

	C	C'	Total
S	350	400	750
S'	100	150	250
Total	450	550	1000

The corresponding probabilities are:

	C	C'	Total
S	0.35	0.40	0.75
S'	0.10	0.15	0.25
Total	0.45	0.55	1.00

From the above table:

(A) $P(C \text{ or } S) = P(C \cup S) = P(C) + P(S) - P(C \cap S)$
$$= 0.45 + 0.75 - 0.35$$
$$= 0.85$$

(B) $P(C' \cap S') = .15$

57. (A) Using the table, we have:

$P(M_1 \text{ or } A) = P(M_1 \cup A) = P(M_1) + P(A) - P(M_1 \cap A)$
$$= .2 + .3 - .05$$
$$= .45$$

(B) $P[(M_2 \cap A') \text{ or } (M_3 \cap A')] = P(M_2 \cap A') + P(M_3 \cap A')$
$$= 0.2 + 0.35 \text{ (from the table)}$$
$$= 0.55$$

59. Let K = "defective keyboard"
and D = "defective disk drive."

Then $K \cup D$ = "either a defective keyboard or a defective disk drive"
and $(K \cup D)'$ = "neither the keyboard nor the disk drive is defective"
$= K' \cap D'$

$P(K \cup D) = P(K) + P(D) - P(K \cap D) = 0.6 + 0.5 - 0.1 = 0.1$

Thus, $P(K' \cap D') = 1 - 0.1 = 0.9$.

61. The sample space S is the set of all possible 10-element samples
selected from the 60 watches, and $n(S) = C_{60,10}$. Let E be the event
that a sample contains at least one defective watch. Then E' is the
event that a sample contains no defective watches. Now, $n(E') = C_{51,10}$.

Thus, $P(E') = \dfrac{C_{51,10}}{C_{60,10}} = \dfrac{\dfrac{51!}{10!41!}}{\dfrac{60!}{10!50!}} \approx 0.17$ and $P(E) \approx 1 - 0.17 = 0.83$.

Therefore, the probability that a sample will be returned is 0.83.

63. The given information is displayed in the Venn diagram:

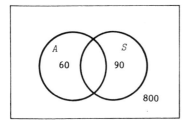

A = suffers from loss of appetite
S = suffers from loss of sleep

Thus, we can conclude that $n(A \cap S) = 1000 - (60 + 90 + 800) = 50$.

$P(A \cap S) = \dfrac{50}{1000} = 0.05$

65. (A) "Unaffiliated or no preference" = $U \cup N$.

$P(U \cup N) = P(U) + P(N) - P(U \cap N)$

$= \dfrac{150}{1000} + \dfrac{85}{1000} - \dfrac{15}{1000} = \dfrac{220}{1000} = \dfrac{11}{50} = 0.22$

Therefore, $P[(U \cup N)'] = 1 - \dfrac{11}{50} = \dfrac{39}{50}$ and

Odds for $U \cup N = \dfrac{11/50}{39/50} = \dfrac{11}{39}$

(B) "Affiliated with a party and prefers candidate A" = $(D \cup R) \cap A$.

$P[(D \cup R) \cap A] = \dfrac{300}{1000} = \dfrac{3}{10} = 0.3$

The odds against this event are:

$$\frac{1 - 3/10}{3/10} = \frac{7/10}{3/10} = \frac{7}{3}$$

67. Let S = the set of all three-person groups from the total group.
Let E = the set of all three-person groups with at least one black.
Let E' = the set of all three-person groups with no blacks.
First, find $P(E')$, then use $P(E) = 1 - P(E')$ to find $P(E)$.

$$P(E') = \frac{n(E')}{n(E)} = \frac{C_{15,3}}{C_{20,3}} \approx 0.4$$

$$P(E) = 1 - P(E') = 0.6$$

EXERCISE 5-2

Things to remember:

<u>1</u>. CONDITIONAL PROBABILITY

For events A and B in a sample space S, the
CONDITIONAL PROBABILITY of A given B, denoted
$P(A|B)$, is defined by

$$P(A|B) = \frac{P(A \cap B)}{P(B)}, \quad P(B) \neq 0$$

<u>2</u>. PRODUCT RULE

For events A and B, $P(A) \neq 0$, $P(B) \neq 0$, in a
sample space S,

$$P(A \cap B) = P(A) \cdot P(B|A) = P(B) \cdot P(A|B).$$

<u>3</u>. INDEPENDENCE

Let A and B be any events in a sample space S.
Then A and B are INDEPENDENT if and only if

$$P(A \cap B) = P(A) \cdot P(B).$$

Otherwise, A and B are DEPENDENT.

<u>4</u>. INDEPENDENT SET OF EVENTS

A finite set of events is INDEPENDENT if, for
each subset $\{E_1, E_2, \ldots, E_n\}$,

$$P(E_1 \cap E_2 \cap \cdots \cap E_n) = P(E_1)P(E_2) \cdots P(E_n).$$

ADDITIONAL TOPICS IN PROBABILITY

1. $P(A) = 0.50$
   See the given table.

3. $P(D) = 0.20$
   See the given table.

5. $P(A \cap D) = .10$
   See the given table for occurrences of both A and D.

7. $P(C \cap D) =$ probability of occurrences of both C and $D = .06$.

9. $P(A|D) = \dfrac{P(A \cap D)}{P(D)} = \dfrac{0.10}{0.20} = 0.50$

11. $P(C|D) = \dfrac{P(C \cap D)}{P(D)} = \dfrac{0.06}{0.20} = 0.30$

13. Events A and D are independent if $P(A \cap D) = P(A) \cdot P(D)$:

    $P(A \cap D) = 0.10$
    $P(A) \cdot P(D) = (0.50)(0.20) = 0.10$

    Thus, A and D are independent.

15. $P(C \cap D) = 0.06$
    $P(C) \cdot P(D) = (0.20)(0.20) = 0.04$
    Since $P(C \cap D) \neq P(C) \cdot P(D)$, C and D are dependent.

17. (A) Let $H_8 =$ "a head on the eighth toss." Since each toss is independent of the other tosses, $P(H_8) = 1/2$.

    (B) Let $H_i =$ "a head on the ith toss." Since the tosses are independent,

    $$P(H_1 \cap H_2 \cap \cdots \cap H_8) = P(H_1)P(H_2) \cdots P(H_8) = \left(\frac{1}{2}\right)^8 = \frac{1}{2^8} = \frac{1}{256}.$$

    Similarly, if $T_i =$ "a tail on the ith toss," then

    $$P(T_1 \cap T_2 \cap \cdots \cap T_8) = P(T_1)P(T) \cdots P(T_8) = \frac{1}{2^8} = \frac{1}{256}.$$

    Finally, if $H =$ "all heads" and $T =$ "all tails," then $H \cap T = \emptyset$ and

    $$P(H \cup T) = P(H) + P(T) = \frac{1}{256} + \frac{1}{256} = \frac{2}{256} = \frac{1}{128} \approx 0.00781.$$

19. Given the table:

e_i	1	2	3	4	5
P_i	0.3	0.1	0.2	0.3	0.1

$E =$ "pointer lands on an even number" $= \{2, 4\}$.
$F =$ "pointer lands on a number less than 4" $= \{1, 2, 3\}$.

(A) $P(F|E) = \dfrac{P(F \cap E)}{P(E)} = \dfrac{P(2)}{P(2) + P(4)} = \dfrac{0.1}{0.1 + 0.3} = \dfrac{0.1}{0.4} = \dfrac{1}{4}$

(B) $P(E \cap F) = P(2) = 0.1$

   $P(E) = 0.4$ and $P(F) = P(1) + P(2) + P(3) = 0.3 + 0.1 + 0.2 = 0.6$

   and

   $P(E)P(F) = (0.4)(0.6) = 0.24 \neq P(E \cap F)$.

   Thus, E and F are dependent.

21. From the probability tree,

  (A) $P(M \cap S) = (0.3)(0.6) = 0.18$

  (B) $P(R) = P(N \cap R) + P(M \cap R) = (0.7)(0.2) + (0.3)(0.4)$
  $$= 0.14 + 0.12$$
  $$= 0.26$$

23. $E_1 = \{HH, HT\}$ and $P(E_1) = \frac{1}{2}$

   $E_2 = \{TH, TT\}$ and $P(E_2) = \frac{1}{2}$

   $E_3 = \{HT, TT\}$ and $P(E_3) = \frac{1}{2}$

  (A) $P(E_1 \cap E_3) = P\{HT\} = \frac{1}{4}$

  $P(E_1) \cdot P(E_3) = \frac{1}{2} \cdot \frac{1}{2} = \frac{1}{4}$

  Thus, E_1 and E_3 *are* independent.

  (B) Two events, A and B , are mutually exclusive if $A \cap B = \emptyset$. Since $E_1 \cap E_3 = \{HT\} \neq \emptyset$, E_1 and E_3 are *not* mutually exclusive.

25. Let E_i = "even number on the ith throw," $i = 1, 2,$ and O_i = "odd number on the ith throw," $i = 1, 2.$

  Then $P(E_i) = \frac{1}{2}$ and $P(O_i) = \frac{1}{2}$, $i = 1, 2.$

  The probability tree for this experiment is:

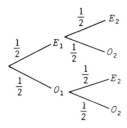

  $P(E_1 \cap E_2) = \left(\frac{1}{2}\right)\left(\frac{1}{2}\right) = \frac{1}{4}$

  $P(E_1 \cup E_2) = P(E_1) + P(E_2) - P(E_1 \cap E_2) = \frac{1}{2} + \frac{1}{2} - \frac{1}{4} = \frac{3}{4}$

27. Let C = "first card is a club,"
  and H = "second card is a heart."

  (A) Without replacement, the probability tree is as shown at the right:

  Thus, $P(C \cap H) = \left(\frac{1}{4}\right)\left(\frac{13}{51}\right) \approx 0.0637.$

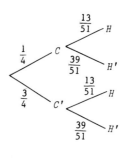

  (B) With replacement, the draws are independent and

  $P(C \cap H) = \left(\frac{1}{4}\right)\left(\frac{1}{4}\right) = \frac{1}{16} = 0.0625.$

29. G = "the card is black" = {spade or club} and $P(G) = \frac{1}{2}$.

H = "the card is divisible by 3" = {3, 6, or 9}. $P(H) = \frac{12}{52} = \frac{3}{13}$

$P(H \cap G)$ = {3, 6, or 9 of clubs or spades} = $\frac{6}{52} = \frac{3}{26}$

(A) $P(H|G) = \frac{P(H \cap G)}{P(G)} = \frac{3/26}{1/2} = \frac{6}{26} = \frac{3}{13}$

(B) $P(H \cap G) = \frac{3}{26} = P(H) \cdot P(G)$

Thus, H and G *are* independent.

31. (A) S = {BB, BG, GB, GG}

A = {BB, GG} and $P(A) = \frac{2}{4} = \frac{1}{2}$

B = {BG, GB, GG} and $P(B) = \frac{3}{4}$

$A \cap B$ = {GG}.

$P(A \cap B) = \frac{1}{4}$ and $P(A) \cdot P(B) = \frac{1}{2} \cdot \frac{3}{4} = \frac{3}{8}$

Thus, $P(A \cap B) \neq P(A) \cdot P(B)$ and the events are dependent.

(B) S = {BBB, BBG, BGB, BGG, GBB, GBG, GGB, GGG}

A = {BBB, GGG}

B = {BGG, GBG, GGB, GGG}

$A \cap B$ = {GGG}

$P(A) = \frac{2}{8} = \frac{1}{4}$, $P(B) = \frac{4}{8} = \frac{1}{2}$, and $P(A \cap B) = \frac{1}{8}$

Since $P(A \cap B) = \frac{1}{8} = P(A) \cdot P(B)$, A and B are independent.

33. (A) The probability tree with replacement is as follows:

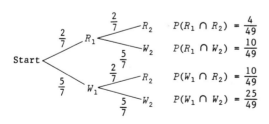

(B) The probability tree without replacement is as follows:

$$P(R_1 \cap R_2) = \frac{1}{21}$$

$$P(R_1 \cap W_2) = \frac{5}{21}$$

$$P(W_1 \cap R_2) = \frac{5}{21}$$

$$P(W_1 \cap W_2) = \frac{10}{21}$$

(Tree: Start branches to R_1 with prob $\frac{2}{7}$ and W_1 with prob $\frac{5}{7}$. From R_1: R_2 with $\frac{1}{6}$, W_2 with $\frac{5}{6}$. From W_1: R_2 with $\frac{2}{6}$, W_2 with $\frac{4}{6}$.)

35. Let E = At least one ball was red = $\{R_1 \cap R_2,\ R_1 \cap W_2,\ W_1 \cap R_2\}$.

(A) With replacement [see the probability tree in Problem 33(A)]:

$$P(E) = P(R_1 \cap R_2) + P(R_1 \cap W_2) + P(W_1 \cap R_2)$$

$$= \frac{4}{49} + \frac{10}{49} + \frac{10}{49} = \frac{24}{49} \checkmark$$

(B) Without replacement [see the probability tree in Problem 33(B)]:

$$P(E) = P(R_1 \cap R_2) + P(R_1 \cap W_2) + P(W_1 \cap R_2)$$

$$= \frac{1}{21} + \frac{5}{21} + \frac{5}{21} = \frac{11}{21} \checkmark$$

37. (A) The probability tree with replacement is as follows:

$$P(A_1 \cap A_2) = \frac{4}{52} \cdot \frac{4}{52} = \frac{1}{169}$$

$$P(A_1 \cap A_2') = \frac{4}{52} \cdot \frac{48}{52} = \frac{12}{169}$$

$$P(A_1' \cap A_2) = \frac{48}{52} \cdot \frac{4}{52} = \frac{12}{169}$$

$$P(A_1' \cap A_2') = \frac{48}{52} \cdot \frac{48}{52} = \frac{144}{169}$$

(Tree: Start branches to A_1 with $\frac{4}{52}$ and A_1' with $\frac{48}{52}$. From A_1: A_2 with $\frac{4}{52}$, A_2' with $\frac{48}{52}$. From A_1': A_2 with $\frac{4}{52}$, A_2' with $\frac{48}{52}$.)

Let E = Exactly one ace = $\{A_1 \cap A_2',\ A_1' \cap A_2\}$.

$$P(E) = P(A_1 \cap A_2') + P(A_1' \cap A_2) = \frac{12}{169} + \frac{12}{169} = \frac{24}{169}$$

(B) The probability tree with replacement is as follows:

$$P(A_1 \cap A_2) = \frac{4}{52} \cdot \frac{3}{51} = \frac{1}{221}$$

$$P(A_1 \cap A_2') = \frac{4}{52} \cdot \frac{48}{51} = \frac{16}{221}$$

$$P(A_1' \cap A_2) = \frac{48}{52} \cdot \frac{4}{51} = \frac{16}{221}$$

$$P(A_1' \cap A_2') = \frac{48}{52} \cdot \frac{47}{51} = \frac{188}{221}$$

(Tree: Start branches to A_1 with $\frac{4}{52}$ and A_1' with $\frac{48}{52}$. From A_1: A_2 with $\frac{3}{51}$, A_2' with $\frac{48}{51}$. From A_1': A_2 with $\frac{4}{51}$, A_2' with $\frac{47}{51}$.)

$$P(E) = P(A_1 \cap A_2') + P(A_1' \cap A_2) = \frac{16}{221} + \frac{16}{221} = \frac{32}{221}$$

ADDITIONAL TOPICS IN PROBABILITY

39. $n(S) = C_{9,2} = \dfrac{9!}{2!\,(9-2)!}$ (total number of balls = 2 + 3 + 4 = 9)

$$= \frac{9 \cdot 8 \cdot 7!}{2 \cdot 1 \cdot 7!} = 36$$

Let A = Both balls are the same color.

$n(A)$ = (No. of ways 2 red balls are selected) + (No. of ways 2 white balls are selected) + (No. of ways 2 green balls are selected)

$$= C_{2,2} + C_{3,2} + C_{4,2}$$

$$= \frac{2!}{2!\,(2-2)!} + \frac{3!}{2!\,(3-2)!} + \frac{4!}{2!\,(4-2)!} = 1 + 3 + 6 = 10$$

$$P(A) = \frac{n(A)}{n(S)} = \frac{10}{36} = \frac{5}{18}$$

Alternatively, the probability tree for this experiment is:

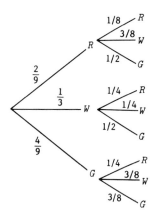

and

$$P(RR,\ WW,\ \text{or}\ GG) = P(RR) + P(WW) + P(GG)$$

$$= \left(\frac{2}{9}\right)\left(\frac{1}{8}\right) + \left(\frac{1}{3}\right)\left(\frac{1}{4}\right) + \left(\frac{4}{9}\right)\left(\frac{3}{8}\right)$$

$$= \frac{2}{72} + \frac{1}{12} + \frac{12}{72}$$

$$= \frac{20}{72}$$

$$= \frac{5}{18}$$

41. The probability tree for this experiment is:

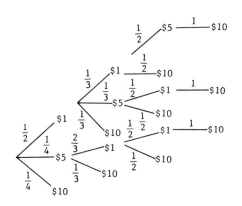

(A) $P(\$16) = \left(\frac{1}{4}\right)\left(\frac{2}{3}\right)\left(\frac{1}{2}\right) + \left(\frac{1}{2}\right)\left(\frac{1}{3}\right)\left(\frac{1}{2}\right) = \frac{1}{12} + \frac{1}{12} = \frac{1}{6} \approx 0.167$

(B) $P(\$17) = \left(\frac{1}{2}\right)\left(\frac{1}{3}\right)\left(\frac{1}{2}\right) + \left(\frac{1}{2}\right)\left(\frac{1}{3}\right)\left(\frac{1}{2}\right) + \left(\frac{1}{4}\right)\left(\frac{2}{3}\right)\left(\frac{1}{2}\right) = \frac{1}{12} + \frac{1}{12} + \frac{1}{12} = \frac{1}{4} = 0.25$

(C) Let $A = \$10$ on second draw." Then

$$P(A) = \left(\frac{1}{4}\right)\left(\frac{1}{3}\right) + \left(\frac{1}{2}\right)\left(\frac{1}{3}\right) = \frac{1}{12} + \frac{1}{6} = \frac{1}{4} = 0.25$$

(D) The payoff table is:

x_i	$10	$11	$12	$15	$16	$17
P_i	0.25	0.167	0.083	0.083	0.167	0.25

Thus,

$E(X) = 10(0.25) + 11(0.167) + 12(0.083) + 15(0.083)$
$\qquad\qquad\qquad\qquad\qquad\qquad + 16(0.167) + 17(0.25)$

$\qquad = \$13.50$

A player should pay $13.50 for the game to be fair.

43. Assume $P(A) \neq 0$. Then $P(A|A) = \dfrac{P(A \cap A)}{P(A)} = \dfrac{P(A)}{P(A)} = 1$.

45. If A and B are mutually exclusive, then $A \cap B = \emptyset$ and $P(A \cap B) = P(\emptyset) = 0$. Also, if $P(A) \neq 0$ and $P(B) \neq 0$, then $P(A) \cdot P(B) \neq 0$. Therefore,

$P(A \cap B) = 0 \neq P(A) \cdot P(B)$,

and events A and B are dependent.

47. (A)

To strike	Hourly H	Salary S	Salary + bonus B	Total
Yes (Y)	0.400	0.180	0.020	0.600
No (N)	0.150	0.120	0.130	0.400
Total	0.550	0.300	0.150	1.000

[Note: The probability table above was derived from the table given in the problem by dividing each entry by 1000.]

Referring to the table in part (A):

(B) $P(Y|H) = \dfrac{P(Y \cap H)}{P(H)} = \dfrac{0.400}{0.550} \approx 0.727$ (C) $P(Y|B) = \dfrac{P(Y \cap B)}{P(B)} = \dfrac{0.02}{0.15} \approx 0.133$

(D) $P(S) = 0.300$

$P(S|Y) = \dfrac{P(S \cap Y)}{P(Y)} = \dfrac{0.180}{0.60} = 0.300$

(E) $P(H) = 0.550$

$P(H|Y) = \dfrac{P(H \cap Y)}{P(Y)} = \dfrac{0.400}{0.600} \approx 0.667$

(F) $P(B \cap N) = 0.130$

(G) S and Y are independent since $P(S|Y) = P(S) = 0.300$

(H) H and Y are dependent since $P(H|Y) \approx 0.667$ is not equal to $P(H) = 0.550$.

(I) $P(B|N) = \dfrac{P(B \cap N)}{P(N)}$

$= \dfrac{0.130}{0.400}$ (from table)

$= .325$

and $P(B) = 0.150$. Since $P(B|N) \neq P(B)$, B and N are dependent.

49. The probability tree for this experiment is:

(A) $P(\$26{,}000) = \left(\dfrac{1}{2}\right)\left(\dfrac{1}{3}\right)\left(\dfrac{1}{2}\right) + \left(\dfrac{1}{4}\right)\left(\dfrac{2}{3}\right)\left(\dfrac{1}{2}\right) = \dfrac{1}{12} + \dfrac{1}{12} = \dfrac{1}{6} \approx 0.167$

(B) $P(\$31{,}000) = \left(\dfrac{1}{2}\right)\left(\dfrac{1}{3}\right)\left(\dfrac{1}{2}\right) + \left(\dfrac{1}{2}\right)\left(\dfrac{1}{3}\right)\left(\dfrac{1}{2}\right) + \left(\dfrac{1}{4}\right)\left(\dfrac{2}{3}\right)\left(\dfrac{1}{2}\right) = \dfrac{3}{12} = \dfrac{1}{4} = 0.25$

(C) Let A = "$20 on third draw." Then

$$P(A) = \left(\frac{1}{4}\right)\left(\frac{2}{3}\right)\left(\frac{1}{2}\right) + \left(\frac{1}{2}\right)\left(\frac{1}{3}\right)\left(\frac{1}{2}\right) + \left(\frac{1}{2}\right)\left(\frac{1}{3}\right)\left(\frac{1}{2}\right) = \frac{3}{12} = \frac{1}{4} = 0.25.$$

(D) The payoff table is:

x_i	$20	$21	$25	$26	$30	$31
P_i	$\frac{1}{4}$	$\frac{1}{12}$	$\frac{1}{6}$	$\frac{1}{6}$	$\frac{1}{12}$	$\frac{1}{4}$

Thus, $E(X) = \frac{1}{4}(20) + \frac{1}{12}(21) + \frac{1}{6}(25) + \frac{1}{6}(26) + \frac{1}{12}(30) + \frac{1}{4}(31)$

$$= \frac{60 + 21 + 50 + 52 + 30 + 93}{12} = \frac{306}{12} = 255$$

and the expected value of the game is $25,500.

51. Let Event A = Adverse reaction was a loss of appetite
and Event B = Adverse reaction was a loss of sleep.

$n(A \cap B) = 1000 - (60 + 90 + 800) = 50$ subjects with both adverse reactions

$n(A) = 60 + 50 = 110$

$n(B) = 90 + 50 = 140$

$P(A) = \frac{n(A)}{n(S)} = \frac{110}{1000} = \frac{11}{100}$

$P(B) = \frac{n(B)}{n(S)} = \frac{140}{1000} = \frac{14}{100}$

$P(A \cap B) = \frac{50}{1000} = \frac{5}{100}$

(A) $P(B|A) = \frac{P(B \cap A)}{P(A)} = \frac{\frac{5}{100}}{\frac{11}{100}} = \frac{5}{11}$ (B) $P(A|B) = \frac{P(A \cap B)}{P(B)} = \frac{\frac{5}{100}}{\frac{14}{100}} = \frac{5}{14}$

(C) $P(B|A') = \frac{P(B \cap A')}{P(A')} = \frac{P(\text{only reaction was loss of sleep})}{1 - P(A)}$

$$= \frac{\frac{90}{1000}}{1 - \frac{11}{1000}} = \frac{\frac{90}{1000}}{\frac{890}{1000}} = \frac{9}{89}$$

(D) $P(A|B') = \frac{P(B \cap S')}{P(B')} = \frac{P(\text{only reaction was loss of appetite})}{1 - P(B)}$

$$= \frac{\frac{60}{1000}}{1 - \frac{14}{1000}} = \frac{\frac{60}{1000}}{\frac{86}{1000}} = \frac{6}{86} = \frac{3}{43}$$

ADDITIONAL TOPICS IN PROBABILITY

53. (A)

	Below 90 A	90–120 B	Above 120 C	Total
Female (F)	0.130	0.286	0.104	0.520
Male (F')	0.120	0.264	0.096	0.480
Total	0.250	0.550	0.200	1.000

[Note: The probability table above was derived from the table given in the problem by dividing each entry by 1000.]

Referring to the table in part (A):

(B) $P(A|F) = \dfrac{P(A \cap F)}{P(F)} = \dfrac{0.130}{0.520} = 0.250$ (C) $P(C|F) = \dfrac{P(C \cap F)}{P(F)} = \dfrac{0.104}{0.520} = 0.200$

$P(A|F') = \dfrac{P(A \cap F')}{P(F')} = \dfrac{0.120}{0.480} = 0.250$ $P(C|F') = \dfrac{P(C \cap F')}{P(F')} = \dfrac{0.096}{0.480} = 0.200$

(D) $P(A) = 0.25$ (E) $P(B) = 0.55$

$P(A|F) = \dfrac{P(A \cap F)}{P(F)} = \dfrac{0.130}{0.520} = 0.250$ $P(B|F') = \dfrac{P(B \cap F')}{P(F')} = \dfrac{0.264}{0.480} = 0.550$

(F) $P(F \cap C) = 0.104$ (G) No, the results in parts (B), (C), (D), and (E) imply that A, B, and C are independent of F and F'.

EXERCISE 5-3

Things to remember:

1. BAYES' FORMULA

Let U_1, U_2, ..., U_n be n mutually exclusive events whose union is the sample space S. Let E be an arbitrary event in S such that $P(E) \neq 0$. Then

$$P(U_1|E) = \frac{P(U_1 \cap E)}{P(E)}$$

$$= \frac{P(U_1 \cap E)}{P(U_1 \cap E) + P(U_2 \cap E) + \cdots + P(U_n \cap E)}$$

$$= \frac{P(E|U_1)P(U_1)}{P(E|U_1)P(U_1) + \cdots + P(E|U_n)P(U_n)}$$

Similar results hold for U_2, U_3, ..., U_n.

$$P(U_1|E) = \frac{\text{Product of branch probabilities}}{\text{leading to } E \text{ through } U_1}$$
$$P(U_1|E) = \frac{}{\text{Sum of all branch probabilities}}$$
$$\frac{}{\text{leading to } E}$$

Similar results hold for U_2, U_3, ..., U_n.

---

1. $P(M \cap A) = P(M) \cdot P(A|M)$
    $= (0.6)(0.8)$
    $= 0.48$

3. $P(A) = P(M \cap A) + P(N \cap A)$
    $= P(M)P(A|M) + P(N)P(A|N)$
    $= (0.6)(0.8) + (0.4)(0.3)$
    $= 0.60$

5. $P(M|A) = \dfrac{P(M \cap A)}{P(M \cap A) + P(N \cap A)}$

    $= \dfrac{0.48}{0.60}$ (see Problems 1 and 3)

    $= 0.80$

7. Referring to the Venn diagram:

    $P(U_1|R) = \dfrac{P(U_1 \cap R)}{P(R)} = \dfrac{\frac{25}{100}}{\frac{60}{100}} = \dfrac{25}{60} = \dfrac{5}{12} \approx 0.417$

    Using Bayes' formula:

    $P(U_1|R) = \dfrac{P(U_1 \cap R)}{P(U_1 \cap R) + P(U_2 \cap R)} = \dfrac{P(U_1)P(R|U_1)}{P(U_1)P(R|U_1) + P(U_2)P(R|U_2)}$

    $= \dfrac{\left(\frac{40}{100}\right)\left(\frac{25}{40}\right)}{\left(\frac{40}{100}\right)\left(\frac{25}{40}\right) + \left(\frac{60}{100}\right)\left(\frac{35}{60}\right)} = \dfrac{0.25}{0.25 + 0.35} = \dfrac{0.25}{0.60} = \dfrac{5}{12} \approx 0.417$

9. $P(U_1|R') = \dfrac{P(U_1 \cap R')}{P(R')}$

    $= \dfrac{\frac{15}{100}}{1 - P(R)}$ (from the Venn diagram)

    $= \dfrac{\frac{15}{100}}{1 - \frac{60}{100}} = \dfrac{\frac{15}{100}}{\frac{40}{100}} = \dfrac{3}{8} = 0.375$

Using Bayes' formula:

$$P(U_1|R') = \frac{P(U_1 \cap R')}{P(R')} = \frac{P(U_1)P(R'|U_1)}{P(U_1 \cap R') + P(U_2 \cap R')}$$

$$= \frac{P(U_1)P(R'|U_1)}{P(U_1)P(R'|U_1) + P(U_2)P(R'|U_2)} = \frac{\left(\frac{40}{100}\right)\left(\frac{15}{100}\right)}{\left(\frac{40}{100}\right)\left(\frac{15}{100}\right) + \left(\frac{60}{100}\right)\left(\frac{25}{60}\right)}$$

$$= \frac{0.15}{0.15 + 0.25} = \frac{15}{40} = \frac{3}{8} = 0.375$$

11. $P(U|C) = \dfrac{P(U \cap C)}{P(C)} = \dfrac{P(U \cap C)}{P(U \cap C) + P(V \cap C) + P(W \cap C)}$

$$= \frac{(.2)(.4)}{(.2)(.4) + (.5)(.2) + (.3)(.6)}$$

[**Note:** Recall $P(A \cap B)$ $= P(A) \cdot P(B|A)$.]

$$= \frac{.08}{.36} \approx 0.222$$

13. $P(W|C) = \dfrac{P(W \cap C)}{P(C)} = \dfrac{P(W \cap C)}{P(W \cap C) + P(V \cap C) + P(U \cap C)}$

$$= \frac{(.3)(.6)}{(.3)(.6) + (.5)(.2) + (.2)(.4)}$$

(see Problem 11)

$$= \frac{.18}{.36} = 0.5$$

15. $P(V|C) = \dfrac{P(V \cap C)}{P(C)} = \dfrac{P(V \cap C)}{P(V \cap C) + P(W \cap C) + P(U \cap C)}$

$$= \frac{(.5)(.2)}{(.5)(.2) + (.3)(.6) + (.2)(.4)}$$

$$= \frac{.1}{.36} = 0.278$$

17. From the Venn diagram,

$$P(U_1|R) = \frac{5}{5 + 15 + 20} = \frac{5}{40} = \frac{1}{8} = 0.125$$

or

$$= \frac{P(U_1 \cap R)}{P(R)} = \frac{\frac{5}{100}}{\frac{40}{100}} = 0.125$$

Using Bayes' formula:

$$P(U_1|R) = \frac{P(U_1 \cap R)}{P(U_1 \cap R) + P(U_2 \cap R) + P(U_3 \cap R)} = \frac{\frac{5}{100}}{\frac{5}{100} + \frac{15}{100} + \frac{20}{100}}$$

$$= \frac{.05}{.05 + .15 + .2} = \frac{.05}{.40} = 0.125$$

19. From the Venn diagram,

$$P(U_3 | R) = \frac{20}{5 + 15 + 20} = \frac{20}{40} = 0.5$$

Using Bayes' formula:

$$P(U_3 | R) = \frac{P(U_3 \cap R)}{P(U_1 \cap R) + P(U_2 \cap R) + P(U_3 \cap R)} = \frac{\dfrac{20}{100}}{\dfrac{5}{100} + \dfrac{15}{100} + \dfrac{20}{100}}$$

$$= \frac{.2}{.05 + .15 + .2} = \frac{.2}{.4} = 0.5$$

21. From the Venn diagram,

$$P(U_2 | R) = \frac{15}{5 + 15 + 20} = \frac{15}{40} = 0.375$$

Using Bayes' formula:

$$P(U_2 | R) = \frac{P(U_2 \cap R)}{P(U_1 \cap R) + P(U_2 \cap R) + P(U_3 \cap R)} = \frac{\dfrac{15}{100}}{\dfrac{5}{100} + \dfrac{15}{100} + \dfrac{20}{100}}$$

$$= \frac{.15}{.05 + .15 + .2} = \frac{.15}{.40}$$

$$= \frac{3}{8} = 0.375$$

23. From the given tree diagram, we have:

$$P(A) = \frac{1}{4} \qquad\qquad P(A') = \frac{3}{4}$$

$$P(B|A) = \frac{1}{5} \qquad\qquad P(B|A') = \frac{3}{5}$$

$$P(B'|A) = \frac{4}{5} \qquad\qquad P(B'|A') = \frac{2}{5}$$

We want to find the following:

$$P(B) = P(B \cap A) + P(B \cap A') = P(A)P(B|A) + P(A')P(B|A')$$

$$= \left(\frac{1}{4}\right)\left(\frac{1}{5}\right) + \left(\frac{3}{4}\right)\left(\frac{3}{5}\right)$$

$$= \frac{1}{20} + \frac{9}{20} = \frac{10}{20} = \frac{1}{2}$$

$$P(B') = 1 - P(B) = 1 - \frac{1}{2} = \frac{1}{2}$$

$$P(A|B) = \frac{P(A \cap B)}{P(B)} = \frac{P(A)P(B|A)}{P(B)} = \frac{\left(\frac{1}{4}\right)\left(\frac{1}{5}\right)}{\frac{1}{2}} = \frac{\frac{1}{20}}{\frac{1}{2}} = \frac{1}{10}$$

Thus, $P(A'|B) = 1 - P(A|B) = 1 - \frac{1}{10} = \frac{9}{10}$.

ADDITIONAL TOPICS IN PROBABILITY

$$P(A|B') = \frac{P(A \cap B')}{P(B')} = \frac{P(A)P(B'|A)}{P(B')} = \frac{\left(\frac{1}{4}\right)\left(\frac{4}{5}\right)}{\frac{1}{2}} = \frac{\frac{4}{20}}{\frac{1}{2}} = \frac{2}{5}$$

Thus, $P(A'|B') = 1 - P(A|B') = 1 - \frac{2}{5} = \frac{3}{5}$.

Therefore, the tree diagram for this problem is as follows:

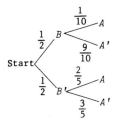

The following tree diagram is to be used for Problems 25 and 27.

```
                1/5 = .2   W (white)
        .5  U₁ (urn 1)<
                4/5 = .8   R (red)
Start<
                3/5 = .6   W
        .5  U₂ (urn 2)<
                2/5 = .4   R
```

25. $P(U_1|W) = \dfrac{P(U_1 \cap W)}{P(W)} = \dfrac{P(U_1 \cap W)}{P(U_1 \cap W) + P(U_2 \cap W)}$

$$= \frac{P(U_1)P(W|U_1)}{P(U_1)P(W|U_1) + P(U_2)P(W|U_2)} = \frac{(.5)(.2)}{(.5)(.2) + (.5)(.6)} = \frac{.1}{.4} = 0.25$$

27. $P(U_2|R) = \dfrac{P(U_2 \cap R)}{P(R)} = \dfrac{P(U_2 \cap R)}{P(U_2 \cap R) + P(U_1 \cap R)}$

$$= \frac{P(U_2)P(R|U_2)}{P(U_2)P(R|U_2) + P(U_1)P(R|U_1)} = \frac{(.5)(.4)}{(.5)(.4) + (.5)(.8)}$$

$$= \frac{.4}{1.2} = \frac{1}{3} \approx 0.333$$

29. $P(W_1|W_2) = \dfrac{P(W_1 \cap W_2)}{P(W_2)} = \dfrac{P(W_1)P(W_2|W_1)}{P(R_1 \cap W_2) + P(W_1 \cap W_2)}$

$\qquad\qquad = \dfrac{P(W_1)P(W_2|W_1)}{P(R_1)P(W_2|R_1) + P(W_1)P(W_2|W_1)} = \dfrac{\left(\frac{5}{9}\right)\left(\frac{4}{8}\right)}{\left(\frac{4}{9}\right)\left(\frac{5}{8}\right) + \left(\frac{5}{9}\right)\left(\frac{4}{8}\right)} = \dfrac{\frac{20}{72}}{\frac{20}{72} + \frac{20}{72}}$

$\qquad\qquad = \dfrac{20}{40} = \dfrac{1}{2}$ or 0.5

31. $P(U_{R_1}|U_{R_2}) = \dfrac{P(U_{R_1} \cap U_{R_2})}{P(U_{R_2})} = \dfrac{P(U_{R_1})P(U_{R_2}|U_{R_1})}{P(U_{W_1} \cap U_{R_2}) + P(U_{R_1} \cap U_{R_2})}$

$\qquad\qquad = \dfrac{P(U_{R_1})P(U_{R_2}|U_{R_1})}{P(U_{W_1})P(U_{R_2}|U_{W_1}) + P(U_{R_1})P(U_{R_2}|U_{R_1})}$

$\qquad\qquad = \dfrac{\left(\frac{7}{10}\right)\left(\frac{5}{10}\right)}{\left(\frac{3}{10}\right)\left(\frac{4}{10}\right) + \left(\frac{7}{10}\right)\left(\frac{5}{10}\right)} = \dfrac{.35}{.12 + .35}$

$\qquad\qquad = \dfrac{.35}{.47} = \dfrac{35}{47} \approx 0.745$

The tree diagram follows:

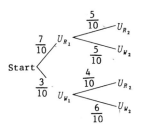

where U_{R_1} is red from urn one,

$\qquad U_{R_2}$ is red from urn two,

$\qquad U_{W_1}$ is white from urn one,

and $\quad U_{W_2}$ is white from urn two.

33.

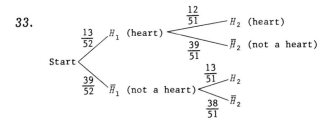

$$P(H_1|H_2) = \frac{P(H_1 \cap H_2)}{P(H_2)} = \frac{P(H_1 \cap H_2)}{P(H_1 \cap H_2) + P(\bar{H}_1 \cap H_2)}$$

$$= \frac{P(H_1)P(H_2|H_1)}{P(H_1)P(H_2|H_1) + P(\bar{H}_1)P(H_2|\bar{H}_1)} = \frac{\frac{13}{52} \cdot \frac{12}{51}}{\frac{13}{52} \cdot \frac{12}{51} + \frac{39}{52} \cdot \frac{13}{51}}$$

$$= \frac{13(12)}{13(12) + 39(13)} = \frac{12}{51} \approx 0.235$$

35. Consider the following Venn diagram:

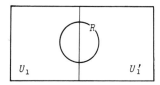

$$P(U_1|R) = \frac{P(U_1 \cap R)}{P(U_1 \cap R) + P(U_1' \cap R)} \quad \text{and} \quad P(U_1' \cap R) = \frac{P(U_1' \cap R)}{P(U_1 \cap R) + P(U_1' \cap R)}$$

Adding these two equations, we obtain:

$$P(U_1|R) + P(U_1' \cap R) = \frac{P(U_1 \cap R)}{P(U_1 \cap R) + P(U_1' \cap R)} + \frac{P(U_1' \cap R)}{P(U_1 \cap R) + P(U_1' \cap R)}$$

$$= \frac{P(U_1 \cap R) + P(U_1' \cap R)}{P(U_1 \cap R) + P(U_1' \cap R)} = 1$$

37. Consider the following tree diagram:

$$
\begin{array}{l}
\text{Start} \\
\quad \underset{.7}{\diagup} S \text{ (satisfactory)} \overset{.9}{\diagup} P \text{ (pass)} \\
\qquad\qquad\qquad\qquad\quad \underset{.1}{\diagdown} NP \text{ (not pass)} \\
\quad \underset{.3}{\diagdown} NS \text{ (not satisfactory)} \overset{.2}{\diagup} P \\
\qquad\qquad\qquad\qquad\qquad\quad \underset{.8}{\diagdown} NP
\end{array}
$$

$$P(S|P) = \frac{P(S \cap P)}{P(S)} = \frac{P(S \cap P)}{P(S \cap P) + P(NS \cap P)} = \frac{P(S)P(P|S)}{P(S)P(P|S) + P(NS)P(P|NS)}$$

$$= \frac{(.7)(.9)}{(.7)(.9) + (.3)(.2)} = \frac{.63}{.69} \approx 0.913$$

39. Consider the following tree diagram:

$$P(A|D) = \frac{P(A \cap D)}{P(D)}, \text{ where}$$

$$P(D) = P(A \cap D) + P(B \cap D) + P(C \cap D)$$
$$= P(A)P(D|A) + P(B)P(D|B) + P(C)P(D|C)$$
$$= (.2)(.01) + (.40)(.03) + (.40)(.20)$$
$$= .002 + .012 + .008$$
$$= .022$$

Thus, $P(A|D) = \dfrac{P(A \cap D)}{P(D)} = \dfrac{P(A)P(D|A)}{P(D)} = \dfrac{(.20)(.01)}{.022} = \dfrac{.002}{.022} = \dfrac{2}{22}$ or 0.091

Similarly, $P(B|D) = \dfrac{P(B \cap D)}{P(D)} = \dfrac{P(B)P(D|B)}{P(D)} = \dfrac{(.40)(.03)}{.022} = \dfrac{.012}{.022} = \dfrac{6}{11}$ or 0.545,

and $\quad\quad P(C|D) = \dfrac{P(C \cap D)}{P(D)} = \dfrac{P(C)P(D|C)}{P(D)} = \dfrac{(.40)(.02)}{.022} = \dfrac{.008}{.022} = \dfrac{4}{11}$ or 0.364.

41. Consider the following tree diagram.

$$P(C|CT) = \frac{P(C \cap CT)}{P(CT)} = \frac{P(C)P(CT|C)}{P(C \cap CT) + P(NC \cap CT)}$$

$$= \frac{P(C)P(CT|C)}{P(C)P(CT|C) + P(NC)P(CT|NC)} = \frac{(.02)(.98)}{(.02)(.98) + (.98)(.01)}$$

$$= \frac{.0196}{.0196 + .0098} = \frac{.0196}{.0294} = 0.6667$$

$$P(C|NCT) = \frac{P(C \cap NCT)}{P(NCT)} = \frac{P(C)P(NCT|C)}{P(C)P(NCT|C) + P(NC)P(NCT|NC)}$$

$$= \frac{(.02)(.02)}{(.02)(.02) + (.98)(.99)} \approx 0.000412$$

43. Consider the following tree diagram.

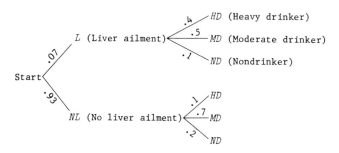

$$P(L|HD) = \frac{P(L \cap HD)}{P(HD)} = \frac{P(L)P(HD|L)}{P(L \cap HD) + P(NL \cap HD)} = \frac{P(L)P(HD|L)}{P(L)P(HD|L) + P(NL)P(HD|NL)}$$

$$= \frac{(.07)(.4)}{(.07)(.4) + (.93)(.1)} \quad \text{(from the tree diagram)}$$

$$= \frac{.028}{.028 + .093} = \frac{.028}{.121} = \frac{28}{121} \approx 0.232$$

$$P(L|ND) = \frac{P(L \cap ND)}{P(ND)} = \frac{P(L)P(ND|L)}{P(L \cap ND) + P(NL \cap ND)} = \frac{P(L)P(ND|L)}{P(L)P(ND|L) + P(NL)P(ND|NL)}$$

$$= \frac{(.07)(.1)}{(.07)(.1) + (.93)(.2)} \quad \text{(from the tree diagram)}$$

$$= \frac{.007}{.007 + .186} = \frac{.007}{.194} = \frac{7}{194} \approx 0.036$$

45. Consider the following tree diagram.

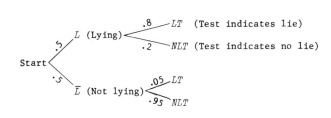

$$P(L|LT) = \frac{P(L \cap LT)}{P(LT)} = \frac{P(L \cap LT)}{P(L \cap LT) + P(\bar{L} \cap LT)}$$

$$= \frac{(.5)(.8)}{(.5)(.8) + (.5)(.05)}$$

$$= \frac{.8}{.86} \approx 0.941 \quad$$ If the test indicates that the subject was lying, then he was lying with a probability of 0.941.

$$P(\bar{L}|LT) = \frac{P(\bar{L} \cap LT)}{P(LT)}$$

$$= \frac{(.5)(.05)}{(.5)(.8) + (.5)(.05)}$$

$$= \frac{.05}{.85} \approx 0.0588 \quad$$ If the test indicates that the subject was lying, there is still a probability of 0.0588 that he was not lying.

EXERCISE 5-4

Things to remember:

1. A TRANSITION MATRIX for a Markov chain is a square matrix such that each entry indicates the probability of a system moving from a given state to another state on the next observation or trial. The sum of the entries in each row is 1. A transition matrix is REGULAR if some power of the matrix has only positive elements.

2. A STATE MATRIX is a matrix of the form

    $$[p_1, p_2, \ldots, p_n],$$

    where each entry indicates the probability of a system being in the state corresponding to the position of the entry and

    $$p_1 + p_2 + \cdots + p_n = 1.$$

    An INITIAL STATE MATRIX is a state matrix in which each entry indicates the initial probability of each event.

3. A state matrix Q is a STEADY-STATE MATRIX relative to a transition matrix P if

    $$QP = Q.$$

1. $MP = [1, 0] \begin{bmatrix} .8 & .2 \\ .4 & .6 \end{bmatrix} = \overset{\textstyle A \qquad B}{[.8 \qquad .2]}$

Initial State

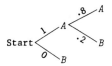

Starting in state A; at the next stage, the probability of being in state A is .8, while the probability of being in state B is .2.

3. $(MP)P = [.8 \quad .2] \begin{bmatrix} .8 & .2 \\ .4 & .6 \end{bmatrix} = [.64 + .08 \quad .16 + .12] = \overset{\textstyle A \qquad B}{[.72 \qquad .28]}$

[Note: MP was computed in Problem 1.]

Starting in state A; at the third stage, the probability of being in state A is .72, and the probability of being in state B is .28.

5. $RP = [.5 \quad .5] \begin{bmatrix} .8 & .2 \\ .4 & .6 \end{bmatrix} = [.4 + .2 \quad .1 + .3] = \overset{\textstyle A \qquad B}{[.6 \qquad .4]}$

The result above can be represented by the following tree diagram:

Initial State

Start with the initial-state matrix R; at the second stage, the probability of being in state A is .6 [$(.5)(.8) + (.5)(.4)$] = .6, while the probability of being in state B is .4 [$(.5)(.2) + (.5)(.6)$] = .4.

7. $(RP)P = [.6 \quad .4] \begin{bmatrix} .8 & .2 \\ .4 & .6 \end{bmatrix} = [.48 + .16 \quad .12 + .24] = \overset{\textstyle A \qquad B}{[.64 \qquad .36]}$

[Note: RP was computed in Problem 5.]

Start with the initial-state matrix A; at the third stage, the probability of being in state A is .64, while the probability of being in state B is .36.

9. To be a transition matrix for a Markov chain, the entries in the matrix must be nonnegative, and the sum of the entries in each row must be 1. Thus,

$.2 + a + .3 = 1 \qquad b + .7 + .1 = 1 \qquad 0 + 0 + c = 1$

$\text{and } a = .5 \qquad\qquad \text{and } b = .3 \qquad\qquad \text{and } c = 1$

11. From **3**, $Q = [m, n]$ is a steady-state matrix for

$$P = \begin{bmatrix} .2 & .8 \\ .7 & .3 \end{bmatrix}$$

if $QP = Q$, i.e., if

$$[m \quad n] \begin{bmatrix} .2 & .8 \\ .7 & .3 \end{bmatrix} = [m, n].$$

This leads to the following pair of linear equations:

$$\begin{array}{ll} .2m + .7n = m \\ .8m + .3n = n \end{array} \quad \text{or} \quad \begin{array}{l} -.8m + .7n = 0 \\ .8m - .7n = 0 \end{array}$$

We also have the equation $m + n = 1$. The system of linear equations:

$$\begin{array}{l} -.8m + .7n = 0 \\ .8m - .7n = 0 \\ m + n = 1 \end{array}$$

is equivalent to the system

$$\begin{array}{l} .8m - .7n = 0 \\ m + n = 1 \end{array}$$

which has the solution $m = .47$ and $n = .53$. Thus, the steady-state matrix is $Q = [.47 \quad .53]$.

13. Again, using **3**, $[m \quad n] \begin{bmatrix} .5 & .5 \\ .3 & .7 \end{bmatrix} = [m \quad n]$

$$[.5m + .3n \quad .5m + .7n] = [m \quad n]$$

Thus, we have the following system of linear equations: $\begin{array}{r} .5m + .3n = m \\ .5m + .7n = n \\ m + n = 1 \end{array}$

Solving the above system, we get $m = .375$ and $n = .625$. Thus, the steady-state matrix $Q = [.375 \quad .625]$.

15. Again, using **3**, $[m \quad n \quad \ell] \begin{bmatrix} .5 & .5 & 0 \\ .25 & .5 & .25 \\ 0 & .5 & .5 \end{bmatrix} = [m \quad n \quad \ell]$

$$[.5m + .25n \quad .5m + .5n + .5\ell \quad .25m + .5\ell] = [m \quad n \quad \ell]$$

Thus, we have the following system of linear equations:

$$.5m + .25n \qquad\quad = m$$
$$.5m + \quad .5n + .5\ell = n$$
$$\qquad\quad .25n + .5\ell = \ell$$
$$m + \quad n + \quad \ell = 1$$

Solving the system above for m, n, and ℓ by using any of the methods discussed in Chapter 1, we get $m = .25$, $n = .5$, $\ell = .25$. The steady-state matrix $Q = [.25 \quad .5 \quad .25]$.

17. (A) Let A = "raining," A' = "not raining." Then the transition matrix is:

Next state

$$\text{Current state} \quad \begin{array}{c} A \\ A' \end{array} \begin{bmatrix} .4 & .6 \\ .06 & .94 \end{bmatrix} = P$$

(B) If it rains on a given Thursday, then the initial state matrix is:

$$\begin{array}{cc} A & A' \\ [1 & 0] \end{array} = N.$$

The states on Saturday are given by:

$$(NP)P = \left([1 \quad 0] \begin{bmatrix} .4 & .6 \\ .06 & .94 \end{bmatrix} \right) \begin{bmatrix} .4 & .6 \\ .06 & .94 \end{bmatrix} = [.4 \quad .6] \begin{bmatrix} .4 & .6 \\ .06 & .94 \end{bmatrix}$$

$$= [.16 + .036 \quad .24 + .564] = [.196 \quad .804] \approx [.2 \quad .8]$$

Thus, the probability of rain on Saturday is .2.

The states on Sunday are:

$$[.2 \quad .8] \begin{bmatrix} .4 & .6 \\ .06 & .94 \end{bmatrix} = [.08 + .048 \quad .12 + .752]$$

$$= [.128 \quad .872] \approx [.13 \quad .87]$$

The probability of rain on Sunday is .13.

(C) To find the steady-state solution, we solve the system

$$[m \quad n] \begin{bmatrix} .4 & .6 \\ .06 & .94 \end{bmatrix} = [m \quad n], \; m + n = 1,$$

which is equivalent to:

$$.4m + .06n = m \qquad\qquad -.6m + .06n = 0$$
$$.6m + .94n = n \qquad \text{or} \qquad .6m - .06n = 0$$
$$m + n = 1 \qquad\qquad m + n = 1$$

The solution of this system is $m = .09$, $n = .91$. Thus, the steady-state solution is [.09 .91].

(D) From the result in (C), the restaurant will be closed 9% of the time.

19. (A) Transition matrix:

Next week

X X'

Current $\begin{array}{c} X \\ X' \end{array} \begin{bmatrix} .8 & .2 \\ .2 & .8 \end{bmatrix}$ X = user of brand
X' = nonusers of brand

(B) Initial-state matrix: X X'

[.2 .8]

Thus, we have the

$$\text{second-state matrix} = \begin{bmatrix} .2 & .8 \end{bmatrix} \begin{bmatrix} .8 & .2 \\ .2 & .8 \end{bmatrix} = \begin{bmatrix} .32 & .68 \end{bmatrix}$$

which shows that 32% will be using brand X one week later. And the

$$\text{third-state matrix} = \begin{bmatrix} .32 & .68 \end{bmatrix} \begin{bmatrix} .8 & .2 \\ .2 & .8 \end{bmatrix} = \begin{bmatrix} .392 & .608 \end{bmatrix}$$

shows that 39.2% will be using brand X two weeks later.

(C) Steady-state matrix Q $(QP = Q)$: $\begin{bmatrix} m & n \end{bmatrix} \begin{bmatrix} .8 & .2 \\ .2 & .8 \end{bmatrix} = \begin{bmatrix} m & n \end{bmatrix}$

$$\begin{bmatrix} .8m + .2n & .2m + .8n \end{bmatrix} = \begin{bmatrix} m & n \end{bmatrix}$$

Thus, we have the following linear equations:

$$.8m + .2n = \qquad\qquad -.2m + .2n = 0$$
$$.2m + .8n = \qquad \text{or} \qquad .2m - .2n = 0$$
$$m + n = 1 \qquad\qquad m + n = 1$$

Thus, $m = .5$ and $n = .5$. And the steady-state matrix $Q = [.5 \quad .5]$, which means that near the end of the season, 50% will be using brand X.

21. To find the steady-state solution, we solve the system

$$[m \quad n \quad \ell] \begin{bmatrix} .5 & .5 & 0 \\ .25 & .5 & .25 \\ 0 & .5 & .5 \end{bmatrix} = [m \quad n \quad \ell], \ m + n + \ell = 1,$$

which is equivalent to:

$$\begin{aligned} .5m + .25n &= m \\ .5m + .5n + .5\ell &= n \\ .25n + .5\ell &= \ell \\ m + n + \ell &= 1 \end{aligned} \quad \text{or} \quad \begin{aligned} -.5m + .25n &= 0 \\ .5m - .5n + .5\ell &= 0 \\ .25n - .5\ell &= 0 \\ m + n + \ell &= 1 \end{aligned}$$

The solution of this system is $m = .25$, $n = .5$, $\ell = .25$. Thus, the steady-state matrix is $Q = [.25 \quad .5 \quad .25]$.

23. (A)

$$\begin{array}{cc} \text{Rapid} & \\ \text{transit} & \text{Auto} \end{array}$$

Initial-state matrix = $[.25 \qquad .75]$

(B) Second-state matrix = $[.25 \quad .75] \begin{bmatrix} .8 & .2 \\ .3 & .7 \end{bmatrix} = [.425 \quad .575]$

Thus, 42.5% will be using the new system after one month.

Third-state matrix = $[.425 \quad .575] \begin{bmatrix} .8 & .2 \\ .3 & .7 \end{bmatrix} = [.5125 \quad .4875]$

Thus, 51.25% will be using the new system after two months.

(C) To find the steady-state solution, we solve the system

$$[m \quad n] \begin{bmatrix} .8 & .2 \\ .3 & .7 \end{bmatrix} = [m \quad n], \ m + n = 1,$$

which is equivalent to:

$$\begin{aligned} .8m + .3n &= m \\ .2m + .7n &= n \\ m + n &= 1 \end{aligned} \quad \text{or} \quad \begin{aligned} -.2m + .3n &= 0 \\ .2m - .3n &= 0 \\ m + n &= 1 \end{aligned}$$

The solution of this system of linear equations is $m = .6$ and $n = .4$. Thus, the steady-state solution is $Q = [.6 \quad .4]$, which means that 60% of the commuters will use rapid transit and 40% will travel by automobile after the system has been in service for a long time.

1. $P(A) = .3$, $P(B) = .4$, $P(A \cap B) = .1$

   (A) $P(A') = 1 - P(A) = 1 - .3 = .7$

   (B) $P(A \cup B) = P(A) + P(B) - P(A \cap B) = .3 + .4 - .1 = .6$

2.   Since the spinner cannot land on R and G simultaneously, $R \cap G = \emptyset$. Thus,

   $P(R \cup G) = P(R) + P(G) = .3 + .5 = .8$

   The odds for an event E are: $\dfrac{P(E)}{P(E')}$

   Thus, the odds for landing on either R or G are:

   $\dfrac{P(R \cup G)}{P[(R \cup G)']} = \dfrac{.8}{.2} = \dfrac{8}{2}$

   or the odds are 8 to 2.

3.   If the odds for an event E are a to b, then $P(E) = \dfrac{a}{a + b}$.

   Thus, the probability of rolling an 8 before rolling a 7 is: $\dfrac{5}{11} \approx .455$.

4. $P(T) = .27$ 5. $P(Z) = .20$ 6. $P(T \cap Z) = .02$ 7. $P(R \cap Z) = .03$

8. $P(R|Z) = \dfrac{P(R \cap Z)}{P(Z)} = \dfrac{.03}{.20} = .15$ 9. $P(Z|R) = \dfrac{P(Z \cap R)}{P(R)} = \dfrac{.03}{.23} \approx .1304$

10. $P(T|Z) = \dfrac{P(T \cap Z)}{P(Z)} = \dfrac{.02}{.20} = .10$

11.   No, because $P(T \cap Z) = .02 \neq P(T) \cdot P(Z) = (.27)(.20) = .054$.

12.   Yes, because $P(S \cap X) = .10 = P(S) \cdot P(X) = (.5)(.2)$.

13. $P(A) = .4$ from the tree diagram.   14. $P(B|A) = .2$ from the tree diagram.

15. $P(B|A') = .3$ from the tree diagram.   16. $P(A \cap B) = P(A)P(B|A)$
                                                            $= (.4)(.2) = .08$

17. $P(A' \cap B) = P(A')P(B|A') = (.6)(.3) = .18$

18. $P(B) = P(A \cap B) + P(A' \cap B)$
            $= P(A)P(B|A) + P(A')P(B|A')$
            $= (.4)(.2) + (.6)(.3)$
            $= .08 + .18$
            $= .26$

19. $P(A|B) = \dfrac{P(A \cap B)}{P(B)} = \dfrac{P(A)P(B|A)}{P(A \cap B) + P(A' \cap B)} = \dfrac{P(A)P(B|A)}{P(A)P(B|A) + P(A')P(B|A')}$

$$= \dfrac{(.4)(.2)}{(.4)(.2) + (.6)(.3)} \qquad \text{(from the tree diagram)}$$

$$= \dfrac{.08}{.26} = \dfrac{8}{26} \text{ or } .307 \approx .31$$

20. $P(A|B') = \dfrac{P(A \cap B')}{P(B')} = \dfrac{P(A)P(B'|A)}{1 - P(B)} = \dfrac{(.4)(.8)}{1 - .26}$ $[P(B) = .26,$ see Problem 18.]

$$= \dfrac{.32}{.74} = \dfrac{16}{37} \text{ or } .432$$

21. $[.3 \quad .7] \begin{bmatrix} .2 & .8 \\ .7 & .3 \end{bmatrix} = \left[[.3 \quad .7] \begin{bmatrix} .2 \\ .7 \end{bmatrix} \quad [.3 \quad .7] \begin{bmatrix} .8 \\ .3 \end{bmatrix} \right]$

$$= [.06 + .49 \quad .24 + .21] = [.55 \quad .45]$$

22. The sum of the entries in each row must be 1 in order for the matrix to be a transition matrix for a Markov chain. Thus,

$.7 + .3 + a = 1 \qquad .2 + b + .2 = 1 \qquad 0 + c + .9 = 1$
$\qquad \quad a = 0 \qquad\qquad\qquad b = .6 \qquad\qquad\qquad c = .1$

23. (A) $P(\text{jack or queen}) = P(\text{jack}) + P(\text{queen}) = \dfrac{4}{52} + \dfrac{4}{52} = \dfrac{8}{52} = \dfrac{2}{13}$

[Note: jack $\cap$ queen $= \emptyset$.]

The odds for drawing a jack or queen are 2 to 11.

(B) $P(\text{jack or spade}) = P(\text{jack}) + P(\text{spade}) - P(\text{jack and spade})$

$$= \dfrac{4}{52} + \dfrac{13}{52} - \dfrac{1}{52} = \dfrac{16}{52} = \dfrac{4}{13}$$

The odds for drawing a jack or a spade are 4 to 9.

(C) $P(\text{ace}) = \dfrac{4}{52} = \dfrac{1}{13}.$ Thus,

$P(\text{card other than an ace}) = 1 - P(\text{ace}) = 1 - \dfrac{1}{13} = \dfrac{12}{13}$

The odds for drawing a card other than an ace are 12 to 1.

24. (A) The probability of rolling a 5 is $\dfrac{4}{36} = \dfrac{1}{9}.$

Thus, the odds for rolling a five are 1 to 8.

(B) Let x = amount house should pay (and return the $1 bet). Then, for the game to be fair,

$$E(X) = x\left(\frac{1}{9}\right) + (-1)\left(\frac{8}{9}\right) = 0$$

$$\frac{x}{9} - \frac{8}{9} = 0$$

$$x = 8$$

Thus, the house should pay $8.

25. The event A that corresponds to the sum being divisible by 4 includes sums 4, 8, and 12. This set is:

$A = \{(1, 3), (2, 2), (3, 1), (2, 6), (3, 5), (4, 4), (5, 3), (6, 2), (6, 6)\}$

The event B that corresponds to the sum being divisible by 6 includes sums 6 and 12. This set is:

$B = \{(1, 5), (2, 4), (3, 3), (4, 2), (5, 1), (6, 6)\}$

$$P(A) = \frac{n(A)}{n(S)} = \frac{9}{36} = \frac{1}{4}$$

$$P(B) = \frac{n(B)}{n(S)} = \frac{6}{36} = \frac{1}{6}$$

$P(A \cap B) = \frac{1}{36}$ [<u>Note</u>: $A \cap B = \{(6, 6)\}$]

$P(A \cup B) = \frac{14}{36}$ or $\frac{7}{18}$ [<u>Note</u>: $A \cup B = \{(1, 3), (2, 2), (3, 1), (2, 6), (3, 5)$ $(4, 4), (5, 3), (6, 2), (6, 6), (1, 5),$ $(2, 4), (3, 3), (4, 2), (5, 1)\}$]

26. (A) $P(\text{odd number}) = P(1) + P(3) + P(5) = .2 + .3 + .1 = .6$

(B) Let E = "number less than 4,"
and F = "odd number."

Now, $E \cap F = \{1, 3\}$, $F = \{1, 3, 5\}$.

$$P(E|F) = \frac{P(E \cap F)}{P(F)} = \frac{.2 + .3}{.6} = \frac{5}{6}$$

27. Let E = "card is red" and F = "card is an ace." Then $F \cap E$ = "card is a red ace."

(A) $P(F|E) = \frac{P(F \cap E)}{P(E)} = \frac{2/52}{26/52} = \frac{1}{13}$

(B) $P(F \cap E) = \frac{1}{26}$, and $P(E) = \frac{1}{2}$, $P(F) = \frac{1}{13}$.

Thus, $P(F \cap E) = P(E) \cdot P(F)$, and E and F are independent.

28. (A) The tree diagram with replacement is:

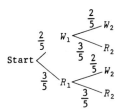

$$P(W_1 \cap R_2) = P(W_1)P(R_2|W_1) = \frac{2}{5} \cdot \frac{3}{5} = \frac{6}{25} \approx .24$$

(B) The tree diagram without replacement is:

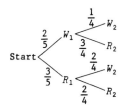

$$P(W_1 \cap R_2) = P(W_1)P(R_2|W_1) = \frac{2}{5} \cdot \frac{3}{4} = \frac{6}{20} = .3$$

29. Part (B) involves dependent events because

$$P(R_2|W_1) = \frac{3}{4}$$

$$P(R_2) = P(W_1 \cap R_2) + P(R_1 \cap R_2) = \frac{6}{20} + \frac{6}{20} = \frac{12}{20} = \frac{3}{5}$$

and

$$P(R_2|W_1) \neq P(R_2)$$

The events in part (A) are independent.

30. (A) Using the tree diagram in Problem 28(A), we have:

$$P(\text{zero red balls}) = P(W_1 \cap W_2) = P(W_1)P(W_2) = \frac{2}{5} \cdot \frac{2}{5} = \frac{4}{25} = .16$$

$$P(\text{one red ball}) = P(W_1 \cap R_2) + P(R_1 \cap W_2)$$
$$= P(W_1)P(R_2) + P(R_1)P(W_2)$$
$$= \frac{2}{3} \cdot \frac{3}{5} + \frac{3}{5} \cdot \frac{2}{5} = \frac{12}{25} = .48$$

$$P(\text{two red balls}) = P(R_1 \cap R_2) = P(R_1)P(R_2) = \frac{3}{5} \cdot \frac{3}{5} = \frac{9}{25} = .36$$

Thus, the probability distribution is:

Number of red balls x_i	Probability p_i
0	.16
1	.48
2	.36

The expected number of red balls is:

$E(X) = 0(.16) + 1(.48) + 2(.36) = .48 + .72 = 1.2$

(B) Using the tree diagram in Problem 28(B), we have:

$P(\text{zero red balls}) = P(W_1 \cap W_2) = P(W_1)P(W_2|W_1) = \dfrac{2}{5} \cdot \dfrac{1}{4} = \dfrac{1}{10} = .1$

$\begin{aligned} P(\text{one red ball}) &= P(W_1 \cap R_2) + P(R_1 \cap W_2) \\ &= P(W_1)P(R_2|W_1) + P(R_1)P(W_2|R_1) \\ &= \dfrac{2}{5} \cdot \dfrac{3}{4} + \dfrac{3}{5} \cdot \dfrac{2}{4} = \dfrac{12}{20} = \dfrac{3}{5} = .6 \end{aligned}$

$P(\text{two red balls}) = P(R_1 \cap R_2) = P(R_1)P(R_2|R_1) = \dfrac{3}{5} \cdot \dfrac{2}{4} = \dfrac{6}{20} = .3$

Thus, the probability distribution is:

Number of red balls x_i	Probability p_i
0	.1
1	.6
2	.3

The expected number of red balls is:

$E(X) = 0(.1) + 1(.6) + 2(.3) = 1.2$

31. The tree diagram for this problem is as follows:

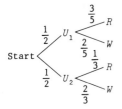

The probability of selecting urn U_1 is .5 and that of selecting urn U_2 is .5.

(A) $P(R|U_1) = \dfrac{3}{5}$ (B) $P(R|U_2) = \dfrac{1}{3}$

(C) $P(R) = P(R \cap U_1) + P(R \cap U_2)$

$\quad = P(U_1)P(R|U_1) + P(U_2)P(R|U_2)$

$\quad = \dfrac{1}{2} \cdot \dfrac{3}{5} + \dfrac{1}{2} \cdot \dfrac{1}{3} = \dfrac{28}{60} = \dfrac{7}{15} \approx .4667$

(D) $P(U_1|R) = \dfrac{P(U_1 \cap R)}{P(R)} = \dfrac{P(U_1)P(R|U_1)}{P(U_1)P(R|U_1) + P(U_2)P(R|U_2)}$

$\quad = \dfrac{\dfrac{1}{2} \cdot \dfrac{3}{5}}{\dfrac{1}{2} \cdot \dfrac{3}{5} + \dfrac{1}{2} \cdot \dfrac{1}{3}} = \dfrac{\dfrac{3}{10}}{\dfrac{7}{15}} = \dfrac{9}{14} \approx .6429$

(E) $P(U_2|W) = \dfrac{P(U_2 \cap W)}{P(W)} = \dfrac{P(U_2)P(W|U_2)}{P(U_2)P(W|U_2) + P(U_1)P(W|U_1)}$

$\quad = \dfrac{\dfrac{1}{2} \cdot \dfrac{2}{3}}{\dfrac{1}{2} \cdot \dfrac{2}{3} + \dfrac{1}{2} \cdot \dfrac{2}{5}} = \dfrac{\dfrac{2}{3}}{\dfrac{16}{15}} = \dfrac{5}{8} = .625$

(F) $P(U_1 \cap R) = P(U_1)P(R|U_1) = \dfrac{1}{2} \cdot \dfrac{3}{5} = .3$

[Note: In parts (A)–(F), we derived the values of the probabilities from the tree diagram.]

26. No, because $P(R|U_1) \neq P(R)$. (See Problem 31.)

33. Let A = "number selected is divisible by 3." Then

$n(A) = \dfrac{200}{3} = 66.67$ or 66.

Let B = "number selected is divisible by 5." Then

$n(B) = \dfrac{200}{5} = 40$.

Now, $A \cap B$ = "number selected is divisible by 3 and 5"
$\quad\quad\quad\quad$ = "number selected is divisible by 15."

Thus, $n(A \cap B) = \dfrac{200}{15} = 13.33$ or 13.

$P(A \cup B) = P(A) + P(B) - P(A \cap B)$

$\quad = \dfrac{66}{200} + \dfrac{40}{200} - \dfrac{13}{200} = \dfrac{93}{200} = .465$

34. The number of numbers between 1 and 30 (inclusive) which are divisible by 4 is:

$\dfrac{30}{4} = 7.5$ or 7

Let A_1 = "first number is divisible by 4"
    A_2 = "second number is divisible by 4"
    A_3 = "third number is divisible by 4."

The tree diagram for this experiment is:

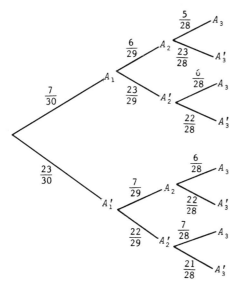

Let B = "at least one number is divisible by 4." Then

$$P(B) = 1 - P(A_1) \cdot P(A_2) \cdot P(A_3) = 1 - \frac{23}{30} \cdot \frac{22}{29} \cdot \frac{21}{28} \approx 1 - .436 = .564.$$

35. $P(\text{second heart} \mid \text{first heart}) = P(H_2 \mid H_1)$

$$= \frac{P(H_2 \cap H_1)}{P(H_1)} = \frac{P(H_1)P(H_2 \mid H_1)}{P(H_1)}$$

$$= \frac{\dfrac{13}{52} \cdot \dfrac{12}{51}}{\dfrac{13}{52}} = \frac{12}{51} \approx .235$$

[Note: One can see that $P(H_2 \mid H_1) = 12/51$ directly.]

36. $P(\text{first heart} \mid \text{second heart}) = P(H_1 \mid H_2)$

$$= \frac{P(H_1 \cap H_2)}{P(H_2)} = \frac{P(H_1)P(H_2 \mid H_1)}{P(H_2)}$$

$$= \frac{P(H_1)P(H_2 \mid H_1)}{P(H_1 \cap H_2) + P(\overline{H}_1 \cap H_2)}$$

(continued)

$$= \frac{P(H_1)P(H_2|H_1)}{P(H_1)P(H_2|H_1) + P(H_1)P(H_2|\overline{H}_1)}$$

$$= \frac{\frac{13}{52} \cdot \frac{12}{51}}{\frac{13}{52} \cdot \frac{12}{51} + \frac{39}{52} \cdot \frac{13}{51}} = \frac{12}{51} \approx .235$$

37. The tree diagram for this experiment is:

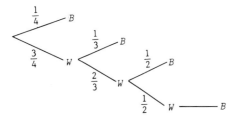

(A) $P(\text{black on the fourth draw}) = \frac{3}{4} \cdot \frac{2}{3} \cdot \frac{1}{2} = \frac{1}{4}$

The odds for black on the fourth draw are 1 to 3.

(B) Let x = amount house should pay (and return the \$1 bet). Then, for the game to be fair:

$$E(X) = x\left(\frac{1}{4}\right) + (-1)\left(\frac{3}{4}\right) = 0$$

$$\frac{x}{4} - \frac{3}{4} = 0$$

$$x = 3$$

Thus, the house should pay \$3.

38. $n(S) = 10 \cdot 10 \cdot 10 \cdot 10 \cdot 10 = 10^5$

Let event A = "at least two people identify the same book." Then A' = "each person identifies a different book," and

$$n(A') = 10 \cdot 9 \cdot 8 \cdot 7 \cdot 6 = \frac{10!}{5!}$$

Thus, $P(A') = \dfrac{\frac{10!}{5!}}{10^5} = \dfrac{10!}{5! \, 10^5}$ and $P(A) = 1 - \dfrac{10!}{5! \, 10^5} \approx 1 - .3 = .7.$

39. $n(S) = C_{30,10} = \dfrac{30!}{10! \, 20!}$

Let A = "at least one defective part." Then A' = "no defective parts," and $n(A') = \dfrac{25!}{10! \, 15!} \cdot$

Thus,

$$P(A) = 1 - P(A') = 1 - \dfrac{\dfrac{25!}{10!15!}}{\dfrac{30!}{10!20!}} = 1 - \dfrac{25!20!}{15!30!} \approx 1 - .109 = .891$$

40. (A)
Nest State

$$\text{Transition matrix} = P = \begin{array}{cc} & X \quad\ X' \\ \begin{bmatrix} .6 & .4 \\ .5 & .5 \end{bmatrix} & \begin{array}{c} X \\ X' \end{array} \end{array} \quad \text{Current State}$$

(B) Initial-state matrix $= \begin{array}{cc} X & X' \\ [.2 & .8] \end{array}$

(C) Second-state matrix $= [.2 \quad .8] \begin{bmatrix} .6 & .4 \\ .5 & .5 \end{bmatrix}$

$$= [.12 + .4 \qquad .08 + .4] = [.52 \quad .48]$$

(D) For the steady-state matrix Q $(QP = Q)$:

$$[m \quad n] \begin{bmatrix} .6 & .4 \\ .5 & .5 \end{bmatrix} = [m \quad n]$$

$$[.6m + .5n \qquad .4m + .5n] = [m \quad n] \text{ and } m + n = 1$$

We have the following linear equations: $\ .6m + .5n = m$ or $m = \dfrac{5}{4}n$

$$.4m + .5n = \quad \text{ or } n = \dfrac{4}{5}m$$

$$m + \quad n = 1$$

Thus, $\dfrac{5}{4}n + n = 1$, $n = \dfrac{4}{9}$, and $m = \dfrac{5}{9}$.

The steady-state matrix $Q = [m \quad n] = \begin{bmatrix} \dfrac{5}{9} & \dfrac{4}{9} \end{bmatrix}$ or $\approx [.56 \quad .44]$

(E) 56% [see part (D)]

41. Let A be the event that a person has seen the advertising and P be the event that the person purchased the product. Given:

$$P(A) = .4 \quad \text{and} \quad P(P|A) = .85$$

We want to find:

$$P(A \cap P) = P(A)P(P|A) = (.4)(.85) = .34$$

42. Let Event NH = individual with normal heart,
Event MH = individual with minor heart problem,
Event SH = individual with severe heart problem,
and Event P = individual passes the cardiogram test.

Then, using the notation given above, we have:

$P(NH) = .82$
$P(MH) = .11$
$P(SH) = .07$

$P(P|NH) = .95$

$P(P|MH) = .30$

$P(P|SH) = .05$

We want to find $P(NH|P) = \dfrac{P(NH \cap P)}{P(P)} = \dfrac{P(NH)P(P|NH)}{P(NH \cap P) + P(MH \cap P) + P(SH \cap P)}$

$$= \dfrac{P(NH)P(P|NH)}{P(NH)P(P|NH) + P(MH)P(P|MH) + P(SH)P(P|SH)}$$

$$= \dfrac{(.82)(.95)}{(.82)(.95) + (.11)(.30) + (.07)(.05)} = .955$$

43. The tree diagram for this problem is as follows:

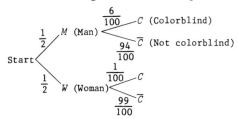

We now compute

$P(M|C) = \dfrac{P(M \cap C)}{P(C)} = \dfrac{P(M \cap C)}{P(M \cap C) + P(W \cap C)} = \dfrac{P(M)P(C|M)}{P(M)P(C|M) + P(W)P(C|W)}$

$$= \dfrac{\dfrac{1}{2} \cdot \dfrac{6}{100}}{\dfrac{1}{2} \cdot \dfrac{6}{100} + \dfrac{1}{2} \cdot \dfrac{1}{100}} = \dfrac{6}{7} \approx .857$$

44. Initial-state matrix = [
$$\begin{array}{cc} \text{Conservative} & \text{Liberal} \\ 1 & 0 \end{array}$$
 ]

Transition matrix =
$$\begin{array}{cc} & \text{Next State} \\ & \begin{array}{cc} \text{Conservative} & \text{Liberal} \end{array} \\ \begin{bmatrix} .7 & .3 \\ .2 & .8 \end{bmatrix} & \begin{array}{l} \text{Conservative} \\ \text{Liberal} \end{array} \end{array}$$ Current

(A) Second-state matrix = $[1 \quad 0]\begin{bmatrix} .7 & .3 \\ .2 & .8 \end{bmatrix} = [.7 \quad .3]$

Third-state matrix = $[.7 \quad .3]\begin{bmatrix} .7 & .3 \\ .2 & .3 \end{bmatrix} = [.55 \quad .45]$

The probability that a conservative couple will have a liberal grandchild is 0.45.

(B) Fourth-state matrix = $[.55 \quad .45]\begin{bmatrix} .7 & .3 \\ .2 & .8 \end{bmatrix} = [.475 \quad .525]$

The probability that a conservative couple will have a liberal great-grandchild is .525.

(C) Steady-state matrix Q $(QP = Q)$:

$[m \quad n]\begin{bmatrix} .7 & .3 \\ .2 & .8 \end{bmatrix} = [m \quad n]$

$[.7m + .2n \quad .3m + .8n] = [m \quad n]$ and $m + n = 1$

We have the following linear equations: $.7m + .2n = m$ or $m = \frac{2}{3}n$

$.3m + .8n = n$ or $m = \frac{2}{3}n$

$m + n = 1, \frac{2}{3}n + n = 1, \frac{5}{3}n = 1$

Thus, $n = .6$ and $m = .4$. The steady-state matrix $Q = [.4 \quad .6]$; 60% of the population will eventually be liberal.

CHAPTER 6   DATA DESCRIPTION
AND PROBABILITY DISTRIBUTIONS

EXERCISE 6-1

Things to remember:

<u>1.</u>   The following techniques are used to graph qualitative data:

(a)   Vertical bar graphs.

(b)   Horizontal bar graphs.

(c)   Broken-line graphs.

(d)   Pie graphs.

---

1.   A vertical bar graph showing the percent of civilian labor force, ages 18-64, with one or more years of college.

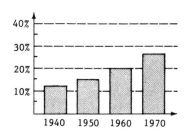

3.   A broken-line graph showing the unemployment rates of three countries.

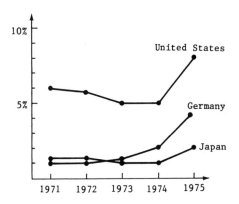

5. A vertical bar graph showing the amounts of pollution emissions in the United States (in millions of tons).

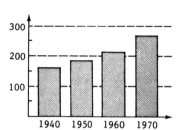

7. A broken-line graph of the data in problem 5.

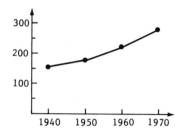

9. A horizontal bar graph showing the immigraion rate to the United States in 1972 (in thousands).

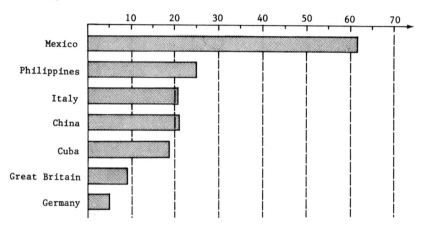

11. A broken-line graph showing the number of illegitimate births per 1000 live births in the United States.

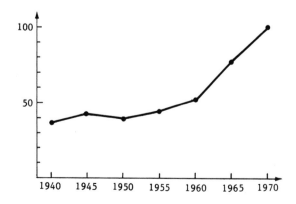

Things to remember:

1. The following techniques are used to depict quantitative data.

   (a) Frequency distribution: a table showing class intervals and their corresponding frequencies.
   (b) Histogram: graphic representation of a frequency distribution.
   (c) Frequency polygon: a broken-line graph of a frequency distribution.
   (d) Cumulative frequency polygon (or ogive): the cumulative frequency is plotted over the upper boundary of the corresponding class.

1. (A) The frequency and relative frequency table for the given data is shown at the right.

Interval	Frequency	Relative frequency
-0.5- 4.5	5	.05
4.5- 9.5	54	.54
9.5-14.5	25	.25
14.5-19.5	13	.13
19.5-24.5	0	.00
24.5-29.5	1	.01
29.5-34.5	2	.02
	100	1.00

(B) The histogram below is a graphic representation of the tabulated data in part (A).

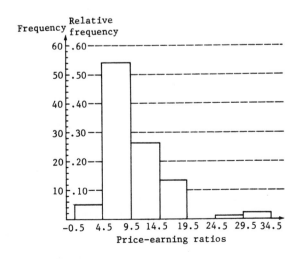

Price-earning ratios

(C) A frequency polygon
    (broken-line graph) for
    the tabulated data in
    part (A) is shown at
    the right.

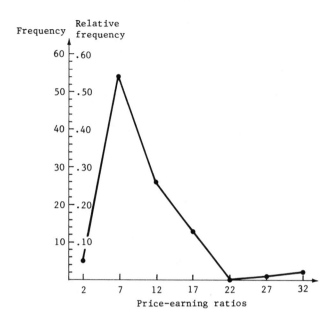

(D) An example of a cumulative and relative cumulative frequency table
    is shown below. From this table, we note that the probability of
    a price-earnings ratio drawn at random from the sample lying between
    4.5 and 14.5 is 0.84 - 0.05 = 0.79.

Interval	Frequency	Cumulative frequency	Relative cumulative frequency
-0.5- 4.5	5	5	.05
4.5- 9.5	54	59	.59
9.5-14.5	25	84	.84
14.5-19.5	13	97	.97
19.5-24.5	0	97	.97
24.5-29.5	1	98	.98
29.5-34.5	2	100	1.00

(E) A cumulative frequency polygon of
    the tabulated data in part (D)
    is shown at the right.

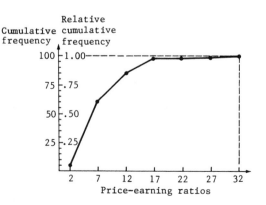

CHAPTER 6

3. (A) The frequency and relative frequency table for the given data is as follows:

Interval	Frequency	Relative frequency
1.95–2.15	21	.21
2.15–2.35	19	.19
2.35–2.55	17	.17
2.55–2.75	14	.14
2.75–2.95	9	.09
2.95–3.15	6	.06
3.15–3.35	5	.05
3.35–3.55	4	.04
3.55–3.75	3	.03
3.75–3.95	2	.02
	100	1.00

(B) A histogram of the tabulated data in part (A) is shown below.

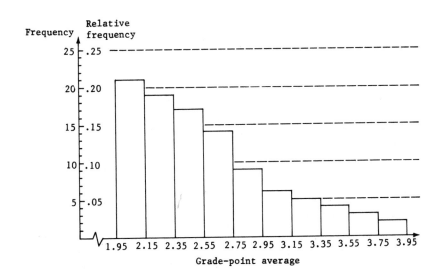

(C) A frequency polygon of the tabulated data in part (A) is shown below.

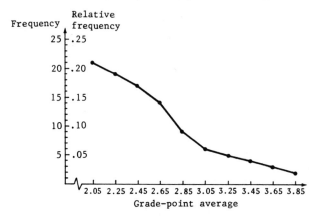

(D) A cumulative and relative cumulative frequency table for the given data is shown below. The probability of a GPA drawn at random from the sample being over 2.95 is 1 - 0.8 = 0.2.

Interval	Frequency	Cumulative frequency	Relative cumulative frequency
1.95–2.15	21	21	.21
2.15–2.35	19	40	.40
2.35–2.55	17	57	.57
2.55–2.75	14	71	.71
2.75–2.95	9	80	.80
2.95–3.15	6	86	.86
3.15–3.35	5	91	.91
3.35–3.55	4	95	.95
3.55–3.75	3	98	.98
3.75–3.95	2	100	1.00

(E) A cumulative frequency polygon for the tabulated date in part (D) is shown below.

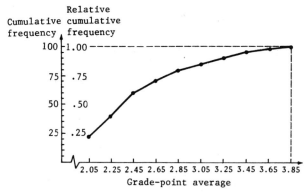

Things to remember:

$\underline{1}$. Given a data set x_1, x_2, $\ldots$, x_n. The MEAN of this set (ungrouped data) is given by:

$$\overline{x} = \frac{\Sigma x}{n} = \frac{x_1 + x_2 + \cdots + x_n}{n}$$

$\underline{2}$. If a data set has been grouped in a frequency table, and x_k is the midpoint of the kth class interval and f_k is the kth class frequency, then the MEAN for the grouped data is:

$$\overline{x} = \frac{\Sigma x f}{N} = \frac{x_1 f_1 + x_2 f_2 + \cdots + x_n f_n}{N},$$

where n is the number of class intervals and $N = \Sigma f$.

$\underline{3}$. Given a data set x_1, x_2, $\ldots$, x_n. Arrange the numbers in either increasing or decreasing order. If n is odd, then the MEDIAN is the middle number; if n is even, then the median is the average of the two middle numbers.

$\underline{4}$. Given a data set x_1, x_2, $\ldots$, x_n. The MODE is the number in the set that occurs most frequently, if there is one. The data set is BIMODAL if there are two values that occur the same number of times and more frequently than any other number. In general, the data set may have several modes or, essentially, no modes.

---

1. Arrange the given numbers in increasing order:

1, 2, 2, 3, $\boxed{3, \ 3,}$ 3, 4, 4, 5

Using $\underline{1}$,

$$\text{Mean} = \overline{x} = \frac{1 + 2 + 2 + 3 + 3 + 3 + 3 + 4 + 4 + 5}{10} = \frac{30}{10} = 3$$

$$\text{Median} = \frac{3 + 3}{2} = 3$$

$$\text{Mode} = 3$$

3. The mean and median are not suitable for these data. The model preference for flavor of ice cream is chocolate.

5. We construct a table indicating the class intervals, the class midpoints x, the frequencies f, and the products xf.

Interval	Midpoint x	Frequency f	Product xf
0.5–2.5	1.5	2	3.0
2.5–4.5	3.5	5	17.5
4.5–6.5	5.5	7	38.5
6.5–8.5	7.5	1	7.5
		$N = \Sigma f = 15$	$\Sigma xf = 66.5$

Thus, $\overline{x} = \dfrac{\Sigma xf}{N} = \dfrac{66.5}{15} \approx 4.433 \approx 4.4$

7. Arrange the given numbers in increasing order.

Number of new one-family homes

Year	Number, x
1969	410,000
1967	430,000
1968	430,000
1970	430,000 = Median
1973	550,000
1971	600,000
1972	650,000
	$\Sigma x = 3,500,000$

$\overline{x} = \dfrac{\Sigma x}{n} = \dfrac{3,500,000}{7}$

$= 500,000 = $ Mean

Mode $= 430,000$

9. Arrange the given numbers in increasing order.

Water pollution, 1971

Major watersheds	Polluted miles, x
Missouri	2,000
Southeast	4,500
Northeast	5,500
Middle Atlantic	5,500
Columbia	5,500 = Median
Great Lakes	8,000
California	8,000
Gulf	12,000
Ohio	24,000
	$\Sigma x = 75,000$

Mean $= \overline{x} = \dfrac{75,000}{9} = 8,333.33$

Mode $= 5,500$

11. Arrange the given numbers in increasing order.

Immigration to U.S., 1972	
Country	Number, x
Jamaica	13,000
India	17,000
Korea	18,000
Cuba	19,000
China	21,000
Italy	21,000
Philippines	25,000
Mexico	62,000
	$\Sigma x = 196,000$

$\left.\begin{array}{l}19,000\\21,000\end{array}\right\} = \text{Median} = \dfrac{19,000 + 21,000}{2} = 20,000$

$\text{Mean} = \bar{x} = \dfrac{196,000}{8} = 24,500$

$\text{Mode} = 21,000$

EXERCISE 6-4

Things to remember:

1. The RANGE for a set of ungrouped data is the difference between the largest and smallest values in the data set. For a frequency distribution, the range is the difference between the upper boundary of the highest class and the lower boundary of the lowest class.

2. The VARIANCE of a data set (ungrouped) $x_1, x_2, \ldots, x_n$ is given by:

$$s^2 = \frac{\Sigma(x - \bar{x})^2}{n - 1}$$
$$= \frac{(x_1 - \bar{x})^2 + (x_2 - \bar{x})^2 + \cdots + (x_n - \bar{x})^2}{n - 1}$$

where $\bar{x}$ is the mean of the data.

3. The STANDARD DEVIATION of the data set $x_1, x_2, \ldots, x_n$ is the square root of the variance, i.e.,

$$s = \sqrt{\frac{\Sigma(x - \bar{x})^2}{n - 1}}$$

x = A measurement
$\bar{x}$ = Mean
n = Total number of measurements

4. The standard deviation for grouped data is given by:

$$s = \sqrt{\frac{\Sigma(x - \overline{x})^2 f}{N - 1}},$$

where x = A class midpoint
f = The corresponding class frequency
$\overline{x}$ = Mean
$N = \Sigma f$ = Total number of measurements

---

1. $\overline{x} = 3$, $n = 10$ (see Problem 1, Exercise 6-3)

$$s = \sqrt{\frac{\Sigma(x - \overline{x})^2}{n - 1}}$$

$$= \sqrt{\frac{(1 - 3)^2 + (2 - 3)^2 + (2 - 3)^2 + (3 - 3)^2 + (3 - 3)^2 + (3 - 3)^2 + (4 - 3)^2 + (4 - 3)^2 + (5 - 3)^2}{10 - 1}}$$

$$= \sqrt{\frac{4 + 1 + 1 + 0 + 0 + 0 + 0 + 1 + 1 + 4}{9}} = \sqrt{\frac{12}{9}} \approx 1.15$$

3.

Interval	Midpoint x	Frequency f	xf	$(x - \overline{x})^2$	$(x - \overline{x})^2 f$
0.5– 3.5	2	2	4	19.36	38.72
3.5– 6.5	5	5	25	1.96	9.80
6.5– 9.5	8	7	56	2.56	17.92
9.5–12.5	11	1	11	21.16	21.16
		$N = \Sigma f = 15$	$\Sigma xf = 96$		$\Sigma(x - \overline{x})^2 f = 87.60$

$$\overline{x} = \frac{\Sigma xf}{N} = \frac{96}{15} = 6.4$$

$$s = \sqrt{\frac{\Sigma(x - \overline{x})^2 f}{N - 1}} = \sqrt{\frac{87.60}{15 - 1}} \approx 2.5$$

5. $\bar{x} = 500,000$ (see Problem 7, Exercise 6-3)

Year	Number, x	$(x - \bar{x})^2$
1967	4.3×10^5	4.9×10^9
1968	4.3×10^5	4.9×10^9
1969	4.1×10^5	8.1×10^9
1970	4.3×10^5	4.9×10^9
1971	6.0×10^5	10.0×10^9
1972	6.5×10^5	22.5×10^9
1973	5.5×10^5	2.5×10^9
		$\Sigma(x - \bar{x})^2 = 57.8 \times 10^9 = 5.78 \times 10^{10}$

$$s = \sqrt{\frac{\Sigma(x - \bar{x})^2}{n - 1}} = \sqrt{\frac{5.78 \times 10^{10}}{6}} \approx 9.815 \times 10^4 = 98,150$$

7. $\bar{x} = 8,333.33$ (see Problem 9, Exercise 6-3)

Major watershed	Polluted miles, x	$(x - \bar{x})^2$
Northeast	5,500	8.03×10^6
Middle Atlantic	5,500	8.03×10^6
Southeast	4,500	14.70×10^6
Great Lakes	8,000	$.11 \times 10^6$
Ohio	24,000	245.44×10^6
Missouri	2,000	40.11×10^6
Gulf	12,000	13.44×10^6
Columbia	5,500	8.03×10^6
California	8,000	$.11 \times 10^6$
		$\Sigma(x - \bar{x})^2 = 338 \times 10^6$

$$s = \sqrt{\frac{\Sigma(x - \bar{x})^2}{n - 1}} = \sqrt{\frac{338 \times 10^6}{8}} \approx 6,500$$

9. $\bar{x} = 24,500$ (see Problem 11, Exercise 6.3)

Country	Number, x	$(x - \bar{x})^2$
China	21,000	12.25×10^6
Cuba	19,000	30.25×10^6
Korea	18,000	42.25×10^6
India	17,000	56.25×10^6
Italy	21,000	12.25×10^6
Jamaica	13,000	132.25×10^6
Mexico	62,000	$1,406.25 \times 10^6$
Philippines	25,000	0.25×10^6
		$\Sigma(x - \bar{x})^2 = 1,692 \times 10^6$
		$= 1.692 \times 10^9$

$$s = \sqrt{\frac{\Sigma(x - \bar{x})^2}{n - 1}} = \sqrt{\frac{1.692 \times 10^9}{7}} \approx 15,547$$

EXERCISE 6-5

Things to remember:

1. A sequence of experiments is called a SEQUENCE OF BERNOULLI TRIALS, or a BINOMIAL EXPERIMENT if:

    (a) Each trial has only two possible outcomes: success S or failure F.

    (b) $P(S) = p$ and $P(F) = 1 - p = q$, $p + q = 1$.

    (c) All trials are independent.

2. The probability distribution of the random variable associated with the number of successes in a binomial experiment is called a BINOMIAL DISTRIBUTION. Let X_n be the random variable which represents the number of successes in n trials. Then

    $$P(X_n = x) = P(x \text{ successes in } n \text{ trials})$$
    $$= C_{n,x} p^x q^{n-x}, \ x \in (0, 1, 2, \ldots, n),$$

    where $C_{n,x}$ is the number of combinations of n objects taken x at a time.

3. BINOMIAL FORMULA

$$(a + b)^n = C_{n,0} \, a^n + C_{n,1} \, a^{n-1}b + C_{n,2} \, a^{n-2}b^2 +$$
$$+ \cdots + C_{n,n} \, b^n$$

$$= \sum_{k=0}^{n} C_{n,k} \, a^{n-k}b^k$$

4. The MEAN μ and STANDARD DEVIATION σ of the random variable associated with a binomial distribution are given by:

Mean: $\mu = np$

Standard deviation: $\sigma = \sqrt{npq}$

---

1. $p = \dfrac{1}{2}$

$q = 1 - \dfrac{1}{2} = \dfrac{1}{2}$

$C_{3,2} \left(\dfrac{1}{2}\right)^2 \left(\dfrac{1}{2}\right)^{3-2} = \dfrac{3!}{2!1!} \cdot \dfrac{1}{8}$

$= \dfrac{3}{8} = .375$

3. $p = \dfrac{1}{2}$

$q = 1 - \dfrac{1}{2} = \dfrac{1}{2}$

$C_{3,0} \left(\dfrac{1}{2}\right)^0 \left(\dfrac{1}{2}\right)^{3-0} = \dfrac{3!}{0!3!} \cdot \dfrac{1}{8}$

$= \dfrac{1}{8} = .125$

5. $p = .4$
$q = 1 - .4 = .6$

$C_{5,3} \, (.4)^3 (.6)^{5-3} = \dfrac{5!}{3!2!}(.4)^3(.6)^2$

$= 10(.064)(.36) = .230$

7. p = probability of getting heads $= \dfrac{1}{2}$

q = probability of getting tails $= \dfrac{1}{2}$

$x = 2, \; n = 3$

$P(2) = C_{3,2} \left(\dfrac{1}{2}\right)^2 \left(\dfrac{1}{2}\right)^{3-2} = \dfrac{3!}{2!1!} \cdot \dfrac{1}{8} = \dfrac{3}{8} = .375$

9. $p = \dfrac{1}{2}, \; q = \dfrac{1}{2}, \; x = 0, \; n = 3$

$P(0) = C_{3,0} \left(\dfrac{1}{2}\right)^0 \left(\dfrac{1}{2}\right)^{3-0} = \dfrac{3!}{0!3!} \cdot \dfrac{1}{8} = \dfrac{1}{8} = .125$

11. $P(\text{at least 2 heads}) = P(x \geqslant 2) = P(2) + P(3)$

$$= C_{3,2} \left(\dfrac{1}{2}\right)^2 \left(\dfrac{1}{2}\right)^{3-2} + C_{3,3} \left(\dfrac{1}{2}\right)^3 \left(\dfrac{1}{2}\right)^{3-3}$$

$$= \dfrac{3!}{2!1!} \cdot \dfrac{1}{8} + \dfrac{3!}{3!0!} \cdot \dfrac{1}{8} = \dfrac{3}{8} + \dfrac{1}{8} = .5$$

13. $P(x) = C_{2,x}(.3)^x(.7)^{2-x}$

x	0	1	2
$P(x)$	.49	.42	.09

The histogram for this distribution is shown at the right.

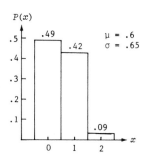

Mean = $np = 2(.3) = .6$ (using 4)

Standard deviation = $\sigma = \sqrt{npq}$ (using 4)

$$= \sqrt{2(.3)(.7)}$$

$$\approx .65$$

15. $P(x) = C_{4,x}(.5)^x(.5)^{4-x}$

x	$P(x)$
0	.06
1	.25
2	.38
3	.25
4	.06

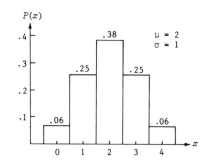

The histogram for this distribution is shown at the right.

$\mu = np = 4 \times .5 = 2$

$\sigma = \sqrt{npq} = \sqrt{4 \times .5 \times .5} = 1$

17. Let p = probability of getting a "2" in one trial = $\frac{1}{6}$,

and q = probability of not getting a "2" in one trial = $\frac{5}{6}$.

$n = 4$, $x = 3$

$$P(3) = C_{4,3}\left(\frac{1}{6}\right)^3\left(\frac{5}{6}\right)^{4-3} = \frac{4!}{3!\,1!}\left(\frac{1}{6}\right)^3\left(\frac{5}{6}\right) \approx .0154$$

19. Let p = probability of getting a "1" = $\frac{1}{6}$,

and q = probability of not getting a "1" = $\frac{5}{6}$.

$n = 4$, $x = 0$

$$P(0) = C_{4,0}\left(\frac{1}{6}\right)^0\left(\frac{5}{6}\right)^{4-0} = \frac{4!}{0!\,4!}\left(\frac{5}{6}\right)^4 \approx .482$$

21. Let p = probability of getting a "6" = $\frac{1}{6}$,

and q = probability of not getting a "6" = $\frac{5}{6}$.

It is actually easier to compute the probability of the complement event, $P(x < 1)$:

$$P(x \geqslant 1) = 1 - P(x < 1) = 1 - P(0)$$

$$= 1 - C_{4,0} \left(\frac{1}{6}\right)^0 \left(\frac{5}{6}\right)^4 = 1 - .4822 \approx .518$$

23. $p = .35, \; q = 1 - .35 = .65, \; n = 4$

  (A) The probability of getting exactly two hits is given by:

  $$P(x = 2) = C_{4,2} \, (.35)^2 (.65)^2 \approx .311$$

  (B) The probability of getting at least two hits is given by:

  $$P(x \geqslant 2) = P(2) + P(3) + P(4)$$

  $$= C_{4,2} \, (.35)^2 (.65)^2 + C_{4,3} \, (.35)^3 (.65) + C_{4,4} \, (.35)^4$$

  $$= .3105 + .1115 + .0150 \approx .437$$

25. $P(x) = C_{6,x} \, (.4)^x (.6)^{6-x}$

x	$P(x)$
0	.05
1	.19
2	.31
3	.28
4	.14
5	.04
6	.004

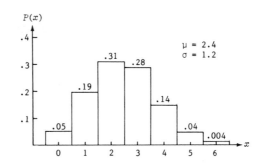

The histogram for this distribution
is shown at the right.

$$\mu = np = 6 \times .4 = 2.4 \qquad \sigma = \sqrt{npq} = \sqrt{6 \times .4 \times .6} = 1.2$$

27. $P(x) = C_{8,x} \, (.3)^x (.7)^{8-x}$

x	$P(x)$
0	.06
1	.20
2	.30
3	.25
4	.14
5	.05
6	.01
7	.0012
8	.0001

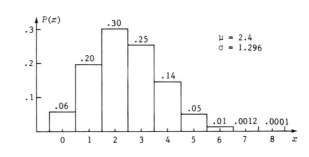

The histogram for this distribution is shown above.

$$\mu = np = 8 \times .3 = 2.4 \qquad \sigma = \sqrt{npq} = \sqrt{8 \times .3 \times .7} \approx 1.296$$

29. Let p = probability of getting heads = $\frac{3}{4}$,

and q = probability of not getting heads = $\frac{1}{4}$.

$n = 5$, $x = 5$

The probability of getting all heads $P(5) = C_{5,5} \left(\frac{3}{4}\right)^5 \left(\frac{1}{4}\right)^0 = .2373$.

The probability of getting all tails is the same as the probability of getting no heads. Thus,

$P(0) = C_{5,0} \left(\frac{3}{4}\right)^0 \left(\frac{1}{4}\right)^5 = .00098$

Therefore,

P(all heads or all tails) $= P(5) + P(0) = .2373 + .00098$
$= .23828 \approx .238$

31. The theoretical probability distribution is obtained by using

$P(x) = C_{3,x} (.5)^x (.5)^{3-x}$

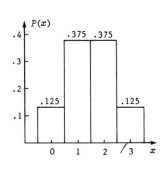

Frequency of heads in 100 tosses of 3 coins			
Number of heads x	$P(x)$	Theoretical frequency $100P(x)$	Actual frequency
0	.125	12.5	(List your
1	.375	37.5	experimental
2	.375	37.5	results
3	.125	12.5	here.)

The histogram for the theoretical distribution is shown above.

33. (A) Let p = probability of completing the program = .7,
and q = probability of not completing the program = .3.

$n = 7$, $x = 5$

$P(5) = C_{7,5} (.7)^5 (.3)^2 = 21(.1681)(.09) = .318$

(B) $P(x \geqslant 5) = P(5) + P(6) + P(7)$
$= .318 + C_{7,6} (.7)^6 (.3) + C_{7,7} (.7)^7 (.3)^0$
$= .318 + 7(.1176)(.3) + 1(.0824)(1)$
$= .3180 + .2471 + .0824 \approx .647$

35. Let p = probability that an item is defective = .06,
and q = probability that an item is not defective = .94.

$n = 10$

$P(x > 2) = 1 - P[x \leqslant 2] = 1 - [P(2) + P(1) + P(0)]$

$\quad\quad\quad\quad = 1 - [C_{10,2}(.06)^2(.94)^8 + C_{10,1}(.06)^1(.94)^9 + C_{10,0}(.06)^0(.94)^{10}]$

$\quad\quad\quad\quad = 1 - [.0988 + .3438 + .5386] = 1 - .9812 \approx .0188$

A day's output will be inspected with a probability of .0188.

37. (A) $p = 0.05$, $q = 0.95$, $n = 6$

The following function défines the distribution:

$P(x) = C_{6,x}(0.05)^x(0.95)^{6-x}$

(B) The following table is obtained by using the distribution function in part (A).

x	$P(x)$
0	.735
1	.232
2	.031
3	.002
4	.0001
5	.000
6	.000

(C) The histogram for the distribution in part (B) is shown at the right.

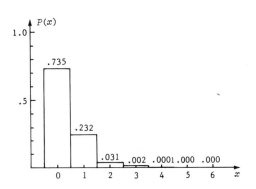

(D) $\mu = np = 6 \times 0.05 = 0.30$

$\sigma = \sqrt{npq} = \sqrt{6 \times (0.05) \times (.095)} \approx 0.533$

39. Let p = probability of detecting TB = .8,
and q = probability of not detecting TB = .2.

$n = 4$

The probability that at least one of the specialists will detect TB is:

$P(x \geqslant 1) = 1 - P(x < 1) = 1 - P(0)$

$\quad\quad\quad\quad = 1 - C_{4,0}(.8)^0(.2)^4$

$\quad\quad\quad\quad = 1 - .0016 = .9984 \approx .998$

41. Let p = probability of having a child with brown eyes = .75,
and q = probability of not having a child with brown eyes (i.e., with blue eyes) = .25.

$n = 5$

(A) $x = 0$ (all blue-eyed children, i.e., no brown-eyed children)

$P(0) = C_{5,0} (.75)^0 (.25)^5 = .00098 \approx .001$

(B) $x = 3$

$P(3) = C_{5,3} (.75)^3 (.25)^2 = .264$

(C) $x \geqslant 3$

$$P(x \geqslant 3) = P(3) + P(4) + P(5)$$
$$= .264 + C_{5,4} (.75)^4 (.25)^1 + C_{5,5} (.75)^5 (.25)^0$$
$$= .2640 + .3955 + .2373$$
$$= .8968 \approx .897$$

43. (A) $p = 0.6$, $q = 0.4$, $n = 6$

The following function defines the distribution:

$P(x) = C_{6,x} (.6)^x (.4)^{6-x}$

(B) The following table is obtained by using the distribution function in part (A).

x	$P(x)$
0	.004
1	.037
2	.138
3	.276
4	.311
5	.187
6	.047

(C) The histogram for the distribution in part (B) is shown at the right.

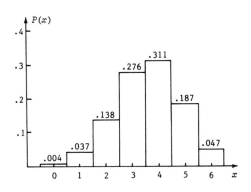

(D) $\mu = np = 6(.6) = 3.6$

$\sigma = \sqrt{npq} = \sqrt{6 \times .4 \times .6} = 1.2$

45. Let p = probability of getting the right answer to a question = $\frac{1}{5}$, and q = probability of not getting the right answer to a question = $\frac{4}{5}$.

$n = 10$, $x \geqslant 7$

$P(x \geqslant 7) = P(7) + P(8) + P(9) + P(10)$

$$= C_{10,7}\left(\frac{1}{5}\right)^7\left(\frac{4}{5}\right)^3 + C_{10,8}\left(\frac{1}{5}\right)^8\left(\frac{4}{5}\right)^2 + C_{10,9}\left(\frac{1}{5}\right)^9\left(\frac{4}{5}\right) + C_{10,10}\left(\frac{1}{5}\right)^{10}$$

$$\approx .000864$$

47. (A) p = probability of answer being correct by guessing = $\frac{1}{5}$ = 0.2, $q = 0.8$, $n = 5$.

The following function defines the distribution:

$$P(x) = C_{5,x}(.2)^x(.8)^{5-x}$$

(B) The following table is obtained by using the distribution function in part (A):

x	$P(x)$
0	.328
1	.410
2	.205
3	.051
4	.006
5	.000

(C) The histogram for part (B) is shown below.

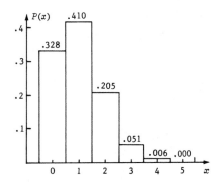

(D) $\mu = np = 5 \times .2 = 1.0$

$\sigma = \sqrt{npq} = \sqrt{5 \times .2 \times .8}$
≈ 0.894

49. Let p = probability of a divorce within 20 years = .60, and q = probability of no divorce within 20 years = .40.

$n = 6$

(A) $P(x = 0) = C_{6,0}(.60)^0(.40)^6 \approx .0041$

(B) $P(x = 6) = C_{6,6}(.60)^6(.40)^0 \approx .0467$

(C) $P(x = 2) = C_{6,2}(.60)^2(.40)^4 \approx .138$

(D) $P(x \geqslant 2) = 1 - P(x < 2) = 1 - [P(0) + P(1)]$

$= 1 - [.0041 + C_{6,1}(.60)^1(.40)^5]$

$= 1 - [.0041 + .0369]$

$= .959$

Things to remember:

1. The properties of a NORMAL CURVE are:

   (a) It is bell-shaped and symmetrical with respect to a vertical line.

   (b) The mean μ is at the point where the axis of symmetry intersects the horizontal axis.

   (c) The shape is completely determined by its mean μ and standard deviation σ.

   (d) Irrespective of the shape, the area between the curve and the x axis is always 1.

   (e) Irrespective of the shape, 68.27% of the area lies within the interval $\mu \pm \sigma$, 95.45% of the area lies within the interval $\mu \pm 2\sigma$, and 99.73% of the area lies within the interval $\mu \pm 3\sigma$.

2. If μ and σ are the mean and standard deviation of a normal curve and x is a measurement, then the number of standard deviations that x is from the mean is given by:

   $$z = \frac{x - \mu}{\sigma}$$

3. A normal distribution provides an adequate approximation to a binomial distribution if the interval $[\mu - 3\sigma, \mu + 3\sigma]$ lies entirely in the interval from 0 to n.

---

1. $x = 65$, $\mu = 50$, $\sigma = 10$

   $z = \dfrac{65 - 50}{10}$ (using 2)

   $= 1.5$

   $x = 65$ is 1.5 standard deviations away from μ.

3. $x = 83$, $\mu = 50$, $\sigma = 10$

   $z = \dfrac{83 - 50}{10}$ (using 2)

   $= 3.3$

   $x = 83$ is 3.3 standard deviations away from μ.

5. $x = 45$, $\mu = 50$, $\sigma = 10$

   $z = \dfrac{45 - 50}{10} = -0.5$

   $x = 45$ is 0.5 standard deviations away from μ.

7. $x = 42$, $\mu = 50$, $\sigma = 10$

   $z = \dfrac{42 - 50}{10} = -0.8$

   $x = 42$ is 0.8 standard deviations away from μ.

9. From Problem 1, $z = 1.5$.

From the table of areas for the normal distribution, we have the area corresponding to $z = 1.5$ is .4332.

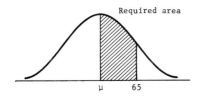
Required area

11. From Problem 3, $z = 3.3$.

From the table, the area corresponding to $z = 3.3$ is .4995.

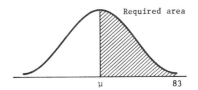
Required area

13. From Problem 5, $z = -0.5$.

From the table, the area corresponding to $z = 0.5$ is .1915.

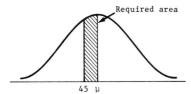
Required area

15. From Problem 7, $z = -0.8$.

From the table, the area corresponding to $z = 0.8$ is .2821.

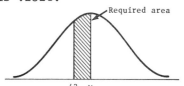
Required area

17. $\mu = 70$, $\sigma = 8$

z (for $x = 60$) $= \dfrac{60 - 70}{8} = -1.25$

z (for $x = 80$) $= \dfrac{80 - 70}{8} = 1.25$

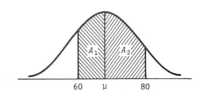

Area $A_1 = 0.3944$ Area $A_2 = 0.3944$.
Total area $= A = A_1 + A_2 = 0.7888$.

19. $\mu = 70$, $\sigma = 8$

z (for $x = 62$) $= \dfrac{62 - 70}{8} = -1.00$

z (for $x = 74$) $= \dfrac{74 - 70}{8} = 0.5$

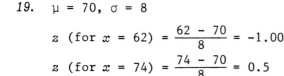

Area $A_1 = 0.3414$.   Area $A_2 = 0.1915$.
Total area $= A = A_1 + A_2 = 0.5328$

21. $\mu = 70$, $\sigma = 8$

z (for $x = 88$) $= \dfrac{88 - 70}{8} = 2.25$

Required area $= 0.5 -$ (area corresponding to $z = 2.25$)
$\qquad\qquad = 0.5 - 0.4878 = 0.0122$

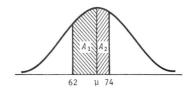
Required area

23. $\mu = 70$, $\sigma = 8$

z (for $x = 60$) $= \dfrac{60 - 70}{8} = -1.25$

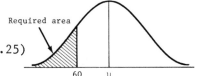

Required area

Required area $= 0.5 -$ (area corresponding to $z = 1.25$)

$= 0.5 - 0.3944 = 0.1056$

60   μ

25. With $n = 15$, $p = .7$, and $q = .3$, the mean and standard deviation of the binomial distribution are:

$\mu = np = 10.5$

$\sigma = \sqrt{npq} = \sqrt{(15)(.7)(.3)} \approx 1.8$

$[\mu - 3\sigma,\ \mu + 3\sigma] = [5.1,\ 15.9]$

Since this interval is not contained in the interval $[0, 15]$, the normal distribution should *not* be used to approximate the binomial distribution.

27. With $n = 15$, $p = .4$, and $q = .6$, the mean and standard deviation of the binomial distribution are:

$\mu = np = 15(.4) = 6$

$\sigma = \sqrt{npq} = \sqrt{15(.4)(.6)} \approx 1.9$

$[\mu - 3\sigma,\ \mu + 3\sigma] = [.3,\ 11.7]$

Since this interval is contained in the interval $[0, 15]$, the normal distribution *is* a suitable approximation for the binomial distribution.

29. With $n = 100$, $p = .05$, and $q = .95$, the mean and standard deviation of the binomial distribution are:

$\mu = np = 100(.05) = 5$

$\sigma = \sqrt{npq} = \sqrt{100(.05)(.95)} \approx 2.2$

$[\mu - 3\sigma,\ \mu + 3\sigma] = [-1.6,\ 11.6]$

Since this interval is not contained in $[0, 100]$, the normal distribution is *not* a suitable approximation for the binomial distribution.

31. With $n = 500$, $p = .05$, and $q = .95$, the mean and standard deviation of the binomial distribution are:

$\mu = np = 500(.05) = 25$

$\sigma = \sqrt{npq} = \sqrt{500(.05)(.95)} \approx 4.9$

$[\mu - 3\sigma,\ \mu + 3\sigma] = [10.3,\ 39.7]$

Since this interval is contained in [0, 500], the normal distribution *is* a suitable approximation for the binomial distribution.

In Problems 33–39, $\mu = 500(.4) = 200$, and $\sigma = \sqrt{npq} = \sqrt{500(.4)(.6)} \approx 10.95$. The intervals are adjusted as in Examples 17 and 18.

33. z (for $x = 184.5$) $= \dfrac{184.5 - 200}{10.95} \approx -1.42$

z (for $x = 220.5$) $= \dfrac{220.5 - 200}{10.95} \approx 1.87$

Thus, the probability that the number of successes will be between 185 and 220

$\quad$ = area A_1 + area A_2
$\quad$ = (area corresponding to $z = 1.42$) +
$\quad\quad$ (area corresponding to $z = 1.87$)
$\quad$ = .4222 + .4693
$\quad$ = .8915
$\quad \approx$ .89

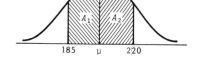

35. z (for $x = 209.5$) $= \dfrac{209.5 - 200}{10.95} \approx .87$

z (for $x = 220.5$) $= \dfrac{220.5 - 200}{10.95} \approx 1.87$

Thus, the probability that the number of successes will be between 210 and 220

$\quad$ = area A
$\quad$ = (area corresponding to $z = 1.87$) −
$\quad\quad$ (area corresponding to $z = .87$)
$\quad$ = .4693 − .3079
$\quad$ = .1614
$\quad \approx$ .16

37. z (for $x = 224.5$) $= \dfrac{224.5 - 200}{10.95} \approx 2.24$

The probability that the number of successes will be 225 or more

$\quad$ = area A
$\quad$ = .5 − (area corresponding to $z = 2.24$)
$\quad$ = .5 − .4875
$\quad$ = .0125
$\quad \approx$ .01

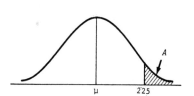

39. z (for $x = 174.5$) $= \dfrac{174.5 - 200}{10.95} \approx -2.33$

The probability that the number of successes will be 175 or less

$\quad$ = area A
$\quad$ = .5 − (area corresponding to $z = 2.33$)
$\quad$ = .5 − .4901
$\quad$ = .0099
$\quad \approx$ .01

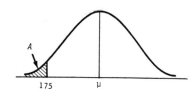

41. $\mu = 200,000$, $\sigma = 20,000$, $x \geqslant 240,000$

$$z \text{ (for } x = 240,000) = \frac{240,000 - 200,000}{20,000} = 2.0$$

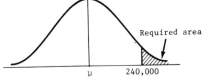

Fraction of the salesmen who would be
expected to make annual sales of $240,000
or more = Area A_1

$\qquad\qquad$ = 0.5 - (area between μ and 240,000)

$\qquad\qquad$ = 0.5 - 0.4772

$\qquad\qquad$ = 0.0228

$\qquad\qquad$ ≈ 0.023

Thus, the percentage of salesmen expected to make annual sales of \$240,000
or more is 2.3%.

43. $x = 105$, $x = 95$, $\mu = 100$, $\sigma = 2$

$$z \text{ (for } x = 105) = \frac{105 - 100}{2} = 2.5$$

$$z \text{ (for } x = 95) = \frac{95 - 100}{2} = -2.5$$

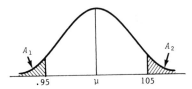

Fraction of parts to be rejected = Area $A_1 + A_2$

$\qquad\qquad\qquad\qquad\qquad$ = 1 - 2(area corresponding to $z = 2.5$)

$\qquad\qquad\qquad\qquad\qquad$ = 1 - 2(0.4938)

$\qquad\qquad\qquad\qquad\qquad$ = 0.0124

$\qquad\qquad\qquad\qquad\qquad$ ≈ 0.012

Thus, the percentage of parts to be rejected is 1.2%.

45. With $n = 40$, $p = .6$, and $q = .4$, the mean and standard deviation of
the binomial distribution are:

$$\mu = np = 40(.6) = 24$$

$$\sigma = \sqrt{npq} = \sqrt{40(.6)(.4)} \approx 3.10$$

$$z \text{ (for } x = 15.5) = \frac{15.5 - 24}{3.1} = 2.74$$

The probability that 15 or fewer households
use the product

$\qquad$ = area A

$\qquad$ = .5 - (area corresponding to $z = 2.74$)

$\qquad$ = .5 - .4969

$\qquad$ = .0031

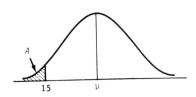

47. $\mu = 240$, $\sigma = 20$

8 days = 192 hours = x

z (for $x = 192$) $= \dfrac{192 - 240}{20} = -2.4$

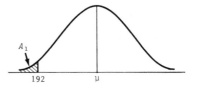

Fraction of people having this incision
who would heal in 192 hours or less = Area A_1

$\qquad\qquad$ = 0.5 - (area corresponding to $z = 2.4$)

$\qquad\qquad$ = 0.5 - 0.4918

$\qquad\qquad$ = 0.0082

Thus, the percentage of people who would heal in 8 days or less is 0.82%.

49. $p = 0.25$, $q = 0.75$, $n = 1000$

$\mu = np = (1000)(0.25) = 250$

$\sigma = \sqrt{npq} = \sqrt{1000 \times 0.25 \times 0.75}$
$\qquad = 13.693 \approx 13.7$

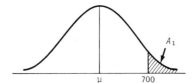

$x = 220$ or less

z (for $x = 220$) $= \dfrac{220 - 250}{13.7} = -2.19$

Probability that 220 or less will have
two girls = Area A

$\qquad\qquad$ = 0.5 - (area corresponding to $z = 2.19$)

$\qquad\qquad$ = 0.5 - 0.4857

$\qquad\qquad$ = 0.0143

51. $\mu = 500$, $\sigma = 100$, $x = 700$ or more

z (for $x = 700$) $= \dfrac{700 - 500}{100} = 2$

Fraction of students who should
score 700 or more = Area A_1

$\qquad\qquad$ = 0.5 - (area corresponding to $z = 2$)

$\qquad\qquad$ = 0.5 - 0.4773

$\qquad\qquad$ = 0.0227

Thus, 2.27% should score 700 or more.

53. $\mu = 70$, $\sigma = 8$

We compute x_1, x_2, x_3, and x_4 corresponding
to z_1, z_2, z_3, and z_4, respectively.

The area between μ and x_3 is 0.2.
Hence, from the table, $z_3 = 0.53$ (approximately).
Thus, we have:

$0.53 = \dfrac{x_3 - 70}{8}$

$x_3 - 70 = 4.24 \quad \left[\underline{\text{Note: }} z = \dfrac{x - \mu}{\sigma}.\right]$

and $x_3 = 74.24$.

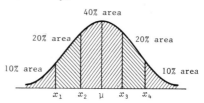

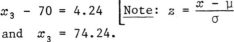

Also, $x_2 = 70 - 4.24 = 65.76$.

The area between μ and x_4 is 0.4.
Hence, from the table, $z_4 = 1.29$ (approximately). Therefore:

$$1.29 = \frac{x_4 - 70}{8}$$

$x_4 - 70 = 8 \times 1.29$

and $x_4 = 70 + 10.32 = 80.32$

Also, $x_1 = 70 - 10.32 = 59.68$.

Thus, we have $x_1 = 59.68$, $x_2 = 65.76$, $x_3 = 74.24$, $x_4 = 80.32$. So, A's = 80.32 or greater, B's = 74.24 to 80.32, C's = 65.76 to 74.24, D's = 59.68 to 65.76, and F's = 59.8 or lower.

EXERCISE 6-7   CHAPTER REVIEW

1. (A)   A bar graph showing imports as a percentage of total new car sales in the U.S.   (B)   A broken-line graph for the data in part (A).

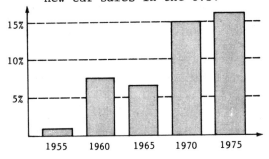
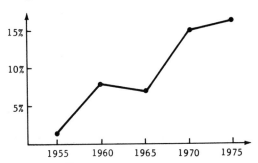

2. A pie graph showing U.S. population in 1970 appears below.

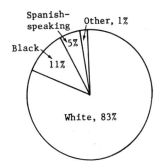

3. (A) $P(x) = C_{3,\,x}(.4)^x(.6)^{3-x}$

(B) $\mu = np = 3(.4) = 1.2$

$\sigma = \sqrt{npq} = \sqrt{3 \times .4 \times .6} \approx .85$

x	$P(x)$
0	.216
1	.432
2	.288
3	.064

A histogram showing this distribution is shown at the right.

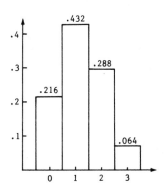

4. (A) Mean $= \overline{x} = \dfrac{1 + 1 + 2 + 2 + 2 + 3 + 3 + 4 + 4 + 5}{10} = \dfrac{27}{10} = 2.7$

(B) Median $= \dfrac{2 + 3}{2}$ (2 and 3 are middle scores)

$= 2.5$

(C) Mode $= 2$

(D) Standard deviation $= \sqrt{\dfrac{\Sigma(x - \overline{x})^2}{n - 1}}$

$= \sqrt{\dfrac{\begin{array}{l}(1 - 2.7)^2 + (1 - 2.7)^2 + (2 - 2.7)^2 + (2 - 2.7)^2 \\ + (2 - 2.7)^2 + (3 - 2.7)^2 + (3 - 2.7)^2 \\ + (4 - 2.7)^2 + (4 - 2.7)^2 + (5 - 2.7)^2\end{array}}{10 - 1}}$

≈ 1.34

5. (A) $\mu = 100,\ \sigma = 10$

z (for $x = 118$) $= \dfrac{118 - 100}{10} = 1.8$

$x = 118$ is 1.8 standard deviations from the mean.

(B) From the table, the required area $A_1 = 0.4641$.

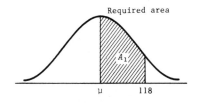

6. (A) The frequency and relative frequency table for the given data is shown below.

Interval	Frequency	Relative frequency
9.5–11.5	1	.04
11.5–13.5	5	.20
13.5–15.5	12	.48
15.5–17.5	6	.24
17.5–19.5	1	.04
	25	1.00

(B) The histogram below shows both frequency and relative frequency scales on the y axis.

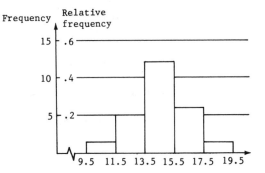

(C) The polygon graph below also shows both frequency and relative frequency scales on the y axis.

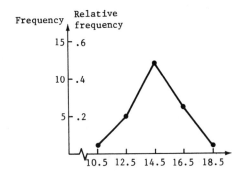

(D) A cumulative and relative cumulative table for the data is given below.

Interval	Frequency	Cumulative frequency	Relative cumulative frequency
9.5–11.5	1	1	.04
11.5–13.5	5	6	.24
13.5–15.5	12	18	.72
15.5–17.5	6	24	.96
17.5–19.5	1	25	1.00

(E) The polygon graph at the right shows both the cumulative frequency and relative cumulative scales on the y axis.

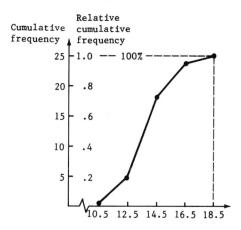

7.

Interval	Midpoint, x	Frequency, f	xf	$(x - \bar{x})^2$	$(x - \bar{x})^2 f$
0.5– 3.5	2	1	2	25	25
3.5– 6.5	5	5	25	4	20
6.5– 9.5	8	7	56	1	7
9.5–12.5	11	2	22	16	32
		$N = 15$	$\Sigma xf = 105$		$\Sigma (x - \bar{x})^2 f = 84$

$$\bar{x} = \frac{\Sigma xf}{N} = \frac{105}{15} = 7$$

$$s = \sqrt{\frac{\Sigma (x - \bar{x})^2 f}{N - 1}} = \sqrt{\frac{84}{14}} \approx 2.45$$

8. (A) $P(x) = C_{6, x} (0.5)^x (0.5)^{6 - x}$

x	$P(x)$
0	.016
1	.094
2	.234
3	.313
4	.234
5	.094
6	.016

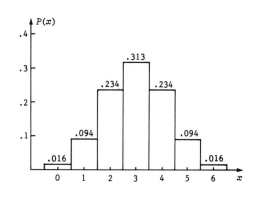

The histogram for this distribution is shown at the right.

(B) Mean = $\mu = np = 6 \times 0.5 = 3$

Standard deviation = $\sigma = \sqrt{npq} = \sqrt{6 \times 0.5 \times 0.5} \approx 1.225$

9. $p = 0.6$, $q = 0.4$, $n = 1000$

$\mu = np = 1000 \times 0.6 = 600$

$\sigma = \sqrt{npq} = \sqrt{1000 \times 0.6 \times 0.4} = \sqrt{240} \approx 15.49$

10. The mean μ and the standard deviation σ for the binomial distribution are:

$\mu = np = 1000 \times 0.6 = 600$

$\sigma = \sqrt{npq} = \sqrt{1000 \times 0.6 \times 0.4} \approx 15.49 \approx 15.5$

Now, we approximate the binomial distribution with a normal distribution.

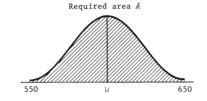

$z \text{ (for } x = 550) = \dfrac{550 - 600}{15.5} = -3.24$

$z \text{ (for } x = 650) = \dfrac{650 - 600}{15.5} = 3.24$

The probability of obtaining successes between 550 and 650 = Area A

$$= 2(\text{area corresponding to } z = 3.24)$$
$$= 2(0.4994)$$
$$= 0.9988 \approx 0.999$$

11. **(A)** $\mu = 50$, $\sigma = 6$

$z \text{ (for } x = 41) = \dfrac{41 - 50}{6} = -1.5$

$z \text{ (for } x = 62) = \dfrac{62 - 50}{6} = 2.0$

Required area $= A_1 + A_2$
$$= (\text{area corresponding to } z = 1.5) +$$
$$(\text{area corresponding to} \cdot z = 2)$$
$$= 0.4332 + 0.4773$$
$$= 0.9105$$

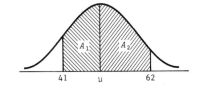

(B) $z \text{ (for } x = 59) = \dfrac{59 - 50}{6} = 1.5$

Required area $= 0.5 - (\text{area corresponding to } z = 1.5)$
$$= 0.5 - 0.4332$$
$$= 0.0668$$

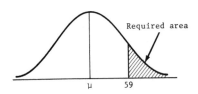

12. (A)

x	Frequency, f	xf	$(x - \overline{x})^2$ ($\overline{x} = 14.6$)	$(x - \overline{x})^2 f$
11	1	11	12.96	12.96
12	2	24	6.76	13.52
13	3	39	2.56	7.68
14	7	98	0.36	2.52
15	5	75	0.16	0.80
16	3	48	1.96	5.88
17	3	51	5.76	17.28
19	1	19	19.36	.19.36
	$N = \Sigma f = 25$		$\Sigma xf = 365$	$\Sigma(x - \overline{x})^2 f = 80$

Thus, $\overline{x} = \dfrac{\Sigma xf}{N} = \dfrac{365}{25} = 14.6$

$$s = \sqrt{\dfrac{\Sigma(x - \overline{x})^2 f}{N - 1}} = \sqrt{\dfrac{80}{24}} \approx 1.83$$

(B)

Interval	Midpoint x	Frequency f	xf	$(x - \overline{x})^2$ ($\overline{x} = 14.6$)	$(x - \overline{x})^2 f$
9.5–11.5	10.5	1	10.5	16.81	16.81
11.5–13.5	12.5	5	62.5	4.41	22.05
13.5–15.5	14.5	12	174.0	0.01	0.12
15.5–17.5	16.5	6	99.0	3.61	21.66
17.5–19.5	18.5	1	18.5	15.21	15.21
		$N = \Sigma f = 25$	$\Sigma xf = 364.5$		$\Sigma(x - \overline{x})^2 f = 75.85$

$\overline{x} = \dfrac{\Sigma xf}{N} = \dfrac{364.5}{25} \quad 14.6$

$$s = \sqrt{\dfrac{\Sigma(x - \overline{x})^2 f}{N - 1}} = \sqrt{\dfrac{75.85}{24}} \approx 1.78$$

13. Let E = "rolling a six." Then $P(E) = \dfrac{1}{6}$, $P(E') = \dfrac{5}{6}$. Thus, $p = \dfrac{1}{6}$, $q = \dfrac{5}{6}$, $n = 5$.

(A) $P(X_5 = 3) = P(\text{exactly three 6's}) = C_{5,3}\left(\dfrac{1}{6}\right)^3\left(\dfrac{5}{6}\right)^2 = \dfrac{5!}{3!2!}\left(\dfrac{25}{6^5}\right) \approx .0322$

(B) $P(\text{at least three 6's}) = P(x \geq 3) = P(3) + P(4) + P(5)$

$$= C_{5,3}\left(\dfrac{1}{6}\right)^3\left(\dfrac{5}{6}\right)^2 + C_{5,4}\left(\dfrac{1}{6}\right)^4\left(\dfrac{5}{6}\right) + C_{5,5}\left(\dfrac{1}{6}\right)^6$$

$$= \dfrac{5!}{3!2!}\left(\dfrac{25}{6^5}\right) + \dfrac{5!}{4!1!}\left(\dfrac{5}{6^5}\right) + \dfrac{5!}{5!0!}\left(\dfrac{1}{6^5}\right) \approx .0355$$

14. The probability of getting a 7 is: $p = \frac{6}{36} = \frac{1}{6}$

Thus, the probability of not getting a 7 is: $q = \frac{5}{6}$

Now, P(at least one 7) $= P(x \geqslant 1) = 1 - P(x < 1)$

$$= 1 - P(0)$$

$$= 1 - C_{3,0} \left(\frac{1}{6}\right)^0 \left(\frac{5}{6}\right)^3$$

$$= 1 - \frac{125}{6^4}$$

$$\approx 1 - .5787 = .4213$$

15. Arrange the given numbers in increasing order:

4, 5, 5, 5, 8, 12, 13, 15, 16, 17

(A) Mean $\overline{x} = \dfrac{4+5+5+5+8+12+13+15+16+17}{10} = 10$

(B) Median $= \dfrac{8 + 12}{2} = 10$

(C) Mode $= 5$

(D) Standard deviation:

$$s = \sqrt{\frac{\begin{array}{c}(4-10)^2 + 3(5-10)^2 + (8-10)^2 + (12-10)^2 \\ + (13-10)^2 + (15-10)^2 + (16-10)^2 + (17-10)^2\end{array}}{10-1}}$$

$$= \sqrt{\frac{36 + 75 + 4 + 4 + 9 + 25 + 36 + 49}{9}} = \sqrt{\frac{238}{9}} \approx 5.14$$

16. The mean and median are not suitable for these data. The modal preference is soft drink.

17. (A) The frequency and relative frequency table is as follows:

Interval	Frequency f	Relative frequency
29.5–31.5	3	0.086
31.5–33.5	7	0.2
33.5–35.5	14	0.4
35.5–37.5	7	0.2
37.5–39.5	4	0.114
	$\Sigma f = 35$	Sum $= 1.00$

(B)

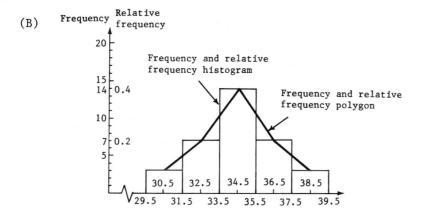

(C)

Interval	Midpoint x	Frequency f	xf	$(x - \bar{x})^2$ ($\bar{x}$ = 34.61)	$(x - \bar{x})^2 f$
29.5–31.5	30.5	3	91.5	16.89	50.67
31.5–33.5	32.5	7	227.5	4.45	31.15
33.5–35.5	34.5	14	483.0	0.01	0.14
35.5–37.5	36.5	7	255.5	3.57	24.99
37.5–39.5	38.5	4	154.0	15.13	60.53
		$N = \Sigma f = 35$	$\Sigma xf = 1211.5$		$\Sigma (x - \bar{x})^2 f = 167.48$

$$\bar{x} = \frac{\Sigma xf}{N} = \frac{1211.5}{35} = 34.61$$

$$s = \sqrt{\frac{\Sigma (x - \bar{x})^2 f}{N - 1}} = \sqrt{\frac{167.48}{34}} = 2.22$$

18. $\mu = 100$, $\sigma = 10$

(A) z (for $x = 91.5$) $= \dfrac{91.5 - 100}{10} = -.85$

z (for $x = 108$) $= \dfrac{108.5 - 100}{10} = .85$

The probability of an applicant scoring between 92 and 108

   = area A
   = 2 · area A_1
   = 2(area corresponding to $z = .85$)
   = 2(.3023) = .6046

Thus, the percentage of applicants scoring between 92 and 108 is 60.46%.

(B) z (for $x = 114.5$) = $\dfrac{114.5 - 100}{10}$ = 1.45

The probability of an applicant scoring 115 or higher

= area A
= .5 - (area corresponding to $z = 1.45$)
= .5 - .4265
= .0735

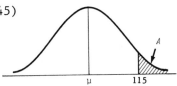

Thus, the percentage of applicants scoring 115 or higher is 7.35%.

19. Based on the publisher's claim, the probability that a person selected at random reads the newspaper is: $p = .7$.

Thus, the probability that a randomly selected person does not read the newspaper is: $q = .3$.

(A) With $n = 200$,

the mean $\mu = 200(.7) = 140$,

and standard deviation $\sigma = \sqrt{200(.7)(.3)} = \sqrt{42} \approx 6.48$.

(B) $[\mu - 3\sigma, \mu + 3\sigma] = [120.76, 159.24]$ and the interval lies entirely in the interval $[0, 200]$. Thus, the normal distribution *does* provide an adequate approximation to the binomial distribution.

(C) z (for $x = 129.5$) = $\dfrac{129.5 - 140}{6.48}$ = $\dfrac{-10.5}{6.48}$ = -1.62

z (for $x = 155.5$) = $\dfrac{155.5 - 140}{6.48}$ = $\dfrac{15.5}{6.48}$ = 2.39

The probability of finding between 130 and 155 readers in the sample

= area A_1 + area A_2
= (area corresponding to $z = 1.62$) +
  (area corresponding to $z = 2.39$)
= .4474 + .4916
= .9390

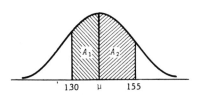

(D) z (for $x = 125.5$) = $\dfrac{125.5 - 140}{6.48}$ = $\dfrac{-14.5}{6.48}$ = 2.24

The probability of finding fewer than 125 readers in the sample

= area A
= 0.5 - (area corresponding to $z = 2.24$)
= 0.5 - 0.4875
= .0125

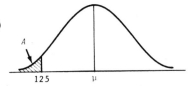

20. $p = .9$, $q = .1$, and $n = 3$

$$P(x \geqslant 1) = 1 - P(x < 1)$$
$$= 1 - P(0)$$
$$= 1 - C_{3,0} \left(\frac{9}{10}\right)^0 \left(\frac{1}{10}\right)^3$$
$$= 1 - \frac{1}{1000}$$
$$= .999$$

CHAPTER 7   GAMES AND DECISIONS

Things to remember:

$\underline{1}$.   If a payoff value is simultaneously a row minimum and a column maximum, then the matrix game is said to be STRICTLY DETERMINED. This value is called a SADDLE VALUE. The optimal strategies are: R should choose any row containing a saddle value and C should choose any column containing a saddle value.

$\underline{2}$.   The VALUE of a strictly determined game is a saddle value.

$\underline{3}$.   If a game matrix has two or more saddle values, then they are equal.

$\underline{4}$.   LOCATING SADDLE VALUES:

(a) Circle the minimum value in each row.
(b) Place squares around the maximum value in each column.
(c) Any entry with both a circle and a square around it is a saddle value.

$\underline{5}$.   A matrix game is said to be NONSTRICTLY DETERMINED if it does not have saddle values.

---

1. $\begin{bmatrix} \boxed{3} & \boxed{②} \\ 2 & ⊖1 \end{bmatrix}$ (using $\underline{4}$)

The game is strictly determined.
(A)   2 (upper right or 1,2 position).
(B) R plays row 1 and C plays column 2.
(C)   The value of the game is 2.

3.   *3.* $\begin{bmatrix} ⊖2 & \boxed{5} \\ \boxed{3} & ⓪ \end{bmatrix}$

The game is not strictly determined.

5. $\begin{bmatrix} \boxed{-3} & 0 \\ \boxed{4} & \boxed{1} \end{bmatrix}$

The game is strictly determined.
(A) 1 (2,2 position)
(B) R plays row 2 and
     C plays column 2.
(C) The value of the game is 1.

7. $\begin{bmatrix} \boxed{2} & \boxed{2} \\ \boxed{2} & \boxed{5} \end{bmatrix}$

The game is strictly determined.
(A) Both 2's in column 1.
(B) R plays either row 1 or row 2
     and C plays column 1.
(C) The value of the game is 2.

9. $\begin{bmatrix} \boxed{2} & -1 & \boxed{-5} \\ 1 & \boxed{0} & 3 \\ -3 & \boxed{-7} & \boxed{8} \end{bmatrix}$

The game is strictly determined.
(A) 0 (in 2,2 position).
(B) R plays row 2 and
     C plays column 2.
(C) The value of the game is 0.

11. $\begin{bmatrix} 3 & \boxed{-2} \\ 1 & \boxed{5} \\ \boxed{-4} & 0 \\ \boxed{5} & \boxed{-3} \end{bmatrix}$

The game is not strictly determined.

13. $\begin{bmatrix} 3 & -1 & \boxed{4} & \boxed{-7} \\ 1 & \boxed{0} & 2 & 3 \\ \boxed{5} & -2 & \boxed{-3} & 0 \\ 3 & \boxed{0} & 1 & \boxed{5} \end{bmatrix}$

The game is strictly determined.
(A) Both 0's in column 2
     (2,2 and 4,2 positions)
(B) R plays either row 2 or
     row 4 and C plays column 2.
(C) The value of the game is 0.

15. $\begin{bmatrix} -3 & m \\ \boxed{0} & 1 \end{bmatrix}$

No; 0 is a saddle value
irrespective of the value of m.

17.

Station C

$1.00 \quad 1.05$

Station R $\begin{array}{c} 1.05 \\ 1.10 \end{array} \begin{bmatrix} \boxed{50\%} & \boxed{70\%} \\ \boxed{40\%} & 50\% \end{bmatrix}$

The saddle value is 50%, as shown in the
upper left corner (1,1 position).

Optimum strategies: R plays row 1 ($1.05)
and C plays column 1 ($1.00).

Store C

		T.C.	I.V.	S.L.T.

$$\text{Store } R \quad \begin{array}{c} \text{T.C.} \\ \text{I.V.} \\ \text{S.L.T.} \end{array} \begin{bmatrix} 50\% & 20\% + \dfrac{50\%}{2} & 20\% + \dfrac{30\%}{2} \\[2ex] 30\% + \dfrac{50\%}{2} & 50\% & 30\% + \dfrac{20\%}{2} \\[2ex] 50\% + \dfrac{30\%}{2} & 50\% + \dfrac{20\%}{2} & 50\% \end{bmatrix} = \begin{bmatrix} 50\% & 45\% & 35\% \\[2ex] 55\% & 50\% & 40\% \\[2ex] 65\% & 60\% & 50\% \end{bmatrix}$$

The optimal strategy for both stores is to locate in South Lake Tahoe and split the basin business equally.

EXERCISE 7-2

Things to remember:

<u>1</u>. Given the game matrix $M = \begin{bmatrix} a & b \\ c & d \end{bmatrix}$.

R's strategy is denoted by a probability row matrix

$$P = [p_1 \quad p_2], \ p_1 \geqslant 0, \ p_2 \geqslant 0, \ p_1 + p_2 = 1.$$

C's strategy is denoted by a probability column matrix

$$Q = \begin{bmatrix} q_1 \\ q_2 \end{bmatrix}, \ q_1 \geqslant 0, \ q_2 \geqslant 0, \ q_1 + q_2 = 1.$$

<u>2</u>. For the game matrix $M = \begin{bmatrix} a & b \\ c & d \end{bmatrix}$ and strategies

$P = [p_1 \quad p_2]$, $Q = \begin{bmatrix} q_1 \\ q_2 \end{bmatrix}$ for R and C, respectively,

the expected value of the game for R is given by

$$E(P, \ Q) = PMQ = ap_1q_1 + bp_1q_2 + cp_2q_1 + dp_2q_2.$$

<u>3</u>. FUNDAMENTAL THEOREM OF GAME THEORY: For every $m \times n$ game matrix M, there exist strategies P^* and Q^* (not necessarily unique) for R and C, respectively, and a unique number v such that:

$$P*MQ \geqslant v \text{ for every strategy } Q \text{ of } C;$$
$$PMQ* \geqslant v \text{ for every strategy } P \text{ of } R.$$

The number v is called the VALUE of the game.

4. For the nonstrictly determined game matrix

$M = \begin{bmatrix} a & b \\ c & d \end{bmatrix}$, the optimal strategies $P*$ and $Q*$

and the value v are given by

$$P* = [p_1^* \quad p_2^*] = \begin{bmatrix} \dfrac{d-c}{D} & \dfrac{a-b}{D} \end{bmatrix},$$

$$Q* = \begin{bmatrix} q_1^* \\ q_2^* \end{bmatrix} = \begin{bmatrix} \dfrac{d-b}{D} \\ \dfrac{a-c}{D} \end{bmatrix}, \text{ and } v = \dfrac{ad-bc}{D},$$

where $D = (a+d) - (b+c)$.

5. RECESSIVE ROWS: A row in a game matrix is said to be recessive and may be deleted if there exists a (dominant) row with corresponding elements greater than or equal to those in the given row.

RECESSIVE COLUMNS: A column in a game matrix is said to be recessive and may be deleted if there exists a (dominant) column with corresponding elements less than or equal to those in the given column.

---

1. $\begin{bmatrix} \boxed{-1} & \boxed{2} \\ \boxed{2} & \boxed{-4} \end{bmatrix}$ The game is not strictly determined.

Using 4: The optimal strategy for R is

$$P* = \begin{bmatrix} \dfrac{d-c}{D} & \dfrac{a-b}{D} \end{bmatrix} = \begin{bmatrix} \dfrac{-4-2}{-9} & \dfrac{-1-2}{-9} \end{bmatrix} = \begin{bmatrix} \dfrac{2}{3} & \dfrac{1}{3} \end{bmatrix}$$

[Note: $D = (a+d) - (b+c) = (-1-4) - (2+2) = -9.$]

The optimal strategy for C is

$$Q^* = \begin{bmatrix} \dfrac{d-b}{D} \\ \dfrac{a-c}{D} \end{bmatrix} = \begin{bmatrix} \dfrac{-4-2}{-9} \\ \dfrac{-1-2}{-9} \end{bmatrix} = \begin{bmatrix} \dfrac{2}{3} \\ \dfrac{1}{3} \end{bmatrix}$$

The value of the game, v, is: $\dfrac{ad-bc}{D} = \dfrac{(-1)(-4)-(2)(2)}{-9} = 0.$

3. $\begin{bmatrix} \boxed{-1} & \boxed{2} \\ \boxed{1} & \boxed{0} \end{bmatrix}$ The game is not strictly determined.

Using $\underline{4}$:

$$P^* = \begin{bmatrix} \dfrac{0-1}{-4} & \dfrac{-1-2}{-4} \end{bmatrix} = \begin{bmatrix} \dfrac{1}{4} & \dfrac{3}{4} \end{bmatrix}$$ [$\underline{\text{Note}}$: $D = (-1+0) - (2+1) = -4.$]

$$Q^* = \begin{bmatrix} \dfrac{0-2}{-4} \\ \dfrac{-1-1}{-4} \end{bmatrix} = \begin{bmatrix} \dfrac{1}{2} \\ \dfrac{1}{2} \end{bmatrix}$$

The value of the game, v, is: $\dfrac{(-1)(0)-(2)(1)}{-4} = \dfrac{1}{2}.$

5. $\begin{bmatrix} \boxed{4} & \boxed{-6} \\ \boxed{-2} & \boxed{3} \end{bmatrix}$ The game is not strictly determined.

Using $\underline{4}$:

$$P^* = \begin{bmatrix} \dfrac{3+2}{15} & \dfrac{4+6}{15} \end{bmatrix} = \begin{bmatrix} \dfrac{1}{3} & \dfrac{2}{3} \end{bmatrix} \qquad Q^* = \begin{bmatrix} \dfrac{3+6}{15} \\ \dfrac{4+2}{15} \end{bmatrix} = \begin{bmatrix} \dfrac{3}{5} \\ \dfrac{2}{5} \end{bmatrix}$$

The value of the game, v, is: $\dfrac{(4)(3)-(-6)(-2)}{11} = 0.$

7. $\begin{bmatrix} \boxed{5} & \boxed{-1} \\ 4 & \boxed{1} \end{bmatrix}$ $P^* = \begin{bmatrix} 0 & 1 \end{bmatrix} \qquad Q^* = \begin{bmatrix} 0 \\ 1 \end{bmatrix}$

The game is strictly determined.   The value of the game, v = saddle value = 1.

9. Using $\underline{5}$, we can eliminate the recessive columns $\begin{bmatrix} 0 \\ 1 \end{bmatrix}$ and $\begin{bmatrix} 2 \\ -1 \end{bmatrix}$. Thus, we obtain the 2×2 matrix:

$$\begin{bmatrix} \boxed{2} & \textcircled{-1} \\ \textcircled{-2} & \boxed{1} \end{bmatrix}$$ The game is not strictly determined.

Now, using $\underline{4}$:

$$P^* = \begin{bmatrix} \dfrac{1 + 2}{6} & \dfrac{2 + 1}{6} \end{bmatrix} = \begin{bmatrix} \dfrac{3}{6} & \dfrac{3}{6} \end{bmatrix} = \begin{bmatrix} \dfrac{1}{2} & \dfrac{1}{2} \end{bmatrix}$$

[$\underline{Note}$: $D = (2 + 1) - (-1 - 2) = 6$.]

$$Q^* = \begin{bmatrix} \dfrac{1 + 1}{6} \\ \dfrac{2 + 2}{6} \end{bmatrix} = \begin{bmatrix} \dfrac{2}{6} \\ \dfrac{4}{6} \end{bmatrix} = \begin{bmatrix} \dfrac{1}{3} \\ \dfrac{2}{3} \end{bmatrix} \text{ or } \begin{bmatrix} 0 \\ \dfrac{1}{3} \\ \dfrac{2}{3} \\ 0 \end{bmatrix}, \qquad v = \dfrac{(2)(1) - (-1)(-2)}{6} = 0$$

11. Using $\underline{5}$, we eliminate the recessive row $[1 \quad -4 \quad -1]$ and the recessive

column $\begin{bmatrix} -1 \\ 0 \\ 2 \end{bmatrix}$. Thus, we obtain the 2×2 matrix: $\begin{bmatrix} \boxed{2} & \textcircled{-3} \\ \textcircled{-1} & \boxed{2} \end{bmatrix}$.

The game is nonstrictly determined. Now, using $\underline{4}$:

$$P^* = \begin{bmatrix} \dfrac{2 + 1}{8} & \dfrac{2 + 3}{8} \end{bmatrix} = \begin{bmatrix} \dfrac{3}{8} & \dfrac{5}{8} \end{bmatrix} \text{ or } \begin{bmatrix} 0 & \dfrac{3}{8} & \dfrac{5}{8} \end{bmatrix}.$$

[$\underline{Note}$: $D = (2 + 2) - (-3 - 1) = 8$.]

$$Q^* = \begin{bmatrix} \dfrac{2 + 3}{8} \\ \dfrac{2 + 1}{8} \end{bmatrix} = \begin{bmatrix} \dfrac{5}{8} \\ \dfrac{3}{8} \end{bmatrix} \text{ or } \begin{bmatrix} \dfrac{5}{8} \\ \dfrac{3}{8} \\ 0 \end{bmatrix}, \qquad v = \dfrac{(2)(2) - (-3)(-1)}{8} = \dfrac{1}{8}$$

13. $\begin{bmatrix} 2 & \textcircled{1} & 2 \\ \boxed{3} & 0 & \textcircled{-5} \\ 1 & \textcircled{-2} & \boxed{7} \end{bmatrix}$ The game is strictly determined.

$P^* = [1 \quad 0 \quad 0] \qquad Q^* = \begin{bmatrix} 0 \\ 1 \\ 0 \end{bmatrix}$

$v = $ saddle value $= 1$

15. (A) $P = \begin{bmatrix} \frac{1}{4} & \frac{1}{4} & \frac{1}{4} & \frac{1}{4} \end{bmatrix}$, $\quad Q = \begin{bmatrix} \frac{1}{4} \\ \frac{1}{4} \\ \frac{1}{4} \\ \frac{1}{4} \\ \frac{1}{4} \end{bmatrix}$

$$PMQ = \begin{bmatrix} \frac{1}{4} & \frac{1}{4} & \frac{1}{4} & \frac{1}{4} \end{bmatrix} \begin{bmatrix} 0 & 2 & 1 & 0 \\ 4 & 3 & 5 & 4 \\ 0 & 2 & 6 & 1 \\ 0 & 1 & 0 & 3 \end{bmatrix} \begin{bmatrix} \frac{1}{4} \\ \frac{1}{4} \\ \frac{1}{4} \\ \frac{1}{4} \end{bmatrix} = \begin{bmatrix} 1 & 2 & 3 & 2 \end{bmatrix} \begin{bmatrix} \frac{1}{4} \\ \frac{1}{4} \\ \frac{1}{4} \\ \frac{1}{4} \end{bmatrix}$$

$\quad$ = 2 or \$2

Since you pay C \$3 to play, the expected value is \$2 - \$3 = -\$1.

(B) The largest of the row minimums is 3 in row 2. Thus, you should play row 2, i.e., $P = \begin{bmatrix} 0 & 1 & 0 & 0 \end{bmatrix}$. Now

$$PMQ = \begin{bmatrix} 0 & 1 & 0 & 0 \end{bmatrix} \begin{bmatrix} 0 & 2 & 1 & 0 \\ 4 & 3 & 5 & 4 \\ 0 & 2 & 6 & 1 \\ 0 & 1 & 0 & 3 \end{bmatrix} \begin{bmatrix} \frac{1}{4} \\ \frac{1}{4} \\ \frac{1}{4} \\ \frac{1}{4} \end{bmatrix} = \begin{bmatrix} 4 & 3 & 5 & 4 \end{bmatrix} \begin{bmatrix} \frac{1}{4} \\ \frac{1}{4} \\ \frac{1}{4} \\ \frac{1}{4} \end{bmatrix}$$

$\quad$ = 4 or \$4

Since you pay C \$3 to play, the expected value is \$4 - \$3 = \$1.

(C) We eliminate the recessive rows [0   2   1   0] and [0   1   0   3], and the recessive columns

$$\begin{bmatrix} 1 \\ 5 \\ 6 \\ 0 \end{bmatrix} \quad \text{and} \quad \begin{bmatrix} 0 \\ 4 \\ 1 \\ 3 \end{bmatrix}.$$

The resulting matrix is: $\begin{bmatrix} \boxed{4} & ③ \\ ⓪ & 2 \end{bmatrix}$ and the game is strictly

determined with a value of 3. You should play row 2 (in the original matrix) and C should play column 2 (in the original matrix). Thus,

$$P = [0 \quad 1 \quad 0 \quad 0] \text{ and } Q = \begin{bmatrix} 0 \\ 1 \\ 0 \\ 0 \end{bmatrix}$$

$$PMQ = [0 \quad 1 \quad 0 \quad 0] \begin{bmatrix} 0 & 2 & 1 & 0 \\ 4 & 3 & 5 & 4 \\ 0 & 2 & 6 & 1 \\ 0 & 1 & 0 & 3 \end{bmatrix} \begin{bmatrix} 0 \\ 1 \\ 0 \\ 0 \end{bmatrix} = [4 \quad 3 \quad 5 \quad 4] \begin{bmatrix} 0 \\ 1 \\ 0 \\ 0 \end{bmatrix}$$

$$= 3 \text{ or } \$3$$

Since you pay C $3 to play, the expected value $3 − $3 = $0.

17. $$PMQ = [p_1 \quad p_2] \begin{bmatrix} a & b \\ c & d \end{bmatrix} \begin{bmatrix} q_1 \\ q_2 \end{bmatrix} = [p_1 \quad p_2] \begin{bmatrix} [a \quad b] \cdot \begin{bmatrix} q_1 \\ q_2 \end{bmatrix} \\ [c \quad d] \cdot \begin{bmatrix} q_1 \\ q_2 \end{bmatrix} \end{bmatrix}$$

$$= [p_1 \quad p_2] \begin{bmatrix} aq_1 + bq_2 \\ cq_1 + dq_2 \end{bmatrix} = [p_1(aq_1 + bq_2) + p_2(cq_1 + dq_2)]$$

$$= [ap_1q_1 + bp_1q_2 + cp_2q_1 + dp_2q_2] = E(P, Q)$$

19. $$P*MQ = \begin{bmatrix} \dfrac{d - c}{D} & \dfrac{a - b}{D} \end{bmatrix} \begin{bmatrix} a & b \\ c & d \end{bmatrix} \begin{bmatrix} q_1 \\ q_2 \end{bmatrix}$$

In Problem 17, substitute $p_1 = \dfrac{d - c}{D}$ and $p_2 = \dfrac{a - b}{D}$. Thus,

$$P*MQ = \frac{a(d - c)}{D} q_1 + \frac{b(d - c)}{D} q_2 + \frac{c(a - b)}{D} q_1 + \frac{d(a - b)}{D} q_2$$

$$= \frac{1}{D}[adq_1 - caq_1 + bdq_2 - bcq_2 + caq_1 - cbq_1 + daq_2 - dbq_2]$$

$$= \frac{1}{D}[(ad - cb)q_1 + (ad - bc)q_2]$$

$$= \frac{ad - cb}{D}[q_1 + q_2] \qquad [\underline{\text{Note}}: q_1 + q_2 = 1.]$$

$$= \frac{ad - cb}{D}$$

Thus,

(A) $P*MQ = \dfrac{ad - cb}{D}$

Similarly, $PMQ* = [p_1 \quad p_2] \begin{bmatrix} a & b \\ c & d \end{bmatrix} \begin{bmatrix} q_1^* \\ q_2^* \end{bmatrix} = [p_1 \quad p_2] \begin{bmatrix} a & b \\ c & d \end{bmatrix} \begin{bmatrix} \dfrac{d - b}{D} \\ \dfrac{a - c}{D} \end{bmatrix}$

$= ap_1\left(\dfrac{d - b}{D}\right) + bp_1\left(\dfrac{a - c}{D}\right) + cp_2\left(\dfrac{d - b}{D}\right) + dp_2\left(\dfrac{a - c}{D}\right)$

$= \dfrac{1}{D}(adp_1 - abp_1 + bap_1 - bcp_1 + cdp_2 - cbp_2 + dap_2 - dcp_2)$

$= \dfrac{1}{D}(adp_1 - bcp_1 - cbp_2 + dap_2) = \dfrac{1}{D}[(ad - bc)p_1 + (da - cb)p_2]$

$= \dfrac{ad - bc}{D}(p_1 + p_2) = \dfrac{ad - bc}{D}$ [Note: $p_1 + p_2 = 1$.]

Thus,

(B) $PMQ* = \dfrac{ad - bc}{D}$

From (A) and (B), we get $v = \dfrac{ad - bc}{D}$, which satisfies $P*MQ \geqslant v$ and $PMQ* \leqslant v$.

21. Given:

$$\begin{array}{c} \\ TV \\ R \\ P \\ M \end{array} \begin{array}{cccc} TV & R & P & M \\ \begin{bmatrix} 0 & -1 & -1 & 0 \\ 1 & 2 & -1 & -1 \\ 0 & -1 & 0 & 1 \\ -1 & -1 & -1 & 0 \end{bmatrix} \end{array}$$

Eliminate the recessive rows $[0 \quad -1 \quad -1 \quad 0]$ and $[-1 \quad -1 \quad -1 \quad 0]$ and

the recessive columns $\begin{bmatrix} 0 \\ 1 \\ 0 \\ -1 \end{bmatrix}$ and $\begin{bmatrix} 0 \\ -1 \\ 1 \\ 0 \end{bmatrix}$ to obtain the 2×2 matrix

$\begin{bmatrix} 2 & -1 \\ -1 & 0 \end{bmatrix}$. The game is not strictly determined.

(A) The optimum strategies for R and C are

$$P* = \begin{bmatrix} \dfrac{0 + 1}{4} & \dfrac{2 + 1}{4} \end{bmatrix} = \begin{bmatrix} \dfrac{1}{4} & \dfrac{3}{4} \end{bmatrix} \qquad [\underline{\text{Note}}: \quad D = 2 + 0 - (-1 - 1) = 4.]$$

and $Q* = \begin{bmatrix} \dfrac{0 + 1}{4} \\ \dfrac{2 + 1}{4} \end{bmatrix} = \begin{bmatrix} \dfrac{1}{4} \\ \dfrac{3}{4} \end{bmatrix}$, respectively.

In terms of the original problem:

$$P^* = \begin{bmatrix} 0 & \frac{1}{4} & \frac{3}{4} & 0 \end{bmatrix} \quad \text{and} \quad Q^* = \begin{bmatrix} 0 \\ \frac{1}{4} \\ \frac{3}{4} \\ 0 \end{bmatrix}$$

The value of the game is: $v = \dfrac{2(0) - (-1)(-1)}{4} = -\dfrac{1}{4}$

(B) $P = \begin{bmatrix} 1 & 0 & 0 & 0 \end{bmatrix} \quad \text{and} \quad Q = \begin{bmatrix} 0 \\ \frac{1}{4} \\ \frac{3}{4} \\ 0 \end{bmatrix}$

$$PMQ = \begin{bmatrix} 1 & 0 & 0 & 0 \end{bmatrix} \begin{bmatrix} 0 & -1 & -1 & 0 \\ 1 & 2 & -1 & -1 \\ 0 & -1 & 0 & 1 \\ -1 & -1 & -1 & 0 \end{bmatrix} \begin{bmatrix} 0 \\ \frac{1}{4} \\ \frac{3}{4} \\ 0 \end{bmatrix} = \begin{bmatrix} 0 & -1 & -1 & 0 \end{bmatrix} \begin{bmatrix} 0 \\ \frac{1}{4} \\ \frac{3}{4} \\ 0 \end{bmatrix} = -1$$

The expected value is -1.

(C) $P = \begin{bmatrix} 0 & \frac{1}{4} & \frac{3}{4} & 0 \end{bmatrix} \quad \text{and} \quad Q = \begin{bmatrix} 0 \\ 1 \\ 0 \\ 0 \end{bmatrix}$

$$PMQ = \begin{bmatrix} 0 & \frac{1}{4} & \frac{3}{4} & 0 \end{bmatrix} \begin{bmatrix} 0 & -1 & -1 & 0 \\ 1 & 2 & -1 & -1 \\ 0 & -1 & 0 & 1 \\ -1 & -1 & -1 & 0 \end{bmatrix} \begin{bmatrix} 0 \\ 1 \\ 0 \\ 0 \end{bmatrix} = \begin{bmatrix} 0 & \frac{1}{4} & \frac{3}{4} & 0 \end{bmatrix} \begin{bmatrix} -1 \\ 2 \\ -1 \\ -1 \end{bmatrix} = -\frac{1}{4}$$

The expected value is $-\dfrac{1}{4}$.

(D) $P = \begin{bmatrix} 0 & 0 & 1 & 0 \end{bmatrix} \quad \text{and} \quad Q = \begin{bmatrix} 0 \\ 0 \\ 1 \\ 0 \end{bmatrix}$

$$PMQ = \begin{bmatrix} 0 & 0 & 1 & 0 \end{bmatrix} \begin{bmatrix} 0 & -1 & -1 & 0 \\ 1 & 2 & -1 & -1 \\ 0 & -1 & 0 & 1 \\ -1 & -1 & -1 & 0 \end{bmatrix} \begin{bmatrix} 0 \\ 0 \\ 1 \\ 0 \end{bmatrix} = \begin{bmatrix} 0 & -1 & 0 & 1 \end{bmatrix} \begin{bmatrix} 0 \\ 0 \\ 1 \\ 0 \end{bmatrix} = 0$$

The expected value is 0.

23.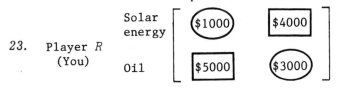

The game is not strictly determined.

Thus, using 4:

$$P^* = \begin{bmatrix} \dfrac{3000 - 5000}{-5000} & \dfrac{1000 - 4000}{-5000} \end{bmatrix} = \begin{bmatrix} \dfrac{2}{5} & \dfrac{3}{5} \end{bmatrix}$$

[Note: $D = (1000 + 3000) - (4000 + 5000) = -5000.$]

$$Q^* = \begin{bmatrix} \dfrac{3000 - 4000}{-5000} \\ \dfrac{1000 - 5000}{-5000} \end{bmatrix} = \begin{bmatrix} \dfrac{1}{5} \\ \dfrac{4}{5} \end{bmatrix}$$

$$v = \frac{(1000)(3000) - (4000)(5000)}{-5000} = \frac{-17,000}{-5} = \$3400$$

This means that you should invest $\frac{2}{5}(10,000) = \$4000$ in solar energy stocks and $\frac{3}{5}(10,000) = \$6000$ in oil stocks. You would then have an expected gain of $3400 no matter how the election turns out.

EXERCISE 7-3

Things to remember:

Given the nonstrictly determined matrix game with payoff matrix

$$M = \begin{bmatrix} a & b \\ c & d \end{bmatrix}.$$

To find $P^* = [p_1 \quad p_2]$, $Q^* = \begin{bmatrix} q_1 \\ q_2 \end{bmatrix}$, and v,

proceed as follows:

STEP 1. If M is not a positive matrix, convert it into a positive matrix M_1 by adding a suitable positive constant k to each element. Let

$$M_1 = \begin{bmatrix} e & f \\ g & h \end{bmatrix}, \quad \begin{array}{l} e = a + k, \ f = b + k, \\ g = c + k, \ h = d + k. \end{array}$$

This matrix game M_1 has the same optimal strategies P^* and Q^* as M, and if v_1 is the value of the game M_1, then $v = v_1 - k$ is the value of the original game M.

STEP 2. Set up the two corresponding linear programming problems:

(A) Minimize $y = x_1 + x_2$

Subject to: $\begin{array}{r} ex_1 + gx_2 \geqslant 1 \\ fx_1 + hx_2 \geqslant 1 \\ x_1, \ x_2 \geqslant 0 \end{array}$

(B) Maximize $y = z_1 + z_2$

Subject to: $\begin{array}{r} ez_1 + fz_2 \leqslant 1 \\ gz_1 + hz_2 \leqslant 1 \\ z_1, \ z_2 \geqslant 0 \end{array}$

STEP 3. Solve each linear programming problem geometrically. [Note: Since (B) is the dual of (A), both problems have the same optimal value, i.e., min y in (A) equals max y in (B).]

STEP 4. Using the solutions in Step 3:

$$v_1 = \frac{1}{y} = \frac{1}{x_1 + x_2} \quad \text{or} \quad v_1 = \frac{1}{y} = \frac{1}{z_1 + z_2}$$

$$P^* = [p_1, \ p_2] = [v_1 x_1 + v_1 x_2]$$

$$Q^* = \begin{bmatrix} q_1 \\ q_2 \end{bmatrix} = \begin{bmatrix} v_1 z_1 \\ v_1 z_2 \end{bmatrix}$$

$$v = v_1 - k$$

$$P*MQ* = v.$$

1. Convert $\begin{bmatrix} 2 & -3 \\ -1 & 2 \end{bmatrix}$ into a positive payoff matrix by adding 4 to each payoff:

$$M_1 = \begin{bmatrix} 6 & 1 \\ 3 & 6 \end{bmatrix}$$

Set up the two corresponding linear programming problems:

(A)   Minimize $y = x_1 + x_2$

Subject to $6x_1 + 3x_2 \geqslant 1$
$x_1 + 6x_2 \geqslant 1$

$x_1 \geqslant 0, \; x_2 \geqslant 0$

(B)   Maximize $y = z_1 + z_2$

Subject to $6z_1 + z_2 \leqslant 1$
$3z_1 + 6z_2 \leqslant 1$

$z_1 \geqslant 0, \; z_2 \geqslant 0$

Solve the linear programming problems geometrically, as shown in the following figures.

(A)

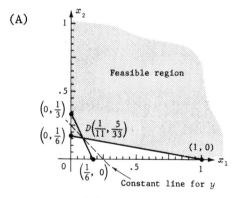

(B)

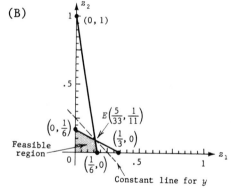

In figure (A), since the minimum $y = x_1 + x_2$ occurs at the point of intersection D, we solve

$6x_1 + 3x_2 = 1$
$x_1 + 6x_2 = 1$

to obtain the coordinates for D: $x_1 = \dfrac{3}{33} = \dfrac{1}{11}$

$x_2 = \dfrac{5}{33}$

In Figure (B), since the maximum $y = z_1 + z_2$ occurs at the point of intersection E, we solve

$6z_1 + z_2 = 1$
$3z_1 + 6z_2 = 1$

GAMES AND DECISIONS

to obtain the coordinates for E: $z_1 = \dfrac{5}{33}$

$$z_2 = \dfrac{3}{33} = \dfrac{1}{11}$$

Thus,

$$v_1 = \frac{1}{x_1 + x_2} = \frac{1}{z_1 + z_2} = \frac{1}{\dfrac{3}{33} + \dfrac{5}{33}} = \frac{33}{8}$$

$$p_1 = v_1 x_1 = \frac{33}{8} \cdot \frac{3}{33} = \frac{3}{8} \qquad\qquad q_1 = v_1 z_1 = \frac{33}{8} \cdot \frac{5}{33} = \frac{5}{8}$$

$$p_2 = v_1 x_2 = \frac{33}{8} \cdot \frac{5}{33} = \frac{5}{8} \qquad\qquad q_2 = v_1 z_2 = \frac{33}{8} \cdot \frac{3}{33} = \frac{3}{8}$$

The value v of the original matrix game is found by subtracting 4 from the value v_1 of M_1. Thus,

$$v = v_1 - 4 = \frac{33}{8} - 4 = \frac{1}{8}$$

The optimal strategies and the value of the game are given by:

$$P\star = \begin{bmatrix} \dfrac{3}{8} & \dfrac{5}{8} \end{bmatrix}, \qquad Q\star = \begin{bmatrix} \dfrac{5}{8} \\[2mm] \dfrac{3}{8} \end{bmatrix}, \qquad v = \frac{1}{8}$$

3. Convert $\begin{bmatrix} -1 & 3 \\ 2 & -6 \end{bmatrix}$ into a positive payoff matrix by adding 7 to each payoff:

$$M_1 = \begin{bmatrix} 6 & 10 \\ 9 & 1 \end{bmatrix}$$

Set up the two corresponding linear programming problems.

(A) Minimize $y = x_1 + x_2$

      Subject to $\;6x_1 + 9x_2 \geqslant 1$

                 $10x_1 + \;\;x_2 \geqslant 1$

                 $x_1 \geqslant 0,\; x_2 \geqslant 0$

(B) Maximize $y = z_1 + z_2$

      Subject to $6z_1 + 10z_2 \leqslant 1$

                 $9z_1 + \;\;\;z_2 \leqslant 1$

                 $z_1 \geqslant 0,\; z_2 \geqslant 0$

The graphs of these inequalities are shown in the following figures.

(A)

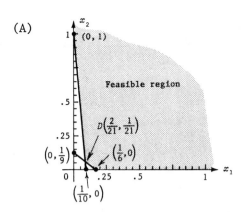

(B)

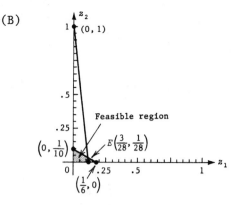

In figure (A), since the minimum $y = x_1 + x_2$ occurs at the point of intersection D, we solve

$6x_1 + 9x_2 = 1$
$10x_1 + x_2 = 1$

to obtain the coordinates for D: $\quad x_1 = \dfrac{2}{21}$

$$x_2 = \dfrac{1}{21}$$

Similarly, in figure (B), since the maximum $y = z_1 + z_2$ occurs at the point of intersection E, we solve

$6z_1 + 10z_2 = 1$
$9z_1 + z_2 = 1$

to obtain the coordinaes for E: $\quad z_1 = \dfrac{3}{28}$

$$z_2 = \dfrac{1}{28}$$

Thus,

$$v_1 = \frac{1}{x_1 + x_2} = \frac{1}{z_1 + z_2} = \frac{1}{\dfrac{2}{21} + \dfrac{1}{21}} = 7$$

$$p_1 = v_1 x_1 = 7 \cdot \frac{2}{21} = \frac{2}{3} \qquad\qquad q_1 = v_1 z_1 = 7 \cdot \frac{3}{28} = \frac{3}{4}$$

$$p_2 = v_1 x_2 = 7 \cdot \frac{1}{21} = \frac{1}{3} \qquad\qquad q_2 = v_1 z_2 = 7 \cdot \frac{1}{28} = \frac{1}{4}$$

The value v of the original matrix is given by $v_1 - 7 = 7 - 7 = 0$.
The optimal strategies and the value of the game are given by:

$$P^* = \begin{bmatrix} \dfrac{2}{3} & \dfrac{1}{3} \end{bmatrix}, \qquad Q^* = \begin{bmatrix} \dfrac{3}{4} \\ \dfrac{1}{4} \end{bmatrix}, \qquad v = 0$$

5. In the game matrix $\begin{bmatrix} 3 & -6 \\ 4 & -6 \\ -2 & 3 \\ -3 & 0 \end{bmatrix}$ row 1 and row 4 are recessive rows and should

be eliminated. Thus, we have $\begin{bmatrix} 4 & -6 \\ -2 & 3 \end{bmatrix}$. We then obtain the positive

payoff matrix by adding 7 to each payoff:

$$M_1 = \begin{bmatrix} 11 & 1 \\ 5 & 10 \end{bmatrix}$$

The linear programming problems corresponding to M_1 are as follows:

(A) Minimize $y = x_1 + x_2$

   Subject to $11x_1 + 5x_2 \geqslant 1$
   $x_1 + 10x_2 \geqslant 1$

   $x_1 \geqslant 0,\ x_2 \geqslant 0$

(B) Maximize $y = z_1 + z_2$

   Subject to $11z_1 + z_2 \leqslant 1$
   $5z_1 + 10z_2 \leqslant 1$

   $z_1 \geqslant 0,\ z_2 \geqslant 0$

The graphs corresponding to the inequalities above are shown in the following figures:

(A)

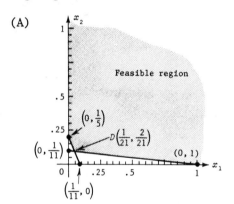

(B)

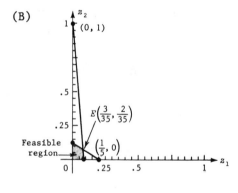

In figure (A), since the minimum $y = x_1 + x_2$ occurs at the point of intersection D, we solve

$11x_1 + 5x_2 = 1$
$x_1 + 10x_2 = 1$

to obtain the coordinates for D: $x_1 = \dfrac{1}{21}$

$x_2 = \dfrac{2}{21}$

Similarly, in figure (B), we solve

$$11z_1 + \quad z_2 = 1$$
$$5z_1 + 10z_2 = 1$$

to obtain the coordinates for E: $z_1 = \dfrac{3}{35}$

$$z_2 = \dfrac{2}{35}$$

Thus,

$$v_1 = \frac{1}{x_1 + x_2} = \frac{1}{z_1 + z_2} = \frac{1}{\dfrac{1}{21} + \dfrac{2}{21}} = \frac{21}{3} = 7$$

$$p_1 = v_1 x_1 = 7 \cdot \frac{1}{21} = \frac{1}{3} \qquad\qquad q_1 = v_1 z_1 = 7 \cdot \frac{3}{35} = \frac{3}{5}$$

$$p_2 = v_1 x_2 = 7 \cdot \frac{2}{21} = \frac{2}{3} \qquad\qquad q_2 = v_1 z_2 = 7 \cdot \frac{2}{35} = \frac{2}{5}$$

The value v of the original matrix is given by $v = v_1 - 7 = 7 - 7 = 0$. Thus,

$$P^* = \begin{bmatrix} 0 & \dfrac{1}{3} & \dfrac{2}{3} & 0 \end{bmatrix}, \qquad Q^* = \begin{bmatrix} \dfrac{3}{5} \\ \dfrac{2}{5} \end{bmatrix}, \qquad v = 0$$

7. Eliminate the recessive rows $[0 \quad -1 \quad -1 \quad 0]$ and $[-1 \quad -1 \quad -1 \quad 0]$,

and the recessive columns $\begin{bmatrix} 0 \\ 1 \\ 0 \\ -1 \end{bmatrix}$ and $\begin{bmatrix} 0 \\ -1 \\ 1 \\ 0 \end{bmatrix}$ to obtain the 2×2 matrix:

$$M = \begin{bmatrix} 2 & -1 \\ -1 & 0 \end{bmatrix}$$

Now, add 2 to each element to get the positive matrix:

$$M_1 = \begin{bmatrix} 4 & 1 \\ 1 & 2 \end{bmatrix}$$

The linear programming problems corresponding to M_1 are as follows:

(A) Minimize $y = x_1 + x_2$ (B) Maximize $y = z_1 + z_2$

    Subject to: $\quad 4x_1 + \quad x_2 \geqslant 1$ Subject to: $\quad 4z_1 + \quad z_2 \leqslant 1$

$$\qquad\qquad\qquad x_1 + 2x_2 \geqslant 1 \qquad\qquad\qquad\qquad z_1 + 2z_2 \leqslant 1$$

$$\qquad\qquad\qquad x_1, \ x_2 \geqslant 0 \qquad\qquad\qquad\qquad\qquad z_1, \ z_2 \geqslant 0$$

The graphs corresponding to the inequalities above are shown on the following page.

(A)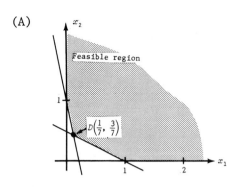

(B)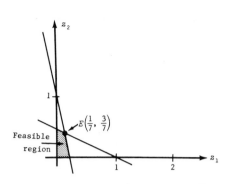

In figure (A), since the minimum $y = x_1 + x_2$ occurs at the point of intersection D, we solve

$$4x_1 + x_2 = 1$$
$$x_1 + 2x_2 = 1$$

to obtain $x_1 = \frac{1}{7}$ and $x_2 = \frac{3}{7}$.

The system in (B) is the same as the system in (A) and so $z_1 = \frac{1}{7}$ and $z_2 = \frac{3}{7}$. Thus,

$$v = \frac{1}{x_1 + x_2} = \frac{1}{z_1 + z_2} = \frac{1}{\frac{1}{7} + \frac{3}{7}} = \frac{7}{4}.$$

$$p_1 = v_1 x_1 = \frac{7}{4} \cdot \frac{1}{7} = \frac{1}{4} \qquad\qquad q_1 = v_1 z_1 = \frac{7}{4} \cdot \frac{1}{7} = \frac{1}{4}$$

$$p_2 = v_1 x_2 = \frac{7}{4} \cdot \frac{3}{7} = \frac{3}{4} \qquad\qquad q_2 = v_1 z_2 = \frac{7}{4} \cdot \frac{3}{7} = \frac{3}{4}$$

The value v of the original matrix is given by

$$v = v_1 - 2 = \frac{7}{4} - 2 = -\frac{1}{4},$$

and $P^* = \begin{bmatrix} 0 & \frac{1}{4} & \frac{3}{4} & 0 \end{bmatrix}$, $Q^* = \begin{bmatrix} 0 \\ \frac{1}{4} \\ \frac{3}{4} \\ 0 \end{bmatrix}$.

Player C (Fate)

Republican   Democrat

9. Player R (You)

	Republican	Democrat
Solar energy	1000	4000
Oil	5000	3000

This game is nonstrictly determined (see Problem 23 in Exercise 7.2). The linear programming problems corresponding to the matrix above are as follows:

(A) Minimize $y = x_1 + x_2$

    Subject to: $1000x_1 + 5000x_2 \geqslant 1$
                       $4000x_1 + 3000x_2 \geqslant 1$
                              $x_1,\ x_2 \geqslant 0$

(B) Maximize $y = z_1 + z_2$

    Subject to: $1000z_1 + 4000z_2 \leqslant 1$
                       $5000z_1 + 3000z_2 \leqslant 1$
                              $z_1,\ z_2 \geqslant 0$

The graphs corresponding to the inequalities above are shown in the following figures:

(A)

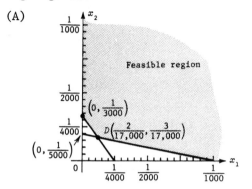

(B)

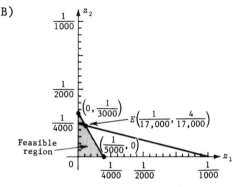

In figure (A), since the minimum $y = x_1 + x_2$ occurs at the point of intersection D, we solve

$1000x_1 + 5000x_2 = 1$
$4000x_1 + 3000x_2 = 1$

to obtain the coordinates of point D:
$$x_1 = \frac{2}{17,000}$$
$$x_2 = \frac{3}{17,000}$$

Similarly, in figure (B), since the maximum $y = z_1 + z_2$ occurs at the point of intersection E, we solve

$1000z_1 + 4000z_2 = 1$
$5000z_1 + 3000z_2 = 1$

to obtain the coordinates of point E:
$$z_1 = \frac{1}{17,000}$$
$$z_2 = \frac{4}{17,000}$$

Thus,

$$v = \frac{1}{x_1 + x_2} = \frac{1}{z_1 + z_2} = \frac{1}{\dfrac{2}{17,000} + \dfrac{3}{17,000}} = \frac{17,000}{5} = 3400$$

$p_1 = vx_1 = 3400 \cdot \dfrac{2}{17,000} = \dfrac{2}{5}$ $q_1 = vz_1 = 3400 \cdot \dfrac{1}{17,000} = \dfrac{1}{5}$

$p_2 = vx_2 = 3400 \cdot \dfrac{3}{17,000} = \dfrac{3}{5}$ $q_2 = vz_2 = 3400 \cdot \dfrac{4}{17,000} = \dfrac{4}{5}$

Therefore,

$$P^* = \begin{bmatrix} \dfrac{2}{5} & \dfrac{3}{5} \end{bmatrix}, \qquad Q^* = \begin{bmatrix} \dfrac{1}{5} \\ \dfrac{4}{5} \end{bmatrix}, \qquad v = 3400 \text{ or } v = \$3400$$

GAMES AND DECISIONS

Things to remember:

Given the nonstrictly determined matrix game M free of recessive rows and columns

$$M = \begin{bmatrix} r_1 & r_2 & r_3 \\ s_1 & s_2 & s_3 \end{bmatrix}.$$

To find $P^* = [p_1 \quad p_2]$, $Q^* = \begin{bmatrix} q_1 \\ q_2 \\ q_3 \end{bmatrix}$, and v,

proceed as follows:

STEP 1. If M is not positive, convert it into a positive matrix M_1 by adding a suitable positive constant k to each element. Let

$$M_1 = \begin{bmatrix} a_1 & a_2 & a_3 \\ b_1 & b_2 & b_3 \end{bmatrix}$$

[Note: If v_1 is the value of the game M_1, then $v = v_1 - k$ is the value of the original game M.]

STEP 2. Set up the two linear programming problems.

(A) Minimize $y = x_1 + x_2$

Subject to: $a_1 x_1 + b_1 x_2 \geqslant 1$
$a_2 x_1 + b_2 x_2 \geqslant 1$
$a_3 x_1 + b_3 x_2 \geqslant 1$
$x_1, \ x_2 \geqslant 0$

(B) Maximize $y = z_1 + z_2 + z_3$

Subject to: $a_1 z_1 + a_2 z_2 + a_3 z_3 \leqslant 1$
$b_1 z_1 + b_2 z_2 + b_3 z_3 \leqslant 1$
$z_1, \ z_2, \ z_3 \geqslant 0$

[Note: (A) is the dual of (B).]

STEP 3. Solve the maximization problem (B) using the simplex method. Since (A) is the dual of (B), this will also produce the solution of (A).

STEP 4. Using the solutions in Step 3:

$$v_1 = \frac{1}{y} = \frac{1}{x_1 + x_2} \quad \text{or} \quad v_1 = \frac{1}{y} = \frac{1}{z_1 + z_2 + z_3}$$

$$P^* = [p_1 \quad p_2] = [v_1 x_1 \quad v_1 x_2]$$

$$Q^* = \begin{bmatrix} q_1 \\ q_2 \\ q_3 \end{bmatrix} = \begin{bmatrix} v_1 z_1 \\ v_1 z_2 \\ v_1 z_3 \end{bmatrix}$$

$$v = v_1 - k$$

STEP 5. The solution found in Step 4 can be checked by showing that

$$P^*MQ^* = v.$$

---

1. Convert $\begin{bmatrix} 1 & 4 & 0 \\ 0 & -1 & 2 \end{bmatrix}$ into a positive payoff matrix by adding 2 to each payoff:

$$M_1 = \begin{bmatrix} 3 & 6 & 2 \\ 2 & 1 & 4 \end{bmatrix}$$

The linear programming problems corresponding to M_1 are as follows:

(A) Minimize $y = x_1 + x_2$

  Subject to $3x_1 + 2x_2 \geqslant 1$
  $\qquad\qquad 6x_1 + x_2 \geqslant 1$
  $\qquad\qquad 2x_1 + 4x_2 \geqslant 1$

  $\qquad\qquad x_1 \geqslant 0, \ x_2 \geqslant 0$

(B) Maximize $y = z_1 + z_2 + z_3$

  Subject to $3z_1 + 6z_2 + 2z_3 \leqslant 1$
  $\qquad\qquad 2z_1 + z_2 + 4z_3 \leqslant 1$

  $\qquad\qquad z_1 \geqslant 0, \ z_2 \geqslant 0, \ z_3 \geqslant 0$

Solve (B) by using the simplex method. We introduce slack variables x_1 and x_2 to obtain:

$$3z_1 + 6z_2 + 2z_3 + x_1 \qquad\qquad = 1$$
$$2z_1 + z_2 + 4z_3 \qquad + x_2 \qquad = 1$$
$$-z_1 - z_2 - z_3 \qquad\qquad\quad + y = 0$$
$$z_1, \ z_2, \ z_3 \geqslant 0, \ x_1, \ x_2 \geqslant 0$$

The simplex tableau for this system is as follows:

$$\begin{array}{cccccc} z_1 & z_2 & z_3 & x_1 & x_2 & y \\ \end{array}$$

$$\begin{bmatrix} ③ & 6 & 2 & 1 & 0 & 0 & | & 1 \\ 2 & 1 & 4 & 0 & 1 & 0 & | & 1 \\ \hline -1 & -1 & -1 & 0 & 0 & 1 & | & 0 \end{bmatrix} \begin{array}{c} \frac{1}{3} \\ \\ \frac{1}{2} \\ \\ \end{array}$$

$$\tfrac{1}{3} R_1 \rightarrow R_2$$

Choose the first column as the pivot column. Then, following the method outlined in Chapter 2, we get the pivot element in the 1, 1 position, indicated by a circle.

$$\sim \begin{bmatrix} 1 & 2 & \frac{2}{3} & \frac{1}{3} & 0 & 0 & \vline & \frac{1}{3} \\ 2 & 1 & 4 & 0 & 1 & 0 & \vline & 1 \\ \hline -1 & -1 & -1 & 0 & 0 & 1 & \vline & 0 \end{bmatrix} \sim \begin{bmatrix} 1 & 2 & \frac{2}{3} & \frac{1}{3} & 0 & 0 & \vline & \frac{1}{3} & \frac{1}{2} \\ 0 & -3 & \boxed{\frac{8}{3}} & -\frac{2}{3} & 1 & 0 & \vline & \frac{1}{3} & \frac{1}{8} \\ \hline 0 & 1 & -\frac{1}{3} & \frac{1}{3} & 0 & 1 & \vline & \frac{1}{3} \end{bmatrix}$$

$R_2 + (-2)R_1 \rightarrow R_2$ and $\frac{3}{8} R_2 \rightarrow R_2$
$R_3 + R_1 \rightarrow R_3$

$$\sim \begin{bmatrix} 1 & 2 & \frac{2}{3} & \frac{1}{3} & 0 & 0 & \vline & \frac{1}{3} \\ 0 & -\frac{9}{8} & 1 & -\frac{1}{4} & \frac{3}{8} & 0 & \vline & \frac{1}{8} \\ \hline 0 & 1 & -\frac{1}{3} & \frac{1}{3} & 0 & 1 & \vline & \frac{1}{3} \end{bmatrix} \sim \begin{array}{cccccc} z_1 & z_2 & z_3 & x_1 & x_2 & y \\ \begin{bmatrix} 1 & \frac{11}{4} & 0 & \frac{1}{2} & -\frac{1}{4} & 0 & \vline & \frac{1}{4} \\ 0 & -\frac{9}{8} & 1 & -\frac{1}{4} & \frac{3}{8} & 0 & \vline & \frac{1}{8} \\ \hline 0 & \frac{5}{8} & 0 & \frac{1}{4} & \frac{1}{8} & 1 & \vline & \frac{9}{24} \end{bmatrix} \end{array}$$

$R_1 + \left(-\frac{2}{3}\right)R_2 \rightarrow R_1$ and $R_3 + \frac{1}{3}R_2 \rightarrow R_3$

The maximum, $y = z_1 + z_2 + z_3 = \frac{9}{24}$, occurs at $z_1 = \frac{1}{4}$, $z_2 = 0$, $z_3 = \frac{1}{8}$. Thus,

$$v_1 = \frac{1}{z_1 + z_2 + z_3} = \frac{1}{y} = \frac{1}{\frac{9}{24}} = \frac{24}{9} = \frac{8}{3},$$

and $q_1 = v_1 z_1 = \frac{8}{3} \cdot \frac{1}{4} = \frac{2}{3}$, $q_2 = v_1 z_2 = \frac{8}{3} \cdot 0 = 0$, $q_3 = v_1 z_3 = \frac{8}{3} \cdot \frac{1}{8} = \frac{1}{3}$.

The solution to the minimization problem (A) can be read from the bottom row of the final simplex tableau for the dual problem above. Thus, from the row

$$\begin{array}{cccccc} & & & x_1 & x_2 & \\ \begin{bmatrix} 0 & \frac{5}{8} & 0 & \frac{1}{4} & \frac{1}{8} & 1 & \vline & \frac{9}{24} \end{bmatrix} \end{array}$$

we conclude that the solution to (A) is:

Min $y = x_1 + x_2 = \frac{9}{24} = \frac{3}{8}$ at $x_1 = \frac{1}{4}$, $x_2 = \frac{1}{8}$.

Also,

$$p_1 = v_1 x_1 = \frac{8}{3}\left(\frac{1}{4}\right) = \frac{2}{3}$$

$$p_2 = v_1 x_2 = \frac{8}{3}\left(\frac{1}{8}\right) = \frac{1}{3}$$

Finally,

$$P^* = \begin{bmatrix} \dfrac{2}{3} & \dfrac{1}{3} \end{bmatrix}, \qquad Q^* = \begin{bmatrix} \dfrac{2}{3} \\[4pt] 0 \\[4pt] \dfrac{1}{3} \end{bmatrix}, \qquad \text{and} \qquad v = \dfrac{8}{3} - 2 = \dfrac{2}{3}.$$

3. Convert $\begin{bmatrix} 0 & 1 & -2 \\ -1 & 0 & 3 \\ 2 & -3 & 0 \end{bmatrix}$ into a positive payoff matrix by adding 4 to each

payoff:

$$M_1 = \begin{bmatrix} 4 & 5 & 2 \\ 3 & 4 & 7 \\ 6 & 1 & 4 \end{bmatrix}$$

The linear programming problems corresponding to M_1 are as follows:

(A)   Minimize $y = x_1 + x_2 + x_3$

Subject to: $4x_1 + 3x_2 + 6x_3 \geqslant 1$
$5x_1 + 4x_2 + x_3 \geqslant 1$
$2x_1 + 7x_2 + 4x_3 \geqslant 1$
$x_1, \; x_2, \; x_3 \geqslant 0$

(B)   Maximize $y = z_1 + z_2 + z_3$

Subject to: $4z_1 + 5z_2 + 2z_3 \leqslant 1$
$3z_1 + 4z_2 + 7z_3 \leqslant 1$
$6z_1 + z_2 + 4z_3 \leqslant 1$
$z_1, \; z_2, \; z_3 \geqslant 0$

We first solve (B) by using the simplex method. Introduce slack variables x_1, x_2, and x_3 to obtain:

$$\begin{aligned}
4z_1 + 5z_2 + 2z_3 + x_1 &= 1 \\
3z_1 + 4z_2 + 7z_3 + x_2 &= 1 \\
6z_1 + z_2 + 4z_3 + x_3 &= 1 \\
-z_1 - z_2 - z_3 + y &= 0 \\
z_1, \; z_2, \; z_3 \geqslant 0, \; x_1, \; x_2, \; x_3 &\geqslant 0
\end{aligned}$$

The simplex tableau for this system is as follows:

$$
\begin{array}{ccccccc}
z_1 & z_2 & z_3 & x_1 & x_2 & x_3 & y \\
\end{array}
$$

$$
\begin{bmatrix}
4 & 5 & 2 & 1 & 0 & 0 & 0 & | & 1 \\
3 & 4 & \boxed{7} & 0 & 1 & 0 & 0 & | & 1 \\
6 & 1 & 4 & 0 & 0 & 1 & 0 & | & 1 \\
\hline
-1 & -1 & -1 & 0 & 0 & 0 & 1 & | & 0
\end{bmatrix}
\quad
\begin{matrix} \frac{1}{2} \\ \frac{1}{7} \\ \frac{1}{4} \\ \\ \end{matrix}
\quad \sim \quad
\begin{bmatrix}
4 & 5 & 2 & 1 & 0 & 0 & 0 & | & 1 \\
\frac{3}{7} & \frac{4}{7} & 1 & 0 & \frac{1}{7} & 0 & 0 & | & \frac{1}{7} \\
6 & 1 & 4 & 0 & 0 & 1 & 0 & | & 1 \\
\hline
-1 & -1 & -1 & 0 & 0 & 0 & 1 & | & 0
\end{bmatrix}
$$

$\frac{1}{7} R_2 \rightarrow R_2$

$R_1 - 2R_2 \rightarrow R_1$, $R_3 - 4R_2 \rightarrow R_3$ and
$R_4 + R_2 \rightarrow R_4$

(continued)

$$\sim \begin{bmatrix} \dfrac{22}{7} & \dfrac{27}{7} & 0 & 1 & -\dfrac{2}{7} & 0 & 0 & \bigg| & \dfrac{5}{7} \\[2mm] \dfrac{3}{7} & \dfrac{4}{7} & 1 & 0 & \dfrac{1}{7} & 0 & 0 & \bigg| & \dfrac{1}{7} \\[2mm] \boxed{\dfrac{30}{7}} & -\dfrac{9}{7} & 0 & 0 & -\dfrac{4}{7} & 1 & 0 & \bigg| & \dfrac{3}{7} \\ \hdashline \\[-3mm] -\dfrac{4}{7} & -\dfrac{3}{7} & 0 & 0 & \dfrac{1}{7} & 0 & 1 & \bigg| & \dfrac{1}{7} \end{bmatrix} \quad \begin{array}{l} \dfrac{5}{7} \div \dfrac{22}{7} = \dfrac{5}{22} \\[2mm] \dfrac{1}{7} \div \dfrac{3}{7} = \dfrac{1}{3} \\[2mm] \dfrac{3}{7} \div \dfrac{30}{7} = \dfrac{1}{10} \end{array}$$

$$\dfrac{7}{30} R_3 \to R_3$$

$$\sim \begin{bmatrix} \dfrac{22}{7} & \dfrac{27}{7} & 0 & 1 & -\dfrac{2}{7} & 0 & 0 & \bigg| & \dfrac{5}{7} \\[2mm] \dfrac{3}{7} & \dfrac{4}{7} & 1 & 0 & \dfrac{1}{7} & 0 & 0 & \bigg| & \dfrac{1}{7} \\[2mm] 1 & -\dfrac{3}{10} & 0 & 0 & -\dfrac{2}{15} & \dfrac{7}{30} & 0 & \bigg| & \dfrac{1}{10} \\ \hdashline \\[-3mm] -\dfrac{4}{7} & -\dfrac{3}{7} & 0 & 0 & \dfrac{1}{7} & 0 & 1 & \bigg| & \dfrac{1}{7} \end{bmatrix}$$

$$R_1 + \left(-\dfrac{22}{7}\right)R_3 \to R_1, \quad R_2 + \left(-\dfrac{3}{7}\right)R_3 \to R_2, \quad \text{and} \quad R_4 + \dfrac{4}{7} R_3 \to R_4$$

$$\sim \begin{bmatrix} 0 & \boxed{\dfrac{24}{5}} & 0 & 1 & \dfrac{2}{15} & \dfrac{11}{15} & 0 & \bigg| & \dfrac{2}{5} \\[2mm] 0 & \dfrac{7}{10} & 1 & 0 & \dfrac{1}{5} & -\dfrac{1}{10} & 0 & \bigg| & \dfrac{1}{10} \\[2mm] 1 & -\dfrac{3}{10} & 0 & 0 & -\dfrac{2}{15} & \dfrac{7}{30} & 0 & \bigg| & \dfrac{1}{10} \\ \hdashline \\[-3mm] 0 & -\dfrac{3}{5} & 0 & 0 & \dfrac{1}{15} & \dfrac{2}{15} & 1 & \bigg| & \dfrac{1}{5} \end{bmatrix} \quad \begin{array}{l} \dfrac{2}{5} \div \dfrac{24}{5} = \dfrac{1}{12} \\[2mm] \dfrac{1}{10} \div \dfrac{7}{10} = \dfrac{1}{7} \\[2mm] \dfrac{1}{10} \div -\dfrac{3}{10} = -\dfrac{1}{3} \end{array}$$

$$\dfrac{5}{24} R_1 \to R_1$$

$$\sim \begin{bmatrix} 0 & 1 & 0 & \dfrac{5}{24} & \dfrac{1}{36} & -\dfrac{11}{72} & 0 & \bigg| & \dfrac{1}{12} \\[2mm] 0 & \dfrac{7}{10} & 1 & 0 & \dfrac{1}{5} & -\dfrac{1}{10} & 0 & \bigg| & \dfrac{1}{10} \\[2mm] 1 & -\dfrac{3}{10} & 0 & 0 & -\dfrac{2}{15} & \dfrac{7}{30} & 0 & \bigg| & \dfrac{1}{10} \\ \hdashline \\[-3mm] 0 & -\dfrac{3}{5} & 0 & 0 & \dfrac{1}{15} & \dfrac{2}{15} & 1 & \bigg| & \dfrac{1}{5} \end{bmatrix}$$

$$R_2 - \dfrac{7}{10} R_1 \to R_2, \quad R_3 + \dfrac{3}{10} R_1 \to R_3, \quad \text{and} \quad R_4 + \dfrac{3}{5} R_1 \to R_4$$

(continued)

$$\sim \begin{bmatrix} z_1 & z_2 & z_3 & x_1 & x_2 & x_3 & y & \\ 0 & 1 & 0 & \dfrac{5}{24} & \dfrac{1}{36} & -\dfrac{11}{72} & 0 & \dfrac{1}{12} \\ 0 & 0 & 1 & -\dfrac{7}{48} & \dfrac{13}{12} & \dfrac{1}{144} & 0 & \dfrac{1}{24} \\ 1 & 0 & 0 & \dfrac{1}{16} & -\dfrac{1}{8} & \dfrac{3}{16} & 0 & \dfrac{1}{8} \\ \hline 0 & 0 & 0 & \dfrac{1}{8} & \dfrac{1}{12} & \dfrac{1}{24} & 1 & \dfrac{1}{4} \end{bmatrix}$$

We obtain: $z_1 = \dfrac{1}{8}$, $z_2 = \dfrac{1}{12}$, and $z_3 = \dfrac{1}{24}$. Thus, $v_1 = \dfrac{1}{\dfrac{1}{8} + \dfrac{1}{12} + \dfrac{1}{24}} = 4$,

and $q_1 = v_1 z_1 = 4 \cdot \dfrac{1}{8} = \dfrac{1}{2}$, $q_2 = v_1 z_2 = 4 \cdot \dfrac{1}{12} = \dfrac{1}{3}$, $q_3 = v_1 z_3 = 4 \cdot \dfrac{1}{24} = \dfrac{1}{6}$.

The solution to the minimization problem (A) can be read from the bottom row of the final simplex tableau for the dual problem above. Thus, from the row

$$\begin{bmatrix} & & & x_1 & x_2 & x_3 & & \\ 0 & 0 & 0 & \dfrac{1}{8} & \dfrac{1}{12} & \dfrac{1}{24} & 1 & \dfrac{1}{4} \end{bmatrix}$$

we conclude that the solution to (A) is:

$$\text{Min } y = x_1 + x_2 + x_3 = \dfrac{1}{4} \text{ at } x_1 = \dfrac{1}{8}, \ x_2 = \dfrac{1}{12}, \ x_3 = \dfrac{1}{24}.$$

Also,

$$p_1 = v_1 x_1 = 4\left(\dfrac{1}{8}\right) = \dfrac{1}{2}$$

$$p_2 = v_1 x_2 = 4\left(\dfrac{1}{12}\right) = \dfrac{1}{3}$$

$$p_3 = v_1 x_3 = 4\left(\dfrac{1}{24}\right) = \dfrac{1}{6}$$

Finally,

$$P^* = \begin{bmatrix} \dfrac{1}{2} & \dfrac{1}{3} & \dfrac{1}{6} \end{bmatrix}, \quad Q^* = \begin{bmatrix} \dfrac{2}{3} \\ 0 \\ \dfrac{1}{3} \end{bmatrix}, \quad \text{and} \quad v = 4 - 4 = 0.$$

5. (A) The matrix for this game is as follows:

$$\begin{array}{c} \\ \text{Paper} \\ \text{Stone} \\ \text{Scissors} \end{array} \begin{array}{ccc} \text{Paper} & \text{Stone} & \text{Scissors} \end{array} \\ \begin{bmatrix} 0 & 1 & -1 \\ -1 & 0 & 1 \\ 1 & -1 & 0 \end{bmatrix}$$

(B) Convert this game matrix into a positive payoff matrix by adding 2 to each payoff:

$$M_1 = \begin{bmatrix} 2 & 3 & 1 \\ 1 & 2 & 3 \\ 3 & 1 & 2 \end{bmatrix}$$

The linear programming problems corresponding to M_1 are as follows:

(1) Minimize $y = x_1 + x_2 + x_3$

Subject to $2x_1 + x_2 + 3x_3 \geq 1$
$3x_1 + 2x_2 + x_3 \geq 1$
$x_1 + 3x_2 + 2x_3 \geq 1$

$x_1 \geq 0, \; x_2 \geq 0, \; x_3 \geq 0$

(2) Maximize $y = z_1 + z_2 + z_3$

Subject to $2z_1 + 3z_2 + z_3 \leq$
$z_1 + 2z_2 + 3z_3 \leq$
$3z_1 + z_2 + 2z_3 \leq$

$z_1 \geq 0, \; z_2 \geq 0, \; z_3 \geq$

Solve (2) by using the simplex method. Introduce slack variables x_1, x_2, x_3 to obtain:

$$2z_1 + 3z_2 + z_3 + x_1 \qquad\qquad = 1$$
$$z_1 + 2z_2 + 3z_3 \qquad + x_2 \qquad = 1$$
$$3z_1 + z_2 + 2z_3 \qquad\qquad + x_3 = 1$$
$$-z_1 - z_2 - z_3 \qquad\qquad\qquad + y = 0$$
$$z_1, \; z_2, \; z_3 \geq 0, \; x_1, \; x_2, \; x_3 \geq 0$$

The simplex tableau for this system is given below:

$$
\begin{array}{ccccccc|c}
z_1 & z_2 & z_3 & x_1 & x_2 & x_3 & y & \\
2 & 3 & 1 & 1 & 0 & 0 & 0 & 1 \\
1 & 2 & ③ & 0 & 1 & 0 & 0 & 1 \\
3 & 1 & 2 & 0 & 0 & 1 & 0 & 1 \\
\hline
-1 & -1 & -1 & 0 & 0 & 0 & 1 & 0
\end{array}
$$

$R_2/3 \to R_2$

$$
\begin{array}{c}
1 \\
\frac{1}{3} \\
\frac{1}{2}
\end{array}
$$

$\sim$

$$
\begin{array}{ccccccc|c}
2 & 3 & 1 & 1 & 0 & 0 & 0 & 1 \\
\frac{1}{3} & \frac{2}{3} & 1 & 0 & \frac{1}{3} & 0 & 0 & \frac{1}{3} \\
3 & 1 & 2 & 0 & 0 & 1 & 0 & 1 \\
\hline
-1 & -1 & -1 & 0 & 0 & 0 & 1 & 0
\end{array}
$$

$R_1 + (-1)R_2 \to R_1, \; R_3 + (-2)R_2 \to R_3$
and $R_4 + R_2 \to R_4$

$$
\begin{array}{ccccccc|c}
\frac{5}{3} & \frac{7}{3} & 0 & 1 & -\frac{1}{3} & 0 & 0 & \frac{2}{3} \\
\frac{1}{3} & \frac{2}{3} & 1 & 0 & \frac{1}{3} & 0 & 0 & \frac{1}{3} \\
⑦\!\!/3 & -\frac{1}{3} & 0 & 0 & -\frac{2}{3} & 1 & 0 & \frac{1}{3} \\
\hline
-\frac{2}{3} & -\frac{1}{3} & 0 & 0 & \frac{1}{3} & 0 & 1 & \frac{1}{3}
\end{array}
$$

$\begin{array}{l} \frac{2}{3} \div \frac{5}{3} = \frac{2}{5} \\ \frac{1}{3} \div \frac{1}{3} = 1 \\ \frac{1}{3} \div \frac{7}{3} = \frac{1}{7} \end{array}$

$\frac{3}{7}R_3 \to R_3$

(continued)

$$\sim \begin{bmatrix} \frac{5}{3} & \frac{7}{3} & 0 & 1 & -\frac{1}{3} & 0 & 0 & \Big| & \frac{2}{3} \\ \frac{1}{3} & \frac{2}{3} & 1 & 0 & \frac{1}{3} & 0 & 0 & \Big| & \frac{1}{3} \\ 1 & -\frac{1}{7} & 0 & 0 & -\frac{2}{7} & \frac{3}{7} & 0 & \Big| & \frac{1}{7} \\ \hline -\frac{2}{3} & -\frac{1}{3} & 0 & 0 & \frac{1}{3} & 0 & 1 & \Big| & \frac{1}{3} \end{bmatrix}$$

$$R_1 + \left(-\frac{5}{3}\right)R_3 \to R_1, \ R_2 + \left(-\frac{1}{3}\right)R_3 \to R_2, \text{ and } R_4 + \frac{2}{3}R_3 \to R_4$$

$$\sim \begin{bmatrix} 0 & \boxed{\frac{54}{21}} & 0 & 1 & \frac{3}{21} & -\frac{5}{7} & 0 & \Big| & \frac{3}{7} \\ 0 & \frac{5}{7} & 1 & 0 & \frac{3}{7} & -\frac{1}{7} & 0 & \Big| & \frac{2}{7} \\ 1 & -\frac{1}{7} & 0 & 0 & -\frac{2}{7} & \frac{3}{7} & 0 & \Big| & \frac{1}{7} \\ \hline 0 & -\frac{3}{7} & 0 & 0 & \frac{1}{7} & \frac{2}{7} & 1 & \Big| & \frac{3}{7} \end{bmatrix} \cdot \quad \begin{array}{l} \frac{3}{7} \div \frac{54}{21} = \frac{1}{6} \\[4pt] \frac{2}{7} \div \frac{8}{21} = \frac{3}{4} \\[4pt] \frac{1}{7} \div -\frac{1}{7} = -1 \end{array}$$

$$\frac{21}{54}R_1 \to R_1$$

$$\sim \begin{bmatrix} 0 & 1 & 0 & \frac{21}{54} & \frac{1}{18} & -\frac{5}{18} & 0 & \Big| & \frac{1}{6} \\ 0 & \frac{5}{7} & 1 & 0 & \frac{3}{7} & -\frac{1}{7} & 0 & \Big| & \frac{2}{7} \\ 1 & -\frac{1}{7} & 0 & 0 & -\frac{2}{7} & \frac{3}{7} & 0 & \Big| & \frac{1}{7} \\ \hline 0 & -\frac{3}{7} & 0 & 0 & \frac{1}{7} & \frac{2}{7} & 1 & \Big| & \frac{3}{7} \end{bmatrix}$$

$$R_2 + \left(-\frac{5}{7}\right)R_1 \to R_2, \ R_3 + \frac{1}{7}R_1 \to R_3, \text{ and } R_4 + \frac{3}{7}R_1 \to R_4$$

$$\begin{array}{ccccccc} z_1 & z_2 & z_3 & x_1 & x_2 & x_3 & y \end{array}$$
$$\begin{bmatrix} 0 & 1 & 0 & \frac{21}{54} & \frac{1}{18} & \frac{5}{18} & 0 & \Big| & \frac{1}{6} \\ 0 & 0 & 1 & -\frac{5}{18} & \frac{7}{18} & \frac{7}{126} & 0 & \Big| & \frac{1}{6} \\ 1 & 0 & 0 & \frac{1}{18} & -\frac{5}{18} & \frac{49}{126} & 0 & \Big| & \frac{1}{6} \\ \hline 0 & 0 & 0 & \frac{1}{6} & \frac{1}{6} & \frac{1}{6} & 1 & \Big| & \frac{1}{2} \end{bmatrix}$$

Thus, $z_1 = \frac{1}{6}$, $z_2 = \frac{1}{6}$, $z_3 = \frac{1}{6}$, $v_1 = \dfrac{1}{z_1 + z_2 + z_3} = \dfrac{1}{\frac{1}{6} + \frac{1}{6} + \frac{1}{6}} = 2$, and

$$q_1 = v_1 z_1 = 2 \cdot \frac{1}{6} = \frac{1}{3}, \quad q_2 = v_1 z_2 = 2 \cdot \frac{1}{6} = \frac{1}{3}, \quad q_3 = v_1 z_3 = 2 \cdot \frac{1}{6} = \frac{1}{3}.$$

The solution to the minimization problem (A) can be read from the bottom row of the final simplex tableau for the dual problem above. Thus, from the row

$$\begin{array}{ccc} x_1 & x_2 & x_3 \end{array}$$

$$\left[\begin{array}{ccccccc|c} 0 & 0 & 0 & \frac{1}{6} & \frac{1}{6} & \frac{1}{6} & 1 & \frac{1}{2} \end{array}\right]$$

we conclude that the solution to (A) is:

$$\text{Min } y = x_1 + x_2 + x_3 = \frac{1}{2} \text{ at } x_1 = \frac{1}{6}, \ x_2 = \frac{1}{6}, \ x_3 = \frac{1}{6}.$$

Also,

$$p_1 = v_1 x_1 = 2\left(\frac{1}{6}\right) = \frac{1}{3}$$

$$p_2 = v_1 x_2 = 2\left(\frac{1}{6}\right) = \frac{1}{3}$$

$$p_3 = v_1 x_3 = 2\left(\frac{1}{6}\right) = \frac{1}{3}$$

Finally,

$$P^* = \left[\begin{array}{ccc} \frac{1}{3} & \frac{1}{3} & \frac{1}{3} \end{array}\right], \quad Q^* = \left[\begin{array}{c} \frac{1}{3} \\ \frac{1}{3} \\ \frac{1}{3} \\ \frac{1}{3} \end{array}\right], \quad \text{and} \quad v = 2 - 2 = 0.$$

7. (A)

$$\begin{array}{c} \text{Economy} \\ \begin{array}{cc} \text{Up} & \text{Down} \end{array} \end{array}$$

$$\begin{array}{c} \text{Delux} \\ \text{Standard} \\ \text{Economy} \end{array} \left[\begin{array}{cc} 2 & -1 \\ 1 & 1 \\ 0 & 4 \end{array}\right]$$

(B) Since the payoff matrix is not positive, we add 2 to each element to obtain the matrix:

$$M_1 = \left[\begin{array}{cc} 4 & 1 \\ 3 & 3 \\ 2 & 6 \end{array}\right]$$

The linear programming problems corresponding to M_1 are:

(A) Minimize $y = x_1 + x_2 + x_3$

Subject to: $4x_1 + 3x_2 + 2x_3 \geqslant 1$
$x_1 + 3x_2 + 6x_3 \geqslant 1$
$x_1, \ x_2, \ x_3 \geqslant 0$

(B) Maximize $y = z_1 + z_2$

Subject to: $4z_1 + z_2 \leqslant 1$
$3z_1 + 3z_2 \leqslant 1$
$2z_1 + 6z_2 \leqslant 1$
$z_1, \ z_2 \geqslant 0$

Solve (B) by using the simplex method. Introduce slack variables x_1, x_2, and x_3 to obtain:

$$
\begin{aligned}
4z_1 + z_2 + x_1 &= 1 \\
3z_1 + 3z_2 + x_2 &= 1 \\
2z_1 + 6z_2 + x_3 &= 1 \\
-z_1 - z_2 + y &= 0
\end{aligned}
$$

The simplex tableau for this system is:

$$
\begin{array}{cccccc}
z_1 & z_2 & x_1 & x_2 & x_3 & y
\end{array}
$$

$$
\left[\begin{array}{cccccc|c}
\boxed{4} & 1 & 1 & 0 & 0 & 0 & 1 \\
3 & 3 & 0 & 1 & 0 & 0 & 1 \\
2 & 6 & 0 & 0 & 1 & 0 & 1 \\
\hline
-1 & -1 & 0 & 0 & 0 & 1 & 0
\end{array}\right]
\begin{array}{c} \frac{1}{4} \\[2mm] \frac{1}{3} \\[2mm] \frac{1}{2} \\[2mm] \end{array}
\sim
\left[\begin{array}{cccccc|c}
1 & \frac{1}{4} & \frac{1}{4} & 0 & 0 & 0 & \frac{1}{4} \\
3 & 3 & 0 & 1 & 0 & 0 & 1 \\
2 & 6 & 0 & 0 & 1 & 0 & 1 \\
\hline
-1 & -1 & 0 & 0 & 0 & 1 & 0
\end{array}\right]
$$

$\frac{1}{4}R_1 \to R_1$

$R_2 + (-3)R_1 \to R_2,\; R_3 + (-2)R_1 \to R_3$
$R_4 + R_1 \to R_4$

$$
\sim
\left[\begin{array}{cccccc|c}
1 & \frac{1}{4} & \frac{1}{4} & 0 & 0 & 0 & \frac{1}{4} \\
0 & \frac{9}{4} & -\frac{3}{4} & 1 & 0 & 0 & \frac{1}{4} \\
0 & \frac{11}{2} & -\frac{1}{2} & 0 & 1 & 0 & \frac{1}{2} \\
\hline
0 & -\frac{3}{4} & \frac{1}{4} & 0 & 0 & 1 & \frac{1}{4}
\end{array}\right]
\begin{array}{c} 1 \\[2mm] \frac{1}{9} \\[2mm] \frac{1}{11} \\[2mm] \end{array}
$$

$\frac{2}{11}R_3 \to R_3$

$$
\sim
\left[\begin{array}{cccccc|c}
1 & \frac{1}{4} & \frac{1}{4} & 0 & 0 & 0 & \frac{1}{4} \\
0 & \frac{9}{4} & -\frac{3}{4} & 1 & 0 & 0 & \frac{1}{4} \\
0 & 1 & -\frac{1}{11} & 0 & \frac{2}{11} & 0 & \frac{1}{11} \\
\hline
0 & -\frac{3}{4} & \frac{1}{4} & 0 & 0 & 1 & \frac{1}{4}
\end{array}\right]
$$

$R_1 + \left(-\frac{1}{4}\right)R_3 \to R_1,\; R_2 + \left(-\frac{9}{4}\right)R_3 \to R_2$

$R_4 + \frac{3}{4}R_3 \to R_4$

(continued)

$$\sim \begin{bmatrix} z_1 & z_2 & x_1 & x_2 & x_3 & y \\ 1 & 0 & \dfrac{12}{44} & 0 & -\dfrac{2}{44} & 0 & \dfrac{10}{44} \\ 0 & 0 & -\dfrac{24}{44} & 1 & -\dfrac{18}{44} & 0 & \dfrac{2}{44} \\ 0 & 1 & -\dfrac{1}{11} & 0 & \dfrac{2}{11} & 0 & \dfrac{1}{11} \\ \hline 0 & 0 & \dfrac{2}{11} & 0 & \dfrac{3}{22} & 1 & \dfrac{14}{44} \end{bmatrix}$$

Thus, max $y = z_1 + z_2 = \dfrac{14}{44} = \dfrac{7}{22}$ occurs at $z_1 = \dfrac{10}{44} = \dfrac{5}{22}$, $z_2 = \dfrac{1}{11}$. Now

$$v = \dfrac{1}{y} = \dfrac{1}{\dfrac{7}{22}} = \dfrac{22}{7}$$

and $q_1 = v_1 z_1 = \dfrac{22}{7}\left(\dfrac{5}{22}\right) = \dfrac{5}{7}$, $q_2 = v_1 z_2 = \dfrac{22}{7}\left(\dfrac{2}{22}\right) = \dfrac{2}{7}$.

The solution to the minimization problem (A) can be read from the bottom row of the final simplex tableau for the dual problem above. Thus, from the row

$$\begin{bmatrix} x_1 & x_2 & x_3 \\ 0 & 0 & \dfrac{2}{11} & 0 & \dfrac{3}{22} & 1 & \dfrac{7}{22} \end{bmatrix}$$

we conclude that the solution to (A) is:

$$\text{Min } y = x_1 + x_2 + x_3 = \dfrac{7}{22} \text{ at } x_1 = \dfrac{2}{11}, \ x_2 = 0, \ x_3 = \dfrac{3}{22}$$

Also,

$$p_1 = v_1 x_1 = \dfrac{22}{7}\left(\dfrac{2}{11}\right) = \dfrac{4}{7}$$

$$p_2 = v_1 x_2 = \dfrac{22}{7}(0) = 0$$

$$p_3 = v_1 x_3 = \dfrac{22}{7}\left(\dfrac{3}{22}\right) = \dfrac{3}{7}$$

Finally, the optimal strategies are

$$P^* = \begin{bmatrix} \dfrac{4}{7} & 0 & \dfrac{3}{7} \end{bmatrix}, \quad Q^* = \begin{bmatrix} \dfrac{5}{7} \\ \dfrac{2}{7} \end{bmatrix};$$

and the value of the game is: $v = v_1 - 2 = \dfrac{22}{7} - 2 = \dfrac{8}{7}$.

(C) Irrespective of what the economy does, the company's budget should be allocated as follows:

$\dfrac{4}{7}$ Delux, 0 Standard, $\dfrac{3}{7}$ Economy

1.
$$\begin{bmatrix} \boxed{-4} & \boxed{6} \\ \boxed{-3} & 1 \end{bmatrix}$$
The game is strictly determined.

(A) Saddle value = 3 (2,1 position).
(B) R plays row 2 and C plays column 1.
(C) The value of the game = -3.

2.
$$\begin{bmatrix} \boxed{-5} & \boxed{2} \\ \boxed{3} & \boxed{-1} \end{bmatrix}$$

The game is not strictly determined.

3.
$$\begin{bmatrix} -3 & -1 & \boxed{5} & \boxed{-8} \\ 1 & \boxed{0} & \boxed{0} & \boxed{2} \\ 3 & \boxed{0} & 1 & \boxed{0} \\ \boxed{6} & -2 & \boxed{-4} & \boxed{2} \end{bmatrix}$$

The game is strictly determined.

(A) The two zeros in column 2 (2,2 and 3,2 positions).
(B) R plays either row 2 or row 3 and C plays column 2.
(C) The value of the game = 0.

4.
$$\begin{bmatrix} 1 & \boxed{-2} & \boxed{3} \\ \boxed{-1} & \boxed{2} & 0 \\ \boxed{3} & 0 & \boxed{-4} \end{bmatrix}$$

The game is not strictly determined.

5. The game matrix $\begin{bmatrix} -2 & 3 & 5 \\ -1 & -3 & 0 \\ 0 & -1 & 1 \end{bmatrix}$ has a recessive row 2 and a recessive column 3. Thus, the reduced game matrix is: $M_1 = \begin{bmatrix} -2 & 3 \\ 0 & -1 \end{bmatrix}$.

6. $M = \begin{bmatrix} -2 & 1 \\ 0 & -1 \end{bmatrix}$

Optimal strategy for $R = P^* = \begin{bmatrix} \dfrac{d-c}{D} & \dfrac{a-b}{D} \end{bmatrix} = \begin{bmatrix} \dfrac{-1-0}{-4} & \dfrac{-2-1}{-4} \end{bmatrix}$

[Note: $D = (a+d) - (b+c)$
$= (-2-1) - (1+0) = -4$.]

$= \begin{bmatrix} \dfrac{1}{4} & \dfrac{3}{4} \end{bmatrix}$

Optimal strategy for $C = Q^* = \begin{bmatrix} \dfrac{d-b}{D} \\[2mm] \dfrac{a-c}{D} \end{bmatrix} = \begin{bmatrix} \dfrac{-1-1}{-4} \\[2mm] \dfrac{-2-0}{-4} \end{bmatrix} = \begin{bmatrix} \dfrac{1}{2} \\[2mm] \dfrac{1}{2} \end{bmatrix}$

Value of the game $= v = \dfrac{ad - bc}{D} = \dfrac{(-2)(-1) - (1)(0)}{-4} = -\dfrac{1}{2}.$

7. Obtain the positive payoff matrix by adding 3 to each payoff:

$$M = \begin{bmatrix} 1 & 4 \\ 3 & 2 \end{bmatrix}$$

The linear programming problems corresponding to M_1 are as follows:

(A) Minimize $y = x_1 + x_2$

      Subject to $x_1 + 3x_2 \geqslant 1$
                      $4x_1 + 2x_2 \geqslant 1$

                 $x_1 \geqslant 0,\ x_2 \geqslant 0$

(B) Maximize $y = z_1 + z_2$

      Subject to $z_1 + 4z_2 \leqslant 1$
                      $3z_1 + 2z_2 \leqslant 1$

                 $z_1 \geqslant 0,\ z_2 \geqslant 0$

8. The graphs corresponding to the linear programming problems given in the solution to Problem 7 are shown below.

(A)

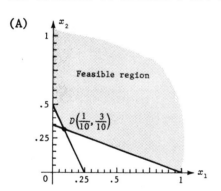

(B)

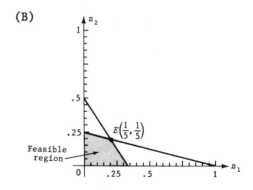

In (A), since the minimum $y = x_1 + x_2$ occurs at the point of intersection D, we solve

$x_1 + 3x_2 = 1$
$4x_1 + 2x_2 = 1$

to obtain the coordinates of D: $\quad x_1 = \dfrac{1}{10} \quad$ and $\quad x_2 = \dfrac{3}{10}.$

Similarly, in (B), we solve

$$z_1 + 4z_2 = 1$$
$$3z_1 + 2z_2 = 1$$

to obtain the coordinates of E: $z_1 = \frac{1}{5}$ and $z_2 = \frac{1}{5}$.

Thus, $v_1 = \dfrac{1}{x_1 + x_2} = \dfrac{1}{\frac{1}{10} + \frac{3}{10}} = \dfrac{10}{4} = \dfrac{5}{2}$, and $v_1 = \dfrac{1}{z_1 + z_2} = \dfrac{1}{\frac{1}{5} + \frac{1}{5}} = \dfrac{5}{2}$.

$$p_1 = v_1 x_1 = \frac{5}{2} \cdot \frac{1}{10} = \frac{1}{4} \qquad\qquad q_1 = v_1 z_1 = \frac{5}{2} \cdot \frac{1}{5} = \frac{1}{2}$$

$$p_2 = v_1 x_2 = \frac{5}{2} \cdot \frac{3}{10} = \frac{3}{4} \qquad\qquad q_2 = v_1 z_2 = \frac{5}{2} \cdot \frac{1}{5} = \frac{1}{2}$$

Therefore, $P^* = \begin{bmatrix} \frac{1}{4} & \frac{3}{4} \end{bmatrix}$, $Q^* = \begin{bmatrix} \frac{1}{2} \\ \frac{1}{2} \end{bmatrix}$, and the value of the game is given by

$$v = v_1 - 3 = \frac{5}{2} - 3 = -\frac{1}{2}.$$

9. First, we solve Problem 7(B). Introduce slack variables x_1 and x_2 to obtain:

$$z_1 + 4z_2 + x_1 \qquad\quad = 1$$
$$3z_1 + 2z_2 \qquad + x_2 \qquad = 1$$
$$-z_1 - z_2 \qquad\qquad + y = 0$$
$$z_1 \geqslant 0,\ z_2 \geqslant 0,\ r \geqslant 0,\ s \geqslant 0$$

$$
\begin{array}{ccccc}
z_1 & z_2 & x_1 & x_2 & y
\end{array}
$$

$$
\left[\begin{array}{ccccc|c}
1 & 4 & 1 & 0 & 0 & 1 \\
③ & 2 & 0 & 1 & 0 & 1 \\ \hline
-1 & -1 & 0 & 0 & 1 & 0
\end{array}\right]
\begin{array}{c} \frac{1}{1} \\ \frac{1}{3} \\ \\ \end{array}
\sim
\left[\begin{array}{ccccc|c}
1 & 4 & 1 & 0 & 0 & 1 \\
1 & \frac{2}{3} & 0 & \frac{1}{3} & 0 & \frac{1}{3} \\ \hline
-1 & -1 & 0 & 0 & 1 & 0
\end{array}\right]
$$

$$\frac{1}{3} R_2 \to R_2 \qquad\qquad\qquad\qquad R_1 + (-1)R_2 \to R_1 \text{ and } R_3 + R_2 \to R_3$$

$$
\sim
\left[\begin{array}{ccccc|c}
0 & ⑩{\over 3} & 1 & -\frac{1}{3} & 0 & \frac{2}{3} \\
1 & \frac{2}{3} & 0 & \frac{1}{3} & 0 & \frac{1}{3} \\ \hline
0 & -\frac{1}{3} & 0 & \frac{1}{3} & 1 & \frac{1}{3}
\end{array}\right]
\begin{array}{l}
\frac{2}{3} \div \frac{10}{3} = \frac{2}{10} \\[4pt]
\frac{1}{3} \div \frac{2}{3} = \frac{1}{2}
\end{array}
$$

$$\frac{3}{10} R_1 \to R_1$$

(continued)

$$
\sim
\begin{bmatrix}
0 & 1 & \frac{3}{10} & -\frac{1}{10} & 0 & \bigg| & \frac{1}{5} \\
1 & \frac{2}{3} & 0 & \frac{1}{3} & 0 & \bigg| & \frac{1}{3} \\
\hline
0 & -\frac{1}{3} & 0 & \frac{1}{3} & 1 & \bigg| & \frac{1}{3}
\end{bmatrix}
\quad
\sim
\quad
\begin{array}{ccccc}
z_1 & z_2 & x_1 & x_2 & y \\
\end{array}
\begin{bmatrix}
0 & 1 & \frac{3}{10} & -\frac{1}{10} & 0 & \bigg| & \frac{1}{5} \\
1 & 0 & -\frac{1}{5} & \frac{2}{5} & 0 & \bigg| & \frac{1}{5} \\
\hline
0 & 0 & \frac{1}{10} & \frac{3}{10} & 1 & \bigg| & \frac{2}{5}
\end{bmatrix}
$$

$$R_2 + \left(-\frac{2}{3}\right)R_1 \to R_2 \text{ and } R_3 + \frac{1}{3}R_1 \to R_3$$

Thus, $z_1 = \frac{1}{5}$, $z_2 = \frac{1}{5}$, $y_{max} = \frac{2}{5}$, $v_1 = \dfrac{1}{z_1 + z_2} = \dfrac{1}{\frac{1}{5} + \frac{1}{5}} = \frac{5}{2}$, and

$$q_1 = v_1 z_1 = \frac{5}{2} \cdot \frac{1}{5} = \frac{1}{2}, \quad q_2 = v_1 z_2 = \frac{5}{2} \cdot \frac{1}{5} = \frac{1}{2}.$$

The solution to the minimization problem (A) can be read from the bottom row of the final simplex tableau for the dual problem above. Thus, from the row

$$
\begin{array}{cccc}
 & x_1 & x_2 & \\
\end{array}
\begin{bmatrix}
0 & 0 & \frac{1}{10} & \frac{3}{10} & 1 & \bigg| & \frac{2}{5}
\end{bmatrix}
$$

we conclude that the solution is:

Min $y = x_1 + x_2 = \frac{2}{5}$ at $x_1 = \frac{1}{10}$, $x_2 = \frac{3}{10}$

Also,

$$p_1 = v_1 x_1 = \frac{5}{2}\left(\frac{1}{10}\right) = \frac{1}{4}$$
$$p_2 = v_1 x_2 = \frac{5}{2}\left(\frac{3}{10}\right) = \frac{3}{4}$$

Finally,

$$P^* = \begin{bmatrix} \frac{1}{4} & \frac{3}{4} \end{bmatrix}, \quad Q^* = \begin{bmatrix} \frac{1}{2} \\ \frac{1}{2} \end{bmatrix}, \quad \text{and} \quad v = \frac{5}{2} - 3 = -\frac{1}{2}.$$

10. $\begin{bmatrix} \boxed{-1} & \boxed{2} & \boxed{8} \\ \boxed{0} & \boxed{2} & \boxed{-4} \\ \boxed{0} & 1 & 3 \end{bmatrix}$ This game is strictly determined.

Also, $P^* = \begin{bmatrix} 0 & 0 & 1 \end{bmatrix}$, $Q^* = \begin{bmatrix} 1 \\ 0 \\ 0 \end{bmatrix}$, and the value of the game, v, equals 0.

11.
$$\begin{bmatrix} \boxed{0} & \boxed{3} & \enclose{circle}{-1} \\ -1 & \enclose{circle}{-2} & \boxed{1} \end{bmatrix}$$ This game is nonstrictly determined.

We obtain a positive payoff matrix by adding 3 to each payoff:

$$M_1 = \begin{bmatrix} 3 & 6 & 2 \\ 2 & 1 & 4 \end{bmatrix}$$

The linear programming problems corresponding to M_1 are as follows:

(A) Minimize $y = x_1 + x_2$

      Subject to $3x_1 + 2x_2 \geqslant 1$
                    $6x_1 + x_2 \geqslant 1$
                    $2x_1 + 4x_2 \geqslant 1$
                          $x_1, x_2 \geqslant 0$

(B) Maximize $y = z_1 + z_2 + z_3$

      Subject to $3z_1 + 6z_2 + 2z_3 \leqslant 1$
                    $2z_1 + z_2 + 4z_3 \leqslant 1$
                      $z_1, z_2, z_3 \geqslant 0$

Solve part (B) by using the simplex method. Introduce slack variables x_1 and x_2 to obtain:

$$3z_1 + 6z_2 + 2z_3 + x_1 \qquad\qquad = 1$$
$$2z_1 + z_2 + 4z_3 \qquad + x_2 \qquad = 1$$
$$-z_1 - z_2 - z_3 \qquad\qquad + y = 0$$
$$z_1, z_2, z_3 \geqslant 0, \ x_1, x_2 \geqslant 0$$

$$
\begin{array}{cccccc}
z_1 & z_2 & z_3 & x_1 & x_2 & y
\end{array}
$$

$$
\begin{bmatrix}
\enclose{circle}{3} & 6 & 2 & 1 & 0 & 0 & 1 \\
2 & 1 & 4 & 0 & 1 & 0 & 1 \\
\hline
-1 & -1 & -1 & 0 & 0 & 1 & 0
\end{bmatrix}
\begin{array}{l} \frac{1}{3} \\ \frac{1}{2} \end{array}
\sim
\begin{bmatrix}
1 & 2 & \frac{2}{3} & \frac{1}{3} & 0 & 0 & \frac{1}{3} \\
2 & 1 & 4 & 0 & 1 & 0 & 1 \\
\hline
-1 & -1 & -1 & 0 & 0 & 1 & 0
\end{bmatrix}
$$

$$\tfrac{1}{3}R_1 \to R_1 \qquad\qquad\qquad\qquad\qquad R_2 + (-2)R_1 \to R_2 \text{ and } R_3 + R_1 \to R_3$$

$$
\sim
\begin{bmatrix}
1 & 2 & \frac{2}{3} & \frac{1}{3} & 0 & 0 & \frac{1}{3} \\
0 & -3 & \enclose{circle}{\frac{8}{3}} & -\frac{2}{3} & 1 & 0 & \frac{1}{3} \\
\hline
0 & 1 & -\frac{1}{3} & \frac{1}{3} & 0 & 1 & \frac{1}{3}
\end{bmatrix}
\begin{array}{l} \frac{1}{3} \div \frac{2}{3} = \frac{1}{2} \\ \frac{1}{3} \div \frac{8}{3} = \frac{1}{8} \end{array}
$$

$$\tfrac{3}{8}R_2 \to R_2$$

(continued)

$$\sim \left[\begin{array}{cccccc|c} 1 & 2 & \frac{2}{3} & \frac{1}{3} & 0 & 0 & \frac{1}{3} \\ 0 & -\frac{9}{8} & 1 & -\frac{1}{4} & \frac{3}{8} & 0 & \frac{1}{8} \\ \hline 0 & 1 & -\frac{1}{3} & \frac{1}{3} & 0 & 1 & \frac{1}{3} \end{array}\right] \sim \begin{array}{c} \begin{array}{cccccc} z_1 & z_2 & z_3 & x_1 & x_2 & y \end{array} \\ \left[\begin{array}{cccccc|c} 1 & \frac{11}{4} & 0 & \frac{1}{2} & -\frac{1}{4} & 0 & \frac{1}{4} \\ 0 & -\frac{9}{8} & 1 & -\frac{1}{4} & \frac{3}{8} & 0 & \frac{1}{8} \\ \hline 0 & \frac{5}{8} & 0 & \frac{1}{4} & \frac{1}{8} & 1 & \frac{3}{8} \end{array}\right] \end{array}$$

$$R_1 + \left(-\frac{2}{3}\right)R_2 \to R_1 \text{ and } R_3 + \frac{1}{3}R_2 \to R_3$$

Thus, $z_1 = \frac{1}{4}$, $z_2 = 0$, $z_3 = \frac{1}{8}$, $y_{max} = \frac{3}{8}$, $v_1 = \dfrac{1}{\frac{1}{4} + 0 + \frac{1}{8}} = \frac{8}{3}$,

$q_1 = v_1 z_1 = \frac{8}{3} \cdot \frac{1}{4} = \frac{2}{3}$, $q_2 = v_1 z_2 = \frac{8}{3} \cdot 0 = 0$, $q_3 = v_1 z_3 = \frac{8}{3} \cdot \frac{1}{8} = \frac{1}{3}$.

Therefore, $Q^* = \begin{bmatrix} \frac{2}{3} \\ 0 \\ \frac{1}{3} \end{bmatrix}$ and $v = v_1 - 3 = \frac{8}{3} - 3 = -\frac{1}{3}$.

The solution to the minimization problem (A) can be read from the bottom row of the final simplex tableau for the dual problem above. Thus, from the row

$$\begin{array}{ccccc} & & & x_1 & x_2 \end{array}$$
$$\left[\begin{array}{ccccc|c} 0 & \frac{5}{8} & 0 & \frac{1}{4} & \frac{1}{8} & 1 & \frac{3}{8} \end{array}\right]$$

we conclude that the solution is:

$$\text{Min } y = x_1 + x_2 = \frac{3}{8} \text{ at } x_1 = \frac{1}{4}, \ x_2 = \frac{1}{8}$$

Now,

$$p_1 = v_1 x_1 = \frac{8}{3}\left(\frac{1}{4}\right) = \frac{2}{3}$$

$$p_2 = v_1 x_2 = \frac{8}{3}\left(\frac{1}{8}\right) = \frac{1}{3}$$

and

$$P^* = \begin{bmatrix} \frac{2}{3} & \frac{1}{3} \end{bmatrix}.$$

12.
$$\begin{bmatrix} -1 & 1 & \boxed{-2} \\ \boxed{0} & \boxed{-2} & \boxed{2} \\ \boxed{-3} & \boxed{2} & -1 \end{bmatrix}$$
This is a nonstrictly determined game.

We obtain the positive payoff matrix by adding 4 to each payoff:

$$M_1 = \begin{bmatrix} 3 & 5 & 2 \\ 4 & 2 & 6 \\ 1 & 6 & 5 \end{bmatrix}$$

The linear programming problems corresponding to M_1 are as follows:

(A) Minimize $y = x_1 + x_2 + x_3$

Subject to $3x_1 + 4x_2 + x_3 \geqslant 1$
$5x_1 + 2x_2 + 6x_3 \geqslant 1$
$2x_1 + 6x_2 + 3x_3 \geqslant 1$

$$x_1, \; x_2, \; x_3 \geqslant 0$$

(B) Maximize $y = z_1 + z_2 + z_3$

Subject to $3z_1 + 5z_2 + 2z_3 \leqslant 1$
$4z_1 + 2z_2 + 6z_3 \leqslant 1$
$z_1 + 6z_2 + 3z_3 \leqslant 1$

$$z_1, \; z_2, \; z_3 \geqslant 0$$

We use the simplex method to solve part (B). Introduce slack variables x_1, x_2, and x_3 to obtain:

$$3z_1 + 5z_2 + 2z_3 + x_1 = 1$$
$$4z_1 + 2z_2 + 6z_3 + x_2 = 1$$
$$z_1 + 6z_2 + 3z_3 + x_3 = 1$$
$$-z_1 - z_2 - z_3 + y = 0$$
$$z_1, \; z_2, \; z_3 \geqslant 0, \; x_1, \; x_2, \; x_3 \geqslant 0$$

$$\begin{array}{ccccccc}
z_1 & z_2 & z_3 & x_1 & x_2 & x_3 & y
\end{array}$$

$$\left[\begin{array}{ccccccc|c}
3 & 5 & 2 & 1 & 0 & 0 & 0 & 1 \\
④ & 2 & 6 & 0 & 1 & 0 & 0 & 1 \\
1 & 6 & 3 & 0 & 0 & 1 & 0 & 1 \\
\hline
-1 & -1 & -1 & 0 & 0 & 0 & 1 & 0
\end{array}\right]
\begin{array}{c} \frac{1}{3} \\ \frac{1}{4} \\ 1 \\ \\ \end{array}
\sim
\left[\begin{array}{ccccccc|c}
3 & 5 & 2 & 1 & 0 & 0 & 0 & 1 \\
1 & \frac{1}{2} & \frac{3}{2} & 0 & \frac{1}{4} & 0 & 0 & \frac{1}{4} \\
1 & 6 & 3 & 0 & 0 & 1 & 0 & 1 \\
\hline
-1 & -1 & -1 & 0 & 0 & 0 & 1 & 0
\end{array}\right]$$

$$\frac{1}{4}R_2 \to R_2$$

$$R_1 + (-3)R_2 \to R_1, \; R_3 + (-1)R_2 \to R_3$$
$$\text{and } R_4 + R_2 \to R_4$$

$$\sim
\left[\begin{array}{ccccccc|c}
0 & ⑦/₂ & -\frac{5}{2} & 1 & -\frac{3}{4} & 0 & 0 & \frac{1}{4} \\
0 & \frac{1}{2} & \frac{3}{2} & 0 & \frac{1}{4} & 0 & 0 & \frac{1}{4} \\
0 & \frac{11}{2} & \frac{3}{2} & 0 & -\frac{1}{4} & 1 & 0 & \frac{3}{4} \\
\hline
0 & -\frac{1}{2} & \frac{1}{2} & 0 & \frac{1}{4} & 0 & 1 & \frac{1}{4}
\end{array}\right]
\begin{array}{l}
\frac{1}{4} \div \frac{7}{2} = \frac{1}{14} \\
\frac{1}{4} \div \frac{1}{2} = \frac{1}{2} \\
\frac{3}{4} \div \frac{11}{2} = \frac{3}{22} \\
\\
\end{array}$$

$$\frac{2}{7}R_1 \to R_1$$

(continued)

$$\sim \begin{bmatrix} 0 & 1 & -\dfrac{5}{7} & \dfrac{2}{7} & -\dfrac{3}{14} & 0 & 0 & \bigg| & \dfrac{1}{14} \\ 1 & \dfrac{1}{2} & \dfrac{3}{2} & 0 & \dfrac{1}{4} & 0 & 0 & \bigg| & \dfrac{1}{4} \\ 0 & \dfrac{11}{2} & \dfrac{3}{2} & 0 & -\dfrac{1}{4} & 1 & 0 & \bigg| & \dfrac{3}{4} \\ \hline 0 & -\dfrac{1}{2} & \dfrac{1}{2} & 0 & \dfrac{1}{4} & 0 & 1 & \bigg| & \dfrac{1}{4} \end{bmatrix}$$

$$R_2 + \left(-\frac{1}{2}\right)R_1 \to R_2, \quad R_3 + \left(-\frac{11}{2}\right)R_1 \to R_3, \quad \text{and} \quad R_4 + \frac{1}{2}R_1 \to R_4$$

$$\begin{array}{ccccccc} z_1 & z_2 & z_3 & x_1 & x_2 & x_3 & y \end{array}$$

$$\sim \begin{bmatrix} 0 & 1 & -\dfrac{5}{7} & \dfrac{2}{7} & -\dfrac{3}{14} & 0 & 0 & \bigg| & \dfrac{1}{14} \\ 1 & 0 & \dfrac{13}{7} & -\dfrac{1}{7} & \dfrac{5}{14} & 0 & 0 & \bigg| & \dfrac{3}{14} \\ 0 & 0 & \dfrac{38}{7} & -\dfrac{11}{7} & \dfrac{13}{14} & 1 & 0 & \bigg| & \dfrac{5}{14} \\ \hline 0 & 0 & \dfrac{1}{7} & \dfrac{1}{7} & \dfrac{1}{7} & 0 & 1 & \bigg| & \dfrac{2}{7} \end{bmatrix}$$

Thus, $z_1 = \dfrac{3}{14}$, $z_2 = \dfrac{1}{14}$, $z_3 = 0$, and $y_{\max} = \dfrac{2}{7}$.

$$v_1 = \frac{1}{z_1 + z_2 + z_3} = \frac{1}{\dfrac{3}{14} + \dfrac{1}{14} + 0} = \frac{14}{4} = \frac{7}{2}. \quad \text{Therefore,}$$

$$q_1 = v_1 z_1 = \frac{7}{2} \cdot \frac{3}{14} = \frac{3}{4}, \quad q_2 = v_1 z_2 = \frac{7}{2} \cdot \frac{1}{14} = \frac{1}{4}, \quad q_3 = v_1 z_3 = \frac{7}{2} \cdot 0 = 0,$$

$$Q^* = \begin{bmatrix} \dfrac{3}{4} \\ \dfrac{1}{4} \\ 0 \end{bmatrix}, \quad \text{and} \quad v = v_1 - 4 = \frac{7}{2} - 4 = -\frac{1}{2}.$$

The solution to the minimization problem (A) can be read from the bottom row of the final simplex tableau for the dual problem above. Thus, from the row

$$\begin{array}{ccc} & x_1 & x_2 & x_3 \end{array}$$

$$\begin{bmatrix} 0 & 0 & \dfrac{1}{7} & \dfrac{1}{7} & \dfrac{1}{7} & 0 & 1 & \bigg| & \dfrac{2}{7} \end{bmatrix}$$

we conclude that the solution is:

$$\text{Min } y = x_1 + x_2 + x_3 = \frac{2}{7} \text{ at } x_1 = \frac{1}{7}, \ x_2 = \frac{1}{7}, \ x_3 = 0$$

Now,

$$p_1 = v_1 x_1 = \frac{7}{2}\left(\frac{1}{7}\right) = \frac{1}{2}$$

$$p_1 = v_1 x_2 = \frac{7}{2}\left(\frac{1}{7}\right) = \frac{1}{2}$$

$$p_3 = v_1 x_3 = \frac{7}{2}(0) = 0$$

and

$$P^* = \begin{bmatrix} \frac{1}{2} & \frac{1}{2} & 0 \end{bmatrix}.$$

APPENDIX A SPECIAL TOPICS

Things to remember:

1. DEFINITION OF a^n, where n is an integer and a is a real number:

(a) For n a positive integer,
$$a^n = a \cdot a \cdot \cdots \cdot a, \; n \text{ factors of } a.$$

(b) For $n = 0$,
$$a^0 = 1, \; a \neq 0, \; 0^0 \text{ is not defined.}$$

(c) For n a negative integer,
$$a^n = \frac{1}{a^{-n}}, \; a \neq 0.$$

[<u>Note</u>: If n is negative, then $-n$ is positive.]

2. PROPERTIES OF EXPONENTS

GIVEN: n and m are integers and a and b are real numbers.

(a) $a^m a^n = a^{m+n}$ $\qquad\qquad$ $a^8 a^{-3} = a^{8+(-3)} = a^5$

(b) $(a^n)^m = a^{mn}$ $\qquad\qquad$ $(a^{-2})^3 = a^{3(-2)} = a^{-6}$

(c) $(ab)^m = a^m b^m$ $\qquad\qquad$ $(ab)^{-2} = a^{-2} b^{-2}$

(d) $\left(\dfrac{a}{b}\right)^m = \dfrac{a^m}{b^m}, \; b \neq 0$ $\qquad\quad$ $\left(\dfrac{a}{b}\right)^5 = \dfrac{a^5}{b^5}$

(e) $\dfrac{a^m}{a^n} = a^{m-n} = \dfrac{1}{a^{n-m}}, \; a \neq 0$ $\qquad$ $\dfrac{a^{-3}}{a^7} = \dfrac{1}{a^{7-(-3)}} = \dfrac{1}{a^{10}}$

3. DEFINITION OF SQUARE ROOT

A number x is a SQUARE ROOT of the number y if $x^2 = y$.

Every positive real number has exactly two square roots, each the negative of the other.

The square root of 0 is 0.

Negative real numbers do not have real number square roots.

4. SQUARE ROOT NOTATION

For a a positive number:

$\sqrt{a}$ is the positive square root of a
$-\sqrt{a}$ is the negative square noot of a

Note: $\sqrt{-a}$ is not a real number.

5. PROPERTIES OF RADICALS

For a and b nonnegative real numbers:

(a) $\sqrt{a^2} = a$

(b) $\sqrt{a}\sqrt{b} = \sqrt{ab}$

(c) $\dfrac{\sqrt{a}}{\sqrt{b}} = \sqrt{\dfrac{a}{b}}$

6. DEFINITION OF THE SIMPLEST RADICAL FORM

An algebraic expression that contains square root radicals is in SIMPLEST RADICAL FORM if all three of the following conditions are satisfied:

(a) No radicand (the expression within the radical sign) when expressed in completely factored form contains a factor raised to a power greater than 1. ($\sqrt{x^3}$ violates this condition.)

(b) No radical appears in a denominator. ($3/\sqrt{5}$ violates this condition.)

(c) No fraction appears within a radical. ($\sqrt{2/3}$ violates this condition.)

---

1. $\quad 2x^{-9} = \dfrac{2}{x^9}$

3. $\quad \dfrac{3}{2w^{-7}} = \dfrac{3w^7}{2}$

5. $\quad 2x^{-8}x^5 = 2x^{-8+5}$
$$= 2x^{-3} = \dfrac{2}{x^3}$$

7. $\quad \dfrac{w^{-8}}{w^{-3}} = \dfrac{1}{w^{-3+8}} = \dfrac{1}{w^5}$

9. $\quad 5v^8v^{-8} = 5v^{8-8}$
$$= 5v^0$$
$$= 5 \cdot 1 = 5$$

11. $\quad (a^{-3})^2 = a^{-6} = \dfrac{1}{a^6}$

13. $(x^6y^{-3})^{-2} = x^{-12}y^6$

$\qquad = \dfrac{y^6}{x^{12}}$

[Note: $(-3)(-2) = 6$]

15. $\sqrt{x^2} = x$

17. $\sqrt{a^5} = \sqrt{a^4 \cdot a}$

$\qquad = \sqrt{a^4}\sqrt{a} = a^2\sqrt{a}$

19. $\sqrt{18x^4} = \sqrt{3^2 \cdot 2x^4} = \sqrt{3^2x^4}\sqrt{2}$

$\qquad\qquad = 3x^2\sqrt{2}$

21. $\dfrac{1}{\sqrt{m}} = \dfrac{1}{\sqrt{m}} \cdot \dfrac{\sqrt{m}}{\sqrt{m}} = \dfrac{\sqrt{m}}{m}$ Rationalizing

23. $\sqrt{\dfrac{2}{3}} = \dfrac{\sqrt{2}}{\sqrt{3}}$

$\qquad = \dfrac{\sqrt{2}}{\sqrt{3}} \cdot \dfrac{\sqrt{3}}{\sqrt{3}}$ Rationalizing

$\qquad = \dfrac{\sqrt{6}}{3}$

25. $\sqrt{\dfrac{2}{x}} = \dfrac{\sqrt{2}}{\sqrt{x}}$

$\qquad = \dfrac{\sqrt{2}}{\sqrt{x}} \cdot \dfrac{\sqrt{x}}{\sqrt{x}}$ Rationalizing

$\qquad = \dfrac{\sqrt{2x}}{x}$

27. $82,300,000,000 = 8.23 \times 10^{10}$

29. $0.783 = 7.83 \times 10^{-1}$

31. $0.000\ 034 = 3.4 \times 10^{-5}$

33. $(22 + 31)^0 = (53)^0 = 1$

35. $\dfrac{10^{-3} \cdot 10^4}{10^{-11} \cdot 10^{-2}} = \dfrac{10^{-3+4}}{10^{-11-2}} = \dfrac{10^1}{10^{-13}}$

$\qquad\qquad = 10^{1+13} = 10^{14}$

37. $(5x^2y^{-3})^{-2} = 5^{-2}x^{-4}y^6 = \dfrac{y^6}{5^2x^4}$

$\qquad\qquad = \dfrac{y^6}{25x^4}$

39. $\dfrac{8 \times 10^{-3}}{2 \times 10^{-5}} = \dfrac{8}{2} \cdot \dfrac{10^{-3}}{10^{-5}}$

$\qquad\qquad = 4 \times 10^{-3+5} = 4 \times 10^2$

41. $\dfrac{8x^{-3}y^{-1}}{6x^2y^{-4}} = \dfrac{4y^{-1+4}}{3x^{2+3}} = \dfrac{4y^3}{3x^5}$

43. $\left(\dfrac{6xy^{-2}}{3x^{-1}y^2}\right)^{-3} = \left(\dfrac{2x^{1+1}}{y^{2+2}}\right)^{-3} = \left(\dfrac{2x^2}{y^4}\right)^{-3}$

$\qquad\qquad = \dfrac{2^{-3}x^{-6}}{y^{-12}} = \dfrac{y^{12}}{2^3x^6}$ or $\dfrac{y^{12}}{8x^6}$

45. $\sqrt{18x^8y^5z^2} = \sqrt{3^2 \cdot 2(x^4)^2(y^2)^2yz^2}$

$\qquad\qquad = 3x^4y^2z\sqrt{2y}$

47. $\dfrac{12}{\sqrt{3x}} = \dfrac{12}{\sqrt{3x}} \cdot \dfrac{\sqrt{3x}}{\sqrt{3x}}$ Rationalizing

$\qquad = \dfrac{12\sqrt{3x}}{3x} = \dfrac{4\sqrt{3x}}{x}$

49. $\sqrt{\dfrac{6x}{7y}} = \dfrac{\sqrt{6x}}{\sqrt{7y}}$

$\qquad = \dfrac{\sqrt{6x}}{\sqrt{7y}} \cdot \dfrac{\sqrt{7y}}{\sqrt{7y}}$ Rationalizing

$\qquad = \dfrac{\sqrt{42xy}}{7y}$

51. $\sqrt{\dfrac{4a^3}{3b}} = \dfrac{2a\sqrt{a}}{\sqrt{3b}}$

$\qquad = \dfrac{2a\sqrt{a}}{\sqrt{3b}} \cdot \dfrac{\sqrt{3b}}{\sqrt{3b}}$ Rationalizing

$\qquad = \dfrac{2a\sqrt{3ab}}{3b}$

53. $\sqrt{18m^3n^4}\sqrt{2m^3n^2} = \sqrt{36m^6n^6}$

$\qquad = \sqrt{6^2(m^3)^2(n^3)^2}$

$\qquad = 6m^3n^3$

55. $\dfrac{\sqrt{4a^3}}{\sqrt{3b}} = \dfrac{2a\sqrt{a}}{\sqrt{3b}} = \dfrac{2a\sqrt{a}}{\sqrt{3b}} \cdot \dfrac{\sqrt{3b}}{\sqrt{3b}} = \dfrac{2a\sqrt{3ab}}{3b}$

57. $\dfrac{9{,}600{,}000{,}000}{(1{,}600{,}000)(0.000\ 000\ 25)} = \dfrac{9.6 \times 10^9}{(1.6 \cdot 10^6)(2.5 \cdot 10^{-7})} = \dfrac{9.6 \times 10^9}{1.6(2.5 \cdot 10^{6-7})}$

$\qquad\qquad = \dfrac{9.6 \times 10^9}{4.0 \times 10^{-1}} = 2.4 \times 10^{9+1} = 2.4 \times 10^{10}$

$\qquad\qquad = 24{,}000{,}000{,}000$

59. $\dfrac{(1{,}250{,}000)(0.000\ 38)}{0.0423} = \dfrac{(1.25 \times 10^6)(3.8 \times 10^{-4})}{4.23 \times 10^{-2}} = \dfrac{1.25(3.8 \times 10^{6-4})}{4.23 \times 10^{-2}}$

$\qquad\qquad \approx 1.1 \times 10^4 = 11{,}000$

61. $\left[\left(\dfrac{x^{-2}y^3t}{x^{-3}y^{-2}t^2}\right)^2\right]^{-1} = \left[\left(\dfrac{x^{-2+3}y^{3+2}}{t^{2-1}}\right)^2\right]^{-1} = \left[\left(\dfrac{xy^5}{t}\right)^2\right]^{-1} = \left[\dfrac{x^2y^{10}}{t^2}\right]^{-1}$

$\qquad = \dfrac{x^{-2}y^{-10}}{t^{-2}} = \dfrac{t^2}{x^2y^{10}}$

63. $\left(\dfrac{2^2x^2y^0}{8x^{-1}}\right)^{-2}\left(\dfrac{x^{-3}}{x^{-5}}\right)^3 = \left(\dfrac{2^2x^{2+1}}{2^3}\right)^{-2}(x^{-3+5})^3 = \left(\dfrac{x^3}{2^{3-2}}\right)^{-2}(x^2)^3 = \left(\dfrac{x^3}{2}\right)^{-2}x^6$

$\qquad = \dfrac{x^{-6}}{2^{-2}} \cdot \dfrac{x^6}{1} = \dfrac{x^{-6+6}}{2^{-2}} = 2^2x^0 = 2^2 = 4$

65. $\dfrac{\sqrt{2x}\sqrt{5}}{\sqrt{20x}} = \dfrac{\sqrt{2x}\sqrt{5}}{\sqrt{2 \cdot 5 \cdot 2x}} = \dfrac{\sqrt{2x}\sqrt{5}}{\sqrt{2}\sqrt{5}\sqrt{2x}} = \dfrac{1}{\sqrt{2}} = \dfrac{1}{\sqrt{2}} \cdot \dfrac{\sqrt{2}}{\sqrt{2}}$ Rationalizing

$\qquad\qquad = \dfrac{\sqrt{2}}{2}$

67. $\dfrac{2}{\sqrt{x-2}} = \dfrac{2}{\sqrt{x-2}} \cdot \dfrac{\sqrt{x-2}}{\sqrt{x-2}}$ Rationalizing

$\qquad = \dfrac{2\sqrt{x-2}}{x-2}$

Things to remember:

1. A sequence of numbers a_1, a_2, a_3, ..., a_n, ..., is called an ARITHMETIC PROGRESSION if there is a constant d, called the COMMON DIFFERENCE, such that

$$a_n - a_{n-1} = d,$$

that is,

$$a_n = a_{n-1} + d$$

for all $n > 1$.

2. If a_1, a_2, a_3, ..., a_n, ..., is an arithmetic progression with common difference d, then

$$a_n = a_1 + (n - 1)d$$

for all $n > 1$.

3. The sum S_n of the first n terms of an arithmetic progression a_1, a_2, a_3, ..., a_n, ..., with common difference d, is given by

(a) $S_n = \frac{n}{2}[2a_1 + (n - 1)d]$

or by

(b) $S_n = \frac{n}{2}(a_1 + a_n)$

---

1. **(A)** is an arithmetic progression; $a_2 - a_1 = a_3 - a_2 = 3$. Thus, $d = 3$, $a_4 = 14$, and $a_5 = 17$.

(B) is not an arithmetic progression, since

$$a_2 - a_1 = 8 - 4 = 4 \neq a_3 - a_2 = 16 - 8 = 8$$

(C) is not an arithmetic progression, since

$$-4 - (-2) = -2 \neq -8 - (-4) = -4$$

(D) is an arithmetic progression; $a_2 - a_1 = a_3 - a_2 = -10$. Thus, $d = -10$, $a_4 = -22$, and $a_5 = -32$.

3. $a_2 = a_1 + d = 7 + 4 = 11$
$a_3 = a_2 + d = 11 + 4 = 15$ (using $\underline{1}$)

5. $a_{21} = a_1 + (21 - 1)d = 2 + 20 \cdot 4 = 82$ (using $\underline{2}$)

$S_{31} = \dfrac{31}{2}[2a_1 + (31 - 1)d] = \dfrac{31}{2}[2 \cdot 2 + 30 \cdot 4] = \dfrac{31}{2} \cdot 124 = 1922$ [using $\underline{3}(a)$]

7. Using $\underline{3}(b)$, $S_{20} = \dfrac{20}{2}(a_1 + a_{20}) = 10(18 + 75) = 930$

9. $f(1) = -1$, $f(2) = 1$, $f(3) = 3$, ... This is an arithmetic progression with $a_1 = -1$, $d = 2$. Thus, using $\underline{3}(a)$,

$f(1) + f(2) + f(3) + \cdots + f(50) = \dfrac{50}{2}[2(-1) + 49 \cdot 2] = 25 \cdot 96 = 2400$

11. Let $a_1 = 13$, $d = 2$. Then, using $\underline{2}$, we can find n,

$$67 = 13 + (n - 1)2 \quad \text{or} \quad 2(n - 1) = 54$$
$$n - 1 = 27$$
$$n = 28$$

Therefore, using $\underline{3}(b)$, $S_{28} = \dfrac{28}{2}[13 + 67] = 14 \cdot 80 = 1120$

13. Consider the arithmetic progression with $a_1 = 1$, $d = 2$. This progression is the sequence of odd positive integers. Now, using $\underline{3}(a)$, the sum of the first n odd positive integers is:

$S_n = \dfrac{n}{2}[2 \cdot 1 + (n - 1)2] = \dfrac{n}{2}(2 + 2n - 2) = \dfrac{n}{2} \cdot 2n = n^2$

15. The yearly salaries from Firm A are: \$24,000, \$24,900, \$25,800, ..., an arithmetic progression with $a_1 = 24,000$ and $d = 900$. Thus, in ten years Firm A will pay

$S_{10} = \dfrac{10}{2}[2(24,000) + 9(900)] = 5(56,100) = \$280,500$

The salaries from Firm B are: \$22,000, \$23,300, \$24,600, ..., an arithmetic progression with $a_1 = 22,000$ and $d = 1300$. Thus, in ten years Firm B will pay

$S_{10} = \dfrac{10}{2}[2(22,000) + 9(1300)] = 5(55,700) = \$278,500$

17. Consider the time line:

The total cost of the loan is: $2 + 4 + 6 + \cdots + 46 + 48$. The terms form an arithmetic progression with $n = 24$, $a_1 = 2$, and $a_{24} = 48$. Thus, using $\underline{3}(b)$,

$S_{24} = \dfrac{24}{2}(2 + 48) = 24 \cdot 25 = \$600$

Things to remember:

<u>1.</u> A sequence of numbers a_1, a_2, a_3, ..., a_n, ...,
is called a GEOMETRIC PROGRESSION if there exists
a nonzero constant r, called the COMMON RATIO,
such that

$$\frac{a_n}{a_{n-1}} = r$$

that is,

$$a_n = ra_{n-1}$$

for all $n > 1$.

<u>2.</u> If a_1, a_2, a_3, ..., a_n, ..., is a geometric pro-
gression with common ratio r, then

$$a_n = a_1 r^{n-1}$$

for all $n > 1$.

<u>3.</u> The sum S_n of the first n terms of a geometric
progression a_1, a_2, a_3, ..., a_n, ..., with common
ratio r, is given by:

(a) $S_n = \dfrac{a_1(r^n - 1)}{r - 1}$, $r \neq 1$,

or by

(b) $S_n = \dfrac{ra_n - a_1}{r - 1}$, $r \neq 1$.

<u>4.</u> If a_1, a_2, a_3, ..., a_n, ..., is a geometric pro-
gression with common ratio r having the property
$|r| < 1$, then $S_\infty = \lim\limits_{n \to \infty} S_n$ exists and is given by:

$$S_\infty = \frac{a_1}{1 - r}, \quad |r| < 1.$$

---

1. (A) is a geometric progression; $\dfrac{a_2}{a_1} = \dfrac{a_3}{a_2} = -2$. Thus, $r = -2$, $a_4 = -8$,
$a_5 = 16$.

(B) is not a geometric progresion, since

$$\frac{a_2}{a_1} = \frac{6}{7} \neq \frac{a_3}{a_2} = \frac{5}{6}$$

(C) is a geometric progression; $\dfrac{a_2}{a_1} = \dfrac{a_3}{a_2} = \dfrac{1}{2}$. Thus, $r = \dfrac{1}{2}$, $a_4 = \dfrac{1}{4}$, $a_5 = \dfrac{1}{8}$.

(D) is not a geometric progression, since

$$\frac{a_2}{a_1} = \frac{2/3}{1/2} = \frac{4}{3} \neq \frac{a_3}{a_2} = \frac{3/4}{2/3} = \frac{9}{8}$$

3. $a_2 = a_1 r = 3(-2) = -6$
   $a_3 = a_2 r = -6(-2) = 12$
   $a_4 = a_3 r = 12(-2) = -24$ (using 1)

5. Using 3(b), $S_7 = \dfrac{-3 \cdot 729 - 1}{-3 - 1} = \dfrac{-2186}{-4} = 546.5$

7. Using 2, $a_{10} = 100(1.08)^9 = 199.90$

9. Using 2, $200 = 100r^8$. Thus, $r^8 = 2$ and $r = \sqrt[8]{2} \approx 1.09$.

11. Using 3(a), $S_{10} = \dfrac{500[(0.6)^{10} - 1]}{0.6 - 1} \approx 1242$

$$S_\infty = \frac{500}{1 - 0.6} = 1250$$

13. (A) $2 + 4 + 8 + \cdots$. Since $r = \dfrac{4}{2} = \dfrac{8}{4} = \cdots = 2$ and $|2| = 2 > 1$, the
    sum does not exist.

    (B) $2, -\dfrac{1}{2}, \dfrac{1}{8}, \cdots$. In this case, $r = \dfrac{-\frac{1}{2}}{2} = \dfrac{\frac{1}{8}}{-\frac{1}{2}} = \cdots = -\dfrac{1}{4}$. Since
    $|r| < 1$,

$$S_\infty = \frac{2}{1 - \left(-\frac{1}{4}\right)} = \frac{2}{\frac{5}{4}} = \frac{8}{5} = 1.6$$

15. $f(1) = \dfrac{1}{2}$, $f(2) = \left(\dfrac{1}{2}\right)^2 = \dfrac{1}{4}$, $f(3) = \left(\dfrac{1}{2}\right)^3 = \dfrac{1}{8}$, $\cdots$. This is a geometric

    progression with $a_1 = \dfrac{1}{2}$ and $r = \dfrac{1}{2}$. Thus, using 3(a),

$$f(1) + f(2) + \cdots + f(10) = S_{10} = \frac{\frac{1}{2}\left[\left(\frac{1}{2}\right)^{10} - 1\right]}{\frac{1}{2} - 1} \approx 0.999$$

17. This is a geometric progression with $a_1 = 3{,}500{,}000$ and $r = 0.7$.
    Thus, using 4,

$$S_\infty = \frac{3{,}500{,}000}{1 - 0.7} \approx \$11{,}670{,}000$$

19. This is a geometric progression with $a_1 = 20{,}000$ and $r = 1.05$. Using 2
    and 3(a), respectively,

$$a_{10} = 20{,}000(1.05)^9 \approx \$31{,}027$$

$$S_{10} = \frac{20{,}000[(1.05)^{10} - 1]}{1.05 - 1} \approx \$251{,}600$$

Things to remember:

<u>1</u>. If n is a positive integer, then n FACTORIAL, denoted $n!$, is the product of the integers from 1 to n; that is,

$$n! = n \cdot (n - 1) \cdot \cdots \cdot 3 \cdot 2 \cdot 1$$

Also, $0! = 1$.

<u>2</u>. If n and r are nonnegative integers and $r \leqslant n$, then,

$$C_{n,r} = \frac{n!}{r!\,(n - r)!}.$$

<u>3</u>. BINOMIAL FORMULA: For all positive integers n,

$$(a + b)^n = C_{n,0}\,a^n + C_{n,1}\,a^{n-1}b + C_{n,2}\,a^{n-2}b^2$$
$$+ \cdots + C_{n,n-1}\,ab^{n-1} + C_{n,n}\,b^n.$$

---

1. $6! = 6 \cdot 5 \cdot 4 \cdot 3 \cdot 2 \cdot 1 = 720$

3. $\dfrac{10!}{9!} = \dfrac{10 \cdot 9!}{9!} = 10$

5. $\dfrac{12!}{9!} = \dfrac{12 \cdot 11 \cdot 10 \cdot 9!}{9!} = 1320$

7. $\dfrac{5!}{2!\,3!} = \dfrac{5 \cdot 4 \cdot 3!}{2 \cdot 1 \cdot 3!} = 10$

9. $\dfrac{6!}{5!\,(6 - 5)!} = \dfrac{6 \cdot 5!}{5!\,1!} = 6$

11. $\dfrac{20!}{3!\,17!} = \dfrac{20 \cdot 19 \cdot 18 \cdot 17!}{3!\,17!}$

$$= \dfrac{20 \cdot 19 \cdot 18}{3 \cdot 2 \cdot 1} = 1140$$

13. $C_{5,3} = \dfrac{5!}{3!\,(5 - 3)!} = \dfrac{5!}{3!\,2!} = 10$ (see Problem 7)

15. $C_{6,5} = \dfrac{6!}{5!\,(6 - 5)!}$

$\qquad = 6$ (see Problem 9)

17. $C_{5,0} = \dfrac{5!}{0!\,(5 - 0)!}$

$\qquad = \dfrac{5!}{1 \cdot 5!} = 1$

19. $C_{18,15} = \dfrac{18!}{15!\,(18 - 15)!} = \dfrac{18 \cdot 17 \cdot 16 \cdot 15!}{15!\,3!} = \dfrac{18 \cdot 17 \cdot 16}{3 \cdot 2 \cdot 1} = 816$

21. Using <u>3</u>,

$$(a + b)^4 = C_{4,0}\,a^4 + C_{4,1}\,a^3b + C_{4,2}\,a^2b^2 + C_{4,3}\,ab^3 + C_{4,4}\,b^4$$

$$= a^4 + 4a^3b + 6a^2b^2 + 4ab^3 + b^4$$

23. Using $\underline{3}$, $(x - 1)^6 = [x + (-1)]^6$

$$= C_{6,0}\, x^6 + C_{6,1}\, x^5(-1) + C_{6,2}\, x^4(-1)^2 + C_{6,3}\, x^3(-1)^3$$
$$+ C_{6,4}\, x^2(-1)^4 + C_{6,5}\, x(-1)^5 + C_{6,6}\, (-1)^6$$
$$= x^6 - 6x^5 + 15x^4 - 20x^3 + 15x^2 - 6x + 1$$

25. $(2a - b)^5 = [2a + (-b)]^5$

$$= C_{5,0}\, (2a)^5 + C_{5,1}\, (2a)^4(-b) + C_{5,2}\, (2a)^3(-b)^2 + C_{5,3}\, (2a)^2(-b)^3$$
$$+ C_{5,4}\, (2a)(-b)^4 + C_{5,5}\, (-b)^5$$
$$= 32a^5 - 80a^4b + 80a^3b^2 - 40a^2b^3 + 10ab^4 - b^5$$

27. The fifth term in the expansion of $(x - 1)^{18}$ is:

$$C_{18,4}\, x^{14}(-1)^4 = \frac{18 \cdot 17 \cdot 16 \cdot 15}{4 \cdot 3 \cdot 2 \cdot 1}\, x^{14} = 3060x^{14}$$

29. The seventh term in the expansion of $(p + q)^{15}$ is:

$$C_{15,6}\, p^9q^6 = \frac{15 \cdot 14 \cdot 13 \cdot 12 \cdot 11 \cdot 10}{6 \cdot 5 \cdot 4 \cdot 3 \cdot 2 \cdot 1}\, p^9q^6 = 5005p^9q^6$$

31. The eleventh term in the expansion of $(2x + y)^{12}$ is:

$$C_{12,10}\, (2x)^2y^{10} = \frac{12 \cdot 11}{2 \cdot 1}\, 4x^2y^{10} = 264x^2y^{10}$$

33. $C_{n,0} = \dfrac{n!}{0!\,(n - 0)!} = \dfrac{n!}{1 \cdot n!} = 1 \qquad C_{n,n} = \dfrac{n!}{n!\,(n - n)!} = \dfrac{n!}{n!\,0!} = 1$

35. The next two rows are:

| 1 | 5 | 10 | 10 | 5 | 1 |

and

| 1 | 6 | 15 | 20 | 15 | 6 | 1, |

respectively. These are the coefficients in the binomial expansions of $(a + b)^5$ and $(a + b)^6$.

1302 Heights Blvd.
1050 Quitman

The Tech-Savvy English Classroom

Sara B. Kajder

Stenhouse Publishers
Portland, Maine

Stenhouse Publishers
www.stenhouse.com

Credits

Page 131: Adapted with permission from "Now That You Know the Basics—Rubrics to Guide Professional Technology Development: Part 1," *Learning & Leading with Technology,* Vol. 28 no. 4, 10–13, 49, copyright © 2000, ISTE (International Society for Technology in Education), 800.336.5191 (U.S. & Canada) or 541.302.3777 (Int'l), iste@iste.org, www.iste.org. All rights reserved. Permission does not constitute an endorsement by ISTE.

Page 134: Reprinted with permission from *National Educational Technology Standards for Students: Connecting Curriculum and Technology,* copyright © 2000, ISTE (International Society for Technology in Education), 800.336.5191 (U.S. & Canada) or 541.302.3777 (Int'l), iste@iste.org, www.iste.org. All rights reserved. Permission does not constitute an endorsement by ISTE. For more information about the NETS Project, contact Lajeane Thomas, Director, NETS Project, 318.257.3923, lthomas@latech.edu.

Page 135: Reprinted with permission from *National Educational Technology Standards for Teachers: Preparing Teachers to Use Technology,* copyright © 2002, ISTE (International Society for Technology in Education), 800.336.5191 (U.S. & Canada) or 541.302.3777 (Int'l), iste@iste.org, www.iste.org. All rights reserved. Permission does not constitute an endorsement by ISTE. For more information about the NETS Project, contact Lajeane Thomas, Director, NETS Project, 318.257.3923, lthomas@latech.edu.

Library of Congress Cataloging-in-Publication Data
Kajder, Sara B., 1975–
    The tech-savvy English classroom / Sara B. Kajder
    p. cm.
    Includes bibliographical references and index.
    ISBN 1-57110-361-9 (alk. paper)
    1. Language arts (Secondary)—Computer-assisted instruction. 2. Educational technology. 3. Information technology. 4. Internet in education. I. Title.
LB1631.K23 2003
428'.0071'2—dc21   2002191215

Cover design by Diana Coe
Cover image from Eyewire/Getting Images

Manufactured in the United States of America on acid-free paper
09 08 07 06 05 04 03 9 8 7 6 5 4 3 2 1

To Phyllis Vestal, the teacher who taught me to ask the big questions and not fear to take on the impossible, learning and laughing throughout the journey.

Tell me and I forget. Show me and I remember. Involve me and I understand.
—Chinese proverb

Every truth has four corners: as a teacher I give you one corner, and it is for you to find the other three.
—Confucius

Contents

Preface

*T*he *Tech-Savvy English Classroom* works to address the serious needs of secondary English teachers who possess the broadest possible range of both technology skill and access to resources. This book is designed to impact the teaching of both the English teacher who has one, nonnetworked, outdated computer in her classroom and the English teacher who is already utilizing networked computers and peripherals with students on a daily basis. It also is a book that addresses the concerns of the teacher who feels that embracing technology in the English classroom leads to the demise of the printed text.

However, this is not a text meant to overpower you with technical jargon. Nor is it a text that will train you in using software products. Instead, the aim is to consider the power that the right technology for a given task can have as a tool in the hands of student learners in the English classroom. We will consider teaching and learning strategies that use several technologies as tools, not how to execute commands in PowerPoint.

This isn't a static text; it is meant to challenge you to continually rethink and grow, no matter your starting point as a technology user or a teacher. This text aims at establishing a space for you to think about your classroom philosophies and practices while doubly acting as a catalyst challenging you to sample new strategies and ways of thinking. It is my hope that you transform the ideas and strategies so that they utilize your resources to richly impact the students in your classrooms.

Lastly, this text is accompanied by a companion Web site, http://www.techsavvyenglish.com, which I maintain as a place for our continued discussion and the sharing of additional strategies and ideas. As the technologies that fill our classrooms continually change and develop, this Web site will allow us to maintain what is "cutting edge" while the philosophies and dialogues in the text will continually root our thinking about technologies as teachers, learners, and users.

Acknowledgments

Thank you to Bill Varner, who saw something in my work and, as a result, inspired and drove the writing of this book.

My students are and will continue to be the center of my work. I am continually asked, Why do you teach? They are each my answer and celebration.

Kathryn Lee started much of this journey by offering a teaching strategy and giving me the space to experiment. Thank you for that spark of inspiration and for believing so strongly in the work that I do.

I have had the privilege of working with so many gifted teachers. Thank you to Phyllis Lucas, who challenged me to teach before I had any inkling of what that could mean. Thank you to Karen Sinning, whose inspiring example and mentoring taught me where to start. Thank you to Kristin Lawrence Shapira, Meredith Jeffcoat Mirkow, and Janelle Keefer for the endless discussions about what really matters in our classrooms. Thank you to the Humanities 8 team (Brad Goldberg, Kathryn Lee, Kristin Lawrence, James Dempsey, Ed O'Neil) for creating a space and a community in which I discovered how exhilarating and empowering it can be to keep learning. We were an incredible team. Estelene Boratenski, Debbie Wilchek, Judy Pearson, Mary Wagner, Carole Goodman, Chris Berry, Sarah Menke-Fish, Rae White—thank you for expecting so much, challenging my thinking, and allowing me room and space to grow. Thank you, Dr. Robyn Jackson, for your courage, your insight, and teaching me to "balance"; I'm working on it. Steve Bedford—thank you for teaching me about what leadership actually means. Dr. Glen Bull—thank you for "kicking it up a notch."

Thank you to my family—Powells and Kajders—for your continuous love and support. I am grateful to my mother for her example and compassion, and for teaching me to find and listen to the voices of my students. My father continually fed my love of books and always set the bar high. My brother, Jim, addressed each pesky "techie question," listened, and continually kept me laughing. You are my home.

Finally, thank you to my husband, Michael. You make all that I do possible. Thank you for anchoring me in what is real.

Introduction

I am continually struck by the emerging and fundamentally essential role that technology plays in both the culture of my classroom and my teaching. From my classroom space to my daily practices as an English teacher, technology permeates my daily work. Take this morning as an example. As I unlocked my classroom door at 6:15 A.M., my briefcase was filled with three books and my two most essential technology tools: my laptop computer and a handheld personal computer (PC). I no longer precariously juggle awkward, overstuffed folders of student work in my arms. Instead, every submission is downloaded from the class digital drop box onto a 32-megabyte chip attached conveniently to my keychain. Once in the classroom, I dodge past the overhead projector that houses the department's coveted LCD projector. When the equipment is available, I share compelling texts, lecture notes, video clips, images, and essential Web sites with my students. I navigate my way to the sole classroom computer, which sits in an accessible corner of the room. I use the opening minutes of the morning to check both my in-school e-mail account and the discussion boards that I maintain for each class on our class Web sites. After calling up any files that I'll need for the day's lessons and updating the class Web sites with homework assignments and .pdf files of notes and handouts, I check online grade and attendance records to plan the student conferences and dialogues that will occur throughout the teaching day. Finally, I turn on the classroom television for the daily live broadcast of announcements.

It's crucial to maintain a sense of balance, noting that my teaching has not always been so technology-laden. Technology infuses my English classroom in dynamic and dramatic ways, all of which would not have been found in my teaching practices and philosophy even three years ago. What changed? What led to such a transformation? It certainly wasn't the availability of resources. I teach in a highly transitory urban-suburban district that serves over 125,000 students representing over 125 different countries and nationalities. Here, there simply isn't enough to go around, and a school is essentially forgotten once it's been "wired" and provided with enough computers to justify the network. The equipment in my classroom is the result of abundant grant writing and supplementing that I do out of my own resources and salary. It certainly wasn't the availability of staff development and training. Instruction-focused training was only found out of district, at state and national conferences, or within the pages of highly coveted journals and books, or in dialogues with colleagues both online and offline. No, the catalyst wasn't the system. It was simply our most essential and fundamental asset. What stimulated the change was the students who filled and continue to enter my classroom each semester.

Not to sound clichéd, but middle and high school students *are* remarkably different now from those who passed through our doors even five years ago. Labeled the "net generation," these students have grown up in a world where computers are always present. An ever-increasing number of them are gaining net access, and most possess some degree of fluency with the digital media—an ability that both excites and frightens teachers who are trying to integrate technology into classroom instruction. This is a generation that is used to tremendous visual stimulus and interactivity when it comes to working with information.

My English classes have always had a constructivist, active foundation. I integrate content standards and acknowledge the continual county, state, and national assessments that keep us "accountable." However, I found that this still wasn't reaching my most needy students. These students weren't learning, and even more troubling was their complete lack of motivation when it came to school.

Two years ago, as I worked to facilitate student learning within a research project, something began to change. I began to recognize that my students no longer saw or appreciated paper as the dominant medium for accessing information. Instead of limiting ourselves to using the text resources in our outdated media center, we went online. I devised a very basic WebQuest, which only came to fruition as a result of hours of assistance from a student who was a master in Web design. We fused the core elements of my already constructivist, problem-based assignment with the dynamic Web sites that held current, compelling data. Students were hooked. Those who had barely lifted their heads from their desks all semester were eagerly working both during the class periods and during optional lunchtime and after-school lab sessions. I knew that I was onto something—and so began the journey that this book encapsulates and extends.

As I began to seek out additional resources and training for meaningfully integrating technology into my classroom teaching, I quickly hit a dead end. My district provided very little training, all of which was focused on software rather than on useful teaching and learning strategies. Very few colleagues had taken this leap, and I instantly felt isolated by a digital divide that had little to do with hardware and much to do with philosophy and support. I actively sought out "digital" colleagues who shared in virtual chats. I attended an extraordinary training program of the Maryland Technology Academy, a partnership between Johns Hopkins University, Towson University, and the Maryland State Department of Education. I read voraciously, never finding a text that emphasized teaching strategies but absorbing what I could about HTML, software programs, and code so that I'd understand what tools would be the most powerful in the hands of my student learners.

The most powerful and essential asset in this journey continues to be my students. Not only do they intuitively embrace the technology I bring into the classroom, but they possess a keen visual eye and a storehouse of knowledge when it comes to the inner workings of software and hardware. It is then up to me as teacher to transform that knowledge into a meaningful classroom experience that takes even my most tech-savvy student further than he or she ever anticipated in understanding and learning.

1 Starting Points

Technology does not necessarily improve education. Take a simple innovation like the pencil: One can use it to write a superlative essay, to drum away the time, or to poke out someone's eye.

—Howard Gardner

What is valuable about what we do is what happens when we read books.

—Richard Lanham

What Is Technology?

According to the *American Heritage Dictionary,* the word *technology* comes from the Greek word *tekhnologiā,* "the systematic treatment of an art or a craft." The further Greek root is *tekhnē,* "skill." To integrate technology meaningfully into the English classroom is just that: a skill, an art, a craft. "Technology" has become the term that we casually use to refer to software, hardware, protocol, or something too technical to name. It's the "hot new thing" that we usually don't yet possess. The haves and have-nots are separated as much by tangible equipment as by the differences in the language that each commands. To be a "techie," you need command over your bits and bytes, RAM and ROM, zips and burners. Dropping terms like these isn't what this book is about, though there is an extensive glossary provided on the companion Web site for those moments when you want to indulge in a little "techno-speak." What is essential is that you understand how we're using the term "technology" as English teachers. Simply defined, technology in the English classroom includes all the tools available in your classroom that when applied with skill can lead you to enrich, extend, and empower student understanding. We will celebrate effective and creative ways of using your computers and "smartboards" as much as we will celebrate how you can use books and pens, all technologies that compose a savvy English teacher's toolkit.

Treacherous Assumptions

I firmly believe that technologies can be used as effective tools when paired with the right task and users who have been trained to use the tools mindfully, effectively, and efficiently. This isn't an earth-shattering idea, and yet in public education this statement simply isn't reflected in what we've spent tremendous resources and time building.

Computers and related technologies have been creeping their way into classrooms for over a decade. School systems across the country have rushed to get classrooms wired and equipment running. However, in the process of getting connected, the choice was made to invest in equipment, not in the human infrastructure within a school. Somewhere, the assumption was made that teachers would instinctively know how to make use of the technologies that are introduced into their classrooms. Again, this isn't an earth-shattering idea. It's one that is painfully obvious to classroom teachers who were "wired" and now are "tired" from years of trying to make sense out of computer technologies on their own. Not only should teachers learn which buttons to click and which menus to open and how to plug in this and compress that. They should also come to see the impact that the resulting interactive multimedia presentations can have on students, and on their role as teachers, and indeed on the nature of their own instructional approach (Golub 1999b).

A high school English teacher came to me the other day, brimming with excitement about the newly "refreshed" equipment that the district was supplying her building. They were to receive three hundred new Pentium IV PCs complete with the latest operating system, MS Office package, and peripherals, all ready to tie into a newer, faster Internet connection. It took only one question for me to pop her bubble: "So, when will you be attending training?" I was met with silence, not surprisingly. What followed was a dialogue where she began to consider the impact that these technologies *couldn't* have, given that the faculty was not only low-skilled but disillusioned from limping along through five years of barely functioning equipment. Instead of empowering teachers, this technology would result in another add-on requiring a serious time commitment when time was already a precious commodity.

I know this place well. Missing from my teacher education program had been any course, unit, or activity challenging me to consider how I'd address technology in the context of a middle or high school English classroom. Missing from my first years of teaching was job-embedded staff development that addressed technology beyond the staff-only e-mail program or the mandatory electronic gradebook. How many schools, even those who have the "blessing" of exciting equipment, pair that with teacher training that focuses on how to use the new tools to enhance and extend student learning? How many teachers have learned how to design and direct technology-infused classroom activities in a challenging and engaging way? We aren't using technology to work smarter. We're just working much, much harder.

A second treacherous assumption holds that because the technology is made available, it must be used. This is the "technology for technology's sake" or "if you build it, they will come" line of thinking. I've worked in schools where the expectation has been that computer labs needed to be utilized every period and that a unit that wasn't tied to our technological resources was weak. These same schools would scrimp in order to buy the latest and greatest equipment simply because it was made available and because it looked great in the Board of Education reports. Technology planning with student and faculty learning at its center wasn't a reality. Again, the loss was time, learning, and ultimately opportunities for our students and colleagues to grow as thinkers, writers, and users of technology.

This leads us to the most treacherous assumption of all—"the software will do it." Especially given the range in teacher comfort and skill levels with computing technologies, it's easy to rely on the computer to walk the student through the learning task. We limit thinking by sitting students in front of drill-and-practice software or by pushing them to create multimedia presentations to the point of "PowerPointlessness" (McKenzie 2000).

This is a safe zone—comfortably using computers as word processors or repackaging the tried-and-true lessons closest to the front of the file cabinet. This is where I started, seeing the computer as a means of energizing my class lectures or as an oversized typewriter that allowed for a different kind of interaction between student writer and text through color, cutting and pasting, and even embedded comments. I celebrate these initial attempts to integrate but now push teachers to consider what it is that we want our students' minds to do in any lesson, activity, or task. The trick is achieving a balance. Just as we need to find a middle ground between teachers who embrace every new thing that comes down the pike and reactionaries who are quick to refuse what's new without investigating what it really means, we must find a balance when it comes to integrating computing technologies usefully and mindfully into our teaching toolkit. The computer isn't a glorified typewriter, and it surely will not transform student learning all by itself. It's more than a simple tool and less than a god (Strickland 1997).

The Reality

We're all in different places, whether in our pedagogies, our philosophies, our students, our communities, or the equipment filling our labs and classrooms. Not only do teachers come into the classroom with dramatically different comfort and skill levels when working with computing technologies, but they face a tremendous range of resources. In a high school in rural Missouri, each academic department has just been granted the funding to add one computer connected to the Internet through a dial-up connection. By contrast, in an affluent middle school in Bethesda, Maryland, each English classroom has a mini-lab of at least twelve computers, all with high-speed Internet access— enough for one computer for each student pair in the class. As teachers, we write grants, seek out community donations, and even bring our own home computers into the classroom to ensure access. To gain the equipment that I currently use in my classroom, I've spent hours researching grant opportunities and writing applications, only occasionally receiving funds. It has taken three years and a transfer to a newly constructed high school with new computers to acquire access to a networked classroom computer with high-speed Internet access and an LCD projector. I use a digital camera acquired through grant funding, and my own laptop and handheld PCs acquired through personal savings. Grants have also funded software purchases and access to several online resources and digital libraries, again supplemented by the rich resources of a newly funded high school media center. But no matter what the tools are, once the funding and equipment are secured and in place, the challenge lies in use and application.

An unexpected finding in current research (Cuban 2001) holds that even when equipment is made available, students aren't using it to extend, enrich, and enhance understanding. They use computers in schools to complete assignments, play games, explore CD-ROMs to find information, and conduct Internet searches. Only on rare occasions did student computer use become of primary importance, as in participating in an online curriculum. We aren't using the tools to do things in innovative, better ways. What Cuban's findings emphasize is that in order for the technology integration to affect students as learners and thinkers, it must bring together the right task, the right tool, and the right student.

That also doesn't mean converting lectures and discussions into glitzy PowerPoint presentations. Perhaps a larger consideration than the equipment at hand is the skill level, practice, and pedagogy of the teacher who wants to integrate technology meaningfully into instruction. It's not the equipment or lack thereof as much as it is the culture of the classroom as established by the teacher from the onset of instruction.

Cuban found that when teachers adopt technological innovations, these changes typically maintain rather than alter existing classroom practices, regardless of the equipment available. Again, this is the comfortable means of adopting something new. The flaw in the logic is that knowledge isn't embedded in the technology. If thinking is stimulated by activity, sitting a student in front of a monitor won't ensure mindful engagement. Learners do not learn from technology; they learn from thinking about what they are doing. Focus has to be placed on learning with the technology rather than learning from or about the technology. Effective integration requires a pedagogical philosophy that concentrates on student-centered instruction where students are actively responsible for their learning. Here, computing technologies are used as a tool in carefully structured lessons/activities where the learner is asked to seek and process information, or to reflect on understandings, beliefs, and thinking processes. Technology can help to make students' thinking processes more visible to the teacher, something that does not happen when students simply turn in a completed assignment for checking and grading. As teachers observe their students working with computer applications, they can see the choices each student is making, stop and ask about the student's goals, and make suggestions for revisions or different strategies (Means and Olson 1997). Teaching and learning are active. The focus is on knowledge construction, not reproduction; conversation, not reception; articulation, not repetition; collaboration, not competition; and reflection, not prescription (Jonassen, Peck, and Wilson 1998). Teachers must learn not only the ways to work with equipment but also the skills for facilitating learning in a technology-rich, constructivist learning environment.

Integration into the English Classroom

Technology in the English classroom is often seen as unnatural and, according to some, will lead to the demise of our beloved books. Birkerts refers to a "language erosion," a flattening of perspectives caused by our reliance on databases rather than texts, with damaging side effects in the realm of personal privacy and individuality (Gilster 1997). However, the computer isn't the enemy of the book. It is the child of print culture, a result of five centuries of organized, collective inquiry and invention that the printing press made possible (J. Murray

2001). As English teachers, we are enraptured by the printed word, and computers paired with the Internet and hypertext are revolutionizing how readers think, process, and understand information. Reading has been transformed into a process that is both up and down and in and out. Students as writers and thinkers need to be taught new processing and evaluation skills for them to grasp, filter, and understand the proliferation of materials now available at their fingertips through a mouse-click or keystroke. Along with our study of great works of literature and writing we must now include both media and digital literacies. Wilhelm (2000) writes that literacy is now defined as "the ability to use the most powerful cultural tools available for making, communicating, and enacting meaning." The change that this demands in the culture of our classrooms is enormous.

Integrating technology into the classroom absolutely requires change in the role of the English teacher. Not only do we need to work to facilitate student learning, but we need to work to develop both our digital literacies and those of our students. In order to construct challenging curriculum- and standards-based activities that effectively integrate technology into English instruction, teachers need to work as *instructional designers*. In this capacity, teachers become *resource managers,* juggling electronic files and resources, hardware and networks. Schools are beginning to support teachers' work by hiring instructional technology specialists or additional media specialists who work as advisers or teammates during technology-infused projects. Innovative programs pair teachers with tech-savvy students who work to maintain the hardware and network needs of the classroom, freeing teacher time for instructional design and student assessment. In other words, you don't have to do it all on your own. Teachers inevitably also act as *researchers,* systematically posing questions, examining when it is appropriate and useful to integrate technology and when it is not, and following through with the implementation and evaluation of technology use (Pope and Golub 2000). Finally, teachers need to work as *communication specialists,* a role natural to English teachers. The Internet allows classrooms to tap into an international network of people, the transformative potential of which allows for the development of exceptional writing and reading skills. Teachers must know both how to tap into this network and how to facilitate experiences that extend students' thinking as writers, readers, and communicators.

What the teacher does not need to become is the technology expert. In order to become tech-savvy, a series of basic skills are required as a foundation. You need to be able to find the "on" switch and to be able to think critically about how you can use the tools available to you to enhance, extend, and empower student learning. You must acknowledge that the computer can both hinder and help create instructional opportunities for students. That's it. The rest can be learned.

Becoming tech-savvy does not require knowing the logistics behind establishing a network or how to repair hardware. You might need to protect yourself from such misplaced expectations once your colleagues learn about the journey you're about to take. The tech-savvy teacher knows how to ask questions and, perhaps more important, whom to ask. This teacher seeks out training and eagerly taps into the knowledge base of media specialists, librarians, computer support specialists, computer science teachers, parents, and especially students. This teacher also has a backup plan for those times when errors occur and equipment fails. As discussed in Chapter 3, becoming a tech-savvy teacher doesn't mean that you have to become a "techie." You don't have to abandon your beloved, tattered copy of Webster's dictionary for the newest online edition available through a handheld PC. Becoming tech-savvy simply means that you will lead students to become digitally literate within the context of your curriculum.

Ending Points

None of these roles should be unnatural for an English teacher. However, they do require change, and as with all changes, we must be critical. What does it mean to integrate technology critically? We question. We probe. We mindfully consider the why behind every attempt to integrate technology into our teaching. With the introduction of computing technologies and the Internet into the English classroom, we open the door to other issues. As Postman (1993) writes, technological change always results in winners and losers. Issues of plagiarism are compounded where cyberpapers and digital resources abound. Students roam the Internet, often finding inappropriate content or suffering from information overload. Most crucial is the loss of time, for instruction and on the part of student researchers as they seek out information.

As teachers, we are used to making choices. We choose the texts we want our students to enjoy and explore. We choose the challenges and exercises we want them to experience as writers. Now we need to choose the most efficient tools for our students as learners. Our toolkit already consists of books, pencils, highlighters, markers, posterboard, three-hole punches, staplers, whiteboards, and paper. The computer is simply another tool, only to be chosen when it is appropriate.

Related Reading

Gilster, Paul. 1997. *Digital Literacy.* New York: Wiley.

Pope, C., and Jeffrey N. Golub. 2000. "Preparing Tomorrow's English Language Arts Teachers Today: Principles and Practices for Infusing Technology." *Contemporary Issues in Technology and Teacher Education* 1 (1): 89–97.

For me, [computers bring] a shift in student attitude that marks a classroom power shift. [The classroom is] not theirs or mine, it's ours.

—Carol Jago

The Beginning

Four years ago, the computer that sat in my classroom was barely used. A graduate of a teacher education program who had yet to make the leap into embracing digital technologies, I was trained to see the computer as a tool that would enhance my personal productivity, not a tool that would meaningfully impact student learning. I maintained the required electronic gradebook and answered e-mail, occasionally tapping into the resources available online to extend lesson resources and, more often than not, sinking hours into finding what it was that I thought I wanted. The computer sat behind my desk, off-limits to the hands and minds of the students in my classroom. This was schoolwide policy, and one that I was commended for routinely practicing.

What changed this limiting, starved pattern was the needs of my students. The change started small as I used the computer to accommodate Phil's requirement for a word processor for writing in class, or as a study tool for Beth, Sahar, and Niko, who were in need of acceleration, or for Rob and Julia, who regardless of their placement in the same class were hungering for enrichment. In the flurry of an engaged class discussion, students would use the computer to research ideas that would add another perspective, adding heat and depth to the dialogue. My ninth-grade English classes participated in Pinsky's online Favorite Poem project, sharing our favorite poems online in an eclectic community of students, teachers, readers, poets, and voices that my students referred to as "unexpected." E-mail accounts available free at Hotmail and Yahoo! allowed us to set up class accounts to correspond with the writers we were reading, parents who were working on dialogue journal assignments, and community members who were serving as interviewees for an oral history assignment. This was a very gradual process, growing as we discovered new uses and new needs for our studies.

For some students, I began to notice an enthusiasm for learning when they were given a task that required use of the classroom computer. These same students would often have days where it was simply too much to lift their heads from the desk, let alone mindfully consider classroom tasks. I saw changes in participation as well as in communication. Students were asking me to take notice of their work; something different was happening. This is reflected in an e-mail from Mike, a student whose habitual absences were going to prevent his graduating on time: "I just wanted to say that even though I'm home sick today, I participated in today's *A Lesson Before Dying* discussion." I took notice, reflected, and spent a great deal of time examining what it was that was happening for those students when we introduced technology into the practices of our classroom. What I discovered wasn't really a change in my students but a change in my practices as a teacher.

In those lessons and experiences where we were using technology, my role in the classroom had changed. I was learning with my students, challenging our technology skills and our skills as readers, writers, and thinkers, and more important, challenging students to learn how to learn. Though our class had always had a student-centered focus, I was now modeling risk taking as we explored what technology could add to our studies. I learned to create more authentic and realistic opportunities for experiential learning and how to provide authentic assessment through experts we could reach online. Papert writes that "the scandal of education is that every time you teach something, you deprive a child of the pleasure and benefit of discovery" (Tapscott 1998). My new role was leading me to see how to tap into that discovery through the creation of engaging, technology-infused activities that challenged my students' abilities and that would work within our English curriculum.

This isn't a change that occurred overnight. It has taken years of experimenting, studying, asking questions, seeking out community, and challenging my own thinking to evolve and grow. I have made mistakes, and the road has been bumpy in unexpected ways. However, the payoff in student engagement and enriched, mindful learning has been well beyond what I could have anticipated.

It all begins by determining two things. First, you need to believe that student thinking is empowered when the right tool is joined with the right task and the right student. Initially, begin with embracing it as a possibility, and use your experiences in your classroom to feed further questioning, learning, and discovery. Second, determine where your skills and experiences lead you to start.

Levels of Integration

Each student brings a different set of skills to the interaction with a computer. Some are savvy in Web design, and others are gaming enthusiasts. Many students, contrary to what teachers might assume, are technophobic, lacking in the very skills that their peers seem to handle effortlessly. Teacher-users bring just as broad a range of skills along with the challenge of discovering what each technology can mean within the context of the classroom. The roles of teacher as user and teacher as instructional designer are inextricably linked. It's impossible to richly explore classroom applications without being able at least to manipulate the basics of the hardware or the software. And it's difficult for the tech-savvy teacher to explore a new or compelling piece of hardware or software without considering the potential classroom uses (and misuses).

Building on the work of Ellen Mandinach and Hugh Cline (1992) and Judith Sandholtz, David Dwyer, and Cathy Ringstaff (1997), I use four "levels" of teacher-integrators throughout the rest of this book, melding the roles of teacher as user and teacher as instructional designer (Sandholtz and Cline 1992). Each level will allow us to establish a community of similarly skilled thinkers and to provide a context for examining both the task at hand and how it can affect and empower student learners. Each level includes teachers who have a range and variety of skills as users and in defining which technologies are used in classroom instruction and how. No level is exclusive, allowing you to move up and down the continuum, depending upon how you choose to integrate technology and the relative effectiveness of those attempts. What follows is a description of what each level might look like in a middle school or high school English classroom. Note that each is accompanied by an icon, which is used throughout the book to denote practices that fit each corresponding level.

The Survivor

Sometimes, finding the "on" switch is a good day for Ms. Powell. Used to technologies that fail her, she limps along, open to bringing in new experiences for her students but lacking the technical skills needed to manipulate those technologies. Students in Ms. Powell's classes use the computer lab for word processing, partly because she recognizes that these are skills her students will need in the workplace and partly because each English class is required to use the lab for a specified number of days per semester. She hasn't explored much of the set of other technologies available to her. Ms. Powell is excited about teaching and learning but has neither the time nor the support in her building to learn about using technology tools or the principles of meaningful classroom technology integration.

Ms. Powell prefers to take a rather formal role in her classroom, especially when it comes to computers. Instruction is teacher-driven and teacher-directed. Much of this formality comes from her desire to tightly manage her class, again emphasized when students are working in the lab. This time is highly structured, and expectations are beyond what can usually be done within the allotted time. Ms. Powell is the first to admit that she lacks the savvy to anticipate problems that might arise and that chaos can often ensue when things do not go according to plan.

Students in these ninth- and tenth-grade English classes do not use the Internet, mostly because Ms. Powell herself has lost hours looking for information online. She isn't willing to sacrifice the instructional time, especially since she isn't sure how to locate good information efficiently when she searches. As a survivor, Ms. Powell is willing to learn new technologies when she is provided with support and resources that won't fail her. She is open to seeing how these tools can help her student learners but has yet to see compelling enough evidence to warrant a significant change in her practices.

Becoming a Master

Mr. Caulfield's classroom is abuzz with activity as students complete an online activity within their unit studying Arthur Miller's *Death of a Salesman* and August Wilson's *Fences*. In this task students work in teacher-assigned teams to explore the Web sites listed on the "hot list" Mr. Caulfield has designed and posted to the school Web server. Each of these sites has been previewed and selected by him for the quality of its content, the accessibility of its design, and its timeliness and relevance. Student teams correspond using the online class discussion board and also post their findings and site evaluations to share with the group. Mr. Caulfield developed this list and included these tools after participating in a three-week summer training program, where he was one of fifty participants selected from a pool of over three hundred applicants.

Mr. Caulfield's classes are provided with the opportunity to weave technology into their classroom studies approximately once every nine weeks. Some attempts at integration challenge students as writers, and others challenge their skills as "information detectives." As a mastery level teacher, Mr. Caulfield clearly sees the need to integrate technology meaningfully into instruction, but he has had limited training and is mostly self-taught apart from what he has learned at the summer training. He can navigate his way intuitively through software and hardware, thinking his way through the technology while slowly experimenting with how it can be used to help students learn. Though willing to learn new skills, he fits in the technology where he can, mostly working with preformatted applications that are quick and effective and that don't require a great deal of tech-specific know-how on his part.

Creating an Impact

Ms. Jackson has worked to integrate technology into her teaching so that it has become a part of the culture of her class. From the start of the school year, she has developed and maintained a class Web site through www.blackboard.com, an online site where she posts homework assignments, class activities, and her first attempt at a WebQuest. The walls of her classroom seem limitless as students enter the online class chat room at all hours to engage in discussions of great works. Technology is woven into most assignments, allowing students to explore electronic libraries in conjunction with the resources in the public library or challenging them to develop spreadsheets of great "openers" and effective subordinate phrases in the texts they read.

As a teacher at the impact level, Ms. Jackson has used her own knowledge as a tech-savvy user to create tools and authentic learning experiences for her students that challenge their understanding and create authentic learning experiences. Working as a facilitator, she prides herself on crafting and then leading students through interactive, technology-infused activities that challenge students as they work through the demands of the high school English curriculum. She taps into her students' digital literacies to extend her own technology learning while leading them to be critical information consumers and users. Often, she uses her students as teachers, asking for tips and help as she learns the basics of Web design or working with new software. As an impact level teacher, she is on the verge of developing and using her own new tools that build on current practices and empower student learning in fresh, new ways.

The Innovator

Mr. Smith's classroom is paperless, requiring students to submit work through the online class drop box. Comments are written electronically into the students' work, allowing for multiple peer responses and critiques. Research integrates online and print sources as well as the development of multimedia components, which are authentically assessed by professionals in the field who are also active members of the class online community. Mr. Smith is experimenting with handheld technologies after receiving a grant from Palm, Inc., to outfit his class with a lab of equipment. Students use these tools to extend and enrich their experiences as writers and readers as well as organizationally in other content area studies. Students in Mr. Smith's class use e-mail and online discussion tools to collaborate with students in English classes across the country as they work on common projects and common texts. Mr. Smith established these connections as he worked with teachers in online communities and in virtual project repositories. He has restructured his curriculum and learning activities while creating a new, rigorous classroom learning environment. As an innovator, he is continually experimenting with new technologies in an attempt to discover new, engaging, transformative means of empowering all student learners in his classroom.

How Do I Know Where I Am?

Integrating technology into your instruction is difficult enough without having to struggle to define where your skills, experiences, and interests place you on the continuum. You more than likely can see yourself in several different "moments" in multiple descriptions. Several rubrics and assessment tools can be found online that measure and weigh your tech savvy. However, I have yet to find one that is centered on the skills needed by the middle or high school English teacher. To that end, I have fused what I know as a teacher and what I focus on as a staff developer into a quick assessment that should help to initially place you on the continuum (see Appendix, "Evaluate Your Tech Savvy"). Before you read further in this chapter, take five minutes to reflect on your practices and skills by completing the assessment. Keep in mind that this is a continuum, leaving great room for growth and skill development at all levels.

The International Society for Technology in Education (ISTE) has identified four similar levels of teacher tech-readiness within a holistic rubric useful when examined against what we've already established (see Appendix, "Planning and Designing Learning Environments and Experiences"). This provides yet another tool for thinking about where you are in the continuum of technology integration. In relation to what we've already seen, the apprentice and the novice in the ISTE assessment are a bit weaker than those teachers we've described so far. The ISTE rubric also considers research and tool selection whereas the earlier assessment focuses on skill, knowledge, and implementation. Ultimately, this holistic rubric provides yet another way of assessing and evaluating your own skills and directions for growth.

Reaching the Standards

No matter what your entry point when it comes to working with technology, this isn't a journey without benchmarks, guidelines, and expectations for where teachers' skills need to be. In 2000, ISTE released National Educational Technology Standards (NETS) for teachers (see Appendix), which, when paired with national and state standards for teaching English, have the potential to lead to tremendous change in the middle and high school English classroom. These standards were written to reflect what all teachers should know about and be able to do with technology in order to prepare students to meet the ISTE National Educational Technology Standards (NETS) for students.

As a teacher, I use the NETS for teachers in two ways. First, I use them as a guide for where my skills need to be when using technology for proficiency as well as to enhance my professional practice. Second, I use them to advocate for training and resources for my department and school. My professional planning is anchored by this document along with the NETS for students, the English Language Arts standards of the National Council of Teachers of English/ International Reading Association (NCTE/IRA), and the Maryland Core Learning Standards for English students. I keep a copy of the NETS for teachers as the third page of my planning binder, and a digital copy is also stored on my handheld PC for additional reference. Just as important, I repeatedly share copies with building administrators to emphasize that these are staffwide needs and anchors.

Especially useful in the NETS document is the notion that there is room for continual growth because the software and hardware tools made available to us in our classrooms change often. Learning doesn't stop because you have mastered the latest version of Microsoft Word or because you have learned how to write HTML code. On the other hand, we really need to fight the impulse to abandon "old" tools that are serving our needs and our students' needs just because something new comes down the pike. Just as we always revisit great novels and explore new ways to teach students about them, technology tools that have become familiar should benefit from rethinking and a fresh perspective.

Teachers as Learners: Boot Camp

So what is it that you actually need to know in terms of basic skills? Where McKenzie (2000) argues that "digital knowledge is only valuable if we have a lot of it," I really feel that to be a tech-savvy English teacher requires only a little bit of digital knowledge that can be leveraged to affect student learning in meaningful and purposeful ways. I start the school year by assessing and evaluating the skills of my students as readers, writers, thinkers, and users of technology only after doing the same for myself. The list of requisite skills is built from my curricular objectives and the NETS for students. My students have dubbed this "boot camp," and I've worked to build a similar set of activities into the beginning-of-the-year activities I share with staff.

Basic Training Technology Skills Checklist

✓ Become knowledgeable about the hardware and peripherals you are using.

✓ Know how to troubleshoot when things don't go as planned.

✓ Use your word processor efficiently. Know its potential.

✓ Be able to work with spreadsheets, databases, multimedia tools, and presentation software, learning each tool with an appropriate and engaging task.

✓ Communicate using e-mail, discussion boards, and online chat rooms.

✓ Be able to use online search tools to efficiently locate and evaluate information.

✓ Know how to locate and manipulate images using available software tools.

✓ Know the laws and rules of the Internet, including those focusing on ethical use and intellectual property.

✓ Be well versed in current "health and safety" concerns.

Working with the basics requires that teachers know how to work with their classroom computer. Whether working with a PC or a Mac, it is essential to be able to save and move files, format disks, and install and use application programs. Especially when you pair students to work with whatever computing technologies are at your disposal, you'll have to know how to troubleshoot—plug in and clean the mouse, select the correct printer, and even hook up a projector. How do you learn the basics? Ask your media specialist. Ask the technology specialists or user support specialists in your building. Ask your students. These are the foundation skills from which you can explore just about everything else, and not knowing the basics ensures chaos when you start actively using technology in your classroom teaching. The bulk of instructional time that I first lost when integrating technology came when I couldn't set up the projector at the beginning of class or wasn't quite sure how to operate the scanner or camera that we were using that day. Consider this to be a fixed part of your lesson plan each and every time you bring any technology into your classroom.

The next step involves learning to use the software technologies available in your classroom. Most computers have a word processor installed, whether it's the most recent edition of Microsoft Word or an older copy of ClarisWorks. As an English teacher, it's critical to know how to use these tools, recognizing that they are much more powerful than an electronic typewriter. You need to understand their capabilities as a word processor, a desktop publisher, and in some cases, even an HTML (hypertext markup language) editor. You have to know the tool before you can expect it to work in your classroom instruction. Though you can usually count on student knowledge of the software, this is an assumption, and as I mentioned in Chapter 1, assumptions about technology can be treacherous. As a rule, you need to know the ins and outs of whatever you bring into your classroom. If not, be prepared to welcome the what-ifs.

English classes can make great use of spreadsheets, databases, multimedia tools, digital imaging tools, and presentation software. The same rules apply: learn the software before you introduce it as an option for student use. Know how to work with the tool and what guidelines frame or bound its potential products. All these tools are discussed in the following chapters within the context of sample lessons. Along with the use of multimedia or Web-editing software comes some knowledge of design principles. I've found the art teachers to be invaluable in helping me navigate through what it takes to make my presentations "play by the rules" while also engaging student interest and providing solid content. Again, tap into the human resources as well as those that require a power strip.

Some knowledge of communication tools has also become a requirement for working with technologies in the English classroom. E-mail, discussion boards, instant messaging, and chat rooms provide their own lexicon, rule systems, and etiquette. Most of these come with time and practice. In my case, it took a lot of practice with chat rooms to be able to use them as an instructional tool. My early attempts led students to be LOL or ROFL (laughing out loud or rolling on floor laughing—chat room abbreviations). I might have been tech-savvy when it came to working in the virtual environment, but I was mostly illiterate when it came to the language and netiquette. What is essential is learning how to navigate efficiently in each of these virtual tools. Most are quite intuitive and use formats similar to those in a word processor.

The introduction of the Internet into classrooms has opened up a wealth of new information, skills, and practices. English teachers must know how to locate information efficiently and evaluate it precisely. My knowledge in this area has been greatly enhanced by instruction from some really savvy media specialists, the best of whom worked alongside me as my students conducted online research or evaluated selected sites. Teachers must know how to navigate the Web but also what the rules are that protect its content. Discussions of ethical use and intellectual property are an indispensable component of classroom dialogue, but they can only occur when teachers are well versed in both the lay of the land and the rules that govern it. Alongside this understanding, teachers need to have a strong sense of "health and safety" issues regarding Internet use. We each need to understand and keep abreast of issues regarding appropriate site content, proper use of student names and pictures, and the dangers of completing surveys and divulging personal information.

Ending Points

Don't feel as if you have to figure this all out right away. As with learning to integrate technologies into your teaching, learning about the software and hardware resources at your disposal takes time. The trick is to work in the technology when it fits what you already need to accomplish. Learn how to use a word processor when you need to write a letter to a parent. Learn how to work with PowerPoint as you approach a professional presentation. Making the technology meaningful to you as a learner will help inspire your learning while pushing you to think about how you can use that tool in your teaching.

If you're lucky, you have resources at your disposal. Sometimes this is as simple as turning to a staff development teacher in your building or—my trustiest resource—the media specialist/librarian on staff. At other times, it can be much more difficult, exhausting the knowledge of the students in your classroom and what you are able to find by searching online. I've had the pleasure of working in buildings where staff development was an engaging part of our daily practice, and I've had the feelings of isolation that come from working in a building where training and resources simply didn't exist. What I've learned to do is keep at it. Use your resources or find new ones. I've shared some of my starting points on this book's Web site for your reference as you need them. Just remember, to be a tech-savvy English teacher absolutely requires being a continual learner.

Related Reading

ISTE (International Society for Technology in Education). 2000. *National Educational Technology Standards for Teachers: Preparing Teachers to Use Technology.* Eugene, OR: ISTE.

3 Tech Boot Camp: Where Are Your Students?

Today's kids are so bathed in bits that they think technology is part of the natural landscape. To them, digital technology is not more intimidating than a VCR or a toaster.

—Don Tapscott

How can we plug in more effectively to kids who are at different stages of development and experience learning in different ways?

—Jane M. Healy

At back-to-school night parents were invited to spend one September evening exploring the building and meeting their students' teachers. I had approximately ten minutes per class period to meet and greet parents of the students in my classes and bring them up to speed on the curricular goals for the semester. Usually, such sessions, at the end of an active teaching day, blur into one another. But I was energized and excited on this particular back-to-school night, at Blake High School, because it marked the unveiling of the class Web site I'd been developing all summer—a repository for students to locate assignments, class notes, handouts, and readings, and a discussion area welcoming parents to enter our classroom community. I had anticipated responses from the parents this evening, but I was not expecting the rich discussions that ensued.

The parents who filled my classroom were eager to hear not just about our formal English curriculum but also about how technology would be used to empower and enrich student learning. Their children, their experiences, my colleagues, and the media had them primed. They wanted to know which books we would read but also what literacies and skills the students would learn when working with computing technologies. Less than 40 percent of these students had access to a computer at home, but all could gain access through school accounts and the extended hours of the school media center. Parents were excited about the resources now at their children's fingertips, but they were deeply concerned about their students as users, thinkers, and learners.

In the second-period class, we noted our ideas on the class whiteboard. This group of parents used the term "digitally anxious" to describe their experiences in working with their children as computer users. Some were curious about their children's online identities, noting that those who had Internet access had more than one e-mail account or instant messaging screen name. Others were concerned about the ease of navigating the Web with good intentions and suddenly landing on a site with inaccurate, offensive, or inappropriate content. To quote one parent, "When my kids are online, all bets are off in terms of what they'll pull up." One outspoken and almost belligerent father wanted to be sure that I knew he felt his son's language skills had been compromised because of the "language" he'd picked up in chat rooms and had started to include in his everyday conversations. Ultimately, unless students were enrolled in specific technology courses or had savvy parents, their skills when working with software, hardware, scanners, cameras, and Web browsers were self-taught, leading parents, as new users, to seek their assistance. Again, the parents' words captured this well. One mother explained, "Now I go to my kids in the same ways I used to go to my own Mom and Dad for help. I'm not sure if that shift is a good thing, but it is clearly here."

The next day, I opened the same discussion with each class of students, asking them about their skills, comfort levels, practices, and understanding when it came to working with computers and related technologies. We talked about many of the same things, having only the prompt "What is technology?" as their trigger. Students talked about the frustrations they felt as they tried to become savvy, skilled technology users while adults were simply more at ease with the more static roles of reader, viewer, and listener. They wanted to try new hardware tools, but adults had a difficult time accepting or even acknowledging their use. Students were excited that they'd managed to teach themselves to use much of what was made available to them—and frustrated that teachers could rarely take their understanding and learning further than where they'd taken them on their own. As much as students were empowered by their independent explorations, they welcomed the opportunity to have experiences in school that would extend their knowledge even further. Students were hungry to complete interactive, engaging tech-infused activities in class and to extend the classroom community beyond our classroom walls through discussions and virtual correspondence with students across the globe. One student put it all into perspective by stating, "Teachers are helping to prepare us for careers that haven't been invented yet—requiring inventive thinking and new technologies. Doesn't that have to be a part of my education as much as Shakespeare and calculus?"

Facts and Figures

So, how wired are our students? Is it accurate to have named them the net generation? The 2000 census found that the majority of students in the United States have computers and Internet access in their homes. This isn't surprising news, but it dramatically affects the way we think about teaching digital literacy in the secondary English classroom. The data indicate that two-thirds of homes with a child aged 6–17 have a computer, with 53 percent of those homes connecting to the Internet (Poftak 2002). The UCLA Internet Project (2002), an ongoing study of the effects of the Internet, reports that students are spending an average of 7 hours, 36 minutes, online at home per week. At school the number drops to 1 hour, 36 minutes. A startling 41 percent of Internet users aged 12–17 think that "about half" of what they find on the Internet is reliable and accurate. On the other hand, 51 percent still believe that "most or all" of the information on the Web can be trusted to be right (Poftak 2002). Not surprising to those of us who work in classrooms, lower-income students continue to lag behind in both access to equipment and the skills needed to use it efficiently.

NETS for Students

Just as English teachers have embraced the English Language Arts standards of the National Council of Teachers of English (NCTE), those of us who have been working to integrate technology meaningfully into our instruction were eager for the development and release of national student technology standards. In 2000 the International Society for Technology in Education (ISTE) released the National Educational Technology Standards (NETS) for students, which focuses on what students should know how to do with technology. The beauty of this document for an English teacher is that it supplies you with specific guidance and expectations for what varying levels of students should be able to do in terms of technology use when presented in the context of learning a specific concept integral to the content area. I use both the NETS for students and the NCTE standards when planning any tech-infused lesson or activity. For example, if I were planning an activity for students to work with a digitized video of poets reading their work, it would target both the NCTE standards, addressing strategies used to comprehend, interpret, evaluate, and appreciate texts (standard 3), and the NETS for students, describing the use of technology tools to enhance learning and promote creativity (standard 3).

As a companion for the general standards developed in NETS for students, grade-specific performance indicators are also included in the standards publications. Teachers are instructed at the start of each indicator that "all students should have opportunities to demonstrate the following performances." This is important to note. Whether you are a middle school English teacher working as part of a collaborative team or a high school English teacher working within a department, students do not have to demonstrate all of these indicators within the bounds of your classroom. Instead, the indicators are meant to be integrated into multiple contexts in multiple disciplines through a period of years. Teachers often look at these documents and become overwhelmed, wondering how it can possibly all be accomplished in 180 days of instruction. The answer is that it does not have to be and that it cannot be. Use the standards and performance indicators to help determine where your students ought to be and where you'd like to take them next. Use them to help lead your colleagues to those same discoveries and discussions. Take it one step at a time.

Boot Camp for Students: Teaching the Basics

I begin each semester with a series of activities that my students have termed "boot camp." These activities center on multiple things: how students work as readers, how they respond to different genres and literary "lenses," how they work as writers of creative and expository texts, how they work as listeners and speakers, and of course, what technology skills they bring to their classroom studies. What follows are some ideas and techniques for assessing and evaluating technology skills of middle and high school level students. Again, it's important to note that with each class of students, the skill level seems to increase. My expectations cannot be the same for eighth graders who entered my classroom last semester and those who are entering this fall; after all, the technologies that they know are often worlds apart. I use the standards as a guide but, most essentially, I listen, watch, and think about what my students tell me from the day that they enter my classroom.

In my middle school classes, I expect students to enter with basic competency skills: the ability to operate PC and Mac computers, navigate through the different operating systems in order to save and locate their work, troubleshoot when things don't work, and figure their way through using a basic digital camera or scanner. I also expect that students have a basic sense of how to work through word-processing and presentation software. Initially, I assessed these understandings through a simple Jeopardy!-style quiz game, complete with buzzers and a quirky host. I wrote the questions in advance, including categories ranging from "Clicks and Clunks" to "Scream Savers." Because class sizes were large, I'd split the class into groups so we'd be running two or three games simultaneously. It never took long for the tech gurus to show themselves, a discovery that was essential when it came to later phases of boot camp.

For my high school students, my expectations were higher. I expected most students to enter with a more sophisticated and efficient set of strategies for working with software and hardware. At this stage, students should be able to pair appropriate tools with tasks and situations. This requires a basic knowledge of how to work with word processors, spreadsheets, databases, presentation software, Web authoring tools, and collaborative tools such as e-mail and discussion boards. The initial assessment took a more advanced form, requiring one day in the English department computer lab. Students would initially rate their skills in six areas: troubleshooting, productivity software, multimedia design, communication tools, research tools, and Web design. I simply asked students to raise the number of fingers in the air that corresponded with their level of understanding: one = basic, finding the "on" switch is a good day; three = moderate, I can navigate and figure through this with relative ease; five = master, I could teach Bill Gates a thing or two. I emphasize that students need to be bluntly honest with themselves at this point in the evaluation, and I find that they are often harder on themselves than their actual skills and work will reflect.

Once students have labeled their appropriate skill levels, they are assigned one of three tasks to complete within the class period. Working as individuals, they must solve a problem or generate a model, each of which corresponds to their skill level. For a student who identifies herself as being at the basic level, I would assign a simple task such as the creation of a brochure. For a student at the mastery level, the task might require evaluation and selection of preselected materials and presentation of findings through a multimedia presentation with required elements. Create tasks that correspond to the types of activities that you'll be asking students to develop later in the semester, just as you would when examining skills in a reading or writing assignment. I maintain records of student levels so that I know which skills I need to teach the full class, which I need to provide as mini-lessons, and which I need to include as online tutorials or activities within a learning center.

The later phases of boot camp for both my middle and high school students require them to demonstrate proficiency using software programs made available in our classroom or department labs. Sometimes this takes the form of a warm-up "race" or a homework assignment. The difficulty here lies in balancing what I need to accomplish in early assessments and what content we need to begin exploring. I try to anchor those assessments and early evaluations to short stories, poems, and other texts that we encounter early in the semester. Again, context is essential.

There have been years where I've relied on less involved assessments. My earliest assessment was built from the teacher skills assessment described in Chapter 2 (see Appendix). Although this can be a reliable tool, I've found that more information regarding students' skills becomes apparent when they are asked to complete specific small tasks in an interactive, sometimes competitive class activity. We all become more invested, and the environment and culture in our classroom begin to take shape.

Another fun assessment to use with students at the beginning of the school year is the betting game (see Appendix). Given specific topics (similar to those used in the Jeopardy!-like game), students write specific questions on the game form. For example, if the category were "saving a file," I would write the question, "What drive would I need to save a document to if I wanted to save to my floppy disk?" Students then exchange the game forms. To answer a question, the student must place a value ($1 to $100) in the corresponding box, reflecting his confidence level when it comes to the question's topic. Questions are revealed only when the bets have been made. Have the students write their answers to each question and then return the completed game cards to the original authors for scoring. These questions and answers provide additional insights for teachers in evaluating students' technology understanding and knowledge.

There are two additional assessments I use when time is tight and I need to quickly determine how to progress (and who the strong students are who are willing to be "tapped"). One is low-stakes, involving only some Post-it notes and a surface upon which they can be placed. List skills or topics on a chalkboard, a whiteboard, or chart paper posted in the classroom or lab. Students write their names on Post-it notes and place them in the column that corresponds with their skill or comfort level. A more social though less accurate means of student self-assessment is the time-honored teaching strategy of simply asking the students to arrange themselves in a line, indicating their comfort with a skill or task according to their place in line.

Simple Management Techniques That Work

When working with students in the computer lab, I use some techniques I've picked up that help to focus attention and use time more efficiently.

- *Monitors off.* Any time you need to give instructions or need students' attention when working with classroom computers or computers in a lab, have students turn their monitors off. Students are distracted by the movement or content of what appears on the screen, sometimes to the point of absorption. Turning the monitor off brings attention to the task and keeps students from clicking around the screen or typing on a keyboard.
- *Tech-tips notebooks.* As students learn a new technology skill, have them record it (and its specifics) in a section of their class notebook or binder allocated specifically for tech tips. This can be supplemented by handouts, including tutorials on skills such as saving and using graphics, manipulating digital images, or Boolean search indicators. If students have access to a handheld computer, I require that they maintain a digital copy of this document for reference and use.
- *Help cards.* Ask students to keep two Velcro-backed notecards near the monitor. One should be green (or have a green stripe) and the other should be red (or have a red stripe). Students should attach the notecard, using the Velcro strip, to the top of the monitor to indicate their comfort level with the task at hand. If they run into trouble or have questions, they should post the red card. If all is well, they need only post the green card.
- *Hands off!* This is a policy that needs to be in place any time that you or another student is helping anyone to work with equipment or tools. No matter how strong the impulse, don't use a student's mouse to demonstrate a task. By removing the student's hand from the mouse, you break the line of contact with her brain. Stuff your hands in your pockets, put them behind you. Just don't touch that mouse.
- *Active monitoring.* This is completely the responsibility of the teacher. Your students need to know that you are savvy. They need to know that you know what they are doing and where they are going. I've worked with teachers who expected time in the lab to be relaxing. It's not. I go home more tired from days in the lab than even from days when we've constructed a set on the stage. This is active teaching, and it requires being actively involved with the work that each student is working to complete. You need to know where in the task your students are at all times. Periodically go around the lab and check which windows students have open (they are collapsed at the base of the screen on a Windows system). Periodically check the Back button of their browser to see what sites they've been on. In the lab, you are a coach and a facilitator, but with some classes you might initially need to be a detective.

- *Prethinking.* Just as you work and plan lessons before students ever sit in front of a computer, students need to organize their thinking before they get to work. Provide students with the assignment and time to storyboard, write, draft, and plan before they begin using the appropriate technologies for the task at hand. Require this work as an entrance ticket into the computer lab. You'll lead students to be more efficient users by ingraining this practice into your work in class, and you'll lose much less instructional time.

- *Model.* This one is simple. Using a projector, model for your students the work or activity that they are about to complete. This provides them with an immediate frame of reference as well as a starting point.

- *Power teams.* This is a simple strategy for working with students who are at dramatically different levels of skill and knowledge when it comes to working with a particular technology tool. Pair your savvy students with those who are struggling, allowing each to test the thinking of the other. Your classroom environment needs to be one of support and teamwork in order for this to be most effective, but it is a strategy that works to boost the knowledge and understanding of both members of the team.

- *"Learn-teach-learn."* This is another strategy straight from what we already know as best practice. One small group is taught how to use a tool by the teacher. That group then teaches the next group, and so on, until each group has acquired the necessary skill or information. Based on some of the same thinking as Power Teams, this strategy reinforces student knowledge by asking them to teach what they know.

Netiquette and Fair Use

The last component of basic training for English students at any level involves working with what my students now refer to as the "rules of the game." Students are often surprised to learn that materials and information posted online are not only subject to questioning and evaluation but are not "free" for the use of all. It's essential that students understand the rules that protect information (including music and graphics) found online before you start any online project or activity.

For starters, always assume that whatever you find online is copyrighted and protected. It's essential to immediately get into the habit of giving credit to the source each time you use an image, a sound, or a bit of text. An increasing number of authors/creators/artists are including information online that specifies guidelines for using the work in question. If explicit guidelines exist, follow them. Sometimes this requires a link to the original site. Sometimes it requires a more formal process. Whenever feasible, ask the owner of the copyright for permission. Keep a copy of your request for permission and the permission received. If students aren't following these practices, they are plagiarizing. Your school should have an acceptable use policy, to which you'll need to continually refer as you address copyright and plagiarism issues in your teaching and as you teach students to follow the rules when working with intellectual property.

In addition to learning about copyright and fair use, it takes some practice for students to learn the systems of etiquette tied to online communication such as e-mail and chats. On the Internet, a system of tacit codes popularly known as netiquette has evolved. In netiquette, as in etiquette, respect for others translates into respect for others' rights (Tapscott 1998). Kathy Schrock (2001) lists the following rules:

Standards of Netiquette
- Don't e-mail what you wouldn't say face-to-face.
- Respect other people's time.
- Spelling, grammar, and punctuation still count in e-mail interactions and discussion board postings. Yes, there is a grammar for some chats, but that needs to be used only in that arena. Don't let it get in the way of expressing meaning.
- Include a meaningful subject line in all e-mails.
- Always include contact information when e-mailing.

Ending Points

A student in my on-level eleventh-grade English class wrote the following letter in an end-of-the-year class evaluation:

Dear Ms. Kajder,
    You'll see a lot of my comments about how I worked as a reader and writer in the questions you have included above. What I want to express wasn't a part of the options. I want to talk about thinking. Coming into your class, I simply didn't know which end was up. We don't have a computer at home and, somehow, I'd worked my way through eleven years of school without having to know anything more

than how to type in Word. It freaked me out that I needed to do better than that in your class—and it's why I didn't do much for the first couple of weeks. I knew I didn't have it—and wasn't sure that I wanted it.

The thing was, you didn't just teach us how to use tools. You taught me to question why I was using them and if they even made sense. We never had a lesson on that, and you really never said it, but that is what I learned. Did you notice that I started to get it later on in the semester? That's because I made the choice but also that I found the answer to the questions. Yeah, I need to know how to use the tools, but I need to know how to use them in order to think through whether or not they make sense for what I want to say and do. Most people don't think about it—and now I do.

You always call us "scholars" in class, and I didn't buy that. I do now. I'm a scholar because I know that I'm thinking not only about my ideas but how I can express them. I'm a scholar because I can write my ideas and choose to simply share them with myself but I also know how to share them with a community. Computers aren't so intimidating anymore—things are flipped. I'm not the one connected to a power strip. My power comes from my questions.

Related Reading

Healy, Jane M. 1998. *Failure to Connect: How Computers Affect Children's Minds—And What We Can Do About It.* New York: Simon and Schuster.

ISTE (International Society for Technology in Education). 2000. *National Educational Technology Standards for Teachers: Preparing Teachers to Use Technology.* Eugene, OR: ISTE.

Poftak, Amy. 2002. "Net-Wise Teens: Safety, Ethics and Innovation." *Technology and Learning* 1 (23): 36–49.

Tapscott, Don. 1998. *Growing Up Digital: The Rise of the Net Generation.* New York: McGraw-Hill.

4 Hypertext in the English Classroom

Hypertext has the potential to change fundamentally how we write, how we read, how we teach these skills, and even how we conceive of text itself.

—Davida Charney

The cursor is a physical means of inserting the reader into the text.

—Richard Lanham

Reading has always been my home, my sustenance, my great invincible companion.

—Anna Quindlen

As a culminating activity at the close of a short story unit, I presented my eighth-grade students with a serious challenge—to break the rules. The task was to create a piece of short, short fiction in which the conventions we'd studied throughout the past four weeks were pushed, tested, and ultimately broken. The objective behind the assignment was for students to demonstrate and continue to discover how character, style, narrative, time, and point of view work together (or in opposition) to convey a story.

Elizabeth's story was like nothing I'd ever seen. Instead of writing in Microsoft Word, she used PowerPoint to create slides that were webbed together, linked by options at the base of each slide. She explained her approach in a reflective journal entry, writing that "stories always command where I go. Sometimes I really like that, but my favorite childhood books were the ones which let me choose my own path." Each slide was linked to at least two options, allowing the reader to select where he wanted to go next. There were multiple possibilities for how the story would unfold and what would happen next. As a reader and as a teacher, I was intrigued by how she'd made an extremely complex, nonlinear story work, and how the technology tool had enabled it to come together. Elizabeth brought hypertext into my classroom and led me to rethink not only how text works to convey meaning but what it now meant to be a reader and a writer in this new environment.

Hypertext Defined

Hypertext has exploded the traditional ideas of writing and authorship. Although it ultimately leaves us where we've been—exploring the words that appear on a page (or screen)—it has fed the reactionaries at both extremes. It has both its champions and its critics, leading to what Sven Birkerts (1994) refers to as a "battle between technology and soul." To some, hypertext marks another step in the evolution of language. We've transitioned from the development of alphabetic print, to the creation of the printing press, to the development of digital text. To others, it represents a demise of the printed text, a devolution back to a mode of communication dependent upon signs, symbols, and pictures, and the utter death of the paragraph.

Hypertext can be defined simply as a set of documents of any kind (images, text, charts, tables, video or audio clips) connected to one another by links (J. Murray 2001). We don't see printed words but text that is simultaneously visible and invisible. Instead of turning pages, links allow the reader to interact with nonlinear, often multimedia text, deciding which pieces of information are important by following a path that she determines. The writer creates a text riddled with paths, knowing that each reader will determine a different way of negotiating the text (Gilster 1997). This directly changes rhetorical patterns as the reader chooses which path to read as well as which links to use from within each screen, card, slide, or lexia (block of text). The relation between sections of text is multidirectional and instant, not simply up or down or across or sequential. Hypertext has the potential to empower student readers; however, it also has the potential to become an indiscernible maze that mystifies and confuses readers. In fact, hypertext can run to either of two extremes, on one hand, being so restrictive that readers find they have no more navigation than they would with linear text, and on the other, providing so many choices that users are simply overwhelmed with options.

Birkerts (1994) cautions that hypertext works to eradicate what we know as literature and literacy, arguing that "the premise behind textual interchange is that the author possesses wisdom, an insight, a way of looking at experience that the reader wants. . . . This is the point of writing and reading." Books, or printed text, are static. They don't change. If I read page three today, I can turn back to page three tomorrow and find the same words printed on the page. Birkerts finds it more perilous when we deal with electronic text: "Words read from a screen or written onto a screen—words which appear and disappear, even if they can be retrieved and fixed onto a place with a keystroke—have a different status and affect us differently from words held immobile on the accessible space on a page." Because the Internet is a dynamic environment, the information found from one day to the next is in a continual state of change, again eroding the meaning encased in the printed word. The "subjective ecology of reading" print text allows Birkerts to feel the power of the words on the page, a power that he emphasizes cannot be felt with hypertext.

What is it to be a reader? What do books do to us and for us? Rosenblatt (1996) explains that through the medium of words, the text brings into the reader's consciousness certain concepts, certain sensuous experiences, certain images of things, people, and actions. Certainly, this degree of mindful interaction is possible whether students are engaging with printed or electronic forms of text. In a list of the lessons that teachers demonstrate about reading through classroom practice, Lucy Calkins writes that through our actions or our words we often convey to students that reading is a waste of English class time; that readers break whole, coherent, literary texts into pieces, to be read and dissected one fragment at a time; and that reading is a serious, painful experience (Atwell 1998). These myths should be targeted and debunked as students work with hypertext in class, actively exploring text by crafting their own journey as they make meaning from the text they choose to encounter with each click of the mouse. Hypertext might even allow us to make more tangible the sometimes nebulous ideas of voice and audience.

Hypertext invariably presents challenges to even the savviest English and reading teachers. Just as Yeats asked, "How can we know the dancer from the dance?" we might ask, How can we tell the reader from the text? Hypertext not only invites readers to participate in the making of text but forces them to do so. That introduces uncertainty regarding authority and authorship. Furthermore, who controls the reading of the hypertext? Can readers select what and how much to read? Can readers create an appropriate reading order? The expectations students have learned through interactions with print text no longer apply when working with most hypertexts. Hypertexts don't have a defined beginning, middle, or end. There are no physical or conceptual end points except for those created by the reader. Navigating through hypertext can take an already ambiguous text and load the reading experience past the understanding of student readers. The same reading strategies used to help students unlock rigorous print texts might be useful in work with hypertext but would require some alteration. Glossing, structuring, image marking, questioning, and connecting have to mean something different within this digital environment. Students need tools for determining how to navigate text, unpack and comprehend meaning, and figure out how they got to that text in the first place. This isn't like students' work in deconstructing a text or interpreting it through personal experience. It's a very different degree of agency and, consequently, security.

One of my many goals when it comes to working with students is to excite them as readers. Most aren't active readers when they enter my classroom. I use every tool at my disposal to engage their thinking, including hypertext. As I've discussed in other sections of this book, the right tool when paired with the right task and the right student can yield tremendous results. Hypertext is often that tool, and my students are eager to take on this medium in English class. As students navigate through hypertext immersing themselves in the sounds, images, and scenes of the Jazz Age prior to reading *The Great Gatsby,* they are engaged, participating readers who are actively bringing text to life and establishing schema needed for interacting with Fitzgerald's text. This doesn't mean that they abandon print text. It simply means they are learning how to navigate, interact with, and think through all that is presented through hypertext. Wilhelm (2000) puts it well: "We live in a hypertextual world and must prepare our students to live in one. This doesn't mean that literature is dead, or that we won't read novels or poetry—it just means that these arts will exist in a new writing space, with new possibilities and permutations, sometimes in conjunction with art and video and sound."

Investigating Student Work

As with most of the technology tools that I have introduced into my classroom teaching, I started slowly when it came to figuring out the best ways to use hypertext. It is essential to introduce this tool only when it fits the task at hand and the students with whom I'm working.

Discussion Tools

My first use of hypertext during the school year involves a close examination of the discourse that we share in using the class discussion board (see Figure 4.1). Outside class, students use the discussion board to post questions and responses to readings. Inside the classroom, we begin by using the discussion board in class to hold "silent" discussions of great works. Sometimes this is set up using the department computer lab, and at other times we use either the stations available in the media center (rotating through in small groups) or the single computer in my class-

Figure 4.1

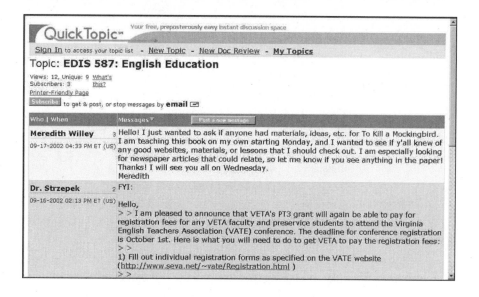

room. The discussions posted can be entered at any point, as opposed to using a chat room, where all players need to be present at the same time in order to participate. Students type their questions, responses, and reactions, establishing a low-stakes entry point for those students who might traditionally be reluctant to enter into a whole-class oral discussion. It's through the work of posting comments to the discussion board that students begin to work with hypertext. The discussion is nonlinear. It does not have a beginning, middle, or end; instead, it is simply a series of interconnected postings that students can enter and explore as they choose.

Once all students have had an opportunity to post their comments to the class discussion board, we examine the fuller "conversation" that occurred. I typically project the online discussion board using an LCD projector so that we can navigate through the postings as a whole class. I ask students to talk about their experiences as writers, speakers, listeners, and participants in this form of a discussion. We talk about where they entered, what strands or threads were the most compelling, how they navigated through the postings, and finally, how they were able to interpret, understand, and build upon the postings that they read. Students have all voiced at some point in this reflective work that the discussion here is much more "natural" than what usually occurs in a teacher-led discussion. Here, they could enter and exit the conversation, leading it in whatever direction they were led by the postings they chose to read, much like the evolution of dialogue in the hallways between a group of friends. Students also tie exploration of hypertext to an exploration of the roles of readers and writers, talking about intended meaning and how reader's choices of links lead to changes in direction.

Annotating Poetry

The next step in our work with hypertext is to use it for annotating poetic texts. Students in my ninth-grade English class typically work to analyze poetry early in the first semester, and that falls soon after we've held the reflective discussion on hypertext on the class discussion board. Naturally, I want to push our thinking further, and to that end, I meld our work with hypertext with my curricular objectives for the study of poetic devices in the work of Wordsworth, Shakespeare, and Dickinson.

Students first select one of six possible poems as the focus of analysis. Given the resources at our disposal, they have the choice of creating their annotated hypertext poem as a HyperCard stack, a PowerPoint slide show, or a Web page. They begin with a typed copy of the poem, selecting the lines, words, or phrases that they want to respond to. These are then converted into links, taking the reader to other windows or slides offering an interpretation, connection, related text, or other idea. Before students begin this work on the computers, I require that they map out the links and write the text. These are then used as checkpoints that we discuss in conferences prior to the students' time working on the computer to craft the hypertext. After students have completed their annotated hypertext poems, we do a "scramble" around the workstations in the computer lab. Students peer-review and critique one another's work using a preformatted response sheet or by opening the word-processing program and typing comments and responses while at the workstation. If you use the electronic response option, simply have different students respond in different colors, leaving the "window" open for other students to add their feedback.

The rigor in this task increases dramatically as students are provided with the opportunity to explain the thinking behind the connections and links that they embed in their work. I've challenged students to do this orally in class presentations, in reflective or expository writing, or even in the annotations that are provided within the poem. When taken to yet another level, students begin to discuss and reflect on how the connections and links all relate to one another, advancing their thinking and meta-cognition another step.

Hyperlinked Essays

Another simple way of using hypertext involves embedding links in student-written essays in place of footnotes or endnotes. Just as a printed book uses footnotes to carry additional information beyond that presented in the regular text, a hypertext document can point to the background information that supplements what we read on the first pass (Gilster 1997). This pertains directly to the purpose of the footnote, to point the reader to additional work that would elucidate and support the writer's argument. Linking to sites on the World Wide Web pushes the possibilities even further: the writer can link to entire pages of related information. Footnotes point to precise sources, whereas Web links can aid exploration and additional evaluation of the information presented at each linked site. Students need to learn to critically evaluate the sites they select as links (see Chapter 5).

Writing Poetry

Once students have learned to construct a basic hypertext, we move to working with their creative texts. Students in my eighth-grade magnet English classes spent one week exploring New York City in a multidisciplinary, experiential field trip. The English components of the experience centered on interview skills and poetry writing. Prior to the trip, we immersed ourselves in texts about the city, ranging from Alfred Kazin's *A Walker in the City,* to Walt Whitman's "Give Me the Splendid Silent Sun," to John Lennon's interviews in *Rolling Stone.* Students then wrote poetry throughout their visit, completing at least eight different texts to eight different prompts or assignments. I added hypertext to this assignment by challenging students to enhance their original poems with images, sounds, and additional descriptions.

Julia, a strong writer, submitted a poem in which she contrasted her views of New York City from above and below, during the day and the night. The first few stanzas read,

New York is
a chameleon at night,
Changing colors and identities,
Resembling a dozen different things.

From above,
New York is
A dress of raven velvet,
Which glitters with the light
Of a million tiny sequins.

From below,
New York is
A contest among the lights—
Each one competes with the other
Trying to burn brighter
And gain more notice.

From above,
New York is
An illuminated blueprint,
A scale model of the city,
Clearly defined
By the outlining lights.

From below,
New York is
Ads in Times Square,
Bursts of color,
Vivid fireworks
Down by the streets.

The hypertext components that she linked to in presenting this poem included photos from her trip, descriptions lifted from her journal notes, anecdotes of things she saw and people she met, and related pieces of text from the poetry and writing we had studied in the days leading up to the trip. For example, the link at "each one competes with the other" included text from her journal and from Thomas Wolfe's "Enchanted City":

> It's exactly as we read in Wolfe's work: "No matter how ugly its parts may be, [the whole city] becomes a proud, passionate Northern place: everything about it seems to soar up with an aspirant, vertical, glittering magnificence to meet the stars." Everything here is intense, even the structures of the buildings. Each seems to compete with the other, not satisfied to be magnificent—reaching for utter brilliance. No wonder everyone under their shadows feels compelled to do the same—no wonder everyone rushes. We want to be just as brilliant.

A link at "blueprint" included a childhood memory involving her father's desk and the fresh smell of the ink and paper blueprints. Julia used her tech skills to

Figure 4.2

New York is
a chameleon at night,
Changing colors and identities,
Resembling a dozen different things.

create an image where a photo she took of the streets of New York during the day morphed into the same shot as it would appear taken at night, much like the chameleon she describes (see Figure 4.2). The visual and textual links provide an extension and enrichment of the poem's text as well as a direct glimpse into the writer's thinking.

Exploring Writing

More involved uses of hypertext in the English classroom ask students to write original fiction in which they explore point of view, description, character development, narrative structure, and genre through the use of linked lexia. Hypertext makes for an interesting collaborative tool, allowing student groups and teams to fuse their writing to tell a larger story or instruct on a concept. I've also used hypertext as an anticipatory activity, assigning teams of students different historical events or geographic locations that are essential to understanding a text we are about to study. We've taken that even further by exploring hypertext as a model through which we reciprocally teach literary devices or grammar rules. The possibilities are really open to be explored. Again, the key is pairing hypertext as an appropriate and rigorous tool with the right task and students whose skills and understanding will be authentically challenged.

Curricular Connections

Reading Skills

Teaching students to read and, more important, to read critically, is essential. When working with hypertext, we are teaching students to read critically while also breaking familiar patterns by now reading in and out, up and down. In hypertext, sequential reading is supported by nonlinear jumps to alternative idea caches, with inevitable repercussions for comprehension (Gilster 1997). Through modeling and close monitoring of student thinking, teachers need to ensure that students have strategies for assembling knowledge and understanding content. I use graphic organizers and structured reading activities in order to monitor not only how students are navigating hypertext but how they understand the information it presents.

For example, students in my eleventh-grade on-level English class study Arthur Miller's *The Crucible.* National Geographic has a tremendous online site, which allows students to learn about the trials while "choosing their path" within the role of a Salem villager in 1692. Students were asked to complete an active reading chart as they read and interacted with the hypertext (see Figure 4.3). The chart is built from a modified K-W-L (know–want to learn–learned) chart (Ogle 1986), asking students to record information before, during, and after reading. I modify the chart to include specific questions, or have students write the questions before starting the activity. In this case, students were asked before reading to record what they already knew about Salem in 1692 and to list questions they would seek answers to while reading. During reading, students were asked to write questions that arose about the contents of the hypertext, questions that would help them make connections to their prior knowledge and any ideas they had as to the information they were looking for. We used the last column to ask questions about the activity, make inferences about what they had read in relation to Miller's text, and note changes in their understanding or thinking. This chart is an invaluable assessment tool when it comes to monitoring student growth and knowledge.

Instructional Design Strategies

For planning student work with hypertext, it is important, as in all lessons that integrate technology, that you consider the tools you'll have access to. Hypertext activities work in a one-computer classroom, a lab that doesn't have Internet access, or an Internet-ready computer lab with workstations for every

Figure 4.3
Organizer: Salem
Witch Trial Activity

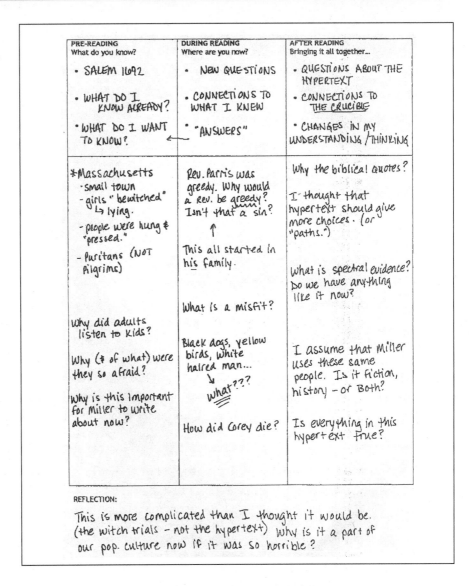

PRE-READING What do you know?	DURING READING Where are you now?	AFTER READING Bringing it all together...
• SALEM 1692 • WHAT DO I KNOW ALREADY? • WHAT DO I WANT TO KNOW?	• NEW QUESTIONS • CONNECTIONS TO WHAT I KNEW • "ANSWERS"	• QUESTIONS ABOUT THE HYPERTEXT • CONNECTIONS TO THE CRUCIBLE • CHANGES IN MY UNDERSTANDING / THINKING
*Massachusetts - small town - girls "bewitched" ↳ lying. - people were hung & "pressed." - Puritans (NOT pilgrims) Why did adults listen to kids? Why (# of what) were they so afraid? Why is this important for Miller to write about now?	Rev. Parris was greedy. Why would a Rev. be greedy? Isn't that a sin? ↑ This all started in his family. What is a misfit? Black dogs, yellow birds, white haired man... ↓ what??? How did Corey die?	Why the biblical quotes? I thought that hypertext should give more choices. (or "paths.") What is spectral evidence? Do we have anything like it now? I assume that Miller uses these same people. Is it fiction, history – or Both? Is everything in this hypertext true?

REFLECTION:
This is more complicated than I thought it would be. (the witch trials - not the hypertext) Why is it a part of our pop. culture now if it was so horrible?

student. Projects can use HyperCard stacks, PowerPoint slides, Web pages, or whatever electronic options you have available.

Teachers do need to be especially careful when structuring hypertext activities. Just as students need to balance content with "splash" in their work, teachers need to balance allowing students to discover with tightly controlling the outcome of their work. Too much discovery can lead to wasted instructional time and loss of student focus and understanding. Too much control leads to students' working down a prescribed path, producing confined work.

Discussion is essential throughout work with hypertext. Be sure to talk about how it affects and defines the roles of both readers and writers. Discuss how writers create effective paths for readers and yet manage the notion that readers will be crafting their own paths and meaning. Focus thinking on how the meaning of a piece of hypertext is shaped by a reader's selection of what and how much to read. This medium changes so much of what we know as readers and writers that these ideas demand thoughtful, reflective thinking.

Student Design

When provided with a multimedia environment and the opportunity to create, students need to practice control. The impulse is to create the flashiest presentation that incorporates the latest interactive software and images that blink, move, and often distract the viewer from the intended meaning in the work. "Visual assault" is the result of lack of guidance or lack of understanding when it comes to the content or requirements. Early projects submitted by my students reflected that the time and attention had been placed in animation rather than thinking. It wasn't unusual for me to open a student file and brace myself for the sensory onslaught that would begin as soon as I clicked the Start button. Together, we learned. The golden rule in my classroom when it comes to any multimedia task is 80 percent content, 20 percent glitz. The 20 percent provides students with just enough room for creativity, keeping the content in the forefront. Students begin to internalize this balance, developing their own criteria for information quality, presentation, and the overall final product.

As with the other design-related activities discussed in this book, it is imperative that students plan prior to setting foot in a computer lab. As an incremental checkpoint in all multimedia-related projects, I require that students submit (and gain approval for) storyboards and design plans before they gain access to a computer. In the case of a hypertext project, students must also have written all the text. Although designs and text are always open to change once students are working with the computer, the plans work as guides. Without that, tremendous amounts of time can be misspent. Generally, a more complex design of a hypertext project indicates deeper student understanding. However, teachers need to closely gauge the design so that the goals do not extend beyond the time allotted or the skills of the group members.

Collaboration

Building hypertext lends itself well to a team or group approach. As in all collaborative activities in my class, students are provided with rubrics and requirements that specify how each student will be held accountable for her work. To that end, I typically make sure that individual students are responsible for specific chunks of text. Students then work to fuse their writing, which challenges them to see their individual words as part of a larger context. Furthermore, this process often requires students to explore point of view and voice as they work to piece the individual texts into a whole.

As in most team activities, group experiences assist in the development of interpersonal skills. The process of having to make it clear to one's peers what one wants to say, what matters about the information, can be very powerful, even if the finished product is more a collection than a fully integrated collaboration. Also, students need to work as a team to manage the specific tasks within the project. If the team members don't work to determine the focus of their writing, dividing it into reasonable, well-focused subtasks, the individual writings won't have meaning when brought together. Again, teachers need to actively monitor, encouraging students to ask critical, reflective questions about the collaborative process, analyze the effects of their choices, and probe their own collective thinking as others interpret and navigate through their product.

Oral Presentation

Hypertext presentations lend themselves quite well to in-class presentations, especially because students are so invested in their work. The presence of a real audience motivates students to go beyond the requirements of an assignment, pushing them to think more deeply and consider their audience's response to their work. Kayla wrote in a journal entry, "Because I have to present this to the class and the tenth graders who are using my work before studying *Night,* I've found myself paying close attention to detail and really thinking about what readers will know after working through this hypertext. It really has increased the challenge. I want this to be useful *and* meaningful." Furthermore, integrating technology into a presentation helps to draw in students who are tech-savvy but not necessarily eager presenters. Broadening the audience by posting the work to the Internet invests students even more.

Ending Points

A close examination of state and national standards reflects that work with hypertext is anchored in those skills and understandings that we are working to develop in students. Hypertext provides a new avenue through which we can explore the roles of readers and writers. We can talk about how meaning is conveyed and constructed. We can talk about how we structure experiences for readers, whether text is linear or nonlinear.

I continually turn to my students' writing as a reflection of the power of matching the right technology tool with the right students and the right task. Krystale, a student writer who struggled with quantity and with conveying her intended meaning, made the following observations at the close of our first hypertext project:

> I could start by thinking about and writing about the fact that class is really different when a teacher is the one asking "How did you do that?" but that is another entry altogether. Instead, I want to think about what this has taught me as a writer. I understand that what I am placing out there for readers is almost as much about navigation as it is about what I have to say, whether it's linear or nonlinear. Hypertext has led me to think about how I communicate my ideas because my earlier linear writing is probably as much of a Web as that which I've done in this project. . . . I was able to add so much—strategically—in using hypertext. It taught me precision and elaboration, voice and audience, and structure and lack thereof. I'm so curious about how this will impact how I write from this point forward.

Related Reading

Birkerts, Sven. 1994. *The Gutenberg Elegies: The Fate of Reading in an Electronic Age.* New York: Fawcett Columbine.

Gilster, Paul. 1997. *Digital Literacy.* New York: Wiley.

Gruber, Sibylle. 2000. *Weaving a Virtual Web: Practical Approaches to New Information Technologies.* Urbana, IL: National Council of Teachers of English.

Murray, Janet H. 2001. *Hamlet on the Holodeck: The Future of Narrative in Cyberspace.* Cambridge, MA: MIT Press.

Patterson, Nancy G. 2000. "Weaving a Narrative: From Tears to String to Hypertext." *Voices from the Middle* 7 (3): 41–48.

Wilhelm, Jeffrey. 2000. "Literacy by Design: Why Is All This Technology So Important?" *Voices from the Middle* 7 (3): 4–14.

5 Reading the Web: Information Literacy

The creation of information about information is the beginning of the new enlightenment.

— Tim Berners-Lee

Your doubts are the strongest asset you bring to the Internet.

— Paul Gilster

We have been slow to acknowledge that every extension of speech—from painting to hieroglyphs to the alphabet to the printing press to TV—also generates unique ways of apprehending the world, amplifying or obscuring different features of reality. Each medium, like language itself, classifies the world for us, sequences it, frames it, enlarges it, reduces it, argues a case for what the world is like.

— Neil Postman

As English teachers, we never expect students to select a book and work their minds through it without first preparing them with strategies, expectations, and tools for unpacking what they might find. Why is it, then, that we allow students to access digital information posted online without similar tools? We know that the Internet presents something dramatically different from what we find in print text. So, why don't we empower students before we set them loose?

I learned this the hard way. I was introduced to the Internet while in college, developing my own means of sorting and sifting the then limited stores of information that it presented. I headed into my first year of teaching confident that I could efficiently use the Internet to find the information I needed and faultily assuming that my students possessed the same skills. After all, they had been a part of a school with abundant resources, complete with an Internet-connected computer in each classroom, not to mention several networked computer labs with high-speed access. Surely, my eighth-grade students had been taught to locate, question, evaluate, and use the information found online.

My first attempt at working with students as researchers in the computer lab occurred early in the school year as we took on our first research project. As a part of an interdisciplinary study of the discovery of the *Titanic,* students in my class were to research the histories of the passengers on the ship. Our goal was to write a persuasive essay addressing whether the remains of the RMS *Titanic* and its passengers should be raised for public sale and viewing. In preparation for the work ahead, I previewed the writing assignment with students, discussing portions of the book by explorer Robert Ballard that they were reading in science class. We didn't talk about the specifics of the research ahead, only that we would meet the next day in the lab.

What I saw as structuring the assignment was really just structuring my classroom. Students were assigned specific seats in the thirty-seat computer lab. I checked which computers were functioning, hanging a sign on those that weren't connected or that had some other problem. I did some quick math, determining which computers would be used for the Internet and which would be used to search the CD-ROM resources available in the media center. After all, I knew our Internet connection was slow enough to prevent twenty-eight students from conducting online searches simultaneously if we actually expected to get anywhere in our forty-five-minute class period. I labeled each computer with a colored 3" x 5" card indicating which research tool that workstation was to be used with. Though this was significant preparatory work, none of it addressed teaching students how to research or how to use the information each tool would make available.

I invited my first-period class into the computer lab from their orderly line in the hallway. Students took their seats, filling all the workstations designated for Internet use and sporadically selecting some of the other resources. I quickly reviewed the assignment, emphasizing that students needed to use their research time efficiently because we only had two days of lab time reserved. They quickly leapt to the task, logging onto their workstations and locating information that met their research needs. Or so I thought.

Carrie was one of the strongest writers in the class, possessing remarkable skills when it came to crafting poetry. She was painfully shy, to the point of barely speaking with her peers and never speaking in class. These students were part of a cohort and had been working together in blocked classes for the past three years. Few had ever heard Carrie speak, but they all respected her intellect and mastery over written words. Yesterday, in class, Carrie had stood in the front of the class and read a few stanzas of an extended metaphor poem she'd written that morning. It was one of those moments where the classroom was hushed in respectful awe, with my students startled and yet supportive of these giant steps being made by one of their own. Carrie's smile as she finished reflected that she understood the leap she'd just made, and I felt as if I might burst with pride and excitement for what was ahead.

As students began their research in the lab, Carrie was seated at a computer that was to be used to access the Internet. She logged on and applied the strategy with which she was accustomed to finding information online. Most Web sites at this early stage of the Internet had their subject matter in the URL (universal resource locator). For example, you could go to www.pets.com if you needed advice on how often to walk your dog, or to www.nbc.com if you were looking for that night's television lineup. Carrie used this same logic to start her search, typing www.titanic.com into the search field in her browser window. Up came a porn site. (Note that this same address now will reach the *Titanic* site correctly.) Like many of these sites, not one window opened but several, causing Carrie to panic as she anxiously clicked to close the windows that continued to open and get increasingly offensive. As if this situation wasn't bad enough, Bob, the student seated next to her, noticed the inappropriate content on her screen and, in a way that reminded me that he was a preteen, called it to the attention of his peers.

I lost Carrie that day. Her confidence and willingness to share aloud in class was shattered by her embarrassment. I had failed her by not ensuring that she knew how to find the information she was looking for. I had failed her by not teaching her to read, search, evaluate, and efficiently locate useful, accurate information. It wasn't a lesson I needed to learn twice. Just because our students are able to cruise through the Internet with speed and what looks like skill doesn't mean they know what they are doing. The Internet can be a tremendously valuable communication and information tool when harnessed in the context of your classroom studies and when you teach students to be savvy users. Missing that step only leaves students to navigate the information superhighway without a map, a tank of gas, and a spare in the trunk.

What Is the Internet?

Simply put, the Internet is a worldwide network of networks. Its essence, though, is how computers send data to each other. The data are transmitted over various carriers, such as telephone lines, cable TV wires, and satellite channels. The data can be text, e-mail messages, sounds, images, or software programs (Berners-Lee 1997). Content online is immediate, interactive, and immersive. We access the Internet in our classrooms or homes using either a network or an access provider and a browser. Physically, the Internet is a worldwide tangle of cables, modems, computers, and other hardware. Teachers are usually less interested in the technical specifics than in the information it makes available. Though documents available online are text-heavy, the Internet is quickly being overrun with images, music, images, video segments, images, animations, and still more images. The World Wide Web (a huge collection of sites made accessible via the Internet), besides having the unique status of being named "word of the year" in 1995, is what, in conjunction with your browser, allows you to access all documents stored using a multimedia format (hypertext transfer protocol) (Baron 1999). Online access in the classroom means immediate access to a tremendous and increasing network of people: writers, great thinkers, parents, community members, and specialists. We communicate through e-mail, discussion boards, chat areas, MOOs (MUDs, object-oriented), and MUDs (multi-user dungeons, from gaming).

The Pew Internet and American Life Project has generated several reports, all of which are focused on how we are using the resources that the Internet makes available to us both in school and at home. The most recent federal research finds that more than 98 percent of U.S. public schools have some kind of Internet access for students (Lenhart and Simon 2001). As most teachers would be quick to point out, having access doesn't mean students are using the Internet to empower their learning. Three-quarters of online teens say the Internet helps them do their schoolwork; half say it helps them a lot (Lenhart and Simon 2001). Students use the Internet to download study tools such as Cliffs Notes, Monarch Notes, and study guides. Seventy-one percent of online teens reported relying mostly on Internet sources for their research with only 24 percent reporting that they use mostly library sources (Lenhart and Simon 2001). Students in my classes agreed, explaining that the Web, when harnessed effectively, has speed and currency on its side, whereas school and local libraries often do not have current materials and are more difficult for students to navigate.

What follows is a discussion of how I teach all students in every one of my classes to mindfully work with information found on the Internet. Though this is sometimes built into the basic training activities at the start of the semester, I often wait to include this once we begin research projects utilizing online sources. The key is that I don't allow students to use online resources for any class projects until we've gone through the basics. Students are sometimes very resistant to acknowledging that they don't know everything when it comes to working online. Perhaps this is because they are so used to working with the technology. Perhaps it is because we often turn to teenage users as "experts." In any case, it's always interesting to note how in the course of the classes we spend on examining the Internet, we all learn something new. Students continually teach me new approaches to searching or show me new search engines. On the flip side, students are grateful to learn strategies that lead them to be more informed, critical, efficient users when they are going online to seek out timely, accurate information. Wilhelm (2000) poses a question when it comes to working with technology in our classrooms: "Will we surf on the crest of the future's breaking wave—which will be exciting, scary and outrageously fun— or will we drown in it?" The goal of these strategies is to, at the very least, provide a flotation device.

Assessing the Basics

Step One: What Do Students Already Know?

As with so many of the activities and studies that we undertake in our classroom, we begin by discussing what we know, what we have experienced, and what questions we have. I ask students about their online history. Who has used the Internet as a research tool? How did that go? Did they find what they needed right away? Who taught them to search? What strategies don't work? Sometimes, students unearth horror stories related to hours spent trying to locate the right information, stumbling onto inappropriate sites, or even including inaccurate, problematic information in class projects, unaware that they were working with a faulty source. These stories build a quick community. As Glen, a junior, wrote, "I thought that I was the only one who hadn't figured out how to really use the Internet for school. Our discussion eased my concerns, piqued my interest, and led me to critically question something that I do now without even thinking."

Step Two: Internet Q&A

We follow our discussion with a quick quiz (see Table 5.1), another assessment tool that allows students to explore what they know and prepare for what is ahead. I have both a PowerPoint and an online version of the quiz, depending on whether we are using a projector and the classroom computer, or the students are working in the lab. My students' favorite use of the quiz is as an active "game show," testing the knowledge of at least two students. Sometimes the quiz is a discussion catalyst, and sometimes I use it simply to trigger their indi-

Table 5.1

Question (True or False?)	Answer
1. All search engines are alike.	1. False. There are meta-searches, megasearches, and even search engines that require sites to pay a fee to come up early in a search list.
2. Search engines search everything on the Web.	2. False. They actually search a limited number of sites. The "deep Web," where most primary sources are located, isn't accessed by most search engines.
3. The most common error when searching is spelling.	3. True.
4. Your goal when you search is to gain the highest number of hits.	4. False, though students will disagree. Searching for "George Bush" last night yielded over 35 million pages. Success?
5. Keywords when searching are essential.	5. True.
6. Sites that end in .gov and .edu are "safer" when it comes to research material.	6. False. There is a lot of other information that a URL will give you that is much more helpful in assessing credibility than just the ending of the address. Government and education sites still have private directories that let people post opinions and inaccurate information.
7. The first site listed after I have completed a search using a search engine is the best.	7. False. The order of the results differs from search engine to search engine. Some list them in order of most popular. Others invite the owners of Web sites to pay a fee, which corresponds to the order of their posting. For example, if I pay $500, mskajder.com can be listed within the first ten hits when a user searches under "Kajder."

vidual, silent thinking. Sometimes I use it as a journal prompt, and sometimes I use it as a written preassessment. No matter how we use it, the questions and responses provide a rich starting point.

Reading a URL

Web sites have addresses that allow you to find specific pages. The URL allows you to point your Web browser to a specific server housing the Web pages and information you are looking for. The server sends an electronic copy of the Web page (or information) to your computer, where your browser software (e.g., Netscape Navigator or Internet Explorer) displays it for you. Learning how to read the URL provides you not only with a clue as to the credibility of the source of the information but some tricks in locating a page when the link doesn't work the first time.

Let's break down the URL of a great Web site and reference tool for English teachers, <http://www.webenglishteacher.com/>.

http://	Hypertext transfer protocol. The set of formal rules describing how to transmit data and information over the Internet.
www	World Wide Web. A collection of sites made accessible by the Internet.
.webenglishteacher	Name of the server.
.com/	Commercial domain.

A word about domains. Though domain names seem to be on the increase, there are just a few that you and your students need to be familiar with:

.gov	government
.edu	education
.org	organization
.net	network
.mil	military
.info	general use
.biz	business

Just because the domain name indicates that the site has a government or education tie doesn't mean that the information is automatically credible. The domain name can give you a tip, but there is still work to be done in order to evaluate the site more fully.

Paul, a colleague who teaches tenth- and twelfth-grade English classes, came to me with a problem this past school year. A student had submitted an essay using several Web sites as references. The problem was that the sites were neither credible nor appropriate, one written by a neo-Nazi and another offering the personal views of an electrical engineer who deemed himself an expert on Holocaust revisionism. Paul had given students a brief how-to for reading the URL of a Web site and felt that they had been prepared prior to starting their online research. I offered a few suggestions after seeing the Web sites his student had selected, pushing him to extend the strategies he provided students when working to evaluate the sites using just the URL.

Paul had instructed students that sites ending in .gov and .edu were usually more credible than those ending in .com or .net. Unfortunately, this advice is a little too general, given all the folders and subdirectories made available for individuals who have rights at government and education (college, school, university) sites. For example, as a graduate student at the University of Virginia, I have online privileges that include a small allocation of Web space. The URL reads <http://www.people.virginia.edu/~sbk8q/>. Another tip when it comes to determining whether a site is personal or "professional" has to do with the tilde (~), which indicates that you are working with a personal subdirectory and personal Web pages. As a rule of thumb, evaluate personal sites closely for accuracy of information and point of view. I don't have to be an expert in the procedure of changing the oil in my car to post "instructions" for this on my personal Web site.

Another tip for working with a URL is to truncate the address to locate additional sites for information, or simply to locate information you were looking for if the immediate link doesn't work. Truncating means deleting a folder or section from the address. For example, if clicking on <http://www.mskajder.com/romeo/lesson> brings up an error page, the URL can be truncated to <http://www.mskajder.com/romeo/> in a new attempt to find that information. This is useful if you are looking for additional information about the site or its author, especially biographical information or information about the larger Web site of which this folder or document is a part.

Paul used these two strategies and found scads of information indicating that the Web sites his student had looked up were problematic, even before he got to the point of reading the text posted to the sites. He conferred with his student, modeled the strategies, and then shared the strategies as part of a mini-lesson to his classes. He explained to me later that "though this doesn't prevent students from stumbling onto a site that isn't appropriate for scholarly research, it gives them more tools to critically investigate the site before they invest the time in reading its content. Starting with the URL is starting at the beginning."

Search Engines

A search engine uses a computer program called a spider or robot to sift through sites on the Web and log the words on the pages it finds. Good search engines will search through the content on the page, and not just the meta-tags that a page's author might have planted for the search engine to immediately pick up.

Search engines don't search every site on the Web, and they don't search Web sites at the moment you enter keywords into their search window. Instead, a search engine searches its own internal database of Web sites. This is why your search can happen so quickly—it's not a live search of the Web. Instead, you're looking through extracts saved on the search engine's server. Because of the sheer size of the Internet, it's not possible for the spiders or robots to find every page. Nor is it possible for a search engine database to be instantly and completely up-to-date.

What this all boils down to is that you cannot literally search the Web. You can only search a snapshot taken by a search engine. What does this mean in terms of your searching? You'll want to use a search engine that is up to speed, houses a large database, and allows you to narrow your search with relative ease.

The foremost database many students and teachers rely on seems to be Google, <http://www.google.com/>. Why? It has the largest database, indexing more than 3 billion Web pages. It turns up those sites that are usually most relevant right from the start. Google uses mathematical formulas to rank a Web page based on the number of "important" pages that link to it. The philosophy is that high-quality Web sites link to other high-quality Web sites. When a search is conducted, Google determines which sites meet the criteria and then lists the most popular sites among the high-quality resources at the top of the list. It also provides local cache access to pages that have disappeared since its last Web crawl or that are otherwise unavailable. (Hint: Click on Cached when you can't get a site to load from Google.)

There are many search engines available online. The key is to know which search engine will yield the results you seek with the least amount of dead time spent as you surf through the listings. As a whole class, we typically explore a range of search engines—some that students regularly use and some from my list of favorites (or not-so-favorites). The trick is to make sure that you examine search engines and not meta-search engines (search engines that search several search engines, such as www.dogpile.com or www.momma.com). I pair students into teams and assign each team two different search engines to examine using the form shown in Figure 5.1. (A blank is provided in the Appendix.)

Using Search Engines

Assigned Search Engine(s): __all the web , yahooligans__

Class Keyword: __SLEEP__

Use the graphic organizer below to record your team's observations in the corresponding columns. Be specific and precise in your observations.

Search Engine (list the name)	Web Address (list the full URL)	Information Display (Is the list categorized? Are the links organized according to a system? How is color used? Are instructions for searching provided? etc.)	Layout and Advertising (Is the site designed in a manner that allows for easy navigation? Do ads distract? Is this a site that would be appropriate for users of all ages?)	Links Listed (Are the listed links described in a way that allows you to scan and select? Are the links that appear after the simple search appropriate and what you are looking for?)
ALL the Web	http:// www. alltheweb.com	Big, open keyword field. "Help" offers instructions but is hard to locate. Color distinguishes between ads, links & description.	- Ads are only up at the top of the page. - "Clean" layout. - "Results" are in a clear list with keywords & a description.	Our keyword is very general, but we did find useful info. many hits, arranged in groups of 10. → Great "news" feature
Yahooligans	http:// www. yahooligans.com	Great graphics. Fun. Color distinguishes between links & description. Lots of "white space." Help comes up after we searched.	- Ads are labelled & off to the right. Very appropriate for school use.	A category is offered for more specific search directions. Hits are all interesting & "classroom appropriate." Again, too many hits. Some answer questions. That would help with research!

Figure 5.1

As a class, we determine a class keyword so that everyone will be using the same search term. I typically make suggestions dealing with topics and great writers from class. "William Shakespeare" and "Mark Twain" have turned up results that stimulate some interesting discussions. You should give this a test run without students, to ensure that the hits found aren't something that you don't want to bring into your classroom. For example, avoid keywords such as "Moby Dick" or "Animal Farm."

Give students time to explore and take note of their findings. I ask students to focus on the layout of the search engine, the speed of the search, the number and arrangements of the hits, the advertising, and the ease of finding and using the search window. Student findings generate a rich discussion, especially when anchored by an examination of these search engines from an educational viewpoint. Which search engines would most likely help students locate effective, credible information in an efficient, easy-to-use manner?

Searching Strategies

Keywords are essential when working with a search engine. Without the right keyword, students use too much time conducting and essentially muddling through the search. However, it isn't just the keyword that is important. Especially when searching for specific documents or information, students need to construct a phrase, searching on multiple phrases while excluding certain other words. The goal is to locate the most relevant information in the shortest amount of time. The key is in preplanning.

Before identifying keywords, students need to consider exactly what information they are looking for. To do this, divide a sheet of paper into three columns: Must, Might, and Mustn't. Brainstorm within these columns those aspects that *must* be located in your search, those that *might* be helpful, and those that *mustn't* enter into the search. Model this for students and then require it as a preplanning organizer or entrance pass to the computer lab.

Once students have identified their topic, have them break it down into key concepts. This is invaluable as they develop a keywords list. Consider the main concepts in the topic, and make sure students know the correct spellings. Once this keywords list is complete, consider how the words can be put together using Boolean operators (AND, OR, NOT) to find more of what students are looking for. To help students visualize how keywords work, I have everyone stand. I begin by asking all of the "television viewers" to remain standing. This typically leaves the entire class still standing. I explain that this is too many students for me to talk with, so I need the "television viewers AND reality TV show fans" to stay standing. This helps to narrow the field some, but it is usually still a pretty large bunch. I again explain that the field is a little large and ask for only the "television viewers AND reality TV show fans NOT *Survivor* fans." I keep narrowing until I have a small group of students. A simple activity, this really is effective in visually demonstrating to students the effect of narrowing the search. It also helps us to start talking about Boolean operators.

Let's start with a simple search. Today, I went into Yahoo! and typed Othello into the search field. I ended with 38,000 hits. Contrary to what students might think, that many hits is not an indication of success. I don't want to scan through 38,000 sites. Instead, I'll work to narrow the list and refine the search using Boolean operators.

To begin, I want to link *Othello* and Shakespeare so that I'm getting Web sites that focus on the play and not a game, a musician, or other unrelated topics. I type Othello AND Shakespeare into the search field. (Boolean operators should always be typed in ALL CAPS.) In some search engines, AND is assumed. In that case, all you need to do is enter Othello Shakespeare. It also works to enter +Othello +Shakespeare. Check the instructions of the search engine to learn the specifics when linking terms.

Let's say that I want to locate information on the play but don't want sites focusing on the Fishburne film released in 1995. I can type +Othello –Fishburne or Othello NOT Fishburne into the search field. This eliminates all the *Othello* sites that have "Fishburne" in their meta-tags.

With some search engines, if I want to find a phrase, I place it in quotation marks. For instance, to find sites featuring Iago's line "I am what I am," I type "I am what I am" into the search field. This also works if you wanted to check a student paper for possible plagiarism. Type the questionable line (with quotation marks) into the search field. This isn't fail-proof, but if the site has been added to the database of the search engine, you'll be able to pull something up.

If I only want to find pages where "Othello" is part of a title, I use the title tag. Type title followed by a colon and the name you are looking for into the search field: title:Othello. This is good when looking for pages that are primarily about one thing and you want a tightly narrowed search.

The link tag is equally useful, especially when evaluating the content of a page or the credibility of its author. Type link followed by a colon and the URL of the site you are searching. In other words, if I want to locate the pages that are linked to www.mskajder.cjb.net, I need to type link:www.mskajder.cjb.net into the search field. You'd find links to the school I used to teach at, Bernie Dodge's WebQuest matrix, www.webenglishteacher.com, and sites of other English teachers around the country. It's a good way to get a better sense of the context of my Web site and my credibility as a source. This tag works exceptionally well in the search engine www.altavista.com.

Keep in mind that each search engine has its own way of searching. Google, for example, does not require a Boolean search; it always works with exactly what you type into the search field. Your best bet—emphasize this to your students—is to read the instructions for the specific search engine that you select. Google has a long, clearly explained help section, a must for any search engine you use in the classroom.

Meta-Searches

Meta-search engines (also known as multithreaded engines) search several major search engines at once. Meta-search engines do not crawl the Web or maintain a database of Web pages. Instead, they act as a middle agent, passing on a query to the major search engines and then returning the results. Because the search engines produce very different results, meta-search engines provide a quick way to determine which engines best match students' needs in terms of research. However, as with anything that yields additional results and ideas, using meta-searches can overwhelm students with options and choices if they aren't set on their topics. I recommend their use only by student researchers who know what they are looking for. The following are some meta-search engines:

www.dogpile.com	Searches fourteen search engines as well as newsgroups, business news, and newswires. Use Boolean operators and phrase searching.
www.c4.com	Displays results from nine search engines, subject directories, and specialty databases. Use Boolean operators and phrase searching.
www.metacrawler.com	Submits queries to nine search engines and subject directories.
www.profusion.com	Searches fourteen engines and subject directories. Use Boolean operators.

The Deep Web

The deep Web (sometimes referred to as the invisible Web) is made up of sites that aren't indexed by search engines. For a search engine to find a site, it needs to be static and linked to other pages. Traditional search engines therefore can't get to those pages that are dynamic or unlinked.

The deep Web is qualitatively different from the surface Web. Deep Web sources store their content in searchable databases that only produce results dynamically in response to a direct request. This is the largest growing category of new information on the Internet. Deep Web sites house images, articles, primary source documents—really specialized content that can be accessed more easily or only by using the Internet. Students need to tap into this in order to benefit fully from a Web search.

Most media centers subscribe to sites that access deep Web resources. Proquest, SIRS Discoverer, SIRS Researcher, and GaleNet offer literary criticism, magazine and journal articles, newspaper articles, charts, maps, digitized sound and video clips, and encyclopedia articles. Your first step needs to be to touch base with your school media specialist or librarian, or your community library, to see what subscription resources are available. Several Web sites also tap into the research resources available online (see the Web site for this book). Search engines are starting to dig deeper or to develop specialized tools that allow users to look through periodicals available online. Google offers a news and periodicals search that my students have found to be tremendously useful when looking for primary sources and other immediately current information. Use the Google link for "news."

Evaluating What You Find

Jim Burke writes in *The English Teacher's Companion* (1998) that when Deng Xiao Ping was asked to allow the people of China to access the Internet, he responded that he would like first to meet with the president of the Internet Corporation. "There is no Internet Corporation," his adviser answered. "Well, then who is in charge of it?" Deng asked. "No one," the adviser answered. That's just it. Anyone can place information online, no matter what its accuracy or content. Although that empowers individuals to post their own content online, it's also a warning that we need to lead students to critically and responsibly choose and evaluate what they find.

McKenzie (2000) writes that students need to become "infotectives," capable of asking good questions about data in order to convert the data into information and eventually into insight. When it comes to working with Web sites, our infotectives need to analyze information about authorship, content, navigability, point of view, purpose, and related links. Students have to be taught to slow down when online. They are used to jumping about from site to site, scanning information, and quickly advancing to the next link. Pushing them to question using a structured rubric and mind-set helps them dissect and analyze what they have found.

In the rubric I use in class, students are given two empty columns, framed by specific information on the right and left sides (see Appendix, "Scoring Rubric for Evaluating Reliability and Credibility of Web Pages"). The design of the rubric is meant to lead students to know what criteria they are looking for and what a good site would contain. I'm quick to emphasize to students that I have yet to find a site (even one I designed) that includes *all* the ideal characteristics in the rubric's right-hand column. The empty columns are for student comments and reflection on the sites they have located, allowing them to record their judgments according to the criteria listed. An electronic copy of the rubric is stored on the hard drives of the computers in our department lab as well as on the hard drive of our classroom computer. I keep paper copies in a box in the front of the classroom and in the writing lab. Students know where to find them, how to use them, and that they are required to evaluate every Web site they use or make reference to in my class.

Burke (2001) writes that "Internet thinking is not inherently reflective; it's hard to think too much about where you are going when you are driving a hundred miles an hour as many do on the Internet." The abundance of information on the Web is just going to grow. Providing students with an evaluation tool that is used actively and discussed regularly in class slows them down, providing some rules for the road that lead them to be mindful, analytical information users.

Ending Points: How to Handle Plagiarism

Inevitably, providing students with access to the volumes of information found online has both positive and negative effects when it comes to how students use what they find. We know that students are natural economizers and that the shortest route through a course is often the most appealing. Just think how many times we're asked, "Will this be on the test?" during the course of the day. Some students have poor time management skills, and others are simply intimidated by the academic or scholarly nature of some of the tasks that they encounter in our classes. No matter what the reason, paper mills and online repositories are deceptive, appealing sites that abound online. Even as I conducted the *Othello* search described in this chapter, I was presented with multiple pop-up windows offering me access to droves of essays written on "popular topics" related to the text, an enticing option for the student who is behind in his work or simply not understanding the reading.

So what does plagiarism look like? In some extreme cases, it is an entire downloaded essay. In others, students cut and paste text from several sources to make one whole essay. Internet plagiarism also occurs when students purchase papers from paper mills (even though I've had scores of discussions with enraged parents who feel that because the paper was purchased it belongs to that student) and when students fake citations. Plagiarism happens when I lift someone else's words without paraphrasing them and don't give credit. Just because text is posted online doesn't mean that it's fair game.

I've seen several obviously plagiarized papers pass over my desk in the past few years. Here are some of the most obvious clues. One student submitted a paper at the bottom of which appeared the line, "This essay is from www.

papermill.com—join today!" Another submitted an essay directly from a Web site that listed the source's URL in the upper right-hand corner. Another paper might come to you with bizarre formatting and layout. The student in this case argued that something happened when he opened the essay in the school computers and that his home printer wasn't working right. Although that can happen, it's rare. Cutting and pasting from online sources with different formats points to direct appropriation.

Other clues to plagiarism are ones we are used to finding in student writing. Perhaps the quality of the writing is remarkably different from the work the student has submitted in the past, or the essay is way off topic. The bibliography is missing, or the essay contains uncharacteristically few grammatical or syntactical errors. I've found vocabulary to be one of the biggest red flags, usually leading me to ask the student to join me for an impromptu quiz on some of the words in the essay.

The foremost thing you can do to prevent plagiarism in your classroom is to educate your students. I make it part of my opening-day presentation, and I emphasize it again and again throughout the year. Make sure that your students know what plagiarism is. Share that definition with parents at back-to-school night. Demonstrate correct and incorrect paraphrases. Make a mini-lesson out of deconstructing an essay you download from a paper mill. Discuss the ethics related to the use of intellectual property. Make it clear that you know what is out there. If your students know that you are savvy, they are less likely to err.

Next, educate yourself. Investigate the Internet paper mills and sites that cater to high school English students. (A current list of active sites is given on the Web site for this book.) Read the sample papers. Put your essay topic into a search engine to see what comes up. Be savvy.

There are other strategies that can simply be incorporated into the design of the task. Clearly state the assignment and your expectations. Provide a narrow list of topics for students to choose from. Unusual topics with a narrow twist allow for unique mindful writing, not a reliance on what has already been said. Require specific components or that students work with specific articles and sources. Require incremental deadlines where students submit outlines, drafts, research material, bibliographies, and so on. I often require oral reports to ensure that my students are familiar with the content of their papers. This includes a classwide question-and-answer period, which generates interesting, testing questions. Last, I pair each written assignment with a written reflection that challenges students to think about what they have learned throughout the task and the writing process. None of this is unfamiliar to us. It is good planning and structured teaching. What works is that it keeps us each accountable and thinking about what is ahead.

Other resources are being developed that are helpful in detecting plagiarized work. Online detectors such as the one available through www.plagiarism .org allow teachers to submit an electronic copy of a student paper that, twenty-four hours later, is returned as a color-coded version of the essay. If text has been found in another source in the database (which is huge), it is changed to a corresponding color. This isn't a free service, but each department I've worked within has been quick to pick up the tab. I would randomly submit student work, and I made students aware of this—not because I was suspicious or didn't trust them but because I recognized the reality of what was available online. Only once did anything turn up.

The most important skill you can have when working with students who might have plagiarized is simply being open to what happened. This isn't an insult toward you; it's a signal that something else is going on. Talk with students. Often, students open up to me in the course of a dialogue, explaining what they didn't understand or how the deadline got the best of them. This is an opportunity for learning on the part of you and your student. This is the most serious academic offense that a student can commit in my class, and one that as members of our classroom community, most of my students take as seriously as I do.

Related Reading

Bushweller, Kevin. 1999. "Generation of Cheaters: Who's Cheating in Schools?" *American School Board Journal* (April). <http://www.asbj.com/>.

Horrigan, John. 2002. "Getting Serious Online." Washington, DC: Pew Internet and American Life Project. <http://www.pewinternet.org/>.

Lenhart, Amanda, and Maya Simon. 2001. *The Internet and Education: Findings of the Pew Internet and American Life Project.* Washington, DC: Pew Internet and American Life Project. <http://www.pewinternet.org/>.

November, Alan. 1998. "Teaching Zack to Think." *High School Principal* (September). <http://www.anovember.com/articles/zack.html>.

Suarez, J., and A. Martin. 2001. "Internet Plagiarism: A Teacher's Combat Guide." *Contemporary Issues in Technology and Teacher Education* 1 (4). <http://www.citejournal.org/vol1/iss4/currentpractice/article2.htm>.

Online Resources

History of the Internet and the World Wide Web.
<http://www.anderbergfamily.net/ant/history/>.
Internet 101. <http://www.Internet101.org/>.
Internet search guide.
<http://www.itrc.ucf.edu/conferences/pres/srchtool.html>.
Kathy Schrock's Guide for Educators (Web site evaluation surveys).
<http://school.discovery.com/schrockguide/eval.html>.
A Web Tutorial. <http://www.webteacher.org/windows.html>.

6

Going Beyond
Word Processing

Writing is the heart of the English class. In one form or another, it is constant: we are reading it, doing it, or preparing to do it.
—Jim Burke

Most people's relationship to the process of writing is one of helplessness.
—Peter Elbow

Words are getting a workout these days. . . . If we think of writing as a conversation, everyone seems to be talking at once.
—Patricia O'Connor

At the start of the school year, I presented my eleventh-grade English students with what I thought was a fairly simple question: "What is English class?" I expected that they would draw on the past years of study and develop an answer that would include some facet of the study of writing, reading, drama, and maybe even grammar and poetry. What I didn't expect was some of their responses. Denise, an articulate student with a strong personality, wrote, "English class is about staring at a blank piece of paper until you can transform it by thinking through your pen." Chris wrote in block letters, "English is about paperwork and what's old." Ben said, "English allows us to work in the computer lab, though it's only to work with the word processor—and even that is confining and restricted. We can only do what the teacher knows to do. English is about just that, restriction. Restricting my ideas and restricting the way in which I can use language or even a computer to express them." And Laura wrote, "English is about reading and writing—reading things that were written by people of different experiences and writing to figure out what those books have to do with me."

Challenged to build from where my students were and where some of them had never been, I aimed to create a rich class experience where writing was transformation of "blank space" and where students were making meaning from text and their own understanding. My goal was to incorporate technology tools and contemporary voices so that students wouldn't be immersed in "paperwork and what's old." I wanted meaningful engagement and understanding, and I wanted to ensure that Ben would be able to express himself using the computer as a creative tool, not as a restrictive device. Like the other attempts at technology integration that we've explored, the trick was both balance and matching the right tool with the right task and the right student.

As any practicing English teacher will tell you, students learn to write by writing. That means we immerse students in the study of existing texts, both great and terrible, and provide them with meaningful opportunities to exercise their own skills as readers and writers. Why add the computer into the equation? Current research and class practice demonstrate that students tend to write more when using a computer, are more willing to take scholarly risks, display more engagement with texts, and gain a clearer sense of voice and audience (Moeller 2002). The computer not only works as a motivator; it also teaches real-world skills and leads teachers and students to work more closely together when addressing and developing student writing.

On the flip side, there are some undeniable challenges. Research and class practice also indicate that working with computers can lead students to confuse editing with revision, to spend time struggling with equipment rather than ideas, and to focus more on the product features of word processing than on the process of writing high-quality text (Moeller 2002). Again, it's about pairing the right tool with the right task and the right student. If one of those elements is missing or even questionable, the pairing simply won't lead students to an enriched or empowered understanding. Instead, it will lead to frustration, much like that voiced by some of the students quoted previously.

Prewriting Strategies

Student writers in my classes have always insisted that getting started is the hardest part. Why? They often question what they have to say. Lucy Calkins (1994) writes, "The powerful thing about working with words is that we are really working with our thoughts. Writing allows us to put our thoughts on the page and in our pockets; writing allows us to pull back and ask questions of our thoughts." Student writers need space to explore their thoughts and to test how they look on paper (or, in this case, on the screen). Writers use prewriting to rehearse mentally, verbally and on paper, to discover the voice and form that will lead them to communicate ideas. Donald Murray (1982) describes prewriting as "everything that takes place before the first draft" and as the phase of writing that "takes about 85 percent of a writer's time." Adding the computer into the mix not only provides additional efficient tools for brainstorming and organizing ideas but lowers the stakes and raises engagement.

Five minutes of monitors off free-write.

Hanging on my classroom wall is a poster displaying Gertrude Stein's mantra "to write is to write is to write is to write is to write is to write is to write." The free-writing activity allows students to do just that. I've heard it called quick writing, invisible writing, or tactile writing. Here, students turn their monitors off and, in a quiet classroom, focus intensely on "screenless" writing. The objective is to help them experience fluency and flow while also lessening the need for control over their practice (Akers 2002). I've seen students who were completely "blocked" open up in this activity, no longer confined or overwhelmed by the blank screen. As Shayla, a ninth-grade ESL student, wrote, "Monitors-off writing allows me to concentrate on my thoughts and figuring out what I have to say. I don't have to worry about translation or grammar or how my work looks—I simply think about what I want to say."

Prewrite collaboratively by exchanging keyboards or roaming to different stations.

When working with a whole-class prompt, students often brainstorm best collaboratively, building ideas from those that are offered by the classroom community. Instead of calling out ideas and listing them on a whiteboard or chalkboard, students think about their writing by writing. As a small-group activity, student teams can simply pass the keyboard while clustered around a workstation. As a whole-class activity when you have access to a computer lab, students can roam to different stations at a cue. My students have likened this to the writer's version of musical chairs—only, now, no one is "out." I've mostly used word-processing software in this activity but have also used *Inspiration* and *Kidspiration* software to generate graphic organizers and mind maps.

Use *Inspiration* software to generate graphic organizers and run brainstorming sessions.

Graphic organizers are an effective way to help students generate nonlinguistic representations and to lead them to think their way through a prompt or writing task (Marzano, Pickering, and Pollock 2001). *Inspiration* (for students in grades 6–12) and *Kidspiration* (for students in grades K–6) are intuitive tools that allow users to easily create concept maps, Venn diagrams, cause-and-effect maps, mind maps, and other visual tools to discover and organize their thinking. Word processors also allow students to move ideas, testing their grouping and trying out relationships. Graphic organizers, when used in the English classroom and in other disciplines, help students visually explain and organize their ideas, think categorically, evaluate information, and understand text. These tools lead students to reveal patterns, interrelationships, and interdependencies. Furthermore, they are a quick tool that I can use, as a teacher, to identify student misconceptions or problem areas.

I use these tools in multiple ways, beginning with a whole-class brainstorm using the rapid-fire feature. Here, I ask a student to be the recorder, challenging both her and the class to generate ideas, which are then projected for whole-class viewing. Students recognize the power of the visual tools, using them not only for their writing but also for work with peers when reciprocally teaching. (This software also works well during staff meetings and staff development sessions for organizing content and responses.)

Use a spreadsheet to collect data for informational writing, brainstorm adjectives for descriptive writing, or list supporting reasons for point of view.

Spreadsheets allow student writers to have a repository of ideas, references, and models. Be creative and flexible with their use. I've used spreadsheets to capture and list great leads, as a tool for recording and then analyzing character traits in a novel, as a reference for student writers to examine rich, sensory description, and even to record progress on writing housed in their electronic portfolios. As a prewriting tool, spreadsheets provide students with a searchable environment in which they can discover, manipulate, and work their way through text and ideas.

Create tables in a word processor to assemble information as a writing reference.

Just as graphic organizers lead students through the organization and evaluation of information, tables created in a word processor will allow for a visual presentation that can also be cut and pasted into a text document.

Construct a story starter picture file using presentation software.

When students enter my classroom, their minds are typically full of whatever happened in the hallway, last period, and even that morning over breakfast. I begin each lesson with an activator in an attempt to lead them to focus on the tasks ahead. A useful prewriting tool is a picture file in PowerPoint (or other presentation software) which, when paired with music and an LCD projector, transports students into another time—particularly useful when we are working with the Jazz Age, the Harlem Renaissance, the American Revolution, and so on. I ask students to journal or free-write as they are presented with images from a period, theme, or specific topic. Often students' thinking is halted when they are dealing with a historical or thematic frame that is outside their experience. Providing them with context lowers the stakes and helps them begin discovery and a thinking process. This is best explained in a quote from Don Murray (1994) that my mentor teacher shared with me: "Writers are born at the moment they write what they do not expect. . . . They are hooked because the act of writing that, in the past, had revealed their ignorance, now reveals that they know more than they had thought they knew." (See examples on the Web site for this book.)

Present a model of the completed assignment and the steps for completion using presentation software.

The pairing of a projector and my classroom computer has yielded tremendous results. Where I'd traditionally relied on the overhead projector and a transparency of the text we were about to examine together, demonstrating takes the discussion to the next level. This provides students with an immediate reference point when they sit in front of their computers. They've seen the steps to the process and immediately know where to begin. As I've said earlier, it's dangerous to assume that all students bring the same tech skills to their classroom studies. By modeling, I demonstrate not only the technologies but also the writing process, thinking process, drafting, and other critical steps toward completing the work. All writers can benefit from strategies that take them beyond conventional drafting routines (Dunn 2001).

Revising and Editing Strategies

Although Donald Murray (1982) argues that writing is rewriting, students often see revision not as an opportunity to develop and improve a piece of writing but as an indication that they have failed to do it right the first time. To student writers, revision means correction. Golub (1999c) writes that "to students, the process of revision usually means to write the composition neater this time and to use only one side of the paper and . . . oh, yes, check the spelling. But using the computer in class to demonstrate the revision process can change a student's perception and understanding suddenly, dramatically, and permanently." It's difficult to lead students to see that revision and editing are separate steps, one involving a rethinking and the other looking at word choice, grammar, semantics, and syntax. Features such as cut and paste, spell check, and grammar check can often be seen as tools for both revising and editing. Using the computer can help students see the differences between the two processes by offering such distinctly different sets of tasks that students complete in the development of each piece.

It is important to note that revising on the computer can sometimes lead student writers to lose sight of the drafting process in that they continually revise using a single copy of the writing. Encourage students to keep track of their drafts so they can later examine how a piece evolved. They can save successive drafts with different version numbers; for example, "newyorkessay1.1," "newyorkessay1.2," and so on. My students find this useful in that they simply add a new number to the version label so that they can see how their text has developed.

Reflect in a writer's journal.

While writing a particular text, students also maintain an additional document that we call their writer's journal. Here, they record ideas for their writing along with reflective pieces on the process of writing a particular text or ideas for its development. In the lab or classroom, I require that students keep open both their writer's journal and the piece they are working on. Reflection allows them to gain additional control over the thinking that runs through their work. The writer's journal reflection allows students to question their own texts and ideas. They can discover "what they're doing well, and what they need to improve, [and] their subsequent performance can incorporate these important insights and lead to greater control" (Golub 1999a).

Do nutshelling.

A poster hanging on my classroom wall features a quote from Maya Angelou which students are always struck by. She writes, "Putting down on paper what you have to say is an important part of writing, but the words and ideas have to be shaped and cleaned as severely as a dog cleans a bone, cleaned until there's not a shred of anything superfluous." The most difficult skill for students in my classes is to learn how to write precisely. They typically have an uncanny knack for writing pages and pages that don't say much of anything. Nutshelling helps them cut through the superfluous text and get to the core of their thinking. To nutshell, students examine their writing, looking for the one sentence that captures the core ideas they want to express. They then begin with that sentence and write from there. Word processors make color coding, cutting, and manipulating text as easy as a keystroke, making this strategy quick and effective.

Locate topic sentences in paragraphs, and format with color. Locate supporting details and elaboration.

When working with a word processor, revising and editing are accessible and efficient. As Strickland (1997) writes, "Real writers can't help but cross out, start over, and move things around, and a computer's word processing facilitates this activity. Only a few keystrokes are needed to delete, copy, move and rearrange text." I require students in my classes to color-code their drafts, highlighting topic sentences in green, supporting details in red, and transitions in blue. This ensures, first, that these elements all exist in the paper, and second, that students are actively thinking about how they are using and identifying these components. Make the colors standard in each piece of writing, and use the strategy in peer reviews and conferences as well.

Use conclusions for introductions.

As a writer, I often have to sit down and write a few pages before I really figure out what I want to say. My students do, too. When it comes to revising their work, I often have them cut the conclusion of their essay and paste it in as the introduction. Typically, this moves the real meat and discovery of the writing to the beginning and allows them to move forward from the best points of their previous draft. Though this is initially met with groans, they later come to see the benefits of the additional labor.

Combine sentences using cut, paste, and copy skills.

When working with a word-processing program, it's easy to manipulate text. Students can work to alter the structure of their sentences, especially since word processors will allow space for adding and deleting from existing sentences. I've used drill and practice ("drill and kill") sentence-combining software with students in the past, but it's much more effective for them to complete activities in the context of their own writing. Have them open their texts, review concepts in a mini-lesson, and then set them loose to examine, manipulate, and enrich the sentences in their own essays.

Create a database of effective transitions and great leads.

Mark Twain explained that "the difference between the right word and the wrong word is the difference between lightning and the lightning bug." To help trigger student writers' thinking and provide a repository of effective words and phrases, have them refer to a class-constructed database of effective transitions, leads, and strong verbs and descriptors.

Use the comments feature in word processors or Adobe Acrobat to annotate writing.

Regardless of whether the feedback is from teachers or peer reviewers, it's difficult for students to take negative comments and spring into revising their work. Instead, they get locked into editing or dismiss the negative comments as a product of an "unfair reading." Atwell (1998) explains, "Writers are vulnerable. Our essential selves are laid bare for the world to see. Writers want response that gives help without threatening." Calkins (1994) recommends that students discuss positive rather than negative aspects of their writings: "Why not ask them to find bits of their writing—words, lines, passages—which seem essential, and then ask them to explore why these sections are so very significant?" Student readers can use the embedded comments feature in word processors or the notes option in Adobe Acrobat to share reactions to others' writing or to annotate their own writing. When student writers start a dialogue with their readers, they start with their own needs and concerns and can progress to being more open to discussion of their own writing.

Use multiple windows for devil's advocate.

Have students open two windows in their word processor, splitting the screen. Post the original essay in one window. Use the other to write the opposite case, pushing the reasoning and logic, and questioning the content of the original piece. The fusion of the two allows students to locate the flaws in their argument, add depth to their original writing, and strengthen their reasoning.

Use interactive multimedia mini-lessons to review writing or content skills.

Student writers all have their own skills and needs. When faced with a class filled with thirty-five different instructional needs, it's easy for a teacher to get overwhelmed. In order to help ensure that all students' needs are met when it comes to writing instruction, I create a bank of interactive gamelike tutorials and mini-lessons using PowerPoint or Flash. This allows students to explore and learn at their own pace, selecting lessons that are often recommended or required based upon their performance on specific writing tasks. This lowers the stakes, allows me to customize student instruction, and works as an effective differentiation tool. (Samples are posted on the Web site for this book.)

Publishing Strategies

Technology makes publishing—linking writers and readers—possible in ways that previously weren't accessible to middle or high school writers. Graves (1983) writes,

> Writing is a public act, meant to be shared with many audiences. When writing was first put to page in alphabetic form, it meant the writer could transcend himself in space and time. It is the poor man's instant replay. With only a writing instrument and material on which to inscribe letters, writers can have an effect on history, on people hundreds or thousands of years hence.

Students write with purpose and passion when they know that people they care about reaching will read what they have to say (Atwell 1998). Publishing in our classrooms, publishing on the Web, and publishing in print and multimedia publications opens all kinds of opportunities when it comes to extending the reach of all our students' voices.

Insert graphics or digital images to enhance presentations.
A simple means of enhancing student work is to add graphics and images, then publish by using a classroom printer or posting on the Web. The trick here is to make sure that the added "bells and whistles" supplement and enrich the content and don't distract readers or lead them down a side path. To insert images and graphics electronically, work with the tool options in your word processor. The low-tech version also works: simply cut and paste, then photocopy or scan the finished product so it now includes the image. Be sure to credit the source if the image or graphic is not created from scratch.

Create brochures, newspapers, and class booklets to share with the community.
An extension of the previous ideas is to produce a print product that is shared with the community outside of your classroom. I assign brochure making as a "during reading" assignment, asking students to create travel brochures for Romeo's Verona or Gatsby's East and West Egg. Students create the *Salem Sentinel* newspaper as an anticipatory activity prior to studying Arthur Miller's *The Crucible*. We compile student poetry and print an electronic and a print edition of a class literary magazine. We collect oral histories of residents of our local community, publishing them with digital images of the interviewees and

the photos and memorabilia that enhance the story. These histories are then shared with the community historical society as well as with the interviewees. Publishing student work in this manner also allows you to teach some basics when it comes to design and layout.

Publish on the Web or through e-mail to share work with others in collaborative online projects.

Though we'll talk more about online collaborative projects in Chapter 8, it's important to note here that one of the most essential features about working with students across the globe is the sharing of final products either through e-mail or by posting student work on the Web. Publishing allows you to extend the dialogue and understanding that grew out of the project while also teaching valuable communication skills. In the case of the Poetry Forge (see the companion Web site), student writers are encouraged not only to post their work but also to discuss the writing process and other student writing in a discussion forum. This allows publishing on multiple levels: publication of student poetry and then publication of thinking and analysis.

Use PowerPoint to publish class slide shows of poetry, letters to the editor, political cartoons.

Time is a scarce commodity in all classrooms, and publishing on the Web can take up a significant amount of it. Therefore, consider publishing student work in a multimedia presentation that is shared with parents at back-to-school night, students in different class periods, and teachers at your department or team meetings. In this way, the objective of sharing student voices and ideas with a larger audience is met. PowerPoint and Flash presentations also can be quickly adapted for uploading on the Web, involving no coding on your part. With simply the click of a button, you can extend the audience as far as you'd like.

Create an electronic portfolio.

I require each of my students to maintain an electronic portfolio using both the school server space and, at the end of each semester, a CD-ROM. Students create their own table of contents, include reflective writing about each piece, add evaluations made by teachers and peers, and include original art, photos, and illustrations. Areas exist for readers to make direct comments, provide feedback, and even include their own writing. These portfolios have been invaluable to students at college interviews while also substituting for a paper portfolio in a large binder that merely stores the work. The electronic portfolio is an organic compilation allowing writers and readers to work interactively through each piece.

Publish on the Web.

By publishing student work online, we extend our classroom community to include parents, other students, telementors, and virtually anyone who browses through the students' Web site. Building a class Web site is discussed more fully in Chapter 9, but it is important to note here that it's no longer necessary to learn HTML (hypertext markup language) in order to develop a Web site. With the introduction of WYSIWYG (what you see is what you get) web authoring software and preformatted sites like www.blackboard.com, teachers and students can develop high-end sites that include, highlight, and celebrate student work. Publishing on the Web extends student ownership and engagement. Jason, a former student who lacked the motivation to complete work successfully in my class, was quick to embrace the chance to create a Web site that featured his writing. To use his words, "No one in my family has ever been an author before . . . but when I took my Mom to the library to see my site, that's what she told me I now was."

Ending Points

I am a strong advocate for using computers as tools in the writing classroom, but I do not feel that all writing needs to be done in front of a computer screen. Instead, students need to learn how to use both sets of tools: computer and keyboard, and pen and paper. Though assessments such as the SAT are "catching up" by allowing students the opportunity to compose using a computer, students still need to know how to write when that tool isn't available. Furthermore, there is something powerful that happens between students, a pen, and a piece of paper. We don't want to lose sight of that. Again, it's about the right tool paired with the right student and the right task. Teachers need to see the computer as a machine that can help students address their writing problems—getting ideas, generating text, manupulating text after reviewing, collaborating with others in the classroom or over a network, editing their documents, and finally publishing hard copy—but that will not magically transform them (Strickland 1997). Ultimately, students are excited to work with computers, and when paired with an engaging and rigorous writing task, technology can enhance the skills of and empower our student writers.

Related Reading

Burke, Jim. 1998. *The English Teacher's Companion.* Portsmouth, NH: Heinemann.

Gleason, Barbara. 2001. "Teaching at the Crossroads: Choices and Challenges in College Composition." *The Writing Instructor.* <http://www.writinginstructor.com/reflections/gleason.html>.

Golub, Jeffrey N. 1999a. *Making Learning Happen.* Portsmouth, NH: Heinemann/Boynton-Cook.

Marzano, Robert J., Debra J. Pickering, and Jane E. Pollock. 2001. *Classroom Instruction That Works: Research-Based Strategies for Increasing Student Achievement.* Alexandria, VA: Association for Supervision and Curriculum Development.

Strickland, James. 1997. *From Disk to Hard Copy: Teaching Writing with Computers.* Portsmouth, NH: Heinemann/Boynton-Cook.

7

Going on a WebQuest

Thus the focus today has shifted from teachers being the gatekeepers of all knowledge and rules to one in which the teacher interacts with the curriculum and the students by designing active learning tasks, designing more authentic types of assessment, and redirecting time and energy.

—Cathy Vatterott

This is the first time I've used the Web, found something useful, and then learned enough to work through reading a piece of "classic" literature—how very cool.

—Sabrina, ninth-grade English student

What Is a WebQuest?

Entering into professional dialogues and toolkits as early as 1995, a WebQuest is an instructional model developed by Bernie Dodge, professor of educational technology at San Diego State University. WebQuests have an immediate connection to the constructivist English classroom in that they are inquiry-oriented and centered on a doable, differentiated, engaging task. The innovative twist, outside of its structure, is that the activity, its resources, and possibly even its product are all found online. Adaptations can be made for the one-computer classroom or those who do not have Internet access in school. Allowing teachers to utilize those sections of the Internet that are most relevant to a given task, the WebQuest is both a research tool and an active, engaging learning activity.

A complete WebQuest consists of an introduction, a task, a process for completing the task, online resources (preselected by the teacher) and an evaluation. Tasks are either short- or long-term. Short-term tasks focus on knowledge acquisition and integration. The task requires that students discover, evaluate, and synthesize new information, ultimately demonstrating understanding through some applied task. Long-term tasks focus on extending and refining knowledge. Here students develop deep understanding of information, communicating and demonstrating that through the creation of a more complex and sophisticated product (Dodge 1997).

Thousands of WebQuests have already been developed and are readily available through a quick online search. However, teachers are far from limited to adapting what has already been created. Working with WebQuests affords teachers the opportunity to generate an entirely new WebQuest from their own curriculum and student base, therefore directly tying to curriculum standards. In doing so, the teacher invariably enters into a professional, curricular dialogue with teachers who form a community of learners. Each of the fifteen WebQuests that I've designed and posted for classroom use has elicited e-mail from teachers across the world who are interested in management techniques, areas for adaptation, and simple reflection after using the activity in the English classroom. Furthermore, WebQuests are a reflective, professional learning tool in that they capture a glimpse of classroom instruction at a given moment. An even higher-level application of the method would challenge students to design their own WebQuests as products.

Curricular Considerations

Implementing WebQuests, like many of the methods and strategies in this book, ultimately requires some "outside-the-box thinking" on the part of teachers. The WebQuest demands that the teacher act as facilitator, designing the learning environment and task for students while ultimately charging them with responsibility for their own learning. An effective WebQuest will take students through all three stages of Silver's learning cycle: exploration, concept development, and concept application (Silver 2000). Teachers need to be familiar with problem-based learning as well as cooperative learning. They need to know how to structure and apply rubrics to evaluate student work. This is a method easily embraced by those who are already following best practice. And implementing a WebQuest might challenge teachers who have never before tried cooperative, problem-based assignments in the English classroom to take on a new hat.

WebQuests are an invaluable component in my classroom instruction for a variety of reasons. First, working with a WebQuest not only immerses my students in the information that I've preselected but also allows them to take responsibility for their own learning while working at their needed pace. The levels and abilities of the students who fill my classroom are strikingly varied, at the very least. In order to address that while planning for classes that average thirty-two students per forty-five-minute period, WebQuesting became a means for me to scaffold, to tap into the natural abilities of each student, and to challenge and push each student to go beyond where he had been before. Furthermore, WebQuests motivate student learners by asking a central question that honestly needs answering. Tom March (2000) writes that "when students are asked to understand, hypothesize, or problem-solve an issue that confronts the real world, they face an authentic task, not something that only carries meaning in a school classroom." When paired with real resources, a genuine question, just enough uncertainty and ambiguity to instill curiosity, and a role that allows them to develop skills, students become motivated, mindful scholars.

WebQuests expand my classroom walls by allowing me to take students anywhere in the world, putting them face-to-face with ancient primary sources as well as experts in any given field. The power is tremendous and the information, if I've done my job in setting up the experience, is current and immediately relevant. Students can pursue topics in significant depth, selecting and owning their learning.

Collaborative learning is a feature of the WebQuest that I have both struggled with and celebrated. Roles within the WebQuest allow students to develop dramatically varying skills and understandings. This is key to the differentiation it allows but also difficult to capture within an assessment rubric that captures both group and individual performance.

Analyzing the Design and Implementation of a WebQuest

I designed the following WebQuest to work within an eleventh-grade thematic unit centered on generating a lengthy research paper. That semester I was working with on-level students who were barely motivated to attend class, let alone complete the thought-provoking research paper that had evolved into a course graduation requirement. Students had learned to work the system and often would fail my course, then take the summer school course, which required no research paper because of time constraints. Using a WebQuest for this research was a natural fit and one that I hoped would motivate students to become the scholars that their potential genuinely indicated. What follows is a discussion of the design and implementation process, which also includes a detailed description of each component of the WebQuest, from introduction to evaluation.

Planning Before Turning on the Computer

Applying the elements of backwards design, I began planning for this WebQuest by considering my content standards and identifying essential questions and enduring understandings that would act as the foundation of the WebQuest:

Essential Questions for Planning

What skills and understandings should all students possess at the completion of this activity?

What related skills and understandings would students need to successfully begin?

How do the skills and understandings fit within the context of the larger unit and course?

The county-produced curricular guide was of little help, listing standards but not the concepts that would lead us there. The curriculum, generated in the mid-1980s, instructed that students were to complete independent research on a self-selected topic while exploring detective stories, which were related only through the "inquiry" theme of the unit. The two tasks were disjointed at best. Furthermore, the research papers were traditionally static documents. Students wrote them. Teachers graded them. The papers were returned and forgotten. My plan was to design a project in which the paper was the foundation for a project that had real-time relevance and value. I wanted to shift the focus from the process of writing the paper to using it to catapult into something that actually contained meaning for both my students and my instruction.

I selected media literacy as the backbone of and "hook" into the assignment. Where literacy involves the ability to understand, analyze, and use print to communicate, media literacy adds the ability to apply these skills to images, sound, and multimedia formats. These were skills that my media-saturated eleventh-grade students simply did not possess. The WebQuest, entitled "Getting the Word Out" (see Figure 7.1), would follow intensive in-class study of media messages grouped into three subcategories: female image, male image, and racial images. Students would choose one of the three subcategories as the subject of their research paper, and the final content of the project would be a team-designed Web site targeting county third-graders and their parents, both of whom would provide authentic assessment.

In terms of logistics, I taught four days of mini-lessons on different media literacy topics, in an attempt to expose students to advertising strategies that tar-

Figure 7.1

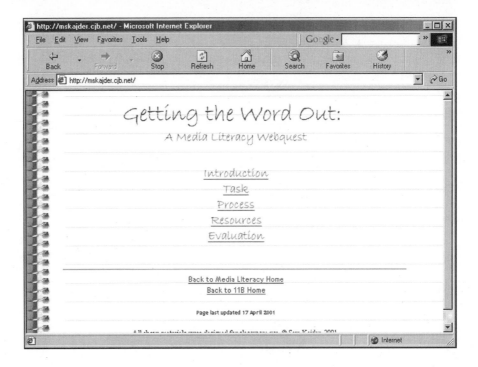

get teens, the holdings of media giants and how they affect what the public sees as news, and the effects of the images depicted in films and magazines. The class was given nine days for research and writing of the research paper. These sessions were held in the school media center, which provided print and non-print resources as well as fifteen networked computers. We then returned to the English classroom for one week of team Web site construction using the classroom computer. Students also were provided with after-school and lunchtime access to the classroom computer for additional work time. One day was then allocated for the presentation of the Web sites as well as debriefing.

Introduction

The purpose of the introduction (see Figure 7.2) is to present students with a lead into the assignment that is both engaging and informative. An effective introduction invites the students into the task while setting this activity apart from others that might have been done within the context of the course.

The introduction for "Getting the Word Out" immediately presents to students in the eleventh-grade class that their research will be the foundation for creating a Web site that could potentially be used by curriculum developers

Figure 7.2

working with Project Media Literacy. This connection was made at a training I attended, held by one of the principal directors of the project, which was in its first year of training teachers. She eagerly embraced the idea of bringing student work onto the program Web site after it had gone through a mutual assessment. This would be conducted in addition to testing the sites with area third-grade students and parents. Again, authentic assessment automatically communicated to students that this was a real-world assignment that would matter outside our classroom.

A structure note: An effective WebQuest will provide links to the different sections from each of its pages. From the introduction, you should be able to directly access the task page. Users should not have to use the Back button on the browser window to access additional pages.

Task

The task page (see Figure 7.3) immediately establishes what students will do to fulfill the project requirements. This is a general description of the end product as well as a continued, high-energy, real-world explanation of what students will complete.

Figure 7.3

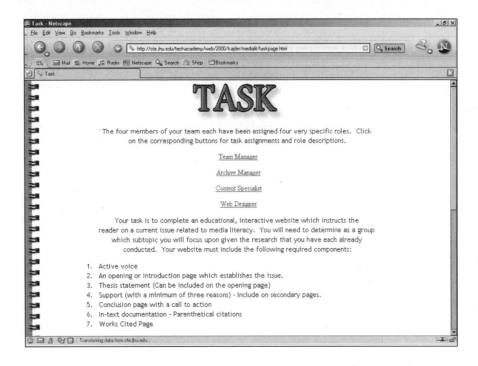

I used the task page to establish student roles as well as give an overview of the requirements for the Web site. Team manager, archive manager, content specialist, and Web designer each had specific instructions, which were accessed by clicking on the corresponding links. In the case of my classes, I assigned specific roles. However, in a class with more autonomy, students could easily and successfully select the roles that they will fill. I selected roles as a differentiation strategy and a means of working past the strict social circles that filled these particular classes. In a classroom that represents thirty-five different students at thirty-five different levels of skill and learning, differentiation strategies are key. However, differentiation isn't a strategy or method. I post this Tomlinson (2000) quote at the top of my lesson planning sheets as a subtle and yet constant reminder: "Differentiation must be a refinement of, not a substitute for, high-quality curriculum and instruction." Using these roles, whether they are teacher-assigned or student-selected, allows for targeted challenges to specific skills of specific students, and ultimately optimal learning.

The task page also delineated expectations for the Web site layout and content. Very few students in this class possessed Web design experience. For this reason, I used the semester preassessment (see Chapter 3) results to assign the Web design roles as well as mini-conferences with students prior to this stage of the WebQuest. All students went through a ten-minute boot camp (see Chapter 3) on the basic elements of Web design prior to the start of the WebQuest activity. The student primarily responsible for crafting the Web site needed to have basic skills. We worked with Netscape Composer, a program that is bundled with the Netscape Communicator package. This software allowed students to design using a WYSIWYG tool instead of coding in HTML.

Process

The process page (see Figure 7.4) breaks down the elements of the assignment, explaining the various steps and deadlines built into the assignment. This is where scaffolding is essential, building from the set roles to include the steps that will need to be taken to complete the assignment. Some WebQuests merge the task and process pages, a choice that often complicates for students the steps related to what they need to complete.

In terms of the scaffolding within my process page, I built a series of additional levels into the project. First, teams, prior to using the class computer for design work, had to complete both an action plan and a design board. The action plan delineates the group's time line and plans for constructing their site. It serves as a tool by which I can gauge their progress as well as an assessment tool during the final evaluation. The design board provides a sketch of the design of each page, again completed prior to a team's use of the classroom computer. I find it invaluable for ensuring that student designers use time productively on the computer rather than brainstorming on-screen.

Journal prompts were required daily and provided via the links on the process page. Here students were given space to reflect on their progress both in synthesizing the information they had collectively researched and in creating their Web site. This provided me with a valuable glimpse into the creative process and inner dynamics of each team.

Team conferences and discussion board postings made up the final component of the process page assignments. Here, we focused on communicating progress not only with me as teacher but with other groups who might be running into similar issues and problems throughout the project. The discussion board was already a common element of our classroom culture, most often utilized as we neared exams or as students struggled through difficult readings. Interestingly, it was a tool that had worked best with honors students prior to this assignment. Once the on-level students saw its immediate benefits to the work that they were completing, postings became an internalized/automatic part of the problem-solving process for most groups.

Figure 7.4

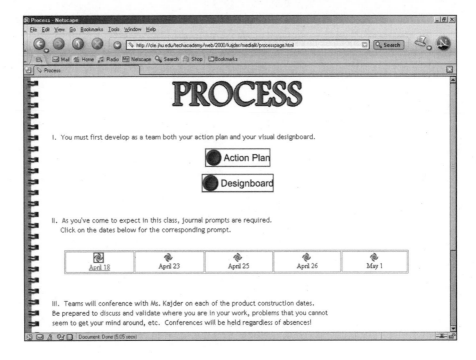

Resources

If the assignment is the heart of the WebQuest, then the online resources (see Figure 7.5) are its energy. Resources are Web sites that the teacher has preselected for educational value, relevance to the assigned topic, and overall effectiveness.

Depending upon the complexity of the assignment posed in the WebQuest, selecting Web sites can be the most time-consuming and difficult part of the development process. For a WebQuest I designed to pair with a unit including *The Crucible,* I went through hundreds of sites dealing with witchcraft and the Salem witch trials. That is the extreme. To locate the sites on "Getting the Word Out" took much less time, for three reasons. First, I knew exactly what I was looking for and already had bookmarked useful sites as I did preliminary research in planning the overall unit. Second, there was much less "garbage" out there because of the relatively scholarly level of the topic. Witchcraft and mass media conglomerates are vastly different topics, which generate very different results in a Web search. Last, my search strategies paid off. I'd learned a great deal since conducting the witchcraft search, and I utilized Boolean operators and searched the deep Web (see Chapter 5). The more efficient I became, the less work I needed to put into locating useful information, a skill that students also develop when taught the strategies needed for successful Web searching.

Figure 7.5

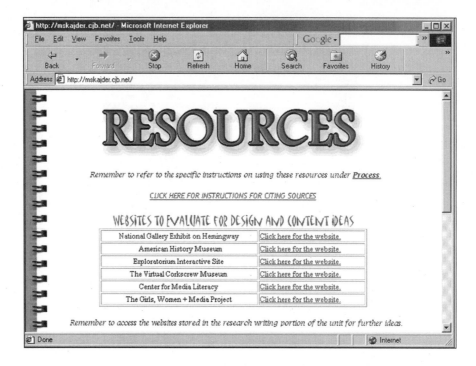

A note about using the resources in this section of the WebQuest: After searching, evaluating, and selecting the sites that would be used, I knew each site quite well. This made it realistic for me to stress to students that these were the only sites that were to be accessed from the class computer and used in the development of their sites. Flexibility was not an option, simply because the search time had already been spent. This is critical to enforce. Countless times, I've observed teachers who don't have a sense of where students really are when they are online. They either ignore or fail to see the diminished window at the bottom of the screen that holds the MTV Web site students were viewing before the teacher turned the corner. Open such windows when monitoring where students are. Use the Back button on the browser. If using Netscape, hold the Back button down to read through the list of sites that students have visited. If you closely and actively monitor, students expect it and stay on task. If you don't, there is little purpose behind the work you spent identifying the sites you want explored.

Evaluation

At the center of assessment in my classroom is the rubric (see Figure 7.6). Often class/student-generated, the rubric is provided at the start of every assignment

Figure 7.6

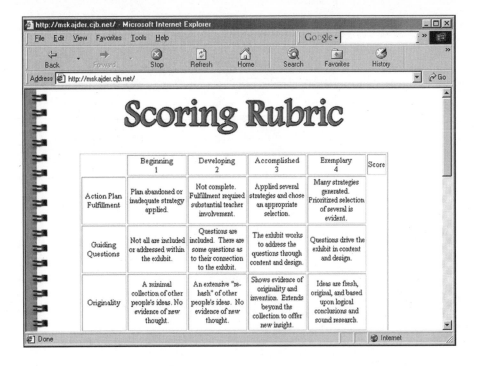

	Beginning 1	Developing 2	Accomplished 3	Exemplary 4	Score
Action Plan Fulfillment	Plan abandoned or inadequate strategy applied.	Not complete. Fulfillment required substantial teacher involvement.	Applied several strategies and chose an appropriate selection.	Many strategies generated. Prioritized selection of several is evident.	
Guiding Questions	Not all are included or addressed within the exhibit.	Questions are included. There are some questions as to their connection to the exhibit.	The exhibit works to address the questions through content and design.	Questions drive the exhibit in content and design.	
Originality	A minimal collection of other people's ideas. No evidence of new thought.	An extensive "re-hash" of other people's ideas. No evidence of new thought.	Shows evidence of originality and invention. Extends beyond the collection to offer new insight.	Ideas are fresh, original, and based upon logical conclusions and sound research.	

so that expectations are immediately made clear from the beginning of the study. This process occurs regardless of how or when technology is integrated into the assignment. Rubrics are a standard element of our classroom culture, and students appreciate and respond to the immediate establishment of expectations and standards for the task at hand. At their best, rubrics are also teaching tools that support student learning and the development of sophisticated thinking skills. In terms of the WebQuest, the rubric is posted electronically from the start of the project, clearly establishing the criteria for excellence or failure. There are various schools of thought as to the effective design of a rubric as an assessment tool. My purpose here is only to talk about its use in the context of the WebQuest assignment, not to discuss the philosophy behind the use or misuse of rubrics.

Although it might seem that the center of this assignment is the product, the student-generated Web site, this rubric targets the process as well as the product. I take into consideration the group's completion of the goals delineated in the action plan and design board. I build in the required presentation skills, allowing students to demonstrate skills learned in earlier units of study. Furthermore, student roles are factored in, allowing for both group and individual assessment—key to the success of any collaborative project.

All rubrics used in my classroom instruction have two features in common. First, they list the criteria for the assignment. Second, they provide gradations of quality, determined from student-generated descriptions of what makes for excellent, adequate, or struggling student work. In this rubric, I describe levels of quality but do not provide a label such as "satisfactory" or "failing." Labeling levels is difficult, and the system has trained students to equate success with the highest number of points. My own use of rubrics has grown; it now strives to include student-generated descriptions of the problems that might be encountered when completing a given task. Students have responded well, indicating that a rubric is almost meaningless when its descriptions are limited to "poor" or "boring."

Choosing and Evaluating a WebQuest

As I said earlier, a simple search online for WebQuests will yield countless hits. It is not critical that a teacher design one from scratch. Instead, you can successfully and efficiently use resources that have been created by teachers from across the globe, extending your classroom and professional community as far as you'd like to reach.

The starting point is to locate a WebQuest that fits your curricular and instructional needs and goals. Just as there are specific search engines or methods for locating primary sources or lesson ideas (see Chapter 5), there are ideal ways of locating effective, classroom-tested master WebQuests.

The WebQuest Matrix

Where better to locate resources than from the originator of WebQuests? Bernie Dodge oversees the WebQuest Page, which lists hundreds of tested WebQuests by content area as well as grade level (see Figure 7.7). Some of the options here are outdated or were developed as a part of early training sessions. However, the list is continually revised and developing; outstanding WebQuests are added as they are submitted.

SCORE CyberGuides

CyberGuides, posted by SCORE (Schools of California Online Resources for Education), are outstanding WebQuest modeled units of instruction centered on core works of literature, grades K–12. Each CyberGuide contains a student and a teacher edition, standards, a task and a process by which it may be completed, teacher-selected Web sites, and a rubric.

Figure 7.7

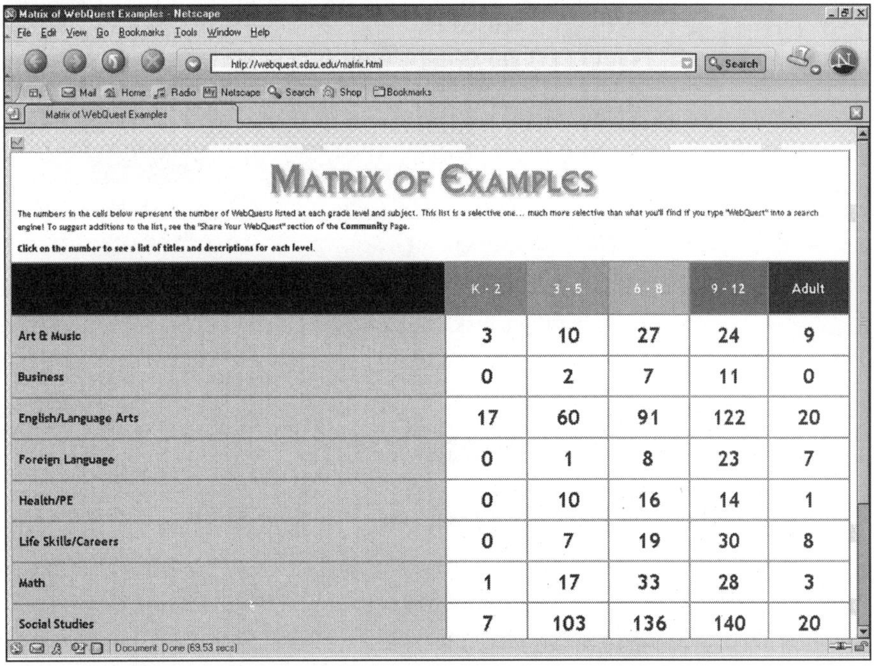

Blue Web'N

Countless educational links are continually added to the Blue Web'N site, a hotbed of resources for teachers and students (see Figure 7.8). Type WebQuest into the search window, and sort through the results. To refine your search, add English or 9-12 in later sorts. Also click on Filamentality to reach an interactive guide that helps teachers pick topics, search the Web, find good Internet sites, and incorporate Web resources into learning activities.

I don't limit my searching to these sites when looking for a WebQuest to implement in classroom instruction. These sites don't actively search the Internet for WebQuests available online. Instead, they depend upon teacher submissions and other review processes. I'm convinced that many teachers who design WebQuests don't think to add them to a matrix or portal. In an attempt to locate those WebQuests, I use search engines, with the types of Boolean and advanced searching techniques discussed in Chapter 5. Using a search engine such as Google requires that you include as many targeted keywords as possible when locating WebQuests. For example, when searching for a WebQuest that uses *Romeo and Juliet* as its central text, I'd include WebQuest and Romeo and Juliet in my search string. This approach to locating an effective WebQuest is

Figure 7.8

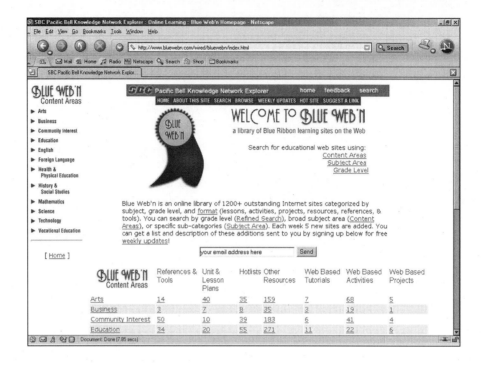

more time-consuming than going to a portal, but you often can locate exactly what you are looking for.

Before we discuss how to evaluate a WebQuest once you've located one that you'd like to consider for classroom use, keep in mind that a central consideration needs to be, Why use the Web for this task? I've watched many teachers use the Web because they feel a pressure to use new technologies, not because it works as a tool for them to extend and enhance student understanding. For example, let's consider a WebQuest that asks students to create a fable or a short story. Clearly, the task requires higher-order thinking and can be structured to make the final product the synthesis of a group process. So far, so good. But sometimes the activities fail to take advantage of benefits afforded by the Internet, such as added information, unusual perspectives, easy collaboration, and challenging contextualization. If these aspects aren't used to empower student learning, we're really using the Web as a means to publish instructions, not to leverage learning (March 2000).

When evaluating WebQuests, there are key aspects to consider, all of which build from other ideas discussed in this chapter. First, does the introduction pose an interesting, engaging task? I find it key here to think like my students: Would this introduction motivate me (as a student) to access the task? Second, does the task pose a challenging, effective question that is appropriate in the context of my curriculum and my classes? Does the task require the fruitful use of the Web? Could it be better accomplished without using the Web? If I respond that this activity does not use the Web in a way that will enhance student learning, I stop. This is critical. Effective use of technology requires using the appropriate technologies for the appropriate task.

From this point, I move on to consider the roles that students are asked to perform along with the thinking skills that the task will require them to exercise. These are both areas that I, as teacher, can continue to manipulate, should I choose to use this WebQuest in my classroom. Often, I have rewritten role requirements, distributing them on 3" x 5" cards and explaining to students how they are to use them to supplement what is found online. It's really important to keep in mind that though you are working with a text that is published online, it is still an adaptable, workable lesson. I've never found a WebQuest that was the immediate right fit for all of my classes. Instead, I work with what is there and adapt it so that it richly challenges and builds on where my students are at that point in time.

It is also important to ensure that the WebQuest taps into timely, accurate resources. Be certain to check the links that are used within the resources. Check every link. Typos happen that might lead to a site that isn't appropriate for your classroom. Also, information that was relevant and timely when the WebQuest was created might not be so when you access it. Generally, it's a good idea to check the links throughout the assignment. URLs change, and you never want to lead students to a site within an educational context that isn't educational in content. I have gone so far as to supplement WebQuest links with an additional printed sheet that students use to investigate sites I have selected to fulfill the original task delineated in the assignment. Again, everything can be adapted or manipulated to fit what works for your classroom and your students.

Online resources aren't just the Web sites that students are sent to explore. The Web is more than a series of networked computers, it's a network of people. A truly effective WebQuest works with that human network to bring additional voices into the English classroom. I use telementors to extend the walls of my classroom by contacting and welcoming the participation of adults around the world. In the "Getting the Word Out" WebQuest, students corresponded electronically with parents, business professionals, and other students, all in an attempt to develop a rich, meaningful product and to continually test their thinking. We utilized discussion boards and chat rooms to facilitate the dialogue and to provide students with a sounding board and work space for their ideas. Communication is key; a rich WebQuest provides students with an opportunity to communicate with a learning community far beyond the walls of the classroom.

Last, you must consider the evaluation mechanisms within the WebQuest. Not all include rubrics, and those that do might not follow a format or standards appropriate for your classroom. I've found great WebQuests online that don't have rubrics. In that case, I simply write one to correspond with our standards and my thoughts on where students need to be by the close of the activity. It's completely appropriate to build from what is there. Also, you might want to e-mail the original author of the site to ask for insights into how the WebQuest has developed since it was originally posted or to ask for evaluation ideas.

Implementing a WebQuest

Teachers continually ask about tips and hints that I have gathered as a result of working with WebQuests over the years. Most of these I've mentioned already. However, there are some that stand out and need further development. First, using a WebQuest in a fully networked computer lab is a big leap for a class of students who are first-time users. In this case, preview the WebQuest with them in the classroom, if at all possible. If not, require that all monitors be off as you preview together in the lab. This blocks the urge for students to type or surf while you are working as a class to figure out the assignment. Be sure to go through each section of the WebQuest, orienting students to those areas that are central to completing the task successfully. This doesn't mean that you need to review each Web site, but it does require that you consider the "building blocks" of the WebQuest. A shorter task is a better bet for classes who aren't familiar with the approach.

WebQuests do lend themselves well to instruction in the one-computer classroom. Here, I typically use the WebQuest as part of a series of learning stations that are set up around the room. This allows teams of students to access the class computer on a rotating basis. When working in a building without Internet access, teachers can save the files using software such as WebWhacker to copy the files to disk. The most recent versions of Microsoft's Internet Explorer Web browser also have this ability. WebQuests can also be extended to be used as a whole-class instructional tool.

WebQuests require that the teacher really act as facilitator. For the "Getting the Word Out" WebQuest, I met with the teams daily but worked more closely with the student project manager than with other team members. I let the project manager handle the logistics of what was happening within the team, relying on me when problems arose or questions were too large for the group to answer on their own. This requires that, as teacher, I give up a great deal of control. However, the nature of the WebQuest isn't one that lends itself to teachers working as the holders of all knowledge. Nor can the teacher be a passive member of the class. Instead, we are thrown into the role of a curricular designer who simply has to allow students to struggle through the task at hand. It isn't easy. And it certainly isn't less work. This is not a time when a teacher can expect to sit at the side of the lab, grading. If anything, I work harder and more actively on days when classes are working on WebQuests than on other days. I go repeatedly from group to group and lead them to unlock their thinking. Though the Web sites are preselected, students still need monitoring and guidance. Keep a close eye on where they are and provide questions that test their thinking. It's good teaching, just more active than some teachers might be used to experiencing.

I've emphasized that a WebQuest should only be used when it enriches and extends student learning in an activity that uses Web resources that makes sound instructional sense. Problem-based learning is often difficult to implement in a high school English class, as we face overcrowded classrooms, overfilled standards-based curricula, and overhyped national and state assessments. However, when well constructed, and given the amount of time needed for students to genuinely explore and learn, problem-based learning allows for a depth of student understanding that rarely happens in other activities, even with the same genuine engagement and insight on the part of my students. As teacher, you need to balance the WebQuest activity with the other facets of your curriculum or school schedule. Allow for the time. This sort of learning needs to unfold; it cannot be pushed.

Ending Points: Student-Designed WebQuests

A rich application of the WebQuest is to allow students to create their own WebQuests—a sort of twist on the ideas behind reciprocal teaching or jigsaw instruction. The tasks of developing a WebQuest are different than those of completing a WebQuest activity. WebQuest developers, whether they are students or teachers, must compose clear explanations, ask essential questions, locate essential and timely Web sites to link to for information, and design the layout and presentation of the Web pages. Clearly, this empowers students to act as both learners and teachers.

After working with WebQuests for over two years, I took the plunge and worked with an eleventh-grade honors English class as the students developed WebQuests that explored the American Dream as they studied Arthur Miller's

Death of a Salesman, Scott Fitzgerald's *The Great Gatsby,* and August Wilson's *Fences.* (Another technique for integrating technology into this unit is discussed in Chapter 8.) The challenge was for each team to develop a WebQuest to teach other students about the American Dream as it was defined in different eras of U.S. history. Students worked in teams of four, with one member trained as the Web designer either through course work in other classes or through tutorial sessions that I held during lunchtime and online. Teams were then to present their work to the class online, allowing other students to discover each era through the other teams' WebQuests.

Flexibility was crucial as we worked on this assignment; the creation of WebQuests required online access that went beyond the one computer in my classroom. Students used most of the classroom instruction time to meet or study the novels. Web design occurred in the school labs outside of class or on the networked computers that a small percentage of students had at home. This project was worth 25 percent of the total points accumulated during the nine-week grading period, requiring substantial flexibility in terms of how we spent time in teaching and exploring the novels. Instead of formally studying the novels, we used them as a springboard into investigating the period in which they were written and the vision and ideas that they expressed. In studying these through the lens of the American Dream, students discussed literary elements, such as symbolism or theme, as these elements shaped the texts.

One area in which I was completely inflexible was with student deadlines. I set multiple incremental deadlines for portions of the assignment: action plan, journal entries, postings to discussion boards and participation in class chat rooms, introduction, task, process, resources, evaluation, periodic correspondence with telementors, and subsequent revisions. The assignment began in January, a month fraught with adjustments due to testing and the unpredictable weather. However, students recognized that the deadlines were solid regardless of what else the schedule might present. This mostly worked, both because of the students' dedication and the flexibility of our media center staff, which kindly provided extended hours for students to complete the design of their WebQuests.

Throughout the design process, students would first work on paper, developing the vision and layout of their sites before they worked on the computer. This was critical in two ways: they needed to balance the "splash" and the content of their sites, and they were ready to implement the design as soon as the computer became available. Students as designers are quick to go for the "bells and whistles," effects that can obscure information with the blinking and motion on the screen. In my classroom, the rule is 80 percent content, 20 percent "splash." This allows students to focus on conveying meaning and information rather than on generating special effects. Furthermore, time spent working with the computers was far more efficiently used when students worked with predeveloped designs, avoiding the process of developing the site from a blank screen.

Working in teams took on a completely different look in this assignment. Student teams were explorers as well as readers, designers as well as viewers, and teachers as well as learners. Consensus had to continually be reached as they considered their interpretation of both history and the text as well as the design of their WebQuest. The roles typically assigned in a WebQuest activity seemed to be taken much more seriously, as students constructed roles for others to follow in their own assignments. Peer review occurred on a daily basis, and like the roles, was taken very seriously, even by those teams with students who were typically less motivated. The teams that were the most successful were those that shared openly throughout the design process and in which all had some significant hand in the design of the WebQuest.

Students were extremely challenged by both the content and the process of this assignment. Startling to me was the discovery that very few of them had ever considered what their own definition of the American Dream was, let alone explored what that had meant in different eras. This posed a significant obstacle, especially when students were being asked to look at the texts in a way that was dramatically different from the way they were used to doing in English class. Traditionally, students were used to unpacking a text by exploring the conventions used by the writer. This assignment asked that they use the text to unpack history and voice, a very different task for the reader. Rather than building basic knowledge, they were able to synthesize and really challenge their own thinking. Furthermore, students were challenged by the medium and the idea of using their WebQuest as a tool for teaching others about the American Dream in their era. The interdisciplinary connections came quite naturally, as students sought out the advice and knowledge of their history teachers. Ultimately, this project certainly led me to explore applications beyond having students utilize a predesigned WebQuest as a learning tool. Instead of thinking "outside the box," I'm now more prone to allowing my students to define the box, and the technology tools that we use in class stem directly from that.

Related Reading

Dodge, Bernie. 1997. "Some Thoughts About WebQuests."
    <http://edweb.sdsu.edu/courses/edtech596/about_webquests.html>.

———. 2002. "A Road Map for Designing WebQuests."
<http://webquest.sdsu.edu/roadmap/index.htm>.

March, Tom. 1998. "Why WebQuests?"
<http://www.ozline.com/webquests/intro.html>.

———. 2000. "The 3 R's of WebQuests."
<http://www.infotoday.com/MMSchools/nov00/march.htm>.

Watson, Kenneth Lee. 1999. "WebQuests in the Middle School Curriculum: Promoting Technological Literacy in the Classroom." *Meridian* 2 (2).
<http://www.ncsu.edu/meridian/jul99/webquest/index.html>.

Online Resources

Blue Web'N. <http://www.kn.pacbell.com/wired/bluewebn/>.

Florida State University Secondary English WebQuests.
<http://www.fsu.edu/~CandI/ENGLISH/web.htm>.

Kathy Schrock's Guide for Educators: WebQuest Resources.
<http://school.discovery.com/schrockguide/webquest/webquest.html>.

SCORE CyberGuides (English 6–12).
<http://www.sdcoe.k12.ca.us/score/cyberguide.html>.

WebEnglishTeacher.com (English 6–12).
<http://www.webenglishteacher.com/>.

WebQuest Design Flow. <http://www.ozline.com/webquests/design.html>.

The WebQuest Page. <http://webquest.sdsu.edu/>.

8 Creating Community: Telecommunication and Teleinformation Tools

The classroom is a community.

—Harvey Daniels

How often do you encounter well-developed people or gain any understanding of why they make the choices they do?

—Don Graves

Instructional Design

There is a world of difference between using a technology tool in a lesson or activity and working as an instructional designer. It is in the area between lesson planning and instructional design that we run into the most trouble, especially when technology tools are thrown into the mix. We are trained in how to write an effective lesson plan. We know how to differentiate, to consider essential questions, and to begin with the end in mind. Our lessons and activities are rich, invite depth of study, and yet are temporary, striving to a fixed close, when we then pick up with something new. What we don't know how to do is provide students with a rich, complex, real-world, sustained experience that balances curricular goals, standards, and skills with multiple possibilities for student action. Furthermore, where does technology fit in? As I've said earlier, the name of the game is to use technology tools to extend and empower student learning while figuring our way through how to construct spaces and experiences for student learning.

E. M. Rogers wrote in *Diffusion of Innovations* (1995) that "new technologies are tools that can be applied in many different ways and for different purposes. Adoption of these innovations is an active process which involves much reinvention." Reinvention is scary because it requires a change from what is familiar and comfortable. It's often uncharted but can yield tremendous growth, challenge, and understanding. Reinvention requires rethinking what we know works in our classroom instruction and changing, growing, redeveloping so that technology tools can lead students to a richer experience.

It's simple. We ask whether a tool enables students to do something they couldn't do before, or could do before but now do it better. Only if the answer is yes do we reinvent. If the answer is no, we move on. Time and learning are too precious to force-fit a technology tool into a lesson or activity if it won't lead to that rigorous, deep experience we are looking to construct.

When it comes to instructional design, we strive to create meaningful spaces for student learning. We want to create real-world experiences for student thinkers, challenging them to tackle authentic problems paired with authentic evaluation and assessment. To do so requires expanding our classroom community while also working with current resources that tap into immediately accessible, real-time information and data. Perhaps we invite writers to correspond with our students, or we challenge students to participate in projects where they collaborate and problem-solve with other students. The twist that technology provides is to amplify our resources, allowing students to dialogue and collaborate with writers, thinkers, students, and communities across the globe in real-time interactions. The purposeful introduction of these tools, when presented in the context of a carefully crafted space and experience for student learning, can lead to amazing results in terms of the leaps that students will make as skillful thinkers, writers, and speakers. As we continually see, the key is to pair the right tool with the right task and the right student.

What follows is an investigation of communication and information technologies, and projects that use them in positive and negative ways. We'll talk about possibilities, learning, design, implementation, assessment, standards, and students. We'll celebrate what works and question what doesn't, all the while keeping in mind whether the use of the tool is leading us to work better together as a community of learners.

Communication Tools

E-mail

E-mail has become ubiquitous. Katie, a freshman in one of my ninth-grade English classes, wrote that "e-mail allows me to share my ideas as they are happening. I can connect with my friends immediately and get their responses just as quick. I can't imagine not having it." Yes, e-mail is a powerful communication tool, and yet it raises interesting questions when we examine how it works, how it is used, and how we might tap into it for classroom study.

It's important to first consider what Katie had to say. E-mail is appealing to students (and teachers) because of its speed, efficiency, ubiquity, and accessibility. Using e-mail, I can attach files to share with colleagues—video, text, photos, and even sounds. This has opened up new worlds when it comes to eliciting feedback on lesson ideas, materials, and student writing. However, the speed and accessibility continue to pose problems. While rushing to send an e-mail (from the cluttered files that seem to result as soon as you open an account), we don't always take time to consider tone, grammar, and conventions such as capitalization and punctuation. Quick e-mail doesn't mean e-mail that is thought-through. The "unsend" feature in my e-mail software is a useful tool, and teachers in my building have often come bursting into my classroom, trying to retract an e-mail that was sent without time, reflection, and serious consideration. E-mail opens up rich classroom dialogues about how language works when using different communication tools and writing to different audiences, but these are often missed opportunities when we are speedily working through our curricular goals.

In teaching students to compose e-mail effectively, it often works best to lead them to compose messages first in a word processor. Students typically take more time to think through content, while also taking advantage of tools such as spell check and grammar check. Then they can copy and paste the completed message into the e-mail program and send it on its way. We also discuss the use of emoticons and the use of words in parentheses in order to convey emotion and tone. It's also helpful for students to learn appropriate ways of replying to unclear messages they might receive in the course of their e-mail correspondence. The more techniques they master, the more effective they will be as users of e-mail. Additional suggestions and links to related resources can be found on the Web site for this book.

E-mail accounts in the classroom can be difficult to manage. Though just about every student with online access has an account with one of the many free options available (e.g., Hotmail, Yahoo!), these aren't necessarily the accounts that you want opened in your classroom. In fact, most schools now have firewalls and other blocking mechanisms to prevent students accessing these accounts from school. While I'm not against using e-mail in the classroom, I'm against using students' personal accounts. I liken this to how I use the account set up through my school system: I use it only for professional activities. My friends and family send e-mail to my personal account, which I set up privately with an Internet service provider. There is a clear dividing line between my professional and personal worlds. I expect the same from my students, whether they are at middle or high school level, when it comes to using e-mail in the classroom. I expect nothing less than a professional and scholarly use of the tool. It's not the time to e-mail your best friend. It's not the time to check the e-mail you just received from the fan club of the hottest new teen idol. We're getting down to business. Period.

That said, student e-mail accounts in my classroom are set up through a schoolwide service (which has only been available in one of the four schools I've worked in) or through an educational Web site such as www.epals.com or www.iecc.org. Epals is a Web site that allows teachers and students from across the globe to communicate. I first saw its use in a foreign language class and have been continually impressed with its ability to connect student readers and writers. My English class students have found pen pals, or as one class called it, think pals, who have provided insight and ideas when we've studied texts from other cultures. Reading Amy Tan's work is more powerful when you can exchange ideas with female students in China. While reading *The Diary of Anne Frank* and *Zlata's Diary,* we corresponded with students in Germany and Eastern Europe, again adding a rich dimension to our study that was real-time, keeping pace with the ideas of my students and those with whom we'd been paired.

Because I use e-mail for students to correspond with teammates, telementors, and other people whom we welcome into our classroom community, it's often easiest to establish the accounts myself. That way I can randomly look into the accounts to ensure that students are following the policies and using the accounts only for scholarly purposes. Yes, it's a bit like Big Brother, but it keeps us all responsible when it comes to using the tool for the reasons that we've brought it into the classroom. There have been times where I've used a Yahoo! or Hotmail account that is established in my name, to protect the identity of my students and yet allow us to tap into the community and resources we want to bring into our studies.

It's important to consider the power of students' writing when using e-mail as a tool. E-mail allows them to communicate their ideas, no matter how shy they might be. Students who are in the process of developing their persona and voice are open to writing and communicating via e-mail, finding comfort in the lower-stakes environment it provides. Dani, an eighth-grade student, wrote, "E-mail allows me to be secure . . . posing my ideas where they will be pushed and extended without my having to be on the line."

Nabe, a student in my eleventh-grade English class, used e-mail to exchange ideas with his telementor at the start of a project examining the

American Dream. Nabe's family had just moved from Nigeria, giving him only two weeks to settle in before the school year started. He spoke English well but was not secure in his writing or in interacting with his peers. He had barely started to think of himself as an American, let alone now as a part of a family pursuing the American Dream.

Frank offered Nabe his own experiences:

> I am a thirty-year-old black male who is now a professional. My Mom raised me alone and cleaned homes to support me. I picked up odd jobs as soon as I was able, just trying to help out. I graduated from college because of the values and supports that my Mom provided. I'm educated, made the most of my opportunities, have a career that I enjoy, and now take care of her. We live better than I'd thought possible, all because of work and hope. Every day I meet someone who came from somewhere else with nothing but some hope. Amazing.

Nabe's response to this reflects not only his growing understanding but major leaps in starting to define who he could now be:

> I know that I won't always have it easy here, but I think that only here can I be who I am. I can rise or fall based upon my effort. The American Dream, to me, means that I have the possibility and the chance. It's up to me now.

Christian (1997) calls this "striving writing," the dazzling moment where the stars are aligned just so, and a young writer finds the right words to create something powerful. E-mail is a tool that allows our student writers to explore identities, voice, and ideas. Yes, we accomplish this through journals and other writing activities that we already use well. However, the introduction of this electronic technology allows us to extend community, deepen experience and voice, and ultimately do it better.

Discussion Boards

As I mentioned in Chapter 4, I regularly use discussion boards in my classroom as a starting point in our exploration of hypertext. Instead of individual discussions occurring through e-mail correspondence, discussion boards allow messages to be posted in a central location with a subject heading, date, time, and author's name or e-mail address. Students post to the nonlinear discussion, selecting those ideas they find to be the most compelling and offering their ideas for response and development. I use discussion boards in class but have found that students also use the boards outside of class to post questions and access our community as they are reading or writing for homework. This allows for learning to occur as students' questions arise, rather than having them retain the question for discussion six or even twelve hours later. Parents also appreciate the discussion area as a tool for monitoring and participating in the class; they often respond to questions or post their own.

Several free services exist online for establishing class discussion areas. I review some here but encourage you to check the current resources available on this book's Web site, because free tools come and go so quickly. You can also find your own space and tools by searching on Google in the directories.

- www.quicktopic.com. This is my current free tool of choice. The site describes itself as "preposterously easy" (see Figure 4.1), and even the lowest-tech teacher that I've worked with has agreed. No ads. Clear, precise instructions. This is a top-notch site.
- www.blackboard.com. Blackboard is free to teachers for a specific interval of time (which keeps changing). Lots of school systems are buying Blackboard server space, so I recommend checking with your technical support staff or library media specialist. The discussion and chat tools bundled in Blackboard work extremely well, especially since they can only be accessed by students or parents with the corresponding password. No ads. Simple interface with really clear instructions.
- www.voy.com and www.server.com. These are two additional tools that teachers have used with great success. They are free and simply require your registration as the manager in order for the discussion tool to be created. You can link to these from your class Web site or simply create a bookmark for student machines. Again, clear directions are offered and only a small investment of time is required in getting these up and running.

Once you have the discussion board set up, it becomes your job to get the initial conversations rolling. I often pass this facilitator role to students as the semester progresses, but we need to get the initial community built and the level of inquiry defined. A few rules to consider:

- The discussion community is not just a forum for individual expression. Students need to have space to test their ideas, but the discussion community also must provide a place where the group's voice is gathered and amplified, so that the group can affirm, question, challenge, and correct the voice of the individual.

- The space should welcome silence and speech. Yes, this discussion is one that should be full of talk and active idea sharing, but it also needs to provide such compelling ideas that students feel welcome to "lurk," free to read, think, and explore without the pressure of continually adding to the conversation.

- Conflict is okay. It allows us to test ideas in the open in an attempt to stretch each other and make better sense of the world. However, this must be a thoughtful, embracing conflict. Students need to learn the difference between sharing and pushing thinking, and an attack.

- The discussion will most likely not facilitate itself. There needs to be at least one person who is paying close attention and asking deliberate questions that challenge the participants' ideas, thinking, and meaning. This is a best practice—one that teachers already embrace. It's only different online insofar as it asks us to think and respond in a different medium. It's easy for teachers to think that the technology itself will lead students to high-level thinking. Not true.

- Last, take advantage of the technology. Link to articles and online texts that will enrich and extend the dialogue. Nourish student minds by providing immediate catalysts.

Chat Rooms

Chats are real-time (synchronous) dialogues between individuals who are all gathered in one location on a Web site (Jonassen, Peck, and Wilson 1998). Comments are captured and posted to a scrolling list that updates on a regular basis. Chat conversations can be difficult to enter and follow, mostly because of the shorthand used and the rate of the updates on the screen. Things move very quickly, and the greater the number of participants, the greater the rate and number of postings.

Because participants also break out into separate rooms, conversations posted to the main area can be redundant or fragmented. Introducing a chat room into classroom study requires that students discuss Internet safety and the use of these communication tools outside of class study. Students need to consider where they chat and how to work in an environment where people may not be who they present themselves to be. Check your school policies to see if students are permitted to access an online chat room or if that will require parental permission. A class chat room can be structured to be an effective tool. Students in my classes must first demonstrate that they can responsibly and mindfully use a discussion board as a communication tool before establishing a class chat. Chats provide an exciting way for students to interact with experts and great writers. They have also allowed us to continue our dialogues even when I need to be out for a presentation. The first time I realized I had crossed over into the realm of "techie" was when I sat in the Denver airport, running a class chat with my third-period class just before boarding my flight.

Again, several free services exist for establishing online chats. I prefer to use those that are password-encrypted, preventing people who are not class members from accessing or participating in our conversations. This is a safety issue that needs to be closely considered. When establishing your chat room, be sure that you have the rights as the organizer. Doing so ensures that you control who may enter the chat room, set the parameters for the hours or times the chat room is available to selected users, and edit/delete posts if they are not appropriate. Each chat room has its own procedures for discussion leaders and organizers. Be sure to read instructions for each tool you use.

There are alternatives to chat rooms that still allow for maintaining synchronous, real-time discussions. Microsoft NetMeeting is an Internet conference tool that allows for synchronous discussion in a protected environment. Here, you can avoid a chat room and simply hold a meeting. All you need is to be working from a Windows system and to know the IP address of the computer you are linking to. Some firewalls can block this feature, so check with your technical support or computer lab staff.

Listservs

A listserv is a twist on e-mail. Using an e-mail account, users subscribe to a listserv on a topic. Once they have successfully joined, they will receive e-mail that is copied to all the list members. Users can post their own messages to the entire membership of the list by simply replying to the full group or including the listserv e-mail as the sending address. Lists have hundreds or thousands of subscribers, which can lead to a flood of e-mail into your account. The National Council of Teachers of English lists are great examples of this. The day after I joined the NCTE-Talk list, I received over one hundred messages. This was an incredible tool, especially early in my teaching career, allowing me to correspond with a community of practicing teachers across the country. I welcomed the flow of ideas that the e-mail flood brought. However, I have joined other listservs that haven't been quite as useful. Be selective about what you join, and be prepared to receive a significant number of messages from the more active groups.

Classes can develop their own listserv by working through a variety of e-mail providers. My current favorite is Yahoo! eGroups. By establishing a listserv here, I can ensure that students or parents receive essential class information or assignments. Again, the tool is about sharing ideas with an eager, supportive, yet critical community.

Online Communities

Teachers have naturally sought out colleagues and peers when working through new ideas, learning new skills, or trying out new activities. We're good at sharing our ideas and eliciting feedback when trying something new. We're hungry to learn from one another, celebrating what's really effective and sharing in the frustration when things don't go as planned. Technology allows us to extend the reach of that community. We no longer have just the members of our department, but we can dialogue with teachers across the country. Online communities of teachers and writers provide a hotbed of information, ideas, support, and feedback.

- www.tappedin.org. The ultimate professional learning community. Participate in (or get the transcripts from) dialogues with education experts and teachers from across the globe. Hold or attend classes online in your virtual office space. Find experts, resources, and colleagues, and read the transcripts from previous discussions and events. A safe, very supportive environment. When you join (free), you'll automatically begin receiving e-mail updates that provide the monthly schedule as well as information and descriptions of the many scheduled events. Community tours are hosted regularly, and the "information desk" is a great resource when you're getting started.
- www.classroom.com. Interact with teachers from across the globe, share lesson plan ideas, set up e-pals between classes of students—the options here are boundless.
- www.learningspace.org. An online network of teachers, students, and experts. You'll find volumes of online collaborative projects, innovative classroom ideas, and colleagues who are eager to talk about how to meaningfully integrate technology into classroom instruction across all content areas.

To locate additional learning communities for teachers, I recommend searching in the Google directory for "online learning communities for teachers." A current list is also posted on the Web site for this book. As an extension of the richness I found in the teacher-centered resources in online communities, I now encourage students to participate in online communities of readers, writers, poets, playwrights, and thinkers. I use the same search technique when looking for "online learning communities for students."

Information and Exploration

The Internet has become a storehouse of powerful resources, electronic texts, and primary sources that can enrich units of study with compelling, real-time content and context. In navigating the available materials, students engage in teleresearch, specifying, locating, sifting, sorting, interpreting, evaluating, synthesizing, and applying information in different learning contexts (Harris 1998a). Virtual museums and virtual field trips provide teachers and students with an accessible entry point when it comes to bringing online resources into classroom study.

Virtual Field Trips

A virtual field trip allows teachers and students to be transported via the Internet into other times and places. Students can "walk" the grounds of Auschwitz or travel along the Chesapeake Bay. These trips lend themselves well to both whole-class experiences and individual learning. I've set up the class computer and an LCD projector, transporting our study into 1920s Harlem. We've also used individual workstations in the computer lab to explore Tibet.

Locating field trips that enhance curricular resources and objectives has become a simpler task with the introduction of several portals and online repositories, for instance, the Global Schoolhouse or Field Guides. These repositories list the best of educational field trips, but there may be times that you will want to extend your search using Google. These repositories typically don't include more general trips, such as Yellowstone National Park or the glaciers in Alaska, but they do come complete with teacher resource guides, lesson plan ideas, experts, and companion readings.

Exploring a virtual field trip lends itself to a host of class experiences, working as an acceleration tool, as a writing prompt, or as a catalyst for the exploration of an essential question to which you've connected novels, short stories, nonfiction, and other texts. I've asked students to respond to photos of cave art as poets. We've written short plays and journals in response to artwork created by children in concentration camps. One team of students examined a virtual field trip to the Chesapeake Bay as research for writing a persuasive speech. Students later delivered the speech to area officials in a symposium addressing protection and conservation efforts. The curricular possibilities are quite open, especially when you consider online field trips through the lens of an instructional designer. Use the field trip experience to lead students into the exploration of authentic questions and problems, challenging their understanding as readers, writers, thinkers, speakers, and perhaps most important, human beings.

Virtual Museums

A virtual museum is an organized collection of electronic artifacts and information resources—virtually anything that can be digitized. Museum exhibits typically present any combination of paintings, drawings, photographs, diagrams, graphs, recordings, video segments, newspaper articles, transcripts of interviews, numerical databases, and a host of other items that may be saved on the museum's file server. They may also offer links to great resources from around the world that are relevant to the museum's main focus.

Scores of virtual museums can be found in a simple Google search, but much of what you find may not be the best fit for your students' needs and your curricular goals. In investigating virtual museums, my students have located everything from a museum on corkscrews to museums celebrating the one-hundredth anniversary of the bottling of Pepsi. Though these served as interesting models, they didn't relate to the core or focus of our studies. Besides conducting an evaluation based on content, consider other factors and indicators when examining a virtual museum for possible classroom use.

First, you want a rich, compelling, and substantial collection. As an example, the National Portrait Gallery has an online version of an exhibit featuring portraits of Hemingway in a variety of stages of his life. The collection offers art, primary sources (letters, journal entries), and portions of his writing. The range and depth of the collection offers students a wealth of ideas, images, and texts to consider. Though an exhibit does not have to be this extensive, it needs to have enough substance for students to be mindfully engaged. The better museums can take multiple visits for users to explore the content fully.

As important as the content is its presentation, especially given the multimedia nature of an online museum. Look for content to be multisensory, multidisciplinary, and dynamic. My all-time favorite exhibits are housed at the

Exploratorium, challenging student skills in perception and visual literacies. The exhibits are interactive, requiring student control and exploration.

Last, I really believe that an effective virtual museum visit increases desire for a real-time visit to the bricks-and-mortar original (if there is one). I had the luxury of teaching in schools located along the D.C. MetroRail, allowing us to explore the exhibits housed in the Smithsonian Institution and the museums that line the National Mall. Student experiences in the virtual exhibits of the Hirshhorn Museum inspired a class visit to the 1999 *What Is Beauty?* collection. Discussions about portraits and how photos tell a story led to a class exploration of the 2000 Annie Lebowitz collection *Women*. Opening the door to a virtual museum opens the door to much more.

Extension and Enrichment

I regularly assign students the challenge of creating their own virtual field trips or virtual museums. I find that the museum format lends itself well to this type of task because students are continually finding new things to archive, and more stories that need telling in the context of an exhibit. My students have created museums that present their understanding of the American Dream (see Chapter 7). We've created museums depicting a collection of oral histories from area residents who are recent immigrants or, at the other end of the spectrum, who have lived in our very transient community for a minimum of twenty-five years. The challenge is for students to create an online space that works to tell a story which is both compelling and related to our class study.

Each museum construction activity is experiential, leading students to work in specific roles to construct a museum that will be authentically assessed and then posted online. It's anchored in a real-world need and poses authentic questions. Let me emphasize that this is a time-consuming activity which only works well when completed within the context of related texts and classwork. If all components of the essential formula (right task, right tool, right student) aren't solidly in place, this activity can be a glorious flop. I've watched colleagues get caught up in the fancy of creating an online museum of Anytown Senior High School only to lose students by creating a detached, extra assignment that had nothing to do with curricular goals. Students are invested when they know they are being challenged and when the work they are completing is rigorous and real. They simply don't buy in when we use technology in ways that lack context and compelling questions.

In my first attempt at leading students through a museum project, student teams were asked to build a virtual museum exhibit that would reflect their

Figure 8.1

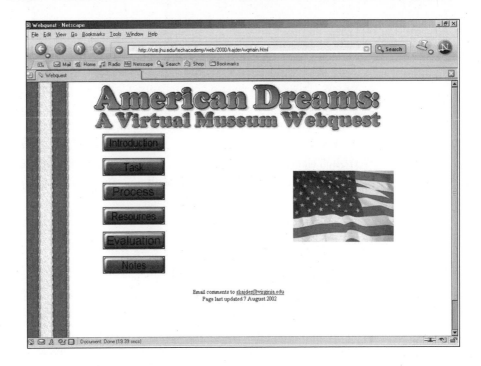

understanding of the American Dream. The work built from an earlier assignment that challenged them to amass a multimedia archive of photos, primary source texts, sound clips, and video which encapsulated what it was to be American and what it was to believe in the American Dream. Set up as a WebQuest (see Figure 8.1), the task was divided into specific segments (action plan, design board, telementor correspondence, design work, presentation), which were to be completed by a team of students each assigned to individual roles (team manager, research manager, production manager, archive manager). Incremental deadlines kept the teams closely in check, as did daily conferences with me. Teams worked during specific lab days but also were challenged to complete their designs while studying additional works in class. Products were assessed by a team of humanities teachers as well as two curators from the Smithsonian Institution. The development of museums allows students to consider how to select, interpret, and arrange artifacts while also considering how to allow for different visitors and kinds of visits. Though this was not a formal requirement, every student exhibit included lines from the texts we'd studied and several related texts that students discovered on their own. The level of synthesis was incredible, especially since the teams were built from both my honors and on-level classes. Sample student work can be found on the Web site for this book.

Collaboration

Through several of the communication tools just discussed, we extend the reach of our classes to include other students, teachers, and experts from across the globe. Community begins with interactions but can be strengthened and defined by the rich encounters that it engenders. We've explored interpersonal exchanges and information collections that are enhanced by communication tools. The next step, and what I argue is often the most advanced melding of collaboration and technologies, is to challenge students through developing online curriculum-based collaborative projects.

Models and Types of Activities

Judi Harris, the guru of collaborative technology-infused projects, has identified seven action "C-Quences" (see Table 8.1) that reflect the types of activities commonly found in effective, challenging online collaborative projects. I use these parameters to explore potential connections and openings within my curriculum, to evaluate potential projects, and to think about the possible online activities I might build for my students.

Selecting a Project

Locating projects has become a rather easy task; it's selecting one that fits best into your curricular framework and classroom community that poses the greatest challenge. I recommend checking the projects posted to the Global Schoolhouse, iEARN, Kidproj, and Blue Web'N for starters. My evaluation process centers on three main ideas: How does this affect my students' curricular needs? How does this challenge their skills and thinking? and Do we have the requisite resources? If I have a difficult time reaching a satisfactory answer for any of those questions, I typically do not explore the project any further. Several secondary questions naturally result, but these three ideas are the core. Effective, rigorous tasks challenge student skills and understandings while taking advantage of the curricular and technology resources available.

When it comes to those secondary questions, it's all pretty familiar territory. These are things that good teachers think about when planning any major activity. What kind of time do you have available when it comes to what you are willing to invest in this project? Will this require new learning on your part for you to even get started? Does your classroom have the kind of community which allows for effective, rich collaborative work? Are students comfortable with the

Table 8.1

C-Quences	Description
Correspond	Students work to create a publication that is reviewed, revised, and eventually shared with a larger audience.
Compete	Students register to participate and then complete work that is submitted to a competition. Feedback is shared by reviewers and other participants.
Comprehend	Students read and evaluate online resources.
Collect/Share/Compare	Students develop work and then add it to a collection of similar pieces, sharing feedback and reviews with other contributors.
Chain	Students complete an activity, generate a product, and then send both along so that other students can do something similar.
Come along	Students shadow experts, communicating throughout the process of work aimed at completing an experience or task.
Collaborate	Students work remotely with others to realize a common goal.

Adapted from Judi Harris, "I Know What We're Doing, But How Do We Do It?" *Learning and Leading with Technology* 26 (1998, no. 6).

technologies this task will require? Are you ready to tackle the technology needs, or will that learning be so mammoth that it poses too great a hurdle? Do you have technical support in case things don't go as planned? There are many projects with substantial appeal. The trick is to balance where you want to take your students with the opportunities provided in the project. Don't be seduced by glitzy online projects full of "splash" and promises. Look instead for solid instructional content, effective planning, and an appropriate use of technology to do something better as a result of the tools that are applied or the opportunity that is created.

Participating and Planning

Each online project should be paired with specific instructions, goals, and directives. To begin, you'll typically register your class as participants, committing to the project and opening the channels of communication with the project director. Read through the directions very closely before you register. Know what you're letting yourself and your students in for. There may be room for some negotiation, but prepare to accommodate if you're really invested in what the project will provide student learners.

Again, the next step is one that is comfortable for good teachers. Taking the instructions and goals of the project, you establish a time line and communicate your expectations to your students. Your time line needs to be different from the one you establish for students. Build in as much time as you need to familiarize yourself with new content and skills. I allow a cushion for delays in e-mail correspondence as well, assuming that not everyone is the e-mail junkie that I have become. I also try to begin correspondence with other teachers or project directors as early into my planning as possible so as to learn personalities and smooth any glitches that might arise. Establish the community and the channels for communication. Send "hello" messages and share these with students. Gather your texts, computers, and whatever else you might need to complete the project. I'll never forget one midnight trip to the local Barnes and Noble's after discovering at the last minute that an online project required the use of an obscure short story to be shared using NetMeeting and our inexpensive class teleconferencing camera with a class in Ontario. Needless to say, that wasn't a lesson I needed to learn twice.

Another key lesson learned was one dealing with student permission. In one school, it was an unspoken rule that students involved in extensive learning projects that used a live Internet connection were to get *written* parental permission. Make sure that your students have all the requisite permissions and accounts needed before starting any project. Check with your building specialists because this differs from school to school. I take this a step further, reviewing netiquette and acceptable use policies with classes, just as a quick reminder. We make it fun through a game show format, but I clearly emphasize that these are scholarly tools with very set expectations.

Once I have things solidified and planned, I open our classroom doors. I announce the project in our schoolwide parent newsletter and post an invitation to participate on the class Web site. If I'm feeling particularly giddy, I invite administrators to observe students working on the project, enriching both my students' opportunities to demonstrate their learning and engagement, and the administration's sense of how technology can be used to empower and enrich student understanding.

While working through the project, there are some additional ideas that I recommend implementing. Have students maintain a reflective journal throughout the activity so that they can examine not only what they are learning in terms of content but what they take away from the collaborative process. If students are participating in real-time video conferencing, record the interactions for later analysis and debriefing. Last, keep closely in touch with other teachers who are involved in the project. Develop a common planning time for an online chat or NetMeeting. Share lesson plans via e-mail. Keep the communication and ideas flowing to help push your thinking and add to your shared community.

There is no such thing as overplanning or taking too long to develop your ideas. A project's success is rooted in its planning and procedures. Even the greatest idea will die a lingering death in cyberspace unless you know exactly what you want to do and communicate it clearly to other participants (Harris 1999).

Designing Your Own Project

I take on the challenge of designing my own online projects when I have specific ideas, curricular needs, and the right group of students. As with most planning and instructional design, I begin with the end. Where do I want students to be by the close of a project? What are the essential questions I want them to probe and discover? What are the outcomes for the project? Does using the technologies collaboratively in this project allow me to challenge, enrich, extend, and empower student learning? What will the product look like? If this project requires specific collaboration, whom do we need to seek out for this to be a success? It's also crucial to ensure that the activity is in alignment with state and national standards for learning.

It's essential to consider two additional factors. First, what will the buy-in be for other participants? Think about why other teachers and classes of students would want to participate in the project. For example, in developing the Poetry Forge, www.poetryforge.org (see Figure 8.2), I rooted my work in thinking about why students and teachers would want to use the site's tools and participate in the accompanying discussion areas. Simply put, you don't have a collaborative project if no one is collaborating.

Second, how will you build and "bill" the activity? Structure the project so that expectations are clear and the time line is ambitious, yet reasonable. It's important to create a challenge but not one that is too limiting. Determine how collaborators will be involved (e-mail, discussion, chat, sharing posted projects/ products) and what their specific roles will require. Once the project is up and running, you need to invite, excite, evoke, and invoke participation. I choose to post projects to established project databases, such as www.telementor.org and

Figure 8.2

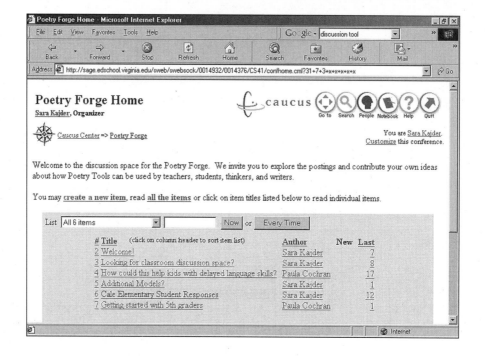

the Global Schoolhouse. I also post invitations on our class Web site and other school resources. The critical aspect of building your project is building an active, invested community.

Ending Points: Building Community

No matter if you are working with discussion tools or participating in a global online collaborative project, the challenge central to building a genuinely rich use lies in the community the work engenders. Building this community is the toughest part of the entire process. At this stage in our growth as technology-literate teachers, no one has found the end-all, be-all formula for success when it comes to building online community. Each experience leads me closer to figuring it out, but I often still feel as if I'm miles away.

The one idea that I'm certain of is that in order for the community to be successful, every participant needs to be mindfully committed to the conversation itself. We need to be aware of our strengths and limits as learners, and we need to be struck by the richness of the text and task. But, ultimately, we need to want to voice ideas, putting them out there for others to consider, question, and build upon. We need to trust. And we need to believe that through the investment of our thoughts, our time, and our work, we'll come out on the other end with something greater. Sometimes this is an understanding. Sometimes this is a relationship and partnership. Sometimes this is a text. Working to nurture, foster, test, and establish a deeply rooted online community requires supreme patience, something difficult enough for me to exhibit when I'm uncomfortable with the silences that periodically fill my classroom. What keeps me poised and willing is the belief that this circular, interactive, dynamic body will take us further, enriching and testing our thinking while pushing us to grow as thinkers, users, techies, readers, writers, and speakers.

Related Reading

Bull, Glen, Paula Cochran, and Sara Kajder. 2002. "The Poetry Forge." *Learning and Leading with Technology* 30 (4).

Harris, Judi. 1998. *Virtual Architecture: Designing and Directing Curriculum-Based Telecomputing.* Eugene, OR: International Society for Technology in Education (ISTE).

Palmer, Parker. 1998. *The Courage to Teach.* San Francisco: Jossey-Bass.

Online Resources

Online Communities for Teachers

Harvard Online Community. <http://www.learnweb.harvard.edu/>.
Tapped in Community for Teachers. <http://www.tappedin.org/>.

Virtual Museums

Exploratorium. <http://www.exploratorium.edu/exhibits/f_exhibits.html>.
Hemingway Portrait Collection. <http://www.npg.si.edu/exh/hemingway/>.
Virtual Corkscrew Museum. <http://bullworks.net/virtual.htm>.

Virtual Field Trips

Anne Frank House. <http://www.annefrank.nl/>.
Bay Trippers. <http://www.mpt.org/learningworks/baytrippers/index.html>.

The Cave of Chauvet-Pont-d'Arc.
<http://www.culture.gouv.fr/culture/arcnat/chauvet/en/index.html>.
Field Guides. <http://www.field-guides.com/trips.htm>.
The Global Schoolhouse.
<http://gsh.lightspan.com/project/fieldtrips/index.html>.

Collaboration

Blue Web'N. <http://www.kn.pacbell.com/wired/bluewebn/>.
The Global Schoolhouse. <http://gsh.lightspan.com/pr/index.html>.
iEARN. <http://www.iearn.org/>.
International Telementor Program. <http://www.telementor.org/>.
Kidproj. <http://www.kidlink.org/KIDPROJ/>.

9 Your-Class.com

I've never had a teacher with his or her own Web site. Using the tools now online, I managed my own learning by scheduling homework, accessing resources, and even "speaking" with actual writers.
—Niko, eleventh-grade English student

Even though I've been absent for the past couple of days, I wanted to be sure that you noted that I participated in the class online discussion of TKAM.
—Stephanie, ninth-grade English student

Three years ago I took yet another leap toward becoming a tech-savvy English teacher when I designed my first class Web site. Inspired by a colleague at another high school, I decided to build a basic class Web site on which I would post homework assignments, class announcements and information, and some limited resources to help students prepare for the coming exams. Over the course of one spring break, I'd managed to read a manual (yes, the *Dummies Guide to Web Design*), create a basic page with one graphic and a whole lot of text, and upload it to some free Web space available at <http://geocities .yahoo.com>. It was almost embarrassingly simple, but I celebrated its content and design as if it were my first born-child. I celebrated as I photocopied in the staff lounge. I celebrated as I said the pledge on the first morning back from break. I celebrated right up until the time when I released the URL to students and projected the page using the departmental LCD projector. When presented to my audience, the page lost its luster, all because of one comment from a student, who rarely contributed in class. "Ms. Kajder," he said, "that's a really good first attempt." My bubble popped. I had seized the challenge, created a masterpiece, and been told not to quit my day job. What happened next transformed my teaching. I asked for help. Elliott, the bubble-popping student, stayed after school each day for the next three weeks, teaching me the basics and patiently revisiting those basics every time I missed an important step. With his help, my site evolved into a four-page collection that I could quickly update and slowly build upon. Teachers, parents, students, and staff began using the site as an informational tool, tapping into the communication resources Elliott added by linking to a discussion board. It was a marvel.

Why was this so important? First, by valuing Elliott's tremendous knowledge base, I brought him into a leadership role in our classroom community. His work after school led him to become more confident in his abilities during class. Good teachers know the transformative powers of such interactions. Second, my classroom community became increasingly informed and solid. Students no longer lined up at my desk after an absence, asking for missed assignments. Instead, they checked the Web site from home, from a friend's house, or from the library. Parent phone calls started to diminish as word spread about the information available online. The questions that I did receive were more informed, asking about student learning rather than specific assignments. The Web resource became a tool that extended learning and community while teaching me to determine how and what to share and how to start nurturing this online community.

I don't think every teacher should build a Web site. It's a tool. Just like the other tools we've explored up to now, it needs to be paired with the right task and the right students. You also need the time and desire to build and maintain the site, an investment I value but that others might not. What follows are steps for establishing a Web presence as well as anecdotes that illustrate how it can be used well or not so well. We need to critically question the use of such Web sites as teaching tools, curricular devices, and motivators or as add-ons and black holes that can absorb an enormous amount of instructional time. Again, we want to use technology to enrich, empower, and extend student learning. How can a class Web site do that?

Goal Setting: Where to Start

A class Web site is an instructional tool. To that end, it must be rooted in your curricular objectives and teaching goals. My primary goal in developing a class Web site is to maximize student learning inside and outside of my classroom. That means I might use the Web site for posting exemplary student work, offering enrichment reading, or structuring acceleration for students who need some preteaching before we begin a new unit. Though the Web site will continually evolve, its foundational goals need to stay mostly static, or else it's easy for it to become disconnected and fragmented.

The secondary goals I considered when first building a class Web site all grew from wanting to develop a site that would empower student learning. I wanted to increase digital literacy by providing an electronic medium for students to navigate. I wanted to develop communication with parents by posting assignments and homework. As the site grew, I wanted to build and nurture the early community that developed. I also started to consider the Web site as an extension of my professional portfolio, allowing me to participate in professional dialogues through the sharing of what happened in my classroom and the resulting ideas about teaching and learning.

It's essential that your goals, whatever their content, stay at the forefront of your work as you develop and then maintain your Web site. The work of a Web site tends to grow beyond what you initially anticipate. What starts as a handful of pages can quickly spiral to twenty or more. It's important to keep that in check, developing only the content that meets your goals. In my case, it became a question of making sure that I only worked to add content that extended what was happening in class rather than developing photo-laden galleries depicting where we had been together, or linking to hundreds of good but unrelated Web sites. Stay focused.

Content: What Do You Include?

Let me first emphasize that you simply must complete this step before you ever sit down to design using your computer. Just as we don't expect student writers to take out a blank piece of paper and write a masterpiece without any preplanning or prethinking, it's easy to get overwhelmed by the blank screen. Furthermore, it seems that an increasing number of sites are subscribing to what my student Elliott calls "the kitchen sink syndrome." Especially when working to develop a class Web site, less is more. You want to be deliberate in what you select to post. Don't allow your site to become a virtual filing cabinet. Ensure that you stick to the goals you established. The easiest way? Make a list. Let it sit for awhile. Then critically revisit and rethink each item. I apply the same thinking to Web sites as I do to most practices in my life: start small, do that bit really well, and build from there.

I look at the content of a site as the element that creates reasons for students, parents, teachers, colleagues, and viewers to visit and participate in our online community. I try to feature student work on the opening page. This provides an immediate context, celebrating the thinking and writing that students produce in class. My class Web site is about my students, first and foremost.

Because I want to develop a site that communicates expectations and provides information, I include homework assignments, .pdf files of assignments we are working on, and electronic grade files. It's crucial, if you are making the commitment to post this kind of information, that you update it regularly. I've seen teacher sites where teachers work on a daily basis to update content and keep it as current as possible. That might be more extreme than what you need, but students certainly should not find November's assignments posted in March.

When thinking about the reasons that students would visit the site, I decided there needed to be something beyond posting what a savvy student might already have mastered. Some students have no need for reprinting class assignment sheets, or perhaps they are excellent record keepers and know exactly where they stand in terms of their grades. Sure, I could post related resources and links, but my goal was to make the site an extension of our classroom, inviting engagement with text as writers and readers, inciting collaboration and discussion, and enriching our course study. This thinking led me to start including interactive components on the site: a discussion area (using a free site), simple JavaScript grammar games, and homework help. What's crucial is to consider what your students need, why they might access the site that you create, and what you can provide that would meet your goals and offer a compelling resource.

Time Out: I'm Not into Design

The great thing about the tools that are becoming increasingly available online and in the market is that you no longer need to know HTML (hypertext markup language) code in order to design Web pages. Working with software such as Microsoft FrontPage, Macromedia Dreamweaver, or Microsoft Word, you can create an HTML document that only requires you to manipulate basic word-processing tools. What you type on the screen is what you get on the page—it's that easy. But perhaps you don't even want to think about designing a page at all. You just want a simple way to communicate class ideas. Not to worry. There are tools for that as well.

The least involved option is to post class information using a free Web site that is preformatted. Teachers have access to such sites through resources such as www.teacherweb.com or www.blackboard.com. Creating your site is as easy as logging on, establishing an account, and then typing your information and attaching any files that you want posted. There are other free hosting services and sites out there, but you need to be wary of advertising.

If you want an even simpler start, consider the merits of creating a list of Web sites that can be used to enrich study of a novel, a period, a genre, or a grammar concept. After doing some Web site evaluation (see Chapter 5), select the sites you want to post. Then create a list of those sites using www.backflip.com or www.ikeepbookmarks.com. These tools keep all of your information in one place while also allowing students, parents, and teachers to access the resources you've selected. The only thing you'll need to do is register an account, and type and submit the URLs of the sites you want to link to.

If and when you're ready and willing, here's a step-by-step guide to developing your site using Web editing software (either free or available on the market).

Layout: What's It Going to Look Like?

Again, we still aren't at a point where you should be sitting down in front of your computer screen. Just as I require students to design and mock up what a Web page, slide, hypercard, or electronic publication will look like, I apply that same strategy to my own work. It keeps you focused and saves time. Surprising to most teachers is that I rarely start by designing the look of a page. Instead, I consider the design of the overall site. I take the list of topics that I want to include and transfer them to sticky notes. I then create a diagram that outlines how the pages will be ordered and linked. Why the sticky notes? Just as in my writing classes, they allow me to rearrange, rethink, and reorder simply by lifting and resticking. They save time and resources. Another idea might be to use *Inspiration* to generate a diagram of the site. What is essential is that you pre-plan as thoroughly as possible.

There isn't a set graphic organizer for the task of designing the interface, or what the pages will look like. Instead, I simply use a blank piece of 8½" x 11" paper and draw a navigation bar that runs either vertically or horizontally, somewhere that allows it to be clear and intuitive. If I'm using a horizontal bar, it's usually right underneath a banner. If I'm using one that is vertical, it's usually flush to the left of the screen. When it comes to navigation bars, I'm reminded of my first computer screen, a whopping 12 inches in length. Why is that important to consider? Well, if I design a page for classroom viewing, I want to make sure that I am building something that is visible to all users regardless of what size screen they have. My 12-inch monitor allowed me to see about half of what might have been initially included or intended. To that end, the left-side navigation bar works really well. Keep in mind that navigation is also about ease of use. If you can easily get around a site and find your way back where you came from without using the Back button on your browser or leaving a breadcrumb trail, the navigation on a site is good. The idea is not to lose anyone, especially when designing for classroom and home use.

Sketch out how you want the pages to look, along with the navigation bar. Include room for the graphics you want to post. Specify what fonts you want to use. Include links to other pages. (Note: Links are what the Web is all about. A page without links is an "orphan," a Web design don't. Link to your school's site. Link to your favorite author's site. Just be sure to link.) Also be sure to include your e-mail address as well as the date the page was last updated. Why? It's really frustrating when students are working with outdated information. A date gives us a frame of reference when considering the information you are sharing. The e-mail link allows teachers, parents, and students to correspond when links break, directions need clarification, or a burning question needs to be voiced. I receive e-mail now from visitors to my Web site from all across the globe, and I delight in the perspective and thought that each one adds to my learning and my teaching. If the Web is just a giant connection of millions of people, you need to be sure that when you are joining that resource you are joining in the conversation.

I know that I just said you should include the graphics and "bells and whistles" when sketching. I'm going to take part of that back now. Include only what is necessary and meaningful. Avoid creating a site that visually assaults those who stumble onto it. A little bit goes a long way, especially when your goals are centered on students and your classroom community. Keep colors and fonts under control, too. Trust me. I too made the initial plunge into "too much." I used every color and font I could find, and the things that blinked didn't do so in unison. The key is to keep it simple, effective, and precise. Keep your goals at the forefront of your work.

When it comes to using images, graphics, sounds, video, and other multimedia elements, you can design your own or use what's available online. The most serious rule of thumb to follow is, give credit where credit is due. Just because something can be found online doesn't mean it's free to be used anywhere, anytime, and by anyone. Not crediting your sources is plagiarism, even when it comes to crediting the Web site that helped you create your banners and buttons.

That said, you certainly don't have to be a graphic designer to build an appealing site. There are plenty of image and graphics repositories available online. You can find backgrounds, fonts, buttons, and even sites that help you to easily make your own graphics. An up-to-date list can be found on the Web site for this book. These tools are continually changing and relocating. I initially used what I found in these free tools and by linking to other sites. Now, I work with Adobe Photoshop and Macromedia Fireworks to create graphics and manipulate my own photos. Maximize your time. Maximize your impact. But, again, keep it in moderation. The rule that I use with students is 80 percent content, 20 percent "splash" or "bells and whistles."

Once your sketches are complete, gather them along with your list of content, your diagram of the overall site, and your goals, and head to the computer. Using any one of the many software products available, create the pages. The Web site for this book offers some tutorials and guides for how to work with some of the conventional software. My personal favorite has become Macromedia Dreamweaver, mostly because of its management options, since my Web site has grown to immense proportions. Again, most tools allow you to work as if you are working in a word-processing program; the most sophisticated will also allow you to work with HTML code. To be honest, I didn't learn to code until the third or fourth version of my site. Until that point, I used Netscape Composer, an editor bundled into Netscape Communicator. I designed pages as if I were designing a handout, and though that made designers cringe, it got the job done. The rest I learned once the process began, and only because I chose to. I sought student help when it came to making my sites more interesting and user-friendly, which led to discoveries using JavaScript and HTML. I worked to learn more as I tried to use code available online to enrich my navigation bar or online form. Again, it was all a matter of choice and of aligning my vision of what I wanted the site to be with the constraints of everything else I was juggling as a teacher and in my life outside the classroom. The early sites effectively met my goals. It's all about finding what works for you.

Meta-Tags: Making Sure Your Site Can Be Found

The one piece of HTML that I strongly recommend teachers learn involves being able to work with the opening section of a page just enough to add meta-tags. A meta-tag allows a search engine (such as Google or Yahoo!) to find your site and to describe it using the words that you actually want. Some search engines do extract text from your pages rather than working from a description, but meta-tags help. Before I added meta-tags to my pages, the description of my index page typically read, "Don't forget to submit tonight's homework assignment as soon as you enter the classroom." This didn't have anything to do with what the site contained, but it was all I provided. Meta-tags provide keywords that you believe apply to your site as well as a brief description.

Meta-tags need to be placed just after the <head> tag at the top of a page. The description tag for an early version of my Web site read

<META NAME="description" CONTENT="This site features the work of students in an eighth-grade honors English class in Silver Spring, Maryland.">

The keyword tag for the site read:

<META NAME="keywords" CONTENT="MCPS, English, Kajder, student, webquest."

For more information on meta-tags, see the Web site for this book, or do a quick search in Google.

Ending Points: Opening Your Work for All

The essential power of the Web is its power to reach everyone regardless of disability. To that end, standards of design have been established that aim at making all sites accessible to viewers with disabilities. Led by Tim Berners-Lee, the inventor of the World Wide Web, the World Wide Web Consortium (W3C) has a Web Access Initiative that provides abundant online resources for Web designers to learn these standards and to know what needs to be done to make a Web site accessible to as wide a community of users as possible. Why is this important when it comes to class Web sites? Simply, the students who enter our classrooms come equipped with dramatically different skill levels, experiences, and even disabilities. Good teachers work to include everyone in their class communities, and that must extend to the Web.

What are main things to consider? W3C offers the following list of tips:

- *Images and animations.* Use the alt attribute to describe the function of each visual.
- *Image maps.* Use the client-side map and text for hotspots.
- *Multimedia.* Provide captioning and transcripts of audio, and descriptions of video.
- *Hypertext links.* Use text that makes sense when read out of context. For example, avoid "click here."

- *Page organization.* Use headings, lists, and consistent structure. Use CSS for layout and style where possible.
- *Graphs and charts.* Summarize or use the longdesc attribute.
- *Scripts, applets, and plug-ins.* Provide alternative content in case active features are inaccessible or unsupported.
- *Frames.* Use the noframes element and meaningful titles.
- *Tables.* Make line-by-line reading sensible. Summarize.
- *Check your work.* Validate. Use tools, checklist, and guidelines at <http://www.w3.org/TR/WCAG/>.

What's most crucial to consider is how you can open your site to all students. I follow these guidelines as closely as possible and regularly submit my sites to the Bobby Scan, available through the Watchfire Corporation. This tool scans a page to identify possible barriers to access by individuals with disabilities. Bobby tests Web pages using the guidelines established by the World Wide Web Consortium's Web Access Initiative as well as Section 508 guidelines from the Architectural and Transportation Barriers Compliance Board (Access Board) of the U.S. federal government. Once a page meets these guidelines, designers are given the opportunity to post a "Bobby-approved" seal on the page to indicate its accessibility. The seal definitely gives a site more credibility when I'm reviewing it for classroom use.

Related Reading

Williams, Robin, and John Tollett. 2000. *The Non-Designer's Web Book.* Berkeley, CA: Peachpit Press.

Online Resources

Bobby Scan Web Site. <http://bobby.watchfire.com/bobby/html/en/index.jsp>.
CSS (Cascading Style Sheets) Layout.
    <http://developer.apple.com/internet/css/introcsslayout.html>.
Web Accessibility Initiative.
    <http://www.w3.org/WAI/References/QuickTips/>.

10 Cyberspace, Innovation, and Imagination

The first step in transforming the world is to begin to see it anew.
—John Willinsky

It should be our delight to watch this turmoil, do battle with the ideas and visions of our own time, to seize what we can use, to kill what we consider worthless, and above all to be generous to the people that are giving shape as best as they can to the ideas within them.
—Virginia Woolf

Perhaps one of the most exciting things about considering what meaningful technology integration can introduce into our classrooms is the fact that we have yet to really know what is to come. I have routinely asked my students what they envision in the classrooms of the not-so-distant future. Some see a classroom where every student is provided with a top-of-the-line super workstation that allows them to instantly connect with an international community. Others see a classroom that is accessed from anywhere, providing rich virtual instruction that taps into the compelling multimedia and primary sources that are finding their home on the Internet. If it takes a generation to unlock the potential of a transformative technology, we certainly are seeing that play out in our classrooms now. The technology is trickling up. When it all shakes out, I honestly believe that the digital divide will no longer be about accessing the tangible equipment but about having the skills needed to mindfully access, probe, extend, launch, and configure the tools at hand.

It's difficult to write about what innovation will look like, especially since that is uncharted ground. There are some definite threads and ideas that have the potential to continue posing the challenge to teachers to rethink and reenvision how we teach, who we teach, and what we teach. Surely, we are approaching a point of ubiquitous technology, where serious tools are accessible to all. Communication is exploding through new media and tools, leading us to question modes of speaking and writing while also providing rich options for class study. And, last, we are on the edge of an open source educational movement, providing many options for study, exploration, and ownership of the technology tools utilized in our classrooms. The challenge is to be ready for that which is ahead, to have mindfully explored where we might head and what we need in order to be prepared.

Ubiquitous Technology: Something for Everyone?

Technology in education is reaching a tipping point, the relatively short period of time where significant change happens because a critical mass has been achieved. How do we get effective, powerful tools into the hands of every student? We build on what has already worked. Countless students have graphing calculators, providing them with a portable computer that until now has only featured math-specific software. This technology hasn't meant a great deal to English teachers, except in those rare moments when an off-task student is busy playing a game on his calculator when he ought to be participating in class. It's a single-subject tool. However, it's a model that some are paying close attention to.

Portable computing is making inroads into the English classroom. At surprisingly low cost for substantial power and options, Palm Pilots and handheld computers have provided interesting options. Several grant options have been presented to classroom teachers who wish to explore the possible applications of these tools in the curriculum. Handheld computers are still not an everyday reality for students, but they have gained our notice, providing students with a multisubject tool with the ability to amplify and extend student thinking, writing, reading, and practice.

The tipping point will be reached when every student has access to a portable, wireless computer that can take their learning physically and metaphorically anywhere. Our students will shift from a paradigm of minutes-per-week access to complete access all day, every day. This, in turn, will permit new instructional paradigms, assessment tools, and management techniques. Even just the introduction of a class set of today's handheld computers that aren't linked to the Internet provides a powerful glimpse into potential options. Using a base model Palm capable of beaming and equipped with Microsoft Word and Excel-like "Documents to Go" software, students can generate and share a reading list; actively collaborate on, critique, and share student drafts; write and read e-books; record voice notes; develop concept maps and graphic organizers; listen to radio addresses, speeches, and music; manipulate and view images; develop and share flashcards; organize assignments; examine language by using a dictionary and thesaurus; send and receive individual questions; keep a journal; access notes from class discussions and readings; and on and on. Imagine where we could go once this tool taps into a wireless network.

Educational computing journals are full of forecasts, each outdoing the other when it comes to predicting the time when each of our students will have immediate, continual access via whatever computing device will provide the right balance of portability, affordability, and power. This innovation requires investment (noting that you can currently purchase numerous well-equipped handheld computers for the cost of one desktop system), exploration, research, and time. Ultimately, it also requires that we add to our rule, fusing together the right tool, the right task, the right students, and the right, visionary teachers.

Starting Points

T. S. Eliot writes in "Little Gidding" that it's only at the end that we can discover the beginning, clearly, and often for the first time. So what does it take to be a tech-savvy English teacher? A little vision. A lot of patience. The openness and willingness to take risks. The belief that students can benefit from a rich and compelling melding of the right tool with the right task. The drive to keep learning from the community of learners within every classroom and every school. I'm reminded of one of my favorite passages from the work of William Blake:

To see a world in a grain of sand
And heaven in a wild flower,
Hold infinity in the palm of your hand
And eternity in an hour.

The tech-savvy English teacher needs to be able to see the world in that grain of sand—whether it has pages, a screen, a wireless connection, a touchpad, or some option that we have yet to discover. We will undoubtedly hold infinity in the palms of our hands. The challenge is to ensure that we use the potential to enrich, extend, and empower our student learners.

I invite you to continue your exploration. Join the online community that is established on the Web site for this book. Share your ideas with your students and the community in your classroom. Keep your expectations high. We're all looking forward to where you help us to go next.

Related Reading

Bull, Glen, Gina Bull, Joe Garofalo, and Judi Harris. 2002. "Grand Challenges: Preparing for the Tipping Point." *Learning and Leading with Technology* 29 (8): 6–11.

Gladwell, Malcolm. 2000. *The Tipping Point: How Little Things Can Make a Big Difference.* Boston: Little, Brown.

Lessig, Lawrence. 2001. *The Future of Ideas: The Fate of the Commons in a Connected World.* New York: Random House.

Appendix

Evaluate Your Tech Savvy

Directions: Carefully read the descriptions listed in each category. Reflect honestly on your skills and your practices. Record the number that most closely reflects your level in the blank at the end of each section. Total your responses to find your current overall level. Keep in mind that this is a continuum, leaving great room for growth and skill development at all levels.

I. Using technology to improve student writing

Level One: I occasionally ask that the final draft of student writing be typed.

Level Two: I regularly require that students submit their work in a typed, specifically formatted manner. I encourage students to compose and edit using the computer and try to provide structured lab-time where we work with drafts.

Level Three: I help students use the computer in all phases of the writing process from using graphic organizers to composing to editing. This includes the use of idea generators, AlphaSmarts, outlining tools, spelling and grammar checkers, desktop publishing tools—all that I can get my hands on. I use technology to help students share their work with a wide audience.

Level Four: I store portfolios of my students' work electronically. I share exemplar units with others through print and electronic publishing and through conference presentations and workshops. I look for specific technology tools to help my students improve their writing skills and work to bring them into our classroom environment.

My closest level is _____.

II. Using technology to improve student reading

Level One: Students rarely have the opportunity to read electronic texts in their classroom.

Level Two: Students work to read and critically evaluate text in my classroom on a fairly regular basis. We work with online texts and apply a class rubric to evaluate its accuracy, timeliness, accessibility and usefulness.

Level Three: We work to develop information literacy while also targeting reading and understanding skills. We work with electronic texts and hypertexts as readers, writers and thinkers. Students use higher-level thinking skills to critique texts, use and site electronic information sources, and communicate ideas within a variety of electronic environments.

Level Four: I am actively involved in curriculum planning teams and advocate for multidisciplinary units and activities that require information literacy skills and close, high-level reading skills. I share successful units with others through print and electronic publishing and through conference presentations and workshops. I look for specific technology tools to help my students improve their reading skills and work to bring them into our classroom environment.

My closest level is _____.

III. Instructional software use

Level One: Students rarely have the opportunity to work with instructional software in my classroom, not because of access but because of time and what I see as important to their instruction.

Level Two: I use a few instructional programs as a supplemental activity, a reward, or to accelerate for students with special needs.

Level Three: I use several programs (e.g., interactive tools, simulations and tutorials) to help all of my students meet specific learning objectives. The software allows me to accelerate, teach or reinforce concepts more effectively than some traditional methods. When it is available, I use the software to help assess student progress and performance.

Level Four: I seek out new programs for evaluation and adoption. I know sources of reviews and keep current on developments in computing technologies through professional reading and conference attendance. I share my findings with other professionals, parents and my students.

My closest level is _____.

IV. Modification of instructional delivery

Level One: I have a few effective methods of delivering content to my students. I do not use technology if it requires that I change my instructional methodology.

Level Two: I am working to develop and implement units or projects that have a technology component, but I am more comfortable working with tasks that involve whole group instruction.

Level Three: I use a variety of instructional delivery methods and student grouping strategies routinely throughout the year. I can design activities and approaches that best fit both the learning objectives and the resources available to me. I can use small groups working cooperatively or in rotation to take advantage of student-to-equipment ratios of greater than one to one.

Level Four: I continuously try new approaches suggested by research or observation to discover the most effective means of pairing the right student with the right task and right tool. I work to both engage students and meet curricular goals. I work with a team of fellow teachers either face to face or online to create, modify, and improve my practices in instructional delivery.

My closest level is _____.

V. Adaptive technologies

Level One: I am not aware of how technology can help students with special learning needs.

Level Two: I work with students who may bring with them special devices that allow them to work and communicate in the classroom.

Level Three: I use technology when appropriate to help students with special learning needs. This includes detailed IEPs and specialized communications devices.

Level Four: I actively read current research and work with special educators to learn about appropriate tools for my students. I work to share what I learn with other professionals.

My closest level is _____.

VI. Professional growth and communication

Level One: I have occasionally researched electronic resources for professional growth and/or communication.

Level Two: I regularly look online to locate lesson plans and research within online databases. I correspond with parents and other teachers using email and other communication devices when appropriate.

Level Three: I use the Internet and other online resources to obtain research, teaching materials, and information related to the content of my classes. I read electronic journals to keep current on educational practice. I participate in electronic discussion groups and chat rooms related to teaching English. I use multimedia presentation software when giving workshops or speaking at conferences. I take part in distance learning opportunities using technology.

Level Four: I organize professional growth opportunities for other teachers and feel comfortable teaching other staff members how to use technology.

My closest level is _____.

Survival Level 0–5 points
Mastery Level 5–10 points
Impact Level 10–15 points
Innovation Level 15–20 points

Adapted from Doug Johnson, "Now You Know the Basics," *Learning and Leading with Technology,* December/January 2000–2001.

Planning and Designing Learning Environments and Experiences

Teachers plan and design effective learning environments and experiences supported by technology:

Distinguished (4)	Proficient (3)	Apprentice (2)	Novice (1)
Consistently and creatively attends to developmental needs and student diversity.	Shows adequate attention to developmental needs and student diversity.	Shows moderate attention to developmental needs and student diversity.	Shows weak attention to developmental needs and student diversity.
Applied current research and theory when planning technology-rich learning activities.	Mentions current research and theory when planning technology-rich learning activities.	Gives minimal attention to current research and theory when planning technology-rich learning activities.	Does not utilize conclusions from current research and theory when planning technology-rich learning activities.
Consistently demonstrates critical thinking in selecting software.	Shows some critical thinking in selecting software.	Shows minimal critical thinking in selecting software.	Rationale for selecting software is weak, lacking evidence of critical analysis.
Anticipates technology-related classroom management issues and plans multiple courses of action.	Anticipates technology-related classroom management issues and plans a course of action.	Anticipates technology-related classroom management issues but does not plan alternative actions.	Does not anticipate technology-related classroom management issues and does not plan alternative actions.
Plans multiple strategies to facilitate students' higher-order thinking, critical thinking about electronic information, ethical sensitivity, and technical skills.	Plans some strategies to facilitate some of the following: students' higher-order thinking, critical thinking about electronic information, OR technical skills.	Plans strategies to facilitate only technical skills or is focused on only one aspect of technology use.	Planning is inconsistent and does not cover any strategy well.

Source: ISTE (International Society for Technology in Education) 2002.

ISTE National Educational Technology Standards (NETS) and Performance Indicators for Teachers

All classroom teachers should be prepared to meet the following standards and performance indicators.

I. TECHNOLOGY OPERATIONS AND CONCEPTS
Teachers demonstrate a sound understanding of technology operations and concepts. Teachers:

A. demonstrate introductory knowledge, skills, and understanding of concepts related to technology (as described in the ISTE *National Educational Technology Standards for Students*).

B. demonstrate continual growth in technology knowledge and skills to stay abreast of current and emerging technologies.

II. PLANNING AND DESIGNING LEARNING ENVIRONMENTS AND EXPERIENCES
Teachers plan and design effective learning environments and experiences supported by technology. Teachers:

A. design developmentally appropriate learning opportunities that apply technology-enhanced instructional strategies to support the diverse needs of learners.

B. apply current research on teaching and learning with technology when planning learning environments and experiences.

C. identify and locate technology resources and evaluate them for accuracy and suitability.

D. plan for the management of technology resources within the context of learning activities.

E. plan strategies to manage student learning in a technology-enhanced environment.

III. TEACHING, LEARNING, AND THE CURRICULUM
Teachers implement curriculum plans that include methods and strategies for applying technology to maximize student learning. Teachers:

A. facilitate technology-enhanced experiences that address content standards and student technology standards.

B. use technology to support learner-centered strategies that address the diverse needs of students.

C. apply technology to develop students' higher order skills and creativity.

D. manage student learning activities in a technology-enhanced environment.

IV. ASSESSMENT AND EVALUATION
Teachers apply technology to facilitate a variety of effective assessment and evaluation strategies. Teachers:

A. apply technology in assessing student learning of subject matter using a variety of assessment techniques.

B. use technology resources to collect and analyze data, interpret results, and communicate findings to improve instructional practice and maximize student learning.

C. apply multiple methods of evaluation to determine students' appropriate use of technology resources for learning, communication, and productivity.

V. PRODUCTIVITY AND PROFESSIONAL PRACTICE
Teachers use technology to enhance their productivity and professional practice. Teachers:

A. use technology resources to engage in ongoing professional development and lifelong learning.

B. continually evaluate and reflect on professional practice to make informed decisions regarding the use of technology in support of student learning.

C. apply technology to increase productivity.

D. use technology to communicate and collaborate with peers, parents, and the larger community in order to nurture student learning.

VI. SOCIAL, ETHICAL, LEGAL, AND HUMAN ISSUES
Teachers understand the social, ethical, legal, and human issues surrounding the use of technology in PK–12 schools and apply that understanding in practice. Teachers:

A. model and teach legal and ethical practice related to technology use.

B. apply technology resources to enable and empower learners with diverse backgrounds, characteristics, and abilities.

C. identify and use technology resources that affirm diversity.

D. promote safe and healthy use of technology resources.

E. facilitate equitable access to technology resources for all students.

The Betting Game

Name:

Part 1:
Read the questions. Use your consultants to answer the questions. Write the answer in that column.

Part 2:
Wait until you are instructed to place your bet for that question. You may bet as much as $100 or as little as $1 based on your commitment to your answer to the first question. Keep a tally as we discuss each question; add if your answer is correct, and subtract if your answer is wrong.

Score - $100	Answer	Question
Bet: Score:	1.	1.
Bet: Score:	2.	2.
Bet: Score:	3.	3.
Bet: Score:	4.	4.
Bet: Score:	5.	5.
Bet: Score:	6.	6.
Bet: Score:	7.	7.
Bet: Score:	8.	8.
Bet: Score:	9.	9.
Bet:	10.	10.
Final Score:		

Using Search Engines

Using Search Engines

Assigned Search Engine(s): _____

Class Keyword: _____

Use the graphic organizer below to record your team's observations in the corresponding columns. Be specific and precise in your observations.

Search Engine (list the name)	Web Address (list the full URL)	Information Display (Is the list categorized? Are the links organized according to a system? How is color used? Are instructions for searching provided? etc.)	Layout and Advertising (Is the site designed in a manner that allows for easy navigation? Do ads distract? Is this a site that would be appropriate for users of all ages?)	Links Listed (Are the listed links described in a way that allows you to scan and select? Are the links that appear after the simple search appropriate and what you are looking for?)

Scoring Rubric for Evaluating Reliability and Credibility of Web Pages

Criteria	No Information	Some Information	Rich and Relevant Information
1. Determine the author's expertise on the topic.			Information includes the author's occupation, experience, and educational background. This is found within the site, not just on the target page.
2. Learn more about the site where the page appears.			Information includes who supports the Web site (an individual's page, an educational site, a commercial site, an organization) and contact information.
3. Check out the links from the author's page to other pages.			The facts/pictures/videos can be substantiated at other sites. Links add to both credibility and resources available. External links are to helpful sites.
4. Find out which Web pages have links pointing to the author's page or to the sponsoring organization's site.			Information from sites that link to the author's page is legitimate and provides documentation for the author's page.
5. Look for "pages on the Web" rather than Web pages about the author or organization.			Information is triangulated—available from more than one source, preferably three—from traditional sources such as newspapers, magazines, or library resources on the Web.
6. Determine how recently the page was published or updated.			Information is included about the date of publication. That date is timely, especially in relation to the content.
7. Assess the accuracy of the information in the document.			Information is included about the accuracy of the content and its presentation (grammar, spelling, punctuation, layout).
8. Look for bias in the presentation of the Web page.			Information includes an examination of the language within the document (extreme, appeal, limited perspective).
9. Assess the evidence presented to support opinions or conclusions expressed in the document.			Information includes evidence to support opinions and conclusions expressed in the document (data-driven, references provided, author contact information).
10. Check to make sure that the information included is complete and, if applicable, cited from a current source.			Information is not "under construction." Copyrighted material is cited and an effort to maintain its timeliness is clearly reflected.
11. Check whether design of the site promotes the information and reflects balanced "splash."			Multimedia, if included, assist in conveying information AND are appropriate. Site follows the 80/20 formula.

References

Akers, William T. 2002. "The Tactility of Writing." *English Journal* 91 (6): 58–62.

Atwell, Nancie. 1998. *In the Middle: New Understandings About Writing, Reading and Learning.* 2d ed. Portsmouth, NH: Heinemann.

Baron, Dennis. 1999. *From Pencils to Pixels: The Stages of Literacy Technologies.* Logan, UT: Utah State University Press.

Berners-Lee, Tim. 1997. *Weaving the Web: The Original Design and Ultimate Destiny of the World Wide Web.* New York: HarperCollins.

Birkerts, Sven. 1994. *The Gutenberg Elegies: The Fate of Reading in an Electronic Age.* New York: Fawcett Columbine.

Bull, Glen, Gina Bull, Joe Garofalo, and Judi Harris. 2002. "Grand Challenges: Preparing for the Tipping Point." *Learning and Leading with Technology* 29 (8): 6–11.

Bull, Glen, Paula Cochran, and Sara Kajder. 2002. "The Poetry Forge." *Learning and Leading with Technology* 30 (4).

Burke, Jim. 1998. *The English Teacher's Companion.* Portsmouth, NH: Heinemann.

———. 2001. *Illuminating Texts.* Portsmouth, NH: Heinemann.

Bushweller, Kevin. 1999. "Generation of Cheaters: Who's Cheating in Schools?" *American School Board Journal* (April).

Calkins, Lucy. 1994. *The Art of Teaching Writing.* Portsmouth, NH: Heinemann.

Charney, Davida. 1994. "The Effects of Hypertext on Processes of Reading and Writing." In *Literacy and Computers: The Complications of Teaching and Learning with Technology,* ed. Cynthia Selfe and Susan Hilligoss. Chicago: Modern Language Association of America.

Christian, Scott. 1997. *Exchanging Lives: Middle School Writers Online.* Urbana, IL: National Council of Teachers of English.

Cuban, Larry. 2001. *Oversold and Underused: Computers in the Classroom.* Cambridge, MA: Harvard University Press.

Daniels, Harvey, and Marilyn Bizar. 1998. *Methods That Matter: Six Structures for Best Practice Classrooms.* Portland, ME: Stenhouse.

Dodge, Bernie. 1997. "Some Thoughts About WebQuests." <http://edweb.sdsu.edu/courses/edtech596/about_webquests.html>.

———. 2002. "A Road Map for Designing WebQuests." <http://webquest.sdsu.edu/roadmap/index.htm>.

Dunn, Patricia. 2001. *Talking, Sketching, Moving: Multiple Literacies in the Teaching of Writing.* Portsmouth, NH: Heinemann.

Elbow, Peter. 1973. *Writing Without Teachers.* New York: Oxford University Press.

Gilster, Paul. 1997. *Digital Literacy.* New York: Wiley.

Gladwell, Malcolm. 2000. *The Tipping Point: How Little Things Can Make a Big Difference.* Boston: Little, Brown.

Gleason, Barbara. 2001. "Teaching at the Crossroads: Choices and Challenges in College Composition." *The Writing Instructor.* <http://www.writinginstructor.com/reflections/gleason.html>.

Golub, Jeffrey N. 1999a. *Making Learning Happen.* Portsmouth, NH: Heinemann/Boynton-Cook.

———. 1999b. "Thoughts Worth Thinking About: Reflections, Connections, Projections." *Virginia English Bulletin* 49 (2): 52–54.

———. 1999c. "Turn on Your Computers, Turn on Your Students." *Notes Plus* (National Council of Teachers of English) (April).

Graves, Donald H. 1983. *Writing: Teachers and Children at Work.* Portsmouth, NH: Heinemann.

———. 1999. *Bring Life into Learning: Create a Lasting Literacy.* Portsmouth, NH: Heinemann.

Gruber, Sibylle. 2000. *Weaving a Virtual Web: Practical Approaches to New Information Technologies.* Urbana, IL: National Council of Teachers of English.

Harris, Judi. 1998a. "Educational Teleresearch: A Means, Not an End." *Learning and Leading with Technology* 26 (3): 42–46.

———. 1998b. *Virtual Architecture: Designing and Directing Curriculum-Based Telecomputing.* Eugene, OR: International Society for Technology in Education (ISTE).

———. 1999. "Taboo Topic No Longer: Why Telecollaborative Projects Sometimes Fail." *Learning and Leading with Technology* 27 (5): 58–61.

Healy, Jane M. 1998. *Failure to Connect: How Computers Affect Children's Minds— And What We Can Do About It.* New York: Simon and Schuster.

Horrigan, John. 2002. "Getting Serious Online." Washington, DC: Pew Internet and American Life Project. <http://www.pewinternet.org/>.

ISTE (International Society for Technology in Education). 2000. *National Educational Technology Standards for Teachers: Preparing Teachers to Use Technology.* Eugene, OR: ISTE.

Jonassen, David, Kyle Peck, and Brent Wilson. 1998. *Learning with Technology.* Upper Saddle River, NJ: Prentice Hall.

Lanham, Richard. 1993. *The Electronic Word: Democracy, Technology and the Arts.* Chicago: University of Chicago Press.

Lenhart, Amanda, and Maya Simon. 2001. *The Internet and Education: Findings of the Pew Internet and American Life Project.* Washington, DC: Pew Internet and American Life Project.

Lessig, Lawrence. 2001. *The Future of Ideas: The Fate of the Commons in a Connected World.* New York: Random House.

Mandinach, Ellen, and Hugh Cline. 1992. "The Impact of Technological Curriculum Innovation on Teaching and Learning Activities." Paper presented at AERA.

March, Tom. 1998. "Why WebQuests?" <http://www.ozline.com/webquests/intro.html>.

———. 2000. "The 3 R's of WebQuests." <http://www.infotoday.com/MMSchools/nov00/march.htm>.

Marzano, Robert J., Debra J. Pickering, and Jane E. Pollock. 2001. *Classroom Instruction That Works: Research-Based Strategies for Increasing Student Achievement.* Alexandria, VA: Association for Supervision and Curriculum Development.

McKenzie, Jamie. 1995. "Crossing the Great Divide: Adult Learning for Integrative and Innovative Use of Technologies with Students." <http://emifyes.iserver.net/fromnow/fnosept95.html#Crossing>.

———. 1998. "Grazing the Net: Raising a Generation of Free Range Students." *Phi Delta Kappan* (September). <http://www.fno.org/text/grazing.html>.

———. 2000. Presentation at Maryland Technology Showcase, December 10.

Means, B., and K. Olson. 1997. *Technology and Education Reform.* Washington, DC: U.S. Department of Education.

Moeller, Dave. 2002. *Computers in the Writing Classroom.* Urbana, IL: National Council of Teachers of English.

Murray, Donald M. 1982. *Learning by Teaching: Selected Articles on Learning and Teaching.* Portsmouth, NH: Heinemann/Boynton-Cook.

———. 1994. "Teach Writing as Process Not Product." In *Rhetoric and Composition: A Sourcebook for Teachers and Writers,* ed. Richard L. Graves. Portsmouth, NH: Heinemann/Boynton-Cook.

Murray, Janet H. 2001. *Hamlet on the Holodeck: The Future of Narrative in Cyberspace.* Cambridge, MA: MIT Press.

November, Alan. 1998. "Teaching Zack to Think." *High School Principal* (September). <http://www.anovember.com/articles/zack.html>.

O'Connor, Patricia. 1999. *Words Fail Me.* San Francisco: Harcourt.

Ogle, D. S. 1986. "K-W-L Group Instructional Strategy." In *Teaching Reading as Thinking,* ed. A. S. Palincsar, D. S. Ogle, B. F. Jones, and E. G. Carr, 11–17. Alexandria, VA: Association for Supervision and Curriculum Development.

Palmer, Parker. 1998. *The Courage to Teach.* San Francisco: Jossey-Bass.

Patterson, Nancy G. 2000. "Weaving a Narrative: From Tears to String to Hypertext." *Voices from the Middle* 7 (3): 41–48.

Poftak, Amy. 2002. "Net-Wise Teens: Safety, Ethics and Innovation." *Technology and Learning* 1 (23): 36–49.

Pope, C., and Jeffrey N. Golub. 2000. "Preparing Tomorrow's English Language Arts Teachers Today: Principles and Practices for Infusing Technology." *Contemporary Issues in Technology and Teacher Education* 1 (1): 89–97.

Postman, Neil. 1993. *Technopoly: The Surrender of Culture to Technology.* New York: Vintage Books.

———. 1998. *Conscientious Objections: Stirring up Trouble About Language, Technology, and Education.* New York: Knopf.

Quindlen, Anna. 1997. *How Reading Changed My Life.* New York: Ballantine.

Rogers, Everett M. 1995. *Diffusion of Innovations.* 4th ed. New York: Free Press.

Rosenblatt, Louise. 1996. *Literature as Exploration.* Chicago: Modern Language Association of America.

Sandholtz, Judith, David Dwyer, and Cathy Ringstaff. 1997. *Teaching with Technology: Creating Student-Centered Classrooms.* New York: Teachers College Press.

Schrock, Kathy. 2001. "Covering the Technology Standards: Part 2." *Creative Classroom* (November).

Silver, Debbie. 2000. "Engaging Students in the Learning Cycle." *Principal* 77 (4): 62–64.

Strickland, James. 1997. *From Disk to Hard Copy: Teaching Writing with Computers.* Portsmouth, NH: Heinemann/Boynton-Cook.

Suarez, J., and A. Martin. 2001. "Internet Plagiarism: A Teacher's Combat Guide." *Contemporary Issues in Technology and Teacher Education* 1 (4). <http://www.citejournal.org/vol1/iss4/currentpractice/article2.htm>.

Tapscott, Don. 1998. *Growing Up Digital: The Rise of the Net Generation.* New York: McGraw-Hill.

Tell, Carol. 2000. "The I-Generation—From Toddlers to Teenagers: A Conversation with Jane M. Healy." *Educational Leadership* 58 (2).

Tomlinson, Carol Ann. 2000. "Reconcilable Differences?" *Educational Leadership* 58 (1).

UCLA Internet Project. 2002. <http://www.ccp.ucla.edu/pages/InternetStudy.asp>.

Veenema, Shirley, and Howard Gardner. 1996. "Multimedia and Multiple Intelligences." *American Prospect* 7 (29). <http://www.prospect.org/print/V7/29/veenema-s.html>.

Watson, Kenneth Lee. 1999. "WebQuests in the Middle School Curriculum: Promoting Technological Literacy in the Classroom." *Meridian* 2 (2). <http://www.ncsu.edu/meridian/jul99/webquest/index.html>.

Wilhelm, Jeffrey D. 2000. "Literacy by Design: Why Is All This Technology So Important?" *Voices from the Middle* 7 (3): 4–14.

Wilhelm, Jeffrey D., Tanya N. Baker, and Julie Dube. 2001. *Strategic Reading.* Portsmouth, NH: Heinemann.

Williams, Robin, and John Tollett. 2000. *The Non-Designer's Web Book.* Berkeley, CA: Peachpit Press.

Index

acceptable use policies, 31
action plans, for WebQuests, 84
active monitoring, 29, 86
adaptive technology, 133
Adobe Photoshop, 123
AlltheWeb.com, 56
Altavista.com, 58
American Dream
    virtual museums, 108–9
    WebQuests, 93–95
AND operator, 57
Angelou, Maya, 70–71
Anne Frank House (virtual field trip), 115
annotated poetry hypertext projects, 38
anticipatory activities, hypertext for, 41
Architectural and Transportation Barriers
    Compliance Board, 125
assessment. *See also* evaluation
    betting game, 28, 136
    Jeopardy!-style game, 26–27
    journal prompts for, 52
    Post-it notes skills listing, 28
    self-assessment by students, 27
    of student technology skills, 26–27, 28,
        51–52
assignments, posted on classroom Web sites,
        17, 23, 119–20
assistance, hands-off rule for, 29
Atwell, Nancie, 72

Backflip.com, 121
Ballard, Robert, 48
Bay Trippers (virtual field trip), 115
Berners-Lee, Tim, 47, 124
betting game, 28, 136
Birkerts, Sven, 9, 34
.biz domains, 53
Blackboard.com, 17, 75, 102, 120
Blake, William, 129
Blue Web'N, 89–92, 110, 116
Bobby Scan, 125
Boolean operators, 57–58

boot camp
    defined, 20
    for students, 26–28
    for teachers, 19–22
brainstorming
    prewriting and, 67–68
    rapid-fire feature, 68
    whole-class, 67, 68
brochures, 73–74
Burke, Jim, 60, 61, 65
business domains (.biz), 53

Calkins, Lucy, 35, 66, 72
cameras, 8
cause-and-effect maps, 67–68
Cave of Chauvet-Pont-d'Arc, The (virtual
        field trip), 116
C4.com, 59
CD-ROMs, for electronic portfolios, 74
Charney, Davida, 33
chat rooms, 103–4
    defined, 103
    establishing, 104
    parent concerns about, 24
    school policies about, 103–4
    teacher learning about, 21
Christian, Scott, 101
class booklets, 73–74
class discussion boards. *See also* discussion
        boards
    effectiveness of, 37
    establishing, 102
    for literature discussions, 36–37
    purposes of, 101–2
    rules for, 102–3
    students as facilitators of, 102–3
class drop box, 1, 17–18
Classroom.com, 105
classroom computers, 13, 20
classroom television sets, 1
classroom Web sites, 1, 117–25. *See also*
        Web sites